American Exceptionalism in Crime and Punishment

American Exceptionalism in Crime and Punishment

Edited by

KEVIN R. REITZ

OXFORD
UNIVERSITY PRESS

OXFORD
UNIVERSITY PRESS

Oxford University Press is a department of the University of Oxford. It furthers the University's objective of excellence in research, scholarship, and education by publishing worldwide. Oxford is a registered trade mark of Oxford University Press in the UK and certain other countries.

Published in the United States of America by Oxford University Press
198 Madison Avenue, New York, NY 10016, United States of America.

Library of Congress Cataloging-in-Publication Data
Names: Reitz, Kevin R., editor.
Title: American exceptionalism in crime and punishment /
[edited by] Kevin R. Reitz.
Description: New York : Oxford University Press, [2018] | Includes index. |
Identifiers: LCCN 2016050137 (print) | LCCN 2017016137 (ebook) |
ISBN 9780190203559 (ebook) | ISBN 9780190203542 (hardback)
Subjects: LCSH: Criminal justice, Administration of—United States. |
Crime—United States.
Classification: LCC HV9950 (ebook) | LCC HV9950 .A44 2017 (print) |
DDC 364.973—dc23
LC record available at https://lccn.loc.gov/2016050137

1 3 5 7 9 8 6 4 2

Printed by Sheridan Books, Inc., United States of America

Contents

List of Figures and Tables vii

List of Contributors xiii

Introduction
American Exceptionalism in Crime and Punishment:
Broadly Defined—KEVIN R. REITZ 1

PART I: *American Exceptionalism: Perspectives*

1. American Exceptionalism in Crime, Punishment, and Disadvantage: Race, Federalization, and Politicization in the Perspective of Local Autonomy—NICOLA LACEY and DAVID SOSKICE 53

2. The Concept of American Exceptionalism and the Case of Capital Punishment—DAVID GARLAND 103

3. Penal Optimism: Understanding American Mass Imprisonment from a Canadian Perspective—CHERYL MARIE WEBSTER and ANTHONY N. DOOB 121

4. The Complications of Penal Federalism: American Exceptionalism or 50 Different Countries?—FRANKLIN E. ZIMRING 181

PART II: *American Exceptionalism in Crime*

5. American Exceptionalism in Comparative Perspective: Explaining Trends and Variation in the Use of Incarceration—TAPIO LAPPI-SEPPÄLÄ 195

6. How Exceptional Is the History of Violence and Criminal Justice in the United States? Variation across Time and Space as the Keys to Understanding Homicide and Punitiveness—RANDOLPH ROTH 272

7. Making the State Pay: Violence and the Politicization of Crime in Comparative Perspective—LISA L. MILLER 298

8. Comparing Serious Violent Crime in the United States and England and Wales: Why It Matters, and How It Can Be Done—ZELIA GALLO, NICOLA LACEY, and DAVID SOSKICE 332

PART III: *American Exceptionalism in Probation, Parole, and Collateral Consequences of Conviction*

9. American Exceptionalism in Community Supervision: A Comparative Analysis of Probation in the United States, Scotland, and Sweden—EDWARD E. RHINE and FAYE S. TAXMAN 367

10. American Exceptionalism in Parole Release and Supervision: A European Perspective—DIRK VAN ZYL SMIT and ALESSANDRO CORDA 410

11. Collateral Sanctions and American Exceptionalism: A Comparative Perspective—NORA V. DEMLEITNER 487

Index 527

Figures and Tables

Figures

I.1	Incarceration Rates, Western Europe and United States, 2000–2016 or Most Recent	4
I.2	American Exceptionalism in Probation Supervision	10
I.3	Per Capita Prison Growth by Sentencing System Type, 1980–2009	16
I.4	Homicide Rates, Seven English-Speaking Countries during "Crime Drop" Decades, 1994–2014 or Most Recent	22
I.5	Crime Spike: Four Serious Violent Crimes, 1962–1974 (Standardized to 100 in 1962)	23
I.6	Homicide Rates, Seven English-Speaking Countries, 1962–1972	24
I.7	Scissors Effect: US Homicide and Prison Rates, 1962–1972	26
I.8	The Homicide "Plateau" in the United States, 1972–1993; Contrasted with Homicide Spike, 1962–1972	28
1.1	Imprisonment Trends in Europe, 1950–2010	54
1.2	Imprisonment Trends in Europe and the United States, 1950–2010	55
1.3	Imprisonment and Homicide Trends, 1950–2010	55
1.4	American Exceptionalism in Adverse Social Outcomes	56
1.5	Levels of Political Decision-Making in Liberal Market Economies	57
3.1	US and Canadian Imprisonment Rates per 100,000 Residents (1955–2013)	122
3.2	US and Canadian Reported Crime Rates per 100,000 Residents (1962–2013)	123

3.3	US and Canadian Homicide Rates per 100,000 Residents (1962–2013)	124
4.1	Aggregate Executions per Million Population, 1976–2012	183
4.2	Imprisonment Rate per 100,000 Population, United States, 1925–2002	186
4.3	2007 Incarceration Rate by State	187
4.4	Incarceration Rate, States and Select Nations	187
4.5	The Almost Bell Curve Distribution of State Imprisonment Growth Rates, 1972–2007	188
4.6	Likelihood of Normal Distribution of State-Level Imprisonment Growth, Two Measures and Two Tests	190
5.1	Incarceration Rates per 100,000 in Europe and the Anglosphere, 2014	198
5.2	Percentage Changes in Incarceration Rates in 100 Nations, 1992–2012	199
5.3	Incarceration Trends in Western Europe, the United States, and the Anglosphere, 1960–2014	200
5.4	Imprisonment Rates in Europe and 50 US States	202
5.5	Incarceration, Reported Crime, and Victimization	206
5.6	Crime and Incarceration, US States	208
5.7	Correlations between Annual Changes (First Differences) in Homicide Rates and Changes in Imprisonment Rates in 1992–2000 in Organisation for Economic Co-operation and Development Countries (Homicide Lagged by 1 Year) and in US States (Homicide Lagged by 4 Years)	211
5.8	Imprisonment Rates and Recorded Crime Rates, 1960–2010: England and Wales and the Nordic Countries, Germany and the Netherlands, the United States and Canada	212
5.9	Homicide and Incarceration Going Together, Then Departing: New Zealand and England and Wales, 1960–2010	214
5.10	Homicide and Incarceration Zigzagging without Clear Trend: Germany and Denmark, 1960–2010	215
5.11	Homicide and Incarceration (Mostly) Going Down Together: Finland and Japan, 1960–2010	215
5.12	Radical Peaks and Drops in Homicide, Incarceration, or Both: Belarus and Estonia, Different Time Periods	216

5.13	Similar Crime Profiles but Radically Different Incarceration Profiles, Canada and the United States, 1960–2010	217
5.14	Changes in Homicide and Incarceration in Canada and the United States, 1960–2010 (Phillips-Type Curve)	218
5.15	Comparison of Incarceration and Crime Rates, 10 High–Prison Growth and 10 Low–Prison Growth US States, 1977–2010	221
5.16	Incarceration and Index Crime, 1977–2010: Missouri versus Minnesota, Louisiana versus Utah	224
5.17	Imprisonment Rates, Index Crime, and Homicide, 1977–2010: Idaho versus Maine, West Virginia versus New York	226
5.18	Income Inequality and Indicators for Welfare Provision, Organisation for Economic Co-operation and Development Nations and US States	232
5.19	Incarceration and Social Trust, Organisation for Economic Co-operation and Development Countries and US States	235
5.20	Punitivity and Imprisonment, Organisation for Economic Co-operation and Development Nations	239
5.21	Fear of Crime and Pro-Control Attitudes, US States	239
5.22	The Style and Level of Democracy, Organisation for Economic Co-operation and Development Nations and the United States	244
5.23	Imprisonment Rates and Elected State Officials (Separately Elected Officials), Cross-Sectionally and by Percentile Groups, 1977–2010	245
6.1	Executions in the United States, 1777–2002	277
6.2	Homicide Rate versus Spending Too Little on Halting Crime in the United States, 1973–2012	283
6.3	Homicide Rate versus Fear of Walking Near Home at Night in the United States, 1965–2012	284
6.4	Homicide Rate versus Support for the Death Penalty in the United States, 1956–2012	285
6.5	Police in 23 Cities and Prisoners in the United States, 1850–1920	286
6.6	Police in Northern and Southern Cities, 1870–1880	287

6.7 Incarceration Rate of Inmates Incarcerated under State and Federal Jurisdiction per 100,000 Population, 1925–2013 288
6.8 Prisoners in the United States by Region in 1860, 1880, and 1910 289
7.1 Extant Frameworks on Democracy and Punishment 303
7.2 Homicide Rates per 100,000 (3-Year Moving Average), Select Countries, 1950–2008 305
7.3 Maximum, Minimum, Average Homicide Rates (3-Year Moving Average) Select Countries, Excluding the United States, 1950–2008 307
7.4 UK Homicide Rate (3-Year Moving Average) Queen's Speeches, "Most Important Problem," and Select Events (Percentages for Crime/Punishment), 1960–2008 308
7.5 US Homicide Rate, Public and Legislative Agendas on Crime (Congressional Hearings and "Most Important Problem"), 1948–2010 309
7.6 Pennsylvania Homicide Rate (3-Year Moving Average), Public ("Most Important Problem") and Legislative Attention to Crime (Governor's Budget Address and Legislative Hearings), 1979–2009 310
7.7 Acts Passed and Spending in Pennsylvania, Select Topics, 1979–2009 319
10.1 Prisoners (Including Jail Populations and Pretrial Detainees), Probationers, and Parolees per 100,000 General Population in the United States and Europe in 2013 419
10.2 Parolees (under Bureau of Justice Statistics Definition) per 100,000 General Population, Selected US States and European Countries (10 Highest and 10 Lowest Rates), Year End 2013 421

Tables

3.1 Ten States with the Lowest and Highest Absolute Change in Imprisonment Rates from 1971–1975 to 2006–2010 128
3.2 Ten Highest and 10 Lowest State Prison Rates in 1971–1975: Change in Imprisonment Rates from 1971–1975 to 2006–2010 130

3.3	Size of the Increase in Imprisonment as a Function of the Imprisonment Rate in the Early 1970s	133
3.4	Social Policies and Imprisonment Rates (Some Examples)	135
3.5	Racial Makeup of the State (2012–2013) and Imprisonment Rates	138
3A.1	Imprisonment Rates for 50 States (1971–1975 and 2006–2010)	179
4.1	Western European and US Pioneers in Permanent Abolition of the Death Penalty	183
5.1	Correlations between Annual Changes (First Differences) in Homicide Rates and Changes in Imprisonment Rates 1960–2013 (OECD) and 1977–2010 (US States)	210
5.2	Indicators of the Level and Distribution of Wealth and Prosperity	230
5.3	Trust and Legitimacy	234
5.4	Punitivity: Fears and Values	236
5.5	Democracy	242
5.6	Demographics	247
5.7	Variables and Intercorrelations: Global Sample (52 nations)	249
5.8	Regression Models: Global Sample	250
5.9	Regression Models: OECD countries	252
5.10	Regression Models: 50 US States	254
7.1	Matrix of Violence and Politicization and Predicted Outcomes Based on Extant Literature	304
7.2	Homicide Rates and Political Salience of Crime: United Kingdom, United States, Pennsylvania, 1948–2010	313
7.3	Speech Mentions and Acts, Crime and Social Welfare Provisions, 1957–2010	318
8.1	The Ratio of Serious Violent Crime and of Homicides, United States, England and Wales, Canada, and New Zealand: Offenses per 100,000 Population	333
8.2	Comparison of Detailed Rules for Recording Violent Offenses in the United States and England and Wales	347

Contributors

Alessandro Corda is Lecturer in Criminal Law at Queen's University Belfast School of Law (United Kingdom) and Fellow at the Robina Institute of Criminal Law and Criminal Justice, University of Minnesota Law School (United States of America)

Nora V. Demleitner is Roy L. Steinheimer, Jr. Professor of Law, Washington and Lee School of Law.

Anthony N. Doob is Professor Emeritus of Criminology, University of Toronto.

Zelia Gallo is Lecturer in Criminal Law and Criminology & Criminal Justice at the Dickson Poon School of Law, King's College London.

David Garland is Arthur T. Vanderbilt Professor of Law and Professor of Sociology, New York University.

Nicola Lacey is School Professor of Law, Gender and Social Policy, London School of Economics and Political Science.

Tapio Lappi-Seppälä is Director, Institute of Criminology and Public Policy, University of Helsinki.

Lisa L. Miller is Professor of Political Science, Rutgers University.

Kevin R. Reitz is James Annenberg La Vea Professor of Criminal Procedure and Co-Director, Robina Institute of Criminal Law and Criminal Justice, University of Minnesota Law School.

Edward E. Rhine is Director, Parole Release and Revocation Project, Robina Institute of Criminal Law and Criminal Justice, University of Minnesota Law School.

Randolph Roth is Professor of History and Sociology, Ohio State University.

David Soskice is School Professor of Political Science and Economics, London School of Economics and Political Science; Research Professor Emeritus of Political Science, Duke University.

Faye S. Taxman is University Professor, Criminology, Law and Society, Center for Advancing Correctional Excellence!, George Mason University.

Dirk van Zyl Smit is Professor of Comparative and International Penal Law, University of Nottingham.

Cheryl Marie Webster is Professor of Criminology, University of Ottawa.

Franklin E. Zimring is William G. Simon Professor of Law and Director, Criminal Justice Studies, University of California, Berkeley Law School.

American Exceptionalism in Crime and Punishment

INTRODUCTION

American Exceptionalism in Crime and Punishment: Broadly Defined

Kevin R. Reitz

IN THE MID- and late twentieth century, the United States diverged markedly from other Western nations first in its high rates of serious violent crime and soon after in the severity of its governmental responses. In the words of historian Randolph Roth, "Since World War II, the United States has stood out from the rest of the affluent world in its violence and in the punitive nature of its criminal justice system" (see Roth, this volume). This has left an appalling legacy of American exceptionalism in crime and punishment (AECP) for the new century.

When the United States is compared with other Western countries and criticized for its exceptionalism in criminal justice, the conversation usually narrows to two subjects: (1) high incarceration rates and (2) the nation's continued use of the death penalty. With respect to both, the United States is seen as operating on an entirely different scale of punitive severity from other developed societies. Adding to the indictment, it has long been known that America's uses of prisons, jails, and the death penalty are racially disproportionate (e.g., *Furman v. Georgia* 1972; Blumstein 1982; Ayers 1984; *McCleskey v. Kemp* 1987; Blumstein 1993; Kennedy 1997; Alexander 2010; Tonry 2011).

One goal of this book is to broaden the scope of AECP inquiry to include sanctions beyond incarceration and the death penalty. From what we know, it is reasonable to hypothesize that the United States imposes and administers probation, parole, economic sanctions, and collateral consequences of conviction with a heavier hand than other developed democracies (see Rhine and Taxman, this volume; van Zyl Smit and Corda, this volume; Demleitner, this volume). Although the inquiries in this book are preliminary, they raise the possibility that AECP extends across many landscapes of criminal punishment—and beyond, to the widespread social exclusion and civil disabilities imposed on people with a conviction on their record (Jacobs 2015; Love, Roberts, and Klingele 2016).

In addition, the book insists that any discussion of AECP should focus on US crime rates along with US penal severity (see Lacey and Soskice, this volume; Lappi-Seppälä, this volume; Miller, this volume; Gallo, Lacey, and Soskice, this volume). More often than not, American crime is discounted in the academic literature as having little or no causal influence on American criminal punishment (see Miller, this volume). This is a mistake for many reasons but is especially unfortunate because it truncates causation analyses that should reach back to gun ownership rates, income inequality, conditions in America's most disadvantaged neighborhoods, and possibilities of joint or reciprocal causation in the production of US crime rates and punitive severity (see Lacey and Soskice, this volume; Lappi-Seppälä, this volume; Miller, this volume; Gallo, Lacey, and Soskice, this volume).

This chapter is divided into three segments. First, it includes a brief tour of the conventional AECP subject areas of incarceration and the death penalty. Second, it will introduce claims that a wider menu of sanction types should be included in AECP analyses.[1] Third, it will speak to the importance of late twentieth-century crime rates to US punitive expansionism.

The Usual Suspects

Incarceration

The subject of mass incarceration entered America's consciousness in a big way when the nation cemented its status as world leader in per capita incarceration—a watershed that occurred around the turn of the century,[2] following a neck-and-neck race with Russia through the 1990s (Sentencing Project 2001, 1; Tkachuk and Walmsley 2001, 15; Kuhn 1995, 56; Mauer 1994; Associated Press 1991).[3] Since then, US prison and jail confinement rates have come under increasing public scrutiny and have been widely impugned as "mass incarceration" (e.g., Blumstein et al. 2000; Garland 2001a; Simon 2012). After several decades of tough-on-crime politics and public sentiment, there has been a profound shift in the way Americans talk about prison policy. By 2010—illustrated by the appearance of a new conservative organization called

"Right on Crime"—the view that US incarceration rates had spiraled out of control had achieved a footing in both major political parties (Gingrich and Nolan 2011; Savage 2011; Dagan and Teles 2016).[4] Despite the outcome of the 2016 presidential election, this bipartisan sentiment has remained alive at the state and local levels, where most criminal justice is dispensed (Hulse 2017; Garrett 2017; Rosenberg 2017).

The basic facts of mass incarceration will be assumed knowledge throughout this book: After 35 years of continuous prison growth, U.S. incarceration rates (counting both prisons and jails[5]) topped out in 2007 and 2008 at 760 per 100,000 general population—a quintupling of 1972 rates—and have since entered a period of modest decline (Kaeble, Glaze, Tsoutis, and Minton 2015: 3 table 2). Near the peak, the Pew Charitable Trusts calculated that "One in 100" American adults were in prison or jail at yearend 2006—or "one in 54" adult males. (Pew Center on the States 2008, 5, table A-6)

As of this writing, America's per capita confinement has inched downward for six consecutive years, but the reductions have been modest. Overall the nation has returned to the confinement rates of the early 2000s—when the term "mass incarceration" was coined—so the punitive era can hardly be declared over. By the US Justice Department's counts, America's combined prison-plus-jail rates in 2014 (477 and 234, respectively) added up to a total incarceration rate of 711 per 100,000. In raw numbers that translated into 2.3 million prison and jail inmates on any one day in 2014 (Carson 2015; Minton and Zeng 2015).

Few nations have ever made it to the "700 Club" (700 or more prisoners per 100,000). Indeed, in contemporary western Europe, there are no nation states at all in the 200 Club, and half cannot even claim membership in the 100 Club (see Lappi-Seppälä, this volume, Figure 5.1; World Prison Brief 2016). By the standards of other developed democracies, the scale of incarceration in America is astounding. Our 2014 incarceration rate was more than 7 times the average in western Europe, 6 times the Canadian rate, more than 4.5 times that in Australia, and almost 3.5 times New Zealand's rate.[6] As of 2014, the United States had left its formal rival far behind, exceeding the Russian incarceration rate by 53 percent (World Prison Brief 2016).[7] For comparisons between the United States and western European states, Figure I.1 displays changes in incarceration rates from 2000 to 2016 (or the latest available year) in 10 countries.

It is useful to assess what it would take for the United States to rejoin the mainstream of the Western world in its incarceration practices. Regression toward the mean is usually not an ambitious goal, but in this case it is positively grandiose. For instance, in order to downsize to the same incarceration

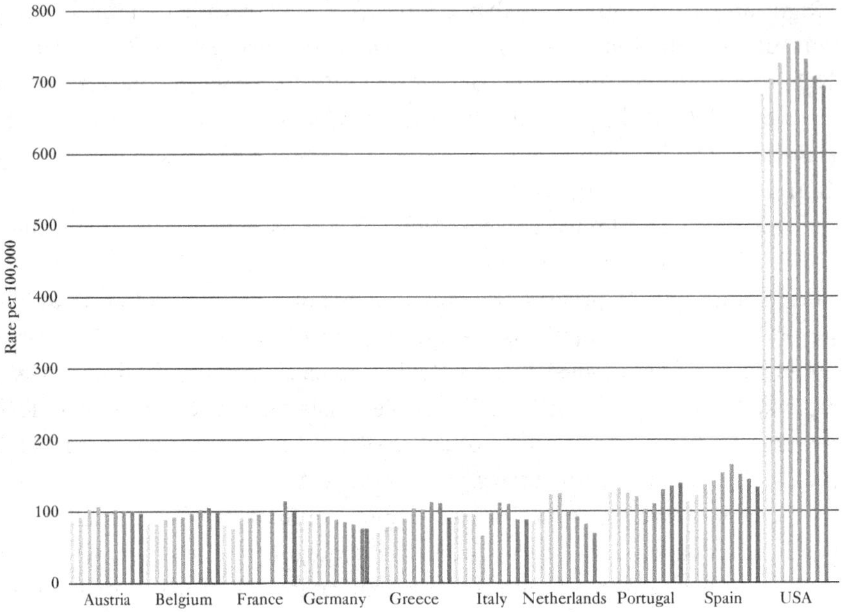

FIGURE 1.1 Incarceration Rates, Western Europe and United States, 2000–2016 or Most Recent (sampling every other year, as available)

Source: Institute for Criminal Policy Research. World Prison Brief. 2017. http://www.prisonstudies.org/world-prison-brief-data.

rate as England and Wales—one of western Europe's leaders in per capita imprisonment—the United States would have to release more than 1.8 million inmates out of a total 2.3 million, leaving 473,000 in the prisons and jails for the entire country.[8] Immense social and political movements would be required to effect such a change.

Compounding problems of the sheer scale of US incarceration are enormous breakdowns in distributive justice. The African American imprisonment rate is nearly 6 times that for whites, the Latino rate is more than 2.5 times the white rate, and the rate for Native Americans—although not regularly reported—has been about 2.5 times the white rate (Carson 2015, 15, table 10; Ruth and Reitz 2003). Pew's "one in 100" report observed that roughly "one in 9" (not a misprint) black men aged 20–34 were in prison or jail on any given day in 2007 (Pew Center on the States 2008, 6).

The Justice Department estimated that a black male child born in 2001 had a 32.2 percent chance of going to prison during his lifetime. (The much greater lifetime probabilities of spending time in jail were not calculable.) For a white male child born the same year, the lifetime probability of imprisonment was 5.9 percent (Bonczar 2003, 8).[9] These statistics are even more startling when interpreted with class in mind. For middle-class blacks, lifetime risk of incarceration is not dramatically different from that for middle-class whites. Therefore, for the most disadvantaged black men, the chances of going to prison during adulthood are much higher than one in three. For example, Steven Raphael estimated that in California "at the end of the 1990s, over 90 percent of black male high-school dropouts . . . have served prison time in the state" (Raphael and Stoll 2009, 10; see also Pettit and Western 2004).

Before leaving the subject of incarceration and racial disparities, I want to point out an acute policy dilemma that is likely to arise if the United States truly enters a prison-downsizing era. Will we think it more important to reduce the "disparity ratio" between black and white incarceration rates or reduce absolute levels of incarceration? In some foreseeable scenarios, it would be impossible to do both. Imagine a hypothetical reform (such as the introduction of actuarial risk assessment at sentencing as a prison diversion tool)[10] that is projected to reduce incarceration rates nationwide by 20 percent, but the measure would reduce white incarceration rates by 25 percent and black incarceration rates by 15 percent.[11] In other words, the probability of a white defendant benefiting from the measure is 66 percent greater than the probability a black defendant will benefit. From a disparity-ratio perspective, this would be a disaster. There's a fair chance it would even be unconstitutional.

Despite the ratio effects, however, the measure would reduce black incarceration rates substantially compared to the status quo. If we forgo the measure on disparity grounds, roughly 150,000 black people would be incarcerated in the United States on any given day, extending into the foreseeable future, who would no longer have been incarcerated if we had adopted the measure.[12] Every year, this would add up to 150,000 *person-years* of confinement for black defendants that could have been avoided. In a mere seven years, the failure to adopt the racially disparate reform would yield more than 1 million additional person-years of black incarceration.

The problem is that the same reform that would buy 1,050,000 fewer person-years of incarceration for black defendants in seven years would yield 1,750,000 fewer incarceration-years for white defendants. What ethical calculus applies?

Capital Punishment

Mass incarceration is a new kid on the block when it comes to comparative embarrassments in American criminal justice policy. As Europe and the Anglosphere abandoned capital punishment in the decades following World

War II, the failure of nationwide abolition in the United States became a leading symbol of American regressivism (e.g., Sellin 1959; Bedau 1964; *Furman v. Georgia* 1972; Black 1974; Zimring and Hawkins 1986; Steiker 2002, 100; Zimring 2003; Garland 2010).

As a purported example of AECP, however, capital punishment in the United States is not in the same league as mass incarceration (see Garland, this volume; Zimring, this volume). America stands alone in the Western world for its retention of capital punishment, but it is far from the planet's leader.[13] While a deeply significant moral issue, the death penalty in America is applied to a vanishingly small percentage of the population, for example, 28 total executions in 2015 (Death Penalty Information Center 2016a). In the same year, there were 2.59 million deaths from all causes (Centers for Disease Control and Prevention 2016). Other comparisons make the same point: less than 1 percent of all offenders convicted of homicide have been executed since 1976 (Zimring 2003). For 2015, the risk of execution was less than one-tenth the risk of being struck by lightning.[14]

In short, unlike mass incarceration (and most other instances of AECP), capital punishment in America is not exceptional because of its scale. Moreover, capital punishment in America is a highly localized phenomenon. Most of the United States can be classified as abolition or nonexecuting territory, in common with other Western democracies (Zimring 2003; Garland 2010). In any recent year, the majority of US states have held zero executions, including abolition states and death-penalty states that rarely carry out the sentence. For example, in 2013, only nine states held executions (a total of 39 executions overall for that year) (Snell 2014b, 1).[15] Even within executing states, a relatively small number of counties are historically where most of a state's death sentences have been imposed and where most executions originate, such as Harris and Dallas Counties in Texas (Death Penalty Information Center 2016d; Texas Department of Criminal Justice 2016).[16] From 1976 to 2013, 2 percent of all counties in America had produced 52 percent of all executions (Dieter 2013, 6). In contrast, from 1967 to 2013, 85 percent of all counties in the United States had produced no executions at all (Dieter 2013, 1).

If racial disproportionality in the use of a criminal punishment is considered an element of AECP, the death penalty qualifies. Racial disparities in the use of the death penalty have been an American disgrace for more than 200 years, especially if one counts vigilante lynchings as a form of capital punishment (Stampp 1956; Wolfgang and Riedel 1973; Higginbotham 1978; Ayers 1984; Kennedy 1997; Cole 1999; Zimring 2003, chap. 5). In the modern era of American capital punishment (post–*Gregg v. Georgia* 1976), large disparities by race of defendant continue to exist—more so in some jurisdictions than others. Nationally, African Americans are 13 percent of the US population yet make up 35 percent of all people executed since 1976—a racial disparity of 3.4 to 1 when compared with the rate of execution for whites (Death Penalty Information Center 2016e; Baldus et al. 1998; Eberhardt et al. 2006; Tabak 2010).

Starting in the 1980s, a growing body of research has shown that the race of the *victim* is a strong predictor of use of the death penalty in individual cases. The most famous study was conducted by David Baldus, who examined thousands of potentially capital murder cases in Georgia during the 1970s. Baldus found that, holding other factors constant, a black defendant who killed a white victim was 4.3 times more likely to be sentenced to death than a black defendant who killed a black victim (*McCleskey v. Kemp* 1987; see also Phillips 2009; Baldus et al. 2009; Baumgartner, Grigg, and Mastro 2015).[17] Somehow, even while accepting the validity of the Baldus study, the US Supreme Court held in *McCleskey* that the race-of-victim finding did not demonstrate did not demonstrate a constitutionally significant risk of racial discrimination in the administration of Georgia's death penalty scheme.[18]

Returning to the issue of the death penalty's scale, the non-Western world includes many other executing jurisdictions (including Israel and Japan[19]). While a world leader in confinement, it is less commonly asked where the United States ranks in the per capita use of capital punishment. To facilitate cross-jurisdictional comparisons, I will use a measure of "executions per 100 million." (You need a big denominator to get American execution rates into the single digits.) Corrected for population, the US execution rate in 2015 was 8.7 per 100 million. Since the 1940s, the peak execution year in the United States was 1999, when there were 98 executions total, or 36 per 100 million.

More usefully, American execution rates may be calculated for individual states: in the four decades after 1976, the most executions carried out by any state in one year was Texas in 2000 with 40 executions, or 191 per 100 million population (Death Penalty Information Center 2016c; US Census Bureau 1998, 2001, 2016). In 2015, Missouri was the nation's leader in per capita executions at 100 per 100 million (6 total). In second place, Texas's 2015 execution rate was down to 47 executions per 100 million (13 total). *Subtracting* Missouri and Texas, the 2015 execution rate for the remaining 48 states was 3.1 per 100 million. For 44 states in 2015, the rate was zero.

Many nations have higher capital punishment rates than the United States as a whole, or any individual state. Iran, lately the most vigorous death-penalty jurisdiction, conducted 1,084 executions in 2015, or 1,364 per 100 million (Kredo 2016; Statista 2016).[20] As recently as 2002, China was estimated to have executed 12,000 people (Dui Hua Foundation 2016), suggesting an "Iran-like" execution rate of 937 per 100 million for that year. The number of executions in China has been falling rapidly in the 2000s, however. The Chinese government executed 2,400 people in 2015, as estimated by the Death Penalty Information Center (2016b). If the estimate is correct, China's rate in 2015 was "only" 178 executions per 100 million population—still 20 times the United States rate for the same year.

What would it take for America to rejoin the mainstream of other Western democracies in the abolition of state-sponsored executions? The task is far less daunting than an unwinding of mass incarceration. David Garland argues that the United States is already on a course toward death penalty abolition—in common with other Western nations; the only qualification is that some American states are moving more slowly (see Garland 2010; Garland, this volume). Indeed, some US states abolished capital punishment well ahead of the post–World War II European wave, dating to the mid-nineteenth century, so the entire nation has not been "behind" the Western curve (Zimring 2003).

In addition, capital punishment in the United States could end with a single stroke via a Supreme Court ruling. The country came close to constitutionally mandated abolition in 1972 and again in 1987 (*Furman v. Georgia* and *McCleskey v. Kemp*). No similar heroic remedy is available for mass incarceration or for any of the other species of AECP examined in this book.

AECP in Broader Focus: Other Criminal Sanctions

Probation

The central hypothesis of this book is that AECP is a phenomenon of unacknowledged breadth—which reaches beyond the familiar monstrosities of mass incarceration and capital punishment. "Mass punishment" may be a better, more embracing, term than mass incarceration. This section introduces the claim that probation supervision across the United States is a full-fledged instance of AECP.

Probation used to be considered an instrument of lenity, not severity. In the not-too-distant past, many people thought that making greater and more imaginative use of probation was the best way to reduce incarceration rates (Morris and Tonry 1990; Byrne, Lurigio, and Petersilia 1992; DiIulio 1997). Probation has often been billed as an "alternative" to prison, implying that, if managed correctly, imprisonment should decline as probation goes up (e.g., Cavanagh and Kleiman 1990; Sigler and Lamb 1995; Anderson 1998).

The history of the late twentieth and early twenty-first centuries does not fit the expected program. Instead of acting as a replacement for prison beds, probation supervision rates have exploded alongside incarceration[21]—and high probation populations have been important feeders of prison and jail populations through the revocation process (Klingele 2013).[22] Recently, the literature has begun to speak of "mass probation" or "mass supervision" (Phelps 2016; McNeill and Beyens 2014). On any day in 2014, nearly 4 million people were serving probation sentences across America (Kaeble, Maruschak, and Bonczar 2015, 1).[23] That is roughly twice the size of the combined US prison and jail populations.

The current scale of probation in the United States is considerably larger than that in eastern and western Europe. As the Robina Institute of Criminal Law and Criminal Justice reported, the average 2013 probation supervision rate across all 50 states was more than five times the average among European countries (Alper, Corda, and Reitz 2016; see Figure I.2).[24] On this measure, America's "exceptional" status in probation is even more dramatic than in its use of prisons and jails. The ratio of US incarceration rates to European rates is about 3.5:1 when counting both eastern and western European countries (see van Zyl Smit and Corda, this volume, Figure 10.1).

Further, the day-to-day experience of being on probation is more difficult than commonly understood (Corbett 2015) and especially painful in the United States when compared with other countries.[25] Rhine and Taxman (Chapter 9) posit that, more than in other advanced democracies, the philosophy of probation supervision in the United States has shifted away from a social work model and toward an orientation of surveillance and control. One expression of this is the imposition of numerous and intrusive conditions that any law-abiding citizen would have difficulty satisfying (Corbett 2015). Making things worse, the focus of some probation departments and private services providers is to collect supervision and program fees from their clientele (Ruhland, Robey, Corbett, and Reitz 2017; American Civil Liberties Union 2010; Human Rights Watch 2014). Across Texas, for example, county probation offices depend on fees from probationers for 50 to 75 percent of their operating budgets. Probation officers spend much of their time and energy collecting supervision fees (Alper and Ruhland 2016a, 2016b). This conflict of interest detracts from probation's original mission of rehabilitation, and appears to be a problem peculiar to the United States (see Rhine and Taxman, this volume).

What would it take for the United States to rejoin the Western mainstream in its approaches to probation supervision? In order to approximate European supervision rates, the total US probation population would have to drop from roughly 4 million to 800,000—a differential of 3.2 million probationers. Large reductions in the number of people placed on probation in the first place would probably be necessary, which would require that lesser penalties somehow become acceptable to courts, prosecutors, victims, politicians, and the public.

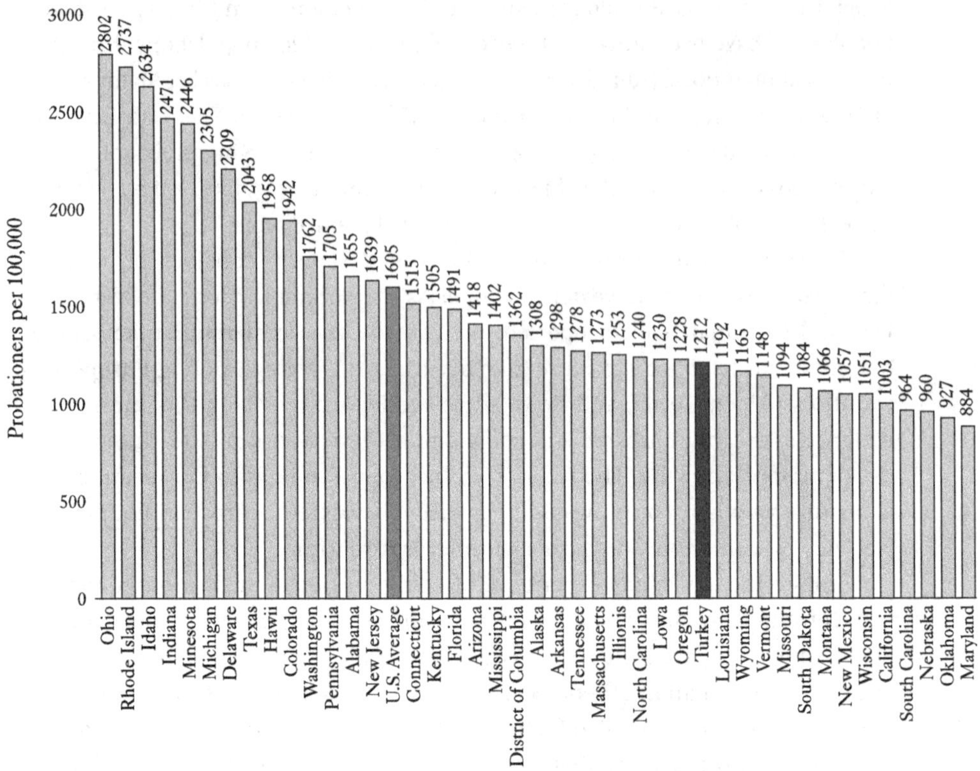

FIGURE 1.2 American Exceptionalism in Probation Supervision
Source: Alper, Mariel, Alessandro Corda, and Kevin R. Reitz. *American Exceptionalism in Probation Supervision*. Minneapolis, MN: Robina Institute of Criminal Law and Criminal Justice, 2016.

Across-the-board efforts would be needed to shorten the average lengths of probation terms, especially in some states, which are considerably longer than those in Europe. There is almost nothing to be gained from a probation sentence longer than two or three years; yet many states mete out probation by the decades, and "lifetime supervision" has become a popular idea for the punishment of sex offenders (American Law Institute 2017, § 6.03 & Comment).

Compared with prison downsizing, large changes in probation strategies across the country would encounter opposition from fewer institutional and economic interest groups. If we monetize probation, it is a much smaller business than incarceration. Probation agencies tend to run on a shoestring, with modest expenditures per client. We do not hear of community corrections unions as major players in state elections, for example, nor does the placement of probation offices drive local economies.

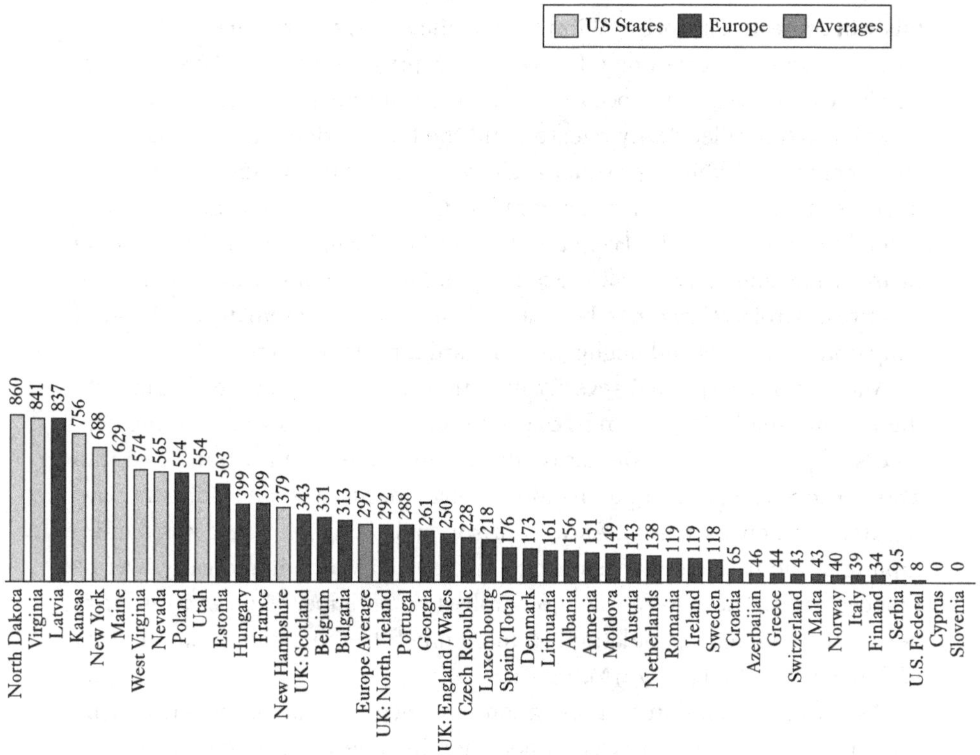

FIGURE I.2 (continued)

On the other hand, probation is the most decentralized of US punishments because it is overwhelmingly administered at the county level. In practical terms, it is difficult to effect meaningful changes across thousands of largely independent government agencies. This is a puzzle that might be solved by new statewide controls imposed through centralization, legislation, or sentencing guidelines. Institutional creativity will almost certainly be needed, not just a change in policy sentiment.

Parole

The weight of the available evidence suggests that parole as administered in the United States is an instance of AECP, at least when compared with arrangements in other Western democracies for prison release, supervision of releasees, and revocations back to prison. Most importantly, changes in parole practices were a major contributor to US prison growth in the late-twentieth and early twenty-first centuries.

For most people—even criminal justice professionals and academics—this will come as a surprise. Within the United States, parole has had a durable reputation of shortening otherwise harsh prison sentences. Discretionary parole release, because it occurs before a maximum prison term has been served, is often called "*early* release"; and the law considers it a "privilege" or an "act of mercy" when a prisoner is allowed to serve the balance of his or her prison sentence in the community rather than behind bars (e.g., *Greenholtz v. Inmates of the Nebraska Penal and Correctional Complex* 1979; *Pennsylvania Board of Probation and Parole v. Scott* 1998). From the public and media perspectives, parole release has been associated with the premature release of dangerous criminals and negligent disregard for public safety.

Markers of exceptional severity in American parole practices begin with the raw numbers. At year end 2014, 856,900 individuals were serving sentences of parole supervision across the United States, which translated into 269 per 100,000 general population (Kaeble, Maruschak, and Bonczar 2015, 1; Bureau of Census 2016a). As with prison and probation, there was a quintupling of the parole supervision rate in the late twentieth and early twenty-first centuries. There were 102,036 parolees under supervision in 1965, or 53 per 100,000 general population—a mere one-fifth the national rate in 2014 (Cahalan 1986, 181, table 7-9A).

As with incarceration and probation, the sheer number of people serving sentences of post-prison-release supervision in America is much greater, correcting for population, than the average among reporting nations in Europe. One recent study concluded that parole supervision rates across the United States in 2013 were at least five times the European average (Corda, Alper, and Reitz 2016).[26] Some of the 5:1 ratio is a direct product of unusually high incarceration rates in the United States, of course. Unsurpassed high American parole supervision rates might thus be seen as an unsurprising side effect of AECP in imprisonment. Even if this simple explanation is correct, postrelease supervision rates have not been included in the usual accountings of AECP. They are a substantial addition to the descriptive balance sheet.

The experience of parole supervision is no picnic. Compared with probationers, prison releasees are a high-risk population; they are generally managed with tighter surveillance, more restrictive conditions, and more of a sense that they "deserve" the pains of supervision. The distinctive American toughness in community supervision is especially present in parole. As summarized by van Zyl Smit and Corda in Chapter 10,

> While in Europe [parole supervision] is mostly structured as a rehabilitative tool aimed at facilitating the re-entry and resettlement of

> the offender in the community, in the United States parole tilts more heavily toward a punitive and managerial intervention, weakening or supplanting a commitment to the ideal of reintegrating parolees into society. . . . In comparison to Europe two distinctive characteristics of US parole are (1) longer terms of supervision and (2) more, and more intrusive, conditions of supervision. The latter add greatly to the burden placed on American parolees.

Parole revocation rates also appear to be high in the United States compared with reporting European countries. For the United States as a whole, 26 percent of all prison admissions in 2014 were due to parole violations (Carson 2015, 10, table 7). Probation revocations are not tracked separately in US national statistics but, filling in a reasonable estimate of prison entries from probation failures, at least 50 percent of American prison admissions are probably attributable to community supervision revocations of all kinds.[27] In contrast, among reporting European countries in 2012, combined revocations (or "recalls") from parole and probation amounted to only 7.4 percent of all prison admissions (Aebi and Delgrande 2015, Table 8).[28]

The legal architecture of parole-release discretion in the United States is by itself a form AECP. Parole-releasing systems are called "indeterminate" because, on the day of judicial sentencing, the actual length of a prison sentence cannot be predicted with reasonable accuracy. The *degree* of indeterminacy in US systems is greater than that in most or all other countries (Reitz 2014).[29] In other words, American prison-release agencies control a greater share of the maximum prison term than in other countries—and the number of prisoners serving sentences with extremely long maximum terms is larger in the United States than elsewhere.

To illustrate the high degree of indeterminacy in many American jurisdictions, in New Jersey, a maximum 10-year prison sentence yields first release eligibility after 23 months. The parole board decides one way or another on more than 80 percent of the possible prison term (New Jersey State Parole Board 2010, 35). In Colorado, many lower-level sex offenses carry prison sentences of one year to life (or two years to life or four years). The percentage of the possible prison term controlled by the parole board is not precisely calculable, but very large (Colo. Rev. Stat. §§18-1.3-1004; 18-1.3-401). At the extremes of indeterminacy, six states empower the parole board for most offenses to release prisoners the day they are admitted to prison, or keep them for their full maximum terms, or anything in between.[30] In this type of system, the courts decide who will be incarcerated and who will not, but the parole board is 100 percent in charge of prison-sentence lengths.

As far as I know, such stunning delegations of power to prison-release decision-makers have not occurred in other countries.

Just as telling as percentage measures of discretionary-release authority is the looseness with which prison-release agencies exercise their power in practice. In the United States, parole-release decisions are unpredictable and patterns of decisions are highly changeable over time.[31] There is no substantive or procedural regularity to speak of. Decision criteria are open-ended, usually allowing the board to readjudicate all the factors originally considered by the sentencing court, plus additional considerations—like the infamously vague question of "readiness for release."

Decisional instruments and parole guidelines, where they exist, are advisory and unenforceable, and the boards' decisions are effectively unreviewable. Indeed, important decision tools such as guidelines or risk assessments are rarely shared with prisoners, who have no meaningful ability to contest the evidence or evaluations in their dossiers. Victim input to parole boards, which research has shown to make denials of release more likely, is generally held confidential, too. In many states, release decisions are made by one or two board members without consultation with each other or with the board as a whole, and it is common knowledge that individual board members have dramatically different approaches when performing their jobs (Rhine, Petersilia, and Reitz 2017; Reitz 2014; Roberts 2012; American Law Institute 2011, appendix B).

American parole boards are supremely powerful institutions. In a recent count, 347 individuals served as members of paroling agencies across the United States as a whole (Paparozzi and Caplan 2009). This small group wields greater power over the duration of prison terms than legislators, judges, prosecutors, corrections officials, or anyone else in the criminal justice system.[32] The long-term prison policy of indeterminate states is thus (and has been) dominated by parole-release decision-making—a fact that has gone almost totally unremarked in the "mass incarceration" literature.[33]

At the same time, parole boards are exceedingly weak agencies in terms of status, political insulation, and members' job security. Most boards are made up of gubernatorial appointments, and members are easily removed by the governor. One member of the Arkansas parole board explained the "most obvious" reality of this setup: "If the governor likes you, you might get to keep your job" (Arkansas Times Staff and Max Brantley 2005). In the vast majority of states, there are no required statutory qualifications for appointment to the parole board (Ruhland, Rhine, Robey, and Mitchell 2017), so members lack the professional standing of other key decision-makers.[34] Turnover rates are high, even among chairs, and only some of this is voluntary. Members or entire boards have been forced to resign after a single high-profile crime committed by a released prisoner. In the wake of episodes like these, firings or no, release rates plummet (Schwartzapfel 2015).[35]

The combination of great discretion to make prison policy and minimal institutional clout has been a formula for disaster. The parole-release decision point across America is dominated by risk aversion, which I sometimes visualize as an oppressive cloud of humidity in every hearing room. A parole board member *never* takes a personal risk by voting to deny release and *always* takes a chance when letting someone out. While this is a long-recognized problem (e.g., Morris 1974), it has gotten worse over the past several decades. In a 2015 national survey, parole board chairs nominated political vulnerability and pressure toward minimization of all risk as one of the most important problems confronting the field today (Ruhland, Rhine, Robey, and Mitchell 2017). Even in states with good-quality decisional and risk-assessment instruments, parole board members depart from recommendations to release far more often than from recommendations to deny release (e.g., Colorado Division of Criminal Justice and Colorado State Board of Parole 2013).

Contrary to the romanticized vision of US parole systems as "giving breaks" to large numbers of offenders, actual practices have run a different course. Indeed, one major cause of mass incarceration was a nationwide shift among discretionary prison-release agencies toward lower release rates. From the late twentieth century, most paroling states have been high-incarceration jurisdictions when compared with "determinate" states that have done away with discretionary release. Nine out of 10 states with the highest prison populations at the peak of the prison boom were paroling states and not determinate states. The indeterminate states also had the greatest increments of prison growth dating back two or three decades (American Law Institute 2011). An American Law Institute report compared the total amount of prison growth experienced by all 50 states from 1980 to 2009, according to the type of sentencing system in each state, as displayed in Figure I.3.

The case of American parole systems as an instance of AECP is largely the story of parole's causal connections to mass incarceration, which derive from a set of legal and institutional arrangements that are peculiarly American. Without the high degree of indeterminacy in prison-release decision making that has existed throughout most of the United States, and the political weakness of parole boards, the nation's overall incarceration rates would be substantially lower today.

What would it take for the United States to rejoin the Western mainstream in parole practices? The task would be easier than for probation because parole-release and revocation decisions are concentrated in single agencies

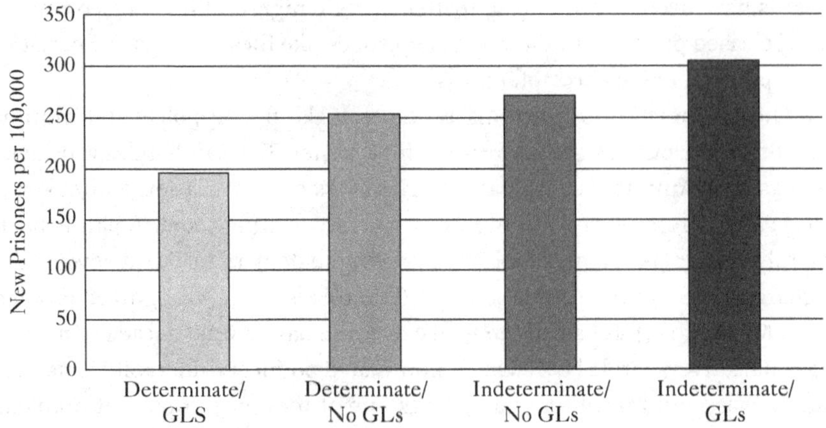

FIGURE 1.3 Per Capita Prison Growth by Sentencing System Type, 1980–2009
Source: Sourcebook of Criminal Justice Statistics Online. Table 6.29. 2012. http://www.albany.edu/sourcebook/pdf/t6292012.pdf.

with only 4 to 14 board members per state. This provides a ready focal point for system change. Outright abolition of discretionary parole release has already been pursued by roughly one-third of the states—an option that has been endorsed by the American Bar Association (1994) and the American Law Institute (2011). Retention of state parole boards with significant reform is also possible but has never been tried. For a comprehensive plan, see Rhine, Petersilia, and Reitz (2016).

Economic Sanctions

Although little noticed, the use and severity of economic criminal penalties in the United States have rocketed upward in the last few decades along with most other forms of criminal punishment. This is a badly under-researched and under-theorized area of American penality.[36] There is no readily available statistic, like an incarceration rate, that indicates the average severity of economic penalties across different states and countries or changes in severity over time. And in order to estimate the practical severity of fines, forfeitures, restitution, costs, and fees we would have to know a great deal more about defendants' means to pay and whether they can pay while still living at a reasonable subsistence level (see American Law Institute 2017, § 6.04(6) & Comment).

Despite a shortage of statistics, there is much suggestive evidence that AECP extends to financial sanctions.

First, we know that economic penalties have been rapidly expanding in the United States since the 1980s, albeit with large variations across states and counties.[37] There has been a sustained uptick in fine amounts, asset forfeitures, and a congeries of costs, fees, and assessments levied against criminal offenders.[38] At least some of the growth is due to the fact that the criminal justice agencies that impose and/or collect these monies are often entitled to keep the funds for their own budgets and expenses, or the funds are used as revenue for their home municipalities. The systematic soaking of the poor in Ferguson, Missouri is only one of many examples (see, e.g., US Department of Justice 2015; Logan and Wright 2014; Alper and Ruhland 2016a).

In addition, across all 50 states, there has been a wave of constitutional and statutory provisions that mandate or authorize victim restitution as part of criminal sentences (Tobolowsky et al. 2010, 155–57). Efforts at collection and enforcement have also intensified, including the piling on of interest and late fees (Bannon, Nagrecha, and Diller 2010).

The ballooning of economic penalties has overlapped with decades of growing income inequality in America. If we imagine a growth curve for the cumulative effect of all these obligations, and their real impact on the already-poor, the slope would be upward with a vengeance for the past three decades or so. And as illustrated in the US Department of Justice's Ferguson Report (2015), disadvantaged minority communities have been hit the hardest. So much fits the AECP pattern.

With caution, we can also posit that other countries do not tax offenders as exuberantly as the United States does.[39] While some European countries have boosted their use of fines in recent decades, this has been a part of efforts to reduce the use of short prison terms.[40] Low probation supervision rates in Europe may also owe something to the use of fines as default punishments for low-level offenses. Scandinavian countries have developed "day fine" systems that assess proportionate financial penalties according to the wealth, earning power, and obligations of each defendant.[41] At least in some legal systems, therefore, the application of monetary sanctions shows greater sensitivity to defendants' means than is commonly true in the United States.

If America is distinctive in the ways described, it does not add up to a good program. Offenders under the jurisdiction of criminal courts may be the worst of all candidates to be designated as special taxpayers, no matter how great the need to make up shortfalls in funding for police, the courts, defense services, and correctional programming. Convicted offenders by and large come from the lowest rungs of the economic ladder and are struggling with the stark employment-market disadvantages that come with criminal convictions.[42] Politically, offenders may be attractive targets for special taxation because they are unpopular, tainted by a finding of guilt, and disenfranchised; but American tax policy is distorted when they are exploited or driven into financial hopelessness. Heavy economic sanctions are regressive taxation taken to an extreme (see American Law Institute 2017, § 6.04 & Comment).

Nor does any of this serve traditional criminal justice priorities. Revenue generation is not a legitimate purpose of criminal law, and it is a goal that is antagonistic to the usual concerns of criminal sentencing. Certainly, rehabilitation and offender reintegration do not play major roles in the creation and administration of financial penalties in the United States.[43]

Several bodies of research into desistance from crime suggest that economic sanctions, when overdone, are criminogenic.[44] Falling behind in payments often leads to further sanctions that deepen the hole for offenders, including suspension of driver's licenses, lengthened periods of community supervision, arrest warrants, and sentence revocations.[45] Unrealistic or heavy financial obligations interfere with offenders' abilities to obtain credit, pay for transportation (often essential to employment), and pursue educational opportunities. Damaged credit can make it hard to find housing or land a job. Processes for the collection of criminal justice debt can also disrupt employment relationships—as when garnishment of wages is used—or may simply reduce the incentives of ex-offenders to earn in the legitimate economy. Also, if the burdens of criminal justice debt make it impossible for a husband or father to contribute his share to household expenses or even his own living expenses, the sentencing system places strain on the bonds of stable family life (Eaglin 2015; Bannon, Nagrecha, and Diller 2010).[46]

The bulk of social science research indicates that decent housing, strong families, and satisfying work are among the most important protective factors associated with desistance from crime.[47] Criminal justice policies that block or dilute these protective factors are profoundly misconceived.

A long list of changes would be needed for the United States to reform its use of economic penalties. Financial sanctions add up to big money for the police, courts, corrections agencies, and private corrections providers. Police and prosecutors will go to the mat to defend asset forfeitures, for example, which are among the worst abuses (American Law Institute 2017, § 6.04D). Victims' rights groups are powerful, and restitution is the most broadly accepted part of their agenda (Ruback 2015). Expect huge resistance—and who politically will stand for criminal offenders, overwhelmingly poor, who are caught in the system?

One large step forward would be to create an enforceable standard of means testing at sentencing, with an across-the-board rule that no economic penalty of any kind may be imposed unless after payment (of the total amount or scheduled installments) the defendant would still have sufficient economic resources to provide reasonable support for himself and his family.[48] This rule was adopted as part of the new Model Penal Code's recommendations to state legislatures nationwide (American Law Institute 2017, § 6.04(6) &

Comment).[49] If implemented, it would be significantly more muscular than the weak "ability-to-pay" protection in constitutional law.[50] Given the financial standing of most defendants in state criminal courts, a "reasonable subsistence" standard would drastically cut back on imposition of financial penalties in the aggregate and would foreclose the worst abuses in states' and local governments' current practices.

Collateral Consequences of Conviction

Across the United States, the number of civil legal consequences of conviction had dwindled to historic lows in the 1960s[51] but soon began to grow by leaps and bounds (Klingele, Roberts, and Love 2013). Today, "[p]eople convicted of crimes are not subject to just one collateral consequence, or even a handful. Instead, hundreds and sometimes thousands of such consequences apply under federal and state constitutional provisions, statutes, administrative regulations, and ordinances" (Chin 2012). As summarized by the American Law Institute (2017, 238),

> [I]n 1962, the primary consequence of conviction was a fine, probation, or a period of incarceration. Collateral consequences were limited in most cases to a temporary loss of the right to vote, hold public office, serve on a jury, and testify in court. Since then collateral consequences have proliferated, and now include mandatory deportation, inclusion on a public registry, loss of access to public housing and benefits, financial aid ineligibility, and occupational licensing restrictions. Some of these consequences last for the duration of the convicted individual's life.

Professor Michael Pinard has said that, "Given the breadth and permanence of collateral consequences, [convicted] individuals are perhaps more burdened and marginalized by a criminal record today than at any point in U.S. history" (2010a, 1219).[52] Nonetheless these sanctions fly below radar because the individual unit of punishment appears minor; they are far from the stuff of television drama.

The vast majority of these collateral sanctions are technically classified as "civil" and "regulatory" measures rather than "criminal punishments"—but they must be included in an overall accounting of the harshness with which Americans are treated after the conviction of a criminal offense. They are laws that make it harder, and often more humiliating, to live—and they persist long after criminal sentences expire.[53] Margaret Love (2015, 250) has observed that "[a]s a practical matter . . . collateral consequences have become more important to many criminal defendants than any penalty likely to be imposed by the court."

Not only have collateral consequences increased in their effects on *individual* offenders but their societal effects have been doubly magnified because the number of people carrying criminal convictions has itself exploded. While something approaching 7 million people are serving a criminal sentence on any given day in the United States, it is estimated that 10 times that number have a record of prior criminal conviction (Jacobs 2015; Rodriguez and Emsellem 2011). With such large numbers, the legal system is not targeting hard-core criminals with its civil restraints. The majority of people who suffer under collateral consequences have never been to prison—a conviction followed by a probationary or suspended sentence also triggers the cascade of sanctions (Chin 2012).

Collateral consequences of conviction in the United States appear to exhibit the hallmarks of AECP: they greatly expanded in the United States in the late decades of the twentieth century, in parallel with prison and jail populations, probation, parole, and economic penalties. They are racially disparate in their effects and hit the poorest and most disadvantaged ex-offenders the hardest (Alexander 2010; Pinard 2010b). If they reflect a criminal justice philosophy, it is one of punishment and incapacitation, with little regard for net effects on recidivism rates and public safety.

While the number of comparative policy analyses is small, they have concluded that America has earned exceptional status in the domain of collateral consequences when compared with other Western democracies (Pinard 2010b; see Demleitner, this volume). As Nora Demleitner puts it in Chapter 11,

> The starkest differences between collateral sanctions in Europe and the United States are the breadth, automaticity, and often the lengths of the consequences that befall offenders in the United States even after they have served a criminal justice sentence. . . . Even though sanctions generally have also become harsher in Europe in recent decades, collateral sanctions remain more narrowly targeted, less comprehensive, usually imposed directly and publicly, not retroactive, and time-limited.

Moreover, legally instantiated collateral consequences float in the community alongside powerful social and economic forces of exclusion that operate privately, without legal mandate or encouragement, as when an employer turns down a job applicant, a parolee cannot rent an apartment, or a person with an arrest or conviction on his or her record cannot find a college willing to admit him or her. All of these informal disabilities are especially *enabled* by American laws, however, which make criminal-record information freely available to the public, including private vendors who gather and maintain databases that cannot practicably be corrected when wrong, or expunged when outdated (Jacobs 2015).

Taken as a broad category, collateral consequences affect more lives in America on a daily basis than any other repercussion of a criminal conviction. If the death penalty is the small-numbers phenomenon of AECP—a relative drop in the bucket—then collateral consequences are a sea. Indeed, they suggest that the greatest and most persistent social impacts of an overgrown criminal justice system may be low on the scale of punitiveness of intervention. Racially stilted stop-and-frisk and traffic stops ("walking" and "driving" while black), fines and fees extracted overwhelmingly from the poor, extraordinarily high community supervision rates with decreasing emphasis on services—these are all low-level uses of governmental coercion when compared with capital punishment and imprisonment, yet they touch many more millions of lives.

While collateral consequences have been on the American criminal law reform agenda for two decades, the tool of comparative analysis has not been exploited. It would be useful to know if *any* other democratic society approaches the United States in the disabilities it imposes on ex-offenders or the degree to which it facilitates private discrimination. If you ask around, at international conferences or when working abroad, the usual answer is "no"; but documentation of America's outlier status would be helpful.

It would be a staggering job to limit or repeal the thousands of statutes, across state and federal codes, that make up the confusing jumble of collateral consequences now in force. The American Bar Association (2016) undertook merely to *compile* the relevant laws in state and federal codes, and it proved a bottomless task. Any program of direct reconsideration of these provisions, one at a time, would make a good example in the legal dictionary under "piecemeal reform."

A more sweeping approach could be to give sentencing judges the power to grant relief from collateral consequences, either at sentencing or at a designated later time (American Law Institute 2017, § 6x.04)—but this is a responsibility many judges do not want or feel qualified to discharge. In fact, for this particular instance of AECP, no one is at the wheel. There is paralyzing uncertainty about who should be professionally responsible for comprehending this subfield of criminal punishment, let alone administering it in a prosocial way.

AECP in Broader Focus: Serious Violent Crime

America has long been an outlier among developed democracies for its high rates of homicide and serious violent offending more generally (see Roth, this volume; Lappi-Seppälä, this volume). This is not true for all crimes across the board. Zimring and Hawkins (1997) drew a distinction between "crime in general" and the small percentage of criminal acts that are lethal or near-lethal in their effects. The United States does not have more "general" crime than other Western societies when corrected for population—but it has considerably more homicides, near-homicides, and serious woundings.

American serious violent crime rates surged from the early 1960s through the early 1970s and then remained at very high levels for two decades—a 20-year period one might call the "high-crime plateau" (Wilson 1995). After 1993 and through 2014, American crime rates dropped or remained stable—the "crime drop" period—returning the United States to lower volumes of crime not seen since the 1960s. Even today, however, American homicide rates remain high by Western standards. To illustrate, Figure I.4 depicts the crime drop in homicide for seven English-speaking countries from 1994 to 2014. Even after 20 years of remarkable decline, the 2014 homicide rate in the

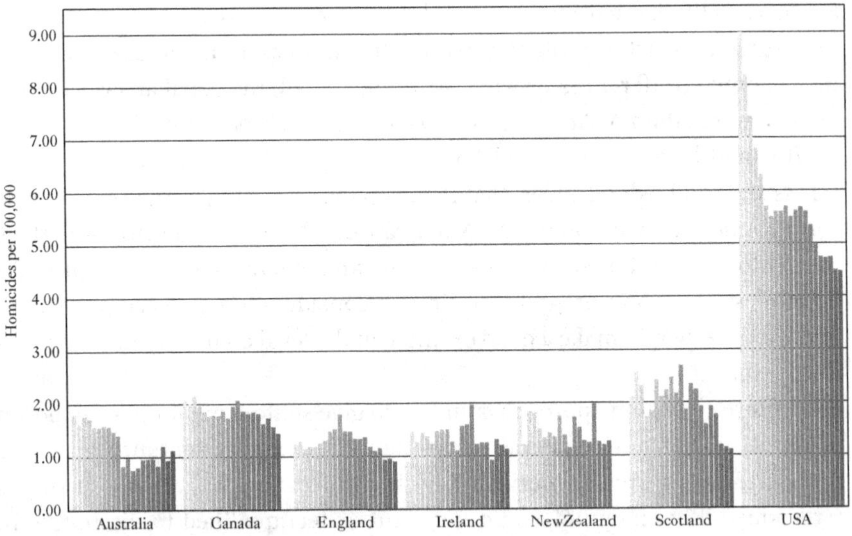

FIGURE I.4 Homicide Rates, Seven English-Speaking Countries during "Crime Drop" Decades, 1994–2014 or Most Recent

Source: Institute of Criminology and Legal Policy, University of Helsinki. 2016. Data provided in personal correspondence by Martti Lehti, June 22, 2016.

United States remained about three to four times that of Australia, Canada, England, Ireland, New Zealand, and Scotland.[54]

In all of American history of crime and punishment, one of the most pivotal decades was the 1960s or, more precisely, the years from the early 1960s through the early 1970s. To understand the American milieu of criminal justice policy through the late twentieth and early twenty-first centuries, this is the critical juncture. I will call it the "crime-spike" period.

US homicide rates doubled in the compressed span of 10 years, which is even worse than it sounds. Homicide trends tend to be a bellwether of trends in other categories of serious violent offending. According to the FBI's yearly Uniform Crime Reports, other frightening crimes were rising even faster than homicide. Figure I.5 examines the changing rates of the four most serious reported crimes from 1962 to 1974. To facilitate comparisons, the 1962 rates

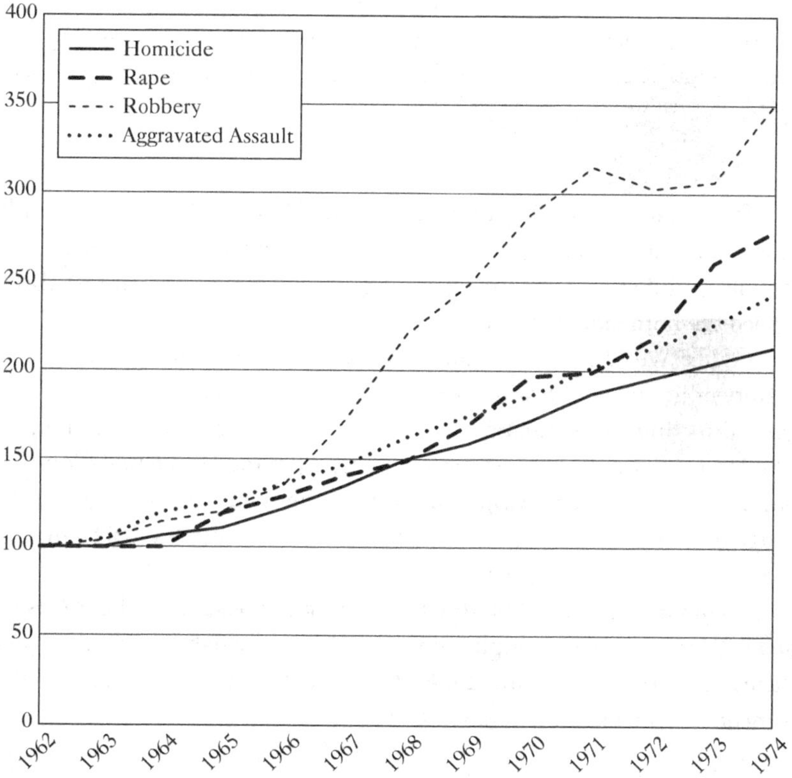

FIGURE I.5 Crime Spike: Four Serious Violent Crimes, 1962–1974 (Standardized to 100 in 1962)

Source: Federal Bureau of Investigation. Uniform Crime Reporting Statistics, UCR Data Online. 2017. https://www.ucrdatatool.gov/Search/Crime/State/RunCrimeStatebyState.cfm.

FIGURE I.6 Homicide Rates, Seven English-Speaking Countries, 1962–1972
Source: Institute of Criminology and Legal Policy, University of Helsinki. 2016. Data provided in personal correspondence by Martti Lehti, June 22, 2016.

of all four offenses are standardized to 100. While homicide increased by a factor of 2.1 over the period, the reported robbery rate increased by much more (3.5 times), while rape (2.75 times) and aggravated assault (2.4 times) also outstripped the homicide increase.[55]

No other Western nation had a comparable experience. Figure I.6 tells the story of homicide rates in seven English-speaking countries from 1962 to 1972. Correcting for population, the annual number of *additional* homicides in the United States from 1962 to 1972 was 4.4 per 100,000 population (rising from 4.6 to 9.0 per 100,000). Among the other countries in Figure I.5, the average increment of change was 0.4 (less than one-tenth the US change); the largest was in Canada: 0.9 per 100,000.

In an ill-fated juxtaposition, the frightening crime spike of the 1960s coincided with a time of wide-ranging liberalization in the nation's criminal justice policies. As surveyed by Ruth and Reitz (2003, 70–72), major markers of this advancement included the following:

- 1960–1972 was one of the rare periods since the invention of American penitentiaries in which the nation's imprisonment rate declined substantially.
- Through the 1960s, the US Supreme Court issued a remarkable series of decisions that asserted federal power over state criminal justice systems

and placed new federal constitutional limits upon state criminal courts, juvenile courts, and police activities nationwide.

- The lower federal courts became significantly involved in overturning state court convictions through federal habeas corpus review.
- The use of capital punishment in the United States dwindled through the 1960s and early 1970s, partly due to Supreme Court intervention, falling to zero executions from 1968 to 1976. Compared with any prior decade in the twentieth century, the 1960s saw the flowering of a death penalty–abolition movement.
- The liberalization of criminal justice policies was strongly associated with the civil rights movement, which itself moved ahead with particular momentum in the 1960s. Charges of racial discrimination in policing, prosecution, and sentencing were broadly voiced and taken seriously by large segments of the American public.
- The gun control movement in America became more visible and assertive than ever before in the nation's history.
- In the early 1970s, the federal courts became active—sometimes to the point of micromanagement—in regulating conditions of confinement in prisons and jails at the federal, state, and local levels.
- Laws against drug possession, public drunkenness, and public order offenses were relaxed in the 1960s and early 1970s, as was the enforcement of those laws. Some were declared unconstitutional by the federal courts.
- Legal changes in case processing and courtroom procedure during the 1960s focused almost exclusively on the rights of criminal defendants and either ignored or worked against the interests of crime victims.
- The 1960s and early 1970s were marked by broad-based enthusiasm, among policymakers and criminological experts, in favor of programs for the rehabilitation of criminals and social welfare programs aimed at poor and crime-ridden communities. The Presidential Crime Commission declared that "Warring on poverty, inadequate housing and unemployment, is warring on crime. A civil rights law is a law against crime. Money for schools is money against crime. Medical, psychiatric, and family-counseling services are services against crime. More broadly and most importantly every effort to improve life in America's 'inner cities' is an effort against crime."[56]

Of course, the convulsions of the 1960s reached far beyond the criminal justice system.[57] Numerous destabilizing forces reared up during that turbulent decade—including many that invited a conservative backlash.[58] Unique in

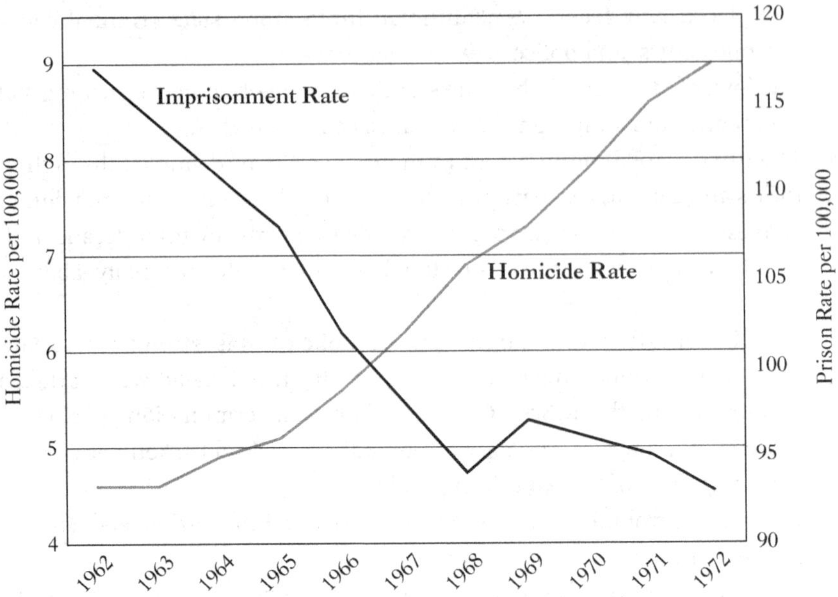

FIGURE I.7 Scissors Effect: US Homicide and Prison Rates, 1962–1972
Source: Bureau of Justice Statistics. *Sourcebook of Criminal Justice Statistics, 1999*. Washington, DC: Government Printing Office, tables 3.120 and 6.26. 2000.

America, however, was the collision between an especially horrific violent crime spike and a robust liberal revolution in criminal justice law and policy. Virtually every element of the leftist reform agenda was moving forward—but the seeming effects were awful.[59]

Figure I.7 gives one graphic illustration of the train wreck. It displays the criss-crossing of prison rates and homicide on the *y* axes. We could just as easily draw similar pictures using other serious violent crimes and alternative indicia of the increasing "softness" of American crime policies.

By the mid-1970s, the pillars of liberal criminal justice ideology collapsed with unceremonial abruptness. Robert Martinson's 1974 meta-analysis of rehabilitative programs concluded that most did not work or had only small effects—and that some programs made criminals worse. The study made a tremendous splash and spawned the "nothing works" outlook that towered over the field for the next 20 or 30 years. In 1975, James Q. Wilson's *Thinking about Crime* repudiated every major tenet of the liberal criminal justice philosophy of the 1960s. The book became the most influential academic work in the history of American crime policy and served as an intellectual blueprint for conservative reaction (Ruth and Reitz 2003). Wilson skewered rehabilitation, promoted deterrence and incapacitation, and declared that his program was firmly on the moral high ground. The book concluded (at p. 209) with the following summation:

> Wicked people exist. Nothing avails except to set them apart from innocent people. And many people, neither wicked nor innocent, but watchful, dissembling, and calculating of their opportunities, ponder our reaction to wickedness as a cue to what they might profitably do. We have trifled with the wicked, made sport of the innocent, and encouraged the calculators. Justice suffers, and so do we all.

Sentiments like these granted permission to conservative leaders and a frightened public to see criminals as unchangeable and evil, or venal and calculating, and fully deserving of harsh treatment when necessary to protect society.

What made everything worse was that, after serious violent crime rates had shot up so precipitously through the early 1970s, they *remained* at those elevated levels for the next 20 years. Figure I.8 compares the homicide crime spike (1962–1972) with the homicide "plateau" (1972–1992). Consistently high rates after 1972 produced more crime and victimization by far than the spike of the 1960s. In addition, persistent high rates can be more conducive of outrage and despair than spiking rates because they suggest a permanent equilibrium. As the crime spike settled into the crime plateau, America's self-image became one of a "high-crime society" (Garland 2001b). In major cities, perceptions of disorder and personal danger were ingrained in daily life (Wilson and Kelling 1982). By the early 1990s, there had been no stretch of time in the past 30 years that did not feature sharply increasing crime rates or rates that were "stuck" at peak levels.

After three decades in the making, it took a while for the high-crime mentality to ease in Americans' psyches. When the crime drop began in 1993, it was the most unanticipated societal transformation since the crime spike, and it did not achieve credibility as a sustained phenomenon for 10 years or so. (This is about the same period of delay as between the beginning of the crime spike in the early 1960s and the solidification of the get-tough orientation in the early 1970s.) Indeed, even as the US crime drop was gaining steam, respected national leaders and criminologists were warning the nation to expect a "bloodbath" through the 1990s and into the 2000s as a large demographic of "juvenile super-predators" aged into the prime of their criminal careers (DiIulio 1995; Fox 1995; Bennett, DiIulio, and Walters 1996; Haberman 2014). *Newsweek* (1995) reported that, "Criminologists are already warning that the United States can expect another wave of violent crime in the coming decade, and some say it will be much worse than the

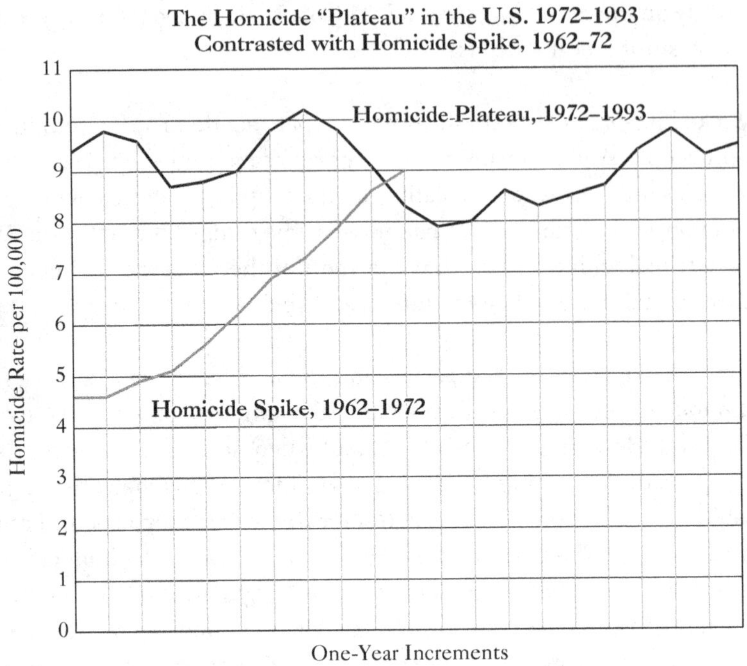

FIGURE 1.8 The Homicide "Plateau" in the United States, 1972–1993; Contrasted with Homicide Spike, 1962–1972

Source: Federal Bureau of Investigation. Uniform Crime Reporting Statistics, UCR Data Online. 2017. https://www.ucrdatatool.gov/Search/Crime/State/RunCrimeStatebyState.cfm.

one that is now subsiding." James Q. Wilson, by then the nation's preeminent political scientist and an adviser of presidents, urged the public to "Get ready" (1995, 507).[60]

By the early 2000s, however, serious people were taking notice of the crime drop. The search for explanations became an academic specialty—including, most famously, the theory that the establishment of women's right to abortion was the most significant factor (Donohue and Levitt 2001; see generally Blumstein and Wallman 2000).

If American exceptionalism in crime was one proximate cause of the country's long season of punitive expansionism, then an era of lower crime rates should create room in political dialogue and public opinion for a loosening of those policies. This is not likely to happen in year-by-year correspondence with drops in homicide and other serious violent offenses, but as the culture gradually assimilates new expectations about criminality and the vulnerability of the average citizen.

Over time, one would expect to see a tentative slowing, stopping, and reversal of the growth in prison, probation, and parole populations and conversation about more of the same. One would expect a nascent awareness of the burdens on the already-impoverished when economic sanctions and collateral consequences of conviction push them further into hopelessness. One would expect a return to the days when the excesses of the criminal justice system were prominently linked in the public mind with issues of racial injustice. One would expect greater and more successful political activism from the inner cities as the majority culture evinces somewhat more willingness to listen. If any of the above things were to happen, they would be good signs.

For those who would advocate major changes, however, one serious problem will be the difficulty of ground-level, unglamorous implementation. As of this writing, there has been a change in the rhetoric of criminal justice reform in the United States, but it is mostly talk. Because of our crazy-quilt federal system and our peculiar empowerment of local governments, there are uncounted efforts to be launched—each requiring calibrated adjustments for local circumstances—and hordes of people to persuade in the microcultural pockets throughout America. Local governments may be particularly hard targets, if Lacey and Soskice (Chapter 1) are right that political realities at the local level lean naturally toward policies that drive crime rates *and* punitive severity upward at the same time. Even with the crime drop fueling changes in politics and public attitudes, the problems of logistics in trying to access so many different fiefdoms should not be underestimated. It is nearly impossible to *overestimate* them.

In addition, pinning reformist optimism to a new "low plateau" of American crime rates is not a wholly defensible way to plan for the future. Just because the nation experienced a historic crime drop from 1993 to 2014 does not mean that we can count on crime to continue going down or even stay where it is. The FBI reports for 2015, for example, show homicide rates rising quickly in many major cities, including Chicago, St. Louis, and Baltimore, with a 10 percent increase in homicide nationwide from 2014 to 2015 (Federal Bureau of Investigation 2016, table 1). Preliminary reports for 2016 foreshadow a continuing upward trend in serious violent offending (Federal Bureau of Investigation 2017, table 1).

What is the plan if we enter a new crime spike? An optimist must hope that Americans have learned something from the societal catastrophes of the past 40 years. *Constructive* strategies to fight crime in the coming years will deserve greater attention than they received during the last panic over rising and sustained crime rates (e.g., policing reform, gun control, early childhood care for those who can't afford it, reinvestment in public schools, renovation of social welfare programs). The 1960s sentiment that "warring on poverty is warring on crime" deserves a more genuine test drive than it received in the twentieth century. We now have reason to believe that successful efforts to "war on crime" will reinforce a "war on mass punishment."

NOTES

1. This is not offered as a full accounting but is broader than the usual and explores relationships between sanctioning policies that may otherwise be missed.
2. Criticism that America's incarceration rates were too high dates back at least to the 1960s and 1970s but was limited to law reformers and academics, some of whom assumed the nation was on a natural and enlightened course to dramatically cut back in the use of prisons and jails (President's Commission on Law Enforcement and Criminal Justice 1967; American Friends Service Committee 1971; National Advisory Comm'n on Criminal Justice Standards and Goals 1973; Frankel 1973). Before the 2000s, concern over incarceration rates had virtually no resonance in public or political discourse—or if it did, it was in the form of stout calls for the *greater* use of imprisonment to reduce crime rates (Wilson 1975; Bennett, DiIulio, and Walters 1996).
3. Technically, America's incarceration rates are not so distinctive if we count countries with populations no larger than a small city. For instance, the World Prison Brief listed Seychelles—an island nation off the coast of East Africa—with a 2014 incarceration rate of 799 per 100,000 (735 prisoners total). At the time, Seychelles had an estimated general population of only 92,000. Another diminutive country within striking distance of world leadership is St. Kitts and Nevis, a Caribbean island nation reported to have 334 prisoners and a prison rate of 607 per 100,000 in 2014—which placed it in third position worldwide for that year (World Prison Brief 2016). It is also doubtful the United States is the world's all-time carceral leader by historic standards. Scholars have documented a higher incarceration rate for Stalinist Russia, at least twice the peak US rate (Belova and Gregory 2009, 465–66; estimating, depending on whom you count, an incarceration rate of 1,558 or 2,605 per 100,000).
4. High-profile members of Right on Crime have included Bob Barr, William J. Bennett, Jeb Bush, Chuck Colson, Monica Crowley, John J. DiIulio Jr., Newt Gingrich, Asa Hutchinson, George Kelling, Edwin Meese III, Pat Nolan, Grover Norquist, and Rick Perry (Right on Crime 2011, 2016).
5. The US "imprisonment rate" captures only inmates in state and federal prisons; more than 30 percent of inmates are held in local jails on any given day (Minton and Zeng 2015; Carson 2015). In American discourse, "incarceration rates" are defined as the sum of prison plus jail confinement rates. In other countries,

"incarceration rates" and "imprisonment rates" tend to be synonymous terms; other jurisdictions do not follow America's idiosyncratic division of confinement populations into prisons and jails or do not bifurcate their reporting of statistics.

6. New Zealand is the Western nation with the highest incarceration rate after the United States (World Prison Brief 2016).
7. Russia has significantly decreased its prison populations and rates in the past 15–20 years. From 1999 to 2001 alone, the Russian incarceration rate fell from 730 per 100,000 to 644, due in part to mass amnesties (Sentencing Project 2001, 1). By 2016, the Russian rate had fallen to 453 per 100,000 (World Prison Brief 2016).
8. England and Wales' total incarceration rate was 146 per 100,000 in 2016 (World Prison Brief 2016). US prison-plus-jail rates in 2014 added up to 711 per 100,000, a total of 2,305,908 incarcerated people on any one day (Carson 2015; Minton and Zeng 2015).
9. This estimate was based on the national prison rate in 2001, which was nearly identical to the national rate in 2014 (see Bonczar 2003, 8; Carson 2015, 8, table 6).
10. Ostrom et al. (2002); Bazelon (2005); American Law Institute (2017, § 6B.09).
11. In fact, one of the most common concerns about the use of risk-assessment instruments as prison diversion tools is that they will benefit whites more than blacks. The ethical dilemma is far worse if risk-assessment technology is used to increase the severity of prison sentences compared to the status quo (Harcourt 2006; Starr 2014). On the other hand, concerns about racial bias in actuarial risk assessment have not often been tested with empirical rigor, and the best study to date indicates that those fears may be exaggerated. Skeem and Lowenkamp (2016, 700) studied the postconviction risk assessment (PCRA) currently used in the federal system and concluded the following:

    > [T]hese results indicate that risk assessment is not "race assessment." First there is little evidence of test bias for the PCRA. The instrument strongly predicts re-arrest for both Black and White offenders. Regardless of group membership, a PCRA score has essentially the same meaning, i.e., same probability of recidivism.

12. Figures are roughly based on current incarcerated populations.
13. With 28 executions in 2015, America fell last in the top five for raw numbers of executions (Amnesty International 2016, 63), but several other countries had *much* higher rates of execution per capita.
14. From 2006 to 2015, the National Weather Service reported that an average of 31 people per year have been killed by lightning strikes and an average of 310 people have been injured or killed each year (National Weather Service 2016).
15. The most executions in the past 70 years occurred in 1999 (98 executions), but still only 19 states participated—and nine of these states held only a single

execution (University at Albany, Hindelang Criminal Justice Research Center 2012, table 6.85.2012).

16. Stephen Bright (2008, 374) reported that "[m]ore people sentenced to death in Harris County [Texas] have been executed than from any state except Texas itself." For reports from other states, see Rosenberg (1995, 22: Pennsylvania), Willing and Fields (1999, A1: Ohio), and Paternoster (2005, A19: Maryland).
17. Little comparable research has been done for noncapital cases, in part because race-of-victim data are rarely included in official records. A handful of studies suggest that the devaluation of black victims relative to whites also occurs in cases of violent and sexual assaults not resulting in death (Spohn and Spears 1996; Walsh 1987; LaFree 1989).
18. *McCleskey* was a 5–4 decision. Justice Lewis Powell, the swing vote and author of the majority opinion, later told his biographer that he regretted his vote in *McCleskey* and would change it if he could (Jeffries 2001, 451).
19. Japan held three executions in 2015, for a rate of 2.7 per 100 million. The 2015 US rate without Texas and Missouri was a "Japan-like" 3.1.
20. Further down the rankings in 2015 were Saudi Arabia (406 per 100 million, 128 total) and Pakistan (170 per 100 million, 326 total).
21. In 1965, the number of probationers in the United States was estimated to be about 432,000, which translated into a probation supervision rate of 222 per 100,000 general population (Ruth and Reitz 2003, 24, figure 1.4; Cahalan 1986, 181, table 7-9A). By 2014, the total number had grown to 3,864,100, or a rate of 1,212 per 100,000—more than a fivefold increase in per capita supervision (Kaeble, Maruschak, and Bonczar 2015, 1). This is uncannily similar to the increase in per capita incarceration over the last several decades.
22. "Revocation," in US terminology, occurs when a probationer is found to have violated one or more of the conditions of his or her probation sentence and on this ground is sent to prison or jail (see Mitchell et al. 2014).
23. American probation populations are racially disparate but not to the same degree as those in prisons and jails. While about 13 percent of the US population, African Americans made up 36 percent of all prisoners in 2014, 35 percent of all jail inmates, and 30 percent of probationers. Similarly, Hispanics accounted for 22 percent of all prisoners, 15 percent of all jail inmates, and 13 percent of probationers. In contrast, whites are more heavily represented among probationers. Whites made up 54 percent of US probation populations in 2014, 34 percent of state prisoners, and 47 percent of jail inmates (Carson 2015; Minton and Zeng 2015; Kaeble, Maruschak, and Bonczar 2015). In other words, as the severity of sanction type increases, so does the relative share of people of color exposed to that sanction, while the exposure of whites declines.
24. This finding is based on statistics from 39 reporting European countries, compiled by the Council of Europe for 2013 (Aebi and Chopin 2015). Depending

on how one interprets the Council of Europe data, the ratio between US and European probation rates is probably closer to 9:1 (see van Zyl Smit and Corda, this volume). The Robina report was based on the most conservative possible calculations of US versus European rates—that is, it counted several ambiguous categories of European offenders who might not meet the US Department of Justice definition of being "on probation" (Alper, Corda, and Reitz 2016) but, for example, might instead be prison releasees or unsupervised pretrial defendants.

25. In some states, it is not unusual for defendants to decline the offer of a probation sentence and opt to serve out their prison time as the easier route to a clean slate. Likewise, some probationers volunteer for revocation in order to "max out" their prison sentence and bypass the difficulties of community supervision (Ruhland, Robey, Corbett, and Reitz 2017).
26. As with the comparative probation study, the calculation of a 5:1 ratio is conservative. All ambiguous categories of offenders in Council of Europe data were "credited" to European post-prison supervision rates if there was any doubt that those offenders would meet a definition of parole supervision comparable to that used in the American Bureau of Justice Statistics counts (Corda, Alper, and Reitz 2016).
27. Probationers are at lower risk of failure than parolees, but there are four times as many probationers. When records are compiled at the state level, it is common to find that over 50 percent of prison admissions stem from parole and probation revocations combined.
28. The compatibility of European and American statistics on this point is open to question. The American figures do not include jail admissions or the numbers of probationers admitted to jails due to sentence violations.
29. This may have been due to excessive American optimism, in the Progressive era, about the prospects for the rehabilitation of prisoners and about the ability of parole boards to detect when rehabilitation had occurred in individual cases (see Webster and Doob, this volume; Rothman 1980).
30. See Ruhland, Rhine, Robey, and Mitchell (2017, 13–15) (in national survey, paroling authorities in six states reported that they held discretion to set minimum terms for violent, property, sex, and public order crimes; parole boards in eight states reported having such power in drug offense cases).
31. One famous study found that parole-release rates declined during state election cycles as the next election approached (cited in Travis 2002). Another study found that parole boards' generosity in granting release dropped significantly as the amount of time since members' last meal increased (Kahneman 2011, 43).
32. In addition to their releasing powers, parole boards preside over revocation decisions (returns to prison for violations of parole). Parole revocations accounted for 28 percent of all prison admissions in 2015 and a much larger percentage of prison admissions in the 1990s and 2000s (Carson and Anderson 2016; Carson

and Golinelli 2013; Jacobson 2005; Petersilia 2003). Unique among American criminal justice players, parole boards hold both "in–out" discretion and "out–in" discretion.

33. If anything, the literature tends to blame the abolition of parole-release discretion in some states as a major factor contributing to prison growth (Reitz 2006; American Law Institute 2011, 142–43 note 88).
34. While the best European systems vest prison-release discretion in judicial officers, such an arrangement is extremely rare in the United States (van Zyl Smit and Spencer 2010).
35. Episodes like this have occurred in Pennsylvania, Massachusetts, and Connecticut. For example, in Massachusetts in 2010, following the killing of a police officer by a parolee, the chair, board members who voted on his release, and the executive director resigned (Reitz 2014; Clear and Frost 2014; American Law Institute 2011, Appendix B).
36. Things may be changing. America's "mass fines" practices gained prominence post-Ferguson, where the police shooting scandal was supplemented with a report revealing "soaking the poor" and "debtors' prison" scandals. The same has been uncovered in more and more jurisdictions (Harris 2016; US Department of Justice 2015; American Civil Liberties Union 2010; Bannon, Nagrecha, and Diller 2010). In 2014, National Public Radio reported on a yearlong investigation into user fees imposed by courts and corrections agencies in a series of broadcasts called "Guilty and Charged."
37. For an excellent compilation and analysis of economic sanctions in Pennsylvania, showing average amounts that differed wildly from county to county, see Ruback and Clark (2011, 770). Ruback and Clark identified 2,629 separate economic sanctions across the state, of which 2,371 were costs and fees imposed by counties and an additional 79 were county fines (p. 767). For a study focused on Washington State, see Beckett and Harris (2008).
38. On the growing number, use, and amounts of financial sanctions in the United States, see Beckett and Harris (2010, 512); Bannon, Nagrecha, and Diller (2010, 1); Corbett (2015); Ruback and Clark (2011, 752–53). On costs, fees, and assessments, see American Law Institute (2017, § 6.04D; recommending their abolition); Ruback 2015 (same). Fines, fees, and forfeited assets often go to the municipality or agency that collects them, such as courts, prosecutors, police departments, community corrections agencies, private corrections providers, or local governments (US Department of Justice 2015; Ingraham 2015).
39. On the rarity of the imposition of criminal justice costs and fees outside the United States, see O'Malley (2011, 547–48): "Fees . . . are much less prominent outside the United States, almost never being levied for imprisonment and only in recent years being levied in some jurisdictions for victim compensation and costs of fine enforcement."

40. In present-day American culture, economic sanctions do not have much "utility" as retributive punishments. That is to say, a judge's pronouncement of a large fine delivers little retributive satisfaction to the American ear. Because of this low retributive valuation, American legal systems have not found it possible to substitute economic penalties for jail or prison terms—and it is likely they do not stand in for probationary sentences either. Instead, in American legal culture, fines, restitution, fees, and surcharges are "add-ons," rarely viewed as adequate sentences in themselves.
41. See Federal Ministry of Justice (Germany) (2007, 81): "In 2004, the sanctions given to 94% of all persons convicted under general criminal law were either fines (80.6%) or suspended prison sentences (13.7%)." Also Morris and Tonry (1990, 143–44; discussing the use of day fines in Scandinavia).
42. A large percentage are also in arrears in child support payments, including at least 20 percent of all prisoners. A collaborative investigative report by The Marshall Project and the *Washington Post* (Hager 2015) interviewed dozens of released fathers and found child support debts ranging from $10,000 to $110,000. The report observed the following:

    > [R]esearch shows that the two most important factors in a former prisoner's successful reentry into the community are employment and positive relationships with family. Both of these are hindered by the aggressive pursuit of child support arrears: Garnishing 65 percent of a father's paycheck, so he is tempted to earn cash off the books; suspending his driver's license so he can't get to work; sending him bills that are so far beyond his capacity to pay that he keeps his distance from his family. . . . "I see it all the time," [Bo] Twiggs [Director of the Upnext Program in New York City] said: "Not reengaging with the family. Noncompliance with parole and child support. Under-the-table efforts at income. Self-defeat, high anxiety, general institutional distrust. All of that is triggered by this absolutely overwhelming, impossible feeling of debt."

43. Almost no one thinks about the proportionality of economic sanctions imposed in the United States, standing alone or in combination with other penalties (American Law Institute 2017, § 6.04 & Comment). In part this is because system actors assume that most offenders will never be able to pay their economic sentence amounts in full, so "pronounced" sentences are regarded as flimsy and of doubtful weight in proportionality analysis.
44. Although there have been very few studies, empirical research suggests the same (Piquero and Jennings 2016; Pleggenkuhle 2012).
45. Under the law, probationers in most states may be revoked to prison for nonpayment (Mitchell et al. 2014), and the threat of revocation is used as a powerful collections tool. Ethnographic and interview data show that some probationers abscond, and go "on the run," when they fall hopelessly behind in their fees. At least some others turn to the criminal economy to meet their financial debts to

the justice system (see Goffman 2014; Ruhland, Robey, Corbett, and Reitz 2017). Needless to say, these are not outcomes the criminal law should be abetting.

46. In addition, when unrealistic economic penalties are visited on offenders, they can inspire feelings of despair and futility or perceptions of courts' sentences as illegitimate. None of these are desirable outcomes.

47. Strong work ties and job stability correlate with lower rates of reoffending (Sampson and Laub 1995, 140–41). The acquisition of a "satisfying job," not just any job, may have an even greater correlation with desistance (Shover 1996, 127). One study found the employment effect greatest for men over the age of 27, with no measurable effect for younger participants (Uggen 2000, 529). On housing, see National Research Council (2007, 54–55): "Released prisoners who do not have stable housing arrangements are more likely to return to prison." One widely cited study found that being married was associated with a 35 percent reduction in risk of reoffending (Sampson, Laub, and Wimer 2006, 465). Other research has discovered similar but smaller effects (Horney, Osgood, and Marshall 1995, 665; Piquero, MacDonald, and Parker 2002, 654). On the importance of family ties more generally, see National Research Council (2007, 44): "Greater contact with family during incarceration (by mail, phone, or in-person visits) is associated with lower recidivism rates. Prisoners with close family ties have lower recidivism rates than those without such attachments."

48. A frequent objection, or reason given for pessimism, is that most courts have no reliable way to find out how much money a defendant has or can be expected to earn (Eaglin 2015). For myself, I would accept the sworn testimony of the defendant on this point unless the government produces evidence to the contrary. As information systems within and across state governments improve, it will become easier to access defendants' tax returns, social welfare records, and the like. Further, because the criminal defendant population is overwhelmingly poor, it makes sense to "slant" the process in the direction of presuming poverty, with the burden of persuasion on the government to debut a defendant's testimony.

49. The new Model Penal Code includes a comprehensive slate of recommendations to reform economic sanctions law across the United States (American Law Institute 2017, § 6.04 et seq.). For another set of far-reaching recommendations for legislative, judicial, and executive reforms in the realm of criminal justice debt, see Criminal Justice Policy Program (2016).

50. *Bearden v. Georgia* (1983): offenders may not be incarcerated for failure to pay a fine or restitution unless they "willfully refused to pay or failed to make sufficient bona fide efforts legally to acquire the resources to pay"; there is an exception, however: offenders without ability to pay may be incarcerated for nonpayment "if alternative measures are not adequate to meet the State's interests in punishment and deterrence." By many accounts, the *Bearden* principle has not been

applied conscientiously by many courts. See American Civil Liberties Union (2010, 5): "Today, courts across the United States routinely disregard the protections and principles the Supreme Court established in *Bearden v. Georgia* over twenty years ago. . . . [D]ay after day, indigent defendants are imprisoned for failing to pay legal debts they can never hope to manage. In many cases, poor men and women end up jailed or threatened with jail though they have no lawyer representing them." See also Bannon, Nagrecha, and Diller (2010, 20); Beckett and Harris (2010, 524–25); Katzenstein and Nagrecha 2011, 565).

51. Civil consequences of criminal conviction have deep historical roots in Roman and Germanic law (see Demleitner, this volume). In England and early America, convicted felons were subject to "civil death" and lost most of their legal and civil rights, including the ability to sue another person in court. The severity of these civil consequences was mitigated, however, by the relative frequency of pardons in those times. Also, record-keeping and information systems were primitive, allowing people to slip between the cracks relatively easily; and civil death applied only in the state in which a person was convicted (Chin 2012).
52. Jacobs points out that informal discrimination against people with criminal histories is more robust in the United States than in many other societies because the United States makes arrest and conviction records more widely available to the public. Jacobs calls this "U.S. criminal record exceptionalism" (2015, 159: "In Europe, individual criminal history records created and held by the police are not available to non-police agencies, much less the media and general public."
53. More than this, the number and severity of collateral consequences may be increased long after the dates of offenders' convictions or after they have completed their criminal sentences. There is no *ex post facto* prohibition on increased punishment in this context because the vast majority of collateral sanctions are deemed civil and regulatory rather than criminal (Chin 2012, 1811; *Kennedy v. Mendoza- Martinez* 1963).
54. US homicide rates were also more than four times the rates in most of western Europe, including Austria, England, France, Germany, Italy, the Netherlands, Portugal, Spain, and Switzerland (Institute of Criminology and Legal Policy, University of Helsinki 2016).
55. The Uniform Crime Reports of this era probably exaggerated the actual increases in robbery, rape, and aggravated assault; but an informed estimate is that rates of all four crimes actually doubled from 1962 to 1974—very close to the curve of the homicide spike (see Ruth and Reitz 2003).
56. President's Commission on Law Enforcement and Criminal Justice (1967, 6).
57. This chapter cannot even sketch a history of the 1960s in America, but here is a list of some of the most memorable disruptions: urban riots across major cities and the assassinations of a president, a national civil rights leader, and a presidential candidate; the Vietnam War and the rise of student protests across

universities; the Cold War; the threat of nuclear holocaust (which was still novel enough to provoke all sorts of irrational behavior); the rise of youth culture and the sexual revolution; the rise of a militant black protest movement; and the unraveling of the 1950s *Leave It to Beaver* model of the stable nuclear family with low divorce rates and stay-at-home mothers. For a rich description, see Garland (2001b).

58. This includes every part of Lyndon Johnson's "Great Society," federal civil rights legislation, and voting rights legislation.
59. I do not personally believe that liberalization of crime policy in the 1960s contributed very much to the upsurge in crime—but I am here mostly concerned with appearances and understandable public perceptions at the time.
60. As Wilson is so quotable, here is the entire passage:

> Meanwhile, just beyond the horizon, there lurks a cloud that the winds will soon bring over us. The population will start getting younger again. By the end of this decade there will be a million more people between the ages of fourteen and seventeen than there are now. . . . This extra million will be half male. Six percent of them will become high rate, repeat offenders-thirty thousand more young muggers, killers, and thieves than we have now.
>
> Get ready.

CASES CITED

Bearden v. Georgia, 461 U.S. 660, 672, 674 (1983).
Furman v. Georgia, 408 U.S. 238 (1972).
Greenholtz v. Inmates of the Nebraska Penal and Correctional Complex, 442 U.S. 1 (1979).
Gregg v. Georgia, 428 U.S. 153 (1976).
Kennedy v. Mendoza- Martinez, 372 U.S. 144, 168 (1963).
McCleskey v. Kemp, 481 U.S. 279 (1987).
Pennsylvania Board of Probation and Parole v. Scott, 524 U.S. 357 (1998).

REFERENCES

Aebi, Marcelo F., and Julien Chopin. *Council of Europe Annual Penal Statistics: SPACE II Survey 2013: Persons Serving Non-custodial Sanctions and Measures in 2013*. Strasbourg, France: Council of Europe, 2015.

Aebi, Marcelo F., and Natalia Delgrande. *Council of Europe Annual Penal Statistics: SPACE I—Prison Populations Survey 2013*. Strasbourg, France: Council of Europe, 2015.

Alexander, Michelle. *The New Jim Crow: Mass Incarceration in the Age of Colorblindness*. New York: New Press, 2010.

Alper, Mariel, Alessandro Corda, and Kevin R. Reitz. *American Exceptionalism in Probation Supervision*. Minneapolis, MN: Robina Institute of Criminal Law and Criminal Justice, 2016.

Alper, Mariel, and Ebony Ruhland. *Probation Revocation and Its Causes: Profiles of State and Local Jurisdictions: Bell County, Texas*. Minneapolis, MN: Robina Institute of Criminal Law and Criminal Justice, 2016a.

Alper, Mariel, and Ebony Ruhland. *Probation Revocation and Its Causes: Profiles of State and Local Jurisdictions: Wharton County, Texas*. Minneapolis, MN: Robina Institute of Criminal Law and Criminal Justice, 2016b.

American Bar Association. *Standards for Criminal Justice: Sentencing*. 3rd ed. Washington, DC: ABA Press, 1994.

American Bar Association. National Inventory of the Collateral Consequences of Conviction. 2016. http://www.abacollateralconsequences.org.

American Civil Liberties Union. *In for a Penny: The Rise of America's New Debtors' Prisons*. New York: American Civil Liberties Union, 2010.

American Friends Service Committee. *Struggle for Justice: A Report on Crime and Punishment in America*. New York: Hill & Wang, 1971.

American Law Institute. *Model Penal Code: Sentencing*. Tentative Draft No. 2. Philadelphia: American Law Institute, 2011.

American Law Institute. *Model Penal Code: Sentencing*. Proposed Final Draft. Philadelphia: American Law Institute, 2017.

Amnesty International. *Death Sentences and Executions: 2015*. London: Amnesty International, 2016.

Anderson, David C. *Sensible Justice: Alternatives to Prison*. New York: New Press, 1998.

Arkansas Times Staff and Max Brantley. "Web Special: Dumond Case Revisited—A Reminder of Huckabee's Role in His Freedom. *Arkansas Times*, September 1, 2005.

Associated Press. "U.S. Has Highest Rate of Imprisonment in World." *New York Times*, January 7, 1991.

Ayers, Edward L. *Vengeance and Justice: Crime and Punishment in the Nineteenth-Century American South*. New York and Oxford: Oxford University Press, 1984.

Baldus, David, Julie Brain, Neil A. Weiner, and George Woodworth. "Evidence of Racial Discrimination in the Use of the Death Penalty: A Story from Southwest Arkansas (1990–2005) with Special Reference to the Case of Death Row Inmate Frank Williams Jr." *Tennessee Law Review* 76 (2009): 555–613.

Baldus, David C., George Woodworth, David Zuckerman, Neil Allen Weiner, and Barbara Broffitt. "Racial Discrimination and the Death Penalty in the Post-Furman Era: An Empirical and Legal Overview, with Recent Findings from Philadelphia." *Cornell Law Review* 83 (1998): 1638–1770.

Bannon, Alicia, Mitali Nagrecha, and Rebekah Diller. *Criminal Justice Debt: A Barrier to Reentry*. New York: Brennan Center for Justice, 2010.

Baumgartner, Frank R., Amanda J. Grigg, and Alisa Mastro. "Race-of-Victim Effects in US Executions, 1976–2013." *Politics, Groups and Identities* 3 no. 2 (2015): 209–21.

Bazelon, Emily. "Sentencing by the Numbers." *New York Times Magazine*, January 2, 2005.

Beckett, Katherine, and Alexes Harris. *The Assessment and Consequences of Legal Financial Obligations in Washington State*. Olympia: Washington State Minority and Justice Commission, 2008.

Beckett, Katherine and Alexes Harris. "On Cash and Conviction: Monetary Sanctions as Misguided Policy." *Criminology & Public Policy* 10 (2010): 509–37.

Bedau, Hugo Adam. *The Death Penalty in America: An Anthology*. Chicago: Aldine, 1964.

Belova, Eugenia, and Paul Gregory. "Political Economy of Crime and Punishment under Stalin." *Public Choice* 140 (2009): 463–78.

Bennett, William J., John J. DiIulio, Jr., and John P. Walters. *Body Count: Moral Poverty . . . And How to Win America's War against Crime and Drugs*. New York: Simon & Schuster, 1996.

Black, Charles L., Jr. *Capital Punishment: The Inevitability of Caprice and Mistake*. New York: W.W. Norton, 1974.

Blumstein, Alfred. "On the Racial Disproportionality of United States' Prison Populations." *Journal of Criminal Law and Criminology* 73, no. 3 (1982): 1259–81.

Blumstein, Alfred. "Racial Disproportionality of U.S. Prisons Revisited." *University of Colorado Law Review* 64 (1993): 743–60.

Blumstein, Alfred, Douglass W. Cassel, Bernardine Dohrn, Mark J. Heyrman, Randolph N. Stone, and Franklin E. Zimring. "Mass Incarceration: Perspectives on U.S. Imprisonment." *The University of Chicago Law School Roundtable* 7, no. 1 (2000): 91–136.

Blumstein, Alfred, and Joel Wallman, eds. *The Crime Drop in America*. Cambridge: Cambridge University Press, 2000.

Bonczar, Thomas P. *Prevalence of Imprisonment in the United States Population, 1974–2001*. Washington, DC: Bureau of Justice Statistics, 2003.

Bright, Stephen B. "The Death Penalty and the Society We Want." *Pierce Law Review* 6 (2008): 369–85.

Byrne, James M., Arthur J. Lurigio, and Joan Petersilia, eds. *Smart Sentencing: The Emergence of Intermediate Sanctions*. Newbury Park, CA: Sage Publications, 1992.

Cahalan, Margaret Werner. *Historical Corrections Statistics in the United States, 1850–1984*. Washington, DC: Government Printing Office, 1986.

Carson, E. Ann. *Prisoners in 2014*. Washington, DC: Bureau of Justice Statistics, 2015.

Carson, E. Ann, and Daniela Golinelli. *Prisoners in 2012, Trends in Admissions and Releases, 1991–2012*. Washington, DC: Bureau of Justice Statistics, 2013.

Carson, E. Ann, and Elizabeth Anderson. *Prisoners in 2015*. Washington, DC: Bureau of Justice Statistics, 2016.

Cavanagh, David P., and Mark A. R. Kleiman. *Cost Benefit Analysis of Prison Cell Construction and Alternative Sanctions*. Washington, DC: National Institute of Justice, 1990.

Centers for Disease Control and Prevention. Deaths and Mortality. National Center for Health Statistics. 2016. http://www.cdc.gov/nchs/fastats/deaths.htm

Chin, Gabriel J. "The New Civil Death: Rethinking Punishment in the Era of Mass Conviction." *University of Pennsylvania Law Review* 160 (2012): 1789–1833.

Clear, Todd R., and Natasha A. Frost. *The Punishment Imperative: The Rise and Failure of Mass Incarceration in America*. New York: New York University Press, 2014.

Cole, David. *No Equal Justice: Race and Class in the American Criminal Justice System*. New York: New Press, 1999.

Colorado Division of Criminal Justice and Colorado State Board of Parole. *Analysis of Colorado State Board of Parole Decisions: FY 2013 Report*. Denver: Colorado Division of Criminal Justice, 2013.

Corbett, Ronald P. Jr. "The Burdens of Leniency: The Changing Face of Probation." *University of Minnesota Law Review* 99, no. 5 (2015): 1697–1732.

Corda, Alessandro, Mariel Alper, and Kevin R. Reitz. *American Exceptionalism in Parole Supervision*. Minneapolis, MN: Robina Institute of Criminal Law and Criminal Justice, 2016.

Criminal Justice Policy Program. *Confronting Criminal Justice Debt: A Guide for Policy Reform*. Cambridge, MA: Harvard Law School, 2016.

Dagan, David, and Steven Teles. *Prison Break: Why Conservatives Turned against Mass Incarceration*. New York and Oxford: Oxford University Press, 2016.

Death Penalty Information Center. "Executions by Year." 2016a. http://www.deathpenaltyinfo.org/executions-year.

Death Penalty Information Center. "Death Penalty Worldwide: China." 2016b. https://www.deathpenaltyworldwide.org/country-search-post.cfm?country=China#f10-2.

Death Penalty Information Center. "Facts about the Death Penalty." 2016c. https://deathpenaltyinfo.org/documents/FactSheet.pdf.

Death Penalty Information Center. "Executions by County." 2016d. http://www.deathpenaltyinfo.org/executions-county.

Death Penalty Information Center. "Race of Death Row Inmates Executed since 1976." 2016e. http://www.deathpenaltyinfo.org/race-death-row-inmates-executed-1976#defend.

Dieter, Richard C. *The 2% Death Penalty: How a Minority of Counties Produce Most Death Cases At Enormous Costs to All*. Washington, DC: Death Penalty Information Center, 2013.

DiIulio, John J., Jr. "The Coming of the Super-Predator." *Weekly Standard*, November 27, 1995.

DiIulio, John J., Jr. "Reinventing Parole and Probation: A Lock-'Em-Up Hardliner Makes the Case for Probation." *Brookings Review* 15, no. 2 (Spring 1997): 40–42.

Donohue, John J., III, and Steven D. Levitt. "The Impact of Legalized Abortion on Crime." *Quarterly Journal of Economics* 116, no. 2 (2001): 379–420.

Dui Hua Foundation. "Criminal Justice: Death Penalty Reform." 2016. http://duihua.org/wp/?page_id=136.

Eaglin, Jessica M. "Improving Economic Sanctions in the States." *Minnesota Law Review* 99 (2015): 1837–70.

Eberhardt, Jennifer L., P.G. Davies, Valerie J. Purdie-Vaughns, and Sheri-Lynn Johnson. "Looking Deathworthy: Perceived Stereotypicality of Black Defendant Predicts Capital-Sentencing Outcomes." *Psychological Science* 17 (2006): 383–86.

Federal Bureau of Investigation. *Crime in the United States 2015*, 2016. https://ucr.fbi.gov/crime-in-the-u.s/2015/crime-in-the-u.s.-2015.

Federal Bureau of Investigation. *Preliminary Semiannual Uniform Crime Report, January–June, 2016*, 2017. https://ucr.fbi.gov/crime-in-the-u.s/2016/preliminary-semiannual-uniform-crime-report-januaryjune-2016.

Federal Ministry of Justice. *Second Periodical Report on Crime and Crime Control in Germany*, Abridged Version. Berlin, Germany: Federal Ministry of Justice, 2007.

Fox, James Alan. "The Calm before the Crime Wave Storm: Homicides: The Rate Will Soar as Baby Boomers' Children Reach Teenhood. We Can Invest in Them Now or Build Prisons Later." *Los Angeles Times*, October 30, 1995.

Frankel, Marvin E. *Criminal Sentences: Law without Order*. New York: Hill and Wang, 1973.

Garland, David, ed. *Mass Imprisonment*. London: Sage, 2001a.

Garland, David. *The Culture of Control*. New York and Oxford: Oxford University Press, 2001b.

Garland, David. *Peculiar Institution: American Death Penalty in an Age of Abolition*. New York and Oxford: Oxford University Press, 2010.

Garrett, Brandon L. "Conservatives Are Leading the Way as States Enact Criminal Justice Reform." *Slate*, March 31, 2017.

Gingrich, Newt, and Pat Nolan. "Prison Reform: A Smart Way for States to Save Money and Lives." *Washington Post*, January 7, 2011.

Goffman, Alice. *On the Run: Fugitive Life in an American City*. Chicago: University of Chicago Press, 2014.

Haberman, Clyde. "Retro Report: When Youth Violence Spurred 'Superpredator' Fear." *New York Times*, April 6, 2014.

Hager, Eli. "For Men in Prison, Child Support Becomes a Crushing Debt." The Marshall Project, October 18, 2015. https://www.themarshallproject.org/2015/10/18/for-men-in-prison-child-support-becomes-a-crushing-debt#.KIPVtiCTt.

Harcourt, Bernard E. *Against Prediction: Profiling, Policing, and Punishing in an Actuarial Age*. Chicago, IL: University of Chicago Press, 2006.

Harris, Alexes. *A Pound of Flesh: Monetary Sanctions as Punishment for the Poor*. New York: Russell Sage Foundation, 2016.

Higginbotham, A. Leon, Jr. *In the Matter of Color: Race in the American Legal Process.* New York and Oxford: Oxford University Press, 1978.

Horney, Julie, D. Wayne Osgood, and Ineke Haen Marshall. "Criminal Careers in the Short-Term: Intra-Individual Variability in Crime and Its Relation to Local Life Circumstances." *American Sociology Review* 60 (1995): 655–73.

Hulse, Carl. "Bipartisan View Was Emerging on Sentencing. Then Came Jeff Sessions." *New York Times*, May 14, 2017.

Human Rights Watch. *Profiting from Probation: America's "Offender-Funded" Probation Industry.* Washington, DC: Human Rights Watch, 2014.

Ingraham, Christopher. "How Philadelphia Seizes Millions in 'Pocket Change' from Some of the City's Poorest Residents." *Washington Post*, June 10, 2015.

Institute of Criminology and Legal Policy, University of Helsinki, 2016. Data provided by personal communication from Martti Lehti June 22, 2016.

Jacobs, James B. *The Eternal Criminal Record.* Cambridge, MA: Harvard University Press, 2015.

Jacobson, Michael. *Downsizing Prisons: How to Reduce Crime and End Mass Incarceration.* New York: New York University Press, 2005.

Jeffries, John C. Jr. *Justice Lewis Powell, Jr.* New York: Fordham University Press, 2001.

Kaeble, Danielle, Lauren Glaze, Anastasios Tsoutis, and Todd Minton. *Correctional Populations in the United States, 2014.* Washington, DC: Bureau of Justice Statistics, 2015.

Kaeble, Danielle, Laura M. Maruschak, and Thomas P. Bonczar. *Probation and Parole in the United States, 2014.* Washington, DC: Bureau of Justice Statistics, 2015.

Kahneman, Daniel. *Thinking Fast, and Slow.* New York: Farrar, Straus and Giroux, 2011.

Katzenstein, Mary Fainsod, and Mitali Nagrecha. "A New Punishment Regime." *Criminology & Public Policy* 10 (2011): 555–68.

Kennedy, Randall. *Race, Crime, and the Law.* New York: Pantheon, 1997.

Klingele, Cecelia M. "Rethinking the Use of Community Supervision." *Journal of Criminal Law and Criminology* 103 (2013): 1015–69.

Klingele, Cecelia, Jenny Roberts, and Margaret Colgate Love. *Collateral Consequences of Criminal Convictions: Law, Policy and Practice*, 2012–2013 ed. New York: Thomson West, 2013.

Kredo, Adam. "Iran Executed 1,084 People in 2015: Led the World in Per Capita Number of State-Sanctioned Executions." *Washington Free Beacon*, January 12, 2016.

Kuhn, André. "Incarceration Rates: Europe versus USA." *European Journal on Criminal Policy and Research* 4, no. 3 (1995): 46–73.

LaFree, Gary D. *Rape and Criminal Justice: The Social Construction of Sexual Assault.* Belmont, CA: Wadsworth, 1989.

Logan, Wayne A., and Ronald F. Wright. "Mercenary Criminal Justice." *Illinois Law Review* 2014 (2014): 1175–1226.

Love, Margaret Colgate. "Managing the Collateral Consequences in the Sentencing Process: The Revised Sentencing Articles of the Model Penal Code." *Wisconsin Law Review* 2015 (2015): 247–87.

Love, Margaret Colgate, Jenny Roberts, and Cecelia Klingele. *Collateral Consequences of Criminal Convictions: Law, Policy and Practice.* Eagan, MN: Thomson West, 2016.

Martinson, Robert. "What Works? Questions and Answers About Prison Reform." *Public Interest* 35 (1974): 22–54.

Mauer, Marc. *Americans behind Bars: The International Use of Incarceration, 1992–1993.* Washington, DC: The Sentencing Project, 1994.

McNeill, Fergus, and Kristel Beyens, eds. *Offender Supervision in Europe.* New York: Palgrave Macmillan, 2014.

Minton, Todd D., and Zhen Zeng. *Jail Inmates at Midyear 2014.* Washington, DC: Bureau of Justice Statistics, 2015.

Mitchell, Kelly Lyn, Kevin R. Reitz, Alexis Watts, and Catherine A. Ellis. *Profiles in Probation Revocation: Examining the Legal Framework in 21 States.* Minneapolis, MN: Robina Institute of Criminal Law and Criminal Justice, 2014.

Morris, Norval, 1974. *The Future of Imprisonment.* Chicago: University of Chicago Press, 1974.

Morris, Norval, and Michael Tonry. *Between Prison and Probation: Intermediate Punishments in a Rational Sentencing System.* New York and Oxford: Oxford University Press, 1990.

National Advisory Comm'n on Criminal Justice Standards and Goals. *Corrections.* Washington, DC: US Government Printing Office, 1973.

National Public Radio. "Guilty and Charged." 2014. http://www.npr.org/series/313986316/guilty-and-charged.

National Research Council. *Parole, Desistance from Crime, and Community Integration.* Washington, DC: National Academies Press, 2007.

National Weather Service. "How Dangerous Is Lightning?" National Oceanic and Atmospheric Administration. 2016. http://origin-www.nws.noaa.gov/om/lightning/odds.shtml.

New Jersey State Parole Board. *The Parole Book: A Handbook on Parole Procedures for Adult and Young Adult Inmates.* 4th ed. Trenton: New Jersey State Parole Board, 2010.

Newsweek Staff. "The Lull before the Storm?" *Newsweek,* December 3, 1995.

O'Malley, Pat. "Politicizing the Case for Fines." *Criminology and Public Policy* 10 (2011): 547–53.

Ostrom, Brian J., Matthew Kleiman, Fred Cheesman II, Randall M. Hansen, and Neal B. Kauder. *Offender Risk Assessment in Virginia: A Three-Stage Evaluation.* Williamsburg, VA: National Center for State Courts, 2002.

Paparozzi, Mario A., and Joel M. Caplan. "A Profile of Paroling Authorities in America: The Strange Bedfellows of Politics and Professionalism." *The Prison Journal* 89, no. 4 (2009): 401–25.

Paternoster, Ray. "Misunderstandings Cloud Death Penalty Findings." *Baltimore Sun*, December 20, 2005.

Petersilia, Joan. *When Prisoners Come Home: Parole and Prisoner Reentry*. New York and Oxford: Oxford University Press, 2003.

Pettit, Becky, and Bruce Western. "Mass Imprisonment and the Life Course: Race and Class Inequality in US Incarceration." *American Sociological Review* 69, no. 2 (2004): 151–69.

Pew Center on the States. *One in 100: Behind Bars in America 2008*. Washington, DC: Pew Charitable Trusts, 2008.

Phelps, Michele S. "Mass Probation: Toward a More Robust Theory of State Variation in Punishment." *Punishment and Society* 19, no. 1 (2016): 53–73.

Phillips, Scott. "Status Disparities in the Capital of Capital Punishment." *Law and Society Review* 43 (2009): 807–38.

Pinard, Michael. "Reflections & Perspectives on Reentry and Collateral Consequences." *Journal of Criminal Law and Criminology* 100 (2010a): 1213–24.

Pinard, Michael. "Collateral Consequences of Criminal Convictions: Confronting Issues of Race and Dignity." *New York University Law Review* 85 (2010b): 457–534.

Piquero, Alex R., and Wesley G. Jennings. "Justice System Imposed Financial Penalties Increase the Likelihood of Recidivism in a Sample of Adolescent Offenders." *Youth Violence and Juvenile Justice* 2016 (2016): 1–16.

Piquero, Alex R., John M. MacDonald, and Karen F. Parker. "Race, Local Life Circumstances, and Criminal Activity." *Social Science Quarterly* 83 (2002): 654–70.

Pleggenkuhle, Breanne. "The Effect of Legal Financial Obligations on Reentry Experiences." PhD diss., University of Missouri–St. Louis, St. Louis, MO, 2012.

President's Commission on Law Enforcement and Criminal Justice. *The Challenge of Crime in a Free Society*. Washington, DC: Government Printing Office, 1967.

Raphael, Steven, and Michael A. Stoll. "Why Are So Many Americans in Prison?" In *Do Prisons Make Us Safer? The Benefits and Costs of the Prison Boom*, edited by Steven Raphael and Michael A. Stoll. New York: Russell Sage Foundation, 2009: 27–72.

Reitz, Kevin R. "Don't Blame Determinacy: U.S. Incarceration Has Been Driven by Other Forces." *Texas Law Review* 84 (2006): 1787–802.

Reitz, Kevin R. "Discretionary Prison Release Systems in the US: A Comparative Framework." In *Offender Release and Supervision: The Role of Courts and the Use of Discretion*, edited by Martine Herzog-Evans. Nijmegen, the Netherlands: Wolf Legal, 2014: 81–107.

Rhine, Edward E., Joan Petersilia, and Kevin Reitz. "The Future of Parole Release." *Crime and Justice: A Review of Research* 46 (2017): 279–338.

Right on Crime. "Jeb Bush Signs the Right on Crime Statement of Principles." September 2, 2011. http://rightoncrime.com/2011/09/jeb-bush-signs-the-right-on-crime-statement-of-principles/.

Right on Crime. Right on Crime Signatories. Accessed July 21, 2016. http://rightoncrime.com/right-on-crime-signatories/.

Roberts, Julian V. "Crime Victims, Sentencing, and Release from Prison." In *The Oxford Handbook of Sentencing and Corrections*, edited by Joan Petersilia and Kevin R. Reitz, 23–52. New York and Oxford: Oxford University Press, 2012.

Rodriguez, Michelle Natividad, and Maurice Emsellem. *65 Million Need Not Apply: The Case for Reforming Criminal Background Checks for Employment.* New York: National Employment Law Project, 2011.

Rosenberg, Tina. "Even in Texas, Mass Imprisonment Is Going Out of Style." *New York Times*, February 14, 2017.

Rosenberg, Tina. "The Deadliest D.A." *New York Times Magazine*, July 16, 1995.

Rothman, David. *Conscience and Convenience: The Asylum and Its Alternatives in Progressive America*. Boston, MA: Little, Brown, 1980.

Ruback, R. Barry. "The Benefits and Costs of Economic Sanctions: Considering the Victim, the Offender, and Society." *Minnesota Law Review* 99 (2015): 1779–1835.

Ruback, R. Barry, and Valerie Clark. "Economic Sanctions in Pennsylvania: Complex and Inconsistent." *Duquesne Law Review* 49 (2011): 751–72.

Ruhland, Ebony L., Edward E. Rhine, Jason P. Robey, and Kelly Lyn Mitchell. *The Continuing Leverage of Releasing Authorities: Findings from a National Survey.* Minneapolis, MN: Robina Institute of Criminal Law and Criminal Justice, 2017.

Ruhland, Ebony L., Jason P. Robey, Ronald P. Corbett, Jr., and Kevin R. Reitz. *Exploring Supervision Fees in Four Probation Jurisdictions in Texas: Summary Report.* Minneapolis, MN: Robina Institute of Criminal Law and Criminal Justice, 2017.

Ruth, Henry, and Kevin R. Reitz. *The Challenge of Crime: Rethinking Our Response.* Cambridge, MA: Harvard University Press, 2003.

Sampson, Robert J., and John H. Laub. *Crime in the Making: Pathways and Turning Points through Life*. Cambridge, MA: Harvard University Press, 1995.

Sampson, Robert J., John H. Laub, and Christopher Wimer. "Does Marriage Reduce Crime? A Counterfactual Approach to Within-Individual Causal Effects." *Criminology* 44, no. 3 (2006): 465–508.

Savage, Charlie. "Trend to Lighten Harsh Sentences Catches On in Conservative States." *New York Times*, August 12, 2011.

Schwartzapfel, Beth. "Life without Parole: Inside the Secretive World of Parole Boards, Where Your Freedom May Depend on Politics and Whim." The Marshall

Project, July 10, 2015. https://www.themarshallproject.org/2015/07/10/life-without-parole#.k8ggEELRX.

Sellin, Thorsten. *The Death Penalty: A Report for the Model Penal Code Project of the American Law Institute*. Philadelphia: American Law Institute, 1959.

Sentencing Project. *U.S. Continues to be World Leader in Rate of Incarceration*. Washington, DC: The Sentencing Project, 2001.

Shover, Neil. *Great Pretenders: Pursuits and Careers of Persistent Thieves*. Boulder, CO: Westview Press, 1996.

Sigler, Robert T., and David Lamb. "Community-Based Alternatives to Prison: How the Public and Court Personnel View Them." *Federal Probation* 59, no. 2 (1995): 3–9.

Simon, Jonathan. "Mass Incarceration: From Social Policy to Social Problem." In *The Oxford Handbook of Sentencing and Corrections*, edited by Joan Petersilia and Kevin R. Reitz, 23–52. New York and Oxford: Oxford University Press, 2012.

Skeem, Jennifer L., and Christopher T. Lowencamp. "Risk, Race, and Recidivism: Predictive Bias and Disparate Impact." *Criminology* 64, no. 4 (2016): 680–712.

Snell, Tracy L. *Capital Punishment, 2013—Statistical Tables*. Washington, DC: Bureau of Justice Statistics, 2014b.

Spohn, Cassia, and Jeffrey Spears. "The Effect of Offender and Victim Characteristics on Sexual Assault Case Processing Decisions." *Justice Quarterly* 13, no. 4 (1996): 649–79.

Stampp, Kenneth. *The Peculiar Institution: Negro Slavery in the American South*. London: Eyre and Spottiswoode, 1956.

Starr, Sonja B. "Evidence-Based Sentencing and the Scientific Rationalization of Discrimination." *Stanford Law Review* 66 (2014): 803–72.

Statista. "Iran: Total Population from 2010 to 2020 (in Million Inhabitants)." 2016. http://www.statista.com/statistics/294102/total-population-of-iran/.

Steiker, Carol S. "Capital Punishment and American Exceptionalism." *Oregon Law Review* 81 (2002): 97–130.

Tabak, Ronald J. "The Continuing Role of Race in Capital Cases, Notwithstanding President Obama's Election." *Northern Kentucky Law Review* 37 (2010): 243–72.

Texas Department of Criminal Justice. "Total Number of Offenders Sentenced to Death from Each County." 2016. https://www.tdcj.state.tx.us/death_row/dr_number_sentenced_death_county.html.

Tkachuk, Brian, and Roy Walmsley. *World Prison Population: Facts, Trends and Solutions*. Helsinki, Finland: European Institute for Crime Prevention and Control, 2001.

Tobolowsky, Peggy M., Mario T. Gaboury, Arrick L. Jackson, and Ashley G. Blackburn. *Crime Victim Rights and Remedies*. 2nd ed. Durham, NC: Carolina Academic Press, 2010.

Tonry, Michael. *Punishing Race: A Continuing American Dilemma.* New York and Oxford: Oxford University Press, 2011.

Travis, Jeremy. *Thoughts on the Future of Parole.* Washington, DC: Urban Institute Justice Policy Center, 2002.

Uggen, Christopher. "Work as a Turning Point in the Life Course of Criminals: A Duration Model of Age, Employment, and Recidivism." *American Sociology Review* 65 (2000): 529–46.

University at Albany, Hindelang Criminal Justice Research Center. "Sourcebook of Criminal Justice Statistics." 2012. http://www.albany.edu/sourcebook.

US Census Bureau. *1997 Population Profile of the United States.* Washington, DC: US Government Printing Office, 1998.

US Census Bureau. *Current Population Reports, Series P23-205, Population Profile of the United States 1999.* Washington, DC: US Government Printing Office, 2001.

US Census Bureau. "Annual Estimates of the Resident Population by Sex, Age, Race, and Hispanic Origin for the United States and States: April 1, 2010 to July 1, 2015." 2016. https://factfinder.census.gov/faces/tableservices/jsf/pages/productview.xhtml?src=bkmk.

US Department of Justice. *Investigation of the Ferguson Police Department.* Washington, DC: US Department of Justice, 2015.

van Zyl Smit, Dirk, and John R. Spencer. "The European Dimension to the Release of Sentenced Prisoners." In *Release from Prison: European Policy and Practice,* edited by Nicola Padfield, Dirk van Zyl Smit, and Frieder Dünkel, 9–48. Portland, OR: Willan, 2010.

Walsh, Anthony. "The Sexual Stratification Hypothesis and Sexual Assault in Light of the Changing Conceptions of Race." *Criminology* 25 (1987): 153–73.

Willing, Richard, and Gary Fields. "Geography of the Death Penalty." *USA Today,* December 20, 1999.

Wilson, James Q. *Thinking about Crime.* New York: Basic Books, 1975.

Wilson, James Q. "Crime and Public Policy." In *Crime,* edited by James Q. Wilson and Joan Petersilia. Ithaca, NY: ICS Press, 1995: 489–507.

Wilson, James Q. "Interview with James Q. Wilson." *Criminal Justice Matters* (Autumn 1996): 4.

Wilson, James Q., and George L. Kelling. "Broken Windows: The Police and Neighborhood Safety." *The Atlantic,* March 1982.

Wolfgang, Marvin, and Marc Riedel. "Race, Judicial Discretion and the Death Penalty." *The Annals of the American Academy of Political and Social Science* 407 (1973): 119–33.

World Prison Brief. "Highest to Lowest—Prison Population Rate." London: Institute for Criminal Policy Research, 2016. http://www.prisonstudies.org/highest-to-lowest/prison_population_rate?field_region_taxonomy_tid=All.

Zimring, Franklin E. *The Contradictions of American Capital Punishment.* New York and Oxford: Oxford University Press, 2003.

Zimring, Franklin E., and Gordon Hawkins. *Capital Punishment and the American Agenda.* Cambridge: Cambridge University Press, 1986.

Zimring, Franklin E., and Gordon Hawkins. *Crime Is Not the Problem: Lethal Violence in America.* New York and Oxford: Oxford University Press, 1997.

PART I

American Exceptionalism

Perspectives

1

American Exceptionalism in Crime, Punishment, and Disadvantage

RACE, FEDERALIZATION, AND POLITICIZATION IN THE PERSPECTIVE OF LOCAL AUTONOMY

Nicola Lacey and David Soskice

Introduction

In key criminal justice indices such as the rate of the most serious violent crime and the imprisonment rate, the United States not only performs differently from other advanced democracies but does so to a startling degree. Moreover these differences have become more extreme over the last half-century. For example, the imprisonment rate, which was double that in England and Wales in 1970, is today five times higher, notwithstanding the fact that the rate in England and Wales has itself more than doubled during that period. And the American homicide rate, while at between four and five times the English level, is broadly comparable today with that in 1950 (when it was nearly six times the English level), it reached 10 times that level in the late 1970s (Figures 1.1–1.3). These differences are widely recognized. What is less often recognized in comparative criminal justice scholarship is that these differences in criminal justice variables sit alongside stark differences in other key social indicators, notably in inequality of educational outcomes and in residential socioeconomic and racial segregation. In these areas, too, the United States produces more extreme outcomes than the other "liberal market economies" which, according to the varieties of capitalism typology (Hall and Soskice 2001), exhibit broadly similar economic, political, and welfare systems (Figure 1.4). The comparison with other "liberal market economies" such

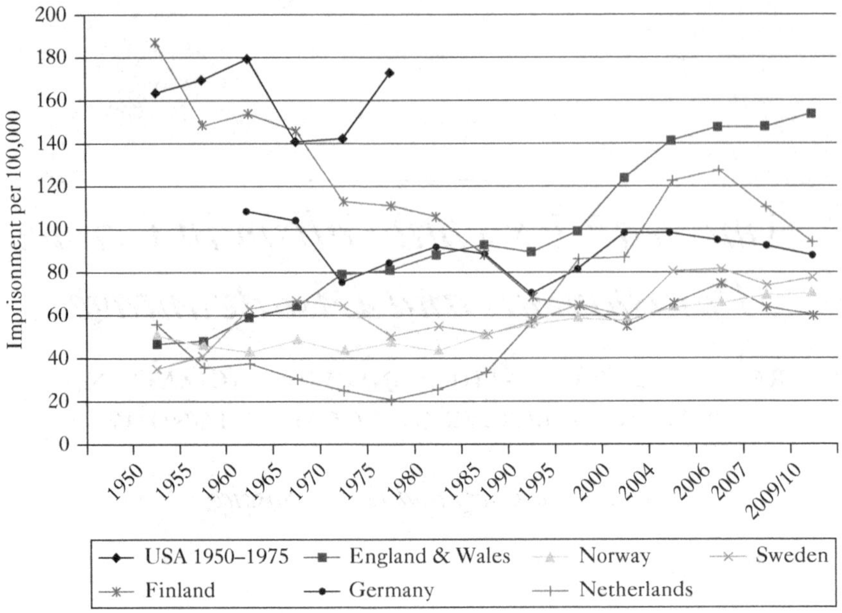

FIGURE I.1 Imprisonment Trends in Europe, 1950–2010
Note: The US trend for 1950–1957 is shown for comparison.
Sources: International Centre for Prison Studies (2010); Pratt (2008 a and b).

as those of the United Kingdom and New Zealand is even more striking in the light of their own inegalitarian outcomes on all these variables as compared to the "coordinated market economies" of northern Europe and Japan.

In a recent article (Lacey and Soskice 2015), we presented a thesis about what explains each of these distinctive American outcomes and how they relate to one another, so as to shape the position of the United States as an outlier in key indices of social polarization and disadvantage. Our core argument focused on the institutional structure of the political system. We suggested that the uniquely decentralized American political system, which accords a distinctive degree of autonomy to localities and which governs a distinctively wide range of decisions about education, zoning, and criminal justice through local electoral politics (Figure 1.5), produces a polarizing dynamic in which it is impossible to garner stable political support for integrative, let alone redistributive, policies. The key "median" voters in local elections are, disproportionately, homeowners, who vote for policies that will maximize their own property values and the quality of services and the environment in their immediate area and who are reluctant to vote for costly public goods whose benefits are not so restricted. In this light, it is rational for local governments to form

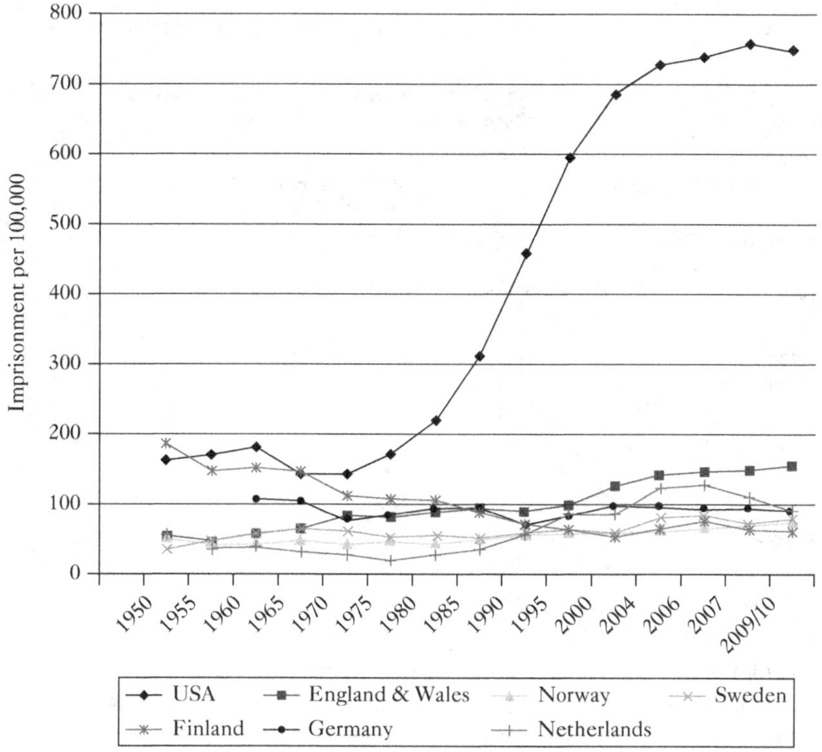

FIGURE 1.2 Imprisonment Trends in Europe and the United States, 1950–2010
Sources: International Centre for Prison Studies (2010); Pratt (2008 a and b).

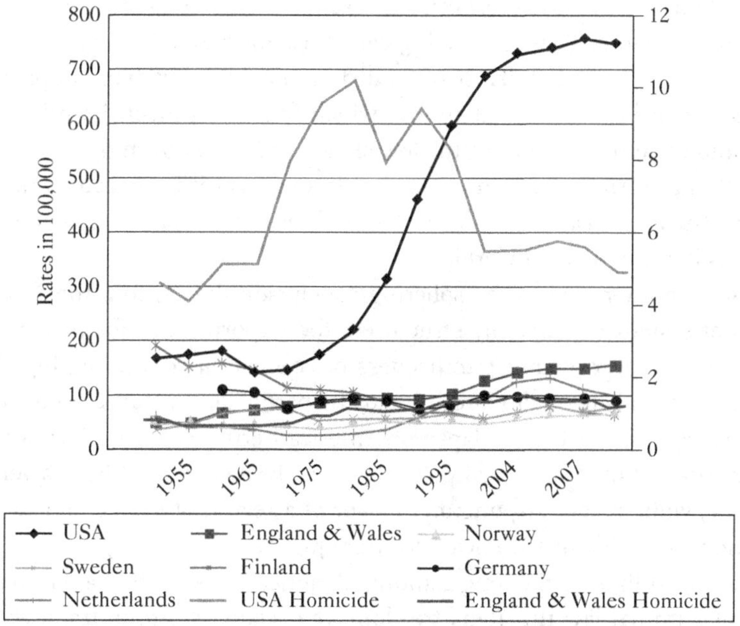

FIGURE 1.3 Imprisonment and Homicide Trends, 1950–2010
Sources: International Centre for Prison Studies (2010); Pratt (2008 a and b).

	United States	*United Kingdom*	*Australia*	*New Zealand*	*Canada*	*Sweden*
Residential Segregation: (Ethnic)	10.8 [11.4] *Black*	1.7 [9.9] *S Asian*	0.1 [2.7] *Asian*	0.0 [19.6] *Maori*	1.4 [11.2] *Asian*	
Prison per cap	701	141	115	155	129	73
Homicide rate	5.0	1.2	1.2	1.5	1.8	1.0
Literacy score 5th percentile	136.7	151.2	145.1	164.8	144.5	214
Child poverty	23.1	12.1	10.9	11.7	13.3	7.3

FIGURE 1.4 American Exceptionalism in Adverse Social Outcomes
Sources: Johnston, Poulsen, and Forrest (2005); International Centre for Prison Studies (2010); Organisation for Economic Co-operation and Development (2013); UNICEF (2012); United Nations Office on Drugs and Crime (2012).

policies based on zoning: whether of good schools, of community policing, of public housing, or—the most extreme example—of offender populations into the prison system. These polarizing dynamics, moreover, have become particularly strong since the collapse of Fordist industrial production,[1] implying the disappearance of many manual jobs which formerly provided a bridge from education to employment for the low-skilled. It follows from the dynamics of decentralized American democracy, we argued, that it is virtually impossible to construct political coalitions at the local level in order to build alternative bridges in a post-Fordist world.

Our argument led to the sobering conclusion that, within the American political system as currently structured, the opportunities for reversing the trend toward ever greater punitiveness or combating continuing high levels of violence and inequality are limited. In particular, our argument implied that a diagnosis of the "collapse of American criminal justice" in terms of the federalization of criminal policy by an activist state is, at best, a very partial one, while recent arguments in favor of a revival of local democracy as a solution to the ills of American criminal justice are seriously misconceived. Ironically, in light of the long-standing American anxiety that a national system of criminal law threatens freedom, the relatively strong framework for

	Police	Prosecutors	Local judges	Zoning	Schools
US	City/ municipal appointment by mayor (sometimes elected)	DA elected county or multicounty district	Most states elected on county or multicounty district	Zoning Boards appointed by locally elected Council/ Mayor	Property tax by elected School Board at School District
Canada	Office of Provincial AG; operating procedures, appointments, training	Provincial AG	Provincial government	Provincial, Federal defined policies	Provincial policies
England and Wales	Home Office appoints Chief Constables	Attorney General (government agency)	Lord Chancellor (Ministry of Justice)	Min Housing rules, right of appeal to Minister	National government policies
NZ	Government appoints (under Minister of Police, prosecution independence)	Attorney General appoints (remain private lawyers) national guidelines	Attorney General	National guidelines	National system (Ministry of Education)

FIGURE 1.5 Levels of Political Decision-Making in Liberal Market Economies

national policy development and implementation in other Anglo-Saxon countries has—notwithstanding their relatively poor performance in comparison with the coordinated countries—provided mechanisms countering some of the polarizing and inegalitarian dynamics of a liberal market system.

In this chapter, we set our argument within the context of a broader literature in the comparative political economy of crime and punishment. We then go on to consider three possible objections to our analysis: the argument that increasing American exceptionalism in the postwar period is to be explained primarily in terms of a distinctive history and politics of race; the argument that it is to be attributed primarily to national policy driven by the federal government; and the argument that it is driven by the interests of political elites who are relatively disconnected from the interests of their electors. Each of these objections can, we suggest, be met. But considering them carefully enables us to refine our hypothesis.

Politics, Crime, and Punishment: The Existing Literature

Notwithstanding the obvious status of punishment as a product of political action and the widespread acknowledgment that crime and punishment moved up the political agenda in the 1970s and 1980s in many countries, interdisciplinary and comparative scholarship has tended to focus its search for explanations of trends in crime and punishment on cultural, demographic, and economic variables rather than on political–institutional ones. Thus far, even in relation to the United States, notwithstanding a pervasive interest in the "politics of law and order" (Beckett 1997; Scheingold 2010) and a recognition that key federal initiatives in criminal justice—notably the War on Drugs—were the product of clear electoral strategies, curiously little has been done to try to understand the impact on criminal justice policymaking of the institutional structure of the contemporary political system.[2] How, if at all, do factors like the electoral system; the availability of citizen-initiated referenda; the relationship between executive, legislature, and judiciary; the status of the expert civil service bureaucracy; federal structures; or the distribution of veto points around the political system affect the formation of criminal policy? These seem obvious questions to pose; and yet, shaped by the prevailing concerns of sociology, on the one hand, and of political economy, on the other, the influence on crime and punishment of factors such as cultural norms oriented to solidarity and altruism or of the structure of labor markets, unemployment rates, and the distribution of wealth has dominated the effort to understand offending behavior and punishment in their full social context (Rusche and Kirchheimer 1969; Garland 1990; de Giorgi 2006). While we share the view that such economic and social variables are of key importance, we see them as profoundly shaped by the political system. Moreover, the political system seems to offer a promising line of inquiry in investigating American exceptionalism, given the very long-standing differences in the nature of the US polity as compared to countries such as the United Kingdom, Canada, or New Zealand—all of them Anglo-Saxon societies differentiated from the rest of the advanced world by deep political–economic similarities.

In a 2008 book, *The Prisoners' Dilemma* (Lacey 2008), one of us made an initial attempt to analyze the question of how political structures affect criminal justice. The book's starting point was the striking fact that, though most advanced countries saw proportionately comparable rises in crime from the early 1970s to the mid-1990s (since when most countries have experienced a very significant drop in crime, with the US decline, which has taken crime back to something like its 1960s levels, particularly dramatic), their reactions in terms of punishment had been markedly different (Figures 1.1 and 1.2).[3] These differences undermined the diagnosis of a burgeoning "culture of control" or "neoliberal penality" grounded in factors such as a common reaction to the economic restructuring following the global economic crisis of the 1970s (Garland 2001; Reiner 2007; Wacquant 2009). Notwithstanding the increasing interdependence of national economies, nation states have maintained striking differences in penal policy. Looking at the trajectory of punishment over time and space, we can see a number of patterns, widely noted in the sociological literature: countries with lower levels of inequality, more generous welfare states, higher levels of unionization, and higher levels of social trust, for example, show consistently lower rates of imprisonment (Sutton 2004; Downes and Hansen 2006; Zimring and Johnson 2006; Savage, Bennett, and Danner, 2008; see Lappi-Seppälä, this volume). The challenge is to move from an observation of these patterns or correlations to an explanation of how they were reproduced over time, even amid common pressures created by a globalizing economy. The institutional structure and modus operandi of political systems are, we suggest, obvious places to look.

Drawing on work by Iversen and Soskice which examines the political underpinnings of different forms of capitalism (Iversen and Soskice 2006, 2009), *The Prisoners' Dilemma* argued that the structure of electoral competition in winner-takes-all, first-past-the-post systems like that of England and Wales or of the United States tends under certain conditions to produce what we might call a law-and-order arms race between the two main parties.[4] This argument about political systems was nested within the "varieties of capitalism" distinction between "liberal" and "coordinated" market economies (Hall and Soskice 2001).[5] A "coordinated market economy" functions in terms of long-term relationships and stable structures of investment, not least in education and training oriented to company- or sector-specific skills, and incorporates a wide range of social groups and institutions into a highly coordinated governmental structure, including a generous welfare state (Esping-Andersen 1990). Such a system is more likely to generate incentives for the relevant decision-makers to opt for a relatively inclusionary criminal justice system. For it is a system that is premised on incorporation, and hence on the need to reintegrate offenders into society and economy—making it structurally less likely to opt for exclusionary stigmatization in punishment. Typically, moreover, the interlocking and diffused institutions of coordination of the coordinated market economies of northern Europe and the Nordic region conduce to an environment of relatively extensive informal social controls, and this in turn supports the cultural mentalities which underpin and help to stabilize a moderated approach to formal punishment.

A "liberal market economy" is typically more individualistic in structure, is less interventionist in economic regulation, depends far less strongly on the sorts of coordinating institutions that are needed to sustain long-term economic and social relations, and features considerably less extensive welfare provisions. In these economies, flexibility and innovation, rather than stability and investment, form the backbone of comparative institutional advantage. It follows that, particularly under conditions of surplus unskilled labor—conditions which liberal market economies are also more likely to produce—the costs of a harsh, exclusionary criminal justice system are less than they would be in a coordinated market economy. Britain and the United States, of course, fit firmly within the typology of an individualistic, liberal market economy.

Where do political systems fit into this account? The organization of political systems varies widely, of course, between both countries and subnational regions (Tonry 2007a, 2007b; Lacey 2008, chaps. 2–4; Barker 2009; McAra 2011). But it is striking that the two families of capitalist system turn out to be distinguished not only by differently structured production regimes and welfare states (Esping-Andersen 1990, 1996) but also by different types of polities. For example, the coordinated market economies feature, without exception, proportionally representative electoral systems, and the liberal market economies, with a small number of exceptions, first-past-the-post, majoritarian systems. This makes a substantial difference to criminal justice in a number of ways. Of indirect but real importance to punishment, the structure of the political system affects the capacity to build coalitions capable of providing stable support for long-term investment in institutions such as the welfare state, the education system, and the more welfarist versions of criminal justice intervention whose benefits are hard to quantify and are realized only in the medium or long term. More directly, the shape of the political system affects the ways in which perceived anxiety about crime or insecurity register in the electoral process. In long-standing proportionately representative systems, to be brief, there are significant constraints on executive power, as well as robust institutional arrangements facilitating coordination between settled interests and underpinning, in Lijphart's terms, a consensus orientation in politics.[6] In "first-past-the-post" systems, by contrast, a typically adversarial and individualistic political culture, along with a decline in electoral turnout, particularly among younger and less advantaged voters, and a reduction in the number of voters who identify consistently with a particular party, have fostered the volatility of law-and-order politics amid an unedifying scramble for the short-term support of the "floating" or the reluctant voter.

Features of political systems, in other words, conduce to—or militate against—support for the economic and social policies that make it easier for governments to pursue inclusionary criminal justice policies. In liberal market economies with majoritarian electoral systems—particularly under conditions of relatively low trust in politicians and declining electoral turnouts, relatively low deference to the expertise of criminal justice professionals,[7] a reduction in the proportion of the electorate who vote on stable party lines, and candidates for office consequently focused on the resultant "floating" (or potentially abstaining) voter—the unmediated responsiveness of politics to popular opinion in the adversarial context of a two-party system makes it harder for governments to resist a ratcheting up of penal severity wherever key voters become concerned about crime (Enns 2014; 2016). These dynamics become particularly strong where both parties take up a law-and-order agenda (Downes and Morgan 2007; Newburn 2007), and where—as in the United Kingdom and the United States over much of the period since the 1970s—economic inequality and insecurity have fed popular anxiety about crime, marking out penal policy as an especially suitable platform on which politicians from all points of the political spectrum may appeal to undecided voters. The result is, loosely speaking, a "prisoners' dilemma" in which neither party can afford, electorally, to abandon its tough stance, while everyone (other than those—not insignificant—groups with a financial interest in the prison buildup) loses from the increasing human and economic costs of an ever more punitive system (Western 2006; Gottschalk 2014).

The Prisoners' Dilemma is not alone in pointing toward the relevance of political–institutional dynamics in producing crime and punishment. Since the mid-1990s, various features of America's political–institutional structure have begun to attract criminological attention. Michael Tonry (1995, 2004, 2007a) has analyzed not only the impact of the politics of race but also that of a constitutional structure which places few restraints on the substance of criminal policy, of the separation of powers, and of the relative insulation from politics of the policymaking process (see also Savelsberg 1999). Consistent with the argument of *The Prisoners' Dilemma*, he has also noted the relevance of Lijphart's (1984, 1999) distinction between consensus-based and competitive political systems, though he has not as yet pursued the point in terms of an integrated analysis of the institutional structure of the US political system. James Whitman (2003) has argued that the distinctive history of the US political system, which never had to effect the decisive rejection of premodern penal practices oriented to status degradation seen in the systems of the continent of Europe in the late eighteenth and early nineteenth centuries, has decisively shaped the trajectory of American punishment toward its current enactment of unduly *Harsh Justice.* Marie Gottschalk (2006) has traced the shifting role of criminal politics in American history, pointing up a gradual accretion of institutional capacity which ultimately underpinned the prison expansion of the late twentieth century, and a political structure in which the preferences of a distinctively punitive victims' movement registered strongly. Lisa Miller (2008) has shown how the dynamics of criminal justice policy-making differ between the federal, state, and local levels of the multitiered American political system.[8] Vanessa Barker's (2009) study of California, New York, and Washington has shown the way in which different governance structures have contributed to large regional disparities in patterns of punishment. Barker shows that, interacting with the history and culture of state politics, those structures shape varying—populist, managerialist, or deliberative—traditions of political participation which imply markedly different capacities for collective agency. Loïc Wacquant (2009) has emphasized the changing balance between "the penal state" and "the welfare state" attendant on the prison buildup and the shift to workfare-based social welfare, interpreting this as a significant transformation of the nature of the American state toward "neoliberalism" (for discussion, see Lacey 2013a). Both David Garland (2001) and Jonathan Simon (2007) have argued that waning confidence in the political capacity to manage the economy, alongside the relatively straightforward process of demonstrating governmental competence through tough law-and-order policy, has helped to accentuate the tendency to "govern through crime" and enhanced the executive power of officials such as prosecutors. And the decentralization of the US political system, which causes problems for any national reform movement, is an important factor in Garland's (2010) analysis of American retention of capital punishment. Franklin Zimring (2007) has studied the impact of local policymaking on the "great crime decline" and has noted that the fact that (most) criminal justice policymaking is divided between local and state levels has implications for how effectively costs, or a reduction in costs, register in the political process: for example, the penal cost savings produced by an effective crime-prevention strategy at the local level will have to be massive before they register with policymakers at the state level (Zimring 2012, app. B). And a developing literature exploring the various links between crime and punishment and politically relevant economic factors such as wage rates (Bound and Freeman 1992; Boggess and Bound 1993; Freeman 1996; Fagan and Freeman 1999; Western and Beckett 1999; Gould, Weinberg, and Mustard 2002; Machin and Meghir 2004) is raising questions about the causal relevance of institutional factors, although studies in this area have tended so far to be monocausal and relatively little attention has been paid to the ways in which individual incentives and motivations may be influenced by institutional structures and settings. These and other examples throw up important elements of a systematic analysis of how political institutions shape crime and punishment, but they remain at a fragmentary level and do not provide the overarching explanation attempted by *The Prisoners' Dilemma*.

From the point of view of understanding crime and punishment in America, however, *The Prisoners' Dilemma* suffered two key drawbacks. First, it was primarily concerned with punishment rather than crime, and hence did not present a systematic argument about how the two might be related.[9] Second, it prompted the question of why the scale of crime (notably homicide and other serious violence; see Gallo, Lacey, and Soskice, this volume) and punishment in the United States had come to dwarf that in other liberal market economies. Certainly, it provided some tools from which such an analysis might be derived. The US majoritarian system has a particularly weak system of party discipline, its bureaucracy has become highly politicized, and its constitutional controls are oriented to due process rather than to the substance of punishment or criminalization. Moreover, the US economy is marked by particularly low levels of unionization, of employment protections, and of industry/union/government coordination and investment in training; it experienced a particularly catastrophic collapse of Fordist industrial production; its welfare system is particularly ungenerous, and this conduces—notwithstanding its reputation as a classless society—to especially high levels of social inequality and polarization, most vividly around the characteristic of race (see Western and Pettit 2000; Sutton 2004; Western 2006; Wacquant 2009; Lerman and Weaver 2014; Goffman 2014).

Even granting the relevance of the argument that the United States amounts to an "extreme case" of a liberal market economy type, however, the scale of the penal disparities are such as to invite a more careful look at the way in which the model applies. While, as Western and his colleagues have argued (Western and Pettit 2000; Western 2006; see also Wacquant 2009), there is a persuasive case for the proposition that increasing social inequality in the United States is strongly associated with the rise in punishment, with prisons gradually replacing, in many states, social welfare as the dominant strategy for "governing social marginality" (Beckett and Western 2001), this sort of analysis begs the question of why political support for the policies that produced these dynamics should have been so strong in the United States—and in certain US states in particular. According to a 2014 Sentencing Project report, the combined jail and imprisonment rate ranged from a high of 1,597 per 100,000 in Louisiana to a low of 262 in Maine, as compared with an overall US rate of 716. Average rates in the South are substantially higher those in the Northeast (Sentencing Project 2014).[10] This variation also applies to racial disparities in incarceration: the rate of black imprisonment in the United States in 2006 ranged from highs of 4,710 and 4,416 per 100,000 in, respectively, South Dakota and Wisconsin, to lows of 851 in Hawaii, 1,065 in Washington, DC, and 1,579 in Maryland (Mauer and King 2007, 8). And analogous differences can be seen in patterns of capital punishment: since the relegalization of the death penalty in 1976, more than 70 percent of all executions have been carried out by the southern states, with Texas alone accounting for more than a third of the executions that took place in the 30 years from 1976 (Garland 2007, 2010). How can we trace the relevant institutional and causal relationships here?

Local Autonomy and the Polarizing Political Dynamics of Punishment

Many existing analyses of the US political system focus on its distinctive range of checks and balances between judicial, executive, and legislative powers, as well as between state and federal powers. By contrast, we argue that these arrangements, and particularly those pertaining to the federal structure, rarely have a decisive impact on the formation of criminal justice policy, even given key federal initiatives in the area of law enforcement (Feeley and Sarat 1980). For the bulk of criminal policy implementation—and along with it, a decisive formation of criminal policy itself—goes forward not merely at the state but at the local level.[11] The most promising lines of inquiry about the impact of the political system, we argue, have rather to do with the nature of the US party system and the highly decentralized nature of its electoral democracy. These factors both lead to a magnification of the "prisoners' dilemma effect" and imply that much policy—not only criminal justice policy but other social policies that shape the interests and preferences of voters in relation to crime and punishment—is strongly affected by local elections in which voters have a relatively constrained view of the relevant externalities—in other words, where voters are unlikely to support investment in policies from which they will not benefit directly. This underlying dynamic of the political system, we argue, provides a crucial missing link in existing analyses of the relationship between crime, punishment, and inequality in the United States. We have set out this argument in detail elsewhere (Lacey and Soskice 2015);[12] for the purposes of this chapter, however, the core of our thesis can be captured relatively briefly.

There are, we argue, three mutually reinforcing sets of dynamics attendant on the decentralized structure of the US political system, each of which has clear consequences for crime, punishment, social polarization, and—crucially—the links between the three.

First, building on the thesis developed in *The Prisoners' Dilemma*, there is strong reason to think that the multiplication of sites of electoral competition in the American political system, particularly when combined with its quality of weak party discipline and under circumstances of significant median voter concern about crime, produces upward pressure on punishment. As compared with the most similar advanced democracies, the diffusion of electoral competitions at the local level in the American system is quite extraordinary. Elections select not only local politicians in the general sense but also a host of roles directly or indirectly involved in the development and execution of criminal justice policy. Not just city or county governors and boards but (subject to local variation) mayors, school boards, district attorneys, county commissioners, treasurers, zoning boards, police chiefs, and judges compete politically for office (Orfield 1997). Moreover even in areas where, for example, mayors or zoning boards are appointed, they owe their appointment to elected officials and are hence indirectly subject to electoral influence. In a system of weak party discipline—and one where many elections at the local level are not fought primarily on party platforms—candidates for office are on the lookout for issues of concern to key voters around which to frame their case for election. Unfortunately, in the wake of rising concern about crime since the 1970s, criminal justice has become one of these issues. Hence, the "arms race" around toughness on crime between the two main political parties witnessed at the national level in other majoritarian liberal market countries in the late twentieth century has been magnified by the diffusion of electoral democracy at the local level in the United States.

This magnification of the "prisoners' dilemma effect" is of particular significance because of another, related feature of the US political system: the extent to which key aspects of criminal justice policy and indeed social policy more generally are developed at the local level. Whereas in comparable liberal market countries such as Britain, Canada, or Australia, the main lines of policy in areas such as policing, sentencing, planning, and education are set down at the national or provincial/state level, in the United States localities such as cities and counties can shape each of these policy areas to a striking degree (Figure 1.5). This makes the prisoners' dilemma effect yet more powerful. Furthermore, it entails a cluster of accountability problems. This may seem surprising given that we tend to think of democratic elections as an effective form of accountability. But amid a diffusion of electoral sites, accountability gaps can be created when a candidate stands for office on the basis of a policy platform the costs of which he or she will not be held electorally accountable for because they are run from, or because voters ascribe primary responsibility for them to, a different level of government (Chubb 1988; Boggess and Bound

1993; Stuntz 2001; Soskice 2009; Campbell 2012, 306; Zimring 2012, app. B). A classic example would be the overall costs of the prison system, which fall at the state level, as compared with the electoral gains for a prosecutor, judge, or police chief standing on the basis of a promise of or reputation for severity. Unsurprisingly, therefore, empirical evidence of these electoral cycle effects on levels of prosecution, on police practices, and on sentencing is plentiful (Levitt 1997; Brooks and Raphael 2002; Huber and Gordon 2004; Dyke 2007; Shepherd 2009; Berdejó and Yuchtman 2013).

But why should political decentralization affect patterns and levels of crime? And why should voters at the local level be less likely than voters at the state or national level to vote for investment in the sorts of public policies which promise less punitive, potentially more effective strategies for dealing with high crime rates and insecurity about crime? This brings us to the second reason for thinking that the location of so much democratic decision-making in the areas of criminal justice, education, and zoning in the United States in the city or county has had decisive and unfortunate consequences for criminal justice policy. The institutional structure of the American political system entails that local autonomy has tremendous power and that decisions reflect the interests and preferences of median voters at the local level. The key point here is that the median voter in local elections, where turnout is relatively low, is likely to be different—and to have different interests—from the median voter at either state or national elections where turnout is higher. The median voter in local elections in political systems with such a degree of local autonomy is likely to be a homeowner with strong concerns to maintain property values (Fischel 2001, 2004). This voter is therefore inclined to segregate the poor residentially—in the suburbs to keep the poor out and in the cities to push the poor into their own enclaves (the middle classes, including the black middle classes, escape or gentrify)—and to keep property taxes low if public schools are bad (*de facto* segregated) or high if they are good. These voters will also be likely to favor effective policing outside disadvantaged, high-crime areas (Sharp 2013), while being indifferent to the need to invest in "community" policing in poor areas (where victims are poor and are not median voters). These areas accordingly experienced either a vacuum of legitimate law enforcement or intensive, stop-and-frisk, or even military-style policing, often on an intermittent basis and invariably poorly tailored to the needs of crime victims (Meares and Kahan 1999). Disadvantaged youths accordingly found themselves in dangerous environments which were in turn extremely difficult—and costly—to police effectively on a consensus basis and in which gangs offered alternative means of social protection (Venkatesh 2008): hence, a self-reinforcing process was at work. Policing is normally determined at the city level for poor inner-city areas (a unified city police force is the rule, even if there are somewhat different policies in different areas of the city). Poor areas are seldom separate cities (and so are unable to determine policing practices), though they would presumably prefer more investment in community policing and other crime-prevention initiatives to spending on mass imprisonment, both for their own safety and to prevent their own young men being imprisoned (Miller 2008).

Locally determined policies on zoning, education, and policing have strong implications for violent crime, both in highly segregated poor (largely black and Hispanic) tracts and via its spillover into middle-class areas. In a powerful study, Krivo and Petersen have shown how violent crime is strongly related to highly segregated poor areas with a high proportion of high school dropouts (Krivo, Peterson, and Kuhl 2009; Peterson and Krivo 2010). Krivo and Peterson also show that middle-class areas in cities with high proportions of such poor, high-violence areas suffer from some spillover of violent crime.

Other areas of cities, therefore, prefer tough sentencing since they regard it as cheaper than effective policing, let alone broader social policy interventions, and because they do not see themselves as benefiting from the greater safety for those in poor areas, which high-quality policing, combined with other social initiatives, can arguably buy (Meares and Kahan 1999). This holds *a fortiori* for housing and education provision in these areas. There are therefore two conditions for investment in effective (and expensive) community policing. The first is economic activity sufficiently strong in poor areas for such policing to be feasible, combined with its being economic for the rest of the city to invest in these areas. (This seems likely to have been one factor in the crime decline in New York, where the small size and high density of Manhattan implied that violence and poverty in Harlem, for example, had palpable citywide effects.[13]) The second is political determination at the state level, preferably realized through a clear legislative framework, to prevent tough sentencing.[14] In many racially and economically diverse urban areas of the United States, these conditions are not met—and were not met to a particularly stark degree in the 1970s and 1980s.

"Homevoters"—people particularly motivated to vote out of concern with ensuring policies that protect the value of their primary asset (Fischel 2001, 2004, 2005)—turn out to vote in much higher numbers than others (Hajnal and Trounstine 2005; see also Enos 2016) and co-opt the local state, which in effect operates in their private interests: the local state is used to insure private assets. But why should this "homevoter" effect be so powerful in the United States, leading to unique levels of residential segregation (Peach 1996; Johnston, Poulsen, and Forrest 2007)? Two considerations are important and may to some extent differentiate the United States from comparable countries such as the United Kingdom. The first has to do with the structure of the labor market and the provision of pensions. The motivation of the median voter is almost certainly strongly affected by concern about property values in other countries where homeownership is widespread, as is the case in most liberal market economies. But in United States the home represents not only the largest personal investment for many middle-class families but also their pension pot as compared with more complete public and occupational pension provision in the less flexibilized liberal market economies. Growing rates of homeownership through the second half of the twentieth century have increased the relevant dynamics (Simon 2010). The second consideration brings us back to local autonomy and follows from the fact that the main mechanism by which segregation is achieved is that of zoning—a key form of autonomous political power at the local level ever since the Supreme Court ruled on the legality of zoning ordinances in 1926.[15] By contrast to the localized basis for zoning, education, and policing decisions in the United States, all the key rules governing zoning, police organization and practice, justice, public prosecution, and the education system are made primarily at the national or provincial level in other liberal market economies such as Canada, the United Kingdom, and New Zealand (Figure 1.5).

The idea that people are more likely to vote for public goods at the national than at the state or local level may seem counterintuitive given evidence that more homogeneous groups are more likely to vote for collective goods (Alesina, Baqir, and Easterly 1999). But it makes sense if one assumes a mobile society in which people vote at the national level for goods from which they will benefit wherever they live. Conversely, at the local level people will be inclined to vote only for things from which they can be guaranteed to benefit—hence voters are less likely to vote for long-term investment, notably in education, where the benefits accruing may then move elsewhere. Local voters, in short, have an incentive to "capture" the benefits of social policy by restricting their support to policies from which they are sure to benefit. Under conditions of relative homogeneity, this becomes a less pressing concern. But the extensiveness of local electoral government means that arrangements which are in the interests of politically powerful swing voters—themselves drawn from more advantaged groups—can more readily be inscribed in public policy.

The final aspect of decentralization which bears on our explanation of America's distinctive problems of criminal violence, punitiveness, and polarizing social policy follows from the second. As the Great Society and New Deal Programs of the mid-twentieth century attest,[16] the United States can on occasion develop significant national policies in areas such as education, housing, and criminal justice. But the federal government can push forward nationwide policy objectives only within certain constitutional constraints and under certain conditions: either where a party with a clear program has control of Congress as well as the presidency or where there is cross-partisan consensus. Where neither of these conditions pertains, everything turns on states or localities. And even when federal initiatives are brokered, implementation largely rests on action at the state and local levels (Feeley and Sarat 1980). In the absence of powerful agencies, implementation furthermore has to be triggered either by legal enforcement, with all its problems of cost, unevenness, delay, and ineffectiveness as a strategic tool (Kagan 2001; Douglas 2005; Pattillo 2007; Aaronson 2014), or by financial incentives—the provision of which has become more problematic in an era of small government ideology and budget deficits. Lessons from school segregation and civil rights history show that while litigation strategies can achieve real progress, they are both costly and divisive: they provide an adversarial framework for policy implementation, while individual case-based legal remedies or even class actions are rarely effective as resolving structural or coordination problems (Kagan 2001; Douglas 2005). Hence, this distinctively American translation of political activism into legal strategy has significant disadvantages. It is no surprise that law has come to assume such dominance in the American system: it makes sense that the more individualistic and fragmented the society, the more likely it will be to resort to legal enforcement which does not depend on compromise and negotiation, hence bypassing structural problems of coordination. But these problems, inevitably, reproduce themselves at the implementation level (Massey and Denton 1993, 14–15, 187, 223–30, 206 ff; Pattillo 2007, 110–14; Peterson and Krivo 2010, chap. 5) and have become more acute in an era of declining funding for agency enforcement (Pierson and Skocpol 2007).

Local Autonomy as Criminogenic?

We have argued that the dynamics of voting and of electoral competition in the decentralized US system have implied powerful polarizing forces. This polarization, and its exclusion of the "truly disadvantaged" (Wilson 1987), also have key implications for comparative levels of violence (Miller 2015, 2016). We have shown elsewhere (see Gallo, Lacey, and Soskice, this volume) that distinctively high US homicide rates are matched by levels of the much larger category of serious violent crime—also significantly higher than those in comparable countries such as England and Wales, Canada, and New Zealand. As Peterson and Krivo (2010)[17] have shown, levels of violence are strongly positively correlated with levels of residential segregation, in terms of both poverty and race—with the criminogenic effects of segregation spilling out across the entire city: violent crime is higher in the most advantaged areas of the most highly segregated cities than in the least advantaged areas of the most integrated cities (Charles 2006; Krivo, Peterson, and Kuhl 2009).

But why should high levels of violence be related to political decentralization? The dominant explanation of the relationship between segregation, poverty, and crime lies in "disorganization theory" (Sampson and Groves 1989; Hagan and Peterson 1995; Sampson and Wilson 1995)—the argument that deprivation and, in particular, concentrations of deprivation undermine the capacity of communities to sustain norms of order. Crucially for our argument, much of that disorganization in the United States is traceable to political decisions at the local level (Massey and Denton 1993, 14, 153–60; Hagan and Peterson 1995, 15, 23–24). As Krivo and colleagues spell out the irony here, the greater the fragmentation and polarization, the greater the need for coalition-building to resolve problems, yet the lower the capacity to engage in it (Krivo, Peterson, and Kuhl 2009). Inadequate or oppositional policing of poor areas plays into the strength of gangs (Hagedorn 1998, 2008), which get involved in legitimate as well as illegitimate social control and team up with institutions like block clubs, community associations, and churches to provide local goods and security—hence with public local support and toleration of their illegitimate activities, albeit within limits (Pattillo-McCoy 1999, chaps. 4 and 5; Venkatesh 2008). Poor policing—and policing that commands little trust within communities—prompts deprived groups to form protection associations which can readily resort to violence and/or turn into gangs, creating violence-promoting boundary disputes (cf. analogous dynamics traced in work on ethnic violence: Fearon and Laitin 2000). In the face of these developments, the middle-class median voter reacts by interpreting crime and indeed poverty as matters of individual responsibility, thus legitimating his or her own resistance to voting for expensive strategies such as the improved housing, better schools, and proactive policing which might hold out some hope of real crime-reductive effects (Royster 2003, 184 ff; Peterson and Krivo 2010; Alexander 2012, 216). In short, the spillover of the effects—material and psychological—of violent crime promotes electoral concerns which foster polarizing policies through the locally controlled mechanisms of education, policing, prosecution, and zoning.

This is not to say, of course, that cultural and economic factors have been unimportant, alongside political dynamics, in shaping crime and punishment in the United States. The collapse of Fordist production in the 1970s, leading to the loss of many unskilled and semiskilled jobs, had a particularly devastating effect, especially in northern and midwestern industrial cities. And, as we shall see in more detail in the next section, it had a particularly severe impact on black workers, coming as it did relatively soon after the Civil Rights Act (Wilson 1987, 1996; Lacey and Soskice 2015). But the fragmentation of America's political system does help to explain both the relative lack of success in motivating support for the long-term project of building educational and other bridges to new forms of employment, as well as providing adequate welfare support, for those who lost out with the demise of the Fordist era. And the resultant economic and social exclusion, exacerbated by stark levels of residential segregation, has produced some distinctive social patterns which themselves both pose problems for and further accentuate some of the dynamics already present in the criminal justice system. Inevitably, disadvantaged people with poor prospects in the legitimate economy looked for other avenues of self-development and earnings. Here, interacting with the impact of local autonomy, the infrastructure of gangs becomes important since the protection, peer approval, and economic activities provided by gangs constitute an alternative, parallel social and economic system for young people but one which is, crucially, a bridge that is hard to recross once it has been traversed (Fagan and Freeman 1999; Venkatesh 2008). In this context, the distinctive ethnic composition of gangs in the United States, as well as their unique scale and geographical reach, acquire real significance in explaining American patterns in crime and punishment and intersect with cultural factors pertaining to both the persisting separation of distinct racial identities in some parts of the population (Pattillo-McCoy 1999) and the widely debated American attachment to guns.

The much discussed crime decline of the 1990s was associated with a decisive upswing in the real hourly wages of men in the bottom economic half of the population and in particular for those in the tenth and twentieth wage percentiles (Austin 2011). This is of particular significance because accumulating scholarship on the relationship between crime and labor market indicators suggests that changes in the average hourly real wage levels of low-skilled workers are much more strongly associated with crime levels than are unemployment rates—the main focus of the criminological literature and hence the basis for widespread skepticism in that literature about the relationship between labor market and other economic indicators and crime (Machin and Meghir 2004). Furthermore, it is arguable that the greatest strides toward racial integration in the United States took place not in the wake of the Civil Rights Act but in the decades of growth from the 1940s to the late 1960s (with more modest gains also seen during the "great moderation" of 1990–2008).

If we look at the development of gangs during this period, it is possible to hypothesize some explanations. Research shows that by the (late) 1970s gangs were strongly established in many of the highest crime areas of the United States and that they were predominantly black or Hispanic (Office of Juvenile Justice and Delinquency Prevention 2013). This period, of course, coincided with the accelerating War on Drugs. Drugs were largely controlled by street gangs. As has been widely acknowledged (Tonry 1995; Stuntz 2001, 2008), arrests on suspicion of drug offenses are often used by the police as convenient proxies for other kinds of law enforcement. Even without discriminatory sentencing norms such as those pertaining to crack until the Fair Sentencing Act of 2010, this would help to explain some part of the disproportionate racial impact of criminal enforcement.[18]

We need to add several further items to this account. First, the consolidation of gang networks within prisons creates a nexus between black/Hispanic imprisonment and continued gang activity postsentence (Skarbek 2014). Second, the growth of gangs in (particularly urban) localities makes it hard for the police to gather intelligence without cooperating with them. Third, social disorganization allows gangs to organize and get a purchase at the local level, while reduced investment in policing in poor areas added to problems of violent crime lead to attenuated networks of information, making effective policing yet more difficult. Fourth, the link between a sense of insecurity and fear of crime and gang activity implied increasing reliance on gangs' alternative protection systems in disadvantaged communities. Data on gangs in the United States moreover suggest a close association between the scale and scope of gang activity and fluctuations in the economy; the collapse of Fordism was associated with the steady growth and diffusion of gangs, while the period of growth from the mid-1990s was associated with a corresponding decline. Gang activity, this suggests, is proto-economic activity, with gangs providing the nexus to "careers" for a substantial number of (particularly black and Hispanic) youth during the 1970s–1990s. With these factors in mind, the patterns of criminalization and punishment become less puzzling. And, crucially from a comparative perspective, nothing equating to the level, intensity, or racial patterning of gang activity existed in the United Kingdom over the same period (Hagedorn 1998, 2008; Office of Juvenile Justice and Delinquency Prevention 2013).

Counterarguments to the Local Autonomy Thesis: The Politics of Race, Federalization, and the Elite Politics of Law and Order

In this section, we consider three possible ripostes to the argument set out above: first, the argument, widely voiced in criminological, sociological, and political science literature, that the key driver of American exceptionalism in crime, punishment, and social inequality is the distinctive American history and politics of race; second, the argument that many of the factors which have driven the increase in American exceptionalism since the 1970s stem from the increasing activism of the federal state in the area of criminal justice; and third, the argument that the prison buildup had little to do with crime but rather was the creation of a political elite motivated ultimately by electoral interests, encapsulated in the "southern strategy" of the Republican Party. In our view, each of these positions offers either a misdiagnosis or, at best, a radically incomplete explanation for the development of US criminal policy from the 1970s on.

The History and Politics of Race

Race and racism have long occupied a central place in explanations of distinctive American patterns of crime and, especially, punishment (Tonry 1995, 2011; Loury 2003, 2010), as indeed of social organization more generally (Wilson 1987; Massey and Denton 1993). And recently, a striking argument has placed race at the heart of the explanation of the prison buildup, suggesting that mass imprisonment is in effect an analogue of the vicious "Jim Crow" system geared to perpetuating the structural exclusion of black Americans from full citizenship in the first half of the twentieth century (Alexander 2012). In this section, while acknowledging that it would be foolish to deny that the history and politics of race have been key contributors to America's distinctive patterns of crime and punishment, we suggest that a comparative analysis undermines the suggestion that race is the primary, let alone the exclusive, explanation for American exceptionalism in crime and punishment. We argue, moreover, that the impact of race has itself been decisively shaped by the dynamics of local autonomy analyzed in the first part of this chapter.

While the overrepresentation of certain ethnic groups, notably young black men, is a marked phenomenon in the criminal justice systems of many countries, with the disproportion in England and Wales, for example, corresponding to that in the United States (Tonry 2014), the much larger population of African Americans in the United States than of black Britons in the

United Kingdom entails a more noticeable impact on overall prison numbers, as well as a larger social and political problem in absolute terms.[19] In 2006, the imprisonment rate for men in the United States was 943 per 100,000; disaggregating by race, this drops to 487 for white males, rising to 1,261 for Hispanic and Latino males and to a staggering 3,042 for black males (Bureau of Justice Statistics 2007, 8). Despite drops in US prison rates beginning in 2010–2014 and some reduction in racial disparities, these remain very stark: in 2014 the national imprisonment rate for males was 890 per 100,000; 465 for white males; 1,090 for Hispanics; and 2,724 for black males (Mauer and King 2007; Bureau of Justice Statistics 2015, 7, table 5). These factors, it might be argued, are in themselves sufficient to lead us to expect that the United States would display especially acute penal severity. Moreover, the War on Drugs has undoubtedly accentuated the racially skewed patterns of law enforcement since the 1980s, not least because of the use of drug arrests as "proxies" for enforcement of more serious offenses that present greater problems of proof (Tonry 1995, 2011; Loury 2003, 2010; Mauer 2006; Stuntz 2011).

But, as James Forman (2012) has persuasively argued, an explanation founded wholly in racial exclusion encounters significant difficulties—not least in explaining the class aspects of racial patterns of crime and punishment (with mass imprisonment, unlike Jim Crow, leaving a substantial black middle class virtually untouched and, conversely, having a significant impact on poor whites and Hispanics: see also Gottschalk 2014, chaps. 6–9); in explaining black political support for tough crime policies, as witnessed by policy choices in the black-majority jurisdiction of Washington, DC (Forman 2012, 38–44); as well as in explaining the role of violent crime—in which black Americans are disproportionately both victims and offenders—in moving crime up the political agenda from the mid-1960s. A comparative analysis reinforces Forman's call for a more nuanced interpretation. For a start, the huge penal disparity between the United States and other liberal market economies at similar levels of economic and political development has become markedly greater since the 1970s, while in the earlier part of the twentieth century American penal practices equated more closely to those of, say, the United Kingdom. Until the mid-1970s, the US imprisonment rate was relatively stable, ranging from a low of 119 in 1925 to 153 in 1974, with moderate fluctuations, and breaching the 200 mark only in a single year—1939.[20] Moreover, the gap between imprisonment rates in the United States and in England and Wales is two and one half times larger today than it was in 1970, notwithstanding a large increase in the English/Welsh rate during that period (Figures 1.1–1.3). And while some of the explanatory factors which we rely on—notably the collapse of Fordism—relate specifically to the more recent period in which those disparities have grown, many of the salient features of the US system—including its relatively high black and Hispanic population and its practices of racial oppression and institutional discrimination—have a much longer history (King and Smith 2011; Alexander 2012). It is true, of course, that black Americans and, to a somewhat lesser extent, Hispanics have suffered particularly acutely from the labor market changes of the 1970s and 1980s, in a tragic collision between economic forces and the continuing legacy of racism, which put African Americans in precisely the wrong place (poor areas in large cities) at precisely the wrong time (during the collapse of industrial production) (Wilson 1987, 1996; see also Allen and Farley 1986). Moreover, the collapse in the industrial economy came hard on the heels of the passage of the Civil Rights Act, arguably underpinning a more radical backlash against the legislation than might otherwise have occurred (Forman 2012, 34).

It is instructive here to compare the United States with New Zealand—a country that has, in its Maori population, a disadvantaged minority of similar relative size[21] and which exhibits similar overrepresentation of that minority in both crime and punishment: while Maori constitute 15 percent of the New Zealand population, they make up 51 percent of its prison population (Pratt and Clark 2005; New Zealand Department of Corrections 2007). Moreover, while never subjected to slavery, the Maori people were expropriated by British colonialism and struggled for over a century for compensation and proper recognition of their culture. Indeed, most serious observers of New Zealand's white culture would regard it as having had significant racist elements, reflected, for example, in its immigration policy through the twentieth century. Yet we see in New Zealand nothing approaching the scale overall of crime, punishment, or segregation that pertains in the United States (Johnston, Poulsen, and Forrest 2005, 2007). Though this does not exclude the possibility that race has an independent impact on the overall pattern and scale of American punishment, it is also worth noting that if we remove blacks from the US imprisonment figures, the rate remains in the region of 450 per 100,000, about three times the level in England and Wales and two and a half times that in New Zealand. Even with Hispanics too removed from the prison figures, the rate remains about 300, double that in England and Wales and one and a half times that in New Zealand. The legacy of a vicious history of racism, even reinforced by continuing worries about discrimination, is, pace many commentators (e.g., Tonry 1995; Alexander 2012), not enough in itself to explain American crime and punishment.

We further argue that the concept of institutional racism which is so frequently invoked in the relevant literature exhibits some ambiguity as between two explanatory positions. The first is the claim that what is at issue is pretextual racism covered up by formally equal institutional structures that are really a proxy for race-based classifications: straightforwardly discriminatory motivations underlie these institutional designs (Massey and Denton 1993; Alexander 2012; Peterson and Krivo 2010, 33). The second is the rather different claim that continuing patterns of racial segregation and disadvantage are an unintended consequence of institutional structures that have evolved in particular ways over time; for example, Wilson's argument (1987) that the timing of desegregation and the Civil Rights Act happened to coincide with the collapse of Fordism and that this hit black Americans hardest because of their recent entry into the labor market on (formally) equal terms. The "pretextual racism" account has retained its appeal and has recently assumed a particular priority thanks to the striking argument of Michelle Alexander's *The New Jim Crow*, which is often couched in the terms of deliberate policy—for example, in her description of poor whites as "collateral damage. . . . Not the real target" (Alexander 2012, 204). Yet in Alexander's book and in much of the relevant literature, it is not absolutely clear which of those two positions is being adopted. For example, while Alexander argues (persuasively) that a "racial caste" system can be sustained without racial animus (Alexander 2012, 183 ff), she also refers to "color-blindness" as a "veil" (p. 204), which appears to imply a strategy (for further examples of this ambiguity, see Massey and Denton 1993, 182–85, 205; Alexander 2012, 223).

If pretextual racism is the favored explanation, it becomes hard to explain the undoubted progress, in economic and social terms, that American blacks made up to the 1970s, particularly after the Second World War, leading to the growth of a substantial black middle class that has not been affected by mass imprisonment in anything like the same way as disadvantaged blacks, Hispanics, or, indeed, whites (Forman 2012, 58 ff). Conversely, the unintended consequences version still begs the question of what explains why the particular form of American institutions had continuing racially patterned effects, notwithstanding some key political efforts—in the White House, in Congress, in the courts, and among social movements—to avoid it. What are their longer-term origins, and what has enabled them to remain stable notwithstanding their adverse effects on the realization of an articulated public policy of equal protection and antidiscrimination (Aaronson 2014)? Evidence from social psychology (Baumeister and Leary 1995) suggests that most people prefer to live in proximity with like-minded neighbors and that more advantaged people show consistent bias against and hostile attitudes toward low-income/low-skill groups unless they behave subserviently. The unfortunate likelihood is that not merely "blacks on the block" but "poor whites on the block" push down middle-class house prices (including those of black homeowners). This is an inference not merely from our argument but from the minutes of zoning boards and case studies in the sociological literature (Pattillo 2007, chap. 5; Matejczyk 2001). Sampson and Wilson (1995) are right to insist that there is "more than just race" at work here: that race and class are inextricably linked in the production of the persisting and devastating disadvantages still encountered by African Americans in criminal justice, education, housing, and beyond (see also Wilson 1987, 2009; and on the effects of inequality in punishment, Western 2006; Lerman and Weaver 2014). Massey and Denton (1993), Charles (2006), and Peterson and Krivo (2010) are right to ascribe primary importance to residential segregation in the production of disadvantage—an effect that feeds into other important dynamics such as social networks; access to education, training, and jobs; and the development of patterns of employment (Boyd 1996). But more work remains to be done if we are to pin down the institutional processes and political motivations that produce that segregation (see also Sampson 2012). King and Smith's account in terms of shifting coalitions forming opposing transformative and antitransformative "racial institutional orders" or "racial institutional alliances" (2005, 2011) provides in our view a promising framework in that it includes a clear description of the role of agency as well as of institutions. But even here, there remains some ambiguity about the extent to which the authors assume the current "antitransformative" coalition—which they argue to operate within the parameters of formal equality but via a negative agenda aimed at opposing "measures (such as affirmative action) explicitly aimed at reducing racial inequalities" (King and Smith 2005, 83)—to be characterized by a deliberate desire to impede progress toward a reduction of substantive racial inequality.

To reiterate, in arguing that race has not been the sole or overriding cause of mass incarceration in America, we are not arguing that the history and politics of race do not have large and continuing effects. The stark facts of racial inequality in the United States, as graphically charted by scholars like Wilson (1987), Massey and Denton (1993), Loury (2003), Western (2006), and Alexander (2012) are clearly direct and indirect consequences of southern racism in (and before) the nineteenth century (Charles 2006, chap. 6; Aaronson 2014) and the continuing echoes of slavery, the Jim Crow regime which replaced it, and a host of associated institutional arrangements, notably in relation to policing (Muller 2012). And we must acknowledge the continuing existence of racist attitudes—which persist of course not just in the United States but also in the United Kingdom and in New Zealand,[22] to take just two broadly comparable cases. The pathologies of racial oppression and discrimination are near-historical constants in the United States as in many other

Western societies, with manifestations and effects that long predate the era of mass incarceration. But continuing segregation, particularly in the industrial cities of the Northeast and Midwest, along with the lack of any real educational escape for the truly disadvantaged, have been consequences of local median voters' choices under conditions of radical local autonomy. And this has been exacerbated by the social disorganization attendant on the demographic implications of mass migration and, later, the gradual exit, whether to suburbs or to contiguous areas (Pattillo-McCoy 1999), of a sizeable number of the black middle class (Wilson 1987). In addition, the centrifugal dynamics set up by local autonomy have driven demographic divisions within as well as between racial groups (Charles 2006), just as they have given local black political leaders disincentives to combat segregation (Massey and Denton 1993, 153–60, 213–15). Once divisions of disadvantage become mapped onto space, the possibilities of reversal[23]—notably through educational achievement—steadily diminish. And these local institutional arrangements that have, often through zoning, fostered the spatial concentration of disadvantage crucially predate the great migrations of black Americans of the early and mid-twentieth century.

The resulting tragedy of entrenched segregation did not happen on the same scale in systems where policing, planning, and education policy are developed at the national level (Figure 1.5). For example, the degree of racial residential segregation in America has been shown to be substantially higher than that in the United Kingdom, Australia, or New Zealand (Johnston, Poulsen, and Forrest 2005, fig. 4, 2007). This can hardly be thought to be because other Anglo-Saxon countries are strangers to racism or indeed to discriminatory public policy. The United Kingdom introduced an implicitly color-based "nationality" (i.e., immigration) act in 1971 and comprehensive race discrimination legislation only in 1976, 12 years after the Civil Rights Act. Australia abolished the last elements of the white Australia immigration policy which had prevailed since the beginning of the twentieth century only in 1973. Perhaps most striking of all, New Zealand, whose Maori population is, as we have seen, roughly comparable to the black American population in terms of both proportionate size and historic social and economic disadvantage and is overrepresented in the prison population to a similar degree (New Zealand Department of Corrections 2007), had an explicitly white New Zealand immigration policy until 1986. Yet Maoris have been integrated into the cities in which they are most populous, notably Auckland, about twice as completely (in terms of residential segregation) as American blacks.

In America's radically decentralized system, it is impossible to frame and find consistent support for political strategies to combat segregation. And without such policies, racial disadvantage will continue to accumulate. Indeed, one might even say that it is not primarily racial dynamics which today cause segregation but rather the segregation-promoting dynamic of local politics that consolidates the problem of black and Hispanic disadvantage. This is consistent with Peterson and Krivo's findings (2010) that higher segregation is accompanied by higher levels of violence across the city. American localism predates, and cannot be argued to have been motivated by, racism; but it has, unfortunately, had particularly striking effects in consolidating the disadvantage of certain groups, notably blacks and Hispanics.

Local autonomy has been a key element in the government of the United States since the early nineteenth century, at least outside the southern states. Moreover, through the nineteenth century, the local autonomy of cities and townships was critical in driving economic development outside the South. This contrasted with the push in the United Kingdom and its settler colonies toward centralization. Equally, the system of ethnic segregation of migrants in the North and the Midwest long predates black migration (Katznelson 1981). Indeed, to the extent that people prefer to live among those they consider to be similar to themselves (Baumeister and Leary 1995), one might see residential sorting as a "normal" response of local democratic autonomy to waves of migration, albeit one which has ill effects. But earlier migrants had significantly higher education and more developed institutions of social organization: the Irish, Poles, and Italians had the hierarchical Roman Catholic Church; Germans and Swedes brought a strong tradition of local associational organization with them to the United States. This in turn made it relatively easy for "city hall" governments to incorporate them into employment and the education system. These groups accordingly found it easier to find a position within the system of "city trenches" which formed the nineteenth-century system of local government in the United States and were gradually integrated in both residential and employment terms. But, as Katznelson (1981) has charted, after the breakdown of city trenches, continuing black segregation made it hard for them to find stable positions in local government; and, as a further complicating factor, in so far as black local politicians have stable power bases, this often depends on residential segregation, hence compromising their commitment to measures to combat segregation (Massey and Denton 1993; Douglas 2005; Pattillo 2007).

The legacy of both slavery and the governmental structure of the South right through to the end of the Jim Crow era accordingly had two effects which are of special importance in explaining why it turned out to be so difficult to achieve real black integration, particularly in the cities of the North and Midwest. First, the southern regime impeded the development of any political structuring of black society—a fact which had significant long-term implications for social disorganization. And second, the southern regime restricted the educational development of blacks. We argue that it is these features, rather than, as Wilson (1987) suggests, the sheer size of the black migration which have had such damaging implications for the chances of black integration in the North. This historical legacy was then magnified by the dynamics set up by strong local autonomy and weak national capacity for policy development and implementation. The collapse of Fordism happened at a disastrous time vis-à-vis black integration, and local autonomy made things decisively worse by allowing the median voter to zone poverty and disadvantage spatially and educationally. This has set up a polarizing dynamic in which the more advantaged have an interest in, and, given local autonomy, the power to, separate themselves ever more completely—spatially, culturally, educationally, economically—from the disadvantaged. Since blacks and Hispanics are markedly overrepresented among the disadvantaged, they suffer especially from these dynamics. In this light, mass imprisonment looks dispiritingly like the extreme policy manifestation of a much more widespread institutional (as well as social) dynamic. Pattillo-McCoy's (1999) refinement of Wilson's (1987) thesis about outmigration of the black middle class—often into liminal areas between white suburbs and inner city—plus the continuing extent of intraracial commerce (Boyd 1996) reinforces the idea that they too would have been more affected than the white middle class by the collapse of Fordism.

The key problem therefore lies in the local political institutions that have driven and sustained socioeconomic segregation and in doing so subverted not only the ideals of the civil rights movement but any real prospect of alleviating poverty and disadvantage in the absence of state or federal initiatives. In the face of these dynamics, the main tools for national policymaking and for the implementation of national policy at the local level—the provision of federal grants to localities, the institution of regulatory agencies to produce and/or monitor standards, and the enforcement of constitutional standards in the courts—have proved weak or even impotent. Local administration of federal grants subjects federal policy to local political dynamics. Regulatory agencies tend to be weak and have in any event become less salient in the wake of the "new federalism" (Feeley and Sarat 1980) and, most recently, of budget cuts. And litigation is protracted, expensive, divisive, uneven in its impact, poorly adapted to tackle broad issues of policy or principle reaching beyond the specific case,[24] and unhelpfully trained on issues of process rather than issues of substance (Kagan 2001). In this context, even criminalization of forms of discrimination often operates merely as symbolic politics, diverting attention from, and having little power to address, structural causes of disadvantage (Aaronson 2014). Key examples of these pathologies of overreliance on legal enforcement include the Gautreaux litigation in Chicago and the drift in litigation challenging state public school financing systems and in particular the impact of the varying tax base on education provision (Massey and Denton 1993, 14–15, 187, 223–30, 206 ff; Pattillo 2007, 110–14; Peterson and Krivo 2010, chap. 5). Since the *Rodriguez* case[25] in which the US Supreme Court in effect diverted this issue to state courts, there has been a gradual shift from a concern with equity to a diluted concern to enforce an obligation merely to provide a baseline of adequate education and a reluctance to treat children in poorer school districts as victims of unequal protection or to subject local education financing to more than deferential scrutiny for the purposes of constitutional review (Nickerson and Deenihan 2002). The racial justice to which the civil rights movement aspired remains all too distant—as social outcomes in education, crime, punishment, and housing all too clearly attest. Our argument is that the decentralization and fragmentation of power in the American political system, and the political sway which this gives to parochial self-interest, is one important reason why that is the case.

The Limited Impact of "Federalization" in the Context of Local Power

Recently, two influential scholars have mounted arguments that speak to political institutional structure and which merit particular attention because they argue against the position we have adopted, in that they attribute the rise in crime and punishment in part to an impoverishment of local democracy. Lisa Miller (2008) has focused on the significance of the differently constituted policymaking environments at the national, state, and local levels. She diagnoses a distortion of political representation at the national and state levels and argues that it has been of great significance in the upswing in punishment as a result of the increasing federalization of criminal policy (see also Stuntz 2001, 2006, 2008, 2011; Husak 2008). In her empirical study, Miller found that local politics in Philadelphia evinced a markedly more complex, less straightforwardly punitive analysis of crime than that which pertained at the national or state level. Her argument is that the distance of state and national politicians from constituents' concerns, in which both criminal victimization and the deleterious social impact of mass imprisonment register rather strongly, and the influence of prosecutors and other pro-victim lobbies have had a decisive impact on the acceleration of punitiveness at those levels.

In similar vein, in his important posthumous book *The Collapse of American Criminal Justice* (2011), William Stuntz noted that local political decision-making produced in many cities a new investment in policing and a rethinking of policing policy that is widely (though not universally: Harcourt 2001) acknowledged to have had some positive impact in reducing crime, increasing a sense of security, and moderating the demand for punishment. State decision-making, by contrast, produced an ever larger and more costly prison system, as well as sentencing frameworks which often (though not universally) facilitated a move to greater severity in sentencing. A greater involvement of local decision-makers in the construction and delivery of policy, he concluded, would lead to a more moderated approach (see also Bibas 2012; Lacey 2013b). Stuntz accordingly argued for the redrawing of electoral constituencies in terms that allowed for the voices of differently constituted—less advantaged, less white—groups of median voters to swing the outcome.

This is, at first sight, an attractive argument. But if we are right about the dynamics of local democracy in the contemporary United States, its appeal is merely superficial. First, even if it was possible to garner the political support necessary for such a structural change, this would have little effect on enhancing equality in the criminal process. For since good-quality criminal justice, like good-quality schools and good-quality housing, costs money, in the absence of redistribution of income via taxation, the zoning of electoral districts within smaller, more "communitarian" units would simply serve to exacerbate the already powerful polarizing and ghetto-producing dynamics of the American political system. And, crucially, issues of redistribution would continue to be decided at levels where the median voter is unlikely to be enthusiastic about paying higher taxes to be used on goods which they do not want, which they do not need, or to which they do not have access.

Our argument, secondly, runs directly counter to Stuntz's conclusion in arguing that, in crucial ways, the check on federal influence at the local level has conduced to volatility in criminal justice policy because the federal median voter has a different view of the relevant externalities from the local median voter. But we also question how important federalization has really been, in comparison with the influence of political dynamics and decisions at the local level. Let us take what is probably the key example for the "federalization" analysis: the War on Drugs. It is incontrovertible that the War on Drugs significantly expanded federal jurisdiction (Tonry 1995; Mauer 2006, 157–76). And while most enforcement was at the state and local levels, this was federally influenced, primarily via financial incentives to states, in terms of both cash incentives to mold legislative or enforcement policy in particular ways and provision of the military-style policing hardware that has recently risen to prominence, with baleful effect, on the streets of Ferguson, Missouri. Many commentators cite these incentives and set out the relevant figures, but they rarely give any careful critical attention to the question of how big these financial incentives really were, in the context of overall state budgets (see, e.g., Alexander 2012, 73 ff; cf. Feeley and Sarat 1980, 36–61). From this comparative point of view, we argue that the federal incentives are unlikely to have been large enough to get states and localities to do what they did not already have substantial reason to do as a result of local political incentives. As an indicative measure, in 1992, the federal Byrne Grant program provided $160 million for multijurisdictional task forces enforcing drug laws: this compares with a total policing expenditure that year of approximately $40 billion. Moreover, the fact that the financial incentives were subject to local administration implied plentiful room for operational interpretive maneuver at the local level.

As Marie Gottschalk (2006, 41–76) has shown, to the (in our view modest) extent that there has been a nationalization of crime policy in the United States, it goes back a long way, at least to the creation of the FBI. Federal policy can be influential when it is backed by the creation of powerful executive agencies such as the FBI. But agency enforcement is not always successful. President Johnson constructed the Law Enforcement Assistance Administration (LEAA) (Beckett 1997, 90–92, 99) in an effort to counter Barry Goldwater's emphasis on crime in the presidential campaign of 1964. It provided modest federal funds to bolster law enforcement at state and local levels backed up by a national agency oriented to the delivery of consistent standards of effective law enforcement (Feeley and Sarat 1980). Though the LEAA was not infrequently used for moderate purposes such as diversion schemes, it is often argued to have set the model for more robust federal intervention via the sorts of financial incentives used in the War on Drugs and prompted the growth of law enforcement agency lobby groups (Beckett 1997). Yet in the long run, the LEAA was a model case study in the limits of federal enforcement powers. These forms of highly visible federal intervention should not blind us to the fact that not only federal but even state control of American criminal justice is dwarfed by local control and implementation: indeed, as both Feeley and Sarat (1980) and Scheingold (2010, 82–83) have argued, this explains the ultimate demise of the LEAA. The recent decline in the funding of agency enforcement in an era of "small government" means that implementation—always the Achilles heel of a system such as the American one in which both the decentralized fragmentation of political institutions and limits on the jurisdiction of federal government imply low capacity for coordinating and seeing through the implementation of policy (Feeley and Sarat 1980; Hacker and Pierson 2007)—has been rendered yet more problematic. Even in the era of so-called activist government, localities were capable of using federal funds to subvert state or federal purposes, as Michael Campbell (2012) has shown in his fascinating account of the Texas public prosecutors' association—precisely the sort of institution the LEAA was designed to encourage and support—which cooperated to subvert moderating state-level penal policies that prosecutors saw as undercutting their autonomy at the local level. While the activist federal state of the mid-twentieth century was an important development, in the long historical sweep it was a relatively short-lived adjustment to a longer-standing American structure of localism, while the comparative perspective which is so often sorely missing from accounts of the American criminal process (and indeed of other American institutions) reveals that its scope, as judged, for example, in terms of spending levels, remained modest in comparison with other liberal market economies.

Moreover, the image of law as a guarantor of common standards, even across single states, is compromised in the United States by the inevitabilities of discretionary implementation accentuated by the profusion of electoral mechanisms. Crucially, it is also compromised by the widespread existence of powers at city and county levels to create, for example, via ordinances, regulatory mechanisms which institutionalize the polarizing dynamics produced by the way in which preferences are shaped by and registered in the local political system. For example, in their recent study of Seattle—hardly the city one would have selected as a key suspect for exclusionary or segregative criminal justice practices—Beckett and Herbert (2009) trace extensions of trespass laws and the creation of civil/criminal hybrids such as park exclusion orders and off-limits laws, most of them used to sanitize middle-class areas of the city or to keep the poor from leisure and retail facilities (cf. Husak 2008). In effect, Beckett and Herbert identify a resurgence of police power at the local level, which has been used to reinvent the loitering and vagrancy laws invalidated by the Warren court in the 1960s and 1970s—a stunning example of the impotence of even the highest level of judicial enforcement to counter underlying political dynamics in the longer term. In a phrase that underlines the effect of those dynamics on crime, punishment, and inequality at the local level, they refer to the upshot of these legal inventions as a form of "banishment," in which the poor or otherwise undesirable—many of them nonwhite—are driven out of "nice" middle-class areas. Our one disagreement with their analysis would be in their description of this process as "counterproductive." Certainly, they are right to emphasize both the cruelty of the process and the fact that it resolves none of the problems that originally created crime, homelessness, or drug and alcohol addiction or that brought the poor onto the streets and into the parks. But in a dark and real sense, our argument implies that "banishment" is far from "counterproductive": on the contrary, it is simply one manifestation of a polarizing logic that increasingly structures American institutions and whose fundamental dynamic is fostered by local autonomy, accentuated by the value that private and commercial property owners attach to their investments.[26]

Recent scholarship on federalization, in particular the work of Lisa Miller (2008, 2010), has been important in highlighting the relevance of the different levels of decision-making to the production of crime and criminal justice policy in America. But, as Miller herself acknowledges,[27] it does not follow that the solution to the problem is a rejuvenation of local democracy, let alone that an increase in direct electoral accountability equates with a better quality of democratic governance. As we have argued, an analysis of the distribution of voter preferences within the decentralized US system in fact leads to the very different conclusion that the diffusion and localization of democracy has been one of the most powerful institutional factors in shaping America's distinctive patterns of crime, punishment, segregation, and indeed social inequality. The "truly disadvantaged" groups, mainly located in inner-city areas, whose victimization at the hands of both crime and criminal justice underpins their more complex view of crime and punishment, are rarely the median or decisive voters in the electoral contests that shape policy (Cutler, Glaeser, and Vigdor 1999; Stucky 2003, 2005a, 2005b; Hajnal and Trounstine 2005). The history of increasing racial and socioeconomic polarization, in both economic and spatial terms, in recent years, much of it driven by zoning regulations and median voter concern with property values, gives the lie to any thought that greater localization spells more equal criminal justice. Radical local autonomy is, in short, one important source of the ills of American criminal justice and not a recipe for its cure.

Elites and Law and Order

We would like, finally, to underline one further argument that is implicit in what has gone before but which perhaps requires some emphasis. In an effort to trace the undoubtedly important political dynamics that have led to the prison buildup in the United States since the 1980s, some scholars have gone as far as to argue that rising crime and the insecurity attendant on fear of crime were either irrelevant to the growth of punishment or merely a political construct manufactured by political elites in pursuit of electoral gain. Stuart Scheingold (2010) and Katherine Beckett (1997) (see also Beckett and Sasson 2004) in particular have argued that a careful analysis of contemporary social attitudes as revealed through surveys does not back up the claim that politicians alighted on crime as a salient issue because of widespread concern about crime among the electorate. Rather, crime in their view presented a convenient platform for adversarial electoral competition and for the furthering of a largely (but covertly) race- and class-based agenda of repression.

We agree with Beckett and with Scheingold that the dynamics of electoral competition have been highly influential in producing American patterns of punishment: indeed, this chapter is an effort to analyze precisely these dynamics and the institutional framework that shapes them. But we do not accept that the aggregate survey data on fear of crime on which they rely supports the conclusions drawn from it. This is for the simple reason that electoral outcomes (and hence politicians' electoral strategies) are shaped not by all voters—let alone by all those eligible to vote, from whom survey recipients are drawn—but by a particular subset of voters. To make the argument that, for example, Scheingold advances, it would have to be shown that this subset of swing voters had the same attitudes to crime as general survey respondents. But in fact there is strong reason to think that rising street and violent crime from the 1970s had a particular impact on swing voters such as blue-collar workers—the white working classes whom the Republicans targeted in their "southern strategy" during the Nixon election campaign of 1968—and later the "Reagan democrats" whose votes were so crucial to the outcome of the 1980 presidential election. For many of them were living in precisely the urban areas that were becoming most directly affected by ghettoization, the concentration of poverty, and the rise in violence (Peterson and Krivo 2010; Miller 2015). It was not irrational for these voters to fear the impact of crime on both their daily lives and the value of their hard-earned assets, and political strategists—particularly those in the Republican Party—astutely exploited these fears. And notwithstanding the social attitudes data cited by Scheingold, there is plenty of other evidence that crime was a salient political issue among particular sectors of the electorate from the mid-1970s on (Gottschalk 2006, chap. 2).

Similarly, Beckett's otherwise powerful argument struggles in our view to explain why political elites saw it as so strongly in their interests to play on or stimulate fear of crime and develop the War on Drugs through exercise of federal power. Her analysis blends aspects of the race conspiracy theory considered and questioned earlier and a median voter argument which should point to the conclusion that crime mattered to swing voters from the mid-1970s on in ways it had not before (Beckett 1997, 85). We share with Beckett and with Scheingold the view that political elites are driven by self-interest. But accounts such as theirs do not fully explain why those interests fell out as they did, and in our view they exaggerate the detachment between the policy platforms of political elites and the interests and preferences of median voters. A key underlying problem is in the tendency of this "politicization of punishment" scholarship—in common with much other criminological work—to underplay the real significance of rising crime in shaping the political preferences of swing voters: a significance that is finally reoccupying its proper place in scholarly efforts to explain the distinctive American penal trajectory (Forman 2012; Miller 2015, 2016; see Miller, this volume; Gallo, Lacey, and Soskice, this volume).

Conclusion

Both the dynamics of race and the impact of the federalization of criminal justice policy, then, have to be understood within the context of a particular form of American exceptionalism: the huge—and distinctive among Anglo-Saxon countries—degree of democratic autonomy ceded to the local level. This autonomy is ceded primarily to incorporated cities but also to counties, school districts, district prosecutors, and judges, as well as other special-purpose districts and including the *de facto* power of unincorporated municipalities within counties to incorporate. While both federal and state governments, as well supreme courts at both levels, have sought at different moments and in different areas to roll back this autonomy, they have seldom attained the desired goals. Gains through litigation have tended to be both fragmentary and fragile in the light of countervailing political dynamics in local government, while the decentralization of law enforcement and the proliferation of locally based ordinances and control measures in civil as well as criminal law have increasingly been called in aid to further and consolidate the centrifugal and polarizing dynamics created by the political system (Beckett and Herbert 2009). The contrast between this radical decentralization and the national frameworks within which planning, education, and criminal justice policy proceed in other liberal market economies can hardly be exaggerated.

Significantly and sharply rising crime rates from the 1960s fostered an increasing sense of insecurity and concern about crime which, through its particular impact on swing voters, itself helped to move crime and punishment up the political agenda. The decentralization and penetration to localities and to a vast variety of roles of competitive electoral politics or political appointment in the American system, along with the homevoter dynamic in local elections in which homeowners concerned about protecting their investments dominate in low-turnout elections (as in other forms of civic activism; Pattillo 2007), helps to explain the radical way in which the increasing political salience of crime led to an upswing in punitiveness and segregation. As Sampson and Wilson (1995), Wilson (1987), and most recently Peterson and

Krivo (2010) have shown, the consequent concentration of poverty and disadvantage has in turn been associated with rising violence (see also Sampson 1987), whose own spatial distribution gives further impetus to the centrifugal dynamic implicit in local autonomy. As long as it remains easier to motivate the local median voter to vote for locally specific goods, for example, security in a particular area, the polarizing dynamics of the localized US system will remain in place—with baleful consequences for the quality of not only criminal justice but also education, housing, and social equality more generally.

It is only a minor exaggeration to say that democratic local autonomy puts *de facto* into the hands of local median voters power over policy and taxation in the areas of public education, zoning, police strategy, prosecution, and sentencing. Homeowners, who, as Fischel (2001, 2004) has noted, have a sharp incentive to participate in local politics, are overrepresented in the ranks of median voters at the local level. Particularly up to 1970, these dynamics were reinforced by white homeowners' willingness to pay a premium to live in segregated areas (Cutler, Glaeser, and Vigdor 1999). This has led to a set of policy and tax choices profoundly inimical to the poor: to the residential segregation of the racially patterned poor; to inadequate policing, particularly of poor black areas; and to their weak educational provision. Caging the poor into inadequately policed segregated tracts, and without the middle-class communicative skills or the socioeconomic networks needed to get stable employment after the collapse of Fordism, has also led to flourishing gangs and violent crime. As violent crime spills over into white-homeowner communities, there is political pressure on police, (elected) district prosecutors, and (often elected) district judges for exclusion of criminals via long imprisonment. This then reinforces the concern of (voting) homeowners to ensure residential segregation of the poor. In this regard, it is significant that the decisive crime decline which growing, economically regenerating cities such as New York has seen since the mid-1990s has not eventuated to the same extent in cities such as Detroit, Baltimore, or Philadelphia, where the effects of deindustrialization are still most strongly felt.

The upside of local autonomy is a high degree of individual freedom; the downside is that only the privileged can use that freedom fully and that they moreover tend to do so to the further disadvantage of the already disadvantaged. In other liberal market economies, greater controls on individual freedom via planning laws and other forms of regulation (e.g., gun control) are regulative institutions that are regarded as a normal part of the political scene. By contrast, the polarizing dynamic in the United States is a strong one because the advantaged have not only greater freedom but also more reason to use their freedom to distance themselves from the disadvantaged the more disadvantaged the latter become. To put the point in the terms used by Bill Clinton at the 2012 Democratic Convention, the localized democratic structure in the United States has already created a society in which the advantaged can opt to "go it alone" whenever "being in it together" doesn't suit them—whether through participation in organizations like churches, by moving to suburbs or gated communities, or by voting to isolate troublesome cohabitants in inner-city ghettos, poor suburbs, or, more extremely, prisons. Conversely, the disadvantaged, locked out from the benefits of being "in it together," become more likely to opt to use their remaining autonomy by participating in alternative political economies (such as profitable crime often backed up by violent informal forms of policing) or by committing to alternative social norms and institutions (such as those fostered by gangs) (Hagedorn 1998; Young 1999; Hale 2005; Venkatesh 2008).

Other Anglo-Saxon countries, all of which have retained central or state/provincial control over policy tools in education, housing, and criminal justice (Figure 1.5), have avoided the levels of fragmentation and polarization that have been influential in producing the uniquely poor social outcomes and levels of inequality exhibited by the United States (Figure 1.4). Central control of these key policy areas represents, we might say, a commitment to some form of collective belonging and mutuality. It is inconceivable, of course, that the United States will scale back local power to any significant degree in the foreseeable future. But the formulation of policies and strategies designed to dilute the polarizing effect of political fragmentation constitutes one of the key challenges for American criminal justice reformers (Orfield 1997), while the costs of American decentralization provide salutary lessons for other jurisdictions tempted to expand local democracy.

Acknowledgments

Our warm thanks go to Lisa Miller for helpful discussion, advice, and feedback; to Kevin Reitz for his wise editorial comments; to audiences at the Robina Institute, University of Minnesota Law School; Oxford University; the London School of Economics (Law Department and Mannheim Centre for Criminology); the Inequality seminar at the Kennedy School, Harvard, and Harvard Law School; to Ely Aaronson, Christopher Jencks, Desmond King, Ian Loader, George Molyneaux, Christopher Muller, Tim Newburn, Robert Reiner, Carol Sanger, Carol Steiker, and Seth Stoughton for comments on earlier drafts; to Zelia Gallo for both comments and research assistance; and to Lea Sitkin and Kate Steward for research assistance.

NOTES

1. Fordist production regimes, pioneered by the Ford Motor Company (Tomkins 2012) but spreading far more widely in the manufacturing sector, standardized tasks so as to create a large number of relatively well-paid and stable jobs for workers with relatively low skills.
2. There are, of course, some honorable exceptions, discussed later in this chapter: see, for example, Miller (2008), Barker (2009), and Campbell (2012).
3. For a comparison of the homicide patterns in the United States and Canada, see Chapter 3, Figure 3.3. Evidently, the very different scale of both serious violent crime (Miller 2016; see Miller, this volume; Gallo, Lacey, and Soskice, this volume) and imprisonment in the United States makes a real difference to the social reach and significance of these phenomena; and these absolute differences—particularly in violence, which appears to be historically persistent (see Roth, this volume)—themselves call for explanation. Nevertheless, proportionate changes have an independent importance, particularly in comparative analysis, where they capture *inter alia* something important about policy and institutional change over time.
4. Since publishing *The Prisoners' Dilemma*, Nicola Lacey has been working on a series of papers seeking to refine this broad argument by using case studies such as the United States, New Zealand, and Scotland to isolate and examine the impact of particular features of political structure, so as to explain differences between (and within) countries with similar forms of electoral system (Lacey 2010, 2011a, 2011b, 2012).
5. The varieties of capitalism framework was developed specifically in relation to the "advanced economies" which made up the original Organisation for Economic Co-operation and Development countries. Its hypotheses require adaptation in relation to the countries of southern Europe, such as Spain, Portugal, Greece, and Turkey, and *a fortiori* in relation to other regions such as Latin America.
6. The qualifier "long-standing" is important: in subsequent work, Lacey has refined the proportionately representative/majoritarian argument by exploring the significant differences between coordinated market economy countries whose proportionately representative systems grew out of and alongside a sectoral system, and liberal market economy countries such as New Zealand and Scotland, which have moved to proportionately representative from a majoritarian system (Lacey 2011b, 2012).
7. On the links between different forms of political system and the status of the expert bureaucracy, see Lacey (2008, 72–75, 191–92); Savelsberg (1994, 1999); Kagan (2001, 10–11, 61–81). Particularly in recent years, the increasing relative importance of political advisers and the concomitant decline in influence of the civil service in the criminal justice field appears to have been driven by growing domination of political parties by their leaders, who multiply

specialist adviser appointments in their own offices to maximize their control over the policymaking process. Again, this is driven by the chase for the swing voter.

8. Of indirect but real relevance, Emily Zackin (2013) has explained the different dynamics and institutional structure of constitutional politics at the state and federal levels—differences which help to explain the generally greater capacity of state constitutions than of the federal constitution to entrench positive rights oriented to redistribution in fields such as education.
9. As pointed out in Tim Newburn's review (2009).
10. Campbell, Vogel, and Williams (2015) have recently argued for a typology differentiating the "sunbelt" states from those of the Northeast and Midwest.
11. The argument that recent criminal justice policy in the United States has been largely shaped by "federalization" is considered, and rejected, below.
12. The following section summarizes the argument of Lacey and Soskice (2015)
13. Again, however, the polarizing dynamic of American politics is evident: for those unable or unwilling to play by the rules of the newly refurbished cities or whose presence promotes feelings of insecurity among residents or those spending money on property investment, retail, or leisure activities, new forms of zoning regulation have been created through civil, criminal, and planning laws to "banish" the troublesome from middle-class areas (Beckett and Herbert 2009).
14. For a case study in the difficulty of implementation at the local level, even given the relevant political determination at the state level, see Campbell (2012).
15. *Village of Euclid, Ohio v. Ambler Realty Co.* (1926), a decision which was made during a period of significant black migration from the South.
16. This was an era, incidentally, which saw drops in the homicide rate (Hall and McLean 2009).
17. See also Charles (2006).
18. Though this point should not be exaggerated: as Forman (2012, 24f5) points out, drug offenders account for only about a quarter of the prison population, while violent offenders make up half—underlining the importance of violent crime for any adequate explanation of American punitiveness: see Miller (2015, 2016); see also Miller, this volume; Gallo, Lacey, and Soskice, this volume.
19. Racial disparities are further magnified in the US incarceration rate, where we include local jails as well as prisons—a calculation which takes the US figures to four times the rate of England and Wales.
20. Incarcerations Rates. USA. Charts. Timelines. http://www.angelfire.com/rnb/y/ratesusa.htm.
21. While the socioeconomic status of Maori, in both absolute and relative terms, has improved through the course of the last century, the gap between their socioeconomic position and that of the white population remains substantial: see, for example, Chapple (2000) and New Zealand Parliament (2000).

22. There are no widely agreed comparative measures of racism. But to take just one compelling example, in his report following the public inquiry on the police investigation of the murder of black teenager Stephen Lawrence in London in 1993, Sir William Macpherson famously diagnosed "institutional racism" in the Metropolitan Police (Macpherson 1999).
23. The spatial concentration of disadvantage is of particular importance given findings not only that perceptions of crime are affected by racial stereotypes (Quilliam and Pager 2001; Chiricos, McEntire, and Gertz 2001) but also that those stereotypes are less powerful in racially heterogeneous neighborhoods (Gilliam, Valentino, and Beckmann 2002).
24. Even class actions, which were designed to overcome some of these difficulties, still encounter them, not least as a result of their extraordinary procedural complexity and the high levels of legal expertise needed to manage them.
25. *San Antonio Independent School District v. Rodriguez* (1973).
26. Our argument here resonates with Jennifer Hochschild's worrying interpretation of the tensions fracturing the "American" dream—tensions which have surely strengthened since her analysis was published (Hochschild 1995).
27. We find Miller's diagnosis of a systematic difference in the framing of criminal justice issues at different levels of government (Miller 2008) persuasive and an excellent example of the ways in which both the size and the fragmentation of the US system have affected its penal policy. But the electoral studies we cite in this chapter nonetheless demonstrate that in the competition for office, law-and-order bidding wars also feature strongly at the local level, hence blocking any inference from Miller's findings about the more sophisticated analyses of crime problems among local residents to the advisability of great diversion of power to the local level. Miller herself (p. 177) is careful to specify that her analysis does not imply a case for localism.

CASES CITED

San Antonio Independent School District v. Rodriguez, 411 U.S. 1 (1973).
Village of Euclid, Ohio v. Ambler Realty Co., 272 U.S. 365 (1926).

REFERENCES

Aaronson, Ely. *From Slave Abuse to Hate Crime: The Criminalization of Racial Violence in American History*. New York: Cambridge University Press, 2014.

Alesina, Alberto, Reza Baqir, and William Easterly. "Public Goods and Ethnic Divisions." *Quarterly Journal of Economics* 114 (1999): 1243–84.

Alexander, Michelle. *The New Jim Crow: Mass Incarceration in the Age of Colourblindness*. New York: New Press, 2012.

Allen, Walter R., and Reynolds Farley. "The Shifting Social and Economic Tides of Black America 1950–1980." *Annual Review of Sociology* 12 (1986): 277–306.

Austin, Algernon. *Reducing Poverty and Increasing Marriage Rates among Latinos and African Americans*. Washington: Economic Policy Institute, 2011.

Barker, Vanessa. *The Politics of Punishment: How the Democratic Process Shapes the Way America Punishes Offenders*. New York: Oxford University Press, 2009.

Baumeister, Roy F., and Mark R. Leary. "The Need to Belong: Desire for Interpersonal Attachments as a Fundamental Human Motivation." *Psychological Bulletin* 117 (1995): 497–529.

Beckett, Katherine. *Making Crime Pay*. New York: Oxford University Press, 1997.

Beckett, Katherine, and Steve Herbert. *Banished: The New Social Control in Urban America*. New York: Oxford University Press, 2009.

Beckett, Katherine, and Theodore Sasson. *The Politics of Injustice: Crime and Punishment in America*. 2nd ed. Thousand Oaks, CA: Sage, 2004.

Beckett, Katherine, and Bruce Western. "Governing Social Marginality." In *Mass Imprisonment: Social Causes and Consequences*, edited by David Garland, 35–50. London: Sage, 2001.

Berdejó, Carlos, and Noam Yuchtman. "Crime, Punishment, and Politics: An Analysis of Political Cycles in Criminal Sentencing." *Review of Economics and Statistics* 95, no. 3 (2013): 741–56.

Bibas, Stephanos. *The Machinery of Criminal Justice*. New York: Oxford University Press, 2012.

Boggess, Scott, and John Bound. "Did Criminal Activity Increase during the 1980s? Comparisons across Data Sources." Working Paper 4431, National Bureau of Economic Research, Cambridge, MA, 1993.

Bound, John, and Richard Freeman. "What Went Wrong? The Erosion of Relative Earnings and Employment among Young Black Men in the 1980s." *Quarterly Journal of Economics* 107 (1992): 201–32.

Boyd, Robert L. "Demographic Change and Entrepreneurial Occupations." *American Journal of Economics and Sociology* 55 (1996): 129–43.

Brooks, R. R., and S. Raphael. "Life Terms or Death Sentences: The Uneasy Relationship between Judicial Elections and Capital Punishment." *Journal of Criminal Law and Criminology* 92 (2002): 609–40.

Bureau of Justice Statistics. *Inmates at Midyear 2006*. Washington, DC: Bureau of Justice Statistics, 2007.

Bureau of Justice Statistics. *Prisoners in 2014*. Washington DC: Bureau of Justice Statistics, 2015.

Campbell, Michael C. "Ornery Alligators and Soap on a Rope: Texas Prosecutors and Punishment Reform in the Lone Star State." *Theoretical Criminology* 16 (2012): 289.

Campbell, Michael, Matt Vogel, and Joshua Williams. "Historical Contingencies and the Evolving Importance of Race, Violent Crime and Region in Explaining Mass Incarceration in the United States." *Criminology* 53, no. 2 (2015): 180–203.

Chapple, Simon. "Maori Socio-Economic Disparity: Paper for the Ministry of Social Policy." September 2000. http://www.nzcpr.com/wp-content/uploads/2014/03/Maori-Economic-Disparity-Simon-Chapple.pdf.

Charles, Camille Zubrinsky. *Won't You Be My Neighbour? Race, Class and Residence in Los Angeles*. New York: Russell Sage Foundation, 2006.

Chiricos, Ted, Ranee McEntire, and Marc Gertz. "Perceived Racial and Ethnic Composition of Neighbourhoods and Perceived Risk of Crime." *Social Problems* 48 (2001): 322–40.

Chubb, John E. "Institutions, the Economy, and the Dynamics of State Elections." *American Political Science Review* 82, no. 1 (1988): 133–54.

Cutler, David M., Edward L. Glaeser, and Jacob L. Vigdor. "The Rise and Decline of the American Ghetto." *Journal of Political Economy* 107 (1999): 455–506.

de Giorgi, Alessandro. *Rethinking the Political Economy of Punishment*. Aldershot, UK: Ashgate, 2006.

Douglas, Davison M. *Jim Crow Moves North: The Battle over Northern School Segregation 1865–1954*. New York: Cambridge University Press, 2005.

Downes, David, and Kirstine Hansen. "Welfare and Punishment in Comparative Perspective." In *Perspectives on Punishment*, edited by Sarah Armstrong and Lesley McAra, 101–18. Oxford: Oxford University Press, 2006.

Downes, David, and Rod Morgan. "No Turning Back: The Politics of Law and Order into the Millennium." In *The Oxford Handbook of Criminology*. 4th ed. Edited by Mike Maguire, Rod Morgan, and Robert Reiner, 201–40. Oxford: Oxford University Press, 2007.

Dyke, Andrew. "Electoral Cycles in the Administration of Criminal Justice." *Public Choice* 133 (2007): 417–37.

Enns, Peter K. "The Public's Increasing Punitiveness and Its Influence on Mass Incarceration in the United States." *American Journal of Political Science* 58, no. 4 (2014): 857–872.

Enns, Peter K. *Incarceration Nation*. New York: Cambridge University Press, 2016.

Enos, Ryan D. "What the Demolition of Public Housing Teaches Us about the Impact of Racial Threat on Political Behaviour." *American Journal of Political Science* 60 (2016): 123–42.

Esping-Andersen, G. *The Three Worlds of Welfare Capitalism*. Cambridge: Polity Press, 1990.

Esping-Andersen, G. *Welfare States in Transition*. London: Sage, 1996.

Fagan, Jeffrey, and Richard Freeman. "Crime and Work." In *Crime and Justice: A Review of Research*. Vol. 25. Edited by Michael Tonry, 225–90. Chicago: University of Chicago Press, 1999.

Fearon, James D., and David D. Laitin. "Violence and the Social Construction of Ethnic Identity." *International Organization* 54 (2000): 845–77.

Feeley, Malcolm, and Austin Sarat. *The Policy Dilemma: Federal Crime Policy and the Law Enforcement Assistance Administration*. Minneapolis: University of Minnesota Press, 1980.

Fischel, William A. *The Homevoter Hypothesis*. Cambridge, MA: Harvard University Press, 2001.

Fischel, William A. "An Economic History of Zoning and a Cure for Its Exclusionary Effects." *Urban Studies* 41 (2004): 317–40.

Fischel, William A. "Politics in a Dynamic View of Land-Use Regulations: Of Interest Groups and Homevoters." *Journal of Real Estate, Finance and Economics* 31, no. 4 (2005): 395–403.

Forman, James, Jr. "Racial Critiques of Mass Incarceration: Beyond the New Jim Crow." *New York University Law Review* 87 (2012): 21–69.

Freeman, Richard B. "Why Do So Many Young American Men Commit Crimes and What Might We Do about It?" *Journal of Economic Perspectives* 10, no. 1 (1996): 25–42.

Garland, David. *Punishment and Modern Society*. Oxford: Oxford University Press, 1990.

Garland, David. *The Culture of Control*. Oxford: Oxford University Press, 2001.

Garland, David. "The Peculiar Forms of American Capital Punishment." *Social Research* 72, no. 4 (2007): 435–66.

Garland, David. *Peculiar Institution: America's Death Penalty in an Age of Abolition*. New York: Oxford University Press; Cambridge, MA: Harvard University Press, 2010.

Gilliam, Franklin D., Jr., Nicholas A. Valentino, and Matthew N. Beckmann. "Where You Live and What You Watch: The Impact of Racial Proximity on Racial Proximity and Local TV News on Attitudes about Race and Crime." *Political Research Quarterly* 55 (2002): 755–80.

Goffman, Alice. *On the Run: Fugitive Life in an American City*. Chicago: Chicago University Press, 2014.

Gottschalk, Marie. *The Prison and the Gallows*. Cambridge: Cambridge University Press, 2006.

Gottschalk, Marie. *Caught: The Prison State and the Lockdown of American Politics*. Princeton, NJ: Princeton University Press, 2014.

Gould, Eric D., Bruce A Weinberg, and David B. Mustard. "Crime Rates and Local Labor Market Opportunities in the United States: 1979–1997." *Review of Economics and Statistics* 84, no. 1 (2002): 45–61.

Hacker, Jacob S., and Paul Pierson. "Tax Politics and the Struggle over Activist Government." In *The Transformation of American Politics: Activist Government and the Rise of Conservatism*, edited by Paul Pierson and Theda Skocpol, 256–80. Princeton, NJ: Princeton University Press, 2007.

Hagan, John, and Ruth D. Peterson. "Criminal Inequality in America: Patterns and Consequences." In *Crime and Inequality*, edited by John Hagan and Ruth D. Peterson, 14–36. Palo Alto, CA: Stanford University Press, 1995.

Hagedorn, John M. *People and Folks: Gangs, Crime and the Underclass in a Rustbelt City*. Chicago: Lake View Press, 1998.

Hagedorn, John M. *A World of Gangs: Armed Young Men and Gangsta Culture*. Minneapolis: University of Minnesota Press, 2008.

Hajnal, Zoltan, and Jessica Trounstine. "Where Turnout Matters: The Consequences of Uneven Turnout in City Politics." *Journal of Politics* 67 (2005): 515–35.

Hale, Chris. "Economic Marginalisation, Social Exclusion and Crime." In *Criminology*, edited by Chris Hale, Keith Hayward, Azrini Wahidin, and Emma Wincup, 325–43. Oxford: Oxford University Press, 2005.

Hall, Peter A., and David Soskice. "An Introduction to the Varieties of Capitalism." In *Varieties of Capitalism*, edited by Peter Hall and David Soskice, 1–68. Oxford: Oxford University Press, 2001.

Hall, Steve, and Craig McLean. "A Tale of Two Capitalisms: Preliminary Spatial and Historical Comparisons of Homicide Rates in Western Europe and the U.S.A." *Theoretical Criminology* 13 (2009): 313–39.

Harcourt, Bernard. *The Illusion of Order: The False Promise of Broken Windows Policing*. Cambridge, MA: Harvard University Press, 2001.

Hochschild, Jennifer L. *Facing up to the American Dream: Race, Class and the Soul of the Nation*. Princeton, NJ: Princeton University Press, 1995.

Huber, G., and S. C. Gordon. "Accountability and Coercion: Is Justice Blind When It Runs for Office?" *American Journal of Political Science* 48, no. 2 (2004): 247–63.

Husak, Douglas N. *Overcriminalisation*. New York: Oxford University Press, 2008.

International Centre for Prison Studies. World Prison Brief. 2010. http://www.prisonstudies.org/world-prison-brief-data.

Iversen, Torben, and David Soskice. "Electoral Institutions and the Politics of Coalitions: Why Some Democracies Redistribute More Than Others." *American Political Science Review* 100 (2006): 165–81.

Iversen, Torben, and David Soskice. "Distribution and Redistribution: The Shadow of the Nineteenth Century." *World Politics* 61, no. 3 (2009): 438–86.

Johnston, Ron, Michael Poulsen, and James Forrest. "Ethnic Residential Segregation across an Urban System: The Maori in New Zealand 1991–2001." *Professional Geographer* 57 (2005): 115–29.

Johnston, Ron, Michael Poulsen, and James Forrest. "The Geography of Ethnic Residential Segregation: A Comparative Study of Five Countries." *Annals of the Association of American Geographers* 97 (2007): 713–38.

Kagan, Robert A. *Adversarial Legalism: The American Way of Law*. Cambridge, MA: Harvard University Press, 2001.

Katznelson, Ira. *City Trenches: Urban Politics and the Patterning of Class in the United States*. Chicago: University of Chicago Press, 1981.

King, Desmond S., and Rogers M. Smith. "Racial Orders in American Political Development." *American Political Science Review* 99 (2005): 75–92.

King, Desmond S., and Rogers M. Smith. *Still a House Divided: Race and Politics in Obama's America*. Princeton, NJ: Princeton University Press, 2011.

Krivo, Lauren J., Ruth D. Peterson, and Danielle C. Kuhl. "Segregation, Racial Structure, and Neighbourhood Violent Crime." *American Journal of Sociology* 114 (2009): 1765–1802.

Lacey, Nicola. *The Prisoners' Dilemma: Political Economy and Punishment in Contemporary Democracies*. Cambridge: Cambridge University Press, 2008.

Lacey, Nicola. "American Imprisonment in Comparative Perspective." *Daedalus* 139, no. 3 (2010): 102–14.

Lacey, Nicola. "Why Globalisation Doesn't Spell Convergence: Models of Institutional Variation and the Comparative Political Economy of Punishment." In *International and Comparative Criminal Justice and Urban Governance*, edited by Adam Crawford, 214–50. Cambridge: Cambridge University Press, 2011a.

Lacey, Nicola. "The Prisoner's Dilemma and Political Systems: The Impact of Proportional Representation on Criminal Justice in New Zealand." *Victoria University of Wellington Law Review* 42, no. 4 (2011b): 1–23.

Lacey, Nicola. "Political Systems and Criminal Justice: The Prisoners' Dilemma after the Coalition." *Current Legal Problems* 65, no. 1 (2012): 203–39.

Lacey, Nicola. "Punishment, (Neo-)Liberalism and Social Democracy." In *The Sage Handbook of Punishment and Society*, edited by Jonathon Simon and Richard Sparks, 260–80. London: Sage Publications, 2013a.

Lacey, Nicola. "Humanising the Criminal Justice Machine." *Harvard Law Review* 126, no. 5 (2013b): 1299–1324.

Lacey, Nicola, and David Soskice. "Crime, Punishment and Segregation in the United States: The Paradox of Local Democracy." *Punishment & Society* 17, no. 4 (2015): 454–81.

Lerman, Amy E., and Vesla M. Weaver. *Arresting Citizenship: The Democratic Consequences of American Crime Control*. Chicago: Chicago University Press, 2014.

Levitt, Stephen D. "Using Electoral Cycles in Police Hiring to Estimate the Effect of Police on Crime." *American Economic Review* 87 (1997): 270–90.

Lijphart, Arend. *Democracies: Patterns of Majoritarian and Consensus Governments in Twenty-One Countries*. New Haven, CT: Yale University Press, 1984.

Lijphart, Arend. *Patterns of Democracy: Government Forms and Performance in Thirty-Six Countries*. New Haven, CT: Yale University Press, 1999.

Loury, Glenn C. *The Anatomy of Racial Inequality*. Cambridge, MA: Harvard University Press, 2003.

Loury, Glenn C. "Crime Inequality and Social Justice." *Daedalus* 139 (2010): 134–40.

Machin, Stephen, and Costas Meghir. "Crime and Economic Incentives." *Journal of Human Resources* 39, no. 4 (2004): 958–79.

Macpherson, Sir William. *The Stephen Lawrence Inquiry*. Cm 4262-I. February 24, 1999. http://www.archive.official-documents.co.uk/document/cm42/4262/4262.htm.

Massey, Douglas S., and Nancy A. Denton. *American Apartheid: Segregation and the Making of the Underclass*. Cambridge, MA: Harvard University Press, 1993.

Matejczyk, Anthony P. "Why not NIMBY? Reputation, Neighbourhood Organisations and Zoning Boards in a U.S. Midwestern City." *Urban Studies* 38 (2001): 507–18.

Mauer, Marc. *Race to Incarcerate*. New York: New Press, 2006.

Mauer, Marc, and Ryan S. King. *Uneven Justice: State Rates of Incarceration by Race and Ethnicity*. Washington, DC: Sentencing Project, 2007. http://www.sentencingproject.org/wp-content/uploads/2016/01/Uneven-Justice-State-Rates-of-Incarceration-by-Race-and-Ethnicity.pdf. For updated figures see the Sentencing Project's interactive map: http://www.sentencingproject.org/map/map.cfm.

McAra, Lesley. "The Impact of Multi-Level Governance on Crime Control and Punishment." In *International and Comparative Criminal Justice and Urban Governance*, edited by Adam Crawford, 276–303. Cambridge: Cambridge University Press, 2011.

Meares, Tracey L., and Dan M. Kahan. *Urgent Times: Policing and Rights in Inner City Communities*. New York: Random House, 1999.

Miller, Lisa L. *The Perils of Federalism: Race, Poverty, and the Politics of Crime Control*. New York: Oxford University Press, 2008.

Miller, Lisa L. "The Invisible Black Victim: How American Federalism Perpetuates Racial Inequality in Criminal Justice." *Law and Society Review* 44 (2010): 805–42.

Miller, Lisa L. "What's Violence Got to Do with It? Rethinking Punishment, Inequality and the Modern State." *Punishment and Society* 17 (2015): 184–210.

Miller, Lisa L. *The Myth of Mob Rule: Violent Crime and Democratic Politics*. New York and Oxford: Oxford University Press, 2016.

Muller, Christopher. "Northward Migration and the Rise of Racial Disparity in America Incarceration, 1880–1950." *American Journal of Sociology* 118 (2012): 281–326.

Newburn, Tim. "'Tough on Crime': Penal Policy in England and Wales." In *Crime, Punishment and Politics in Comparative Perspective: Crime and Justice: A Review of Research*. Vol. 36. Edited by Michael Tonry, 425–70. Chicago: University of Chicago Press, 2007.

Newburn, Tim. "Review of Lacey (2008)." *Modern Law Review* 72 (2009): 510–13.

New Zealand Department of Corrections. *Over-Representation of Maori in the Criminal Justice System: An Explanatory Report*. Wellington: New Zealand Department of Corrections, 2007.

New Zealand Parliament. *"Gaps" between Ethnic Groups: Some Key Statistics*. June 1, 2000. Accessed January 7, 2015. http://www.parliament.nz/resource/mi-nz/00PLSocRP00101/dd813ed30474d07ed48b8da60257af8bac15a7df.

Nickerson, Brian J., and Gerard M. Deenihan. "From Equity to Adequacy: The Legal Battle for Increased State Funding of Poor School Districts in New York." *Fordham Urban Law Journal* 30 (2002): 1341–92.

Office of Juvenile Justice and Delinquency Prevention. Highlights of the 2011 National Youth Gang Survey. September 2013. http://www.ojjdp.gov/pubs/242884.pdf.

Orfield, Myron. *Metropolitics: A Regional Agenda for Community and Stability*. Washington, DC: Brookings Institution Press, 1997.

Pratt J. "Scandinavian Exceptionalism in an Era of Penal Excess: Part I The Nature and Roots of Scandinavian Exceptionalism." *British Journal of Criminology* 48 (2008a): 119–37.

Pratt J. "Scandinavian Exceptionalism in an Era of Penal Excess: Part II Does Scandinavian Exceptionalism Have a Future?" *British Journal of Criminology* 48 (2008b): 275–92.

Pattillo, Mary. 2007. *Black on the Block: The Politics of Race and Class in the City*. Chicago: Chicago University Press, 2007.

Pattillo-McCoy, Mary. *Black Picket Fences: Privilege and Peril among the Black Middle Classes*. Chicago: Chicago University Press, 1999.

Peach, Ceri. "Does Britain Have Ghettos?" *Transactions of the Institute of British Geographers* 21 (1996): 216–35.

Peterson, Ruth D., and Lauren J. Krivo. *Divergent Social Worlds: Neighbourhood Crime and the Racial–Spatial Divide*. New York: Russell Sage, 2010.

Pierson, Paul, and Theda Skocpol. *The Transformation of American Politics: Activist Government and the Rise of Conservatism*. Princeton, NJ: Princeton University Press, 2007.

Pratt, J., and M. C. Clark. "Penal Populism in New Zealand." *Punishment and Society* 7, no. 4 (2005): 303–22.

Quilliam, Lincoln, and Devah Pager. "Black Neighbours, Higher Crime? The Role of Racial Stereotypes in Evaluations of Neighbourhood Crime." *American Journal of Sociology* 107 (2001): 717–67.

Reiner, Robert. *Law and Order: An Honest Citizen's Guide to Crime and Control*. Oxford: Polity Press, 2007.

Royster, Deidre A. *Race and the Invisible Hand: How White Networks Exclude Blacks from Blue Collar Jobs*. Berkeley and Los Angeles: University of California Press, 2003.

Rusche, Georg, and Otto Kirchheimer. *Punishment and Social Structure*. New York: Russell Sage, 1969. First published 1939.

Sampson, Robert J. "Urban Black Violence: The Effect of Male Joblessness and Family Disruption." *American Journal of Sociology* 93 (1987): 348–82.

Sampson, Robert J. *Great American City: Chicago and the Enduring Neighbourhood Effect*. Chicago: Chicago University Press, 2012.

Sampson, Robert J., and W. Byron Groves. "Community Structure and Crime: Testing Social-Disorganisation Theory." *American Journal of Sociology* 94 (1989): 774–802.

Sampson, Robert J., and William Julius Wilson. "Toward a Theory of Race, Crime and Urban Inequality." In *Crime and Inequality*, edited by John Hagan and Ruth D. Peterson, 37–54. Palo Alto, CA: Stanford University Press, 1995.

Savage, Joanne, Richard R. Bennett, and Mona Danner. "Economic Assistance and Crime: A Cross-National Investigation." *European Journal of Criminology* 5, no. 2 (2008): 217–38.

Savelsberg, Joachim. "Knowledge, Domination, and Criminal Punishment." *American Journal of Sociology* 99 (1994): 911–43.

Savelsberg, Joachim. "Knowledge, Domination and Criminal Punishment Revisited." *Punishment and Society* 1 (1999): 45–70.

Scheingold, Stuart A. *The Politics of Law and Order: Street Crime and Public Policy*. New Orleans: Quid Pro Books, 2010. First published 1984.

Sentencing Project. Website Interactive Data Tool. 2014. http://www.sentencingproject.org/map/map.cfm.

Sharp, Elaine. "Politics, Economics, and Urban Policing: The Postindustrial Thesis and Rival Explanations of Heightened Order Maintenance Policing." *Urban Affairs Review* 50 (2013): 340–65.

Shepherd, Joanna M. "The Influence of Retention Politics on Judges' Voting." *Journal of Legal Studies* 38 (2009): 169–206.

Simon, Jonathon. *Governing through Crime: How the War on Crime Transformed American Democracy and Created a Culture of Fear*. New York: Oxford University Press, 2007.

Simon, Jonathan. "Consuming Obsessions: Housing, Homicide, and Mass Incarceration since 1950." *University of Chicago Legal Forum* 2010 (October 2010): 141–80.

Skarbek, David. *The Social Order of the Underworld: How Prison Gangs Govern the American Penal System*. New York: Oxford University Press, 2014.

Soskice, David. "American Exceptionalism and Comparative Political Economy." In *Labor in the Era of Globalization*, edited by Clair Brown, Barry Eichengreen, and Michael Reich, 51–93. New York: Cambridge University Press, 2009.

Stucky, Thomas D. "Local Politics and Violent Crime in U.S. Cities." *Criminology* 41 (2003): 1101–36.

Stucky, Thomas D. "Local Politics and Police Strength." *Justice Quarterly* 22 (2005a): 139–69.

Stucky, Thomas D. *Urban Politics, Crime Rates, and Police Strength*. New York: LFB Scholarly Publishing, 2005b.

Stuntz, William J. "The Pathological Politics of Criminal Law." *Michigan Law Review* 100 (2001): 505–600.

Stuntz, William J. "The Political Constitution of Criminal Law." *Harvard Law Review* 119 (2006): 781–851.

Stuntz, William J. "Unequal Justice." *Harvard Law Review* 121 (2008): 1969–2040.

Stuntz, William J. *The Collapse of American Criminal Justice*. Cambridge, MA: Harvard University Press, 2011.

Sutton, John. "The Political Economy of Imprisonment in Affluent Western Democracies, 1960–1990." *American Sociological Review* 69 (2004): 170–89.

Tomkins, Beth. *The Making of Black Detroit in the Age of Henry Ford*. Chapel Hill: University of North Carolina Press, 2012.

Tonry, Michael. *Malign Neglect: Race, Crime and Punishment in America*. New York: Oxford University Press, 1995.

Tonry, Michael. *Thinking about Crime: Sense and Sensibility in American Penal Culture*. New York: Oxford University Press, 2004.

Tonry, Michael. "Determinants of Penal Policies." In *Crime, Punishment and Politics in a Comparative Perspective. Crime and Justice: A Review of Research*. Vol. 36. Edited by Michael Tonry, 1–48. Chicago: University of Chicago Press, 2007a.

Tonry, Michael, ed. *Crime, Punishment and Politics in a Comparative Perspective. Crime and Justice: A Review of Research*. Vol. 36. Chicago: University of Chicago Press, 2007b.

Tonry, Michael. *Punishing Race: A Continuing American Dilemma*. New York: Oxford University Press, 2011.

Tonry, Michael. "Race, Crime, Ethnicity, and Immigration." In *The Oxford Handbook of Race, Crime, and Immigration*, edited by Sandra M. Bucerius and Michael Tonry, 1–20. New York and Oxford: Oxford University Press, 2014.

UNICEF. *Measuring Child Poverty. New League Tables of Child Poverty in the World's Richest Countries*. Innocenti Report Card 10. Peter Adamson UNICEF Innocenti Research Centre, 2012.

United Nations Office on Drugs and Crime. Homicide statistics. 2012. http://www.unodc.org/unodc/en/data-and-analysis/homicide.html.

Venkatesh, Sudhir. *Gang Leader for a Day*. New York: Penguin Press, 2008.

Wacquant, Loïc. *Punishing the Poor: The Neoliberal Government of Social Insecurity*. Durham, NC: Duke University Press, 2009.

Western, Bruce. *Punishment and Inequality in America*. New York: Russell Sage, 2006.

Western, Bruce, and Katherine Beckett. "The U.S. Penal System as a Labour Market Institution." *American Journal of Sociology* 104 (1999): 1030–60.

Western, Bruce, and Becky Pettit. "Incarceration and Racial Inequality in Men's Employment." *Industrial and Labour Relations Review* 54 (2000): 3–16.

Whitman, James Q. *Harsh Justice*. Oxford: Oxford University Press, 2003.

Wilson, William Julius. *The Truly Disadvantaged: The Inner City, the Underclass and Public Policy*. Chicago: Chicago University Press, 1987.

Wilson, William Julius. 1996. *When Work Disappears: The World of the New Urban Poor*. New York: Knopf, 1996.

Wilson, William Julius. *More than Just Race*. New York: W.W. Norton, 2009.

Young, Jock. *The Exclusive Society*. London: Sage, 1999.

Zackin, Emily. *Looking for Rights in All the Wrong Places*. Princeton: Princeton University Press, 2013.

Zimring, Franklin E. *The Great American Crime Decline*. Oxford: Oxford University Press, 2007.

Zimring, Franklin E. *The City that Became Safe*. Oxford: Oxford University Press, 2012.

Zimring, Franklin E., and David Johnson. "Public Opinion and the Governance of Punishment in Democratic Political Systems." *Annals of the American Academy of Political and Social Science* 605 (2006): 266–80.

2

The Concept of American Exceptionalism and the Case of Capital Punishment

David Garland

THE CONCEPT OF "American exceptionalism" is so frequently evoked in American political discourse that it is easy to assume we all know what it means. But the idea of American exceptionalism comes loaded with several different meanings and a number of historical and comparative claims, each of which may be presented in stronger or weaker versions. My aim in this chapter will be to distinguish these various meanings and thereby clarify what we might mean when we invoke this phrase, as well as to discuss what the American exceptionalism concept implies for the study of crime and punishment. Following a preliminary discussion of the concept and its meanings, I proceed to examine American exceptionalism by means of a close analysis of a specific penal phenomenon that is often invoked as proof that the United States is, indeed, exceptional: America's retention of capital punishment into the twenty-first century.

To be clear at the outset about the implications of my analysis, I do not claim that the death penalty is a crucial test of the theory of American exceptionalism in any of its variants. An analysis might demonstrate that America's death penalty is *not* an instance of American exceptionalism and yet leave the general conception more or less intact. But I do claim that the close analysis of a particular application of the theory can be an effective means of specifying what the general theory entails and what kinds of facts will and will not support it.

Exceptionalism and Other Contrastive Concepts

In the course of my analysis I will make the following theoretical and methodological points:

First, I will stress the importance of internal variation. America is a union of 50 states and several distinct regions which, despite 200 years of joint government, remains in many respects heterogeneous and diverse. Comparative claims about "America" that are pitched at a cross-national level may have to be qualified by reference to internal variation at the subnational level.

Second, I will point to the importance of historical variation. Cross-national comparisons change over time. The historical paths taken by America and by other nations have sometimes converged, sometimes diverged, and sometimes run parallel along separate tracks. We ought not to assume that a difference that exists at the present time has always existed or will always exist.

Third, it follows that, as well as comparing static indicators at one point in time, we should compare trends, trajectories, and processes of change. And these comparative trends ought to be considered over the long and medium terms as well as in the short run.

Fourth, it is important to be precise about the phenomena that we are describing as "exceptional," whether these are institutions, practices, values, social characteristics, or something else. We typically say that America "has the death penalty" while other nations do not. But, as I will show, "having" capital punishment turns out to be a complicated and variable state of affairs (Garland 2010). Much American exceptionalism literature claims that America "lacks social democracy" or has never established a "proper welfare state" (Shafer 1991; Lipset 1996; Madsen 1998; Lockhart 2003; for critiques of this approach, see Baldwin 2009; Hodgson 2009; Foner 2013), but these phenomena also need to be better specified if we are to develop accurate and appropriate comparisons. Similarly, if we are to claim that America's penal system is somehow exceptional, it will be important to specify which aspects of US penality should and which aspects should not be characterized as "exceptional."

Fifth, it follows from this that we ought to be more precise about which aspects of American society are supposedly exceptional. Is the claim that its culture is exceptional? Its economy? Its legal and political institutions? Its ethnic heterogeneity? Its history of racialized slavery? Its popular attitudes? Its religious beliefs? Its social divisions? Some combination of these? All of these? Analyses that invoke American exceptionalism often invoke metaphoric notions of the "character" or "condition" of the nation and its people—but essentialist notions of that kind possess little analytical power.

Sixth, we need to be more precise about the contrastive concepts we use to think about America's distinctiveness and its relation to the nations with which it is being compared. In particular, we ought to differentiate between the following kinds of claims:

a. The claim that America is, in some specified respect, *exceptional*. This is the strongest of the contrastive claims I will describe. To make such a claim requires that we also specify the general norm, pattern, or standard from which America deviates and against which it is an "exception." What would count as a general historical norm of this kind? The best-known candidate would undoubtedly be the Marxist theory of historical development (Marx 1971; McLennan 1981), which asserts that there is a standard pattern of historical development dictated by the laws of historical materialism.[1] Other candidates might include the modern European pattern of death penalty abolition (Garland 2010; Hammel 2010) or the European pattern of welfare state development (Flora and Heidenheimer 1981; Garland 2015); and there may be others—though historians will generally be skeptical of claims that insist there is a single pattern of change that fits all, or all but one, cases. For a claim about "exceptionalism" to be intelligible, some general norm must exist from which the "exceptional" nation somehow deviates. Too often, the claim that the United States is exceptional proceeds with scant attention to robustness of the norm from which it purportedly departs.

b. The claim that America is, in some specified sense, *unique*. This is a weaker claim, insofar as it merely asserts that the United States is different from all other nations, each of which may also be unique in its own way. (At a certain level of specificity, each and every nation might be described as unique.) Unlike the exceptionalism claim, the uniqueness claim carries no implication that all other nations conform to a single standard or a uniform pattern.

c. The claim that America is in some specified sense an *outlier* in a larger set or class of nations. This claim entails the assertion that other nations cluster together in the specified respects while the United States stands at a marked distance from the group.[2]

d. The claim that America, in some specified sense, *occupies an extreme position* on a spectrum of difference or a continuum of variation. This is a weaker claim than that of "outlier" since it may imply only a short distance between the United States and other nations located next to it on the continuum.
e. The claim that America is, in some specified sense, *distinctive*. Given that every nation is undoubtedly distinctive in certain respects, this is the weakest of these contrastive claims.

Attending to these distinctions should increase the precision of our claims and help us pose better research questions. To illustrate—and to anticipate the analysis that I set out in this chapter—we can make the following comparative claims about American capital punishment.

Some of the institutional arrangements that form part of America's capital punishment system are, indeed, unique and exceptional: no other nation elects its judicial officers (county prosecutors and state judges); no other nation links criminal justice so closely to electoral politics; and no other nation allows juries to pass death sentences. Some other aspects of the system are unusual—few other nations devolve criminal lawmaking to the local level. In other respects the American system may be said to be an outlier—e.g. in the timing of death penalty abolition. In yet other respects, it is in the mainstream of social development—e.g. in the pattern of reform that has shaped its historical development. And of course, the American death penalty has always been distinctive in certain respects—e.g. America's evolving sequence of execution technologies, the degree of local control over capital prosecution and sentencing, and so on (see generally Garland 2010).

A *seventh* methodological observation concerns the importance of specifying the phenomenon that is being compared, whether it is defined as "exceptional," "distinctive," or different in some lesser degree. Cross-national comparison is difficult for all sorts of reasons, but it is especially difficult when the thing being compared is complex and is interwoven with other social practices and cultural meanings. A comparative analysis of something relatively simple and discreet, such as capital punishment, presents the fewest challenges. Much more difficult is the comparison of highly complex entities such as "penal systems" or "criminal punishment." It can be done—comparative research on the welfare state has successfully addressed many of the key issues, and penological comparatists can learn a great deal from that field—but it requires a great deal of care in specifying the phenomenon in its various dimensions and in developing appropriate typologies, metrics, and data by means of which the phenomenon can be described and compared.

An *eighth* and final point of clarification: In the present volume, the idea of American exceptionalism is chiefly used in its descriptive sociological sense, that is, as a *sociological* or *historical* claim that America is in important respects different, distinctive, and set off from the standard pattern of Western development. But there is a second usage of the phrase "American exceptionalism" that features prominently in political discourse, though less so in sociology: an *ideological* or *evaluative* usage that claims America is somehow *superior* in virtue, character, or performance (Gingrich 2011; Soderlind and Carson 2011). This is American exceptionalism as a component of American nationalism, a form of patriotic self-regard. I will have little to say about the second usage, other than to note that it has recently taken on a new and more negative meaning—pointing to America's distinctive *vices* instead of its virtues—and that US penal practice, especially death-penalty retention and mass imprisonment, is nowadays often invoked as evidence of this negative exceptionalism (Downes 2001; Ignatieff 2005). We might also notice that the normative and the descriptive usages are often entangled: the allegedly special virtues (or the special vices) of the United States are assumed to be an aspect of the nation's exceptional social or cultural characteristics. To the extent this is the case, a critical examination of the descriptive claims should have implications for the normative claims based upon them.

The particular topic I address—America's retention of capital punishment—is a phenomenon that features in both the evaluative and the descriptive registers mentioned. And in connection with the evaluative version, the American death penalty neatly illustrates the double-sided character of the American exceptionalism idea as it operates today: the conservative (positive) version and the progressive (negative) version.

For many commentators, the kind of exceptionalism capital punishment involves is a *negative* one: a stain on the nation's character which—like the nation's exceptional stance on human rights treaties such as the Convention on the Rights of the Child, which it has refused to ratify; climate change agreements, which it has declined to sign; or the International Criminal Court, which it has refused to recognize (Ignatieff 2005)—reveals the dark side of the nation's distinctiveness. Instead of marking the nation's special virtue, the exceptional retention of capital punishment is a sign of moral failing and of America's distance from standards of progressive civilization that have taken hold elsewhere.

For other, pro–death penalty commentators, America's retention of capital punishment is proof of a normatively *positive* exceptionalism—a mark of the nation's faithfulness to abiding values that other countries have somehow let slide. So, the pro–death penalty activist Dianne Clements writes that "The

United States stands alone on many issues. That does not make us wrong" (quoted in Garland 2010, 183). And Supreme Court Justice Antonin Scalia—perhaps capital punishment's most prominent supporter—writes that "There exists in some parts of the world sanctimonious criticism of America's death penalty as somehow unworthy of a civilized society. I say sanctimonious because most of the countries to which these finger-waggers belong had the death penalty themselves until recently—and indeed many of them would still have it if the democratic will prevailed" (*Kansas v. Marsh* 2006).

These are instances of an evaluative use of American exceptionalism: of claims about the American people's status as morally superior or inferior, about our special virtue or our distinctive vice. In the remainder of this chapter I will concentrate on the other, more descriptive meaning of "American exceptionalism"—America as an empirical exception to the standard paths of Western historical development. And I will focus on the death penalty's retention as a prime example of what that supposedly "exceptional" history entails.

America's Death Penalty in Comparative Perspective

The United States is nowadays the only Western nation that still uses capital punishment. Elsewhere in the West, the death penalty has been decisively abolished. Most Western nations stopped executing offenders for ordinary crimes by the 1960s—some of them long before then—though it took until the 1990s for many of them to abolish it for wartime offenses and crimes against the state.

The divergence between America and other Western nations began in 1976 when the Supreme Court (in *Gregg v. Georgia* and several associated cases) upheld a series of new capital punishment statutes, having invalidated all existing ones four years previously in the case of *Furman v. Georgia*. That divergence increased further in the 1980s and 1990s. Among Western nations, abolition became the new standard, embraced by the Council of Europe, the European Union, and increasingly the United Nations, making most of the Western world a "death-free zone" (for details, see Hood and Hoyle 2015). In the United States, by contrast, capital statutes proliferated at the state and federal levels, the penalty's constitutionality was affirmed, and executions became more frequent. In the years since 1999, US death sentences and executions have declined from more than 300 sentences and close to 100 executions per year to fewer than 100 sentences and 50 executions—this in a nation with around 14,000 homicides in recent years and many more in the 1990s.

Seven further states have abolished the penalty in the last 10 years, bringing the number of death-penalty states to 31. But the fact that America retains capital punishment at all is strikingly at odds with the abolitionism of comparable nations.[3]

This state of affairs, in which the United States is an exception to an established pattern, has prompted scholars and commentators to invoke the sociological theory of "American exceptionalism" as an explanatory resource. At the start of the twenty-first century, articles by Carol Steiker (2002) and Tony Poveda (2000) began to develop this claim at length—the first exploring the theme in a tentative and noncommittal way, the second asserting it as part of a critique of America's long history of race and class oppression. Other writers (e.g., Downes 2001; Braithwaite 2003; Feeley 2003) invoke the idea casually, as if the assertion is self-evident and needs no further argument. Two major books on American punishment—one by Franklin E. Zimring (2003) and the other by James Q. Whitman (2003)—develop the same thesis, albeit with different claims about precisely what it is that marks American culture as "exceptional" and how this culture gives rise to capital punishment. Finally, I again mention Justice Antonin Scalia, who outlines his own, faith-based version of the exceptionalism thesis when he writes that "the more Christian a country is, the less likely it is to regard the death penalty as immoral. Abolition has taken its firmest hold in post-Christian Europe, and has least support in the church-going United States" (Scalia 2002, 20).

To invoke the idea of American exceptionalism like this—as a way of understanding America's retention of capital punishment—is to say more than that the United States is, as a comparative matter, "anomalous" or "on its own." The sociological language of exceptionalism suggests that America's current use of capital punishment is no transient phase of penal policy but is, instead, anchored in a kind of sociocultural bedrock, a set of defining institutions and values that underlie the American nation and shape its historical choices. Viewed in an exceptionalist perspective, capital punishment is not a judicial sanction that might be ended by act of law so much as a cultural disposition that will persist until the American nation changes in some more fundamental way, which is more or less exactly what these authors say (see Zimring 2003, 127; Whitman 2003, 207).

The idea that America was somehow "exceptional" was first suggested by Alexis de Tocqueville in the 1830s (Tocqueville 2004), but it was given its modern sociological meaning by writers such as Hartz (1955), Sombart (1976), and Lipset (1996), who developed the concept of "American exceptionalism" to explain the strength of America's liberal tradition and the weakness of working-class radicalism in the United States. And that theory is still used today to explain distinctive features of contemporary America by reference to an underlying set of "organizing principles"—especially US political and religious institutions—which are taken to be qualitatively different from those of other Western nations.

What are America's "exceptional" characteristics? The answer to this question depends on which source you consult, but the one I will quote here is fairly representative. According to Seymour Martin Lipset, America is distinguished by

> its relatively high level of social egalitarianism, economic productivity, and social mobility . . . [by] the strength of religion, the weakness of the central state, the earlier timing of electoral democracy, ethnic and racial diversity, and [by] the absence of feudal remnants, especially fixed social classes. (Lipset and Marks 2000, 16)

These characteristics are said to have given rise to a distinctive and abiding value system, the "American creed," with its stress upon "liberty, egalitarianism, individualism, populism and laissez-faire." Elsewhere Lipset sums up by stating that, in addition to being more religious, "Americans remain much more individualistic, meritocratic . . . and anti-statist than peoples elsewhere" (Lipset 1996, 61).

When criminologists claim that the death penalty is an instance of American exceptionalism, the implication is that that there is an essential relationship of some kind between America's culture and institutions, on the one hand, and capital punishment, on the other. The death penalty persists in the United States and nowhere else because, it implies, the United States is different in some deep and continuing sociocultural sense.

In my view, this application of the theory of American exceptionalism to capital punishment is an inappropriately deep and deterministic way to understand a difference in penal policy that is actually much more recent and much more contingent than this analysis suggests. Despite its undoubted rhetorical appeal—about which more later—the argument that capital punishment is a product of American exceptionalism is, in my view, misconceived.

The mistake is not in the identification of underlying cultural or value characteristics that help maintain the death penalty—these are clearly involved. Indeed, capital punishment in America today is largely an expressive measure, held in place chiefly by emotionally and culturally charged political considerations rather than by more instrumental concerns such as deterrent crime control. The mistake is not the turn to culture but the invocation of cultural traditions that are supposedly unopposed and unchanging constituents of the

American way. By invoking deep and relatively timeless explanations, these writers remove the institution of capital punishment from the specific history and political events that have actually produced it. As a theory, American exceptionalism directs attention to the wrong historical period and the wrong historical processes. Far from being an abiding element of the American condition, America's twenty-first-century death penalty in all its "distinctiveness" is actually a product of the last few decades, not the last few centuries.

As an account of capital punishment's conditions of existence, an American exceptionalist theory gives too much weight to supposedly timeless cultural values and too little attention to the ways in which cultural meanings change over time and interact in unpredictable ways with political structures and legal decisions. The continued existence of the death penalty is certainly an affront to American liberals, an international human rights scandal, and a moral outrage to anyone who objects to killing offenders. But we ought not to confuse moral salience with sociological significance.

Sociological explanations of punishment need to avoid the twin fallacies of misplaced depth and cultural determinism. I argue that it is much more plausible to view the continued existence of capital punishment as the contingent (and perhaps temporary) outcome of a series of political and legal decisions rather than as an expression of America's underlying character. To the extent that the outcomes of these political and legal decisions were shaped by structural constraints—and they were so shaped, even though the decisions could have been otherwise—the structures in question were political and legal ones and had little to do with any peculiarly American value system or distinctive underlying culture.

How to Think More Clearly about America's Death Penalty

Let me set out this critique in more detail by taking a moment to describe how we conventionally talk about America's death penalty, especially when the discussion turns to international comparisons.

Our standard way of discussing this question is to assert a simple opposition between abolition and retention—"the West" (or "Europe") has *abolished* the death penalty, while America has *retained* it—and then to suggest an explanation that accounts for this stark contrast. The trouble with this oppositional trope is that if the phenomenon to be explained is presented as a simple, binary contrast, then the explanations that come to mind tend also to be simplified, binary ones: "Americans" are punitive—or Puritan, or vigilante, or racist, or individualistic—and Europeans are not. (These, of course, are the oppositions cited by the system's critics, but death-penalty supporters offer their own preferred oppositions: for them, the explanation of the contrasting death-penalty positions between America and Europe is that America is truly democratic and Europe is not or that Americans continue to be God-fearing while Europeans have lost their faith.)

But these crude, simplified oppositions are misleading, quite apart from the dubious explanations that they propose. By aggregating "America" and "Europe," they collapse important internal distinctions, for example, between states such as Michigan, Wisconsin, and Rhode Island, which have been abolitionist since the mid-nineteenth century, and others such as Texas, Oklahoma, and Virginia, which still regularly put offenders to death. Similarly, they fail to distinguish between European nations such as Portugal, which abolished capital punishment for ordinary crimes in 1867, and others such as Britain, Spain, and France, which did not repeal their death-penalty laws until over a century later (Hood and Hoyle 2015).

The opposition between American retention and European abolition also collapses historical time, relying upon a snapshot comparison at a particular moment—the contemporary moment—that may be misleading. Consider, for example, that in 1972 the US Supreme Court ruled all existing capital statutes unconstitutional (in the case of *Furman v. Georgia*), while the French authorities decapitated Claude Buffet and Roger Bontems in the courtyard of La Santé Prison. Or consider that abolition usually occurs, when it does, not as the abrupt cessation of an unquestioned policy of routine executions but instead as the final stage of a long-term historical process in which the death penalty is incrementally restricted, restrained, and displaced by other penal sanctions. Major historical change usually takes the form of a process rather than an event. It is therefore a mistake to juxtapose "abolition" and "retention"—a binary distinction better suited to moral argument than to historical analysis.

This too-stark dichotomy prompts us to think of the American institution as the *opposite* of Western abolition, as if America is altogether unrestrained in its use of the death penalty, like the Stuart monarchs of seventeenth-century Britain or Nazi Germany's criminal courts. But if we view the American system of capital punishment historically and comparatively, on a continuum of death-penalty practices that ranges from the most spectacular, widespread, and intense to the most restricted, reformed, and restrained, then it seems clear that the contemporary United States is much closer to the minimalist pole than the maximalist pole.

American jurisdictions still permit the death penalty, and this is, of course, a significant moral and political fact that properly commands our attention.

But the actual execution of this penalty is comparatively infrequent and largely confined to one region of the country. Its use is subject to close regulation and restraint. And its existence is a matter of legal and political controversy. Such facts ought not to be ignored.

Taken together, the point of view of the present and the rhetoric of normative debate are powerful influences, and they push us to regard the US situation as diametrically opposed to that of Europe. But a more historical perspective suggests that, in many important respects, the two are not so far apart. Perhaps an image might help: if we visualize the full range of death-penalty practices as a line of continuous variation, we would picture the European nations (as well as other Western countries such as Canada, Australia, and New Zealand) as having gradually moved to the minimalist end of the continuum and then finally stepped off altogether, while the United States, which has made exactly the same journey, now hovers close to that same end.

In making these comparative and historical points I am not seeking to make America's death penalty disappear or to deny its distinctiveness. In the Western world, contemporary America is clearly an outlier in terms of the death penalty as well as other aspects of penal policy. Other Western nations share much of the punitive trajectory and culture of control (Garland 2001; Wacquant 2009) that emerged in late twentieth-century America, but no other Western nation exhibits the harsh sentencing tariffs, mass imprisonment, collateral consequences, and capital punishment that now characterize the United States.

Framing the Question

So America is different from other Western nations in important respects, and a central aim of current research is to explain these differences. That there are differences is not at issue. The question is, how best to frame an inquiry that can explain them?

Talk of American exceptionalism usefully reminds us of the need for a comparative perspective and of the distinctive institutional structures and cultural practices that constitute the American polity. It also reminds us that Americans often think of themselves as "exceptional" and care little for international opinion. But as an analytical matter, American exceptionalism is an unhelpful way of framing things, particularly when it employs undifferentiated, ahistorical, and essentialist conceptions of "American culture" or the "American condition."

America is not a single place for penological purposes, any more than is "Europe" or "the West." There are major regional and state-level differences within the United States—including differences between the 32 so-called death-penalty states—which make talk of "American" capital punishment somewhat misleading.

Until recently there were also major differences among the capital-punishment practices of the European nations, though the fact that all of them are now abolitionist has obliterated these contrasts. Like Tolstoy's families, abolitionist nations all now seem alike, but every retentionist nation retains the death penalty in its own way. But the European Union's contemporary abolitionism hides a variety of different histories, many of them very bloody indeed. Each of the European nations was previously a death-penalty nation, and each deployed the death penalty using distinctive national forms (the noose, the axe, the guillotine, or the garrote) in a context of specific local meanings.

There is no constant difference between America and other Western nations that persists through time. If the comparisons were made in the 1830s or 1840s (when the mildness of American punishments impressed European visitors such as Charles Dickens and Alexis de Tocqueville) or in the early 1940s (when American execution rates began their long decline and Nazi Germany moved rapidly toward "assembly line" executions) or even in the mid-1970s (at which point the French authorities were still decapitating offenders while the United States had gone nearly 10 years without a single execution), the ratios would look quite different. Instead of a constant contrast, the historical record shows commonalities and differences, generic developments, and distinctive variants. America is in historical motion, as are each of the European nations with which it is being compared; and its relationship to them varies over time, growing now closer, now further apart.

American exceptionalism is a theory developed to explain long-term, widespread and persistent phenomena by reference to structural and cultural features of the American nation that are also long-term and persistent. An analytical framework of that kind cannot be plausibly applied to a phenomenon—America's retention of the death penalty following abolition in the other Western nations—that is less than 40 years old, is unevenly distributed across the nation's states and regions, and may yet prove to be transient rather than persistent over the medium to long term.

If we replace our conventional dichotomy ("capital punishment retained" and "capital punishment abolished") with a more refined sense of variation along a continuum, then the causal picture alters accordingly. Instead of supposing that qualitatively different effects must have qualitatively different causes, we can think in terms of general causal processes producing varied outcomes in different settings and circumstances.

We might then hypothesize that the reasons for death-penalty abolition in Europe are much the same as the reasons for death-penalty reform in the United States—state building and rationalization, the refinement of social and penal controls, liberalism and democracy's humanism and civilized manners, the welfare state, and so on—except that America's anti–death penalty movement, the social forces that propelled it, and the political processes that give it legal expression were somehow weakened, countered, or constrained in their operation, particularly in the final stages of the movement toward abolition.

Instead of thinking in conventional terms of an exceptional history and all that this entails, we ought to think of America as a specific variant within a general set: an outlier on some dimensions, in the central tendency on others, but not different in kind. This approach leads away from myopic talk about "exceptions" toward more detailed and more nuanced historical comparisons.

Viewed in the long term, the historical trajectory of the American institution looks remarkably similar to that of other Western nations. At the beginning of the modern period capital punishment was in widespread use everywhere, enjoying unquestioned legitimacy, imposed in simple and aggravated forms, drawing upon religious as well as secular rationales, targeting many kinds of offense and offender, and executed in public. From the seventeenth century onward, the institution underwent a slow, centuries-long, process of modification, diminution, and abolition.

Historians have described the key stages of this decline as follows: (1) a reduced range of capital offenses and eligible offenders; (2) the abolition of aggravated death sentences such as burning at the stake and of postmortem punishments such as gibbetting, dismemberment, and dissection; (3) the removal of executions from the public gaze; (4) the adoption of technologies such as the guillotine or the trap-door gallows designed to speed death and reduce pain; (5) the emergence of a normative discourse challenging the institution; (6) the development of more formalized legal procedures and safeguards; (7) a secular decline in the frequency of death sentences and executions; and (8) a movement to complete abolition, first *de facto* and then *de jure* (see Garland 2010 for details).

This trajectory of decline, with minor variations, occurred in the United States just as it did throughout the Western world (Banner 2002). Throughout the nineteenth and twentieth centuries, the United States—or, more precisely, certain regions thereof—appeared to be firmly on the abolitionist trajectory and not in the least exceptional. States such as Michigan, Wisconsin, and Rhode Island were in the vanguard of the movement, each having abolished capital punishment in the 1840s and 1850s, long before most European nations considered doing so. In twentieth-century America, the number of executions steadily declined from a peak of 199 per year in 1933 to a handful per year in the 1960s and eventually to zero in 1967. During the period from 1967 to 1976, no one was put to death and the Supreme Court's *Furman* decision in 1972 struck down all of the states' capital-punishment statutes as unconstitutional. It is only in the last four decades, from 1976 to the present, that the United States looks significantly different.

Nor is there anything especially anomalous about the American death penalty other than the fact that it is still in use. In its form, its targets, its techniques, its staging, and its rationales, the institution is not outside the modern Western mainstream. It is true, of course, that the legal and administrative systems that impose and deliver capital punishments in the United States reflect the distinctive complex of institutions, legislation, criminal procedure, and case law that produced it: in that restricted sense, there is a distinctively "American way of death." But this distinctiveness of detail—which is a characteristic of every legal system, each of which imposes and inflicts penalties in its own unique way (Sarat and Boulanger 2004)—does not detract from the broad similarities that link the United States and other Western nations.

Unlike Saudi Arabia or the Sudan where beheadings are staged in public, often for moral or religious offenses, sometimes at the hands of crime victims or their survivors, the American way of death is recognizably modern and Western. Indeed, the widespread use of lethal injections designed to minimize pain (or at least the appearance thereof) and the elaborate framework of legal procedures and appellate reviews designed to minimize arbitrariness and mistake (or at least the appearance thereof) suggest that the American death penalty has been shaped by the same kinds of values and sensibilities that operated in other nations that ultimately became abolitionist.

Opinion poll data suggest that public support for the death penalty is no more extensive or intense in the United States than in several European nations—particularly in those where the death penalty was only recently abolished. (In most nations, capital punishment was abolished *despite* public opinion, not because of it.) Nor is there any evidence that justifications for its use in the United States are significantly different from those that were standardly used in western Europe until recently. When we inspect the actual data about American attitudes to capital punishment, there is no direct evidence of any cultural predisposition. The only evidence we have of "American exceptionalism" is that the penalty is still used: claims about exceptional cultural attitudes are inferential rather than direct.

Capital punishment in America today is the residual trace of a penalty that was once standard in every Western nation. The distinctiveness that scholars set out to explain relates entirely to the pace and completeness of the process of abolition: a matter of timing not trajectory. What this means is that the relevant dependent variable in these analyses is not the death penalty itself but rather the date of its abolition.

When viewed in these terms, the issue looks quite different. Every distribution has extreme data points. Every series has a first and a last. And the fact that American states have been the first (e.g., Michigan) as well as the last (e.g., Texas) in this historical series ought to discourage hasty generalization. American tardiness in enacting complete national abolition is the real issue here, not deeper-than-normal American commitment to the institution.

If the thing to be explained is the persistence of American capital-punishment laws and sentencing in the last 40 years, then reaching back into previous centuries—as American exceptionalism explanations prompt us to do—is unnecessary and inappropriate. We do not need to seek for deep, long-term cultural traditions and value orientations that might explain present-day practices. Instead, we need to look at recent history—at the political and legal struggles that shaped events, at the choices and decisions made by key actors, and at the political, legal, and cultural circumstances that shaped these decisions.

If we wish to understand today's capital punishment—the public attitudes that support it, the values to which it is linked, and the symbolic meanings that it conveys—the history we most need to understand is not that of the eighteenth or the nineteenth century but the history of the last 40 years.

That history unfolded within a context that was structured and constrained by America's distinctive political institutions of federalism, popular democracy, and constitutional review—and to that extent, the American exceptionalism literature has something important to teach us. But the events that mattered, and that made the difference between retention and abolition, were shaped by political choices of a contingent nature rather than by the operation of any deep-seated, long-term national characteristics. And to the extent that cultural values played a part in shaping these political choices—and they did—it was not the age-old values of a "city set upon a hill" but rather a new cultural formation that emerged in the 1970s around issues of race, crime, social change, and social order (Garland 2001, 2010)—together with the conservative legal culture of the Supreme Court in the 1980s and 1990s that shaped the court's legal choices (Weisberg 1983; Liebman 2007; Garland 2010).

In short, America's current stance on capital punishment may be anomalous in international terms, but it is not an instance of American exceptionalism. And examining this specific phenomenon in detail helps clarify precisely what is entailed when we invoke American exceptionalism as a theoretical explanation of twenty-first-century American institutions.

Conclusion

My account of America's death penalty and its largely unexceptional history and character answers one set of questions but also raises another set, and I will end by posing these questions for readers to consider:

First, would we reach the same results if we were to examine, in a similarly detailed way, other alleged instances of American exceptionalism—such as the welfare state, social democracy, or the labor movement?

Second, might American exceptionalism claims be more sustainable—in respect of the death penalty and other practices—if we were to narrow the scope of our theoretical claims and think not in terms of an American exceptionalism in general but instead of a more narrowly drawn "southern exceptionalism" focused on the distinctiveness of the American South?

Third, is it generally the case, as my specific analysis might be taken to suggest, that the most significant distinctive features of the American nation for comparative purposes are not American values or American culture but instead the structure of the American polity, its legal institutions, and the eighteenth-century constitution that sustains them?

NOTES

1. One of the first accounts of American exceptionalism was developed in the late 1920s by members of the American Communist Party seeking to explain why the prospects for revolution were less developed in America.
2. Specified in statistical terms, a data point can be described as an "outlier" in a distribution if it is more than two standard deviations removed from the mean value.
3. It should be said, in the interests of exactitude, that India still executes offenders (though it does so rarely and mostly as a punishment for political assassination) and Japan does too. So there are other democracies in which capital punishment persists. But if the comparison is with "Western nations" then the United States stands alone.

CASES CITED

Furman v. Georgia, 408 U.S. 238 (1972).
Gregg v. Georgia, 428 U.S. 153 (1976).
Kansas v. Marsh, 548 U.S. 163 (2006).

REFERENCES

Baldwin, Peter. *The Narcissism of Minor Differences: How America and Europe Are Alike*. New York: Oxford University Press, 2009.

Banner, Stuart. *The Death Penalty: An American History*. Cambridge, MA: Harvard University Press, 2002.

Braithwaite, John. "What's Wrong with the Sociology of Punishment?" *Theoretical Criminology* 7, no. 1 (2003): 5–28.

Downes, David. "The Macho Penal Economy: Mass Incarceration in the United States—A European Perspective." In *Mass Imprisonment: Social Causes and Consequences*, edited by David Garland, 51–69. London: Sage, 2001.

Feeley, Malcolm M. "Crime, Social Order and the Rise of Neo-Conservative Politics." *Theoretical Criminology* 7, no. 1 (2003): 111–30.

Flora, Peter, and Arnold J. Heidenheimer, eds. *The Development of Welfare States in Europe and America*. New Brunswick, NJ: Transaction Press, 1981.

Foner, Eric. "American Exceptionalism, American Freedom." *Montreal Review*, January 2013. http://www.themontrealreview.com/2009/American-Exceptionalism-American-Freedom.php.

Garland, David. *The Culture of Control: Crime and Social Order in Contemporary Society*. Chicago: University of Chicago Press, 2001.

Garland, David. *Peculiar Institution: America's Death Penalty in an Age of Abolition*. Cambridge, MA: Harvard University Press, 2010.

Garland, David. *The Welfare State: A Very Short Introduction*. Oxford: Oxford University Press, 2015.

Gingrich, Newt. *A Nation Like No Other: Why American Exceptionalism Matters*. Washington, DC: Regnery Publishing, 2011.

Hammel, Andrew. *Ending the Death Penalty: The European Experience in Global Perspective*. London: Palgrave MacMillan, 2010.

Hartz, Louis. *The Liberal Tradition in America*. New York: Harcourt, Brace, 1955.

Hodgson, Godfrey. *The Myth of American Exceptionalism*. New Haven: Yale University Press, 2009.

Hood, Roger, and Carolyn Hoyle. *The Death Penalty: A Worldwide Perspective*. 5th ed. Oxford: Oxford University Press, 2015.

Ignatieff, Michael, ed. *American Exceptionalism and Human Rights*. Princeton, NJ: Princeton University Press, 2005.

Liebman, James S. "Slow Dancing with Death: The Supreme Court and Capital Punishment 1963 to 2006." *Columbia Law Review* 107 (2007): 1–130.

Lipset, Seymour Martin. *American Exceptionalism: A Double Edged Sword*. New York: W.W. Norton, 1996.

Lipset, Seymour Martin, and Gary Marks. *It Didn't Happen Here: Why Socialism Failed in the United States*. New York: W.W. Norton, 2000.

Lockhart, Charles. *The Roots of American Exceptionalism: Institutions, Culture and Policies*. New York: Palgrave, 2003.

Madsen, Deborah L. *American Exceptionalism*. Jackson: University of Mississippi Press, 1998.

Marx, Karl. "1857 Introduction" and "1859 Preface." In *A Contribution to a Critique of Political Economy*, edited by Maurice Dobb. London: Lawrence & Wishart, 1971.

McLennan, Gregor. *Marxism and the Methodologies of History*. London: Verso, 1981.

Poveda, Tony G. "American Exceptionalism and the Death Penalty." *Social Justice* 27, no. 2 (2000): 252–67.

Sarat, Austin, and Christian Boulanger. *The Cultural Lives of Capital Punishment: Comparative Perspectives*. Stanford, CA: Stanford University Press, 2004.

Scalia, Antonin. "God's Justice and Ours." *First Things*, May 2002. http://www.firstthings.com/article/2002/05/gods-justice-and-ours.

Shafer, Byron E., ed. *Is America Different? A New Look at American Exceptionalism*. New York: Oxford University Press, 1991.

Soderlind, Sylvia, and James Taylor Carson, eds. *American Exceptionalism: From Winthrop to Winfrey*. Albany: State University of New York Press, 2011.

Sombart, Werner. *Why Is There No Socialism in the United States?* New York: International Arts & Sciences Press, 1976.

Steiker, Carol S. "Capital Punishment and American Exceptionalism." *Oregon Law Review* 81 (2002): 97–125.

Tocqueville, Alexis de. *Democracy in America*. New York: Library of America, 2004.

Wacquant, Loïc. *Prisons of Poverty*. Minneapolis: University of Minnesota Press, 2009.

Weisberg, Robert. "Deregulating Death." *Supreme Court Review* 1983 (1983): 305–95.

Whitman, James Q. *Harsh Justice: Criminal Punishment and the Widening Divide between America and Europe*. New York: Oxford University Press, 2003.

Zimring, Franklin E. *The Contradictions of American Capital Punishment*. New York: Oxford University Press, 2003.

3

Penal Optimism

UNDERSTANDING AMERICAN MASS IMPRISONMENT FROM A CANADIAN PERSPECTIVE

Cheryl Marie Webster and Anthony N. Doob

The American, by nature, is optimistic. He is experimental, an inventor and a builder who builds best when called upon to build greatly.

JOHN F. KENNEDY

Introduction

Particularly for those who have kept abreast of the rates of imprisonment of Western countries since the mid-1970s, it is likely that few people would disagree with the characterization of American mass incarceration as "exceptional." Indeed, the US imprisonment rate began its steady climb in the early 1970s, increasing by a factor of roughly 5 over the next four decades from approximately 96 adult prisoners per 100,000 residents in state and federal prisons in 1970 to 497 in 2010 (or, including an estimate of the jail population for 1970,[1] from 146 in 1970 to 731 in 2010) (Bureau of Justice Statistics 2015) before beginning to decline slowly. The United States currently holds the (in)famous status of imprisoning its citizens at a rate that exceeds almost every other nation in the world.[2] In fact, any academic debate surrounding this phenomenon appears to be rooted primarily (if not almost exclusively) in the various theories which have been proposed to explain it (see, for example, the differing explanations of Bottoms 1995; Ruth and Reitz 2003; Cavadino and Dignan 2006; Simon 2007; Wacquant 2011). Several of the more compelling explanations have been developed through a comparison of the United States with comparable nations (e.g., Garland 1990, 2001; Roberts et al. 2003; Whitman 2003; Tonry 2004). Within this context, Canada may arguably be well suited to shed light on America's dramatic prison boom.

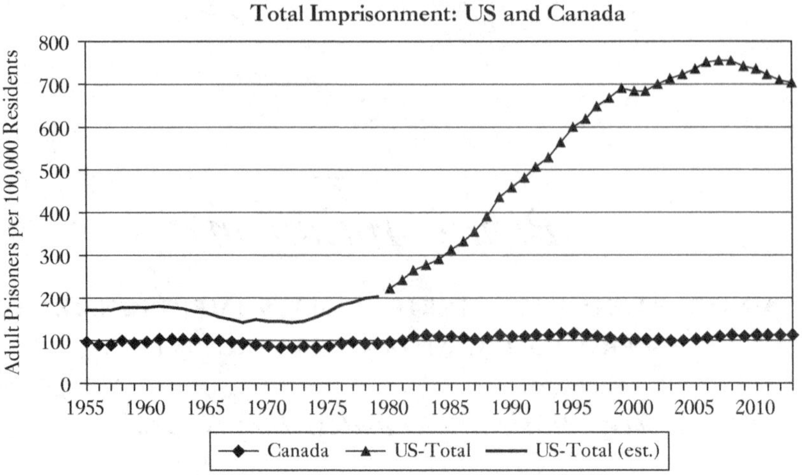

FIGURE 3.1 US and Canadian Imprisonment Rates per 100,000 Residents (1955–2013)

In striking contrast with the United States, Canadian levels of incarceration have remained relatively stable over the last half-century (Doob and Webster 2006; Webster and Doob 2007, 2011, 2012). Further, the current imprisonment rate in Canada—112 per 100,000 general population in 2015—is roughly one-sixth that of the United States (Figure 3.1).

Having said this, Canada is arguably America's closest comparator. The affinities between these two countries are not only geographical, historical, cultural, and economic in nature but also criminological. Canada has experienced a crime culture similar to that found in the United States since the 1960s. While the crime *rates* of the two countries may be somewhat different (and certainly the manner in which national crime figures are estimated in Canada and the United States is considerably different), the *patterns* of growth and decline in levels of crime are remarkably similar—both for crime generally (Figure 3.2)[3] and for homicide in particular (Figure 3.3).[4]

The same can be said for the levels of incarceration of these two nations before 1970 (Figure 3.1). Although the estimated "total" imprisonment rate in the United States (including federal and state prisons as well as the jail populations) is likely to have been about 50 percent higher than that in Canada, both countries showed relative stability from 1930 to 1970.[5]

Methodologically, one has the ingredients of an (*ex post facto*) pseudonatural experiment. That is, one has two broadly comparable groups whose imprisonment rates paralleled each other for at least 50 years (Blumstein, Cohen,

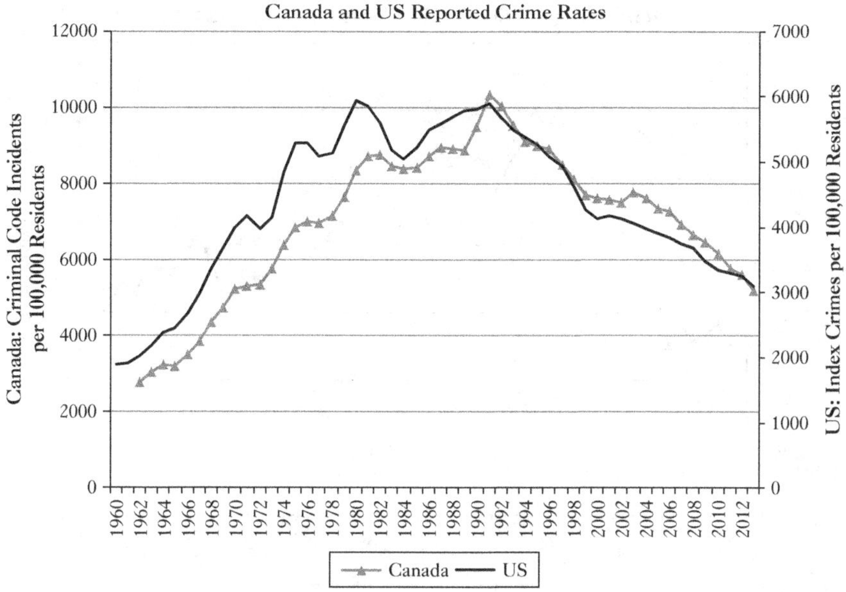

FIGURE 3.2 US and Canadian Reported Crime Rates per 100,000 Residents (1962–2013)

Sources: Sourcebook of Criminal Justice Statistics (2004) (http://www.albany.edu/sourcebook; US Bureau of Justice Statistics, http://www.fbi.gov/about-us/cjis/ucr/crime-in-the-u.s/2013/crime-in-the-u.s.-2013/tables/1tabledatadecoverviewpdf/table_1_crime_in_the_united_states_by_volume_and_rate_per_100000_inhabitants_1994-2013.xls); Statistics Canada, CANSIM. (http://www5.statcan.gc.ca/cansim/a33?lang=eng&spMode=master&themeID=2693&RT=TABLE).

and Nagin 1977; Webster and Doob 2012, Figure 4.1) before diverging dramatically in the mid-1970s. While Canada's levels have remained relatively stable until the present, those of the United States have skyrocketed. One simply needs to identify the independent variable (or set of variables) that occurred in the United States but not in Canada at the time of the divergence as a means of exploring possible (additional) explanations for America's mass incarceration.

The impetus for this chapter derives from this loose methodology. Specifically, we set out to use the Canadian experience as a foil to that of the United States in order to better understand American exceptionalism as it relates to the dramatic growth in its levels of imprisonment since the mid-1970s. Although methodologically simple in design, the identification of the illusive "experimental treatment" proved to be considerably more difficult. The irony, it turns out, is that the most valuable clue was contained in its very name (read *treatment*). While one's attention is naturally drawn to the

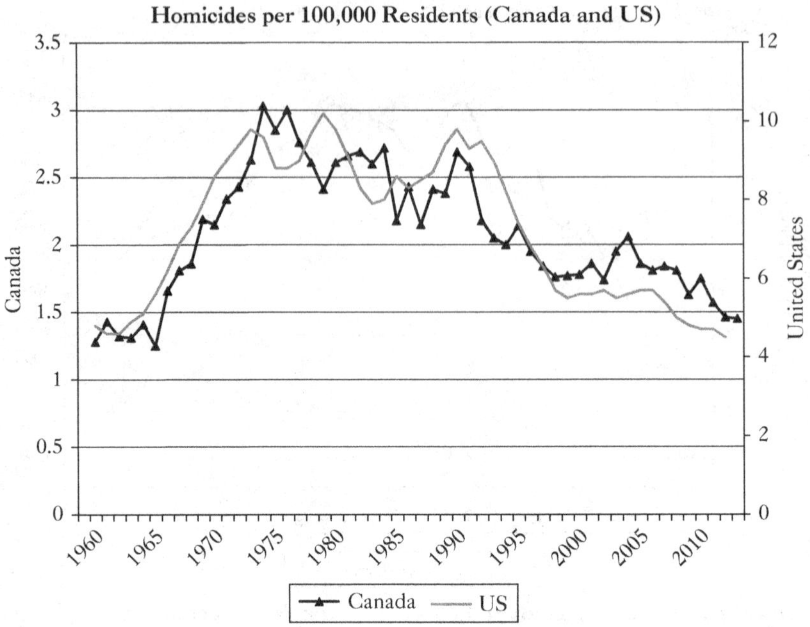

FIGURE 3.3 US and Canadian Homicide Rates per 100,000 Residents (1962–2013)
Sources: Sourcebook of Criminal Justice Statistics (2004) (http://www.albany.edu/sourcebook; US Bureau of Justice Statistics, http://www.fbi.gov/about-us/cjis/ucr/crime-in-the-u.s/2013/crime-in-the-u.s.-2013/tables/1tabledatadecoverviewpdf/table_1_crime_in_the_united_states_by_volume_and_rate_per_100000_inhabitants_1994-2013.xls); Statistics Canada, CANSIM. (http://www5.statcan.gc.ca/cansim/a33?lang=eng&spMode=master&themeID=2693&RT=TABLE).

mid-1970s as the era which must contain the source of the divergence in Canadian and American patterns of incarceration rates, a closer examination of the preexisting trends in imprisonment of these two countries—decades prior to the 1970s—reveals the deceptive nature of their similarity. Although they clearly paralleled each other for over a half-century, they were rooted in fundamentally different conceptualizations of the role of the criminal justice system in controlling crime.

Most obviously, most US states had what is now commonly referred to as an "indeterminate sentencing system" whereby judges—when incarcerating an offender—set broad ranges of possible sentences and administrative bodies (e.g., parole authorities) largely determined when, if ever, the prisoner would be released (see Reitz 2012). The philosophical underpinnings of this sentencing structure were firmly (if not exclusively) entrenched in a rehabilitative model and reflected the optimism of the American policy elite in the ability of the criminal justice system to control crime. During the high-indeterminate era (which began to crumble in the 1970s), the standard narrative in US corrections was that most prisoners were on the path to rehabilitation and that parole boards could detect when individual prisoners had reached that goal and were safe to release (American Law Institute 1962; Frankel 1973). Even if one were to consider the post-1970s era, in which indeterminate sentencing was replaced by more determinate punishment systems, the same utilitarian optimism would appear to be embraced, albeit now rooted predominantly in an incapacitation (and deterrence) model.

In sharp contrast, sentences (other than for murder) would be considered—using the definition given by van Zyl Smit and Corda (see van Zyl Smit and Corda, this volume)—determinate in Canada during the pre-1970s era whereby judges handed down fixed-length (or maximum-term) sentences (although prisoners could be released on parole after serving at least one-third of the sanction). The guiding principle at the root of this sentencing system was proportionality. Notably, this punishment structure has been maintained until the present. In fact, proportionality as the fundamental principle in the determination of sanctions was formally codified in the *Criminal Code* of Canada in 1996 and has been virtually constitutionalized by the Supreme Court of Canada in *Ipeelee* (paragraphs 37–39). In contrast with the United States, the Canadian government and those responsible for developing criminal justice policy have generally been pessimistic about the ability of the criminal justice system to solve society's crime problems.

This distinction raises the possibility that American exceptionalism in the growth of imprisonment since the mid-1970s is rooted, at least in part, in its long-standing belief that crime can be controlled through criminal justice interventions. Optimism in the effectiveness of either rehabilitation or incapacitation/deterrence as a justification of punishment places few natural limits or constraints on the use of criminal law generally and prison in particular (Rothman 1980; Allen 1981; Zimring and Hawkins 1995). In contrast, Canada's long-standing pessimism concerning the utilitarian purposes of sentencing and its corresponding focus on proportionality as the guiding principle may serve a restraining function on the recourse to punishment and, by extension, imprisonment as an appropriate state response to crime.

This chapter explores this hypothesis of penal optimism. To this end, it begins by addressing the methodological issue of the "unit of analysis." Given the American federal structure and its 51 separate criminal justice jurisdictions, it is entirely possible that America's mass incarceration is not actually a "national" phenomenon. Rather, it could be the result of political actions or structures of particular (especially punitive) states, suggesting the need for a more "local" explanatory focus. The second part tests our hypothesis by comparing the broad intellectual histories of American punishment philosophy preceding and following the mid-1970s with a focus on the (optimistic) role of the criminal justice system vis-à-vis crime control. The third part extends this hypothesis testing to Canada, where its broad currents of intellectual thought and policy approach surrounding crime and appropriate responses to it are compared with those of the United States. The chapter concludes with a brief discussion of the implications of our findings, particularly as they relate to explanations of American exceptionalism and the core values underlying it.

Exceptionalism or Exceptionalisms?

Prior research on Canadian imprisonment rates (see, for example, Sprott and Doob 1998; Tucker 2009) has highlighted not only considerable variability across provinces/territories but also diverging trends over time.[6] In particular, levels of incarceration of some provinces/territories have shown a long-term increase, while others have shown a decline. Within the context of explaining Canada's (overall) relative stability in imprisonment rates over the past half-century, macro- or national-level theories have some difficulty in taking this "local" variation into account.

A similar concern arises when attempting to understand "American" exceptionalism. As various authors (see, for example, Zimring and Hawkins 1991; Zimring and Johnson 2006; Zimring 2010) have reminded us, the particular American federal structure is an important consideration when attempting to explain mass imprisonment in the United States. This perspective is consistent with the detailed work of others (Miller 2008; Barker 2009; Lynch 2010; Campbell 2014) who have suggested that to understand exactly how imprisonment changed in the United States one needs to examine the political actions or structures in each state. Within this context, it is not implausible—certainly when viewed from the Canadian context—that America's dramatic growth in levels of incarceration since the mid-1970s could be driven primarily by certain states, with other states theoretically displaying diverging patterns. In this case, although it would not be incorrect to talk of "American" exceptionalism, explanations for this phenomenon would arguably need to be more "locally" grounded.

To explore this question of the limits of one particular unit of analysis (country) over another (state), we examined change in levels of incarceration at the state level. Table 3.1 lists the states with the smallest and the largest absolute change in imprisonment rates (in effect, the data used to form the fourth column in Table 3.1). It also displays the incarceration rate in the early 1970s, the rate in the late 2000s, as well as the difference between these two rates and, for the sake of completeness, the ratio of the two rates.[7]

From the perspective of our macro-level hypothesis, the absolute change in imprisonment rates from 1971–1975 (immediately prior to the increase in mass incarceration and henceforth referred to as the early 1970s rates) to 2006–2010 (the peak of mass incarceration and henceforth referred to as the late 2000s rates) shows very clearly that *every* state—without exception—increased its levels of incarceration over this 35-year period. Further, the increases were nontrivial in size.[8] Ignoring jails and federal imprisonment, the smallest increases in state prison populations occurred in Maine, Minnesota, and Nebraska, whose rates rose by 100, 144, and 174 per 100,000 residents, respectively. Notably, these three "low-increase" states had imprisonment rates—in the early 1970s—of 49, 38, and 69, respectively. From any normal perspective, these *smallest* increases were huge. Simply as a relevant comparator, Canada's increase of 25.4 per 100,000 residents was dramatically less (in absolute or relative terms) than that of any US state.

Having said this, one cannot also help but notice the enormous variation across states in the size of the increase in state imprisonment rates. Judged by absolute numbers, a comparison of the smallest increases (Maine with 100 and Minnesota with 144) with the largest increases (Mississippi with 616 and Louisiana with 749 *additional* state prisoners on an average day per 100,000 residents) tells the story. The contributions of the states to America's prison binge are remarkably uneven. Nonetheless, we argue that when 50 out of 50 states (as well as the federal prisons) show huge increases in their prison systems (without even including nationwide increases in jail populations), there is *something* exceptional and distinctly American that is worth exploring that is *not* state-specific. Simply put, the universality of the large increases in imprisonment in the United States is truly exceptional and deserving of its own explanation.

But we hasten to add that an examination of America as a unified jurisdiction does not tell the whole story. Another way of ordering the 50 states is to compare the states that, in the early 1970s, had the lowest imprisonment rates to those that had the highest levels during this same period. Table 3.2 presents the data.

By world standards, the rates for the "low" states were low in 1971–1975. Even adding in the *average* federal rate for the period (10.6) and multiplying this sum by 1.52 to take into account the missing jail populations, these rates were very low.[9] The same cannot be said for the 2006–2010 rates, especially if one were to add the jail and federal rates. At the same time, both this table as well as Table 3.1 show striking variability across states. A simple comparison

Table 3.1 Ten States with the Lowest and Highest Absolute Change in Imprisonment Rates from 1971–1975 to 2006–2010

Ten States with Lowest and Highest Absolute Change in Imprisonment Rates, 1971–1975 to 2006–2010	Average Imprisonment Rate, 1971–1975	Average Imprisonment Rate, 2006–2010	Absolute Change in Imprisonment Rate between 1971–1975 and 2006–2010	Ratio of 2006–2010 Imprisonment Rate to 1971–1975 Imprisonment Rate
Maine	49.12	149.6	100.48	3.0
Minnesota	37.56	182	144.44	4.8
Nebraska	69.16	243.4	174.24	3.5
Rhode Island	41.9	217	175.1	5.2
New Hampshire	30.34	212.8	182.46	7.0
North Carolina	182.8	366.2	183.4	2.0
Washington	83.76	271.2	187.44	3.2
Utah	49.86	237.4	187.54	4.8
Massachusetts	37.02	224.6	187.58	6.1
North Dakota	24.54	222.8	198.26	9.1
Delaware	63.14	464.6	401.46	7.4
Idaho	57.92	477.4	419.48	8.2
Arkansas	89.62	514.4	424.78	5.7
Missouri	82.18	509.2	427.02	6.2

Arizona	89.44	556.4	466.96	6.2
Texas	143.62	657.4	513.78	4.6
Alabama	109.86	628.4	518.54	5.7
Oklahoma	125.36	660.2	534.84	5.3
Mississippi	87.22	703	615.78	8.1
Louisiana	113.44	862.4	748.96	7.6
Canada	84.9	110.3	25.4	1.3

Source: Sourcebook on Criminal Justice Statistics (University at Albany, School of Criminal Justice), http://www.albany.edu/sourcebook/pdf/t31062012.pdf; US Bureau of Justice Statistics, http://www.bjs.gov/index.cfm?ty=tp&tid=11; Statistics Canada, CANSIM, http://www5.statcan.gc.ca/cansim/a01?lang=eng.

Table 3.2 Ten Highest and 10 Lowest State Prison Rates in 1971–1975: Change in Imprisonment Rates from 1971–1975 to 2006–2010

Ten States with Lowest and Highest Imprisonment Rates, 1971–1975	Average Imprisonment Rate, 1971–1975	Average Imprisonment Rate, 2006–2010	Absolute Change in Imprisonment Rate between 1971–1975 and 2006–2010	Ratio of 2006–2010 Imprisonment Rate to 1971–1975 Imprisonment Rate
North Dakota	24.54	222.8	198.26	9.1
New Hampshire	30.34	212.8	182.46	7.0
Massachusetts	37.02	224.6	187.58	6.1
Minnesota	37.56	182	144.44	4.8
Hawaii	38.08	325.4	287.32	8.5
Rhode Island	41.9	217	175.1	5.2
Montana	42.8	368.8	326	8.6
Vermont	43.86	264.8	220.94	6.0
South Dakota	45.94	417.4	371.46	9.1
Maine	49.12	149.6	100.48	3.0
Alabama	109.86	628.4	518.54	5.7
Louisiana	113.44	862.4	748.96	7.6
Oklahoma	125.36	660.2	534.84	5.3
Nevada	129.28	485	355.72	3.8

Texas	143.62	657.4	513.78	4.6
South Carolina	145.22	515	369.78	3.5
Florida	145.7	543.2	397.5	3.7
Maryland	146.44	394.4	247.96	2.7
Georgia	177.82	533.2	355.38	3.0
North Carolina	182.8	366.2	183.4	2.0
Canada	84.9	110.3	25.4	1.3

Source: Sourcebook of Criminal Justice Statistics (2004), http://www.albany.edu/sourcebook; US Bureau of Justice Statistics, http://www.fbi.gov/about-us/cjis/ucr/crime-in-the-u.s/2013/crime-in-the-u.s.-2013/tables/1tabledatadecoverviewpdf/table_1_crime_in_the_united_states_by_volume_and_rate_per_100000_inhabitants_1994-2013.xls; Statistics Canada, CANSIM, http://www5.statcan.gc.ca/cansim/a01?lang=eng.

of the two states with the lowest imprisonment rates—North Dakota (25 per 100,000 residents) and New Hampshire (30)—with the two states with the highest imprisonment rates—Georgia (178) and North Carolina (183)—shows that large state variation already existed before the "great increase" in American levels of incarceration.

More importantly for our current discussion surrounding units of analysis, it is clear that a "national" explanation for American mass incarceration will seemingly do very little or nothing to explain, for example, why six states (Massachusetts, Minnesota, Hawaii, Rhode Island, Montana, and Vermont) with almost identical 1971–1975 imprisonment rates (ranging from 37 to 43) ended up, 35 years later, with imprisonment rates ranging from 182 to 369. On the contrary, this variability suggests additional explanatory factors above and beyond any national explanation for American exceptionalism in its growth in incarceration. Each of the American states is, in some way, exceptional. The question is simply one of differing degrees.

However, what happened between the early 1970s and the late 2000s is exceptional in yet another way. In a certain statistical sense, the comparison of state prison incarceration rates in the early 1970s and late 2000s is intriguing because it appears to describe an unusual relationship. First of all, we have a perfectly intuitive finding. Treating each of the 50 states as a unit, there is a reasonably high correlation between the imprisonment rate of the states in the early 1970s and their imprisonment rate 35 years later ($r = +.61$). In other words, states with relatively high imprisonment rates in the early 1970s had relatively high imprisonment rates in the late 2000s. This finding is hardly surprising: if every state were to increase its imprisonment rate by roughly 350 prisoners per 100,000 residents, there would be a very high relationship between early 1970s rates and late 2000s rates.

What is more interesting is the correlation between the imprisonment rate in the early 1970s and the *size of the increase* in imprisonment rates (between the early 1970s and the late 2000s). The relationship is positive and large ($r = +.41$). If these 50 states were conceptualized as part of the same population, one might expect what is typically called "regression to the mean" whereby states that started this period with low rates would show greater increases than would states that started already high. In intuitive terms, while all states might increase, a state that was anomalously low for some reason in the early 1970s would be expected to increase more than a state that was already very high simply because it had, after all, more "room" to increase. In contrast, a state that was already very high might be expected to increase less as it was already imprisoning large numbers of people.

This statistical phenomenon is *not* what happened. As Table 3.3 shows, states with low rates in the early 1970s tended to increase less than states with high rates in the early 1970s.

From Table 3.3, one can see that those 17 states with, initially, low imprisonment rates tended to increase *relatively* little. Only two of them showed high rates of imprisonment in 2006–2010. On the other hand, 10 of the 17 states that had high imprisonment rates in the early 1970s had large increases in imprisonment over the next 35 years. In numerical terms, the average state imprisonment rate increase for all states was 327 adult prisoners per 100,000 total residents. However, for those states that had low imprisonment rates in the early 1970s, the increase was only 255. In contrast, those with high rates in the early 1970s increased an average of 399. In brief, the states with low imprisonment rates in the early 1970s did not seem to be as likely to implement policies to increase imprisonment as did those states with already (relatively) high imprisonment rates.

When considered within the context of state variability in levels of incarceration, all signs point to there being a second consideration. Specifically,

Table 3.3 Size of the Increase in Imprisonment as a Function of the Imprisonment Rate in the Early 1970s

		Increase in State Imprisonment Rate from the Early 1970s to Late 2000s (in *Additional* Prisoners per 100,000 Residents)			Total
		Low (100–248)	Medium (248.1–370)	High (370.1–749)	
Early rate (average state prison imprisonment rate, 1971–1975)	Low (24.5–58)	9 (53%)	6 (35%)	2 (12%)	17 (100%)
	Medium (58.1–89.5)	5 (31%)	6 (38%)	5 (31%)	16 (100%)
	High (89.6–182.8)	2 (12%)	5 (29%)	10 (59%)	17 (100%)

Chi squared = 10.17, degrees of freedom = 4, $p = .036$.

Source: Sourcebook of Criminal Justice Statistics (2004), http://www.albany.edu/sourcebook; US Bureau of Justice Statistics, http://www.fbi.gov/about-us/cjis/ucr/crime-in-the-u.s/2013/crime-in-the-u.s.-2013/tables/1tabledatadecoverviewpdf/table_1_crime_in_the_united_states_by_volume_and_rate_per_100000_inhabitants_1994-2013.xls; Statistics Canada, CANSIM, http://www5.statcan.gc.ca/cansim/a01?lang=eng.

states seem to vary in a systematic way in their contribution to this aspect of American exceptionalism. Once again though, we hasten to point out that this finding is hardly surprising. Indeed, one does not need to be an American to look at the 10 states with the highest "early" state imprisonment rates (1971–1975) and the 10 lowest "early" rates (Table 3.2)—or, for that matter, the 10 states with the highest and lowest increases in state imprisonment rates between 1971–1975 and 2006–2010 (Table 3.1)—and quickly conclude that these two groupings of states represent very different societies.[10]

Most obviously, the lowest rates are generally found in northern states, while the highest rates are generally located in southern or western states. However, the distinctions are not only geographic in nature. Rather, these two distinct groups of states remind us of similar alignments that emerged in earlier work (Doob and Webster 2006; Webster and Doob 2007, 2012) in which we reported that US states in the regions with the most "Canadian-like" values—based on a classification developed by Adams (2003) from polling data—had the lowest imprisonment rates (see final panel of Table 3.4).[11] Given that Canada—in contrast with the United States as a whole, as well as with every state (and the federal jurisdiction)—has had a relatively stable rate of adult imprisonment (roughly 100 ± 20 adult prisoners per 100,000 overall residents) since the late nineteenth century and most notably since the 1970s, this relationship provides some support for the notion that levels of incarceration are, in part, a function of underlying value systems. Specifically, Canadian culture appears to be rooted in more nonviolent, communitarian values that may not be as supportive of increasing punitive responses to criminal behavior.

To be clear, we are not suggesting that this relationship is, in any sense, causal in nature. Rather, our point is twofold. On the one hand, variation in levels of incarceration across states does not appear to be random. On the other hand, high imprisonment appears to be embedded in wider social values, particularly (but certainly not exclusively) as they relate to broad orientations toward offenders. Table 3.4 explores the relationship between imprisonment rates and other social policies.

The first panel of Table 3.4 examines capital punishment—the most extreme form of ostracism/social exclusion of the offender who is seen, one might argue, as expendable or beyond hope/redemption. As one can observe, those states that have retained capital punishment (at least until 2012) tended to have higher imprisonment rates both in the early 1970s and in the late 2000s. Further, notwithstanding the fact that they started with higher rates than the abolitionist states, the states that retained capital punishment increased their imprisonment rates to a greater extent than those states

Table 3.4 Social Policies and Imprisonment Rates (Some Examples)

Dimension	Type of State (Number of States in Parentheses)	Average State Imprisonment Rate, 1971–1975	Average State Imprisonment Rate, 2006–2010	Change (Late–Early)
Capital Punishment in 2012	No (17)	55	304	249
	Yes (33)	95*	462*	368*
Felon Disenfranchisement	No (39)	77	385	308
	Yes (11)	97	491*	395*
Imposition of cash assistance and food stamp bans on certain ex-felon drug offenders	None/almost none (14)	68	330	261
	Mixed (26)	81	420	339
	Full or almost full bans (10)	99	488*	390*
Minimum wage	Above federal rate (19)	73	371	298
	At federal rate (20)	78	379	301
	Below federal rate (11)	99	526*	426*
State is in region with Canadian-like attitudes	Yes (17)	66	344	279
	Somewhat (19)	63	359	295
	No (14)	123*	554*	430*

*$p < .05$.

without capital punishment. Within this context, it may not be coincidental that Canada executed its last offender in 1962 and formally abolished capital punishment in 1977. Even in 1987, when the Canadian House of Commons voted on a resolution to reinstate capital punishment, the resolution failed. Similarly, a 2001 unanimous Supreme Court of Canada decision (*United States v. Burns* 2001) refused to allow two people charged with murder in the United States to be extradited for trial until the state gave an undertaking that they would not face the death penalty if convicted.

The second panel considers felon disenfranchisement. The view that former offenders are no longer "real" members of the community can be made quite explicit by removing what might normally be seen as a right of citizenship: the right to vote. Eleven states in the late 2000s did not allow those who have been convicted of a felony to vote, even after their sentences have been completely served (Uggen and Shannon 2012). Although the 1971–1975 average imprisonment rates of the states that had felon disenfranchisement laws in the late 2000s did not differ from those of states that did not have these laws, there were significant differences in 2006–2010. Furthermore, those states with felon disenfranchisement laws in the twentieth century experienced the largest increases in imprisonment rates between the early 1970s and the late 2000s. Notably, Canadian ex-offenders never had special restrictions on their ability to vote. However, federal prisoners were not allowed to vote while in prison until 2002 when the Supreme Court (*Sauvé v. Canada* 2002) decided that prohibiting prisoners from voting was not a reasonable restriction on Canada's constitutional guarantee of the right to vote. Despite being incarcerated, prisoners were still considered full citizens.

Taking away the right to vote from former offenders is one way of reminding them that they have forfeited their (full) citizenship. Taking away welfare and access to affordable food would appear to be an attempt to communicate that offenders are not fully human, sentient creatures (or, at the very least, that they are not worthy of compassion and assistance). The third panel assesses US President Clinton's welfare "reform" bill—which became law in 1996—under which offenders convicted of certain drug offenses were made ineligible *for life* to receive federally supported welfare payments (cash assistance under the Temporary Assistance for Needy Families program and/or the federal Food Stamp program (Mauer and McCalmont 2014)). However, the law allowed states to opt out completely or in part (Mauer and McCalmont 2014) from these punitive provisions. Fourteen states opted out completely or almost completely from the federal policy of not providing the necessities of life to those who were ex-drug offenders and indigent, while another 26 had mixed policies. Clearly, the states that removed welfare benefits from offenders were more likely than those states that (partially or completely) opted out of this policy to have high imprisonment rates in the late 2000s and experience the greatest increases in their incarceration rates during the 35 years of imprisonment growth in the United States.

The only similar provision that we are aware of in Canada was in place briefly in the late 1990s in one province (Ontario). In this case, the provision imposed a lifetime prohibition on receiving welfare payments to anyone convicted of fraud involving welfare. It was instituted by a very socially conservative government that was in power in the province from 1995 to 2003. The regulation came into effect in 2000 and was quietly ended when the Conservatives lost to the Liberals in 2003. In terms of its view of the disadvantaged generally and of offenders in particular, this prohibition was seen as being a break from both previous Conservative governments in Ontario and with the then federal conservatives.

The fourth panel looks at minimum wage. Although it does not relate directly to offenders or imprisonment, it might be seen as an indication of a state's concern about some of its less fortunate citizens (i.e., those who are forced to work for minimum wage). Many states apparently tie their state minimum wage rate to the federal rate. However, those that explicitly set their minimum wage below that of the federal government had higher imprisonment rates in 2006–2010. Further, these states also increased their imprisonment rates to a greater extent between 1971–1975 and 2006–2010 than those states with rates on par with the federal government.

In brief, it appears that high imprisonment is related not only to other punitive criminal justice policies but also to broader social policies such as the minimum wage. This finding is not unexpected. In fact, it corroborates other criminological research. At a macro level, similar relationships between welfare and imprisonment rates were found by Beckett and Western (2001) in the context of the United States and by Downes (2012) who looked at the percent of gross domestic product spent on welfare across European countries and their respective penal policies. Even more broadly, Lappi-Seppälä (2011) surveyed 30 European and English-speaking nations and reported that countries with low rates of economic disparity, with generous social welfare policies, and in which the population is generally more prosperous tend to have low imprisonment rates.

At a more micro level, there is a substantial literature that demonstrates that punitive attitudes (e.g., the view that people who offend should be treated harshly) are related to other social values. For example, Johnson (2009) found that people who support the most punitive approaches to offending tend to be the most fearful and the most angry about crime. Pickett and Chiricos (2012) also noted that punitiveness toward juvenile offenders tends to be concentrated among those who blame blacks for violent crime. This finding is consistent with various other studies (Chiricos, Hogan, and Gertz 1997; Johnson 2009; Pickett and Chiricos 2012) which have suggested that, for some people, "black" and "crime" are associated. More importantly, those people who make the link in their minds between these two constructs tend to be more punitive. Particularly those who feel most threatened by African Americans hold the most punitive attitudes (Pickett, Tope, and Bellandi 2014).

While we prefer to leave the discussion of race and imprisonment in the United States to others who have more expertise than we do, it nonetheless appears notable to us that the proportion of African American residents in a state (in 2012–2013) correlates much more highly with state imprisonment rates in the early 1970s and the late 2000s and the size of the increase (+.65, +.62, +.52, respectively) than does the proportion of Hispanic or "other races" in a state (correlations range from +.07 to +.21). Specifically, if people in states with a high proportion of African Americans are more likely to blame African Americans for crime, it is not surprising that it is those states that have high imprisonment rates for both the period 1971–1975 and 2006–2010 and large increases in imprisonment over this 35-year period (Table 3.5).

As Table 3.5 shows, in those states currently with high proportions of African American residents, the imprisonment rate not only started off higher than in the states with lower proportions of African American residents but increased more and ended up higher.

Table 3.5 Racial Makeup of the State (2012–2013) and Imprisonment Rates

Proportion of 2012–2013 Population That Is African American	Average Overall Imprisonment Rate (Adult Prisoners per 100,000 Residents)			Number of States
	Early 1970s	Late 2000s	Increase (Late–Early)	
Low (<3.5%)	54.7	316.5	261.8	16 (100%)
Medium (3.6%–11.5%)	78.1	413.9	335.9	17 (100%)
High (11.6%–37.9%)	108.7**	489.3**	380.6*	17 (100%)

*$p < .05$, **$p < .01$.

In brief, we would argue that broader social values are not merely correlated with imprisonment rates. Rather, levels of incarceration also appear to reflect—as well as reaffirm—underlying core values regarding offenders (especially as regards the nature of citizenship and the rights, privileges, and protections inherent in it) and appropriate state responses to crime. Most notably, there would seem to have been a moral shift—beginning in the late 1970s—in the value system of Americans (particularly in those states with high imprisonment) which began privileging notions of exclusion, ostracism, ambivalence, and severity—to borrow from Tonry (2013)—vis-à-vis their offenders. Indeed, perceptions of the offender as an outlaw—an individual (physically, legally, and psychologically) excluded or separate from society and whose illegal actions reflect an underlying immoral character that is beyond hope or reintegration—appear to justify particularly harsh state responses of intolerance and ambivalence from law-abiding citizens.

Clearly, "state-specific exceptionalism"—to adapt an expression of Lappi-Seppälä (2011, 324)—is a component of American mass incarceration. The enormous variability across states in their past and present state imprisonment rates (as well as the magnitude of their increases across time) speaks to the need to consider more "localized" explanations. However, the systematic nature of the changes in state levels of incarceration over our 35-year period also suggests that more macro-level factors may be equally legitimate and valuable. Further, the association between high state imprisonment rates and other punitive punishment policies points to the role that the criminal justice system is expected to play vis-à-vis crime control as a potential starting point of investigation. By extension, its relationship to broader social values (particularly linked to citizenship) may provide an intriguing bridge between the two levels of analysis.

Within this framework, the juxtaposition of Canada's currents of thought and policy approach to crime and imprisonment with those of the United States (both before and after the mid-1970s) takes on new meaning. One of the fundamental differences between these two countries resides in their different conceptualizations of the role of the criminal justice system—and, in particular, imprisonment—in addressing crime. We propose that American exceptionalism in its growth in incarceration since the early 1970s can be tied—one might say, ironically—to its penal optimism. That is, the optimism in the ability of the criminal justice system—primarily (but not exclusively) through recourse to prison as an instrument of effective crime policy *writ large*—to control crime. Prior to the mid-1970s, this optimism took the form of a strong belief in the system's capacity to rehabilitate offenders. Subsequent to this era, optimism took the form of a strong faith in the system's ability to bring down crime rates through brute incapacitation and deterrence. In contrast, Canada has always shown deep skepticism that crime could be controlled by the criminal justice system.

American Optimism
Progressive Era

Through a Canadian lens, it would seem that the intellectual history of punishment philosophy of the United States is rooted largely in the belief/acceptance that crime rates and levels of incarceration are related. Specifically, criminal activity can be controlled—if not eliminated—through greater recourse to the criminal justice system, in general, and prison, in particular. We would argue that this utilitarian optimism has been a feature of American penal policy since the beginning of the Progressive era in the early part of the twentieth century. Certainly until the early 1970s, this faith in the criminal justice system as at least a partial solution to crime is most commonly associated with the indeterminate sentencing system which prioritized the rehabilitative ideal. Prison was the site par excellence to cure or reform "lost" or "sick" offenders who would be incarcerated until such time as they were deemed to be reformed.

Indeed, it was believed that crime could be controlled by careful and thoughtful individualized treatment. As Rothman (1980, 5) notes, the American Progressives "aimed to understand and to cure crime, delinquency, and insanity through a case-by-case approach." But to accomplish this task, they needed flexibility—not only in terms of being able to move offenders to the location best able to cure their offending but also (and especially) in terms of being able to hold the offender for a relatively indefinite period of time. The indeterminate sentence was ideal at providing these prerequisites. For Progressives, "the fixed sentence was retributive, crude, and unfair" (Rothman 1980, 68). It made no more sense, they argued, than it would to hospitalize all people with a given disease for a fixed length of time and to release them whether or not they were cured.

In fact, it was just a question of time. The Progressives did not have a single "theory" about crime. Whether criminal behavior was caused by environmental or biological factors did not matter. The goal was unquestionably attainable. One simply had to identify what had gone wrong and "fix" it. And, of course, the state was ideally suited to accomplish this goal: Progressives trusted the state to do good (Rothman 1980, 60). Not surprisingly, they were perfectly willing to give the state significant—if not almost unlimited—power to intervene in the lives of citizens. As Rothman notes,

> Progressives never paused to reckon with their own limitations. They never considered whether, given their knowledge, they should move more cautiously and circumspectly in implementing their policies. . . . Reformers, to a fault, were enthusiasts, so certain of their ability to achieve success that they were unwilling to qualify or to moderate their programs, to protect the objects of their wisdom from the coercion of their wisdom. (p. 8)

Similarly, for those who proved to be incorrigible, the psychiatrist-criminologist Bernard Glueck is quoted by Rothman (1980, 71–72) as suggesting that this group of offenders "had to be dealt with in only one way, and that is permanent segregation and isolation from society." Whether the offender was imprisoned for treatment or for the protection of the public, coercion and often striking violations of any notion of proportionality characterized this era. Having said this, the underlying notion that prisoners can (and should) be held in custody until such time (if ever) that they are safe to be released was justified morally by the genuinely benevolent intentions underlying the rehabilitative ideal. It is difficult to fault a criminal justice system that is rooted in such values as hope, compassion, redemption, and reintegration. In fact, this moral high ground may have also permitted—if not encouraged—the perpetuation of this sentencing system despite the evidence of its ineffectiveness which was mounting even early in the twentieth century.

This same optimism in the ability of the state to solve the problem of crime was also adopted on a broader scale. According to President Lyndon Johnson, criminal behavior could be eliminated from society through effective crime prevention. Rather than cure offenders after the fact, President Johnson proposed a frontal attack on the root causes of crime. Specifically, he declared war against poverty. Indeed, "the war on poverty . . . is a war against crime and a war against disorder" (Johnson 1964). The rallying call was to support "the war on poverty . . . the Civil Rights Act, and . . . major educational bills" as well as "educate your children . . . take care of the delinquent . . . [and] get out and work and vote and fight and give and do something about [poverty]" (Johnson 1964).

As part of this declaration of war, Johnson created the President's Commission on Law Enforcement and Administration of Justice in 1965, chaired by Nicholas deB. Katzenbach. Its 1967 report is a landmark in the intellectual history of criminal justice in the United States. Rhetorically, and because of its presidential imprimatur, it is a high-water mark for the belief that the criminal justice system could successfully "cure" criminals and that these efforts (combined with President Johnson's Great Society and initiatives in the inner cities) would transform society for the better (Ruth and Reitz 2003).

In itself, the commission's final report, *The Challenge of Crime in a Free Society*, makes for interesting reading in the early twenty-first century. Perhaps because the orientation of the commission as a whole was toward its mandate—"law enforcement and administration of justice"—and its task was to look at crime and the system set up to respond to it, the greatest part of the report appears to be what generally would be regarded as liberal proposals to improve various parts of the criminal justice system. Nonetheless, about 24 (pp. 55–78) of its 291 pages focused on what might be described as the social causes of crime—the factors *outside of* the criminal justice system responsible for crime. Recommendations were made with which few, today, would disagree. They included calls to "Re-examine and revise welfare regulations so that they contribute to keeping the family together; Improve housing and recreation facilities" (p. 66) or intensify "[e]fforts, both private and public . . . to prepare youth for employment . . . [and] Create new employment opportunities" (p. 77). In the five pages spent dealing with sentencing, the commission identified a number of problems and advocated for more realistic maximum sentences, the elimination of mandatory minimum sentences, and the creation of mechanisms to deal with disparity in sentencing. They recommended that the orientation of prisons be on rehabilitation and that there be more attention spent on controlled reintegration of prisoners.

The rallying call to improve the correctional system was rooted in the urgency of reform—both of the institution and, by extension, of the lives of the prisoners:

> The costs of action are substantial. But the costs of inaction are immensely greater. Inaction would mean, in effect, that the Nation would continue to avoid, rather than confront, one of its most critical social problems; that it would accept for the next generation a huge, if now immeasurable, burden of wasted and destructive lives. Decisive action, on the other hand, could make a difference that would really matter within our time. (p. 185)

The enormity of the endeavor was not lost on the commission, which noted, realistically, that "this report on crime and criminal justice in America must insist that there are no easy answers" (p. 291). However, they did not shy away from their task of "controlling crime and improving criminal justice" (p. 291). Rather, their more than 200 specific recommendations expressed their "deep conviction that if America is to meet the challenge of crime it must do more, far more, than it is doing now. . . . It must resist those who point to scapegoats, who use facile slogans about crime by habit or for selfish ends" (p. 291).

Indeed, optimism was at the root. As the report affirmed, "Controlling crime in America is an endeavour that will be slow and hard and costly. But America can control crime if it will" (p. 291). What was needed, the commissioners apparently believed, was only the will to implement reasonable policies. America had made itself a promise to put a man on the moon before the end of that decade. Surely it could solve the problem of crime on earth.

But time was running out. As one last gasp of extreme liberal optimism of its kind, Ramsey Clark (US attorney general 1967–1969) returned to the battle cry of the War on Poverty as the solution to the crime problem. Although he was not the only prominent American who continued to express optimism about the government's ability to solve the crime problem during the last years of the Progressive era, he is arguably one of the most eloquent. To win the war, he saw the need to make fundamental changes in American society:

> If the challenge of change seems staggering, our capacity to meet it is overwhelming. There was never a people that so clearly had the means to solve their problems as Americans today. Movers, builders, doers—we have proven the ability of man to dramatically change his destiny. Now we must show that we can control that destiny. A nation that doubled its productive capacity in four years during World War II can supply the needs of its people. (Clark 1970, 341)

While Clark's call for fundamental change in American society was heard, the response was certainly not in the form that Clark was eliciting. The 1970s brought with them a completely different approach to crime and punishment.[12] Gone would be the optimism of the Progressives in a rehabilitation model whereby crime could be resolved through either individualized treatment, the War on Poverty, or reform of criminal justice institutions (and social programs). But in its place would emerge a different form of optimism—what some might suggest as a defeatist's form of optimism—that is rooted in an incapacitation and deterrence model based fundamentally on high incarceration.

Post-Progressive Era

On January 3, 1973, New York's governor Nelson Rockefeller placed one large nail in the coffin of the prior liberal strategy to criminal justice when he introduced his new approach to the use of illegal drugs with the following words:

> It is time for brutal honesty regarding narcotics addiction. . . . In this state, we have allocated over $1 billion to every form of education against drugs and treatment of the addict through commitment, therapy, and rehabilitation. But let's be frank—let's tell it as it is: We have achieved very little permanent rehabilitation—and have found no cure. (quoted by Kohler-Hausmann 2010, 71)

Rockefeller joined with an ever-increasing chorus of Americans in highlighting the failure of rehabilitation. More importantly, he advocated a new role of incarceration which focused on its capacity—par excellence—to segregate offenders from society as a form of physical warehousing for the purpose of containing—if not eliminating—crime. As he explained,

> I, therefore, will ask for legislation making the penalty for all illegal trafficking in hard drugs a life sentence in prison. To close all avenues for escaping the full force of this sentence, the law would forbid acceptance of a plea to a lesser charge, forbid probation, forbid parole, and forbid suspension of sentence. (quoted by Kohler-Hausmann 2010, 71)

This solution was likely rooted in Rockefeller's belief in the relationship between Japan's very low drug addiction rate and the life sentences that were being handed down in this country for drug pushers (Kohler-Haussman 2010, 79). He saw the targeting of small-time drug pushers as a way of protecting society whereby "the young people who are sharing and selling relatively small amounts of heroin" are removed from the community "and isolated like carriers of a dangerous contagion" (Rockefeller, quoted by Kohler-Haussmann 2010, 81). The analogy was clear. Kohler-Haussmann quotes a doctor at the Community Medicine Department of the State University of New York as noting that,

> Governor Rockefeller's new proposals for dealing with the drug problem by attacking sellers are strongly supported by epidemiological theory. . . . Thus heroin addiction is similar in many ways to diseases such as malaria with its identifiable vector, the mosquito. Malaria has

> been controlled in many parts of the world, not by treating sick individuals and not by warning people against swamps, but by eliminating swamps and mosquitoes. Governor Rockefeller, having previously tried treatment . . . and education programs for heroin addiction and seen them fail to control its spread, has opted for a public health approach which . . . has some real chance of success. (Kohler-Haussmann 2010, 82)

This optimism in the ability of the state to control drug crime through sheer containment of offenders arguably opened the floodgates to more punitive responses to crime (i.e., more frequent and longer prison sentences). In fact, in the 10 years following the passing of the "Rockefeller drug laws" in 1973, 48 states added mandatory minimum penalties to their drug laws (Kohler-Haussmann 2010). Perhaps more notably, Blumstein and Beck (1999) suggest that the incarceration of drug offenders was not only a major contributor to the growth in imprisonment between the early 1970s and the late 2000s. Rather, it also contributed "in an important way to the extreme representation of African-Americans in prison" (p. 54). Both phenomena—Kohler-Haussmann (2010, 82) argues—reflect a new perception that cast drug pushers as not only "anti-citizens, but as non-humans whose fate was utterly irrelevant."

The second decisive nail in the coffin of the rehabilitative model came shortly after Rockefeller announced his new battle plan to solve (drug) crime. Martinson's highly influential 1974 paper in *The Public Interest* was seen by many Americans as sounding the death knell for rehabilitation programs generally. While others have noted (see, for instance, Ruth and Reitz 2003, 83–84) that Martinson was not alone in his rather pessimistic assessment of the ability of the criminal justice system to stave off crime through the rehabilitation of offenders, the motto "nothing works" became the rallying cry for a new approach to crime control. Indeed, if the Katzenbach Report is the best intellectual marker of transformative liberal optimism, the Martinson Report is arguably (one of) the most influential work(s) that punctured that balloon. Given America's heavy investment in rehabilitative policies until this point as *the* solution to crime, the acceptance of the apparently unequivocal failure of this approach produced nothing less than a seismic shock in the United States.

In a search for other responses to crime, it appeared that by the mid-1970s Lyndon Johnson's approach to solving the crime problem—by winning the war on poverty—had been forgotten. Nixon had come and gone as president. And since crime was no longer believed to be "curable" through rehabilitation, the other side of the Progressives' crime coin had to be invoked: society simply needed to be protected from offenders. As Rockefeller had already pointed out, the criminal justice system was well placed to accomplish this task. Brute incapacitation was America's new savior.

To bring about this change, the indeterminate sentence was certainly not the answer. By the early 1970s, many groups had lost confidence in this sentencing structure. However, "determinate" sentences had no logical connection with crime rates. But what they did do was give legislatures the power to do something about crime if one believed—as did Rockefeller and those who were influenced by him—that punishment would solve the crime problem. In a carefully argued account of the changes that took place in California, Campbell (2014) suggests that although the original determinate sentencing law in this state (passed in 1976) was not especially harsh, "[w]hat was radical was that [the law] restructured the institutional processes that would establish sentencing ranges in the legislature where they were immediately subject to interest group activism and, ultimately, populist pressures" (p. 394). Particularly after experiencing increases in serious crimes in the late 1970s (Webster, Doob, and Zimring 2006), these Californian bodies began increasing sentencing severity for these crimes (e.g., Proposition 8 in 1982), believing that they had the power to reduce crime through incapacitation and deterrence simply by voting for more punitive sanctions.

By 1981, California's Democratic governor clearly linked crime reduction to tough sentencing measures, such that, as Campbell (2014, 398) points out, "at one point, nearly *one-third* of all bills introduced were crime related." Furthermore, legislators appeared to be willing to pay for increased imprisonment. As one noted, "sometimes we just have to bite the unpalatable bullet on essential issues" (quoted by Campbell 2014, 398). Equally notable, the drop in crime in California in the early 1980s was attributed—by politicians and later by conservative economists (e.g., Kessler and Levitt 1999)—to the new harsh penalties. Campbell (2014) notes that "The [California] Governor essentially redefined overcrowded prisons as an indicator of success, not correctional failure or penal excess" (p. 401). In the early 1980s, the growth in imprisonment required "a solution that repudiated fiscal conservatism in the name of controlling crime. California Governor Deukmejian summed up the logic well [in 1983]: 'Let's never forget that getting more criminals off our streets and into prison is our goal" (Campbell and Schoenfeld 2013, 1399). Only 12 years earlier, Governor Ronald Reagan had celebrated the 32 percent drop in imprisonment that had occurred between 1968 and 1971, noting that,

> With the entire nation plagued by runaway crime rates and bulging prisons, our major California cities report a reduction in crimes of

> violence. Our rehabilitation policies and improved parole system are attracting nationwide attention. Fewer parolees are being returned to prison at any time in our history and our prison population is lower than at any time since 1963. (quoted in Gartner, Doob, and Zimring 2011, 311)

While the criminal justice system was still seen by the political elite as the principal institution responsible for controlling crime, the association of crime rates to imprisonment had been turned upside down. As society could no longer rely on the rehabilitation of offenders into law-abiding, peaceful citizens, society was left exposed—if not defenseless. In fact, Ruth and Reitz (2003, 84) further observe that "[t]he intellectual collapse of optimism in rehabilitation theory occurred at the exact historical moment when the high crime spike of the 1960s, and the scissors effect of rising crime and declining punishment had reached their most dramatic juncture." This coincidence arguably exacerbated a sense of vulnerability of Americans. Perhaps not surprisingly, the perception of offenders changed—now seen as "bad" or morally corrupt individuals who threatened the safety, security, and well-being of "good" people. Exclusion—in the sense of the offender's complete "excommunication" from society and from the rights and protections inherent in its citizens—became the obvious solution.

The leading intellectual justification for this renewed—albeit reoriented—faith in the ability of the criminal justice system to control crime came in 1975. There are two books by Americans with the title *Thinking about Crime*. The first, written by James Q. Wilson, appeared in 1975. Whether he influenced criminal justice policy during the last quarter of the twentieth century or his book merely reflected the dominant—or developing—view of the justice system during this period (or both) is not important for our purposes. His analysis, however, is of consequence.

Wilson rejected the criminologist's belief in the social causes of crime, popular during the early 1970s, not so much because he disagreed with what they said but because he felt that this approach did not lead to policies that would actually reduce crime. The problem, according to Wilson, is that the criminologist's assumption that "the causes of crime are determined by attitudes that in turn are socially derived, if not determined" requires long-term strategies which target these attitudes. As "behaviour is easier to change than attitudes," society's focus should be on "alter[ing] behaviour in the short run." To this end, "the policy analyst is led to assume that the criminal acts *as if* crime were the product of a free choice among competing opportunities and constraints. The radical individualism of Bentham and Beccaria may be scientifically questionable but prudently necessary" (Wilson 1975, 55–56, emphasis in the original).

Wilson substantiated his attack on the criminologist's crime-control approach not only by pointing out that rehabilitation programs in prison did very little to reduce the amount of crime but also by presenting data showing very high recidivism rates in the United States. Indeed, Ruth and Reitz (2003, 84) noted that "[e]ver since [the publication of Martinson's evaluation of correctional rehabilitation in 1974], conservatives like Wilson have stood on the empirical high ground when asserting, not necessarily a nihilistic view of reformist possibilities, but a pessimistic view that rehabilitation is difficult, uncertain, expensive, and can at best reach a minority of all offenders." As a more immediate solution to the crime problem, Wilson suggested that the correctional system's proper role might be seen as serving different functions: to isolate and to punish. In fact, Wilson was optimistic that crime could be effectively dealt with through the criminal justice system (and sentencing, in particular) with almost instantaneous results. As a justification for what was to become implicit American policy, he explained that,

> The purpose of isolating—or more accurately, closely supervising—offenders is obvious: whatever they may be doing when they are released, they cannot harm society while confined or closely supervised. The gains from merely incapacitating convicted criminals may be very large. . . . If much or most serious crime is committed by repeaters, separating repeaters from the rest of society, even for relatively brief periods of time, may produce major reductions in crime rates. (Wilson 1975, 172–73)

In brief, Wilson was unwilling to suggest that Americans should have to wait for "long-term" changes in society to reduce crime. In his view, one can either worry about why crime exists in our society or do something to get rid of it today, whatever its causes. That was the choice. To the extent, then, that this kind of optimistic thinking informed politicians and policy at the time, Wilson gave people reason to believe that America could, if it truly wanted to, get rid of its crime problem. Moreover, while this approach might "strike many enlightened readers [at the time] as cruel, even barbaric," Wilson explained that it was not. Rather, "[i]t is merely a recognition that society at a minimum must be able to protect itself from dangerous offenders . . . [as well as] a frank admission that society really does not know how to do much else" (Wilson 1975, 172).

The mechanisms were simple and effective. On the one hand, Wilson argued that harsh penalties would act as a deterrent. To substantiate this claim, he noted that "[t]he deterrent capacity of criminal penalties is supported by statistical data for large numbers of offences over long periods of time" (Wilson 1975, 177). On the other hand, he contended that more punitive sanctions whereby offenders would be imprisoned for longer periods would also reduce crime. This optimism was supported by a study of the (projected) consequences for New York's crime rate, had a harsher sentencing regime been implemented. Wilson cites the authors as concluding that,

> the rate of serious crime would be only *one-third* what it is today if every person convicted of a serious offence were imprisoned for three years. This reduction would be less if it turned out (as seems unlikely) that most serious crime is committed by first-time offenders, and it would be much greater if the proportion of crimes resulting in an arrest and conviction were increased (as also seems unlikely). The reduction, it should be noted, would be solely the result of incapacitation making no allowance for such additional reductions as might result from enhanced deterrence or rehabilitation. (Wilson 1975, 201, emphasis in the original)

It was "conservative optimism"—to use an expression of Ruth and Reitz (2003, 89)—at its best. In fact, these scholars describe this form of hubristic certainty as "rivalling anything in the annals of rehabilitative optimism."

Perhaps the pinnacle—or at least one of the more amusing high points—of American penal optimism in the incapacitation model proposed by Wilson occurred in 1987 with the release of a US National Institute of Justice report entitled *Making Confinement Decisions* (see Zimring and Hawkins 1988) Through an assessment of the costs and benefits of increasing levels of incarceration, this document demonstrated the dramatic economic savings which would result from the prevention of crime through the mechanisms of incapacitation and marginal general deterrence. Specifically, this report presented an economic model of the impact of long prison sentences on crime rates which estimated that, although imprisonment of one year would involve total social costs of roughly $25,000, the social costs averted by this incarceration (through incapacitation alone) would be approximately $430,000. As Zimring and Hawkins (1988, 426) underline, the cost–benefit ratio which would result from longer prison sentences—over 17 times as great—is clearly beyond anything yet seen in the annals of public administration.

In fact, this economic model could also be used to predict the number of crimes averted through incapacitation. Taking advantage of the natural experiment running in the United States since the early 1970s whereby imprisonment rates had been increasing continuously and substantially, Zimring and Hawkins (1988) applied the estimates generated in *Making Confinement Decisions* to these trends. Using 1977 as their starting point, they calculated—employing the methods used by the US National Institute of Justice report—the total volume of crime during this year to be approximately 40 million reported crimes. By extension, it was determined that the incarceration of roughly 230,000 additional offenders "should reduce crime to zero on incapacitation effects alone" (p. 429). Given that the US prison population increased, in fact, by a total of 237,000 between 1977 and mid-1986, these scholars demonstrated quite convincingly that the theoretical model of this report predicted that there would be *no* crime whatsoever in America by 1987.

It is hard to imagine a more optimistic prediction than this one. Perhaps more revealing than the model's faulty predictive value was the continued (if not expanded) optimism in the ability of the criminal justice system—through harsher sanctions—to solve the crime problem despite this type of debunking.[13] Indeed, while the model may have some glitches, the theory is unassailable. Zimring and Hawkins (1988, 436) provide a compelling explanation for this apparent incongruity:

> As long as levels of crime are high enough to generate substantial anxiety, those who view increased imprisonment as a solution will continue to demand more prisons and will do so in terms that do not change markedly at any level of incarceration. Indeed, the more attenuated the link between the malady and the proposed remedy, the more insatiable will be the demand for more of the remedial measure.

And so it went in America, with ever-increasing recourse to incarceration in the continuing faith that crime would eventually be solved through incapacitation and deterrence. One might be tempted to argue that this form of penal optimism—like its Progressive predecessor—appears to be relatively impervious (at least over an extended period of time) to criticism which calls into question its effectiveness.[14] In fact, such (unshakable) faith in utilitarian mechanisms seemingly provides few inherent limits to the recourse to prison as the sanction par excellence. Indeed, even ethical restraints appeared not to be an obstacle. We would suggest that Americans had little moral difficulty with the notion defended by Wilson—as well as those who followed his suggestions or at least acted in a manner that was consistent with them—of imprisoning people for crimes that they might commit in the future. Similarly, they saw no reason to be concerned about the use of those who have offended as a resource to deter others who might offend. Implicitly, the justification was clear: offenders had shown themselves beyond reasonable doubt to be inherently "bad" people. Their liberty—Wilson told us—needed to be sacrificed for the good of the law-abiding members of the community. Their crimes justified the forfeiture of their rights and protections as full citizens.

Canadian Pessimism

In sharp contrast with the United States, the intellectual history of punishment philosophy of Canada is rooted largely in the general acceptance that levels of incarceration have little to do with crime rates. Specifically, there has never been a strong or consistent belief that criminal activity can be controlled—if not eliminated—through greater recourse to the criminal justice system, in general, and prison, in particular. On the contrary, penal pessimism—that is, the lack of strong faith in the ability of sentencing and imprisonment to serve utilitarian goals such as rehabilitation, incapacitation, and deterrence—has been the predominant leitmotif traversing Canada's broad currents of intellectual thought and policy approach to crime since the nation's birth in 1867.

Adopting the European definition of determinacy (see van Zyl Smit and Corda, this volume), Canada's sentencing system is one of "determinate" sentences.[15] Judges hand down sentences with a fixed maximum term.[16] Further, while a parole board *may* release offenders handed down prison sentences of six months or more on parole under certain conditions, it is notable that this possibility is only available to a small proportion of sentenced prisoners. Specifically, although approximately 33 percent of those *found guilty* in Canada are sentenced to prison, only about 18 percent of those *sent to prison* get sentences in which they have a right to a parole hearing (sentences of six months or more). Even in terms of this small percentage of parole-eligible prisoners, most are not, in fact, paroled (Doob, Webster, and Manson 2014). As such, the vast majority of offenders with prison sentences are released virtually automatically at the two-thirds point in their sentences. In other words, though there is certainly some indeterminacy in Canada's imprisonment system, it is not a central feature.[17]

As Canada's governments have never, apparently, had much confidence that the problem of crime could be solved through the criminal justice system, the fundamental principle of sentencing has largely been that of proportionality. This guiding framework was formally enshrined in legislation in 1996 when sentencing provisions were brought into place which explicitly required judges to sentence proportionately. Canada's *Criminal Code*[18] states relatively clearly[19] that,

> **718.1.** A sentence must be proportionate to the gravity of the offence and the degree of responsibility of the offender.

However, proportionality is not a new addition to Canadian sentencing. In a recent Supreme Court of Canada decision, it was acknowledged that proportionality "was not borne out of the 1996 amendments to the Code but, instead, has long been a central tenet of the sentencing process" (*R. v. Ipeelee* 2012). More importantly for our current purposes, the court underlined that this principle,

> also has a constitutional dimension, in that s. 12 of the *Canadian Charter of Rights and Freedoms* forbids the imposition of a grossly disproportionate sentence that would outrage society's standards of decency. In a similar vein, proportionality in sentencing could aptly be described as a principle of fundamental justice under s. 7 of the *Charter*. (*R. v. Ipeelee*, para. 36)

Clearly, proportionality is also conceived as serving a limiting or restraining function. Indeed, this decision reminds us that "[w]hatever weight a judge may wish to accord to the various objectives and other principles listed in the *Code*, the resulting sentence must respect the fundamental principle of proportionality" (*R. v. Ipeelee*, para. 37).

Not surprisingly, sentencing in Canada is based on the offense (and criminal record of the offender). Though governments have tried, for more than a century, to "correct" offenders when they end up being incarcerated (or with community sanctions), no one ever seemed convinced that this response was going to solve the problem of crime. Further, harsher sanctions for the purposes of deterrence or incapacitation were generally viewed with significant skepticism. On the one hand, Canada never fully believed that they would reduce crime. On the other hand, the harsher sanctions generally associated with these goals ran counter to Canadian conceptions of those who commit crime as well as appropriate state responses to them. In particular, the perception of the offender as a continuing member of society (with all of the rights, privileges, and duties inherent in citizenship) who should ultimately be reintegrated into the community placed substantial restrictions on degrading or exclusionary measures.

Progressive Era Canadian-Style

Penal pessimism emerged as early as 1848—19 years before Canada became a country—in the valorization of certainty rather than severity of punishment when considering the overall deterrent effect of the criminal law. As the chief justice of Upper Canada noted,

> An occasional offence, however flagrant, occurring in a large and populous District can never be justly regarded as a reproach to its inhabitants; it only verifies the certain truth of the imperfection of human nature. . . . What the law alone can do for preventing the increase of crime must depend on the steadiness, activity and intelligence with which it is administered, for it is a true maxim that it's not so much the severity as the certainty of punishment, which deters offenders and makes the law respected. (quoted in Beattie 1977, 51–52)

A similar statement was made by Canada's first prime minister, John A. Macdonald (who, among other things, practiced criminal law before going into politics). Specifically, he affirmed that "Certainty of punishment, and more especially certainty that the sentence imposed by the judge will be carried out, is of more consequence in the prevention of crime than the severity of the sentence" (Gwyn 2011, 160). Harsher sanctions—it would seem—have never been seen in Canada as a solution to crime.

Equally notable, the same chief justice of Upper Canada (quoted in Beattie 1977, 51–52) recognized that despite any value that certainty of punishment may have in controlling crime, "it is on other means of prevention, more slow in their operation, but more secure and more general in their effects, that we must depend. I mean, of course, the religious and moral instruction of the people." It would also seem that the criminal justice system was never perceived to be well placed to stop crime.

That is not to say that rehabilitation of offenders was not a central concern of corrections. However, Canada's early experience with penitentiaries did not provide a great deal of comfort for those who would argue that these institutions would be effective tools to reduce crime. Canada's first penitentiary, opened in 1835, was subject to a major review and investigation starting in 1848, in large part because of reports of unduly harsh treatment of inmates. In 1914, the (federally established) Royal Commission on Penitentiaries reported on, among other things, the results of its inquiry into "the conduct and administration of penitentiaries, including such methods as may conduce to the permanent reformation of the convicts, and, without prejudice to the punishment which convicts should properly undergo and without undue burden upon the public funds, tend to mitigate as far as may be found possible sufferings entailed by their confinement upon those dependent upon them" (Canada 1914, 5). Since this last statement was in the terms of reference of the Commission of Inquiry, it is clear that concerns about the collateral harms of imprisonment were already part of the government's thinking. Importantly, the commission's recommendation that indeterminate sentences be instituted for those sent to penitentiary was not adopted.

Similar negative views of Canada's penitentiaries were expressed 24 years later by another royal commission. Prisons were seen as criminogenic institutions. With clear concern, the report of the Royal Commission to Investigate the Penal System of Canada states,

> The undeniable responsibility of the state to those held in its custody is to see that they are not returned to freedom worse than when they were taken in charge. This responsibility has been officially recognized in Canada for nearly a century but, although recognized, it has not been discharged. The evidence before the Commission convinced us that there are very few, if any, prisoners who enter our penitentiaries who do not leave them worse members of society than when they entered them. (Canada 1938, 100)

Equally notable, the report of the Joint Committee of the Senate and House of Commons on Capital Punishment, Corporal Punishment, and Lotteries (Canada 1956) raised skepticism about the effectiveness of the deterrent impact of these penalties. Although this committee chose not to recommend the abolition of capital punishment, Canada's last offender was executed only six years after the report was completed.[20] In contrast, the committee did recommend the abolition of corporal punishment—in this case the whipping of penitentiary prisoners—both as a sanction and as a disciplinary punishment in prison.[21] This decision reflected not only doubts about its (general and specific) deterrent effect but also the view of the commissioner of penitentiaries (and others) that it hurt the chances of reform and rehabilitation and "did positive harm by embittering some offenders" (p. 44) as well as the perception of others that it was "out of step with modern penal theory" (p. 45).[22]

Certainly one could argue that, during these historical periods, it would not have been surprising to see similar statements coming from comparable groups in the United States. What is important, however, is that the sentencing structure that existed in Canada at the time in which reports such as that of the Joint Committee of the Senate and House of Commons on Capital Punishment, Corporal Punishment, and Lotteries were being written was, in all important respects, the same as it is now. Obviously, the details of the *Criminal Code* have changed in important ways. And sentences have changed. But, for the most part, judges appointed by the provincial or federal governments hear cases prosecuted by prosecutors who are civil servants appointed under normal rules for government employees. The sentences that they hand down to those found guilty appear to be—and generally are—"fixed" sentences. The purposes of sentences are chosen from a menu, and, for the most part, sentences are supposed to be proportionate to the offense and the offender's responsibility for the offense.

By 1969, crime had already started to rise in Canada and the United States. What was to become a landmark document (Canadian Committee on Corrections 1969) was released. Statements reflecting its pessimism about the ability of sentencing to solve the crime problem—particularly through deterrence and incapacitation—are peppered throughout the report:

> Relatively little is known as to the effectiveness of the deterrent techniques and at present protection by way of segregation is, in general, both erratic and irrational in that it is imposed by way of fixed sentences at the end of which the offender, however dangerous, must be set free. Existing legislative provision for indefinite segregation does not appear to us either in theory or in practice to have protected Canadian society from the dangerous offender. (p. 189)

Given these views, it is not surprising that when the committee turned to sentencing, it advocated restraint in the use of prison. Specifically, "in all cases where there has been no finding of dangerousness, sentences of imprisonment should be imposed only where protection of society clearly requires such penalty" (p. 190). Indeed, the committee wished to emphasize,

> the danger of overestimating the necessity for and the value of long terms of imprisonment except in special circumstances. The serving of a long term imposes an enormous financial burden upon society and at the same time greatly reduces the chance of the inmate on release assuming a normal, tolerable, role in society and may indeed result in the creation of a social cripple. (p. 190)

This committee set the tone for formal government statements about sentencing for the next several decades when it concluded that "the Committee maintains that imprisonment or confinement should be used only as an ultimate resort when all other alternatives have failed" (p. 204).[23]

We are not suggesting that by 1969 Canada had rejected "deterrence" and "incapacitation"—or, for that matter, "rehabilitation"—as sentencing purposes. It should be recalled that these provisions are *still* within Canada's *Criminal Code*. Rather, persistent skepticism in the ability to achieve these utilitarian goals has limited their adoption as the principal or guiding purposes of sentencing. For instance, Canada has a long tradition in its commitment to the rehabilitation of offenders.[24] Even within the context of prison, extensive programming and treatment have long been a mainstay. Notwithstanding this focus, Canada has never sentenced offenders to prison *for* rehabilitation, nor has Canada ever adopted an indeterminate model—despite multiple calls for it—whereby the prison-release system depended on a correctional officer's finding of an inmate's successful rehabilitation. While the rehabilitation of an offender is obviously a desired goal in the Canadian *correctional* system, a rehabilitative model of sentencing—particularly within a custodial setting—has never been seen as an effective mechanism of crime control.

Further, Canada's prioritization of proportionality as the guiding principle when handing down sanctions clearly limits or restrains a rehabilitation—or, for that matter, a deterrence or incapacitation—model of sentencing. However, we would add that the perception of offenders within Canada also restricts the types (and degrees) of state response to them. In a statement made in the House of Commons in 1971 suggesting that the government would take seriously its responsibility to rehabilitate those who were housed in its penitentiaries, the (Liberal) minister responsible for these correctional institutions noted that,

> Even nowadays, too many Canadians object to looking at offenders as members of our society and seem to disregard the fact that the correctional process aims at making the offender a useful and law abiding citizen, and not any more an individual alienated from society and in conflict with it. . . . An inmate is always a citizen who, sooner or later, will return to a normal life in our society and as such, is basically entitled to have his human rights as a citizen respected by us to the largest possible extent. (Goyer 1971)

Crime policy put forward by the Liberals was—for the most part, until 2006—indistinguishable from Conservative crime policy. In his response that same day to the minister's statement, the Conservative justice critic stated that,

> He says . . . that the inmate is always a citizen who sooner or later will return to a normal life in our society and is basically entitled to retain his human dignity. . . . I want to congratulate the minister for realizing at last that crime is not just a sordid happening but rather a result of human behaviour brought about by our economic and social conditions which we have failed to change. (Woolliams 1971)

Indeed, offenders in Canada have traditionally been perceived as retaining all of the rights and protections of citizenship. Despite their crimes, they are believed to merit re-entry into the community once their sentence has been fulfilled. Inclusion—rather exclusion—has long been the central goal.

Post-Progressive Era Canadian-Style

In 1973, the same year that Rockefeller proposed an incapacitation approach to solve the "drug problem" in America, Canada responded to its own concerns surrounding increasing drug use in a quintessentially Canadian way. Specifically, it solicited a report of the Commission of Inquiry into the Non-Medical Use of Drugs (more typically referred to as the Le Dain commission, after its Chair, Gerald Le Dain). The commissioners were not optimistic about the use of criminal law, noting that "the effective application of the criminal law in the field of non-medical drug use is subject to many difficulties" (p. 53). After looking at the evidence that had been brought to them, the commission predictably concluded that "[t]he rate of success with law enforcement against both distribution and simply possession (or use) is relatively disappointing. . . . The actual risk of apprehension, which is the essential basis of deterrence, is not very great" (p. 54).

While the committee did not condone the nonmedical use of drugs, it was concerned about the enthusiasm that some had for "stamping out" the use of drugs with the criminal law. In particular, it pointed out that "[u]ndoubtedly, the prohibition against simple possession has some effect on use. The question is whether the effect it has justifies the various costs which it entails" (p. 56). It subsequently proceeded to list and discuss these costs: creating an illicit drug market, inhibiting people from seeking treatment, distorting or limiting the messages that could be given in drug education programs, the demand that a prohibition model puts on law enforcement resources, the stigma of a criminal conviction, and finally the effect of imprisonment. Particularly in terms of this latter cost, the committee was clear:

> The adverse effects of imprisonment, including the physical violence to which inmates are exposed, have been described many times. They are well known. Perhaps the chief objection to imprisonment is that it tends to achieve the opposite of the result which it purports to seek. Instead of curing offenders of criminal inclinations it tends to reinforce them. . . . These adverse effects of imprisonment are particularly reflected in the treatment of drug offenders. (pp. 58–59)

The interim report had recommended maintaining—albeit lowering—the then existing penalties for marijuana (e.g., removing the mandatory minimum penalty for importing marijuana). However, the most notable recommendation was as follows:

> The costs to a significant number of individuals, the majority of whom are young people, and to society generally, of a policy of prohibition of simple possession are not justified by the potential for harm of cannabis and the additional influence which such a policy is likely to have upon perception of harm, demand and availability. We, therefore, recommend the repeal of the prohibition against the simple possession of cannabis. (Commission of Inquiry into the Non-Medical Use of Drugs, 1973, 10)

By the time that the final report was transmitted to the government of Canada (in December 1973), Rockefeller's drug bill had become law.

In 1974, the Martinson Report was published. In contrast with the United States, Canada did not experience the same seismic impact when digesting it. On the one hand, Canadians would not have been shocked by the findings in the report. The deleterious effects of the recourse to criminal law, in general, and to imprisonment, in particular, had repeatedly been recognized by formal government and nongovernment documents throughout the century (Webster and Doob 2012). Indeed, several of the concerns expressed by the Commission of Inquiry into the Non-Medical Use of Drugs a year earlier merely reflect this long-standing recognition of the limited effectiveness of utilitarian sentencing objectives in reducing crime. On the other hand, Canada's early appreciation of the limits of rehabilitation as a sentencing goal stands in sharp contrast to the stubborn persistence of the rehabilitative ideal of the Progressives in the United States during this same era. By extension, the Canadian sentencing system was never built on a full rehabilitative model. As such, the policy elite in Canada saw no need to change their orientation toward imprisonment in the wake of the Martinson Report.

In 1976, just as American imprisonment rates were beginning to rise and an incapacitation/deterrence model was being established, Canada turned in the opposite direction. Restraint in the use of imprisonment became the rallying cry. While deterrence was always in the background, no one seemingly believed that increased use of long sentences would reduce crime. In its first report to Parliament entitled *Our Criminal Law*, the Law Reform Commission of Canada (1976, 24–25) recommended that,

> The cost of criminal law to the offender, the taxpayer and all of us must always be kept as low as possible. . . . The harsher the punishment, the slower we should be to use it. . . . The major punishment of last resort is prison. . . . As such it must be used sparingly. . . . Positive penalties like restitution and community service orders should be increasingly substituted for the negative and uncreative warehousing of prison.

A year later, a House of Commons subcommittee chaired by a future minister of justice looking into the penitentiary system in Canada emphasized that "Society has spent millions of dollars over the years to create and maintain the proven failure of prisons. Incarceration has failed in its two essential purposes—correcting the offender and providing permanent protection to society" (Canada 1977, 35). Noncustodial sanctions were recommended as a more effective means of responding to prohibited behavior. In arguably the clearest statement yet of Canadian pessimism in the ability of incarceration to solve the problem of crime, the report concluded that,

> It is apparent that the penitentiary system is not an effective means for dealing with a significant proportion of the criminality that exists in Canada. If we continue to conceive of imprisonment as a sort of universal solvent to the problems of crime in our society, we will do nothing more than repeat old prescriptions for failure. The penitentiary system should be relied on to do only what it is capable of doing and not be expected to accomplish the impossible task of solving complex social, behavioural and economic problems using steel bars, gas, walls, clubs, repression and isolation as its methods. . . . In addition to financial losses, the damage done to the individual's familial and social relationships, and to his employment future, must also be taken into account. The drastic changes incarceration introduces into his life may

> often make it impossible for him to ever re-establish himself in society. (Canada 1977, 35–36)

In 1982, the then deputy attorney general of Canada developed a document described as "set[ting] out the policy of the Government of Canada with respect to the purpose and principles of the criminal law" (Canada 1982, preface). This report constituted the first comprehensive and fundamental statement of the government regarding its view of the philosophical underpinnings of criminal law policy. Beyond containing the now typical statements of the need for restraint in the use of the criminal law, as well as the importance of proportionality and the use of the least restrictive alternative, this policy explicitly called attention to the fact that,

> It is not so much the law, nor even the agencies of the justice system that have the major impact on creating a just, peaceful and safe society—a society in which we want to live. Rather, justice and peace are functions of the attitudes and behaviour of individual citizens, and the understanding and support they give to the institutions that, after all, exist only for the sake of the collectivity of citizens we call society. (p. 69)

Notably, the document was released under the signature of the (Liberal) minister of justice and future prime minister Jean Chrétien but was reprinted and released by the Conservative government seven years later (though the preface with the Liberal justice minister's signature was carefully removed).

Two years later (1984), Mark MacGuigan, as minister of justice, released a report on sentencing. It noted with displeasure that,

> Statistics are often cited showing that Canada incarcerates, on a per capita basis, more people than almost any other western democracy except the United States. Indeed, Canada's incarceration rate looks relatively restrained only in comparison to that of the United States, and such other countries as the Soviet Union and the Union of South Africa. (Canada 1984, 8)

This report gave a very weak endorsement of deterrence through sentencing, suggesting that there was "ambiguous or inconclusive evidence" (p. 35) at present to support the conclusion that public safety could be achieved by way of deterrence. More important perhaps was the view that "[w]hile it is undeniable that the physical security of the public is protected from inmates while they are incarcerated, it does not follow that non-carceral or community-based sanctions cannot equally serve the purpose of protection of society" (p. 34).

In 1987, the Canadian Sentencing Commission (appointed in 1984 by the Liberals) reported and unambiguously suggested that by handing down proportionate sentences (by way of presumptive guidelines), Canada's imprisonment population could be contained. Once again, proportionality was to be the primary principle determining sentences. Judges would be forbidden to imprison people for the purposes of rehabilitation. Denunciation, deterrence, and the other traditional purposes of sentences could be given "consideration" but only within the limits defined by proportionality, and the restrictions on the use of imprisonment.

A parliamentary committee in 1988 (chaired and dominated by Conservatives) examined the recommendations from the Sentencing Commission. Although it did not endorse several of the Sentencing Commission's more radical recommendations (e.g., presumptive sentencing guidelines, the abolition of discretionary parole for ordinary sentences, and reduced legislated maximum sentences), the parliamentary committee did not challenge any of its major recommendations on the purpose and principles of sentencing. It recommended alternatives to imprisonment (through victim–offender reconciliation programs or alternative sentencing planning) and endorsed the recommendation that "a term of imprisonment should not be imposed, nor its duration determined, solely for the purposes of rehabilitation" (Canada 1988, 247). More generally, restrictions were to be placed on the use of imprisonment.[25]

Two years later (1990), a set of three integrated policy papers on sentencing and corrections released by the Conservative ministers of justice and the solicitor general referred favorably to the (Liberal) 1982 statement of principles on the criminal law and the (Liberal) statement about sentencing. Perhaps the most important recommendations were that sentences be proportionate and that a term of imprisonment should be imposed only under a restricted set of circumstances.[26] In acknowledging the past, the justice minister noted that,

> Although Canada does not imprison as large a portion of its population as does the United States, we nevertheless imprison more people than most other western democracies. Imprisonment is expensive and it accomplishes very little, apart from separating offenders from society for a period of time. [Recent commissions] have urged that imprisonment should be used as a last resort and reserved only for those convicted of the most serious offences. (Canada 1990, 17)

This set of reports—constituting the last major integrative report on Canada's (adult) justice system—not only noted the importance of an integrated examination of the sentencing and corrections systems but also attempted to be honest about what was possible. At the same time, a more pessimistic view of the ability of the punishment system to reduce crime would be hard to find. As a general or overall summary of Canada's position, it was emphasized that,

> We do not at present have the means or the knowledge to drastically reduce crime or rehabilitate all offenders. We can, however, seek to reduce or mitigate the social costs of crime, punish offenders, and create programs, opportunities, and incentives for treatment for those we think might respond so that they are not an ongoing burden to society. (Canada 1990, 8)

This acknowledgment of the limited power of the criminal justice system in solving the problem of crime was reiterated within the context of the perceived ability of imprisonment, in particular to reduce criminal activity. With no ambiguity, it was affirmed that "[i]mprisonment is generally viewed as of limited use in controlling crime through deterrence, incapacitation and reformation, while being extremely costly in human and dollar terms" (Canada 1990, 10). By extension, the overuse of prison was—yet again—condemned. In fact, we were reminded that "[v]irtually all official reports on sentencing and corrections have declared that we rely too heavily in Canada on imprisonment as a criminal sanction" (p. 10). In particular, incarceration continues to be seen as criminogenic in that it "may decrease rather than increase the chances of reforming individual offenders" (p. 8). Within this context, the report underlines that "[w]e need to develop effective alternative methods for punishing and reforming offenders, and where imprisonment is used, we must better prepare offenders for safe reintegration into the community (p. 8). As an overall approach to sentencing, the report is equally clear: "Criminal penalties should be applied in proportion to the degree of responsibility of the offender. . . . On the other hand, the principle requires that punishment be limited by the requirement not to sacrifice the individual accused to the common good" (p. 12).

Importantly, consensus between Canada's two major (federal) political parties was clear throughout this period. Sentencing and imprisonment were important. But if one was interested in reducing crime, one had to look elsewhere. When a Conservative-dominated House of Commons committee looking into crime prevention released its report in 1993, there was as close to a complete rejection of imprisonment as a crime-prevention technique as one could imagine. The committee noted, with smug satisfaction, that,

> If locking up those who violate the law contributed to safer societies, then the United States should be the safest country in the world. In fact the United States affords a glaring example of the limited impact that criminal justice responses may have on crime. . . . Evidence from the U.S. is that costly repressive measures alone fail to deter crime. (Canada 1993, 2)

In 1993 when this report was released, Canada's imprisonment rate had grown to 114 (per 100,000 residents—almost exactly what it was in 2012–2013). The American rate (including jails) in 1993 was 528. In 2012, it had fallen (from a high of 756) to 711.

When the Liberal government did finally put detailed sentencing legislation into the *Criminal Code* in 1996, the main sentencing provisions received almost no public attention. The forces of Canadian pessimism about the ability of the criminal justice system to solve the problem of crime had been well established by that point. Indeed, there was no controversy then[27]—and little since then—on any part of the restrictions on imprisonment other than the last nine words of 718.2(e), which were codified for the first time but had been repeatedly affirmed in the past.[28] We doubt that we need to remind readers of the moves during this same period in the United States toward various forms of "three strikes" legislation as well as other approaches (e.g., the federal guidelines) which were designed to increase imprisonment.

Canadians during the 1990s steadfastly maintained their pessimism that crime could be solved through criminal law. This belief was well enough established that Allan Rock, then minister of justice, affirmed in a public and subsequently published speech that just as "war is too important to be left to the generals. . . . Crime prevention is too important to be left to the lawyers, or the justice ministers, or even the judges. . . . In the final analysis, crime prevention has as much to do with the [minister of] . . . Finance, [the minister of] . . . Industry, and [the minister of] . . . Human Resources Development, as it does with the [minister of] Justice" (Rock 1996, 191–92).[29] Policies related to sentencing and imprisonment had, at that point in Canada's history, been successfully separated from crime prevention.

Equally notably, this pessimism in the ability of the criminal justice system (and imprisonment, in particular) to solve crime was widely held. Beyond the federal level of government, the provinces/territories also showed considerable concern that incarceration rates were creeping up (the 1994 rate of about

116 was an all-time high). In January 1995, the Federal/Provincial/Territorial Ministers Responsible for Justice met to discuss this matter. In response, they asked their deputies and the heads of corrections "to identify options to deal effectively with growing prison populations" (Federal/Provincial/Territorial Ministers Responsible for Justice 1996, i).

In May 1996, they were presented with a policy paper "that would assist in managing and countering the pressures of prison population growth" (Federal/Provincial/Territorial Ministers Responsible for Justice 1997, i). Their statement of principles—apparently endorsed by all ministers at that 1996 meeting—was clear. In particular, it not only stipulated that "[t]he best long-term protection of the public results from offenders being returned to a law abiding life style in the community" but also that "[f]air, equitable and just punishment that is proportional to the harm done and similar to like sentences for like offences is a legitimate objective of sentencing." Finally, it was (re)affirmed that "Incarceration should in most cases be used only where public safety so requires and we should seek alternatives to incarceration if safe and more effective community sanctions are available" (Federal/Provincial/Territorial Ministers Responsible for Justice 1997, annex C, 2). Not surprisingly, the ministers' concern about countering rising imprisonment rates received, as far as we can tell, almost no publicity. Furthermore, we were unable to find—in the public documents—any concern that by "containing" prison populations, crime would be affected.

Discussion/Conclusions

As a natural experiment, our exercise in identifying a possible explanation for the dramatically different trends in imprisonment between Canada and the United States since the mid-1970s is obviously flawed. While Canada is almost certainly the most comparable nation to the United States, there is clearly a multitude of other plausible factors that distinguish the two countries and which might shed light on American mass imprisonment. Moreover, the interaction between broad national explanations and more localized state-level structures and practices renders any macro-level exploration of US criminal justice and sentencing systems considerably more complex.

Within this context, our study should be seen as exploratory in nature. We are not experts on American criminal justice policy or its intellectual history. Our contribution to the discussion is simply to bring to the table a different point of view. Indeed, this chapter reflects our attempt to use the Canadian experience (both before and after the early 1970s) as a lens through which to understand American exceptionalism in its growth in incarceration. Further, the associations we suggest are not meant to be seen as causally determined. Rather, they are intended as "food for thought" for those who have much greater expertise in the subject matter of all that is distinctly American.

With these caveats in mind, one of the most striking contrasts between the United States and Canada seemingly resides in the degree of faith that each nation has placed in the ability of the criminal justice system, generally, and prison, in particular, to reduce—if not eliminate—the problem of crime in society. On one extreme, Canada may be described as portraying considerable penal pessimism. Successive Canadian politicians—starting with Canada's first prime minister over a century ago—as well as numerous government-appointed bodies have had little confidence that the criminal justice system is well placed to control crime, through either rehabilitation, incapacitation, or deterrence. Crime has traditionally been seen as being a product of larger forces in society, and to the extent that it can be affected by government policies, it is government social policies that are seen as important.

Within this context, prisons have largely been seen as a "bad thing." Given their recognized criminogenic features, they have generally been perceived as a cause of crime rather than a solution to it. As such, prisons are viewed simply as a necessary evil whose use should be minimized as much as possible and whose effectiveness in reducing crime is viewed with deep skepticism. Simultaneous to this conceptualization of prison, Canadian governments, other than the Conservative Party in power between 2006 and 2015, have traditionally maintained that offenders—despite their crimes—remain full citizens. As such, they continue to be afforded the rights and privileges inherent in citizenship. Compassion and support—rather than degradation and ostracism—are the guiding responses. Reintegration is the principal goal. Precisely because offenders almost always return to society under Canada's fixed sentencing system, the exclusion of prisoners from Canadian society has never been seen as an effective solution to crime.

On the other extreme, the United States may be described as embracing considerable penal optimism. Dating back to the early 1900s, Americans have shown strong faith in the ability of the criminal justice system—and imprisonment in particular—to significantly reduce, if not eradicate, crime. During the Progressive era, it was believed that the problem of crime could be solved through rehabilitation. By professional examination, treatment, and assessment, the offender could be "cured" of his or her criminal tendencies and return to lead a law-abiding life in the community. Prisons were seen as appropriate locations in which to carry out the rehabilitative techniques, and the indeterminate sentencing system provided the flexibility to administer treatment until such time as the offender has been reformed. Although benevolence was clearly at the root of this sentencing model, the offender was perceived as "sick" and in need of assistance, justifying the violation of many of his or her rights as a citizen in the form of coercive treatment and disproportionate sanctions.

Since the early 1970s, penal optimism continued to characterize the American approach to crime. However, the focus shifted from a strong belief in rehabilitation to an equally powerful faith in incapacitation and deterrence as effective crime-control strategies. It was believed that brute incapacitation would solve the problem of crime not only by removing offenders from society for lengthy periods of time but also by deterring (potential as well as actual) offenders from committing criminal acts in fear of such harsh penalties. Prison continued to be seen as the location par excellence to accomplish this task as it ensured the (long, if not permanent) segregation of offenders from law-abiding citizens. Indeed, Americans' response to offenders hardened whereby ambivalence replaced benevolence and severity substituted for compassion. The offender came to be seen as morally corrupt and either beyond hope or undeserving of assistance. He or she was stripped of the status of full citizen, becoming—in a certain sense—an outlaw. Indeed, exclusion from society (and its protections) became the rule.

From the view of outsiders, one of the defining characteristics of the American model of either the rehabilitation or the incapacitation/deterrence persuasion is the apparent lack of limits that such optimism places on the state's response to crime. Given the spectacular end result—that is, solving the problem of crime in society—as well as the genuine belief that such a laudable goal was attainable, considerable liberties could (justly) be taken on the part of the state in its response to offenders. Perhaps the only remaining restraining factor was that of simple moral palatability. But even in this case, it appears that Americans were able to take the moral high ground—either through the conviction in the sheer benevolence at the root of rehabilitation or the necessity of protecting "good" citizens from dangerous criminals through segregation.

We might suggest that it is not coincidental that one notes—in the first part of this chapter—evidence suggesting that a moral shift occurred in the United States. Beginning in the late 1970s, the core values of Americans appear to have changed whereby notions of exclusion, ostracism, ambivalence, and severity began to be privileged as appropriate state responses to offenders. Equally notable, this new value system was especially evident in states with high imprisonment rates.

This association is not particularly surprising. One does not need to be a philosopher to realize that general deterrence (or, more specifically, deterrence through increased use of imprisonment) and incapacitation—as purposes of sentencing or as justifications for imprisonment—require different moral rationalizations or value systems from prison sentences designed to improve the life chances of an offender. In the case of imprisonment for deterrence purposes, offenders are being used, by the state, as a resource to reduce the burden of crime on society generally. No one needs to justify the sentence in terms of what it does for or to the offender; offenders are simply being sacrificed for the rest of the community. It is acceptable to use them as resources because they are "bad people," the evidence being that they have done bad things (i.e., they were convicted of crime).

In the case of incapacitation—a justification once described informally by Frank Zimring as "having the advantage of having no moving parts"—it is even more simple. Offenders are not being punished for what they have done or to "fix" them. They have, in effect, lost their rights of full membership in society because they have offended and are, in effect, banished. In that sense, they no longer are full citizens in terms of protective obligations on the part of the state. And there is no need to worry about whether it is fair to imprison them or consider principles like proportionality in sentencing (see Zimring and Hawkins 1995). The new three-strikes sanctions say it all. The only difference is that the offender (versus the baseball player) is "out" of a much bigger game.

As Tonry (2004) would say, "sensibilities" changed. Each expression of optimism in the United States seemingly has a corresponding set of core values which gives meaning and justification to the state's principal strategies to resolve the crime problem. The difference between the Canadian and the American approaches may reside—at least to some extent—in the combination of these two elements. Canadian core values of communitarianism, inclusiveness, acceptance, and nonviolence (Adams 2003) have arguably reflected as well as reaffirmed our long-standing restraint in the use of imprisonment and our commitment to inclusionary philosophies regarding the nature of citizenship and the limits of state intervention. Reminiscent of Whitman's (2003) argument, Canada may simply be closer—in punishment strategies—to European countries like France and Germany with their "deep commitment to the proposition that criminal offenders must not be degraded—that they must be accorded *respect* and *dignity*" (p. 8, emphasis in original) than to the United States.

Obviously, it is speculative on our part to suggest that the different Canadian values and approaches to sentencing and imprisonment that have existed for more than a century are *responsible* for the fact that in 2011 the overall US rate of imprisonment was more than six times that of Canada. However, it is intriguing to consider the possibility. While penal optimism and exclusion, on the one hand, and pessimism and inclusion, on the other hand, may seem—at least at first glance—to be odd bedfellows, they suggest that the differences between Canada and the United States in criminal justice policies may go far beyond the relative size of their prison populations.

NOTES

1. Jail figures for the US states are not apparently available reliably until approximately 1980. However, between 1980 and 2010 the *prison* population (state and federal) constituted an average of about 66 percent of the total (prison plus jail) population (range 63 percent–70 percent). Hence, it is plausible, we assume, to estimate that the "total" US imprisonment rate for the pre-1980 period was about 1.52 times the prison rate.
2. The International Centre for Prison Studies on October 8, 2014, listed only Seychelles as having a higher imprisonment rate than the United States (868 vs. 707). http://www.prisonstudies.org/highest-to-lowest/prison_population_rate?field_region_taxonomy_tid=All. Notably though, Seychelles is a country of 155 islands (off the coast of Africa) with a total population of roughly 90,000. While this nation had a total of 786 prisoners in 2014, the United States had an estimated prison and jail population of 2,228,424 in 2012, the most recent year available to the compilers of that list at the time it was downloaded (November 2014).
3. For Canada, total crime includes all offenses considered to be criminal. For the United States, it is only those offenses that are considered to be "index crimes." Most notably, the Canadian measure involves large numbers of minor crimes that are not counted as "index crimes" in the United States (e.g., administration of justice offenses, minor thefts, and minor assaults). As such, any attempt at comparing absolute values for the two countries is meaningless.
4. Note that this figure (and the previous figure) use different scales for the United States and Canada. Homicide rates in the United States are typically about three times the Canadian rate.
5. This pre-1975 stability was, of course, the basis of Blumstein and colleagues' (Blumstein and Cohen, 1973; Blumstein, Cohen, and Nagin, 1977) idea that "stability" in imprisonment needed to be explained (when it was known that crime rates had varied over time).
6. It is important to note that provincial/territorial imprisonment rates only reflect custodial sentences of less than two years. In Canada, criminal law is a federal responsibility, while the provinces/territories are responsible for the administration of justice. Responsibility for corrections is split whereby the federal government is responsible for those sentenced to two years or more and the provinces/territories are responsible for those sentenced to less than two years in prison (and remand prisoners) as well as most community sanctions. This "division of

criminal labor" finds no parallel with the American federal system in that each US state (as well as the federal government) has its own criminal law and its own prison system, which operate largely independently of each other.

7. We include the "ratio" of the two rates for the sake of completeness. However, we do *not* believe that it is a very useful figure, in large part because it is driven so much by the starting rate in the early 1970s. This limitation is best illustrated by looking at the data for North Dakota—the state with the lowest 1971–1975 rate. Its "absolute change" in imprisonment is also fairly small (column 4). In fact, it has the tenth smallest increase in imprisonment in this 35-year period. But the *ratio* of the late 2000s rate over the early 1970s rate is the second largest in the United States. This description does not seem to portray what happened in North Dakota when one considers that its rate was the fifth smallest for the period 2006–2010 (222.8). The full set of data for all 50 states can be found in Appendix 3A.1.
8. We calculated the average of each state's rates of imprisonment for each period of interest. Specifically, we compared the average state increases in the period 1971–1975 (before the "great increase") with those in the period 2006–2010 (at the peak of the "great increase").
9. See note 1. Direct comparisons of these state prison rates with Canada should not be made. The "Canada" rate includes all adult prisoners (those serving sentences in federal and provincial institutions as well as those in presentence custody). Canadian federal imprisonment rates broken down by the province in which the offender was sentenced are not available. Hence, a true "provincial" rate cannot be calculated (just as a true overall rate cannot be calculated for US states because of federal imprisonment rates). Canadian rates also vary by province. Using the federal Canadian penitentiary average for the single year 1971 (34.1 prisoners per 100,000 residents), some Canadian provincial rates for 1971 are comparable to these low US state rates (for 1971–1975) including Newfoundland (60), Nova Scotia (64), and Quebec (55). However, these estimates are problematic as the use of federal penitentiaries appears to vary dramatically across provinces (Sprott and Doob, 1998). Including the federal US imprisonment rate and our estimate of the jail population (see note 1) results in comparable estimates for North Dakota (53.4), New Hampshire (62.2), and Massachusetts (72.4). Using these estimates, in 1971 Vermont's total imprisonment rate would have been about that of Canada as a whole (82.7 in 1971).
10. For a different interpretation, see Zimring (2010). Using a different measure and analytic framework, this scholar concludes that "there are . . . no indications . . . of anything other than fifty different outcomes of a uniform process" (p. 1237). Our analysis in Table 3.3 (as well as in Tables 3.4 and 3.5) would suggest that there are, in fact, clusters of states with different growth rates, as well as related characteristics.
11. Adams' classification of US states in terms of how "Canadian-like" they are was based on a two-dimensional value structure on which individuals (or groups)

can be placed. Canadians were more likely than Americans to hold such attitudes as a willingness to accept nontraditional views of the family or to consider oneself a "citizen of the world" before a "citizen of one's community and country." Canadians were also found to be more likely than Americans to indicate that they are comfortable in adapting to the uncertainties of modern life and were not threatened by the changes and complexities of society today. In contrast, individuals who fell into the quadrant most unlike the preponderance of Canadians were more likely to endorse such views as that "there are rules in society and everyone should follow them" or that "immigrants who have made their home in [this country] should set aside their cultural backgrounds and blend in." It was also found that those least like Canadians were more likely to endorse "confidence that, in the end, people get what they deserve as a result of the decisions they make, both positively and negatively."

12. As Rothman (1980, 12) notes, the perspective of the Progressives "was substantially different from that of the 1970's, so different that I am comfortable in taking the period of 1900–1965 as one, labelling it 'Progressive' and conceiving of the post-1965 period, our own, as post-Progressive—indeed anti-Progressive." While we would agree that the Progressive era is substantively different from its successor, we might quibble with the truncated upper demarcation of this former period. More importantly, we would argue that the categorization of the latter era as "anti-Progressive" misses the continuity between these two broad currents of intellectual thought and policy approach to crime and the role of the criminal justice system.
13. For skeptical readers needing quantitative evidence, Zimring and Hawkins (1988, 230, fig. 1) provided data from the US Department of Justice showing that crime had not, in fact, hit zero by early 1987.
14. One need only think of the extensive research on the marginal deterrent effect of harsher sanctions on crime rates. Despite over 40 years of studies, there continues to be no consistent and plausible evidence to support this form of general deterrence (Doob and Webster 2003, Webster and Doob 2012). The literature on the ineffectiveness of specific deterrence is even stronger (Nagin, Cullen, and Jonson, 2009).
15. Though true now, this was not strictly true in the twentieth century. In some provinces (Ontario, for example), indeterminate sentences (with a maximum of two-year duration) could be handed down. This practice was ended in the 1970s without much fanfare (since, among other things, it involved neither long sentences nor sentences for the most serious crimes).
16. An exception to this generalization is life sentences (and those given indeterminate sentences as "dangerous offenders").
17. An average, in recent years, of roughly 170 offenders per year are admitted on a life sentence (almost all for murder) or an indeterminate sentence (as dangerous

offenders). About 89,000 offenders per year are admitted to Canada's prisons with "fixed" sentences.

18. As noted earlier, criminal law is a federal responsibility. Hence, there is only one criminal law for all of Canada. We have argued previously that the distancing and insulating of the federal government (with its powers to modify the criminal law) from both the administration of most criminal law and individual crimes may act as a protective factor against increased imprisonment (Webster and Doob, 2007, 337–41).
19. Nonetheless, this explicit requirement is muddied somewhat by the fact that all of the usual sentencing purposes, plus a few, are listed as being relevant to the handing down of sanctions. Specifically, Section 718 of the Canadian *Criminal Code* reads,

    The fundamental purpose of sentencing is to protect society and to contribute, along with crime prevention initiatives, to respect for the law and the maintenance of a just, peaceful and safe society by imposing just sanctions that have one or more of the following objectives:

    (*a*) to denounce unlawful conduct;
    (*b*) to deter the offender and other persons from committing offences;
    (*c*) to separate offenders from society, where necessary;
    (*d*) to assist in rehabilitating offenders;
    (*e*) to provide reparations for harm done to victims or to the community; and
    (*f*) to promote a sense of responsibility in offenders, and acknowledgment of the harm done to victims and to the community.

20. However, it is notable that legislation abolishing the practice did not come into effect until 1977.
21. In fact, whipping was imposed by the courts only about 30 times a year or 1.5 percent of the time when it was available between 1950 and 1955—a rather large decline from the period 1930–1934 when it was administered about 116 times a year, representing 9.7 percent of the convictions for which it was available (Canada 1956, 43).
22. In case their recommendation was not accepted by Parliament, they proposed that "uniform specifications for the construction and use of the strap should be made and enforced" (Canada 1956, 47). Whipping of prisoners (in the privacy of one's own penitentiary, of course) was not immediately abolished. Though it was available as part of a sentence and as an institutional disciplinary punishment, it appears that it was mostly used at the end for disciplinary purposes. Correctional Service Canada reports that "[b]etween 1957–67, there were 333 instances of corporal punishment inflicted on offenders for breaching institutional rules, whereas in 1968, only one occurrence is recorded. It appears that October 15, 1968 was the last recorded application of its use as a disciplinary measure in federal penitentiaries. Instances of offenders being sentenced to

corporal punishment by the courts likewise declined: in 1954, for example, corporal punishment was ordered only 14 times." It was officially abolished in 1972 (http://www.csc-scc.gc.ca/text/pblct/rht-drt/05-eng.shtml; downloaded April 3, 2013).

23. More specifically, the committee explicitly recommended that

    Legislation be framed to encompass the principles contained in section 7 of the [1962 draft American Law Institute] Model Penal Code . . . which . . . provides that: "(1) The Court shall deal with a person who has been convicted of a crime *without imposing sentence of imprisonment unless*, having regard to the nature and circumstance of the crime and history, character and condition of the defendant, it is of the opinion that his imprisonment is necessary for the protection of the public because

    (*a*) there is undue risk that during the period of a suspended sentence or probation the defendant will commit another crime; or

    (*b*) the defendant is in need of correctional treatment that can be provided most effectively by his commitment to an institution; or

    (*c*) a lesser sentence will depreciate the seriousness of the defendant's crime." (Canada 1977, 191)

24. For illustrations, see Gaes et al. (1999). In addition, as noted in a government statement of policies and goals for corrections, "The fundamental goal of the correctional system is to contribute to the maintenance of a just, peaceful, and safe society through the safe custody and control of offenders and their reintegration into the community as law-abiding citizens" (Canada 1990).

25. Interestingly, there were some recommendations for harshness as well. In what looks like a compromise for their statement that "the committee does not generally support the introduction of further mandatory minimum sentences" (Canada 1988, 70), mandatory minimum sentences of 10 years were recommended for "all offenders convicted of a second or subsequent offence for sexual assault involving violence." As the committee itself noted, this mandatory minimum sentence "would apply to a narrowly defined class of offenders in narrowly defined circumstances for a very grave offence" (p. 71). That year, there were 791,355 criminal incidents "cleared by charge" and presumably (mostly) ending up in court. Our estimate is that 762 of these charges might have been sexual assaults involving violence, and probably no more than 5–20 percent of these accused (or 38–152) would have been people who were there for a second similar offence. It seems likely that even if their recommendation had been implemented, it would not have created a significant increase in imprisonment since these offenders would have received very long sentences anyway.

26. Specifically, "a term of imprisonment should be imposed only (1) to protect the public from crimes of violence, (2) where any other sanction would not sufficiently reflect the gravity of the offense or the repetitive nature of the criminal conduct of an offender or adequately protect the public or the integrity of the administration of justice, or (3) to penalize an offender for willful noncompliance

with the terms of any other sentence that has been imposed on the offender where no other sanction appears adequate to compel compliance." (Canada 1990, 16).

27. This is not strictly accurate. The bill originally had an exhaustive list of factors that could be the basis of "hate motivated" crime (which was listed as an aggravating factor in sentencing). These included "sexual orientation" among other listed factors. This elicited enormous outcry from conservative politicians, focusing much of their attention related to the bill on those two words. Eventually, the list was made nonexhaustive, which had little impact on the shrill voices of the opposition. But "sentencing" per se was mostly ignored. Also receiving essentially no public scrutiny were provisions allowing for "alternative measures" rather than prosecution of cases (s. 717).
28. Section 718.2 reads, "A court that imposes a sentence shall also take into consideration the following principles . . . (*e*) all available sanctions other than imprisonment that are reasonable in the circumstances and consistent with the harm done to victims or to the community should be considered for all offenders, with particular attention to the circumstances of Aboriginal offenders."
29. It should not be assumed that "tough-on-crime" issues did not arise. In 1996—in a bill which introduced Canada's now defunct "long gun registry"—a provision of four-year mandatory minimum sentences for violent offenses carried out with a firearm was introduced. This legislation was almost certainly seen as an attempt to appease those who were against the gun registry. We estimated (Webster and Doob, 2007, 317, n. 23) that the mandatory minimum had little impact on actual sentences. In interviews with senior people in the Department of Justice at the time, there was clearly concern about the increase. One official told us that the department had estimated that it would have a measurable impact on federal imprisonment counts, while another told us that the department had estimated that it would have little impact on prison counts for reasons outlined in our 2007 chapter.

CASES CITED

R. v. Ipeelee, 2012 SCC 13, [2012] 1 S.C.R. 433.
United States v. Burns, [2001] 1 S.C.R. 283.
Sauvé v. Canada (Chief Electoral Officer), [2002] S.C.C. 68.

REFERENCES

Adams, Michael. *Fire and Ice: The United States, Canada, and the Myth of Converging Values*. Toronto: Penguin Canada, 2003.
Allen, Francis A. *The Decline of the Rehabilitative Ideal: Penal Policy and Social Purpose*. New Haven, CT: Yale University Press, 1981.

American Law Institute. *Model Penal Code.* Philadelphia: American Law Institute, 1962.

Barker, Vanessa. *The Politics of Imprisonment.* New York: Oxford University Press, 2009.

Beattie, John M. *Attitudes towards Crime and Punishment in Upper Canada, 1830–1850.* Toronto: Centre of Criminology, University of Toronto, 1977.

Beckett, Katherine, and Bruce Western. "Governing Social Marginality: Welfare, Incarceration, and the Transformation of State Policy." *Punishment & Society* 3, no. 1 (2001): 43–59.

Blumstein, Alfred, and Allen J. Beck. "Population Growth in U.S. Prisons, 1980–1996." In *Crime and Justice: A Review of Research.* Vol. 26. Edited by Michael Tonry and Joan Petersilia, 17–62. Chicago: University of Chicago Press, 1999.

Blumstein, Alfred, and Jacqueline Cohen. "A Theory of the Stability of Punishment." *Journal of Criminal Law and Criminology* 64 (1973): 198–207.

Blumstein, Alfred, Jacqueline Cohen, and Daniel Nagin. "The Dynamics of a Homeostatic Punishment Process." *Journal of Criminal Law and Criminology* 67 (1977): 317–34.

Bottoms, Anthony E. "The Philosophy and Politics of Punishment and Sentencing." In *The Politics of Sentencing Reform,* edited by Chris Clarkson and Rod Morgan, 17–50. Oxford: Clarendon Press, 1995.

Bureau of Justice Statistics. Total Correctional Population. 2015. http://www.bjs.gov/index.cfm?ty=tp&tid=11.

Campbell, Michael C. "The Emergence of Penal Extremism in California." *Law & Society Review* 48 (2014): 377–409.

Campbell, Michael, and Heather Schoenfeld. "The Transformation of America's Penal Order: A Historicized Political Sociology of Punishment." *American Journal of Sociology* 118, no. 5 (2013): 1375–1423.

Canada. *Royal Commission on Penitentiaries. Report.* Ottawa: J. de L. Taché, Printer to the King's Most Excellent Majesty (George V), 1914.

Canada. *Royal Commission to Investigate the Penal System of Canada. Report.* (Mr. Justice Joseph Archambault, Chairman). Ottawa: J. O. Patenaude, Printer to the King's Most Excellent Majesty, 1938.

Canada. *Reports of the Joint Committee of the Senate and House of Commons on Capital Punishment, Corporal Punishment, and Lotteries.* Ottawa: Queen's Printer and Controller of Stationery, 1956.

Canada. *Sub-Committee on the Penitentiary System in Canada (Mark MacGuigan, Chairman). Report to Parliament (2nd session, 30th Parliament).* Ottawa: Minister of Supply and Services, 1977.

Canada. *Criminal Law in Canadian Society.* Ottawa: Minister of Supply and Services, 1982.

Canada. *Sentencing.* Ottawa: Supply and Services Canada, 1984.

Canada. *Taking Responsibility: Report of the Standing Committee on Justice and Solicitor General on Its Review of Sentencing, Conditional Release and Related Aspects of Corrections.* (David Daubney, Chair). Ottawa: House of Commons, 1988.

Canada. *Directions for Reform: A Framework for Corrections and Conditional Release.* Ottawa: Solicitor General of Canada, 1990.

Canada. *Crime Prevention in Canada: Toward a National Strategy. 12th Report of the Standing Committee on Justice and the Solicitor General (3rd session, 34th Parliament).* Ottawa: House of Commons, 1993.

Canadian Committee on Corrections. *Toward Unity. Criminal Justice and Corrections.* Ottawa: Queen's Printer, 1969.

Canadian Sentencing Commission. *Sentencing Reform: A Canadian Approach.* Ottawa: Supply and Services Canada, 1987.

Cavadino, Michael, and James Dignan. *Penal System: A Comparative Approach.* London: Sage, 2006.

Chiricos, Ted, Michael Hogan, and Marc Gertz. "Racial Composition of Neighbourhood and Fear of Crime." *Criminology* 35, no. 1 (1997): 107–29.

Clark, Ramsey. *Crime in America: Observations on Its Nature, Causes, Prevention and Control.* New York: Simon & Schuster, 1970.

Commission of Inquiry into the Non-Medical Use of Drugs. *Final Report* and *Interim Report.* Ottawa: Information Canada, 1973.

Doob, Anthony N., and Cheryl Marie Webster. "Sentence Severity and Crime: Accepting the Null Hypothesis." In *Crime and Justice: A Review of Research.* Vol. 30. Edited by Tonry, Michael, 143–95. Chicago: University of Chicago Press, 2003.

Doob, Anthony N., and Cheryl Marie Webster. "Countering Punitiveness: Understanding Stability in Canada's Imprisonment Rate." *Law & Society Review* 40, no. 2 (2006): 325–67.

Doob, Anthony N., Cheryl Marie Webster, and Allan Manson. "Zombie Parole: The Withering of Conditional Release in Canada." *Criminal Law Quarterly* 61, no. 3 (2014): 301–28.

Downes, David. "Political Economy, Welfare, and Punishment in Comparative Perspective." In *Resisting Punitiveness in Europe: Welfare, Human Rights, and Democracy*, edited by Sonja Snacken and Els Dumortier, 23–34. Abingdon, UK, and New York: Routledge, 2012.

Federal/Provincial/Territorial Ministers Responsible for Justice. *Corrections Population Growth: Report for Federal/Provincial/Territorial Ministers Responsible for Justice.* Ottawa, Canada: Solicitor General of Canada, May 1996.

Federal/Provincial/Territorial Ministers Responsible for Justice. *Corrections Population Growth: First Report on Progress for Federal/Provincial/Territorial Ministers Responsible for Justice.* Ottawa, Canada: Solicitor General of Canada, February 1997.

Frankel, Marvin E. *Criminal Sentences: Law without Order.* New York: Hill & Wang, 1973.

Gaes, Gerald G., Timothy J. Flanagan, Lawrence L. Motiuk, and Lynn Stewart. "Adult Correctional Treatment." In *Crime and Justice: A Review of Research*. Vol. 26. Edited by Michael Tonry and Joan Petersilia, 361–426. Chicago: University of Chicago Press, 1999.

Garland, David. *Punishment and Modern Society*. Chicago: University of Chicago Press, 1990.

Garland, David. *The Culture of Control: Crime and Social Order in Contemporary Society*. Chicago: University of Chicago Press, 2001.

Gartner, Rosemary, Anthony N. Doob, and Franklin E. Zimring. "The Past as Prologue? Decarceration in California Then and Now." *Criminology and Public Policy* 10, no. 2 (2011): 287–325.

Goyer, Jean-Pierre. Solicitor General of Canada, Thursday October 7, 1971. Ottawa: House of Commons, 1971. Cited from Debates (Hansard), House of Commons, Canada. http://www.lipad.ca/full/1971/10/07/1/.

Gwyn, Richard. *John A.: The Man Who Made Us*. Vol. 1, *The Life and Times of John A. Macdonald: 1815–1867*. Toronto: Vintage, 2011.

Johnson, Devon. "Anger about Crime and Support for Punitive Criminal Justice Policies." *Punishment and Society* 11, no. 1 (2009): 51–66.

Johnson, Lyndon B. "Remarks on the City Hall Steps, Dayton, Ohio." The American Presidency Project. October 16, 1964. http://www.presidency.ucsb.edu/ws/?pid=26621.

Kessler, Daniel, and Stephen D. Levitt. "Using Sentence Enhancements to Distinguish between Deterrence and Incapacitation." *Journal of Law and Economics* 42 (1999): 343–63.

Kohler-Hausmann, Julilly. "'The Attila The Hun Law': New York's Rockefeller Drug Laws and the Making of a Punitive State." *Journal of Social History* 44, no. 1 (2010): 71–95.

Lappi-Seppälä, Tapio. "Explaining Imprisonment in Europe." *European Journal of Criminology* 8, no. 4 (2011): 303–28.

Law Reform Commission of Canada. *Our Criminal Law*. Ottawa: Law Reform Commission of Canada, 1976.

Lynch, Mona. *Sunbelt Justice: Arizona and the Transformation of American Punishment*. Stanford, CA: Stanford Law Books, 2010.

Martinson, Robert M. "What Works? Questions and Answers about Prison Reform." *Public Interest* 35 (1974): 22–54.

Mauer, Marc, and Virginia McCalmont. *A Lifetime of Punishment: The Impact of the Felony Drug Ban on Welfare Benefits*. Washington, DC: Sentencing Project, 2014.

Miller, Lisa. *The Perils of Federalism: Race, Poverty, and the Politics of Crime Control*. Oxford: Oxford University Press, 2008.

Nagin, Daniel S., Francis T. Cullen, and Cheryl Lero Jonson. "Imprisonment and Reoffending." In *Crime and Justice: A Review of Research*. Vol. 38. Edited by Michael Tonry, 115–200. Chicago: University of Chicago Press, 2009.

Pickett, Justin T., and Ted Chiricos. "Controlling Other People's Children: Racialized Views of Delinquency and Whites' Punitive Attitudes toward Juvenile Offenders." *Criminology* 50, no. 3 (2012): 673–710.

Pickett, Justin T., Daniel Tope, and Rose Bellandi. "'Taking Back Our Country': Tea Party Membership and Support for Punitive Crime Control Policies." *Sociological Inquiry* 84, no. 2 (2014): 167–90.

President's Commission on Law Enforcement and Administration of Justice. *The Challenge of Crime in a Free Society*. Washington, DC: US Government Printing Office, 1967.

Reitz, Kevin R. "The 'Traditional' Indeterminate Sentencing Model." In the *Oxford Handbook on Sentencing and Corrections*, edited by Joan Petersilia and Kevin Reitz, 270–98. New York: Oxford University Press, 2012.

Roberts, Julian V., Loretta J. Stalans, David Indermaur, and Mike Hough. *Penal Populism and Public Opinion: Lessons from Five Countries*. New York: Oxford University Press, 2003.

Rock, The Honourable Allan. "Keynote Address: Crime, Punishment and Public Expectations." In *Public Perceptions of the Administration of Justice–Papers Presented at a Conference Held in Banff, Alta, Oct. 11–14, 1995*, edited by Jean Maurice Brisson and Donna Greschner, 185–94. Montreal: Editions Themis, 1996.

Rothman, David. *Conscience and Convenience*. Boston: Little Brown, 1980.

Ruth, Henry, and Kevin R. Reitz. *The Challenge of Crime: Rethinking Our Response*. Cambridge, MA: Harvard University Press, 2003.

Simon, Jonathan. *Governing through Crime: How the War on Crime Transformed American Democracy and Created a Culture of Fear*. New York: Oxford University Press, 2007.

Sprott, Jane, and Anthony N. Doob. "Understanding Provincial Variation in Incarceration Rates." *Canadian Journal of Criminology* 40, no. 3 (1998): 305–22.

Tonry, Michael. *Thinking about Crime: Sense and Sensibility in American Penal Culture*. New York: Oxford University Press, 2004.

Tonry, Michael. "Sentencing in America, 1975–2025." In *Crime and Justice: A Review of Research*. Vol. 42. Edited by Michael Tonry, 141–98. Chicago: University of Chicago Press, 2013.

Tucker, E. Shannon. Instability within Stability: Conflicting Trends Beneath Canada's Aggregate Incarceration Rate. Unpublished Master of Arts Thesis. University of Ottawa. 2009.

Uggen, Christopher, and Sarah Shannon. *State-Level Estimates of Felon Disenfranchisement in the United States, 2010*. Washington, DC: Sentencing Project, 2012.

Wacquant, Loic. *Deadly Symbiosis: Race and the Rise of Neoliberal Penality*. Oxford: Polity Press, 2011.

Webster, Cheryl Marie, and Anthony N. Doob. "Punitive Trends and Stable Imprisonment Rates in Canada." In *Crime and Justice: A Review of Research*. Vol. 36. Edited by Michael Tonry, 297–369. Chicago: University of Chicago Press, 2007.

Webster, Cheryl Marie, and Anthony N. Doob. "Explaining Canada's Imprisonment Rate: The Inadequacy of Simple Explanations." In *International and Comparative Criminal Justice and Urban Governance: Convergence and Divergence in Global, National and Local Settings*, edited by Adam Crawford, 304–30. Cambridge: Cambridge University Press, 2011.

Webster, Cheryl Marie, and Anthony N. Doob. "Maintaining Our Balance: Trends in Imprisonment Policies in Canada." In *Canadian Criminal Justice Policy*, edited by Karim Ismaili, Jane Sprott, and Kimberly Varma, 79–109. Oxford: Oxford University Press, 2012.

Webster, Cheryl Marie, Anthony N. Doob, and Franklin E. Zimring. "Proposition 8 and Crime Rates in California: The Case of the Disappearing Deterrent." *Criminology and Public Policy* 5, no. 3 (2006): 417–47.

Whitman, James Q. *Harsh Justice: Criminal Punishment and the Widening Divide between America and Europe*. New York: Oxford University Press, 2003.

Wilson, James Q. *Thinking about Crime*. New York: Basic Books, 1975.

Woolliams, Eldon M. Member of Parliament, Calgary North. Thursday October 7, 1971. Ottawa: House of Commons, 1971. Cited from Debates (Hansard), House of Commons, Canada. http://www.lipad.ca/full/1971/10/07/1/.

Zimring, Franklin E. "The Scale of Imprisonment in the United States: Twentieth Century Patterns and Twenty-First Century Prospects." *Journal of Criminal Law & Criminology* 100, no. 3 (2010): 1225–45.

Zimring, Franklin, and Gordon Hawkins. "The New Mathematics of Imprisonment." *Crime and Delinquency* 34, no. 4 (1988): 425–36.

Zimring, Franklin E., and Gordon J. Hawkins. *The Scale of Imprisonment*. Chicago: University of Chicago Press, 1991.

Zimring, Franklin, and Gordon Hawkins. *Incapacitation: Penal Confinement and the Restraint of Crime*. New York and Oxford: Oxford University Press, 1995.

Zimring, Franklin E., and David T. Johnson. "Public Opinion and the Governance of Punishment in Democratic Political Systems." *Annals of the American Academy of Political and Social Science* 605 (2006): 266–80.

Appendix 3A.1 Imprisonment Rates for 50 States (1971–1975 and 2006–2010)

	Average 1971–1975	Average 2006–2010	Absolute Change	Ratio: End/ Beginning
Alabama	109.9	628.4	518.5	5.7
Alaska	59.2	407.2	348.0	6.9
Arizona	89.4	556.4	467.0	6.2
Arkansas	89.6	514.4	424.8	5.7
California	90.9	462.0	371.1	5.1
Colorado	80.8	459.2	378.4	5.7
Connecticut	56.7	393.4	336.7	6.9
Delaware	63.1	464.6	401.5	7.4
Florida	145.7	543.2	397.5	3.7
Georgia	177.8	533.2	355.4	3.0
Hawaii	38.1	325.4	287.3	8.5
Idaho	57.9	477.4	419.5	8.2
Illinois	56.4	354.6	298.2	6.3
Indiana	69.9	432.0	362.1	6.2
Iowa	52.5	295.8	243.3	5.6
Kansas	72.8	311.0	238.2	4.3
Kentucky	92.9	480.4	387.5	5.2
Louisiana	113.4	862.4	749.0	7.6
Maine	49.1	149.6	100.5	3.0
Maryland	146.4	394.4	248.0	2.7
Massachusetts	37.0	224.6	187.6	6.1
Michigan	100.1	480.0	379.9	4.8
Minnesota	37.6	182.0	144.4	4.8
Mississippi	87.2	703.0	615.8	8.1
Missouri	82.2	509.2	427.0	6.2
Montana	42.8	368.8	326.0	8.6
Nebraska	69.2	243.4	174.2	3.5
Nevada	129.3	485.0	355.7	3.8
New Hampshire	30.3	212.8	182.5	7.0
New Jersey	73.4	299.2	225.8	4.1
New Mexico	70.0	318.2	248.2	4.5
New York	73.6	308.2	234.6	4.2
North Carolina	182.8	366.2	183.4	2.0
North Dakota	24.5	222.8	198.3	9.1
Ohio	85.5	442.6	357.1	5.2
Oklahoma	125.4	660.2	534.8	5.3

(continued)

Appendix 3A.1 continued

	Average 1971–1975	Average 2006–2010	Absolute Change	Ratio: End/ Beginning
Oregon	89.8	368.2	278.4	4.1
Pennsylvania	53.8	384.0	330.2	7.1
Rhode Island	41.9	217.0	175.1	5.2
South Carolina	145.2	515.0	369.8	3.5
South Dakota	45.9	417.4	371.5	9.1
Tennessee	90.4	428.2	337.8	4.7
Texas	143.6	657.4	513.8	4.6
Utah	49.9	237.4	187.5	4.8
Vermont	43.9	264.8	220.9	6.0
Virginia	107.6	480.8	373.2	4.5
Washington	83.8	271.2	187.4	3.2
West Virginia	60.4	337.4	277.0	5.6
Wisconsin	53.8	379.8	326.0	7.1
Wyoming	76.7	390.2	313.5	5.1
Arithmetic (unweighted) average of states	81.0	408.4	327.4	5.5
Federal institutions	10.6	59.8	49.2	5.6
State (overall) only	88.8	442.2	353.4	5.0
State and federal (combined)	99.4	502.0	402.6	5.1
Canada	84.9	110.3	25.4	1.3

4

The Complications of Penal Federalism

AMERICAN EXCEPTIONALISM OR 50 DIFFERENT COUNTRIES?

Franklin E. Zimring

THE POLITICAL STRUCTURE of government power in the United States presents an important challenge to those who wish to make generalizations about penal policy, including students of what they call "American exceptionalism." While the penal policies of the national government control when in conflict with state legislation, for the most part, the national government leaves issues regarding crimes and punishments to the separate determination of 50 different states. The extent of penal federalism in the United States is much greater than in other formally federal governments. In the People's Republic of China and India, the forms of federalism are important, but every execution in each nation is an act of national government (Johnson and Zimring 2009). In the United States, there were 1,320 executions between 1976 and the end of 2012, and 1,317 of these were conducted by state governments carrying out the enforcement of state criminal laws—99.8 percent of the most severe punishments are therefore determined at the state level of government (Death Penalty Information Center 2013). State and local governments also dominate the administration of penal confinement. About 85 percent of all persons in prisons and more than 90 percent of all persons locked up in prisons and jails are the responsibility of state governments and their political subdivisions. In this important sense, the United States is not one country but

50 different countries. Under these circumstances, does it make any sense to discuss "American exceptionalism" in penal practice?

It may, but only if close attention is paid to the diversity as well as the uniformity that can be observed in subnational penal practices in the United States. There indeed may be occasions when observing state-to-state uniformity and noting state-to-state variation can help to determine the causes of penal practices that are distinctively American. This essay will discuss two punishments most often mentioned as examples of American exceptionalism—capital punishment and imprisonment. In each setting, there are huge variations among American states. In both cases, the study of interstate variation is a useful method of investigating the causes of penal difference. In the case of imprisonment trends over time, there may also be a nearly uniform pattern that teaches us about the influences of culture and public opinion on penal policy.

Capital Punishment as a Case Study in American Exceptionalism

No penal practice currently sets the United States apart from other developed nations as much as the death penalty. The United States is the only Western developed nation that has experienced any executions in the past generation and one of two developed democracies that regularly conducts executions (the other is Japan). But the critical level of government for capital punishment policy is state, and there is tremendous variation in the United States. In the first place, a substantial number of American states have long-standing and consistent credentials as abolitionists. Table 4.1 compares five of the earliest US states to abolish the death penalty with the vintage of six western European abolitions. Michigan permanently abolished the death penalty before *any* western European nation, as did Wisconsin. Minnesota and North Dakota both abolished the death penalty four decades before Germany and Italy.

Even among those states that have conducted executions, the rate of state execution over the years 1976–2012 has varied tremendously, as shown in Figure 4.1.

Even restricting the states reported to those which actually conducted executions (states like New York, New Jersey, and Massachusetts had a death penalty on their books for part of that era but didn't execute), the rates of execution are very different. The four highest rate-to-population states had a cumulative average execution rate of 19.54 per million citizens, while the four lowest execution states had an average of .266 per million. The rate difference is 74 to 1.

Table 4.1 Western European and US Pioneers in Permanent Abolition of the Death Penalty

	United States	Western Europe
Before 1900	Michigan (1846)	Portugal (1867)
	Wisconsin (1853)	The Netherlands (1870)
	Maine (1887)	
1901–1950	Minnesota (1911)	Italy (1944)
	North Dakota (1915)	Germany (1949)
1951–2000		United Kingdom (1965)
		France (1981)

Sources: Zimring and Hawkins (1987, 29, table 2.1); for France, see Zimring (2003, 23, table 2.1).

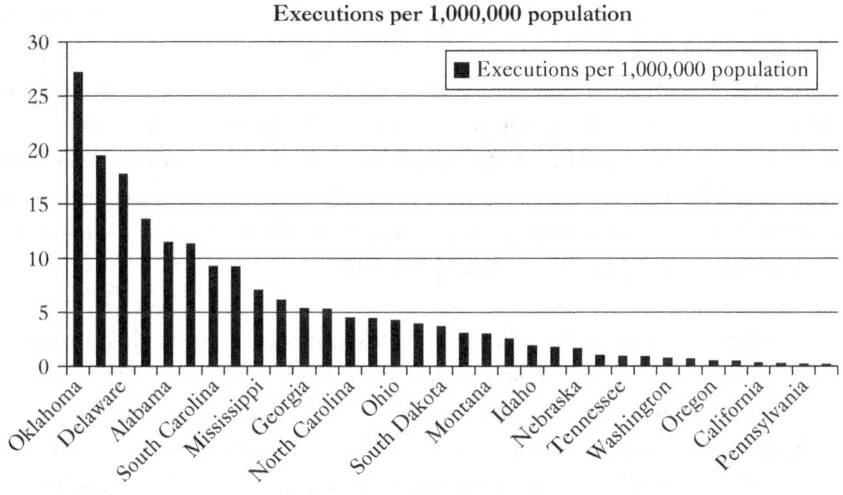

FIGURE 4.1 Aggregate Executions per Million Population, 1976–2012

So how do these data intersect with questions of American penal exceptionalism? Minnesota is as different from Texas in its stable policy toward the death penalty as Norway is from Iraq. Yet Minnesota is just as American as Texas, and it displays an immunity to capital sanctions for a century. What is the character of capital punishment exceptionalism that includes two such diametrically opposed policies?

The radical penal decentralization of the American federal system turns out to be one important substantive element of American exceptionalism.

If a British or Chinese scholar wonders why the United States has been the scene of over 1,300 executions, the power of state-level government to make life-and-death decisions is a big part of the story. If the only government that could authorize and conduct executions were the national government, it is quite probable that the total number of executions for the era after 1976 would only be a fraction, perhaps even a small fraction, of the 1,320 total that the decentralized federal system actually produced. So the same peculiarity of decentralized political authority that made Michigan and Minnesota pioneers in penal reform also left plenty of extra dead bodies in southern states in the 35 years after *Gregg v. Georgia*. Delegating authority to provincial governments increases variance and may also increase aggregate levels of punishment. Penal federalism is an important part of penal exceptionalism.

There is a second respect in which the peculiar distribution of executions in US states provides a methodology for studying what causes executions in some American states and thus also generates important substantive clues about what produces executions on American soil in the twenty-first century. The distribution of executions among the 50 American states is anything but random, with southern states generating more than four-fifths of national execution totals (see Zimring 2003). One methodology of searching for causes is thus looking for features of culture, history, and governance in states like Texas and Virginia that are absent in Minnesota and other nonexecution environments. My 2003 study suggested using "the federal laboratory" to discover the roots of capital punishment exceptionalism:

> The patterned differences between states and regions are both a puzzle and an opportunity. With so much variation between American governmental entities, why not use the 50 United States as a laboratory to test hypotheses about which elements in American character or government might explain the persistent attachment to the death penalty and the different ways in which the penalty is viewed? There is good reason to suppose that theories capable of explaining variations within the United States might also explain differences between the recent career of the executioner in the United States and in other developed countries.
>
> The two central policy puzzles of the past quarter-century are the persistence of the death penalty in the United States when other developed nations have rejected it, and the absence of fear of government as political motive for opposing capital punishment. Perhaps understanding the differences between Texas and Virginia, on the one hand, and Ohio and Michigan, on the other hand, can help explain why so many American states retain and use a death penalty. The assumption is that

> what makes Virginia so much more likely to execute will also explain why so many U.S. states differ from other Western governments. (Zimring 2003, 86)

My own conclusions about the substantive implications of the peculiar patterns of execution in US states can be found in the fifth chapter of *The Contradictions of American Capital Punishment* (Zimring 2003). But the deeper strategic point is that explaining the known differences between American states is a powerful method of exploring the reasons why the United States differs from other nations.

Uniformity and Variations in Rates of Imprisonment

If the death penalty is exhibit A in complaints about American penal exceptionalism, the major emphasis in recent years has come from the nation's extraordinary rates of penal confinement. Here again, the dominant influence on rates of penal confinement is state government, so the federal system must be a major influence on what sets US policy apart from that of other developed nations. But while long-standing policy differences dominated the first section's discussion of capital punishment, the moving parts in the story of mass imprisonment in the United States show a much more dynamic pattern over time.

Figure 4.2 begins my story by showing, at the national level, rates of imprisonment by year from 1925 to 2000. The pattern in Figure 4.2 over time breaks into two distinct eras. For the first 47 years after 1925, rates of imprisonment are quite stable, hovering around 100 per 100,000. For the 35 years after 1972, however, the pattern is one of consistent and substantial increase. Rates of imprisonment go up every year for a generation, and at the end of this time series the rate of imprisonment is five times the rate of the early 1970s.

There are two technical issues relating to the discussion of American exceptionalism that concern the data in Figure 4.2. The first point is that the US national rate was on the high side for developed nations in the first 45 years of Figure 4.2's record but was not what statisticians call an "outlier." The United States was near the top of peer comparison national rates but did not occupy its own statistical stratosphere (see Lappi-Seppälä, this volume). What came to be called "mass imprisonment" in the United States was largely the product of policy and rate changes after 1970.

The second technical point about Figure 4.2 is that this national data set is precisely the kind of "aggregation error" that the introduction to this chapter

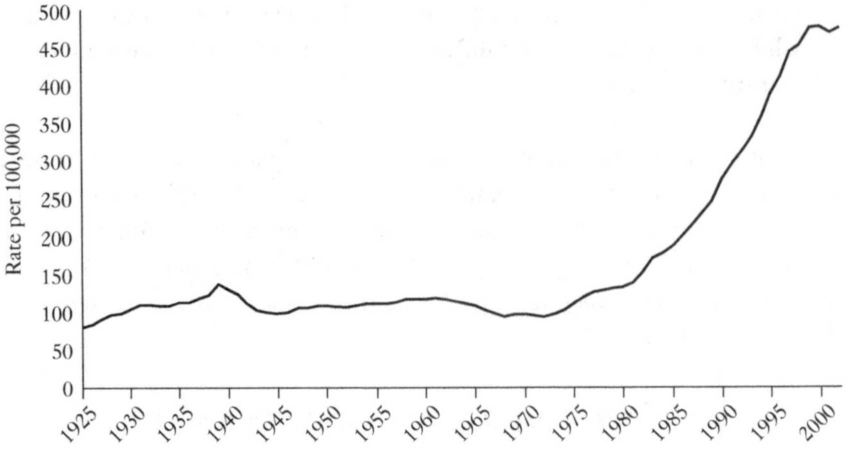

FIGURE 4.2 Imprisonment Rate per 100,000 Population, United States, 1925–2002

put under sustained attack. In a discussion organized around the penal powers of 50 different states, why begin with a national trend that combines all the states into a single total for each year? My justification for showing the aggregate trends is that this sharp an aggregate increase is exactly what *shouldn't* happen when 50 different governments control 85 percent of the process. The sharp trend in the aggregate total means that most of the independent systems that feed into the aggregate are going very much in the same direction.

This trend over time, however, does not mean that rates of imprisonment in the 50 states end up at similar levels. They don't. Figure 4.3 shows the distribution of imprisonment rates for the states for 2007, at the end of the 35-year run-up.

The range of rates in US states is substantial—with three states (Maine, Massachusetts, and Minnesota) under 200 per 100,000, while Louisiana and Delaware incarcerate at rates in excess of 800 per 100,000. There are no obvious differences in population density to account for this more than four to one difference, and these differences between US states are as great as some of the international comparisons on national-level rates that put the US aggregate at the pinnacle of the imprisonment scale. Figure 4.4 adds four foreign nations into the mix of individual state totals to illustrate what disaggregation can teach.

Using 2007 data, it turns out that Latvia reports a rate of imprisonment per 100,000 greater than New Jersey and quite close to that of New York. Thailand uses its prisons more than Washington and Utah, and the Czech Republic has a higher rate of incarceration than Minnesota. To be sure, all

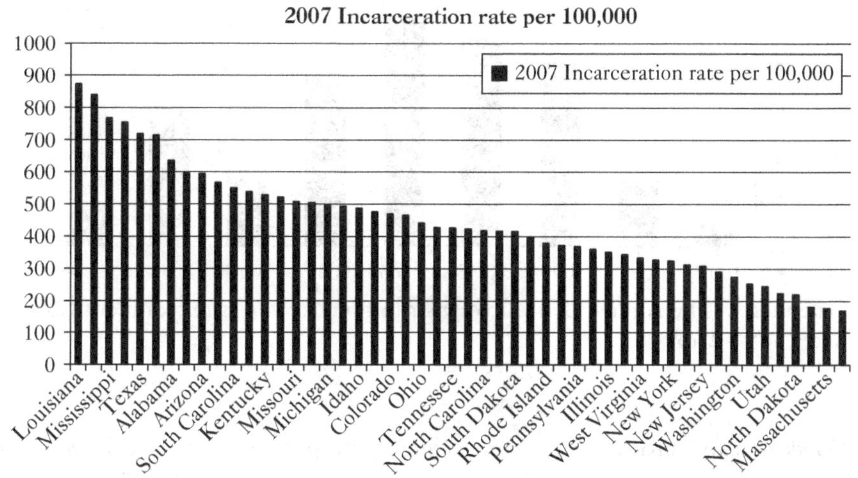

FIGURE 4.3 2007 Incarceration Rate by State

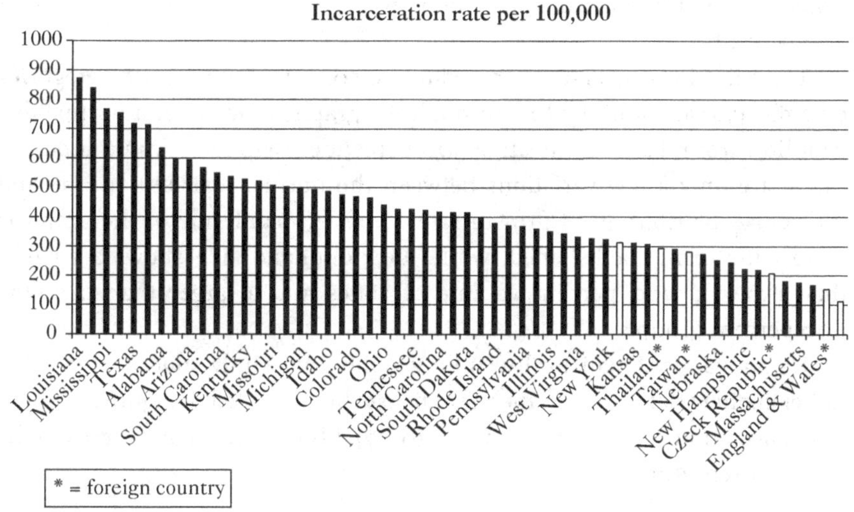

FIGURE 4.4 Incarceration Rate, States and Select Nations

the American states report higher imprisonment than Italy or England and Wales; but even at the end of the explosive growth in imprisonment documented in Figure 4.2 the 50 states are very broadly different in rates of imprisonment, and many states are not that far off the imprisonment rates found in non-US nations.

But while the cross-sectioned differences between US states are quite substantial both at the beginning of the imprisonment growth (Zimring and

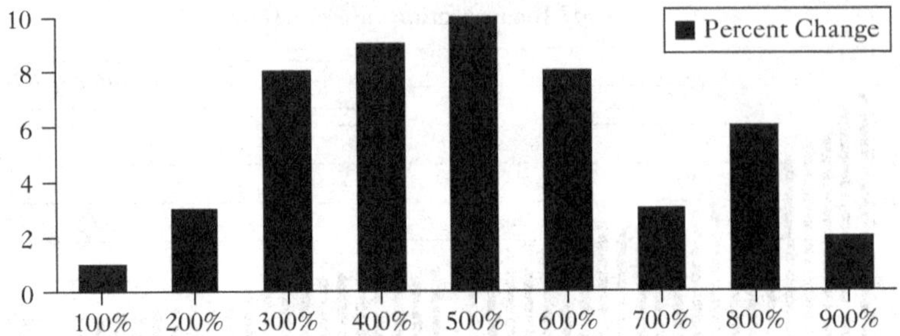

FIGURE 4.5 The Almost Bell Curve Distribution of State Imprisonment Growth Rates, 1972–2007

Hawkins 1991, 149, fig. 6.1) and currently, the pattern of growth in rates of imprisonment is much closer to being uniform. Figure 4.5, taken from a study I published in 2010, compares the percentage growth in state rates of imprisonment over the 35 years after 1972 to the distribution of growth rates one would find with a normal distribution around a single mean growth rate of 400 percent.

The solid bars in Figure 4.5 divide the 50 states into growth categories over the 35 years, and the line through the graph shows what a normal distribution around a 2007 mean of 500 percent of 1972 rates would produce. There are only a few variations between the normal distribution line and the actual distribution of growth rates. The left-hand side of the graph is almost uniformly bell-shaped, while the right-hand side shows a smaller than expected 700 percent volume of states and a larger than expected 800 percent group.

Using standard statistical techniques, the 2010 study suggested that the rather slight variations from the normal distribution noted in Figure 4.5 might be chance variations (Zimring 2010, 1236–37). My conclusion in 2010 from the data bear repeating:

> The smaller the probability that this is a fifty-case sample from a normal distribution, the more likely the pattern of difference observed is not normal, with a probability of 0.05 or less a usual benchmark for strong statistical evidence of non-normal distribution. But using a Shapiro-Wilk test produces a probability of normal distribution of 0.31151 and the Shapiro-Francia test probabilities 0.46612. The question these tests address is "how likely" it is that a distribution like that being tested could be the outcome of sampling fifty readings from a normal distribution. The answer is "pretty likely." There are thus no indications

> in these analyses of anything other than fifty different outcomes of a uniform process. (Zimring 2010, 1237)

If the circumstantial evidence of Figure 4.5 is correct, the 35-year increase in imprisonment might have been 50 different units of government participating in a single process. Whatever the diversity in rates of incarceration at the beginning, the growth process was essentially similar in the different states. And if this uniquely large growth process is the major cause of the current outlier status of American imprisonment, then it may make sense to call mass imprisonment an American national phenomenon.

But any uniformity in prison growth over the generation after 1972 would have had to be the product of nongovernmental circumstances and influences. There was no federal program to encourage prison growth of any kind prior to the federal crime-control legislation of 1994 and only a weak federal prison incentive after 1994 (Reitz 1996). What kinds of cultural or media influence might inspire 50 different political systems to march in the same direction at more or less the same speed?

It is tempting to think that concern over crime or changing attitudes toward punishing offenders might be the driving influence of a single growth process. But this thesis is awfully hard to test in a rigorous way. And it's worth remembering that these same hardening attitudes being nominated as the cause of a 50-state growth in imprisonment produced no changes whatsoever in the substantial number of states that had long rejected the death penalty (see Table 4.1). Indeed, the few states to change their legal position on the death penalty during this period shifted in the direction of abolition or moratorium. And many retentionist states approximated abolition simply by carrying out fewer executions or none at all (Figure 4.1). This fragmented pattern of death-penalty acceptance and use, with small steps in the direction of lenity, does not resemble at all the United States' "national" journey to mass incarceration.

Two other chapters in this book address the question of the pattern of expansion in state imprisonment (see Webster and Doob, this volume; Lappi-Seppälä, this volume), and each raises the question of whether the best measure of growth in scale of imprisonment is percentage change in rate of imprisonment (which I used) or instead the increase in number of prisoners per 100,000 not tied to any base rate for each state.

Webster and Doob (Chapter 3) use a different measure of state growth, contrasting each state's average imprisonment for 1971–1975 with its average rate in 2006–2010, with the multiyear averages meant to avoid single-year aberrations. This yields the "absolute change in imprisonment rate" for each

Percentage Change in State-Level Imprisonment 1971–1975 to 2006–2010	Shapiro-Wilk p. value .5568	Shapiro-Francia p. value .6975
Absolute Change in State-Level Imprisonment per 100,000 1971–1975 to 2006–2010	Shapiro-Wilk p. value .0248	Shapiro-Francia p. value .018

FIGURE 4.6 Likelihood of Normal Distribution of State-Level Imprisonment Growth, Two Measures and Two Tests

state from the earlier to the later period. Webster and Doob claim that the absolute-change measure is superior to the "ratio" approach, which tracks percentage change in imprisonment rates over time, because (in their view) the ratio method "is driven so much by the starting rate in the early 1970s." Because the two calculations rank states differently in comparative prison growth stature, it is useful to give the absolute-change approach a test drive. Figure 4.6 uses Webster and Doob's data to test again for the likelihood of a normal distribution.

The contrast between using percentage growth and incremental change in incarceration rates is dramatic. Both tests show that a normal curve for the 50-state pattern is quite likely for percentage growth (56 percent and 70 percent). Both tests show that the growth in imprisonment rate for each of the 50 states is, when not normed to prior imprisonment, extremely unlikely to be a normal distribution (2.5 percent and 1.8 percent likelihood). So the normal appearance of the percentage growth pattern is strengthened and confirmed, but the distribution of growth numbers unconnected to prior rate is not a bell curve.

So which approach to changes in the scale of imprisonment is correct? One can assume that the percentage growth method would be uncontroversial if all 50 states had started with identical imprisonment rates in the early 1970s. Argument ensues because those beginning rates were so varied—by Webster and Doob's calculation, the state with the highest incarceration rate over 1971–1975 had a rate of roughly six times the lowest incarceration state (see Chapter 3, Table 3.1). By the late 1980s, the spread was ten to one (Zimring and Hawkins 1991, 148). The error in Webster and Doob's argument is that they take the importance of starting rates of incarceration as a *weakness* of the ratio measure as a gauge of comparative experience over time. When the growth in each state's rate of incarceration is not linked to previous rates of incarceration, however, an important measure of the long-term propensity and capacity to imprison is taken off the table. The percentage change adds more information and is thus presumptively preferable. Would we rather measure the growth in per capita income as a percentage of its base or just the size of a dollar increase with no information on base rate?

But what was the mysterious nongovernmental process that pushed all the states to radical increases? It is almost more plausible to assume that the appearance of uniformity or a single process produced in Figure 4.5 is misleading, that prison growth in the states wasn't a single process after all, than it is to imagine the type of changes in the software of citizen opinion that could create an orderly single progression of huge magnitude over a generation.

But whatever the eventual interpretation of the puzzling uniformity in imprisonment growth, a substantial knowledge of the American federal system is a necessary tool for an informed discussion of what might have influenced prison growth in the years after 1972. Any real single trend in those years was not the result of a common government. And if this was the result of shifts in attitude or opinion, they must have been very specific prison-based attitudes rather than a more general shift to a hard line. The evidence here is the fixed propensities of noncapital punishment states.

Conclusion

So the available data on state penal power and patterns of the two most prominent issues implicated in discourse about American penal exceptionalism point in different directions. For the death penalty, state penal power over life and death is itself one important reason why executions continue in the United States. But it is also true that embrace of state killing is not nationwide. Michigan and Wisconsin are in effect different nations from Texas and Oklahoma in relation to state killing as a criminal sanction.

For mass imprisonment, the evidence of nationwide growth in imprisonment is more substantial, but the cross-sectional differences in current rates of incarceration are very large. A state like Minnesota is closer to the Czech Republic and England and Wales in prison levels than to Alabama and Delaware. And if the growth patterns after 1972 are nearly uniform in the states, there is no obvious explanation of the cause.

The puzzles we confront when examining the patterns of penal outcome at the state level are more than substantial. But any responsible empirical research on American punishment must confront these patterns and may yet discover some essential truths about punishment in the United States by sorting out the mysteries of federalism.

CASE CITED

Gregg v. Georgia, 428 U.S. 153 (1976).

REFERENCES

Death Penalty Information Center. Number of Executions by State and Region since 1976. 2013. http://www.deathpenaltyinfo.org/number-executions-state-and-region-1976.

Institute for Criminal Policy Research. World Prison Brief. Prison Population Rate—Europe. 2013. http://www.prisonstudies.org/info/worldbrief/wpb_stats.php?area=europe&category=wb_poprate.

Johnson, David T., and Franklin E. Zimring. *The Next Frontier: National Development, Political Change, and the Death Penalty in Asia.* New York: Oxford University Press, 2009.

Reitz, Kevin R. "The Federal Role in Sentencing Law and Policy." *Annals of the American Academy of Political and Social Science* 543 (January 1996): 116–29.

US Census Bureau. 2010 Census: Interactive Population Map. 2013a. http://www.census.gov/2010census/.

US Census Bureau. Population Estimates. Vintage 2007: State Tables. 2013b. https://www.census.gov/govs/www/state07nslist.html .

US Department of Justice, Bureau of Justice Statistics. *Sourcebook of Criminal Justice Statistics 1990.* Washington, DC: Government Printing Office, 1990.

US Department of Justice, Bureau of Justice Statistics. Sourcebook of Criminal Justice Statistics Online. 2016. http://www.albany.edu/sourcebook/pdf/t6282012.pdf.

West, Heather C., and William J. Sabol. "Prisoners in 2007." *Bureau of Justice Statistics Bulletin* (December 2008). http://bjs.ojp.usdoj.gov/content/pub/pdf/p07.pdf.

Zimring, Franklin E. *The Contradictions of American Capital Punishment.* New York: Oxford University Press, 2003.

Zimring, Franklin E. "The Scale of Imprisonment in the United States: 20th Century Patterns and 21st Century Prospects." *Journal of Criminal Law & Criminology* 100 (2010): 1225–45.

Zimring, Franklin E., and Gordon Hawkins. *Capital Punishment and the American Agenda.* New York: Cambridge University Press, 1987.

Zimring, Franklin E., and Gordon Hawkins. *The Scale of Imprisonment.* Chicago: University of Chicago Press, 1991.

PART II

American Exceptionalism in Crime

5

American Exceptionalism in Comparative Perspective

EXPLAINING TRENDS AND VARIATION IN THE USE OF INCARCERATION

Tapio Lappi-Seppälä

Introduction

In the 1970s criminal justice took a new punitive course in the United States. This change started to attract critical attention in the 1980s (for example, Zimring and Hawkins 1988). From the mid-1970s to the early 1990s, when Nils Christie warned about the rise of a "gulag Western style" (Christie 1993) and Anthony Bottoms coined the term "populist punitiveness" (Bottoms 1995), US incarceration rates increased from below 200 to 500 per 100,000 general population. When David Garland published his epochal work on the growth of the "culture of control" (Garland 2001), the US rate had climbed to 680. And when Loïc Wacquant (2009) argued that penal expansion was linked with the ascendancy of neoliberalism, the figure had reached the all-time record of 750. The expansion of penal control in America had become a widespread subject of scholarly concern, as a phenomenon unto itself and as a possible contagion. While the magnitude of changes in the United States was not mirrored in any other nation, punitive expansionism was seen in some quarters as a global trend—something that was happening elsewhere, or would be, in the foreseeable future.

To some extent, this grim prediction turned out to be true. Over the past several decades, the intensity of crime control expanded in several parts of Europe as well as in countries like Australia and New Zealand. However, there were many divergent trends and country-specific deviations. Scandinavian countries were an important counterexample, as were Germany, Switzerland, France, and Belgium, not to mention Canada in North America. Comparativists began to search for explanations for these different trajectories, designed to take into account national and regional differences as well as specific cultural contexts (see Tonry 2007; Lappi-Seppälä 2007, 2008, 2011a; Green 2008; Pratt 2008; Nelken 2010; Snacken and Dumortier 2012; Hamilton 2014).

This chapter continues that discussion by examining "American penal exceptionalism" in a wider cross-national perspective than previous studies and by disaggregating the US data so that the experiences of individual states may be included in the comparative analysis. The first part describes trends and differences. How do incarceration trends in the US differ from those in other developed countries, and where does the United States fit today in a global comparison? The second part examines these trends and differences in light of crime data as a first step in the search for explanations. Are increasing incarceration rates natural reflections of increasing crime, or are other factors involved? The third part widens the search of explanations to socioeconomic, political, and cultural variables. For example, can we explain the specific position of the United States by using the same factors that have been found to explain variation in imprisonment in Europe or in other Organisation for Economic Co-operation and Development (OECD) countries? And, understanding that the United States is not a unitary jurisdiction but 50 (one) different "countries" (Zimring and Hawkins 1991), does the cross-national model explain differences *among* US states? In other words, are the drivers of penal policy similar in kind across both sides of the ocean? One major finding of the chapter is that the predictors of incarceration rates developed from multinational samples, mostly in Europe, are largely replicated when building models to predict the incarceration rates of individual American states. This is important confirmation of earlier empirical research and provides a new framework for understanding the large variations in incarceration practices across US jurisdictions.

All analyses proceed in two stages. First, the chapter compares the United States against other nation states. Second, it compares American states among themselves.[1]

Incarceration Profiles

In this chapter, the word "incarceration" will be used when comparing total confinement in the United States with that in other countries. This word choice avoids possible confusion. American "incarceration rates" are defined as the sum of prison and jail confinement rates. In the United States, more than 30 percent of inmates are held in jails on any given day (Minton and Zeng 2015; Carson 2015). The US "imprisonment rate" therefore captures only 70 percent of the country's incarcerated population. For other countries, "incarceration rates" and "imprisonment rates" are equivalent terms; they do not follow America's idiosyncratic division of incarcerated populations into state prisons and local jails or do not bifurcate their reporting of statistics.

Incarceration in 2011–2013: Global Overview

The International Centre for Prison Studies has assembled incarceration data from 222 countries for the years 2011–2013. In this large global sample, the overall unweighted mean of national incarceration rates (per 100,000 population) was 170,[2] with rates in individual countries varying from lows of 20–30 to over 700. The United States holds the lead. From 2011 to 2013, there were six countries with incarceration rates exceeding 500 per 100,000 inhabitants (Cuba, Virgin Islands [US], Russian Federation, St. Kitts and Nevis, Seychelles, and the United States).[3]

Figure 5.1 displays regional comparisons for 2014 within Europe, the United States, and other major English-speaking countries (Canada, Australia, and New Zealand). The figure suggests distinct regional patterns in incarceration use. Taken as a whole, Nordic countries have the lowest level of prisoners in Europe, with the Netherlands on the same level. Incarceration rates in individual Scandinavian countries vary from 47 to 73 per 100,000, with an unweighted average of 60. The corresponding figures for other regions include western Europe, 59–119 (average 95); southern Europe, 89–142 (125); British Isles, 83–150 (121); southeastern Europe, 66–198 (127); eastern Europe, 122–204 (173); and Baltic countries, 225–305 (257). The former Soviet Union region ranks the highest, ranging 132–467 (Russia), with an unweighted average of 254.[4]

Most countries in the Anglosphere fit within the regional incarceration rates seen in Europe, albeit in the more punitive European sectors. Canada (106) and Australia (152) locate on the south European spectrum and New Zealand (202) on the east European scale. The United States is a stark exception; in 2014, it had 3.7 times the incarceration rate of its nearest "competitor" in the Anglosphere (New Zealand). Indeed, the United States would be an outlier in *any* of the regions displayed in Figure 5.1. For example, the United States has more than 10-fold the average incarceration rate of Scandinavia, seven times that of western European and two to three times that of the Baltic countries. The increment of difference between rates in the United States and the "second-place" incarceration system in Figure 5.1 (the Russian Federation)

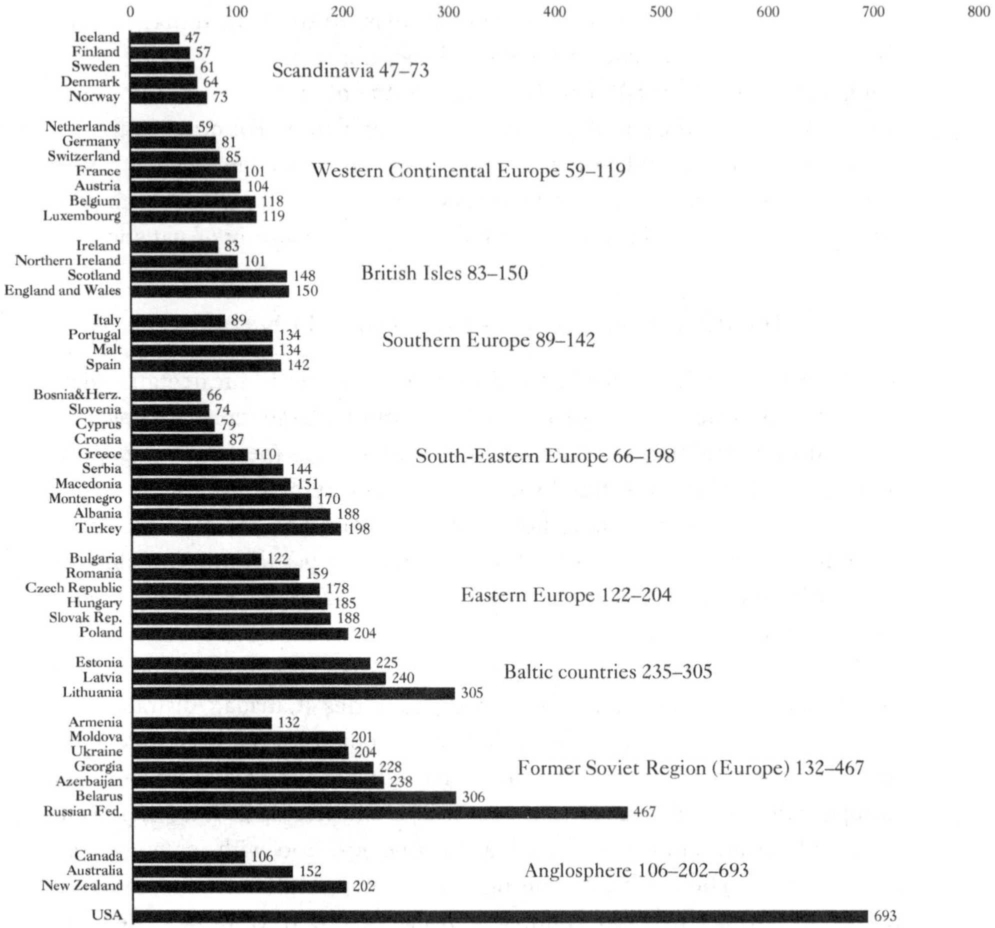

FIGURE 5.1 Incarceration Rates per 100,000 in Europe and the Anglosphere, 2014
Sources: Council of Europe Annual Penal Statistics, Annual Report 2014, Space I (http://wp.unil.ch/space/space-i/annual-reports/); International Centre for Prison Studies (http://www.prisonstudies.org).

is by itself greater than the imprisonment rate of any European country outside the Baltic region.

Prison Trends 1960–2013 in Western Europe, the United States, and the Anglosphere

From 1992 to 2012, comparing data for the top 100 nations on the United Nations Human Development Index (UN HDI), five out of six countries experienced growth in incarceration rates. At the high end, a few countries tripled their incarceration rates over those two decades. A majority increased their rates by at least 50 percent. Only a handful saw decreasing prison rates from

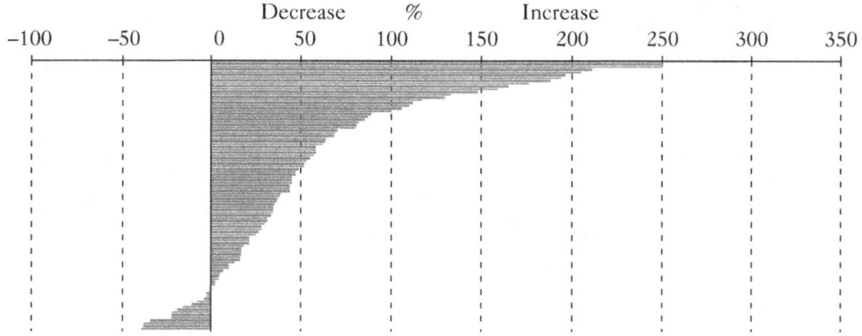

FIGURE 5.2 Percentage Changes in Incarceration Rates in 100 Nations, 1992–2012
Source: Compiled from International Centre for Prison Studies (http://www.prison-studies.org).

1992 to 2012. Figure 5.2 shows the variation in prison-growth experience, without identifying each country, in order to illustrate the wide diversity of national experience.

Figure 5.3 focuses on prison-growth patterns for specific countries, grouped into six regional and cultural clusters.[5] The figure displays incarceration rates from the early 1960s to 2014, thus offering more historical sweep than Figure 5.2. Once again, we see considerable national variation—together with strong evidence of regional patterns.

Within the Nordic cluster, imprisonment rates in Denmark, Sweden, and Norway have remained relatively stable since 1960, with rates bounded between 40 and 70 per 100,000. Finland has followed a different course, proving that "region is not destiny" in prison policy. In 1960, Finland's prison rate exceeded that of any other Scandinavian country by more than a factor of 2. For the next 40 years, while Denmark, Sweden, and Norway experienced modest changes, Finland reduced its prison rate dramatically, from 160 per 100,000 to a little over 60. This is a rare case of a multidecade decline in the use of imprisonment, not seen in other developed societies.[6] By the turn of the century, Finland had "joined" the other Nordic nations and may have settled into regional norms. In the early 2000s all four Nordic countries have experienced a short upward spurt in imprisonment rates, followed by a smooth drop.

Patterns of regional alignment can also be seen in Germany, Austria, and Switzerland, where prisoner rates have remained fairly stable since the 1960s. Germany started from a rate of around 100 per 100,000 in 1962 but experienced two short-term declines, one in the late 1960s and one in the early 1980s. Both periods of decline were followed by a nearly equivalent period of growth. Despite such oscillations, Germany had about the same incarceration rate in 1971, 1992, and 2013. Currently, the three German-speaking countries all have roughly comparable prison rates, within a bandwidth of 75 to 100 per 100,000.

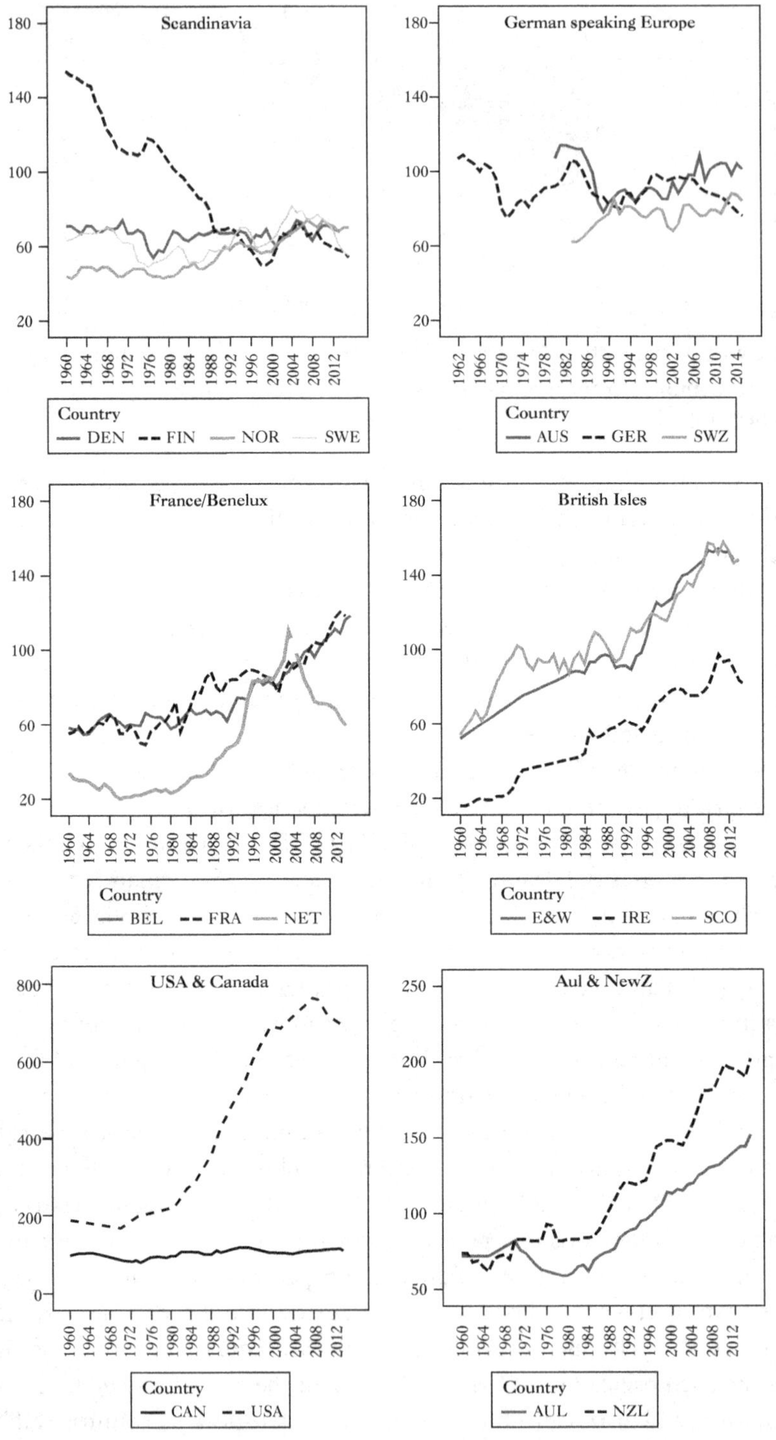

FIGURE 5.3 Incarceration Trends in Western Europe, the United States, and the Anglosphere, Rates per 100,000 1960–2014

The France–Benelux grouping collates prison rates in Belgium, France, and the Netherlands. Over the last 50 years, all three countries have seen a substantial increase in incarceration, although their paths have been somewhat different. France and Belgium witnessed a slow but steady increase from around 60 to 90 or 100 in a period of 50 years. More radical swings in prison policy took place in the Netherlands. After a relatively long period of very low rates (around 20–30 prisoners per 100,000), the Netherlands saw an accelerating pace of growth starting in the 1980s to the early 2000s, peaking at a rate around 110, followed by a sharp decrease back to the level of around 60.[7] Near the turn of the century, Belgium, France, and the Netherlands briefly shared the same rate of incarceration. Since then Belgium and France have continued their smooth, decades-long increases, while rates in the Netherlands lurched sharply upward and then sharply downward. Despite differences in peaks and valleys, the long-term changes in prison practices in these three countries follow a common slope.

The fourth region depicted in Figure 5.3, the British Isles, has seen constant and ongoing increases in prison populations. Over the full 50-year history, there is visible similarity among the three countries displayed. In very recent years, Scotland and Ireland seem to have been able to slow or halt this increase. The curve from England and Wales shows weak tendencies in the same direction.

Outside Europe, New Zealand and Australia both increased their incarceration rates from 1960 to 2013. Since the mid-1980s, New Zealand has tripled its rates from around 70 to 200, and Australia's rates has more than doubled, from 60 to 150. The trend lines in the Oceanic countries closely resemble those of the British Isles, half a world away.

Finally, it must be conceded that North America does not support the theory of regional patterning in incarceration rates. Rather, North America

---

FIGURE 5.3 continued

Sources: Scandinavia: von Hofer et al. (2012) and Kristofferssen (2014).

United States: US Department of Justice, Office of Justice Programs, Bureau of Justice Statistics (http://www.bjs.gov).

Australia and New Zealand: International Centre for Prison Studies (http://www.prisonstudies.org).

Canada: Data provided by Antony Doob (compiled from original sources from Statistics Canada; personal communication May 16, 2016).

All other: 2001–2015, annual reports for Space I (http://wp.unil.ch/space/space-i/annual-reports/); 1995–2000, European Sourcebooks editions II–V (http://wp.unil.ch/europeansourcebook/); earlier data, United Nations World Surveys on Crime Trends and Criminal Justice Systems I–V. (http://www.icpsr.umich.edu/icpsrweb/NACJD/studies/02513) and International Centre for Prison Studies (http://www.prisonstudies.org).

is the home of two outlier nations—and they are outliers in entirely different ways. While the US curve shares an upward slope with many other nations, the amplitude of America's incarceration "explosion" was unparalleled over most of the 50-year history depicted in Figure 5.3 (or in any historical period). Absolute incarceration rates in the United States have become singularly high. Canada, in contrast, is an outlier for its *nonparticipation* in the multijurisdictional thrust toward punitive expansionism from 1960 to 2013. In contrast to all other Anglo-American countries, Canada maintained incarceration rates at a stable level of around 100 per 100,000 across the entire period. "Canadian exceptionalism" from 1960 to 2013 may be just as fruitful an object of study as "American exceptionalism."[8]

The United States and Europe in a State-Level Comparison

There has long been enormous variation in the use of incarceration across different US states (Zimring and Hawkins 1991). Figure 5.4 gives a visual portrait of 2013 incarceration rates disaggregated for all 50 states and adds comparisons with 2013–2015 prison rates in Europe.[9] Including both prisons and

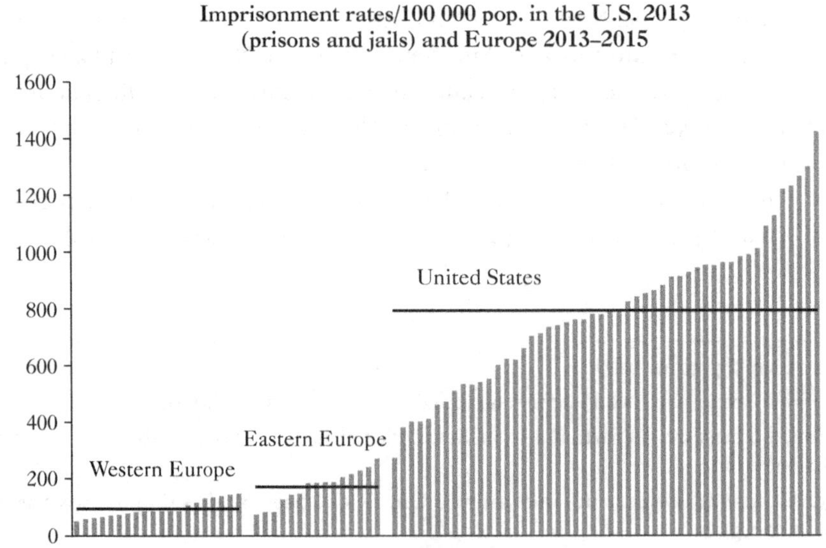

FIGURE 5.4 Imprisonment Rates in Europe and 50 US States

Sources: Aebi, Tiagode, and Burkhardt (2017); Kaeble, Glaze, Tsoutis, and Minton (2015). Rates in the figure are counted relative to total population of all age-groups, for both European and American jurisdictions.

jails, American "incarceration" rates in 2013 ranged from a low of 350 (Maine) to a high of 1,420 (Louisiana). As Franklin Zimring has observed, "these differences between US states are as great as some of the international comparisons" commonly used to establish America's world "leadership" in penal confinement (see Zimring, this volume).

In some ways, Figure 5.4 supports the charge of American exceptionalism in incarceration rates. The figure shows that even the most lenient US states surpassed all European countries in per capita use of confinement. Strikingly, the US figures start roughly from the point where the European ones leave off. It is worth trying to understand why this is so. Just as importantly, it would be useful to know why some US jurisdictions have been more "exceptional" than others.

Crime and Incarceration

One possible explanation for cross-national and cross-state variations in the scale of incarceration is that each jurisdiction must respond to its own unique crime problem. It would be surprising if crime rates were the *sole* driving factor (no human society is that simple), but crime may be one among other important contributors to cross-jurisdictional differences in punitivity (see Gallo, Lacey, and Soskice, this volume; Miller, this volume). This section tests this hypothesis from many angles, using data from a large sample of American and European jurisdictions.[10]

General Remarks

Volume and Policy Effects

Two different types of causal linkages might exist between a society's experience of crime and the size of its prison system. First, crime could influence incarceration rates directly, as a function of its volume. For example, if higher crime rates are translated into rising numbers of arrests, convictions, and sentences, then, all else being equal, incarceration rates will be driven upward by the force of numbers.[11] This can be called a "volume effect." But changes in crime could also create "policy effects" that influence a jurisdiction's incarceration rate. An increase in crime may lead to greater fear of crime in the community, for example, or a general increase in the political salience of crime and punishment (Zimring and Hawkins 1997; Ruth and Reitz 2003; Forman 2012; see Miller, this volume). If such dynamics lead to the adoption of tough anticrime policies, there has been a "policy effect" (Lappi-Seppälä 2011a, 308).

Volume and policy effects are not dependent on the same factors. Upswings in rates of especially serious crimes like homicide or serious sexual assaults can have substantial policy effects, even though they are a tiny fraction of all criminal offending (Zimring and Hawkins 1997). Indeed, punitive policy effects can occur when actual crime volumes are unchanging or in decline. A single high-profile crime can create policy reverberations throughout law enforcement, prosecution, sentencing, and prison-release practices. Volume effects, in contrast, are produced solely by numbers of cases. An upward volume effect can occur even though the crimes on the rise are not especially serious. Meaningful changes in the numbers of basic property offenses, drunk driving, or low-level assaults can have large volume effects on prison populations—and may occur without any notable public discussion.

Studies have found little statistical connection between crime and incarceration rates across jurisdictions. Belief in the absence of a relationship might be called the "disconnectedness" hypothesis. Most commentators (for example, Greenberg 1999; von Hofer 2003; Sutton 2004) tend to agree that prisoner rates are largely unrelated to victimization rates as well as trends in reported crime. These studies, however, have searched foremost for volume effects rooted in objectively measurable changes in crime. They do not purport to investigate policy effects that may bear little or no relationship to crime rates per se.[12]

Data Availability and Reliability

Cross-national comparisons of crime rates are usually based on recorded crime statistics, due in part to the scarcity of survey-based trend data (van Dijk 2008). The problems of official crime statistics are well known and must be noted as a caveat concerning the analysis to follow. Recorded crime covers only a fraction of actual crime, and the fraction varies across crime types and jurisdictions. Units that measure the number of crimes (and offenders) differ across countries. Only lethal violence, measured by mortality statistics, avoids most of these difficulties.[13]

The deficiencies of comparative crime measures are potentially harmful to efforts to observe the policy effects of crime rates on incarceration because each society's direct experience of criminal victimization cannot be accurately determined. The problems of measurement become less serious, however, when we are interested in the impact of crime volume on the use of imprisonment. In that case, it is precisely the detected—not the undetected—crime that is essential.[14]

In recent years, crime surveys conducted by the European Sourcebook group (the fifth edition was published in 2014; see Aebi et al. 2014) have produced comparative data series that have undergone a validation process and have been improved by efforts to harmonize and clarify the applied definitions and concepts. These have been substantial contributions to cross-comparative analyses. They also provide a larger selection of complementing indicators for measuring the levels of crime and the functions of criminal justice.

Crime and Incarceration: Cross-Sectional Snapshots

The scatter graphs in Figure 5.5 test the "connectedness" hypothesis that incarceration rates are related to crime rates, using nation states as the unit of analysis.

The first (bifurcated) chart in Figure 5.5 displays global data from more than 140 countries with populations of more than 500,000, comparing countries' average homicide rates over an eight-year period (2004–2012) with their incarceration rates lagged ahead several years.[15] The chart is bifurcated to display OECD and non-OECD nations separately. For the non-OECD sample, the overall correlation between lethal violence and incarceration is effectively zero. However, when the regression lines are counted separately for OECD countries, there is a strong positive correlation.

This suggests that further analysis is warranted into a possible homicide–incarceration link among developed countries. However, the data are forceful that this linkage is not universal. Moreover, any posited homicide–incarceration relationship cannot adequately explain the extraordinarily high incarceration rate of the United States. While America's nationwide homicide rate places it within the "top" 12 percent of OECD countries, its incarceration rate is roughly three times as high as expected based on the full OECD sample.

The second chart in Figure 5.5 turns away from homicide to test the possibility of a relationship between more "general" crime rates and incarceration policies. The chart is based on crime victim survey data for 10 common crimes from a sample of 29 mostly Western countries, including the United States. Survey data are drawn from the International Crime Victims Survey (ICVS). A comparison of this "general" crime measure with incarceration rates reveals no meaningful correlation at the national level. The United States is visibly an outlier—not for especially high general crime rates—but for its extraordinary high incarceration rate. Higher general crime rates than in the United States are shown, for example, for Denmark, England and Wales, the Netherlands, Switzerland, and New Zealand. Yet none of these "higher-crime" jurisdictions approach the scale of US incarceration; at most, they are modestly distinguishable in their use of imprisonment from "lower-crime" jurisdictions in the 29-nation sample.

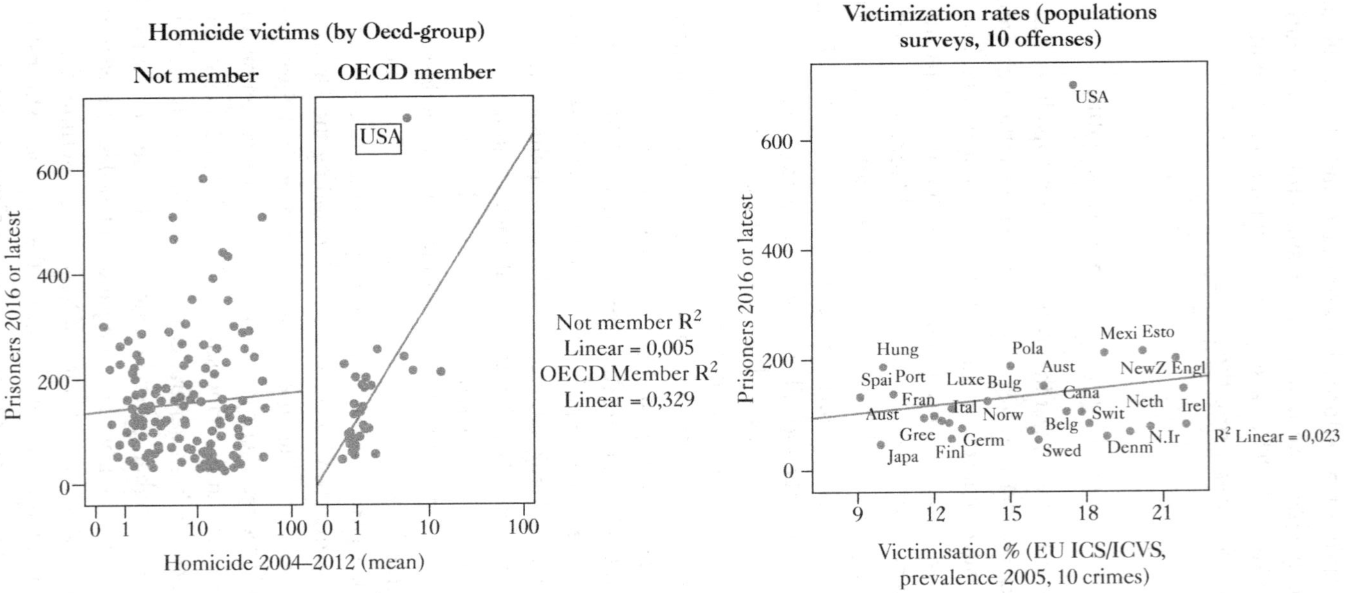

FIGURE 5.5 Incarceration, Reported Crime, and Victimization, per 100,000 population

Sources: Prisoners: International Centre for Prison Studies (http://www.prisonstudies.org).

Victimization: van Dijk (2008).

Homicide: Compiled from Lehti (2013).

The data in Figure 5.5 support the theory of disconnectedness between general-crime volume and incarceration. This comports with earlier research that has failed to find a volume effect linking raw numbers of criminal acts with imprisonment scale. On the other hand, the strong association between homicide and incarceration rates in the OECD sample suggests a policy–effect linkage that operates in some settings, although discernible across non-OECD nations. If we were to draw conclusions from Figure 5.5 alone, we might say that there is no visible evidence of volume-driven connectedness and that the evidence is mixed with respect to policy-driven connectedness.

Figure 5.6 shifts focus from nation states to individual states within the United States.[16] Here, the message is somewhat different. The first chart in Figure 5.6 compares homicide rates and incarceration rates for all 50 states (counting prisons and jails) and shows a substantial positive correlation between the two (R^2 = .556). The second chart compares total violent and property crimes (per the Uniform Crime Reports) with incarceration rates in every state and finds a weaker—but still positive and substantial—correlation (R^2 = .391). In contrast with Figure 5.5, a construct of "general" crime for individual US states is a fair predictor of prison rates.

These results (joining the findings for OECD countries in Figure 5.5) raise the possibility that high homicide rates might generate policy effects that extend to the punishment of crimes other than murder.[17] Such policy effects might occur, for example, because the better-informed members of the public are frightened by troubling homicide statistics, because murders receive more—and more prurient—media coverage than other offenses, or because citizens' life experiences are more often touched by homicides or near-lethal assaults among friends, family members, neighbors, coworkers, and acquaintances. As Randolph Roth (see Chapter 6) has pointed out, a constant homicide rate of 9 per 100,000 inhabitants—the rate that persisted in the United States for most of the twentieth century—means that, on average, 1 of every 141 children born on a given day will be murdered at some point.

With respect to volume effects (not supported by Figure 5.5), Figure 5.6 makes it difficult to rule out the possibility that differences in rates of reported "general" crime are partly responsible for variations in incarceration rates among the 50 US states. However, the correlations shown in Figure 5.6 do not establish causation. It could be that higher rates of incarceration cause higher rates of general crime (Useem and Morrison Piehl 2008) or that some third factor drives up both general crime and incarceration (Lacey and Soskice, this volume). We cannot be confident that higher levels of crime are an important cause of higher confinement rates, and the static data in Figure 5.6 say

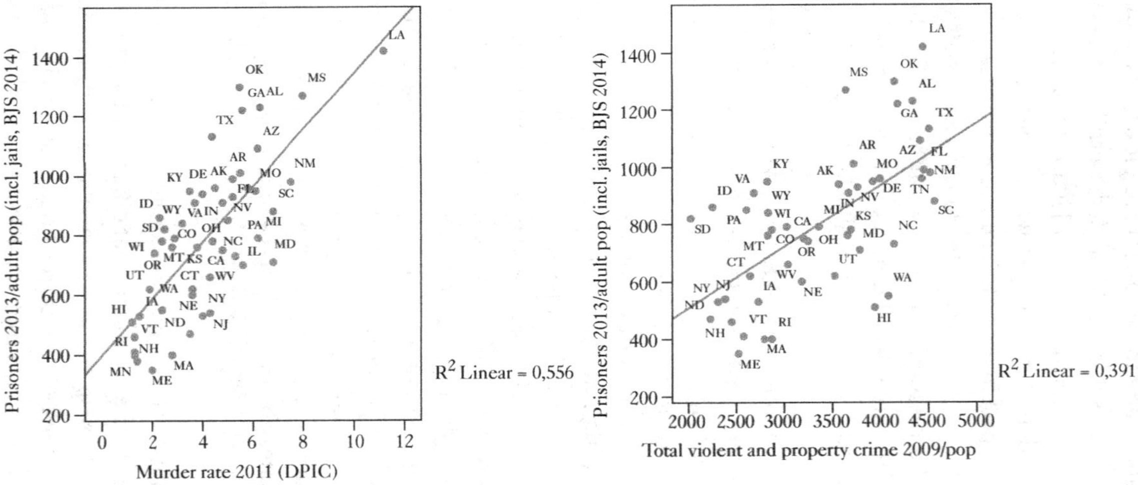

FIGURE 5.6 Crime and Incarceration, US States, per 100,000 population

Sources: Prisoners: Glaze and Kaeble (2014) (http://www.bjs.gov/content/pub/pdf/cpus13.pdf).

Violent and property crime: FBI (https://www.fbi.gov/stats-services/crimestats).

Murder: FBI (https://www.fbi.gov/about-us/cjis/ucr/crime-in-the-u.s/2011/crime-in-the-u.s.-2011/tables/table-4).

nothing about whether increases or decreases in incarceration rates have been associated with changes in crime—a subject that will be addressed in the following section.

Levels and Changes in Lethal Violence and Incarceration: Correlational Analyses

Table 5.1 investigates the relationship between incremental changes in homicide rates and incarceration rates over three time spans in 34 OECD countries and 50 US states. The time periods for the OECD countries are 1960–1991, 1992–2000, and 2001–2013; and those for the 50 US states are 1977–1991, 1992–2000, and 2001–2010. Correlations are counted between annual changes, not between absolute values. We examine whether year-by-year changes (first differences) in homicide and incarceration move in tandem.[18]

Since the hypothesis is that changes in crime rates are reflected in subsequent changes in prisoner rates, we need also to decide the assumed time lag during which this effect should take place. In the following we use one-year and four-year time lags. Thus, Table 5.1 tests whether a change in a jurisdiction's homicide rate in year (x) is associated with a change in confinement rate in year ($x + 1$) or year ($x + 4$).

Correlations in the upper part of Table 5.1 (one-year lag) are weak and nonsignificant, with two exceptions. In 1992–2000, changes in crime rates and imprisonment rates pointed in different directions in the OECD countries (correlation –.140). In 2001–2010 both were pointing in the same direction in the US states (correlation .106). The correlations in the lower part (four-year lag) are also predominantly insignificant, with one exception. In 1992–2000 changes in homicide and incarceration rates were pointing in the same direction in the United States with a moderately strong correlation (.178).[19]

The two strongest correlations point in the opposite direction and are from different samples but from the same period 1992–2000 (OECD with one-year lag and the United States with four-year lag). Profiles for both are illustrated in a scatter form in Figure 5.7.

Difference analyses give only partial and (at best) weak support for the connectedness hypotheses.[20] This remains true despite the fact that high incarceration rates correlate strongly and positively with high homicide rates in a cross-sectional US snapshot above (see Figure 5.6). The failure to find lagged effects over one year or four years does not rule out the existence of diffuse connections that play out over decades rather than years—but theories of this kind take us into speculative territory that can neither be proven nor falsified by the statistical tools employed here.

Table 5.1 Correlations between Annual Changes (First Differences) in Homicide Rates and Changes in Imprisonment Rates 1960–2013 (OECD) and 1977–2010 (US States)

	OECD			50 US States		
Homicide lagged 1 year	Period	Correlation	Significance	Period	Correlation	Significance
	1960–1991	.061	(.154)	1977–1991	.004	(.928)
	1992–2000	−.140*	(.023)	1992–2000	−.043	(.367)
	2001–2013	−.008	(.875)	2001–2010	.106*	(.019)
Homicide lagged 4 years						
	1960–1991	.050	(.262)	1977–1991	.004	(.921)
	1992–2000	.056	(.366)	1992–2000	.178*	(.000)
	2001–2013	−.012	(.816)	2001–2010	−.033	(.470)

*Correlation is significant at the .05 level (two-tailed).

OECD, Organisation for Economic Co-operation and Development.

Sources: Prisoners: Institute for Criminal Policy Research (http://www.prisonstudies.org).

Victimization: van Dijk (2008).

Homicide: Compiled from Lehti (2013).

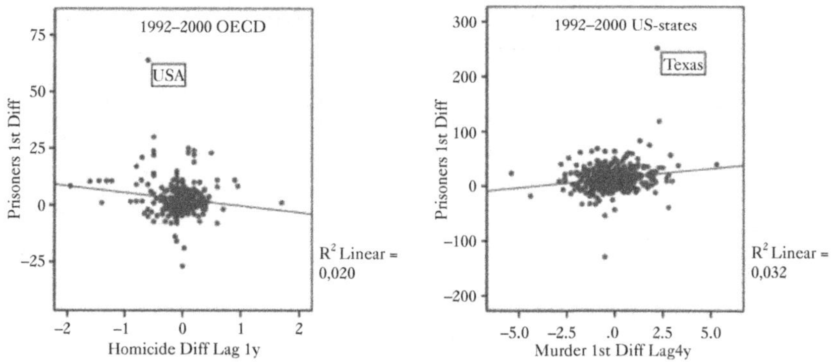

FIGURE 5.7 Correlations between Annual Changes (First Differences) in Homicide Rates and Changes in Imprisonment Rates in 1992–2000 in Organisation for Economic Co-operation and Development Countries (Homicide Lagged by 1 Year) and in US States (Homicide Lagged by 4 Years), per 100,000 population

Sources: Prisoners: International Centre for Prison Studies (http://www.prisonstudies.org).
Victimization: van Dijk (2008).
Homicide: Compiled from Lehti (2013).

Crime Trends and Prison Trends

Comparing Overall Crime Trends

If there were a connectedness between reported general crime rates and prison rates across human societies, one would assume that jurisdictions with similar crime trends would exhibit similar incarceration trends. However, it is easy to find illustrations that this has not been the case. Figure 5.8 includes three rows of charts; each row compares countries with similar general crime trends from 1960 to 2010 (shown in the chart on the left), while also showing those countries' incarceration trends over the same period (in the chart on the right).

The first pair of charts juxtaposes crime and imprisonment in England and Wales, Finland, and the three Nordic countries (Denmark, Sweden, and Norway). Over five decades, the crime rates of all these jurisdictions seem to follow the same pattern—mostly up from 1960 through the early 1990s, then modest overall declines to 2010. Their incarceration trend lines, however, have almost nothing in common—suggesting that almost any prison policy is possible despite parallel experiences of crime. In Finland from 1960 to 2010, incarceration rates dropped in most years, resulting in an overall picture of dramatic decline. In England and Wales, we see roughly the opposite trajectory: prison rates were going up in most years from 1960 to 2010 just as steeply as those in Finland were dropping.[21] Indeed, over

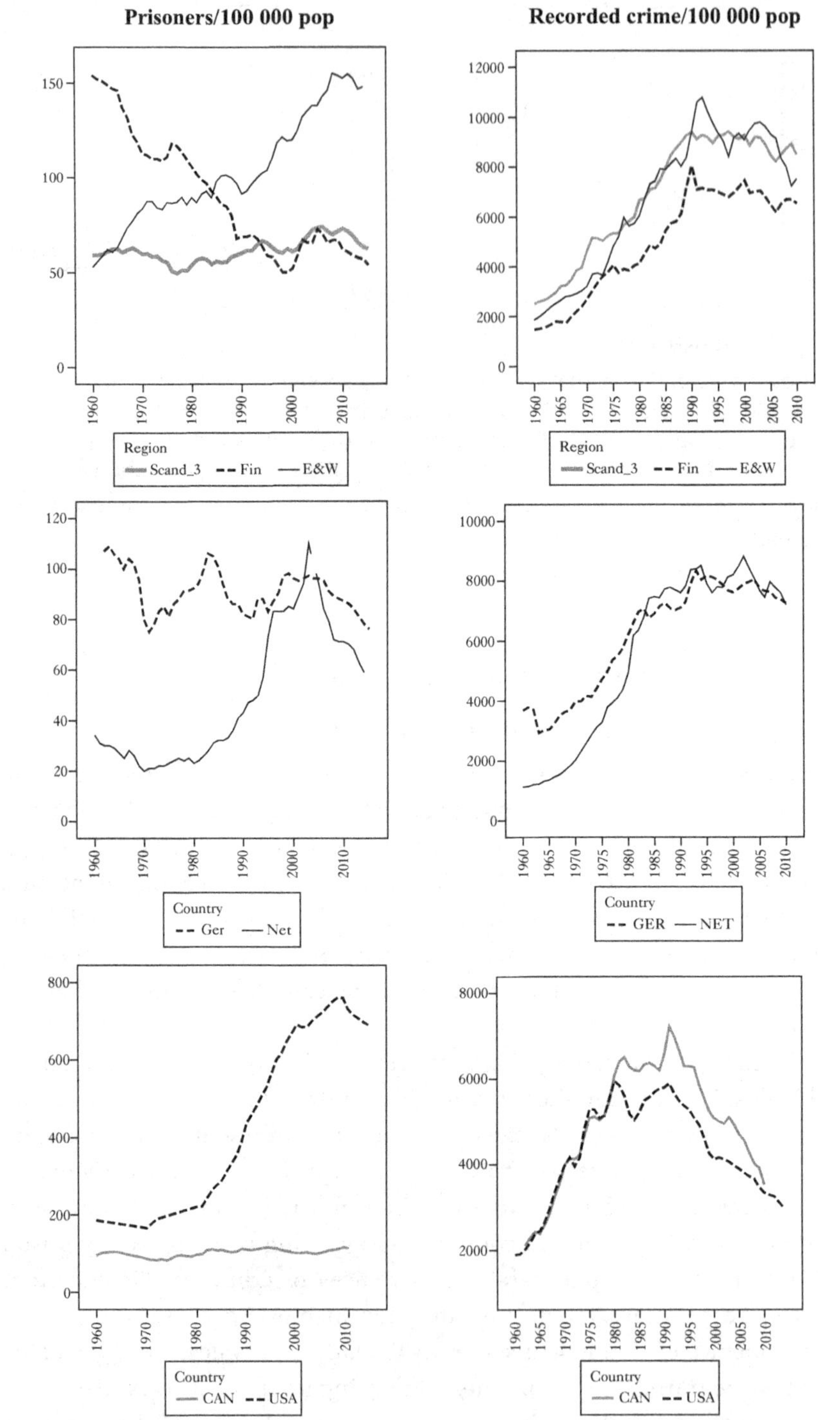

FIGURE 5.8 Imprisonment Rates and Recorded Crime Rates, 1960–2010: England and Wales and the Nordic Countries, Germany and the Netherlands, the United States and Canada, per 100,000 population

the full 50 years, the two countries "switched places" at or near the top of European prison rates. And in the Scandinavian nations, we see a third long-term slope in incarceration practice: their 50-year history has been one of relative stability.

The second and third rows of Figure 5.8 feature more illustrations of apparent disconnectedness between crime and imprisonment trends. Germany and the Netherlands have pursued entirely different prison policies despite parallels in their general crime rates over five decades. The most striking comparison is found between the United States and Canada, noted earlier. The total property and violent crime curves for the two neighboring countries are similar, yet there are stark differences in prison trends (see also Webster and Doob, this volume).

Figure 5.8 is corroborative of our earlier supposition that general crime rates—and volume effects arising from movement in those rates—do not seem to bear much relationship to nations' uses of incarceration. We focus our next longitudinal inquiries on the crime of homicide—the most accurately recorded of all offenses.

FIGURE 5.8 continued

Sources for crime data: Scandinavia: Offenses against the criminal code (minor traffic offenses excluded, drunk driving included). von Hofer et al (2012).

Germany and the Netherlands, all offenses (minor traffic offenses not included): 1960–1994, United Nations World Surveys on Crime Trends and Criminal Justice Systems; 1995–2014, European Sourcebook.

England and Wales: all offenses (motoring offenses not included): (http://webarchive.nationalarchives.gov.uk/20160105160709/; https://www.gov.uk/government/statistics/historical-crime-data)

Canada: All violent and property index offenses: crime 1962–2003 Canadian Crime Statistics 2003, Canadian Centre for Justice Statistics, catalogue no. 85-205-XIE (http://publications.gc.ca/Collection-R/Statcan/85-205-XIE/0000385-205-XIE.pdf). Police-reported crime statistics in Canada 2012 by Samuel Perreault Canadian Centre for Justice Statistics, released on July 25, 2013. Component of Statistics Canada, catalogue no. 85-002-X. (http://www.statcan.gc.ca/pub/85-002-x/2013001/article/11854-eng.pdf). Data for the period 1962–2010 are based on the first Uniform Crime Reporting Survey classifications. See for recent data (http://www23.statcan.gc.ca/imdb/p2SV.pl?Function=getSurvey&SDDS=3302&lang=en&db=imdb&adm=8&dis=2#a2).

United States: All violent and property index offenses: FBI Uniform Crime Reporting figures (https://www.fbi.gov/stats-services/crimestats; http://www.disastercenter.com/crime/uscrime.htm).

For sources for imprisonment data, see the sources in figure.

Trends in Homicide and Incarceration: Nation States

Homicide rates since the 1960s in well-developed industrialized countries have followed a fairly consistent overall pattern: homicide generally increased from 1960 to around 1990 and then fell into an equally regular decline, continuing to the present (Lappi-Seppälä and Lehti 2015). However, incarceration trends from nation to nation have shown a great deal of variation. Figures 5.9 through 5.13 offer a host of single-country case studies from 1960 to 2010 and yield little evidence of a connection between trends in homicide and incarceration. Given roughly similar homicide curves over half a century, we see examples of prison rates going up, going down, remaining steady, and zigzagging inexplicably.

Figure 5.9 gives two examples: New Zealand and England and Wales, with marked increases in incarceration rates over the entire period. Homicide rates and prison rates appear to increase together from 1960 until sometime in the 1990s or early 2000s, but afterward incarceration continues to rise as before—even though homicide has turned significantly downward.

Figure 5.10 includes Germany and Denmark, where prison rates fluctuate quite a bit but with no apparent connection to changes in homicide rates and no common pattern.

In some countries, periods of declining incarceration have coincided with drops in homicide rates. This is the case for Finland (since the mid-1970s) and for Japan from 1960 to 2000, as shown in shown in Figure 5.11.

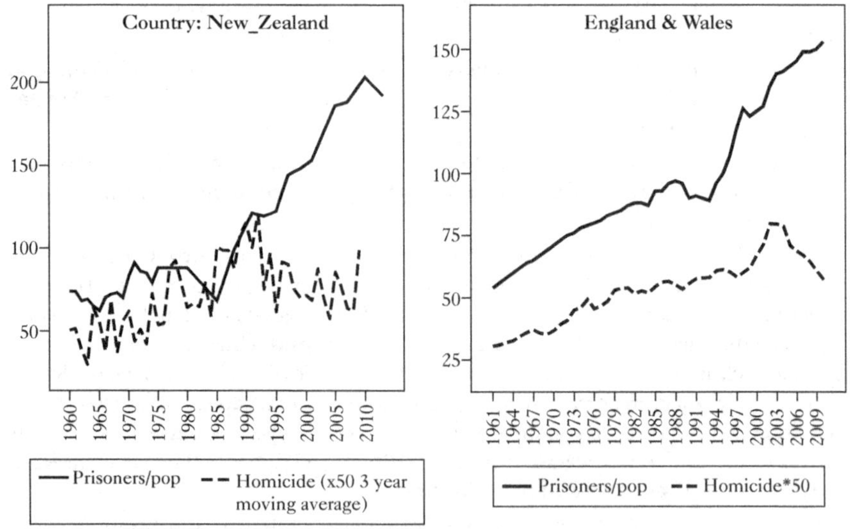

FIGURE 5.9 Homicide and Incarceration Going Together, Then Departing: New Zealand and England and Wales, 1960–2010, per 100,000 population

Sources: For prisoners, see Figure 5.3. Homicide data from Lehti (2013).

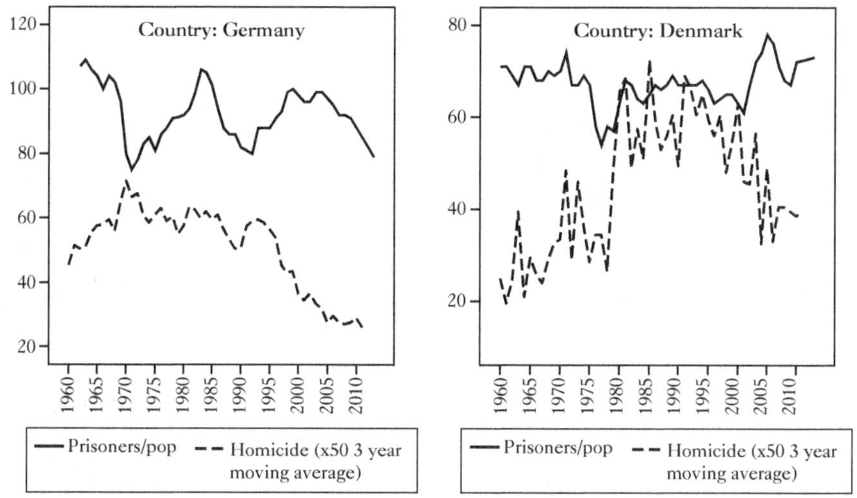

FIGURE 5.10 Homicide and Incarceration Zigzagging Without Clear Trend: Germany and Denmark, 1960–2010, per 100,000 population

Sources: For prisoners, see Figure 5.3. Homicide data from Lehti (2013).

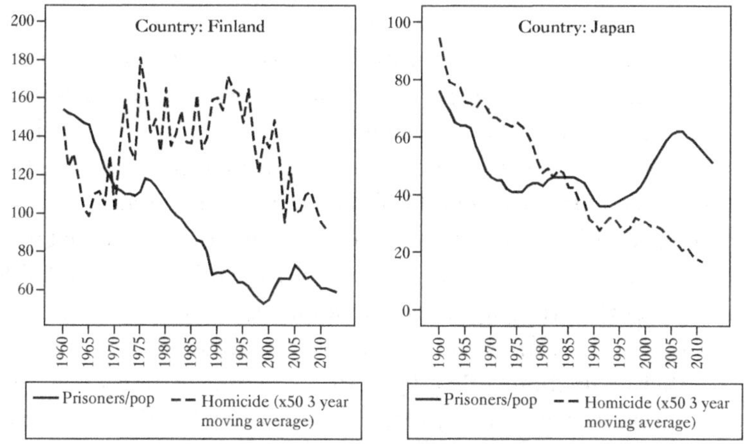

FIGURE 5.11 Homicide and Incarceration (Mostly) Going Down Together: Finland and Japan, 1960–2010, per 100,000 population

Sources: For prisoners, see Figure 5.3. Homicide data from Lehti (2013).

The comparison in Figure 5.12 covers two countries that have undergone deep political transformations. In these jurisdictions, we see higher scales for both homicide and imprisonment—and more radical changes. In Belarus (as in most former Soviet countries), there is an apparent "fit" between lethal violence and imprisonment. However, this is not the case with Estonia.

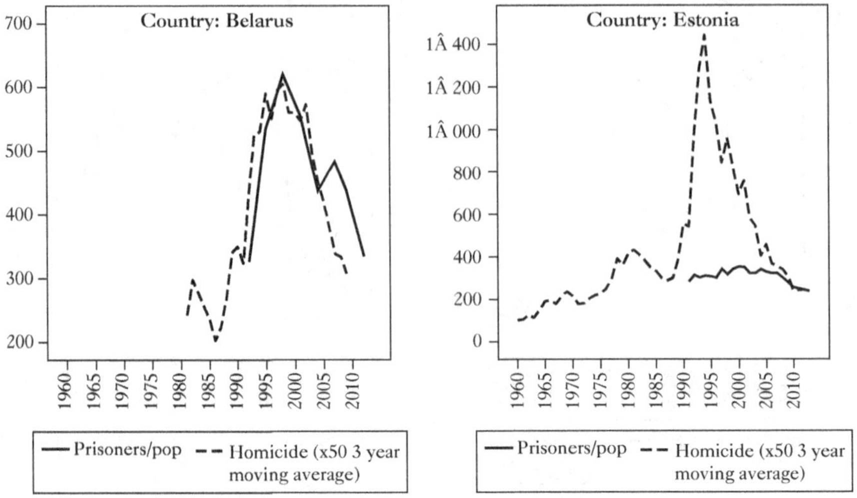

FIGURE 5.12 Radical Peaks and Drops in Homicide, Incarceration, or Both: Belarus and Estonia, Different Time Periods, per 100,000 population

Sources: For prisoners, see Figure 5.3. Homicide data from Lehti (2013).

Last, Figure 5.13 compares the homicide–incarceration profiles of the United States and Canada from 1960 to 2010. The message remains the same as in the previous comparison between those countries (see Figure 5.8). Homicide trends strongly resemble each other across much of the period: lethal violence increased twofold to threefold from 1960 to the mid-1970s. After that followed a period with two "humps" in homicide rates in the early 1980s and early 1990s. There are some differences here in that the three peaks in Canadian homicide incline downward, while in the United States they all "top out" at roughly the same level. Also, the American homicide rates are roughly three times the Canadian rates throughout the period examined. Another distinction is that, by 2010, US homicide levels had returned to the lower levels of the early 1960s, while Canadian homicide rates had not dropped quite so far and stood where they were in the early 1970s.

These differences in homicide trends are overshadowed, however, by the greater differences in incarceration in Canada and the United States. American incarceration rates declined somewhat from 1960 to the early 1970s, while murder rates almost tripled. In Canada there is also a downward trend in incarceration during a period of greatly increasing homicide but in 1965–1975, a little later than in the United States. Afterward, the United States entered a sustained period of incarceration growth, uninterrupted from 1972 until 2009. From the mid-1980s until 2000, one might call this an incarceration "explosion." It is important to note that the period of dramatic prison

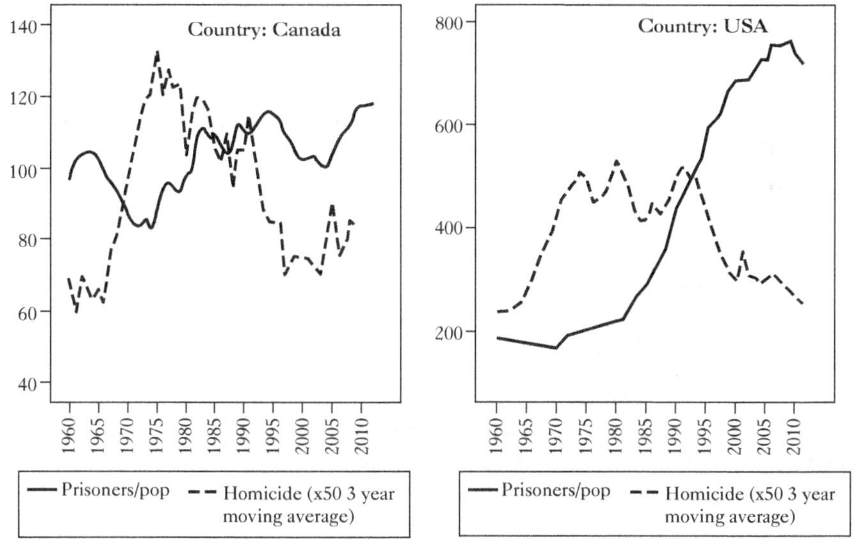

FIGURE 5.13 Similar Crime Profiles but Radically Different Incarceration Profiles, Canada and the United States, 1960–2010, per 100,000 population
Sources: For prisoners, see Figure 5.3. Homicide data from Lehti (2013).

growth in the United States overlapped times of increasing—*and decreasing*—homicide rates. The United States might be cited as "exhibit A" for the proposition that homicide and incarceration rates do not move in tandem.

Canadian imprisonment rates, in contrast, remained relatively stable, around the same level of 100 to 120 prisoners per 100,000, with upswings and downswings. While the US incarceration rate in the 2000s was nearly four times that of 1960, the oscillating Canadian rates never amounted to uninterrupted, let alone "explosive," growth. Canadian imprisonment rates of the 1960s were seen again in the 1980s, 1990s, and 2000s. Overall, Canadian homicide rates were in decline from the mid-1970s through the early 2000s, yet Canadian prison rates oscillated without any apparent relationship to lethal violence.

Another way of analyzing the relationship between crime and incarceration over time is to superimpose a temporal dimension onto a traditional two-dimensional scatter diagram (see von Hofer and Lappi-Seppälä 2014, app. 2). The "Phillips-type" curve in Figure 5.14 gives an overview of how the relation between American and Canadian murder and incarceration rates evolved from 1960 to 2010 and in what direction. This analysis is conducted separately for the United States (left; prisons plus jails) and Canada (right).

A straightforward connection between rising homicide and rising imprisonment would appear on the Phillips curve as a line sloping upward as it

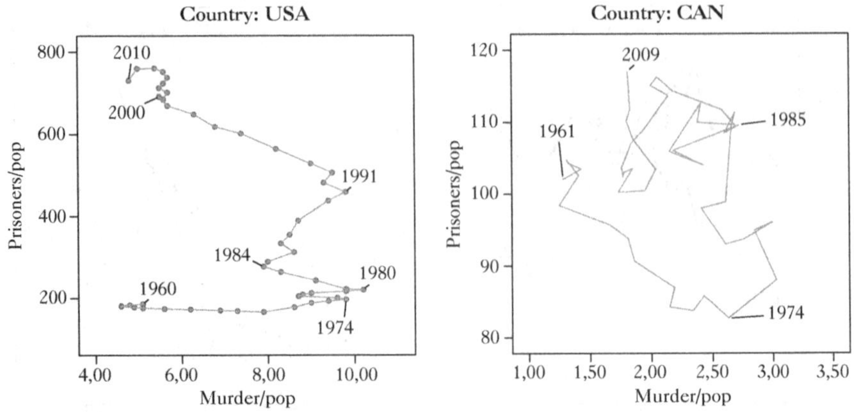

FIGURE 5.14 Changes in Homicide and Incarceration in Canada and the United States, 1960–2010 (Phillips-Type Curve), per 100,000 population
Sources: See sources in Figure 5.3.

moves from left to right (such as in the United States in most years from 1984 to 1991 or in Canada from 1974 to 1975). For lines moving right to left, connectedness theory would predict a downward slope (as in the United States from 2009 to 2010 or in Canada from 1997 to 1999). In Figure 5.13, for both countries, the trend lines defy these expectations more often than they satisfy them.

US incarceration levels fell somewhat through the 1960s, then rose modestly during the early 1970s, never exceeding a rate of 200 per 100,000. Meanwhile, the murder rate more than doubled, from 4.6 to 10. Afterward, the American murder rate followed a switchback pattern, reversing directions in 1974, 1976, 1980, 1984, and the early 1990s. Incarceration rates from 1972 through 2009 increased regardless of the direction in which homicide rates were moving. If incarceration were directly connected with homicide, there should have been a more or less steady increase in incarceration throughout the 1960s and into the 1990s (but interrupted in the early 1980s). After 1992 or so, prisoner rates should have taken a sustained downward curve. Altogether, the Phillips curve for the United States moves in the "wrong" direction for two-thirds of the period covered by Figure 5.14 (1960–1972, 1980–1984, 1992–2009).

However, this may still leave open the possibility of "lagged policy effects." Perhaps it took more than 10 years for American political systems to react to the crime surge of the 1960s. Once the reaction occurred, it may have been sustained by consistently high homicide rates (between 8 and 10 per 100,000) and consistently high violent crime of other kinds, which did not return to early-1960s levels until the 2000s.[22] And perhaps there was a 17-year delay between the steep downturn in homicide, which began in the early 1990s, and the "policy effects" of eventual flattening and modest declines in national incarceration rates.

If this was the case for the United States, it was not replicated to the north. In Canada, incarceration rates came down as homicide was increasing (1961 to mid-1970s). After that, homicide rates remained stable, but imprisonment rates were increasing (1974–1985). From there on, both have oscillated without apparent rhyme or reason. Any theory of lagged policy effects in American incarceration must explain why Canada, which experienced similar crime trends (albeit absolute homicide rates at one-third the US levels), followed such a different course (Webster and Doob, this volume).

Comparing US States

All American states have increased their imprisonment rates since the 1970s but not in lockstep.[23] From 1977 to 2010, the steepest increase took place in Louisiana, where the imprisonment rate grew from around 170 to 870 per 100,000 population. This represents growth of 420 percent—or absolute growth of 710 inmates per 100,000 population. At the other end of the spectrum, incarceration rates in Maine increased "only" from around 60 to 150 (150 percent, or 90 inmates per 100,000 population).[24]

COMPARING "HIGH RISERS" AND "LOW RISERS"

One way of testing the connectedness hypothesis is to compare developments in crime and incarceration among two groups of American states: those that experienced the most incarceration growth from 1977 to 2010 ("high risers") versus those with the least growth ("low risers").

Counterintuitively, it is no simple matter to produce such rankings. The most common approach for the quantification of prison growth, expressed as a single value, has been to calculate the percentage growth in prison rates over a specified period of time. Thus, growth in prison rates from 50 to 75 per 100,000 residents is stated as a 50 percent increase, as is growth from 200 to 300 (see Zimring, this volume). Some researchers have preferred an alternative measure, focused on the absolute change in incarceration rates over time (American Law Institute 2011, 150–54; Reitz 2006, 1796–97). With this method, change from 50 to 75 is expressed as the addition of 25 prisoners per 100,000 residents; change from 200 to 300 is an incremental change in the incarceration rate of 100 per 100,000.

The use of one measure versus another makes an enormous difference. Under the percentage measure, the two hypothetical jurisdictions above would be said to have had the same "amount" of prison growth and would be ranked in identical positions in a multistate array of high and low risers. Under the incremental approach, the second jurisdiction would be assigned a per capita prison-growth value that is four times the prison growth of the first—so that their relative positions on a multistate continuum would be far apart.

Webster and Doob (Chapter 3) distinguish these two measures as the "ratio" approach versus the "absolute-change" approach. They consider the absolute-change approach to be more useful in longitudinal evaluations of incarceration rates, while Zimring (Chapter 4) argues for the superiority of the ratio approach. Without attempting to adjudicate the disagreement, the main point to be made here is that the choice of statistical descriptors of prison growth matters a great deal. Both measures have their benefits, and neither should be used with blind confidence.

Using the alternative sampling methods, Figure 5.15 examines whether the crime curves in high risers and low risers evolved in a similar manner. The charts display average changes in incarceration rates among the 10 low-riser states from 1977 to 2010 together with average changes in their rates of homicide, violent crime, and property crime. The top two charts in Figure 5.14 include states selected by absolute-change ranking, while the lower two charts include states ranked by percentage growth in prison rates.

The following analyzes the histories of the 10 highest-growth and 10 lowest-growth states in America from 1977 to 2010, selected according to absolute change in prison rates. These are the states with the most and the least per capita prison growth from 1977 to 2010.[25] The highest-rising state, identified by this method, is Louisiana, with an imprisonment rate of 152 per 100,000 in 1977, which rose to 867 in 2010 (+715, +470 percent growth). The lowest-rising state was Maine, which saw changes in prison rates from 61 to 148 (+87, +143 percent).[26]

Prison Growth—Comparing high risers with low risers, we see the same directionality of prison-rate change across the entire 33-year period: nearly always upward. This is not surprising. All 50 states participated in this trend. However, we see large differences in the pace and sheer magnitude of prison growth: while low-riser states increased their imprisonment rates—averaged for the whole group—from 84 to 239 per 100,000 (absolute change of +155, "ratio" change of +185 percent), the high-risers increased their rates from 114 to 600 (absolute change of +486, "ratio" change of +426 percent). The high risers started out in 1977 with an average prison rate 25 percent higher than the low risers and ended with a rate that was 109 percent higher in 2010. The spread between high- and low-riser prison rates was 30 per

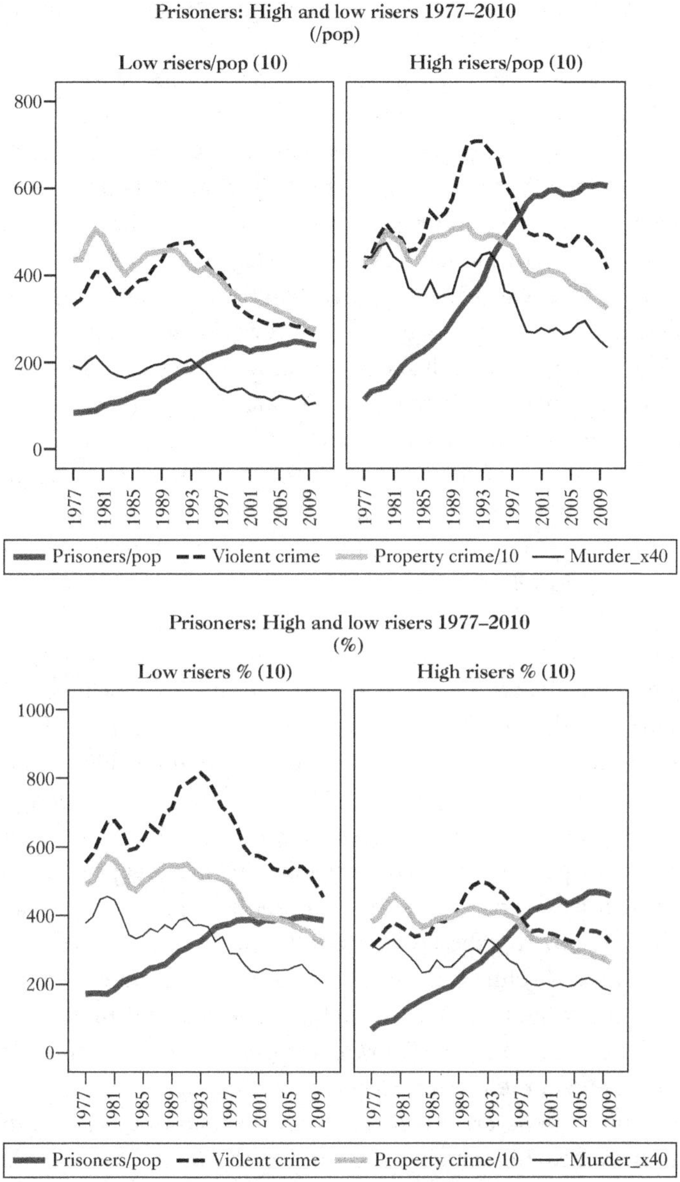

FIGURE 5.15 Comparison of Incarceration and Crime Rates, 10 High–Prison Growth and 10 Low–Prison Growth US States, 1977–2010, per 100,000 population

Sources: Prisoners: Glaze and Kaeble (2014) (http://www.bjs.gov/content/pub/pdf/cpus13.pdf).

Violent and property crime: FBI (https://www.fbi.gov/stats-services/crimestats).

Murder: FBI, (https://www.fbi.gov/about-us/cjis/ucr/crime-in-the-u.s/2011/crime-in-the-u.s.-2011/tables/table-4).

100,000 in 1977 and expanded to a difference of 361 per 100,000 in 2010—a 12-fold increase.

It is also informative to compare our 20 sample states with national (weighted) average changes in prison use. In 1977, the average prison rate among low risers was 28 percent lower than the national average rate among all states combined (84/116), while the high risers started out almost exactly at the national mean (114/116). By 2010, the prison rate in low-rising states was 46 percent lower than the national average (239/442); and among high risers, prison rates were 36 percent higher than the national average (600/442). In absolute change, low risers grew by 171 fewer prisoners per 100,000 than the national average across all states (155/326), while high risers grew by 160 more prisoners per 100,000 than the national average (486/326) (Flanagan and Maguire 1991, table 6.56; Guerino, Harrison, and Sabol 2011, app. table 9).

In sum, the slopes of prison-growth curves for high risers versus low risers are markedly different. Visually in Figure 5.14 (top row), prison growth was far more "explosive" in the high-rising states after 1977, until growth for both groups began to flatten in the 2000s.

Homicide—From 1977 to 2010, the directionality of homicide trends was similar in high- and low-rising states. For both groups of states, peak homicide rates occurred in the early 1980s, followed by several years of decline and then a second, lower peak in the early 1990s. Since then, homicide rates have been stable or declining for both groups. Over the entire period, homicide rates declined by 48 percent in high-riser states and 44 percent in low-rising states. Viewed from the perspective of connectedness theory, it appears that even vast divergences in prison-rate trend lines cannot be explained by notable differences in the year-by-year directionality of homicide-rate trends.[27]

However, the absolute scale of homicide rates was much greater in high risers throughout the period. Average homicide rates for high risers in 1977 were more than double those for low risers (11.1/4.8) and remained more than double at the end of the 33-year period in 2010 (5.3/2.1).

These observations are consistent with a version of connectedness theory: that sustained higher absolute rates of homicide are associated with higher prison rates and faster prison growth.[28] If so, it is the area between homicide-rate curves that matters when predicting incarceration practices across jurisdictions, not year-by-year similarities or dissimilarities in the slopes of homicide trend lines.

Violent Crime—In 1977, the average violent-crime rate among low risers was 79 percent the average rate among high risers (331/417). As with homicide, the directionality of violent-crime trend lines through 2010 is similar for both groups. However, the high-riser states experienced much steeper absolute increases in the late 1980s and early 1990s (+300 per 100,000) than low risers (+130) and much steeper violent-crime drops thereafter (–300 versus –170). The endpoint in violent-crime rates is also higher for the high-riser states (416) than for low risers (291). Overall, violent-crime rates for high risers began and ended in the same place, 1977–2010. For low risers, violent crime was 12 percent lower in 2010 than in 1977.

For low risers, violent crime remained below 500 per 100,000 throughout the period. Nonetheless, violent-crime rates doubled between 1977 and 1991, while imprisonment rates also doubled (84 to 180). From 1991 to 2010, violent crime dropped back below its 1977 levels but imprisonment rates continued to climb (180 to 239). For high risers, violent-crime rates rose quickly above 500 and remained there through almost the whole period. As with low risers, high risers' average prison population rate increased during times of growing violent crime, as well as times of steep declines.

As with homicide, these findings suggest that the area between violent-crime curves may help sort high- and low-prison-growth states, while similarities or differences in the slopes of violent-crime curves has no predictive power.

Property Crime—Property-crime trends among high- and low-riser states are closely similar for the groups selected by absolute change in prison rates. The low risers had a nominally higher average starting point in 1977 (4350/4300) and a somewhat lower endpoint in 2010 (2700/3200). Combining these observations, low risers had a somewhat greater drop in property-crime rates over the full period (–1,650 per 100,000, –38 percent) than high risers (–1,100, –26 percent). With respect to the connectedness hypothesis, these findings suggest that near-identical property-crime curves (in directionality and absolute levels) have no predictive value concerning the amount or speed of prison growth experienced in different jurisdictions. If crime rates have anything to do with state-by-state incarceration levels, the effect would seem to be limited to violent offenses.

Low risers selected by the percentage-change method are notable for their relatively high prison rates in 1977. Since prisoner rates were already high, there may have been less need—and less room—for a stronger increase. States with originally smaller penal populations, on the other hand, could reach high percentage changes more easily, with less money and fewer investments. It is easier and cheaper to double prison capacity from a level of 100 than from a level of 300.

COMPARING INDIVIDUAL STATES

Evidence of disconnectedness between crime and incarceration rates may also be gathered through comparison of the particular histories of selected states. It is easy to find states with similar crime profiles (in terms of both trends and levels) but markedly different prison profiles.

Looking first to rates of index crime and incarceration, Figure 5.16 presents two pairwise comparisons of states with similar histories of overall crime from 1977 to 2010 but different trajectories of incarceration policy. In the first pairing of states, we see that index crime in Missouri declined from around 550 per 100,000 to about 400 over a 33-year period and that incarceration rates grew from 100 to 500—a growth increment of 400 per 100,000 (+400 percent).

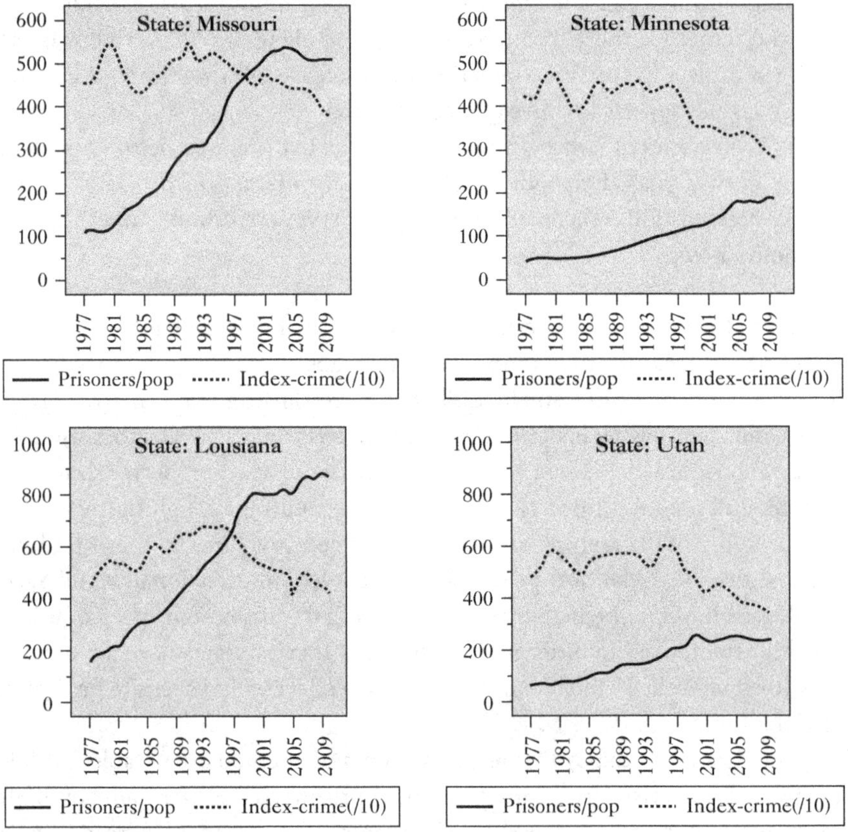

FIGURE 5.16 Incarceration and Index Crime, 1977–2010: Missouri versus Minnesota, Louisiana versus Utah, per 100,000 population

Sources: Prisoners: Glaze and Kaeble (2014) (http://www.bjs.gov/content/pub/pdf/cpus13.pdf).

Index crime: FBI (https://www.fbi.gov/stats-services/crimestats).

In Minnesota, index crime fell from around 450 to 300 but incarceration rates grew from 50 to a little below 200—a growth increment of 150 (+300 percent).

In the second row of Figure 5.16, high-imprisonment state Louisiana is compared with the much lower-incarceration state of Utah. Both states had a stable or slightly increasing crime rates from 1977 to the early or mid-1990s, followed by relative steady dropoffs for the remainder of the period. In Louisiana, however, imprisonment rates skyrocketed from 111 to 540 (+387 percent, +429 inmates per 100,000 population). In Utah, despite its similar crime profile, incarceration rates grew from about 64 to only 238 (+272 percent, +174 inmates per 100,000).

To address doubts about the accuracy of index crime statistics over time, the same exercise can be performed with homicide-rate curves. Pairwise comparisons among states with similar homicide trends yield examples of wildly varying incarceration curves. In the first row of Figure 5.17, Idaho and Maine are both seen to have fairly smoothly declining murder rates from 1977 to 2010 but strikingly different incarceration profiles. While Idaho lifted its prisoner rate from 87 to 474, incarceration rates in Maine increased only from around 61 to little over 148.

In the second row of Figure 5.17, we see that West Virginia had relatively stable murder rates until the early 1990s (with a short drop in the mid-1980s), but the state's use of incarceration leaped upward in the early 1990s, just as homicide was falling and then stabilizing at a new, reduced level. In contrast, New York experienced comparable trends in homicide rates but a far different prison profile.[29] New York had more rapid incarceration growth than Utah from 1977 through the mid-1990s and a radically different course in the new century, when its confinement rates began to drop substantially, while West Virginia's continued to shoot upward.

It is hardly possible to explain different trends in incarceration rates by differences in the levels or trends of index crime—even homicide. Sometimes crime trends and prison trends walk hand in hand, sometimes not. This does not mean that crime is irrelevant for penal policy, however. While there is little evidence of a strong "volume" effect (at least globally), it is still possible that "policy" effects can help explain the variance in the incarceration practices of different jurisdictions. For example, many low-riser states in the United States experienced less of a "homicide surge" in the late 1980s and early 1990s than high-riser states.[30] This could have triggered more punitive reactions in high-riser states, even if homicide had little "volume" impact on incarceration rates, due to its relative rarity. Policy effects are mediated by more than raw numbers of crimes. They respond to other social, cultural, economic, and political drivers of penal policy. Many of these will be discussed in the following section.

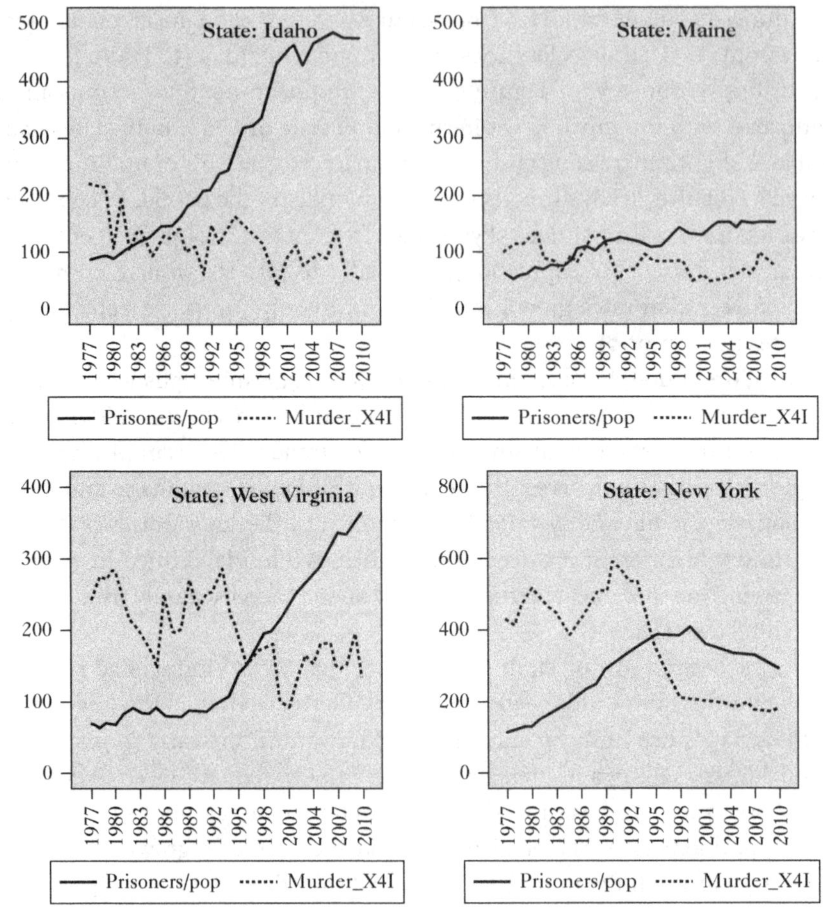

FIGURE 5.17 Imprisonment Rates, Index Crime, and Homicide, 1977–2010: Idaho versus Maine, West Virginia versus New York, per 100,000 population

Sources: Prisoners: Glaze and Kaeble (2014) (http://www.bjs.gov/content/pub/pdf/cpus13.pdf).

Index crime: FBI (https://www.fbi.gov/stats-services/crimestats).

Correlates of Incarceration Rates Worldwide: Is the United States Exceptional?

Data and Methods

This section builds on a body of previous research on penal variation among nation states (see Lappi-Seppälä 2008, 2011a, and 2013). One primary ambition of this chapter is to extend that series of studies to the United States, considered both as a nation state and as a federation of dozens of largely autonomous state criminal justice systems. Earlier studies in the series found that country-level differences in the use of imprisonment are associated with structural differences in nations' political economies and democratic processes, the extent of their welfare states and provision of socioeconomic security, the social values of their populaces, and the breadth of social and institutional trust that exists in their societies.

The earlier findings make intuitive sense. A highly developed public welfare system reflects values of solidarity and social equality. A society of equals, whose citizens show concern for the well-being of others, is less willing to impose heavy penalties upon its comembers. This stands in contrast with cultures of great social distances, where punishments apply chiefly to "others" and the underclass. Widespread inequality in a society is also linked with increased fears and punitive demands, which are reflected in penal policies.

Welfare states also tend to invest in alternatives to imprisonment as means to achieve a low-crime society. Extensive social service networks function as crime-prevention measures, even if that is not their primary intent (for example, universal day care and parental training, a strong public education system that provides equal opportunities, unemployment benefits). Welfare networks affect crime and punishment through enhanced social and economic security, lower levels of fear, lower punitive reflexes, and higher social trust and political legitimacy. In short, there are many reasons that nations with strong welfare institutions, social equality and security, and trust and legitimacy should experience lower incarceration rates.

This section examines whether American incarceration practices "fit" within the general explanatory model summarized above, which was developed for nation states largely across the ocean from the United States. The question will be addressed for the United States as a whole and—more importantly—extended to the 50 states as jurisdictions unto themselves.[31] The analysis will test whether individual states' incarceration practices are associated with the same variables that correlate with prison policies elsewhere in the world, especially the Western world. To the extent that common factors are at work, America is in that limited sense not "exceptional." To the extent that the United States has responded to identified predictors of punitivity with uncommon severity, America is in that defined sense "exceptional."

The analysis works with two samples. Cross-national comparisons are drawn from a global sample of 211 countries. This group is divided into two subsamples. One consists of the 34 countries in the OECD,[32] and the other (177 nations) consists of non-OECD countries. OECD analyses are performed both with the United States included and the excluded (OECD + USA and OECD – USA). This is done because the United States is such an extreme outlier in incarceration policy. As we will see, inclusion of America in the correlation analysis can obscure the strength of associations that exist among the other 33 nation states. The larger global sample is kept in the picture to test differences between developed and less developed countries.

For the global samples, imprisonment rates are from 2016 or the latest available year (usually from 2013 to 2015). The US state sample covers prisoners in state prisons in 2011 (leaving out the District of Columbia).[33] Because the United States is an outlier with incarceration rates nearly two and one-half times that of any other OECD country (United States 698, Chile 290 in second position), several of the country-level correlations and scatter graphs use logarithmic scales for incarceration rates.

The remainder of this section is broken into six subsections. Most of these rely on correlational analyses. Correlations are examined between incarceration rates and four sets of socioeconomic, political, and cultural variables: the first set relates to welfare, prosperity, and social security; the second relates to indicators of social values, trust, and legitimacy; the third relates to measures of democracy and political stability; and the fourth relates to correlations between demographic composition and incarceration. The last subsection consists of cross-sectional regression analyses.

Welfare Policy and Social Inclusion

This subsection uses multiple measures of welfare policy and social inclusion across national and state boundaries. The indicators measure differences in both levels and (fair) distribution. For OECD countries, level indicators of well-being and prosperity include gross domestic product (GDP) and the UN HDI (which includes GDP but adds other indicators related to health, education, and general well-being). Within the sample of US states, general welfare development is measured by the American Human Development Index (American HDI), which uses somewhat different indicators from the UN HDI. This better reflects the US context and maximizes the use of available data.[34]

Distributive social welfare policy and investments in social support are measured among OECD countries by social expenditures as a share of GDP.[35] Income inequality is measured in both samples by the Gini index.[36] Public investments in education, educational achievement, and equal opportunities are measured among OECD countries by the Legatum Prosperity Index of Educational Performance (school enrollment rates, educational expenditures, average years of schooling, and female educational participation).[37] Corresponding US indicators for social expenditures are the maximum monthly Temporary Assistance for Needy Families (TANF) benefit for a family with three children and a composite index of social spending.[38] Educational attainment and investment in education in the United States are measured by the percentage of the population with a high school (or higher) diploma (US Department of Health and Human Services 2008).

Table 5.2 shows that all welfare indicators correlate strongly with incarceration rates in both the OECD – USA and American-state samples. Higher social welfare investments, lower income differences, better educational achievement, higher human development, and the level of overall well-being all go with lower incarceration rates.

However, if the United States is included in the OECD sample, the correlations turn weaker and many of them become statistically insignificant. This is because the United States is so much more punitive than it "should be" according to most robust predictive factors of incarceration rates drawn from the OECD – USA sample.

For example, general increases in wealth (GDP) and development (UN HDI) go together with decreasing incarceration rates in the OECD – USA group.[39] The United States is well above other OECD countries in both measures (GDP 38,165 USD/person in the United States and 20,761 USD/person in the OECD; HDI value .937 in the United States and .879 in the OECD). These ratings "should" have taken the US incarceration rates below the OECD average (127), instead of the top rating of 698.

Other indicators, such as income inequality and social expenditures, locate the United States in the "right direction" in multinational comparisons but much more punitive than one would expect. For example, income inequalities are associated with increasing incarceration rates, and income inequalities are greater in the United States than the OECD – USA average (GINI 41.1 United States and 32.8 OECD).

Level indicators reveal an important difference between the OECD – USA and non-OECD countries. While welfare, prosperity, and general development correlate negatively with imprisonment in the first group, the relationships turn positive in the latter group. This is an important reminder of the fact that the same factors may have opposite effects and consequences in different environments. Prisons are expensive, and in point of development, an increase in economic resources may simply enable the governments to incarcerate more, whereas in other contexts the resources may be invested otherwise.

Figure 5.18 includes visual depictions of 4 of the 12 correlations shown in Table 5.2, to illustrate how the country- and state-specific data array across scatter graphs. The first two charts in the figure use logged values for incarceration rates, which mutes the appearance of the United States as an outlier

Table 5.2 Indicators of the Level and Distribution of Wealth and Prosperity

	Global			United States	
	OECD – USA	OECD+ USA	Not OECD	50 US States	
Indicator	Correlation	Correlation	Correlation (*n*)	Correlation	Indicator
Levels					
GDP per capita ppp 2006 (WB)	–.667**	–.157	.102 (148)	–.300*	GDP 2010
HDI 2012 (UNDP)	–.625**	–.159	.472** (151)	–.636**	American Human Development Index 2010
Education (LPI)	.703**	.236	–.450** (72)	–.560**	High school or higher 2004 (%) (US census)
Distribution					
Public social expenditures 2002–2007, % of GDP (IMF)	–.569**	–.491**	.194 (43)	.673**	Social spending rank (Wall St. 24/7)
Gross public social expenditures 2011 (Socx)	–.627**	–.397**	—	–.629**	TANF benefits (NCCP)
Gini 2010–2013 (WB)	.615**	.516**	.204* (111)	.375**	Gini
					High school or higher 2004 (%) (US census)

*Correlation is significant at the .05 level (two-tailed).

**Correlation is significant at the .01 level (two-tailed).

GDP, gross domestic product; HDI, Human Development Index; IMF, International Monetary Fund; NCCP, National Center for Children in Poverty; OECD, Organisation for Economic Co-operation and Development; TANF, Temporary Assistance for Needy Families; UNDP, United Nations Development Programme; WB, World Bank.

Sources:

Global

- GDP per capita purchasing power parity (ppp) 2006 (WB): World Bank database. (http://data.worldbank.org).
- HDI 2012 (UNDP): United Nations Development Programme, Human Development Reports database (http://hdr.undp.org/en/data).
- Public social expenditures 2002–2007: percent of GDP (International Monetary Fund) (http://www.ilo.org/dyn/sesame/ifpses.socialdbexp).
- Gross Public Social Expenditures 2011: OECD Social Expenditures Database (SocX). (http://www.oecd.org/social/expenditure.htm).
- Gini 2010–2013 (WB): (http://data.worldbank.org).
- Education (LPI): Legatum Institute Prosperity Index (http://www.prosperity.com).

United States

- GDP 2010/population ($): US Bureau of Economic Analysis (http://www.bea.gov).
- American Human Development Index (HDI) 2010: (http://www.measureofamerica.org/human-development/).
- Gini: US Census Bureau (http://www.census.gov).
- Maximum monthly TANF benefit for a family with three children (NCCP): National Center for Children in Poverty database (http://www.nccp.org).
- Social spending rank: Stockdale, Sauter, and Allen (2011).
- Educational attainment (high school or higher): Secretary of Health and Human Services, 2008 Indicators of Welfare Dependence: Annual Report to Congress 2008 (http://aspe.hhs.gov/hsp/indicators08/apa.shtml#ftanf2).

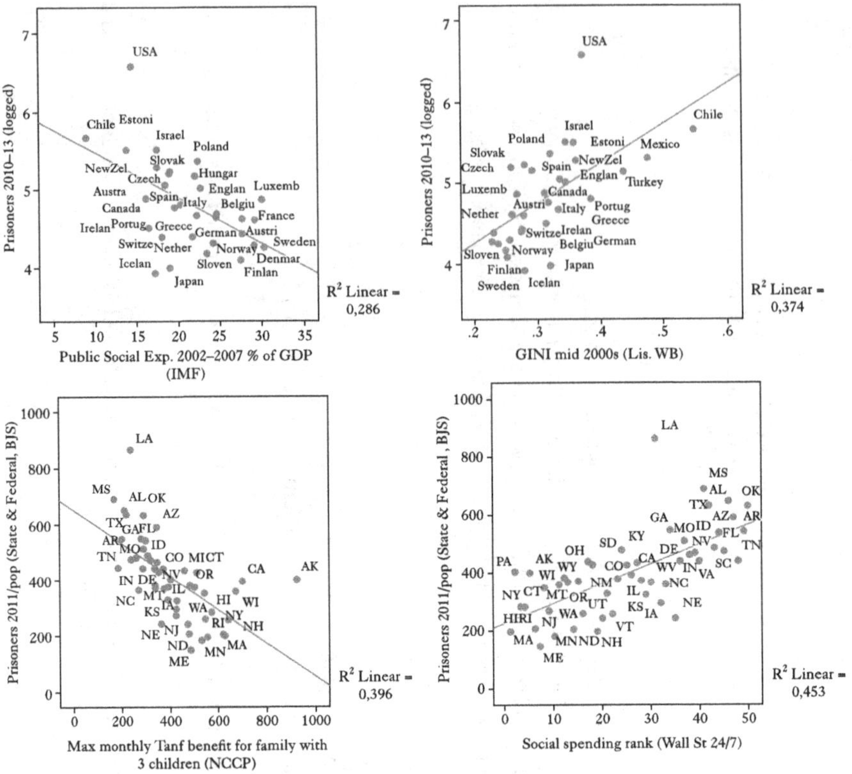

FIGURE 5.18 Income Inequality and Indicators for Welfare Provision, Organisation for Economic Co-operation and Development Nations and US States
Source: See sources for Table 5.2.

in confinement rates. They show that the United States is among the nation states with the highest income inequalities and the lowest investments in welfare (other examples include the Baltic countries, Portugal, and New Zealand). These factors would predict a high position in imprisonment statistics. However, based on the collective experiences of other countries in the OECD sample, one would predict that the US incarceration rate "should be" in the range of 250–300 per 100,000—far below the country's actual rate.

Looking to the 50 US states (in the bottom row of Figure 5.18), there is again a strong and consistent correlation between social spending and imprisonment rates, with Louisiana as an outlier. Indeed, the state-by-state analysis produces somewhat stronger correlations than the country-level OECD sample. This is strong confirmation of one dimension of the explanatory model originally developed for European countries (see Lappi-Seppälä 2008, 2011a, and 2013).

Trust and Legitimacy

Table 5.3 and Figure 5.19 explore the relationships between incarceration rates and societal attitudes such as levels of trust in other people and belief in the legitimacy of institutions.[40] Measurements of trust and legitimacy come from public opinion surveys, although the available measures differ somewhat for OECD nations and American states. At the country level, social and institutional trust (trust in people, in police, in the justice system, etc.) have been measured cross-nationally since 1980 by the World Values Survey and from 2002 by the European Social Survey (ESS).[41]

For the sample of 50 American states, the DDB Needham Lifestyles Survey measured social trust (trust in people) and trust in the criminal justice system.[42] Social trust was measured by asking whether respondents agreed with the statement, "Most people are honest." Trust in justice was measured inversely by the statement, "I have little faith in the criminal justice system."[43]

In both the OECD and US samples, incarceration rates show a fairly strong negative correlation with levels of social trust and faith in the legitimacy of criminal justice institutions. Figure 5.19 includes scatter plots for social trust in OECD countries and the United States. As we saw with welfare investment, the predictive model applied to OECD countries shows comparable strength when applied to the 50 American states. Social trust also correlates strongly with lower incarceration on a US state–level comparison. However, including the United States in the OECD sample weakens the findings, and they lose their statistical significance. As was the case with welfare-level indicators above, these associations do not hold among the less developed nations outside the OECD.

Fears and Punitivity

Fears are the flip side of mistrust: those we do not trust, we easily fear. Attitudes of punitivity and fear of crime are also interconnected since public demands for stiffer penalties may be fueled by a desire to be protected from crime. By hypothesis, public demands influence the content of penal policy, including the use of incarceration.

Table 5.4 distills survey data from several sources on punitive attitudes, fears, and values across different jurisdictions. For OECD nation states, measures of punitive attitudes are derived from the ICVS and the ESS. The ICVS asked respondents to select what they believed to be an appropriate punishment for a recidivist burglar who stole a television set from an apartment. The percentage of prison versus nonprison dispositions was measured, together

Table 5.3 Trust and Legitimacy

Indicator	Global			United States	
	OECD –USA	OECD+ USA	Not OECD	50 US States	
	Correlation	Correlation	Correlation (*n*)	Correlation	Indicator
Social trust (WVS 2005)	–.586**	–.299	–.143 (46)	–.633**	Most people are honest (DDB: 1 disagree, 6 agree)
Confidence in police (WVS)	–.506**	–.194	–.211 (43)	.379**	I have little faith in CJS (DDB: 1 disagree, 6 agree)

**Correlation is significant at the .01 level (two-tailed).

OECD, Organisation for Economic Co-operation and Development; WVS, World Values Survey.

Sources:

Global

- Trust in people: World Values Survey database (http://www.worldvaluessurvey.org).
- Trust in police: World Values Survey database (http://www.worldvaluessurvey.org).

United States

- Most people are honest: DDB Needham Lifestyles Survey (http://www.icpsr.umich.edu/icpsrweb/instructors/icsc/datasets.jsp).
- I have little faith in Criminal Justice System: DDB Needham Lifestyles Survey (http://www.icpsr.umich.edu/icpsrweb/instructors/icsc/datasets.jsp).

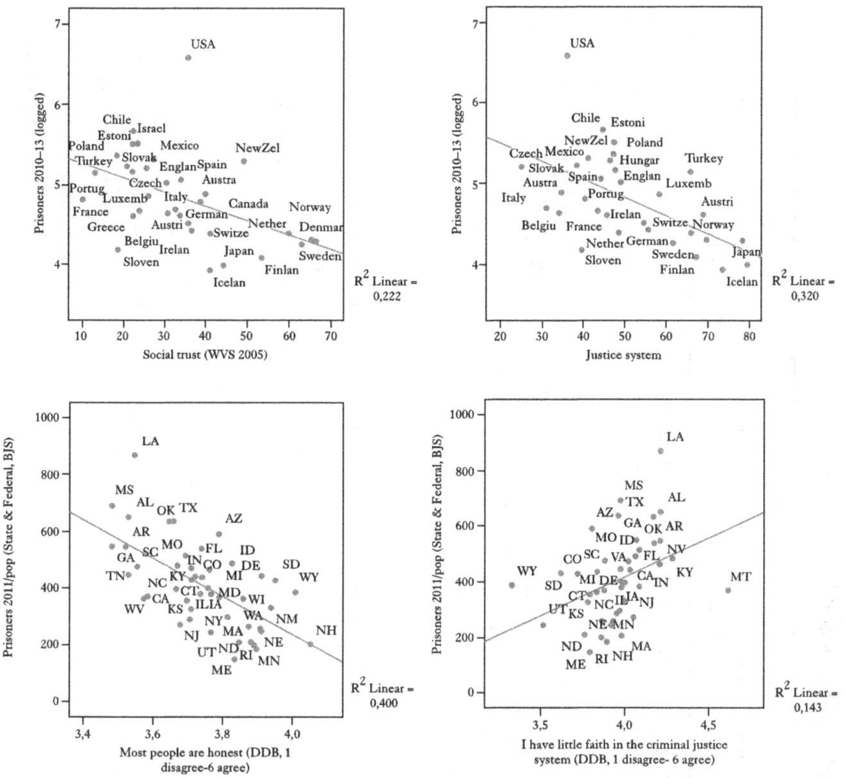

FIGURE 5.19 Incarceration and Social Trust, Organisation for Economic Co-operation and Development Countries and US States
Source: See sources for Table 5.3.

with the length of proposed prison terms. Fear of crime was measured by asking whether respondents felt safe walking in their neighborhoods after dark. In addition, drawing from both the ICVS and the ESS, a combined measure of attitudinal punitivity was constructed (see Lappi-Seppälä 2013).

State-level US attitudinal data come from the DDB Needham Lifestyles Survey. Fear of crime was measured by the assertion, "I worry a lot about myself or a family member becoming a victim of crime." For individual US states, there are no punitivity indicators comparable to those in the ICVS and ESS. However, the Needham survey did test for support of the death penalty ("I am in favor of the death penalty").

Table 5.4 also includes indicators of respondents' views on authoritarian and disciplinary measures in maintaining social order and governing the country. The US respondents were asked to give their views of the assertions, "There should be a gun in every home," and "Police should use whatever force

Table 5.4 Punitivity: Fears and Values

Indicator	Global			United States	
	OECD – USA	OECD+ USA	Not OECD	50 US States	
	Correlation	Correlation	Correlation (n)	Correlation	Indicator
Punitivity and fear of crime					
Prison for burglars (ICVS 2005 or latest)	.474** (31)	.394* (32)	−.294 (43)	.228	In favor of death penalty (DDB)
Prison term (ICVS 2005 or latest)	.724** (31)	.465** (32)	.127 (43)		
Punitive attitudes (ESS and ICVS combined)	.664** (26)	.603** (27)			
Feeling safe after dark (ICVS latest)	−.635** (30)	−.175 (31)	−.560** (30)	.521**	Worry about being a victim of crime (DDB)
Authoritarian vs. democratic values: It is essential for a democracy that . . . (1 Not, 6 Yes)					**"Pro-control" attitudes**
The army takes over when government is incompetent (WVS)	.615** (21)	.434* (22)	−.078 (55)	.543**	Police should use whatever force is necessary to maintain law and order (DDB: 1 disagree, 6 agree)

People obey their rulers (WVS)	.694** (14)	.388 (15)	–.26 (44)	.629**	There should be a gun in every home (DDB: 1 disagree, 6 agree)
Religious authorities interpret the laws (WVS)	.783** (21)	.396 (22)	–.241 (55)		

*Correlation is significant at the .05 level (two-tailed).

**Correlation is significant at the .01 level (two-tailed).

ESS, European Social Survey (http://www.europeansocialsurvey.org/) ; ICVS, International Crime Victim Survey (https://english.wodc.nl/onderzoeksdatabase/icvs-2005-survey.aspx); OECD, Organisation for Economic Co-operation and Development; WVS, World Values Survey.

Sources:

Global

- Prison for burglars % (ICVS 2005).
- Prison term (ICVS 2005).
- Joint punitivity index (ESS and ICVS).
- Fear of crime (ICVS 2005).
- The army takes over when government is incompetent (WVS, http://www.worldvaluessurvey.org)
- People obey their rulers (WVS, http://www.worldvaluessurvey.org)
- Religious authorities interpret the laws (WVS, http://www.worldvaluessurvey.org)

United States

- In favor of death penalty
- Worry about being a victim of crime
- Police should use whatever force is necessary to maintain law and order
- There should be a gun in every home
- Source for all: DDB Needham Lifestyles Survey (http://www.icpsr.umich.edu/icpsrweb/instructors/icsc/datasets.jsp).

is necessary to maintain law and order." These may be interpreted as measures of "pro-control" attitudes. For OECD countries, a rough counterpart may be found in the fifth wave of World Values Survey, where respondents were asked what they thought would be essential for, or fatal to, democracy. The scenarios included "The army takes over when the government is incompetent," "People obey their rulers," and "Religious authorities interpret the laws." This dimension is defined as authoritarian versus democratic values.

The results displayed in Table 5.4 are impressive, and the findings of earlier research outside the United States (Lappi-Seppälä 2008, 2011a, and 2013) appear to be confirmed almost entirely when applied to the US-state sample.

Among OECD nations and American states, fear of crime and attitudinal punitivity tend to correlate strongly with incarceration rates, with the exception of support for the death penalty in US states as measured by the Needham survey[44] (see Table 5.4). Across American states, there is only a weak and nonsignificant positive correlation between support for the death penalty and incarceration rates. This does not mean that public punitivity is irrelevant to incarceration rates; the indicator used may just not be the proper one.

For the OECD countries, authoritarian values are closely linked with more extensive use of imprisonment, as are pro-control attitudes in the United States (Table 5.4).

Analysis of global data for 30–55 countries outside the OECD shows no strong or statistically significant correlations on any of the measures in Table 5.4 except one: fear of crime as measured by the ICVS—a variable for which only 30 non-OECD countries had provided information.

Figures 5.20 and 5.21 provide visual examples of the correlations collected in Table 5.4, while also indicating the position of individual jurisdictions. Among nation states (Figure 5.20), the United States remains an outlier in these comparisons. Based on measures of punitive attitudes, one would expect the United States to be among the countries with the largest incarceration rates, but the US position is much higher than would be predicted by the correlational data from other nations.

Figure 5.21 shows that indicators of fear of crime and pro-control attitudes are also good predictors of interstate variations in incarceration within the United States. Once again, Louisiana is something of an outlier (see also Figure 5.19), with higher incarceration rates than expected from the patterns seen in other states. Overall, on dimensions of public fearfulness and punitivity, analysis of the American state-by-state sample provides confirmation of analyses based on nation state data.

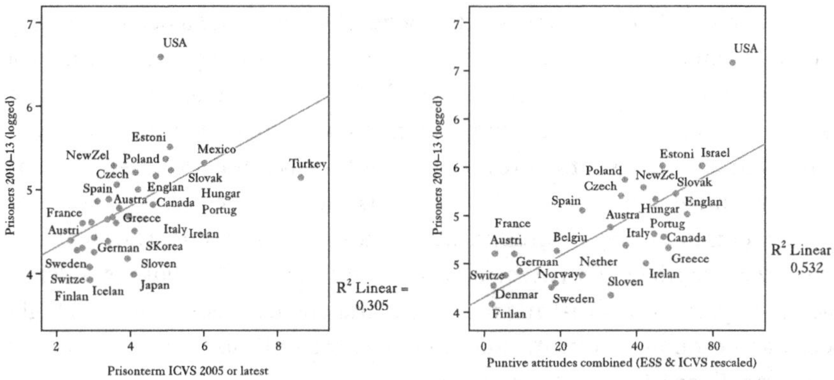

FIGURE 5.20 Punitivity and Imprisonment, Organisation for Economic Co-operation and Development Nations

Source: See sources for Table 5.4.

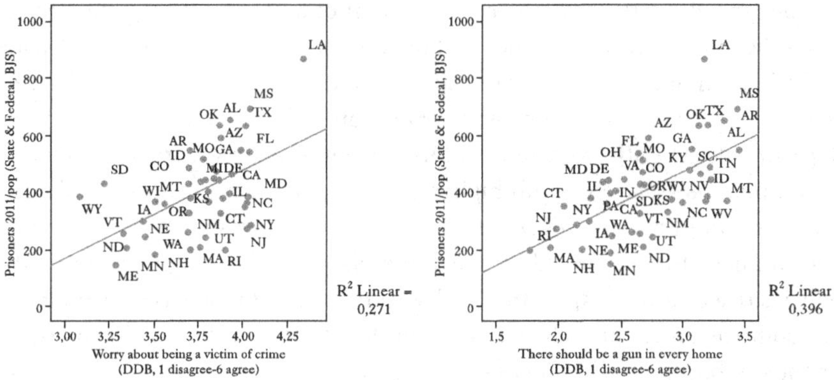

FIGURE 5.21 Fear of Crime and Pro-Control Attitudes, US States

Source: See sources for Table 5.4.

Political Structures and Democracy

This subsection uses correlational analyses to test the proposition that the political structures of jurisdictions have predictable relationships with their incarceration policies. One obvious comparison is democratic versus nondemocratic nation states. Democracies have many different configurations, however, with potential effects on criminal justice policies (see Zimring, Hawkins, and Kamin 2001; Norris 2011; Karstedt 2013). A fundamental distinction has been drawn between "consensual" and "majoritarian" democracies. As defined by Arend Lijphart (2012), consensual democracies are characterized by multiparty systems, coalition versus one-party governments, proportional representation, integration of interest groups into the political system, and a decision-making process premised on negotiation and compromise. In Lijphart's words, consensual democracies are "kinder and gentler" than winner-take-all majoritarian systems, which are based on confrontation and competition (p. 219). Justice policies in consensus structures tend toward deliberation, long-term consistency, and incremental change.[45] Consensual democracies are also characterized by centralized wage coordination and strong labor unions. They tend to be more "welfare-friendly" than majoritarian democracies. The consensus democracies' support for welfarist and more egalitarian policies associates with higher social and economic security and more tolerant and moderate penal policies (see Lappi-Seppälä 2008).[46]

In contrast, in majoritarian democracies there is more crisis talk, criticism, short-term thinking, and political responsivity to public demands. Other dimensions of democracy may be related to punitiveness in criminal justice as well. Especially relevant within the United States, states' democratic structures can be graded by degrees of decentralization of authority. The United States cedes the bulk of criminal justice authority to the states—and individual states differ in their allocations of state and local powers. Greater degrees of decentralization pass authority downward from state officials to local judges, police departments, sheriffs, and prosecutors. By some theories, fragmentation of government is associated with higher punitivity (Barker 2009; Garland 2010; see Lacey and Soskice, this volume). Frequent elections at the state, county, and municipal levels provide an "endless platform" for tough law-and-order policies (Lacey 2011, 245). At the local level measures to increase prison terms are both electorally attractive and politically costless as the financial cost of prisons is borne by the states—a phenomenon called the "correctional free lunch" by Zimring and Hawkins (1991).

Democracies also differ in the extent to which power is apportioned among elected and appointed officials. In America, for example, local prosecutors are elected in every state (but not in the federal system)—an arrangement that distinguishes the United States from nearly every other nation in the world (Tonry 2004, 9–10). Because this is a universal practice in all 50 states, it does not provide a means to distinguish among them. Judicial selection processes, however, do vary widely from state to state. In some jurisdictions, judges are appointed and must stand periodically for retention in uncontested elections. The appointment process is sometimes limited by nominating commissions and sometimes not. In other states, judges must win and retain their seats through contested elections, which have become increasingly partisan (Kritzer 2007). By hypothesis, states with highly political judicial selection and retention systems will be more responsive to public demands for punitive sentences than states in which judges' job security is more insulated from political pressures (Bright 1997; Berdejó and Yuchtman 2013).

Table 5.5 summarizes a number of correlational analyses to test some of these assumptions.

For global samples, the level and "quality" of democracy are measured by five measures.

The Polity IV index and the Freedom House Index are the two most widely used measures of democracy. The Polity index focuses on the control of elites and on the classification of political systems on a scale between the extremes of autocracy and democracy.[47] The Freedom House Index (see Freedom House 2008) scores countries on a scale from 1 to 7 (where 1 is the most democratic) on two dimensions: political rights and civil liberties. The benefits of the Polity index include a large coverage of nations with data dating back to the 1800s but with only very few and formal indicators. Both indexes have been criticized for formality and for omitting the actual realization of rights. Subsequent research has developed more substantive indicators, including the index of "effective democracy" developed by Alexander, Inglehart, and Welzel (2011). The index of the Economist Intelligence Unit (EIU) is also broader and more "substantial," focusing on the elements of political culture and the realization of rights. The Lijphart Executive-Parties (or "joint-power") index, in turn, measures power sharing and the consensus–conflict dimension of political culture.[48]

For the sample of American states, the variables are divided into two blocks. First block ("Bipolarization") deals with the dividing features of the US political landscape. The impact of party politics is measured by grouping states into Republican, Democratic, and "swing" states. The other variable is the geographical division of states between the South and the North.[49]

Second block deals with elements related to localized democracy and decentralization. The judicial selection indicator measures whether judges are selected by nomination (with or without a commission) or through elections (partisan or nonpartisan).[50] The second indicator measures governor's institutional powers (GIP; see Beyle 2004).[51] The SEP indicator measures the number of separately elected executive branch officials. While being a subindex of GIP, SEP is a convenient measure of decentralization and, first and foremost, of the impact of US-specific local electoral systems.[52]

Global Samples

Outside the United States, the Polity IV indicator is unrelated to incarceration in all samples.[53] The same applies very much also to the Freedom House index. However, both the EIU index and effective democracy (Alexander, Inglehart,

Table 5.5 Democracy

Indicator	Global			United States	
	OECD – USA	OECD + USA	Non-OECD	50 US States	
	Correlation	Correlation	Correlation (*n*)	Correlation	Indicator
Democracy				**Bipolarization**	
Democracy, Economist 2008 (EIU)	–.743**	–.413*	.195* (125)	–.554**	Partisan politics (1 Republican –2 swing–3 Democrat)
Effective democracy 2000–2006	–.597**	–.245	.251** (139)	.675**	Region (1 North–2 West–3 South)
Freedom House rating of democracy 2008	.085	–.001	–.139 (147)		
Democracy, Polity IV, constitutional democracy	–.067	.013	–.062 (115)	**Localism and Decentralization**	
				.358*	Judicial selection (2001)
Lijphart's executive-parties index (consensual–conflict)	–.305	–.287	–.558 (12)	–.323*	Governor's institutional powers
				–.553**	SEP ("localized democracy," elected state officials)

*Correlation is significant at the .05 level (two-tailed).

**Correlation is significant at the .01 level (two-tailed).

EIU, Economist Intelligence Unit; OECD, Organisation for Economic Co-operation and Development; SEP, separately elected officials.

Sources:

Global

- Democracy, Economist 2008: Economist Intelligence Unit Database (http://www.eiu.com).
- Effective democracy 2002–2006: Alexander, Inglehart, and Welzel (2011).
- Freedom House Rating of Democracy (2008): Freedom House Database (http://www.freedomhouse.org).
- Constitutional democracy: Polity IV Project database (http://www.systemicpeace.org/polity/polity4.htm).
- Lijphart's executive-parties index (Lijphart 2012)

United States

- Party politics (1 Republican–2 swing–3 Democrat): (http://www.americanthinker.com/blog/2012/07/blue_red_and_swing_states.html).
- Region (1 North–2 West–3 South): (http://thomaslegion.net/uscensusbureauregionsthewestthemidwestthesouthandthenortheast.html). Northeast: Connecticut, Maine, Massachusetts, New Hampshire, New Jersey, New York, Pennsylvania, Rhode Island, Vermont. West/Midwest: Alaska, Arizona, California, Colorado, Hawaii, Idaho, Illinois, Indiana, Iowa, Kansas, Michigan, Minnesota, Missouri, Montana, Nebraska, Nevada, New Mexico, North Dakota, Ohio, Oregon, South Dakota, Utah, Washington, Wisconsin, Wyoming. South: Alabama, Arkansas, Delaware, Florida, Georgia, Kentucky, Louisiana, Maryland, Mississippi, North Carolina, Oklahoma, South Carolina, Tennessee, Texas, Virginia, West Virginia.
- Judicial selection (Behrens and Silverman 2002).
- Governor's institutional powers (Beyle 2004).
- SEP ("localized democracy, elected state officials) (Beyle 2004).

and Welzel 2011) correlate strongly and negatively in the OECD – USA group (–.743, EIU). However, among the less developed nations the correlation is positive (.195, EIU). Including the United States in the OECD sample weakens the correlation (but it is still negative and significant). Both patterns (reverse correlations in the OECD – USA and non-OECD groups and weakening correlations for OECD + USA) follow the logic discovered already in Table 5.2.

The Lijphart index includes also elements of political economy, the relations of executives, political parties, and labor unions. Consensual democracies—as contrasted with more bipolarized majoritarian political systems—seem to incarcerate less.[54] Figure 5.22 illustrates the associations with two substantial indicators (EIU index and Lijphart's executive-parties index).

US States

In the United States, Republican states incarcerate more than Democratic ones and northern states less than southern ones. Judicial selection methods correlate moderately with incarceration (.358). States with appointed judges have fewer prisoners that states with (partisan) elections. A similarly moderate correlation exists between states' GIP index and their incarceration rates, but this correlation was based predominantly on the subindex of SEP (measuring the share of elected officials). Incarceration rates are higher in states that elect a large number of state-level officials by public elections compared to states where more offices are filled by nominations (–.553). As seen in Figure 5.23, incarceration rates varied in the former group around 600 prisoners per 100,000 residents and in the latter from 200 to 300.

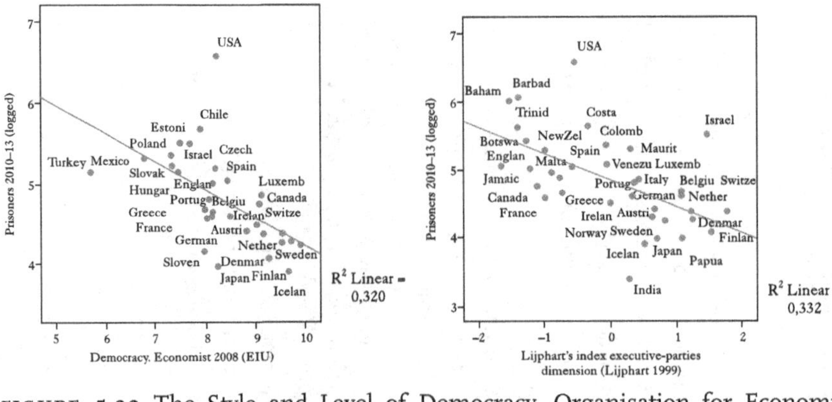

FIGURE 5.22 The Style and Level of Democracy, Organisation for Economic Co-operation and Development Nations and the United States

Source: See sources for Table 5.5.

Note: The Lijphart index is with a different country sample (Lijphart 2012).

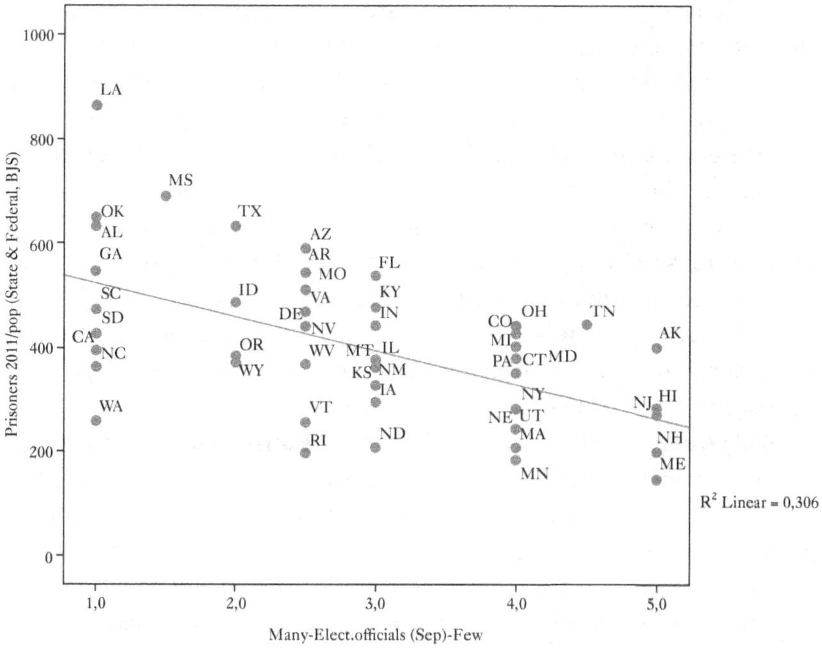

FIGURE 5.23 Imprisonment Rates and Elected State Officials (Separately Elected Officials), Cross-Sectionally and by Percentile Groups, 1977–2010, per 100,000
Source: See sources for Table 5.5.

In sum, hypothesized connections between characteristics of democracies and incarceration policies are in evidence among the 50 US states, just as in the global samples, especially the OECD – USA sample. Individual American states differ from one another in ways that resemble the differentiations seen among developed nation states elsewhere in the world.

Demographics

It is a well-known fact that the composition of the US prison population is demographically skewed. African Americans are imprisoned at nearly six times, and Hispanics more than double, the rate of whites (Carson 2015, 15, table 10). The role of race in US crime policy has been extensively analyzed and is sometimes posited as the primary factor in American punitive exceptionalism (for example, Kennedy 1997; Mauer 2006; Frase 2009; Alexander 2010; Tonry 2012; Forman 2012; Wilson 2012). The following will not add to earlier cultural and historical analyses. However, stark demographic variations demand that factors of race and ethnicity be included in any statistical analysis of American incarceration rates. Moreover, powerful interplays between incarceration rates and race/ethnicity are not unique to the United States, with immigration status also a determinant of disparities in punishment (Bucerius and Tonry 2013). For example, disparities in incarceration even greater than the current 6:1 black:white ratio in the United States have been documented in Canada, England and Wales, and New Zealand (Tonry 1994; Lacey and Soskice, this volume). According to the "minority-threat hypothesis," increases in population heterogeneity result in a greater use of formal social control and imprisonment (Ruddell 2005). Consequently, explanations for differences in penal policies have often been sought from demographic factors. For example, the low imprisonment rates in Scandinavia, and especially in Finland, have been explained by reference to population homogeneity (von Hofer 2003; Ruddell 2005).

Table 5.6 examines these assumptions in raw statistical terms. Demographic composition in the global sample is measured by ethnic fractionalization (measuring linguistic, religious, and ethnic differentiation; see Alesina et al. 2002). Comparisons between American states are based on the percentage share of African American population in each state's total population.

Ethnic fractionalization and incarceration correlate positively (.366) among the OECD – USA nations but negatively among the 145 less developed states. A closer examination of the correlation profiles reveals a clear reverse *U*-shaped curve: countries at both ends of the fractionality scale incarcerate the least. From the global sample, it is hard to reach general conclusions about the relationship between ethnic composition and levels of penal repression.

Within the United States, states' imprisonment rates and the percentage of African Americans in their populations are strongly correlated, with high statistical significance (.607). Whether this is a result of race as such, factors related to race, or third causes unrelated to race cannot be decided without further analyses.

Regression Analyses

We have established strong correlations between incarceration rates and a number of socioeconomic, political, cultural, and demographic variables. Correlations with crime, especially homicide, also exist; but the findings are uneven. These correlations have been detected among developed industrialized nation states in previous research. This chapter establishes that they are similarly present at the subnational level when sorting among the 50 US states.

The questions remain: Which of these interrelated factors play the "key roles" in incarceration policy? What is the relative weight of crime within

Table 5.6 Demographics

Indicator	Global			United States	
	OECD – USA	OECD + USA	Not OECD	50 US States	
	Correlation	Correlation	Correlation (*n*)	Correlation	Indicator
Ethnic fractionalization	.366*	.385*	−.284* (145)	.607**	African American population 2010 (%)

*Correlation is significant at the .05 level (two-tailed).

**Correlation is significant at the .01 level (two-tailed).

OECD, Organisation for Economic Co-operation and Development.

Sources:

Global

- Ethnic fractionalization: Alesina et al. (2002).

United States

- African American population 2010 (%) :US Census Bureau (http://www.census.gov).

a composite explanatory model? To what extent do racial demographics by themselves determine incarceration policy, especially within the United States? Some of these questions can be addressed with the help of the regression analyses presented. We will begin with the global sample and then shift concentration to the American states.

Some caveats must be stated. For the global sample, regressions will be drawn from seven (hypothetically) key variables: data on human development, income inequality, democracy, punitivity (measured by suggested prison term), social trust, ethnic fractionalization, and homicide. These are chosen partly for pragmatic reasons because data spanning a large number of countries are available for only a handful of indicators. The more variables, the fewer observations. Out of the original sample of over 211 nations, only 52 had data for all seven variables.[55] In addition, variables strongly associated with prison rates tend to be interconnected. This presents further challenges to regression analysis. Table 5.7 shows how strongly intercorrelated the seven variables are in the 52-nation sample. Finally, the relevance of different factors could depend on a nation's general level of development, which must be taken into account in interpretation. It follows that truly global statistical explanations are hard, if not impossible, to find. However, we are not after "the final global model." The aim is more modest: to illustrate the relative weight of different factor combinations in countries on different levels of economic and human development.

Linear regression results for the 52-nation sample are in Table 5.8. Results are shown for the entire sample, and then three subsamples are broken down by region. The seven-variable model explains 68 percent of the variance for all 52 nations. The strongest predictor for incarceration rates is human development, followed by homicide, democracy, punitivity, and social trust. Ethnic fractionalization and income inequality did not pass the significance test ($p > .05$).

The picture changes when analyses are run by regions. For subsample 1, composed of 21 western European countries, the model explains 51 percent of the variance in imprisonment rates, but the only significant factor is income inequality. For subsample 2, covering 13 eastern European countries, the model explains 46 percent. However, the model itself doesn't pass the significance test, and the only significant factor is democracy. For subsample 3 (17 non-European nations), the seven-variable model explains 51 percent of the variance. This time the role of the main predictor is given to human development.

When the same seven-variable list was tested with a subsample of only OECD – USA countries, the model failed to pass the collinearity test due to

Table 5.7 Variables and Intercorrelations: Global Sample (52 nations)

	1	2	3	4	5	6	Prisoners 2016 or Latest
HDI 2012 (UNDP)							–.171
Democracy, Economist 2008 (EIU)	.692**						–.487**
Gini 2010–2013 (WB)	–.487**	–.261					.364*
Punitivity, prison term (ICVS)	–.628**	–.757**	.439**				.588**
Social trust (WVS 2005)	.394**	.395**	–.360*	–.533**			–.598**
Ethnic fractionalization	–.566**	–.289	.382**	.334*	–.345*		.282
Homicide 2004–2012 (logged)	–.641**	–.491**	.561**	.579**	–.443**	.562**	.564**

n = 52.

*Correlation is significant at the .05 level (two-tailed).

**Correlation is significant at the .01 level (two-tailed).

EIU, Economist Intelligence Unit; HDI, Human Development Index; ICVS, International Crime Victims Survey; UNDP, United Nations Development Programme; WB, World Bank; WVS, World Values Survey.

Sources: See sources for Tables 5.2–5.6 and Lehti (2013).

Table 5.8 Regression Models: Global Sample

Regression Analyses, Prisoners 2016 or Latest, Logged values.	**Entire Sample**		**Subsample 1**		**Subsample 2**		**Subsample 3**	
	Total (n = 51)		**Western Europe (n = 21)**		**Eastern Europe (n = 13)**		**Not Europe (n = 17)**	
	β-adj. (R^2)	**Significance**	**β-adj. (R^2)**	**Significance**	**β-adj. (R^2)**	**Significance**	**β-adj. (R^2)**	**Significance**
Model R^2 (adj.), significance (F test)	**(.679)**	**.000**	**(.505)**	**.021**	(.458)	.108	**(.526)**	**.031**
Variables								
HDI 2012 (UNDP)	**1.066**	**.000**	.499	.148	.562	.252	**.889**	**.013**
Homicide 2004–2012 (logged)	**.428**	**.001**	.198	.392	.364	.192	.147	.672
Democracy, Economist 2008	**–.397**	**.005**	–.265	.434	**–.665**	**.049**	–.271	.316
Prison term (ICVS)	**.395**	**.003**	.195	.452	.186	.744	.131	.585
Social trust (WVS 2005)	**–.339**	**.002**	–.211	.538	.007	.987	–.363	.157
Ethnic fractionalization	.099	.395	.156	.437	–.064	.816	.185	.458
Gini 2010-13 (WB)	.140	.188	**.622**	**.016**	.382	.228	.355	.227

Bolded: $p < .05$.

HDI, Human Development Index; ICVS, International Crime Victims Survey; UNDP, United Nations Development Programme; WB, World Bank; WVS, World Values Survey.

Sources: See sources for Tables 5.2–5.6 and Lehti (2013).

intercollinearity (variance inflation factor [VIF] values exceeding 4.5). The problem was addressed by reducing the number of variables in the model. It turned out that all models work better with OECD – USA countries compared with non-OECD countries. It also seems that any combination of two to three factors from each key group (economic, social, values and attitudes, and political) can explain 50–60 percent of the variation. Table 5.9 examines, with four models of two to three variables each, whether the introduction of the United States into the sample of developed nations makes a difference.

Model 1, with social trust, social expenditures, and homicide, explains 59 percent of national variations in imprisonment rates without the United States and 53 percent when the United States is added to the sample. Including the United States increases the weight of crime and reduces the role of other social variables.

Model 2, with democracy ($\beta = -.627$) and homicide ($\beta = .345$), explains 63 percent of the variance among OECD nations without the United States and 58 percent when the United States is included. Bringing in the United States lifts homicide to the same level as democracy ($\beta = -.489$ and .470).

Fears and punitivity (model 3) explain 59 percent without the United States, dropping to 53 percent with the United States included. Again, adding the United States to the sample raises the importance of crime; in model 3 with the OECD + USA sample, homicide is the prime predictor ($\beta = .478$).

Model 4 explains 66 percent of the variance in imprisonment rates, with democracy, trust, and homicide all being of comparable strength. Inclusion of the United States drops the overall explanatory power of model 4 to 58 percent and lifts homicide to first position as a predictor.

Thus, the presence of the United States in the OECD sample diminishes the explanatory power of all four models in Table 5.9. This follows from the fact that the US incarceration rate is substantially higher than anticipated, according to the predictors in the models.

Bringing the United States into the analysis also underlines the explanatory importance of homicide rates in some international comparisons. This is consistent with the fact that the mean homicide rate in 2004–2012 was 1.8 per 100,000 residents in the OECD – USA countries but more than three times higher (5.7) in the United States. There are good reasons to believe that exceptionally high US incarceration rates are partly explainable by higher homicide rates compared to other OECD countries—and homicide will be seen to have similar importance in predicting the incarceration practices of individual states within the United States. The amount of "credit" that should be given to homicide as an explanatory variable is impossible to say. The correlation between homicide and incarceration is globally weak and varies across

Table 5.9 Regression Models: OECD countries

	OECD – USA		OECD + USA	
	β-adj. (R^2)	Sig.	β-adj. (R^2)	Sig.
Model 1. Social	(.592)	.000	(.532)	.000
Social trust (WVS 2005)	–.465	.001	–.365	.009
Gross public social expenditure 2011	–.323	.035	–.222	.158
Homicide 2004–2012 (logged)	.256	.080	.419	.008
Model 2. Political	(.629)	.000	(.577)	.000
Democracy. Economist 2008 (EIU)	–.627	.000	–.489	.000
Homicide 2004–2012 (logged)	.345	.006	.470	.001
Model 3. Fears and Punitivity	(.587)	.000	(.534)	.000
Feeling safe after dark (ICVS latest)	–.417	.013	–.219	.183
Prison term ICVS 2005 or latest	.292	.083	.334	.057
Homicide 2004–2012 (logged)	.359	.008	.478	.001
Model 4. Combination: Trust and Democracy	(.656)	.000	(.584)	.000
Democracy, Economist 2008 (EIU)	–.393	.039	–.327	.106
Social trust (WVS 2005)	–.296	.106	–.205	.292
Homicide 2004–2012 (logged)	.349	.005	.476	.001

EIU, Economist Intelligence Unit; ICVS, International Crime Victims Survey; OECD, Organisation for Economic Co-operation and Development; WVS, World Values Survey.

Sources: See sources for Tables 5.2–5.6 and Lehti (2013).

different regions, which prevents the further construction of reliable statistical models.

Table 5.10 assembles similar linear regression analyses for the US states, using five alternative multivariable models to tease out the most important factors. The first three models are without the crime factor, while models 4 and 5 test different combinations with crime included. Due to the pivotal role of race and demographics, all five models were assembled twice—with and without the variable of race (share of African Americans in a state's population).

Model 1 ("social") includes social spending, Gini, and the American HDI. The model explains 60 percent of the variation in state incarceration rates, with roughly similar weight for each predictor. The inclusion of racial demographics increases the explanatory power to 65 percent but drops income inequality off the model.

Fears and pro-control attitudes (model 2) explain 63 percent. The introduction of racial demographics makes no substantial difference in the predictive power of this model.

Politics and geography explain 52 percent (model 3). Introducing racial demographics increases the explanatory power to 61 percent and drops the geographical dimension out of the model.

The addition of the variable of states' homicide rates produces the models with the greatest power to predict states' incarceration rates. The combination of crime and social variables (model 4) explains 68 percent of the variation in state incarceration rates, with homicide the strongest single predictor (.486). Introducing racial demographics does not improve the model.

Model 5 combines crime with social spending, fears, and politics (party politics and localized democracy). This model is the most successful of the five, explaining 77 percent of the variation in state incarceration rates. Homicide remains the most important indicator (.350). However, all other variables are also statistically significant and of roughly equal weight (.213–.290). The addition of racial demographics makes no difference.

The general conclusion about the role of race is that the share of black population improves the models (more black people, more prisoners) only when combined with relatively weak predictors. Once the model is strong enough and once the variable of homicide rates has been introduced, the share of black population no longer has independent relevance.

Taken together, the regression models give strong results, especially with the US data. On the other hand, they are hardly able to provide us with the "final truth" in a form of simple explanation. This may be partly due to defects

Table 5.10 Regression Models: 50 US States

	A (Without Race)		B (Including Race)	
	β-adj. (R^2)	Significance	β-adj. (R^2)	Significance
Model 1. Social	(.596)	.000	(.645)	.000
Social spending rank (Wall St. 24/7)	.392	.002	.291	.015
Gini	.299	.002	.153	.140
US Human Development Index 2010	–.384	.002	–.374	.001
African American population (% 2010)			.302	.009
Model 2. Fears and attitudes	.628	.000	(.655)	.000
Worry about being a victim of crime (DDB)	.498	.000	.330	.007
There should be a gun in every home (DDB)	.611	.000	.558	.000
African American population (% 2010)			.255	.039
Model 3. Politics and region	(.521)	.001	(.614)	.000
Party politics (1 Republican–2 swing–3 Democrat)	–.233	.057	–.324	.005
Elected officials (SEP), many—few	–.256	.032	–.229	.034
Region (1 North–2 West–3 South)	.414	.003	.152	.278
African American population (% 2010)			.390	.001
Model 4. Crime and social	(.677)	.004	(.681)	.000
Murder rate 2011 (DPIC)	.486	.000	.369	.008
Social spending rank (Wall St. 24/7)	.282	.012	.256	.024
US Human Development Index 2010	–.23	.035	–.262	.019
African American population (% 2010)			.156	.213

Table 5.10 Continued

	A (Without Race)		B (Including Race)	
	β-adj. (R^2)	**Significance**	**β-adj. (R^2)**	**Significance**
Model 5. Crime, social fears, and politics	(.774)	.000	(.769)	.000
Murder rate 2011 (DPIC)	.350	.001	.348	.005
Social spending rank (Wall St. 24/7)	.218	.020	.218	.021
Worry about being a victim of crime (DDB)	.213	.030	.212	.048
Party politics (1 Republican–2 swing–3 Democrat)	–.290	.001	–.289	.001
Elected officials (SEP) Many—Few	–.213	.011	–.212	.013
African American population (% 2010)			.005	.965

DPIC, Death Penalty Information Center; SEP, separately elected officials.
Sources: See sources for Tables 5.2–5.6 and Lehti (2013).

in data availability; data covering all important dimensions are available only from a small number of developed countries. But this is not the only, or even the main, reason. As the analyses with subsets of nation states indicated, predictors changed positions according to region. Correlation analyses also showed how different factors had different weight—sometimes even reverse effects—in different surroundings.[56] A model that seems to work with developed countries does not necessarily work with poorer countries. But confining the analyses only to developed countries does not seem to solve the problem either. Here we saw that all key-variable groups seemed to be relevant and that two to four variables from each main group (economic, social, values, political, crime) explained around 60 percent of the variance (usually a little less in the less developed nations, with the US data even more). Furthermore, many of these variables are interconnected, and some are even interchangeable. One could be replaced by another without much happening in the end result. Does this all imply a zero result? We think not. Rather, this may well be the way the things are. Factors influencing penal policy are interconnected and present at the same time. They are working together, influencing, supporting, and sustaining each other. And at the same time, they may have an independent and more direct influence in the formation of national penal policies.

Conclusion

US incarceration rates remain exceptional in terms of levels. The present national imprisonment rate of about 700 per 100,000 population is several times higher than in any comparable developed democracy. The proportionate growth of incarceration in the United States is also exceptional—but not wholly unique. A 275 percent increase from 200 to 750 is certainly high, but there have been similar percentage increases elsewhere. In Europe, the Netherlands increased incarceration rates sixfold from a low of 20 to a high of 120 in 1970 to 2005. Ireland increased its prison population rates from around 20 in 1960 to 90 in 2010 (+350 percent), and rates in England and Wales and in Scotland rose from around 50 to 150 (+200 percent). Distinct from the United States, however, all of these countries started their prison growth from extremely low levels (around 10–20 percent of then-existing US levels). After the growth period, their rates remained lower than the *starting* levels in the United States in the 1970s.

In most countries, increases remained much more modest. Some countries have kept their rates stable over the last several decades, and some have even experienced decline. In worldwide comparison, what is most unique about the United States is the combination of a high base level in 1970, followed by an unusually steep increase in both absolute and percentage terms. Explanations for American exceptionalism should address both of these features.[57]

There is no clear-cut answer to the question of whether and to what extent incarceration rates are guided by crime trends, through either volume or policy effects. The only firm conclusion is that, in global comparison, the extraordinary high US incarceration rate cannot be explained by a higher victimization rate or by a higher homicide rate.

However, different sources and methods seem to point in different directions, cross-sectionally and over time. Cross-sectional comparisons using state-level data from the United States reveal strong positive correlations between violent crime and imprisonment rates. These correlations are enough reason to assume that differences in crime levels and trends are indeed reflected in imprisonment rates, but they are not proof of causality. More precisely, we cannot conclude from the fact that high crime rates coincide with high imprisonment across the United States that high crime rates are the cause of high prisoner rates, just as we cannot conclude on the basis of this same evidence that high prisoner rates are the cause of high crime rates (even if the latter conclusion is intuitively more plausible). The first obstacle to such a conclusion is the possibility that crime and incarceration rates are determined by external third factors (see Lacey and Soskice, this volume). This is more than a theoretical possibility. A growing body of research—now including this study—confirms that indicators of social equality, poverty, trust, and legitimacy explain both national levels of interpersonal violence and the use of imprisonment (Lappi-Seppälä and Lehti 2015; see Roth, this volume).

This study searched for further evidence of a crime–imprisonment connection from trend analyses and cross-sectional regression analyses. The latter method did provide some evidence in favor of a "connectedness" hypothesis, in that homicide remained a key variable in the most successful regression models. However, trend analyses based on comparisons between changes in crime rates and prisoner rates failed to confirm the connection.

This may not be the end of the story, however. It can be claimed with some justification that short-term analyses are unable to capture longer-term causal dynamics. Perhaps long-term experiences of increasing and high crime trends trigger reorientations in criminal justice policy, which eventually result in substantial changes in national prison populations. Partial support for this version of the connectedness hypothesis was found in those US states that experienced the steepest absolute increases in incarceration rates; those states also had substantially higher homicide rates than "low-riser" states. In addition, aggregated US crime data over long periods of increasing crime from the mid-1950s to the late 1970s, followed by a steep increase in imprisonment rates when crime had stabilized or was oscillating at high levels, support this hypothesis (see Introduction to this volume). Similar crime–imprisonment profiles can be detected in several developed countries but not in all. Clear exceptions include Canada and the Nordic countries.

The mixed results imply that, while there evidently exists a weak "average" causal connection (either through policy effect or volume effect) from crime levels to imprisonment levels, the nature and strength of the connection seem to vary over regions, countries, and time. In the face of this diversity, it is hard to avoid the conclusion that imprisonment rates—in the end—are determined not by crime but by other forces and factors that have led countries to adopt different penal policies. The goal of the final sections of this chapter was to examine such factors.

Answers were sought first with correlational analyses. Incarceration rates were reflected against a number of selected socioeconomic, political, and cultural variables. Similar comparisons were conducted between both nation states (OECD countries) and the 50 individual US states. The results were surprisingly similar, even taking into account the differences in the indicators used. Comparisons with nation states indicate that outcome is dependent on interacting socioeconomic and political factors, which both associate with social and cultural values. The same applies to intra-US penal variation, with its own specificities.

In cross-national comparisons, models developed to predict European incarceration rates placed the United States in the "right direction" or the "right quadrant" of the graph, but actual US imprisonment rates were generally about 250–300 percent higher than predicted. In both the European and US samples, incarceration rates correlated strongly with measures related to welfare and social policy (social spending, income differences, and investments in education). Almost equally strong correlations were found with factors related to social values, including social and institutional trust, fears, and punitivity.

The most important goal of this chapter was to test whether associations between levels of penal repression and key socioeconomic factors prevail in jurisdictions on both sides of the Atlantic. This they clearly did—a finding that underlines the importance of the associations detected in earlier studies and brings new light to policy debate strictly within the United States.

In attempts to identify the "best" explanation, giving weight to multiple independent variables, this chapter developed several regression models. The conclusions were less than definitive. All tested key variables proved to be relevant; they also proved to be highly interconnected and sometimes even interchangeable. Different factors carried different weights, depending on context. Thus, for example, the most powerful predictive models for developed countries did not perform well when applied to poorer countries.

Even in the absence of a single "magic formula," however, there are discernable patterns that tie together the main variable groups and explain the logic of detected correlations, without claiming the existence of strong causal relations. Favorable conditions for an "inclusive" and "liberal" penal policy consist of elements such as negotiating political structures and cultures that support welfarist and egalitarian social policies, social and economic security, trust, legitimacy, and lower fears. Contextual risk factors for an "exclusionary" and "punitive" penal policy, in turn, are that combinations of polarized and conflictual political cultures, which heighten controversies and favor simple solutions for complicated problems, are less favorable for solidarity-driven social policy reforms, trust, and institutional legitimacy and allow public pressures and political self-interest a more direct influence on the administration of crime and justice (a feature most visible in the United States).[58]

Criminal justice policy is formed within societal constraints that are to a surprising degree identifiable and measurable. Choices of ruling penal policies are partly determined by their context, yet knowledge of this reality may help create the freedom and the will to choose otherwise.

NOTES

1. An early version of this chapter was presented at a conference on American exceptionalism in crime and punishment organized by the Robina Institute of Criminal Law and Criminal Justice, University of Minnesota Law School, in 2013. The chapter has subsequently experienced several transformations, thanks to editor Kevin Reitz, who has compelled me to check and recheck my claims and conclusions. I'd like to express my gratitude to Kevin, who chose to invest so much of his time to enlighten me on the peculiarities of US penal practices and whose patience made it possible to transform my raw draft into a chapter eligible for publication.
2. Global and regional incarceration rates may be measured using either an unweighted average (each country is given the same weight in the calculus) or a weighted average (countries are weighted by population size). The former method is more apt, for example, when testing whether state policies follow the same "regional" pattern. In such cases, nations are the unit of analysis, and each state should be given equal weight. Weighted comparisons are more suited when one wishes to know the "overall impact" of incarceration in a certain region or globally. In the latter case, large countries like China and India, with fairly low (reported) incarceration rates (for India 30 and for China 122), will have a strong effect on the results.
3. The positions of the small Caribbean islands can change significantly year by year. The most recent updating of the World Prison List (International Centre for Prison Studies website, http://www.prisonstudies.org/world-prison-brief-data, visited March 24, 2016) places Seychelles on the top (799), with the United States following (698). Other participants in the latest "over 500 group" are St. Kitts and Nevis (607), Turkmenistan (583), Virgin Islands (US) (542), Cuba (510), and El Salvador (509).
4. Subregions in the Americas range from 201 in South America to 291 in the Caribbean and to 700 if the United States is separated from the North American region. Regional rates in both Asia (143) and Africa (119) are relatively low. In Asia, central Asia rates the highest (207). In Africa, the top position is occupied by southern Africa (227). Oceania (165) consists of a large variety of small islands, Australia (152), and New Zealand (202).
5. The groupings of countries will vary in the text, depending on the issue at hand.

6. The downward trend in Finland was mainly due to a long-term decarceration program initiated in the late 1960s and continuing to the mid-1990s (Lappi-Seppälä 2011b).
7. Counting rules for the Dutch prisoner rates have undergone changes that complicate comparisons over time. Older data included groups that are, in most countries, excluded from national prison population statistics, such as foreigners detained on the basis of aliens legislation, mental health patients, and young offenders placed in juvenile detention centers. Excluding these groups reduces the national incarceration rate for the Netherlands by around 20 percent. The Space I project has done work toward standardization, and recent annual reports contain both nonadjusted and adjusted (standardized) figures. Also, older Dutch rates were recounted until 2001 (see Aebi and Delgrande 2014, 58) The non-adjusted peak year for the Dutch prisoner rates in 2005 was 134, but the corresponding adjusted rate was 109. The graphs in the text are based on adjusted figures.
8. For a close comparison of incarceration history in Canada and the United States, see Webster and Doob, this volume.
9. These are divided roughly into western and eastern blocks, and countries with fewer than half a million inhabitants were excluded.
10. The relationship between crime and incarceration can be viewed from two opposite ends: We may wish to know what effect crime has on incarceration rates. Or we may wish to know the effects of incarceration on crime rates (e.g., Pew Charitable Trusts 2014; Donahue 2009). The discussion here focuses only on the former question.
11. This is not necessarily a linear relationship. "Stability" theories of prison policy (formerly) posited that actors throughout legal systems would make unconscious adjustments to maintain "homeostasis" in incarceration rates (e.g., Blumstein and Cohen 1973).
12. Long-term statistical analyses from Finland and Sweden, covering more than 200 years, provide evidence of policy effects (crime influencing penal policies) but no evidence of policies affecting crime rates (von Hofer and Lappi-Seppälä 2014).
13. According to some commentators, lethal violence is also a fairly reliable proxy for serious assaults or other serious violent crimes that create a genuine risk of death. If so, measurement of homicide is also measurement of the "penumbra" of near-lethal crimes (Zimring and Hawkins 1997; Ruth and Reitz 2003).
14. Unrecorded crime may, at most, have an indirect impact on public attitudes and penal demands through increased experiences of victimization (but, as often found, fears and punitive demands are largely unrelated to actual victimization experiences).

15. Homicide data come from the University of Helsinki, Institute of Criminology and Legal Policy data set (see Lehti 2013; Lappi-Seppälä and Lehti 2015). In order to neutralize short-term changes, homicide is measured as total averages for the data available from 2004–2012. Imprisonment rates are the latest available single-year figures (usually from 2013–2015).
16. In the absence of survey data at the state level, the US comparisons are based on reported crime (FBI Uniform Crime Reports) relative to 100,000 population. See https://ucr.fbi.gov/.
17. For an extended comparative argument, see Zimring and Hawkins (1997).
18. The use of annual changes (and not absolute values) eliminates the impact of the level differences between the states in terms of incarceration and homicide. These differences could well override the effects of (more modest) changes within the individual states and lead to a fallacious conclusion known as "Simpson's paradox." The paradox can arise in correlations in which two variables appear to have, say, a positive correlation toward one another, when in fact they have a negative correlation, the reversal having been brought about by a "lurking" confounder. In this case, the lurking confounder would be the level differences between the individual states (and the reasons explaining these level differences). For details, see Pearl (2014).
19. The negative correlation in OECD for 1992–2000 was mainly influenced by the United States, where increasing prisoner trends were combined with decreased homicide rates. The positive correlation within the US states in 1992–2000 was, in turn, much influenced by the radical increase in imprisonment rates in Texas during the early 1990s.
20. The results were tested also with fixed-effects linear regression models (we are obliged for this analyses to Dr. Mikko Aaltonen, Institute of Criminology and Legal Policy). Both variables were log-transformed (natural logarithm). All models included dummies for panels (state or country) and time (year). The models were fitted using both variables as outcomes and lagging the independent variable by either one or four years. The models were fitted separately for the three time periods. The fixed-effects results corresponded roughly to those from difference analyses as presented in text. The US data gave three significant positive coefficients as follows: homicide lagged by one-year period 2001–2010 = .032 (above .106), homicide lagged four years 1977–1991 = .073 (above .004), and 1992–2000 = .055 (above .178). These coefficients can also be interpreted as percentage changes. For instance, a coefficient of .05 means that a 100% increase in the independent variable (crime) is associated with a 5 percent increase in incarceration rates.
21. It is true that recorded crime rates in England and Wales did not go into smooth decline starting in the 1990s but went up from the mid-1990s to around 2005 to a new and higher peak. On "connectedness" theory, one might argue that some

of the prison increase in England and Wales is explained by this second crime peak, which did not occur in Finland or the Scandinavian countries. However, the steady upward growth of English incarceration rates had been under way for three decades *before* its "second crime peak," and there was no change in long-term prison growth when crime rates went into sharp decline after 2005. In addition, English crime-recording practices changed early in the 2000s, and this may have produced an artificial peak that was the product of new rules of classification of offenses rather than any genuine upswing in offending. For details, see Berman (2008).

22. Ruth and Reitz (2003, 73–80) argue that America experienced a "crime spike" from the late 1950s through the 1960s and a sustained "high-crime plateau" from the early 1970s through the early 1990s. They say that these back-to-back phenomena contributed to an entrenched set of cultural and political attitudes that took root in the 1970s. These included heightened fear of crime, willingness to regard criminals as evil rather than disadvantaged, frustration with government's helplessness to reduce crime, and impatience for stronger and more effective responses.
23. This section is partly cowritten by Kevin Reitz.
24. All state-level trend comparisons in this section (and elsewhere in this chapter) are based on prison statistics (covering sentences of at least one year or more) because jail numbers are not available on an annual basis going back into the 1970s.
25. The ratio approach and the absolute-change approach are complementing perspectives on the same phenomenon. The latter has been chosen here for practical reasons and from the point of view of the question analyzed. The focus will be in comparisons between crime trends and prison trends, and in this issue the absolute-change approach seems to have more to offer. In other instances the ratio-change perspective could well be more advisable. This is the case, for example, with comparisons that wish to convey a correct message about the relative magnitude of policy changes in two jurisdictions conducting very dissimilar penal policies. Thus, an increase of 50 prisoners per 100,000 inhabitants would signify only a modest increase for the United States, but in Finland it would double the number of prisoners. For a US reader an absolute change of 50 prisoners/population would not be deemed worth mentioning. An increase of 100 percent (only 50 prisoners/population) would mean a total catastrophe for the Finnish prison service, whereas in the United States this probably would be a matter of minor adjustment. For other benefits of the ratio approach, see Zimring, this volume.
26. High risers include Alabama, Arizona, Arkansas, Idaho, Kentucky, Louisiana, Mississippi, Missouri, Oklahoma, and Texas. Low risers include Maine, Maryland, Massachusetts, Minnesota, Nebraska, New Hampshire, New York, North Carolina, Rhode Island, and Washington.

27. We have seen more than once in this chapter that year-by-year changes in a jurisdiction's homicide rates bear no discernible relationship to year-by-year changes in incarceration rates.
28. This may be evidence of connectedness via policy effects: that rough perceptions of the raw amount of serious violence in a society are important drivers of incarceration policies. However, further investigation into earlier time periods, pre-1977, would be needed to explain how high risers and low risers could start out with roughly similar imprisonment rates in 1977, despite large preexisting differences in homicide rates. There was a major surge in homicide in the United States as a whole from the late 1950s into the mid-1970s—not to mention dislocations in the nation's culture, law, politics, demographics, family configurations, race relations, gender relations, economic inequalities, urban conditions, and foreign policy (Garland 2001)—but no one has closely analyzed the disaggregated crime-and-incarceration histories of the 50 states during this period of turmoil (for gestures in this direction, see Stuntz 2001).
29. It is important to note that in the second row of Figure 5.17 the scales of the *y* axes are much different for the two states. New York's homicide rates across the full period were double or nearly double those of West Virginia—and until the 2000s the New York prison rate was more or less double that in West Virginia.
30. See Figure 5.14, top two charts. The illustration given above is based on the experiences of low and high risers selected according to absolute changes in their incarceration rates from 1977 to 2010.
31. Data for explanatory variables come from different sources for nation states and for the US states and do not measure exactly the same thing. In some instances, there is a close similarity between the country-level and US state-level indicators (for example, the Gini coefficient as a measure of income differences). Even when the match is less precise, the indicators have been chosen to measure, at least roughly, the same phenomena.
32. OECD members are Australia, Austria, Belgium, Canada, Chile, the Czech Republic, Denmark, Estonia, Finland, France, Germany, Greece, Hungary, Iceland, Ireland, Israel, Italy, Japan, Korea, Luxembourg, Mexico, the Netherlands, New Zealand, Norway, Poland, Portugal, the Slovak Republic, Slovenia, Spain, Sweden, Switzerland, Turkey, the United Kingdom, and the United States.
33. Since the main focus is on the differences in state policies, the following uses figures from state and federal institutions. However, results were also counted using 2013 total prison population populations (jails included, data from Glaze and Kaeble 2014). No notable difference could be detected.
34. On the construction of the American HDI, see http://www.measureofamerica.org/the-measure-of-america-2010-2011-book/.
35. Source for non-OECD countries is public social expenditures 2002–2007 percent of GDP (International Monetary Fund) (http://www.ilo.org/dyn/sesame/ifpses.socialdbexp) (more data available from http://www.ilo.org/global/

statistics-and-databases/lang--en/index.htm) and for OECD countries, gross public social expenditures 2011 from OECD social expenditures database (http://www.oecd.org/social/expenditure.htm).

36. Source for global sample for Gini 2010–2013 is World bank database (http://data.worldbank.org) and the US Census Bureau (http://www.census.gov). Because the Gini index is sensitive to changes at the top of the income scale, alternative measures were also tested. Comparisons for 78 nations between the poorest and the richest percentiles of the population (10 and 20 percent) yielded practically identical results.
37. Data for educational performance came from the Legatum Institute Prosperity Index (http://www.prosperity.com).
38. The index is published by an information service, *24/7 WallSt.* Items in the index include unemployment benefits, state spending on education per student, income inequality (Gini coefficient), Medicaid spending per recipient, average state employee pension benefits, welfare cash assistance to families with dependent children (TANF), and costs of living. For details, see Stockdale, Sauter, and Allen (2011).
39. However, among the less developed countries this association is the reverse (see the discussions on this in conclusion).
40. In this connection legitimacy is understood in empirical (attitudinal) terms. Normative aspects of legitimacy are discussed briefly in Lappi-Seppälä 2011a and from more broader perspectives in Tankebe and Liebling (2013).
41. The data are available from http://www.worldvaluessurvey.org/wvs.jsp. Social trust was measured by asking whether respondents agreed with the statement, "Most people can be trusted." Trust in police was measured by the statement, "How much confidence do you have in the police (justice, etc.)." Data for the ESS are available from www.europeansocialsurvey.org/.
42. The Needham Survey measured Americans' values, attitudes, and ways of living, annually from 1975 to 1996. Most measurements were based on a 6-point scale depending on the degree to which the respondents agreed or disagreed with statements presented in the survey. Surveys were conducted in each state with a national total sample of 3,500–4,000 respondents (see https://www.icpsr.umich.edu/icpsrweb/instructors/icsc/datasets.jsp). Because this would leave sample sizes in small states too low, results have been counted from cumulative (pooled) data from surveys conducted between 1988 and 1996.
43. One important caveat is that the Needham survey was discontinued after 1996, so the data are 20 years or more old. Unfortunately, no similarly comprehensive survey data exist on the state-by-state level for the time period after 1996, so the Needham survey is the best available source. If meaningful associations exist between contemporary prison policy and the Needham survey, it is because people's attitudes in one state as opposed to another are reasonably persistent over

time. We must assume a degree of cultural stability that differentiates Minnesota from California from New York, etc.

44. As explained earlier, including the United States in the OECD comparisons weakens the correlations—true in this case, especially with respect to fear of crime.
45. As shown in Barker's (2009) case studies of the states of Washington, New York, and California, some of the consensual and negotiating characteristics associated with Nordic consensual democracies may well be of relevance in explaining internal differences in the United States.
46. The related measures of (normative) legitimacy of political order, including political stability, rule of law, and control of corruption, have been discussed in more detail in Lappi-Seppälä (2011a) and Lappi-Seppälä and Lehti (2015).
47. The Polity index consists of six component measures that refer to key qualities of "executive recruitment," "constraints on executive authority," and "political competition" (Marshall and Cole 2008, 4). The EIU index is developed on the basis of expert evaluations of 60 factors from five areas (election process, civil rights, government capability, participation, and political culture, see http://www.eiu.com and Kriesi et al. 2013). For a comparisons between different measures, see Campbell (2008).
48. The index covers the first five of Lijphart's democracy variables (for details, see Lijphart 2012).
49. For the classification, see http://www.americanthinker.com/blog/2012/07/blue_red_and_swing_states.html.
50. The coding is based on Behrens and Silverman 2002 appendix on state judicial selection laws.
51. Barker (2009) treats the GIP indicator as a measure of centralization. The scores of the 5-point GIP index are derived from six categories: separate elected state-level officials, tenure potential (term limits), appointment power, budget control, veto power, and party control (Beyle 2004, 210–18). Thus, the higher the scores, the stronger the governor's position.
52. See Beyle (2004). Since the SEP is directly linked to the number and powers of *elected officials*, it may well be more important for our purposes than GIP. The SEP index was given values from 1 to 5 in the following order: 5 = only governor or governor/lieutenant governor team elected statewide; 4.5 = governor or governor/lieutenant governor team, with one other elected official; 4 = governor/lieutenant team with some process officials (attorney general, secretary of state, treasurer, auditor) separately elected; 3 = governor/lieutenant governor team with some process officials and some major and minor policy officials elected; 2.5 = governor (no team) with six or fewer officials elected, but none are major policy officials; 2 = governor (no team) with six or fewer officials elected, including one major policy official; 1.5 = governor (no team) with six or fewer officials elected, but two are major policy officials; 1 = governor (no team) with seven

or more process and several major policy officials elected. Thus, the lower the value, the larger the number of officials who are elected separately.

53. Regarding the OECD – USA group, this is understandable since the Polity IV measure ranks almost all of those countries in the highest category. But it also seems that the dimensions measured by this indicator are irrelevant for sanction practices among the less developed nations.
54. While the correlation remains insignificant among the OECD countries, it needs to be noted that Lijphart's sample of 36 democracies covered only two out of three of the OECD countries. Including all original 36 countries in the analyses, the correlation would increase to –.429 with the United States included and to –.581 with the United States excluded.
55. Only countries with data from all variables have been included. Statistical software tools would provide means of dealing with missing values (for example, by replacing missing values with group averages). We have not used this option due to the obvious risks involved (there are no guarantees that countries with missing values represent average cases; one would assume the contrary).
56. For example, increases in economic resources in poorer countries that are just building their criminal justice system will have a different (usually increasing) effect on incarceration rates compared with the impact of economic growth in well-developed welfare states that are investing in education and social services (and less on the expansion of prison services).
57. Factors discussed in this chapter had more to say about the post-1970s changes and much less about the factors behind high starting rates. This discussion would have required wider historical comparisons.
58. More elements (including media cultures and judicial structures) should be added in order to complement the story. This, however, goes beyond the tasks of this chapter.

REFERENCES

Aebi, Marcelo F., Galma Akdeniz, Gordon Barclay, Claudia Campistol, Stefano Caneppele, Beata Gruszczyńska, Stefan Harrendorf, Markku Heiskanen, Vasilika Hysi, Jörg-Martin Jehle, Anniina Jokinen, Annie Kensey, Martin Killias, Chris G. Lewis, Ernesto Savona, Paul Smit, and Rannveig Þórisdóttir. *European Sourcebook of Crime and Criminal Justice Statistics 2014*. 5th ed. Publication Series 80. Helsinki, Finland: European Institute for Crime Prevention and Control, 2014.

Aebi, Marcelo F., and Natalia Delgrande. *Council of Europe Annual Penal Statistics: Space I—Prison Populations. Survey 2013*. Strasbourg, France: Council of Europe, 2014.

Alesina, Alberto, Arnaud Devleeschauwer, William Easterly, Sergio Kurlat, and Romain Wacziarg. "Fractionalization." NBER Working Paper 9411, National

Bureau of Economic Research, Cambridge, MA, 2002. http://www.nber.org/papers/w9411.

Alexander, A. C., R. Inglehart, and C. Welzel. "Measuring Effective Democracy: A Defense." World Values Research 4, no. 1 (2011): 1–40. http://www.worldvaluessurvey.org/WVSPublicationsBooks.jsp?PUB=90.

Alexander, Michelle. *The New Jim Crow: Mass Incarceration in the Age of Colorblindness*. New York: New Press, 2010.

American Law Institute. *Model Penal Code: Sentencing*. Tentative Draft No. 2. Philadelphia: American Law Institute, 2011.

Barker, Vanessa. *The Politics of Imprisonment: How the Democratic Process Shapes the Way America Punishes Offenders*. New York: Oxford University Press, 2009.

Behrens, Mark, and Cary Silverman. "The Case for Adopting Appointive Judicial Selection Systems for State Court Judges." *Cornell Journal of Law and Public Policy* 11, no. 2 (Spring) (2002): 273–360.

Berdejó, Carlos, and Noam Yuchtman. "Crime-Punishment, and Politics: An Analysis of Political Cycles in Criminal Sentencing." *Review of Economics and Statistics*, 95, no. 3 (2013): 741–56.

Berman, Gavin. *Changes in Crime Recording Practices*. Standard Note SN/SG/2607. London: House of Commons Library, 2008.

Bert, Useem, and Anne Morrison Piehl. 2008. *Prison State: The Challenge of Mass Incarceration*. New York: Cambridge University Press, 2008.

Beyle, Thad. "The Governors." In *Politics in the American States: A Comparative Analyses*. 8th ed. Edited by Virginia Gray and Russell L. Hanson, 194–231. Washington, DC: CQ Press, 2004.

Blumstein, Alfred, and Jacqueline Cohen. "A Theory of the Stability of Punishment." *Journal of Criminal Law and Criminology* 64, no. 2 (1973): 198–207.

Bottoms, Anthony. 1995. "The Philosophy and Politics of Punishment and Sentencing." In *The Politics of Sentencing Reform*, edited by Chris Morgan Clarkson and Rod Morgan Clarkson, 17–49. Oxford: Clarendon Press.

Bright, Stephen B. "Political Attacks on the Judiciary: Can Justice Be Done Amid Efforts to Intimidate and Remove Judges for Unpopular Decisions?" *New York University Law Review* 72 (1997): 308–36.

Bucerius, Sandra M., and Michael Tonry, eds. *The Oxford Handbook of Ethnicity, Crime, and Immigration*. New York and Oxford: Oxford University Press, 2013.

Campbell, David F. J. *The Basic Concept for the Democracy Ranking of the Quality of Democracy*. Vienna, Austria: Democracy Ranking, 2008. http://www.democracyranking.org/downloads/basic_concept_democracy_ranking_2008_A4.pdf.

Carson, E. Ann. *Prisoners in 2014*. Washington DC: Bureau of Justice Statistics, 2015.

Christie, Nils. *Crime Control as Industry. Towards GULAGS, Western Style*. Abingdon, UK, and New York: Routledge, 1993.

Donahue, John J., III. "Assessing the Relative Benefits of Incarceration: Overall Changes and the Benefits on the Margin." In *Do Prisons Make Us Safer? The Benefits and Costs of the Prison Boom*, edited by Steven Raphael and Michael A. Stoll, 269–342. New York: Russell Sage Foundation, 2009.

Flanagan, Timothy J., and Kathleen Maguire. *Sourcebook of Criminal Justice Statistics, 1990*. Washington, DC: Bureau of Justice Statistics, 1991.

Forman, James, Jr. "Racial Critiques of Mass Incarceration: Beyond the New Jim Crow." *New York University Law Review* 87 (2012): 21–69.

Frase, Richard S. "What Explains Persistent Racial Disproportionality in Minnesota's Prison and Jail Populations?" *Crime and Justice* 38 (2009): 201–80.

Freedom House. *Freedom in the World 2008*. New York and Washington, DC: Freedom House, 2008. https://www.freedomhouse.org/report/freedom-world/freedom-world-2008.

Garland, David. *The Culture of Control: Crime and Social Order in Contemporary Society*. New York and Oxford: Oxford University Press, 2001.

Garland, David. *The Peculiar Institution: America's Death Penalty in an Age of Abolition*. New York and Oxford: Oxford University Press, 2010.

Glaze, Lauren E., and Danielle Kaeble. *Correctional Populations in the United States, 2013*. Washington, DC: Bureau of Justice Statistics, 2014.

Green, David A. *When Children Kill Children: Penal Populism and Political Culture*. Oxford: Oxford University Press, 2008.

Greenberg, David F. "Punishment, Division of Labor, and Social Solidarity." In *The Criminology of Criminal Law, Advances in Criminological Theory*, edited by William S. Laufer and Freda Adler, 283–361. New Brunswick, NJ: Transaction Publishers, 1999.

Guerino, Paul, Paige M. Harrison, and William J. Sabol. *Prisoners in 2010*. Washington, DC: Bureau of Justice Statistics, 2011.

Hamilton, Claire. *Reconceptualising Penality: A Comparative Perspective on Punitiveness in Ireland, Scotland and New Zealand*. Farnham, UK: Ashgate Publishing, 2014.

Karstedt, Susanne. "Democracy and the Project of Liberal Inclusion." In *Crime, Justice and Social Democracy: International Perspectives*, edited by Kerry Carrington, Matthew Ball, Erin O'Brien, and Juan Tauri, 16–33. London: Palgrave MacMillan, 2013.

Kennedy, Randall. *Race, Crime, and the Law*. New York: Pantheon Books, 1997.

Kriesi, Hanspeter, Sandra Lavenex, Frank Esser, Jörg Matthes, Marc Bühlmann, and Daniel Bochsler. *Democracy in the Age of Globalization and Mediatization*. London: Palgrave MacMillan, 2013.

Kristofferssen, Ragnar. *Correctional Statistics of Denmark, Finland, Iceland, Norway and Sweden 2009–2013*. Kriminalforsorgen. Correctional Services of Norway Staff Academy. Report No. 1/2014. Oslo.

Kritzer, Herbert M. "Law Is the Mere Continuation of Politics by Different Means: American Judicial Selection in the Twenty-First Century." *Depaul Law Review* 56 (2007): 423–67.

Lacey, Nicola. "Why Globalisation doesn't Spell Convergence: Models of Instituional Variation and the Comparative Political Economy of Punishment." In *International and Comparative Criminal Justice and Urban Governance*,edited by Adam Crawford, 214–250. Cambridge: Cambridge University Press, 2011.

Lappi-Seppälä, Tapio. "Penal Policy in Scandinavia." In *Crime and Justice: A Review of Research*. Vol. 36. Edited by Michael Tonry, 217–295. Chicago: University of Chicago Press, 2007.

Lappi-Seppälä, Tapio. "Trust, Welfare, and Political Culture: Explaining Difference in National Penal Policies." In *Crime and Justice: A Review of Research*. Vol. 37. Edited by Michael Tonry, 313–387. Chicago: University of Chicago Press, 2008.

Lappi-Seppälä, Tapio. "Explaining Imprisonment in Europe." *European Journal of Criminology* 8, no. 4 (2011a): 303–28.

Lappi-Seppälä, Tapio. "Changes in Penal Policy in Finland." In *Punitivity. International Developments*. Vol. 1, *Punitiveness—A Global Phenomenon?* Edited by Helmuth Kury and Evelyn Shea, 251–88. Bochum, Germany: Universitätsverlag Dr. Brockmeyer, 2011b.

Lappi-Seppälä, Tapio. "Imprisonment and Penal Demands: Exploring the Dimensions and Drivers of Systemic and Attitudinal Punitivity." In *The Routledge Handbook of European Criminology*, edited by Sophie Body-Gendrot, Mike Hough, Klara Kerezsi, René Lévy, and Sonja Snacken, 295–336. Abingdon, UK, and New York: Routledge, 2013.

Lappi-Seppälä, Tapio, and Martti Lehti. "Cross-Comparative Perspectives on Global Homicide Trends." In *Crime and Justice: A Review of Research*. Vol. 43. Edited by Michael Tonry, 135–230. Chicago: University of Chicago Press, 2015.

Lehti, M. NRILP Comparative Homicide Time Series (NRILP-CHTS). National Research Institute of Legal Policy Research Brief 32/2013. Helsinki, Finland: National Research Institute of Legal Policy, 2013.

Lijphart, Arend. *Patterns of Democracy: Government Forms and Performance in Thirty-Six Countries*. 2nd ed. London: Yale University Press, 2012.

Marshall, Monty G., and Benjamin R. Cole. "Global Report on Conflict, Governance and State Fragility 2008." *Foreign Policy Bulletin* 18 (2008): 3–21. http://www.systemicpeace.org/vlibrary/GlobalReport2008.pdf.

Mauer, Marc. *Race to Incarcerate*. rev. ed. New York: New Press, 2006.

Minton, Todd D., and Zheng Zeng. *Jail Inmates at Midyear 2014*. Washington, DC: Bureau of Justice Statistics, 2015.

Nelken, David. *Comparative Criminal Justice: Making Sense of Difference*. London: Sage, 2010.

Norris, Pippa. *Democratic Deficit: Critical Citizens Revisited*. Cambridge: Cambridge University Press, 2011.

Pearl, Judea. "Understanding Simpson's Paradox." *American Statistician* 68 no. 1 (2014): 8–13. http://ftp.cs.ucla.edu/pub/stat_ser/r414.pdf.

Pew Charitable Trusts. *Most States Cut Imprisonment and Crime*. Washington, DC: Pew Charitable Trusts, 2014.

Pratt, John. "Scandinavian Exceptionalism in an Era of Penal Excess. Part I: The nature and Roots of Scandinavian Exceptionalism." *British Journal of Criminology* 48 (2008): 119–37.

Reitz, Kevin R. "Don't Blame Determinacy: U.S. Incarceration Growth Has Been Driven by Other Forces." *Texas Law Review* 84, no. 7 (2006): 1787–1802.

Ruddell, Rick. "Social Disruption, State Priorities, and Minority Threat: A Cross-National Study of Imprisonment." *Punishment and Society: The International Journal of Penology* 7, no. 1 (2005): 7–28.

Ruth, Henry, and Kevin R. Reitz. *The Challenge of Crime: Rethinking Our Response*. Cambridge, MA: Harvard University Press, 2003.

Snacken, Sonja, and Els Dumortier. *Resisting Punitiveness in Europe? Welfare, Human Rights and Democracy*. London and New York: Routledge, 2012.

Stockdale, Charles B., Michael B. Sauter, and Ashley C. Allen. "The States Doing the Most (and Least) to Spread the Wealth." 24/7 Wall St. November 11, 2011. http://247wallst.com/investing/2011/11/11/the-states-doing-the-most-and-least-to-spread-the-wealth/#ixzz329VXPnXR.

Stuntz, William J. *The Collapse of American Criminal Justice*. Cambridge, MA: Belknap Press, 2001.

Sutton, John R. "The Political Economy of Imprisonment in Affluent Western Democracies 1960–1990." *American Sociological Review* 69 (2004): 170–89.

Tankebe, Justice, and Alison Liebling, eds. *Legitimacy and Criminal Justice: An International Exploration*. Oxford: Oxford University Press, 2013.

Tonry, Michael. "Racial Disproportion in U.S. Prisons." *British Journal of Criminology* 34 (1994): 97–115.

Tonry, Michael. *Thinking about Crime. Sense and Sensibilities in American Penal Culture*. Oxford: Oxford University Press, 2004.

Tonry, Michael. "Determinants of Penal Policies." In *Crime and Justice: A Review of Research*. Vol. 36. Edited by Michael Tonry, 1–48. Chicago: University of Chicago Press, 2007.

Tonry, Michael. *Punishing Race: A Continuing American Dilemma*. Studies in Crime and Public Policy. New York: Oxford University Press, 2012.

US Department of Health and Human Services. *Indicators of Welfare Dependence*. Annual Report to Congress. Washington, DC: Office of Human Services Policy, 2008.

van Dijk, Jan. *The World of Crime: Breaking the Silence on Problems of Security, Justice and Development across the World*. Thousand Oaks, CA: Sage, 2008.

von Hofer, Hanns. "Prison Populations as Political Constructs: The Case of Finland, Holland and Sweden." *Journal of Scandinavian Studies in Criminology and Crime Prevention* 4 (2003): 21–38.

von Hofer, Hanns, Tapio Lappi-Seppälä, and Lars Westfelt. *Nordic Criminal Statistics. Summary of a report. 8th revised edition.* Stockholms universitet. Kriminologiska institutionen. Rapport 2012:2. Stockholm.

von Hofer, Hanns, and Tapio Lappi-Seppälä. "The Development of Crime in Light of Finnish and Swedish Criminal Justice Statistics, Circa 1750–2010." *European Journal of Criminology* 11, no. 2 (2014): 169–94.

Wacquant, Loïc. *Punishing the Poor: The Neoliberal Government of Social Insecurity.* London: Duke University Press, 2009.

Wilson, William Julius. *The Truly Disadvantaged: The Inner City, the Underclass, and Public Policy.* 2nd ed. Chicago: University of Chicago Press, 2012.

Zimring, Franklin E., and Gordon Hawkins. "The New Mathematics of Imprisonment." *Crime and Delinquency* 34, no. 4 (1988): 425–36.

Zimring, Franklin E., and Gordon Hawkins. *The Scale of Imprisonment.* Chicago: University of Chicago Press, 1991.

Zimring, Franklin E., and Gordon Hawkins. *Crime Is Not the Problem: Lethal Violence in America.* New York and Oxford: Oxford University Press, 1997.

Zimring, Franklin E., Gordon Hawkins, and Sam Kamin. *Punishment and Democracy. Three Strikes and You're Out in California.* Oxford: Oxford University Press, 2001.

6

How Exceptional Is the History of Violence and Criminal Justice in the United States? Variation across Time and Space as the Keys to Understanding Homicide and Punitiveness

Randolph Roth

SINCE WORLD WAR II, the United States has stood out from the rest of the affluent world in its violence and in the punitive nature of its criminal justice system. Its homicide rate has been extraordinary, especially during the crime boom from the mid-1960s through the early 1990s, when its rate was 4 to 10 times higher than rates in other affluent nations. If the homicide rate that prevailed in the United States for two-thirds of the twentieth century were to return and persist (roughly 9 per 100,000 persons per year), 1 of every 141 children born today would be murdered; and if the rate that prevailed in the mid-twentieth century and since the mid-1990s were to persist (roughly 6 per 100,000 persons per year), 1 of every 211 children would be murdered (Gartner 1990; Eckberg 1995; Zimring and Hawkins 1997, 3–72; Roth 2009a, 3–8).[1] The rate of incarceration in the United States has also been extraordinary since the mid-1970s. At its peak in 2008, more than 1 in every 100 adults were incarcerated—2.4 million Americans—and an additional 5 million Americans were on probation or parole. The United States employed another 2.4 million people in the criminal justice system—law enforcement, courts, and corrections—to put suspects in jail and punish those found guilty, at a cost of $212 billion (Perkinson 2010, 1–3).[2] And the United States stands alone with Japan among affluent nations in its use of the death penalty, although 18 states and the District of Columbia have abolished the practice. Two-thirds of Americans continue to support the death penalty, and over 1,300 Americans have been executed since its reinstitution in 1976 (Banner 2002, 267–305; Gallup 2015).[3]

It would be a mistake, however, to think that the United States has always been more violent and punitive than other affluent nations. At times the United States has been exceptional for its low rates of imprisonment, execution, and homicide. The question of "exceptionalism," like all comparative historical questions, seldom has a simple answer. Which nations are exceptional? When, and in what ways? Once the question of exceptionalism is asked over a long span of time, its answer is almost always fluid and complicated. That is one of the benefits of comparative historical research. Social scientific research is too often confined to the present or near-present, which constrains the range of variation across time and space and makes it difficult to identify the historical circumstances in which phenomena like homicide and punitive penal policies are most likely to appear. Comparative historians cannot perform controlled experiments, but they can engage in the wide-ranging, nonexperimental empirical research that can isolate the most important causes of such phenomena by showing that those causes recur again and again in the presence of certain phenomena (Lieberson 1985). That is how my colleagues in social science history are trying to identify the causes of violence and punitiveness.

Turning first to violence, the United States has not always had the highest rate of homicide in the affluent world, even during the past century. Many European nations had higher homicide rates in the first half of the twentieth century, particularly during the interwar period and toward the ends of World War I and World War II. The homicide rate in the United States fluctuated within a fairly narrow range in the twentieth century, as did rates in Great Britain, Canada, Australia, and New Zealand, even though the US rate—6–10 per 100,000 persons annually—was much higher than the 1–2.5 per 100,000 in those four nations (Chenais 1981; Archer and Gartner 1984). The United States also experienced a sustained drop in its homicide rate from the early 1930s to the mid-1950s, reaching a low of 4.5 per 100,000. By 1956–1957, the rate for "white" Americans had dropped from 6 per 100,000 to only 2.3 per 100,000—a rate comparable to those in postwar Europe, Canada, Australia, and Japan. Rates for racial minorities were higher: 2.9 for Asian Americans, 16.5 for Native Americans, and 23.7 for African Americans. But the rate for

African Americans was half what it had been in 1933, and the rate for Asian Americans was only an eighth. Only the rate for Native Americans was persistently high (Roth 2009a, 435–52).

Looking further back in history, homicide rates in the northern United States and the mountain South were extraordinarily low from the 1790s into the early 1840s—perhaps the lowest in the Western world. They ranged from 1 per 100,000 adults annually in northern New England and parts of the rural Midwest to just over 6 per 100,000 in New York City. Those rates were comparable to rates in Canada, Sweden, and the Low Countries and lower than rates in the rest of Europe. When we consider that roughly half of all homicide victims in that era would have survived with the help of modern emergency services, antiseptics, antibiotics, fluid replacement, surgery, and wound care, the homicide rate in the early nineteenth century was truly exceptional because the weapons at hand—knives, axes, pistols, muskets, hand tools, fists, and feet—were as lethal as today's. The victimization rate for African Americans was comparable to the rate for European Americans, but African Americans—particularly those who were enslaved—were less likely to commit murder than European Americans. Today's pattern of higher rates of commission by African Americans appeared only at the end of the nineteenth century. Homicide rates in the slave South were higher after the Revolution than they had been before and were elevated compared to rates in most of western and central Europe. But they were comparable to rates in southern and eastern Europe—10–15 per 100,000 adults annually—except on contested frontiers like Florida and Texas, where homicide rates ran to 40–80 per 100,000 adults annually or higher. Homicide rates and patterns were quite different in the early nineteenth century from those of today, although most of the American South already had higher homicide rates than the Northeast or the Midwest.[4]

Comparable historical data have not been gathered for criminal justice systems, so it is not yet possible to compare with precision the punitiveness of the system in the United States with that of other systems over time. The prison movement began in Europe, of course, in the late eighteenth and early nineteenth centuries; and a number of prisons were built in local jurisdictions in England and elsewhere. But paradoxically, the United States was the first nation in the world to commit itself wholeheartedly to building prisons, even though those institutions housed only a tiny proportion of the population, particularly in the South, where slaves were punished by other means: corporal punishments, executions, or transportation to the Caribbean. Eight states established prisons between 1785 and 1799 for the long-term incarceration of felons, and most other states followed suit in the early nineteenth century (Lewis 1965; Hindus 1980; Rothman 1980; Ayres 1984, 34–72; Rafter 1985;

Hirsch 1992; Morris and Rothman 1995, 111–226; Meranze 1996; Colvin 1997; Pestritto 2000; Ward and Rogers 2003; Kahn 2005; Cusac 2009; Perkinson 2010, 47–82).

States did not build the first prisons because of a crime problem (rates for most violent and nonviolent felonies were moderate or low) but because prisons appeared ideally suited to punishing and rehabilitating felons in a democratic society. Prior to the Revolution, older forms of punishment—shaming, whipping, branding, maiming, and execution—made sense in a society in which 75–85 percent of the population had embraced Reformed theology and the idea of innate depravity. Most colonists believed that people who were not predestined to receive the gift of God's grace could never be reformed—they were wanton sinners bound for hell who would follow the Ten Commandments only out of fear of public humiliation, physical pain, or death. But after the Revolution, Reformed theology died away quickly, replaced by theologies that emphasized the ability of people to reform (or be reformed) through hard work, discipline, prayer, and the freely given gift of God's grace (no more predestination). Prisons suddenly made sense because they promised to rehabilitate felons and transform them into productive, law-abiding citizens. Prisons could isolate felons from bad influences, minister to their souls, teach them marketable skills, and educate them in the proper ways of society.

It would be a mistake, of course, to think of the new nation's prisons as benign. They were also meant to punish and to serve as a deterrent. The worst penalty in a free society, after all, was not the infliction of physical pain, or even death, but the denial of freedom. And the treatment of prisoners within prisons turned out to be harsher than reformers intended. Prisoners were humiliated. Guards shaved their heads, dressed them in particolored clothing (like contemporary clowns), and forced them to live and work largely in silence. Prisoners were forced to labor against their will, forging nails, weaving cloth, making shoes, or quarrying stone. Corporal punishment did not disappear: it retreated behind prison walls. Prisoners were subjected to severe physical punishments for resistance or disobedience, including whipping, beating, chaining, and solitary confinement. Prisoners were isolated from their loved ones. Visitors other than chaplains were rare or forbidden. And living conditions were often terrible, particularly in states that were hard-pressed financially. Overcrowding, poor diets, poor sanitation, poor medical care, and premature deaths from disease or malnutrition were commonplace. No wonder suicides, riots, escape attempts, and attacks on guards were frequent. It was no accident that violence erupted when persons who once enjoyed freedom suddenly found themselves socially "dead," to invoke Orlando Patterson's phrase for describing the social condition of slaves—subject to general dishonor and coercion and forcibly alienated from their families, ancestors, and heirs (Patterson 1982, 38–45; Roth 1994; Edgerton 2004; Perkinson 2010, 47–82).

The apparatus for treating felons punitively was thus in place in the United States by the early nineteenth century. But it was used sparingly, not only because crime rates were moderate or low but because Americans and their courts tended to be lenient in the nineteenth century toward persons suspected of serious crimes, or at least toward white suspects. The state of Ohio, for instance, imprisoned only 33 persons per 100,000 in its state penitentiary in the early nineteenth century—a fraction of the 500 per 100,000 in the United States today—and inmates served an average of only 3.3 years.[5] The criminal justice system was lenient even when it came to murder. Fewer than half of all homicide suspects of European descent were found guilty or murder or manslaughter (or not guilty by reason of insanity). In northern New England, only 43 percent of known homicides by white suspects ended in a sanction of any kind; in rural Illinois and Ohio, 29 percent; and in rural Georgia, 23 percent. In most cases, suspects fled or were never identified, indictments were not brought, charges were dropped, or suspects were found not guilty, usually on the grounds of provocation, mutual combat, or self-defense. The low homicide rates in the North and mountain South and the moderate rate in the slave South were not caused by deterrence (Roth 2009b).

Capital punishment was also rare for whites, particularly in the North, where the movement to abolish the practice was strongest. The data that scholars have gathered on legal executions are still incomplete, particularly for slave and frontier states; but they show that the execution rate declined steeply after the Revolution, reaching a low point in the early 1840s (Figure 6.1). Three states abolished capital punishment altogether by the Civil War, and other northern states abolished it in fact as a result of decisions by northern judges, juries, legislators, and governors to hand down prison sentences for murderers or issue commutations or pardons. Before the Civil War, Maine executed no one after 1837, Vermont no one after 1839, and New Hampshire only one person after 1843. Public officials like Governor Samuel Crafts of Vermont were so confident of America's future that they thought crime—especially violent crime—would soon be a thing of the past, thanks to the blessings of freedom, democracy, and enlightened laws. "All experience shows that crime has not increased, but diminished, as the criminal laws of a country have become less barbarous and vindictive. Retaliatory punishments have in a measure ceased, and the only sound and substantial reasons for the infliction of punishment are based upon the reformation of the criminal and the security of

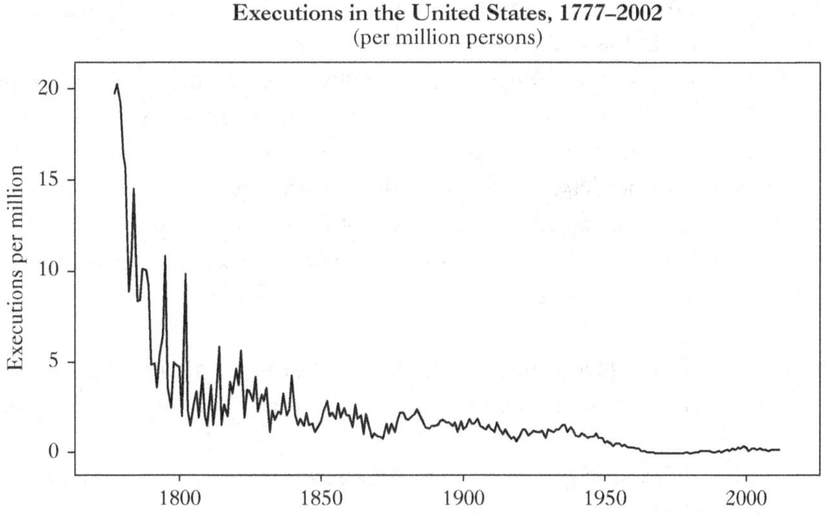

FIGURE 6.1 Executions in the United States, 1777–2002
Sources: Espy and Smykla (2004) and Death Penalty Information Center (2016).

the public." It was time in Crafts' opinion to "demand a commutation or mitigation of punishment," especially in cases of murder or treason (Blaine 1986; Roth 1997, 16–17; Banner 2002, 88–143).[6]

Law enforcement was rudimentary as well, except in the South, where most rural counties had regular slave patrols staffed by armed, mounted citizens and where five cities had military-style police departments by the mid-1830s to control slaves and prevent rebellions. Most local and county governments across the nation spent little to prevent crime or apprehend criminals among the free population. County sheriffs might have had a few deputies, and towns might have had a few part-time constables and watchmen; but modern police were absent from all but three northern cities in the 1830s and 1840s, and those three forces, in Boston, New York, and Philadelphia, were designed primarily to deter riots, not crime, and to ensure that those cities' burgeoning working-class neighborhoods remained orderly. Few citizens feared violence, except from slaves. Americans of the early nineteenth century would be shocked to know how violent and punitive their society would become and how massive and expensive their criminal justice system would be (Lane 1967; Ayres 1984, 73–137; Roussey 1996; Miller 1999; Hadden 2001).

How can we account for the great differences in the United States over time in violence, punitiveness, and deterrence? Why at some times (but not others) has violence been so common, the will to punish so severe? And why has the comparative ranking of the United States among nations changed over time? These are central questions for criminal justice historians and historians of violence in the United States.

The answers to these questions are hotly debated. But as Gary LaFree, Manuel Eisner, Roger Gould, and I discovered independently in the 1990s, homicide rates among unrelated adults in modern and early modern nation states appear to be determined by feelings toward government and society (LaFree 1998; Eisner 2001; Gould 2003; Roth 2009a). As I put it in my own work, there have been four correlates of low rates in North America and western Europe over the past 450 years:

1. The belief that government is stable and that its legal and judicial institutions are unbiased and will redress wrongs and protect lives and property.
2. A feeling of trust in government and the officials who run it and a belief in their legitimacy.
3. Patriotism, empathy, and fellow feeling arising from racial, religious, or political solidarity.
4. The belief that the social hierarchy is legitimate, that one's position in society is or can be satisfactory, and that one can command the respect of others without resorting to violence.

These are the key elements, as historians will be quick to recognize, of successful nation building. When these elements are in place, humans are more willing to cooperate and sacrifice for the good of the whole, and homicide rates are low. But when these elements are not in place and humans sense that their political system is in disarray, that their lives and property are in jeopardy, that their government does not have their interests at heart, that they have little in common with many of their fellow citizens, and that they have little hope of attaining or maintaining their proper place in society, humans are more contentious and, in the extreme, power-hungry and predatory. In such circumstances, homicide rates can reach catastrophic levels. Homicide, intentional or premeditated, political or apolitical, is thus in the aggregate a consequence of the adaptation of humans to group living. When nations—the primary social group for most humans today—falter or fail, aggression and struggles for dominance proliferate until new or more successful nations emerge from the conflict (Roth 2009a, 16–26, 2011).

The correlation between political stability, legitimacy, and everyday homicides has been evident at many times and in many places. Every period of political instability in nineteenth-century France—1830–1831, 1848–1850, 1870–1871—saw a spike in homicide, not just in places that were engulfed in revolutionary violence but in places remote from such violence. As Roger Gould discovered, the homicide rate spiked in the same years even on the island of Corsica, where there were no politically motivated homicides, only an increase in feud violence and honor killings. In England, the frustration of the democratic aspirations of working people in the wake of the Napoleonic wars led to a doubling of the homicide rate after the massacre of voting rights demonstrators at Peterloo in 1819 and to a sustained high rate through the years of Chartist agitation. But when the Second Reform Act passed in 1867, enfranchising propertyless household heads in urban areas, the homicide rate fell suddenly by half; and when the Third Reform Act passed in 1884, enfranchising propertyless household heads in rural areas, the homicide rate fell suddenly by half again. Such patterns have appeared time and again in the history of Western nations over the past 450 years, so often that they show that the relationship between nation building and homicide is causal, even though few homicides are motivated directly by political conflict or political feelings (Chenais 1981, 73–85; Gould 2003, 150–61; Roth 2009a, 243–49, 297–99, 436–37; Nivette and Eisner 2013).

The correlations among feelings, beliefs, and homicides among unrelated adults can be quantified, now that data are available that can be used as proxies for studying changes in political stability, legitimacy, and fellow feeling. Consider, for instance, the rapid drop in the homicide rates among European colonists in British North America between 1675 and 1693, to one-third of their previous levels in Virginia and Maryland and to one-sixth of the previous level in New England. That sudden decline occurred at a time when, as humanistic historians have argued, European colonists banded together along racial lines in the wake of the disastrous Indian wars of the late seventeenth century and racial slavery emerged as a dominant force in American society and when colonists became more patriotic and politically content in the wake of the Glorious Revolution of 1688. The numbers bear this out. The number of individuals banished, exiled, or executed for treason or sedition—a measure of political instability and of challenges to the legitimacy of government—fell to near zero, as did the number of deadly riots and rebellions involving contests for political power or protests against the abuse of power by the government or its officials. The number of individuals banished, exiled, or executed for heresy, witchcraft, or moral offenses (adultery, bestiality, pederasty, etc.)—a measure of hostility, division, and distrust within communities—also fell to near zero, as did deadly riots that sought to regulate the behavior of members of the community. The proportion of new counties named for notable British citizens—a sign of patriotic solidarity—jumped from 40 to 80 percent (Roth 2009a, 61–107, 2012, 197–216). These correlations persisted in the United States through the nineteenth century. The murder rates rebounded with every increase in divisive speech and deadly riots and rebellions and with every decline in the use of patriotic symbols. Political stability, legitimacy, and solidarity—and the feelings and beliefs that sustained them—mattered.

These patterns can help us make sense of America's "exceptional" homicide rates, including the low rates in the North and mountain South in the early nineteenth century and the high rates from the mid-1960s through the early 1990s. The early nineteenth century was a time of great political stability, as indicated by the small number of deadly riots and rebellions in the decades after the Revolution. Riots and political demonstrations involving fisticuffs and property damage were numerous; but they almost always stopped short of lethal violence, and their participants viewed them as legitimate vehicles for protest in a democratic society. It was also a period of great patriotism and national unity. The proportion of new counties named for national heroes peaked in the 1820s and 1830s at nearly 50 percent, and hate speech—including the use of racially and politically charged words like the *N* word or phrases like "slave power"—were rarely used in public discourse (Roth 2012).

But perhaps most important, the Revolution also fostered a belief in the unique promise of the new nation. America would be a country where everyone had a chance to be economically independent. The abolition of slavery, the extension of voting rights, increased toleration for religious dissenters, and high levels of homeownership and self-employment convinced the vast majority of northerners that they were on their way toward putting an end to the oppression, prejudice, and abject poverty that had kept people down for centuries in aristocratic and monarchical societies. Obviously, there was room for improvement in their society, but most people believed that now everyone could get married, set up a household, and own a shop or farm. The sole requisite for success was hard work. Even the poor, Catholics, and former slaves shared that belief, despite the financial obstacles and social prejudices they faced. The social hierarchy that emerged in the North after the Revolution was thus perceived as more legitimate than any that had preceded it. The hostile, defensive, and predatory emotions that lay behind the murders of friends, acquaintances, and strangers were supplanted by the feeling that everyone in America could participate in this grand social and political experiment (Roth 2009a, 180–249). For most people this faith in the social and political order of the post-revolutionary North was justified. By the end of the War of 1812, 60 percent of all adult men in the North owned their own shops or farms. That figure was closer to 80 percent for men in their mid-30s and older. Most of those who did not own shops or farms at least owned homes or headed independent households. Owning a house or shop or farm was the standard by which people were judged. Those who owned property had a sense of accomplishment, greater resilience in the face of disappointments, and a strong bond with other property owners (Montgomery 1967, 25–31; Wilentz 1984, 61–103; Roth 1987, 117–41).

The same sense of promise and opportunity was common in the mountain South, where homicide rates were also extraordinarily low. The slave South, however, had a higher homicide rate in the decades after the Revolution than it had had in the mid-eighteenth century because the Revolution had delegitimized its social hierarchy. Revolutionary ideas and aspirations wrought havoc with the status hierarchy of slave society in a number of ways. Poor and middle-class whites were increasingly frustrated by their inability to rise in a society that remained class-bound and hierarchical. Prominent whites were subjected to the rough and tumble of democracy and were infuriated by the way they were treated by their peers and by social inferiors. Blacks despaired over the failure of the abolition movement in the South, and whites were more fearful than ever of black rebellion. As a result, impatience with restraint and sensitivity to insult were more intense in the slave South, and during this period the region saw more than its share of deadly quarrels, property disputes, duels, and interracial killings (Roth 2009a, 199–233).

People in the slave South were also less likely than people in the North or the mountain South to trust the federal government and to identify with the new nation. Distrust blossomed in the 1820s and 1830s as proslavery southerners realized that the federal government had turned against them on a number of vital issues, including the admission of new slave states and territories and the suppression of abolitionist speech. The distrust may not have been strong enough to raise the homicide rate, but it was strong enough to nullify the dampening effect that the patriotism of the post–War of 1812 period should have had on the homicide rate among whites. In those decades, when American nationalism reached its nineteenth-century peak, identification with national heroes was weaker in the South than in the nation as a whole. The difference was so strong that a higher percentage of places were named in the North than in the South for the South's national heroes, including Washington, Jefferson, and Jackson. Regional differences in national loyalty would become even more marked in the 1860s, of course, and again in the 1890s (Zelinsky 1988, 119–43). But they were substantial enough in the post-revolutionary period to help raise the homicide rate above the levels of the mid- eighteenth century. The slave South thus became the first region of the United States to deviate from the long-term trend toward lower homicide rates in North America and western Europe. But its homicide rate was nonetheless moderate compared to rates in much of southern and eastern Europe.

The question remains, how did the homicide rate in the United States come to stand out among affluent nations by the late twentieth century? The deep-seated cause was the nation's catastrophic failure at nation building in the mid-nineteenth century, which set the United States on its homicidal path. No Western nation suffered a national breakdown in the nineteenth century as severe or as violent as the United States did between the Mexican War and the end of Reconstruction, when the rate of politically motivated homicides and nonpolitical homicides spiked. The United States has not yet recovered from that political crisis, which left in its wake racial and regional animosities that have made it difficult for Americans to build a strong sense of national unity and a deep-seated distrust of government, especially among whites in the former Confederacy, that has made it impossible for many Americans to accept the legitimacy of the federal government, particularly when politicians they support are out of power. The hatred, fear, and distrust are not as intense as they were during the Civil War era, nor is the homicide rate as high. But those feelings persist (Roth 2009a, 297–385).

Homicide rates have fluctuated, however, since the Civil War era. They reached a low point in the mid-1950s when, as Gary LaFree observes, trust in government and faith in public officials were at their highest in the post–World War II era. That trust and faith grew out of the successes of the New Deal, victory in World War II, and the strength of the postwar economy, which persuaded the majority of Americans, especially among the poor, that the federal government was competent, legitimate, and interested in the welfare of all. Patriotism and national solidarity were also at their post–World War II peaks because of the Cold War and the gradual integration of Asian Americans and African Americans into mainstream society (LaFree 1998; Roth 2009a, 440–52).

Feelings toward government and society changed rapidly, however, in the mid-1960s and 1970s as the struggle for civil rights turned divisive, as the war in Vietnam became unpopular, and as deindustrialization made it difficult for the poor who had not finished high school to rise into the middle class. Once again, the homicide rate rose, but it tracked differently for blacks and whites. The black homicide rate peaked between 1971 and 1974, when black trust in government reached a post–World War II low. The white homicide rate peaked in 1980 during the final year of the Carter administration, when white trust in government reached its postwar low because of accumulated anger over busing, welfare, affirmative action, the defeat in Vietnam, and the seizure of American hostages in Iran. That rate—7 per 100,000 white persons

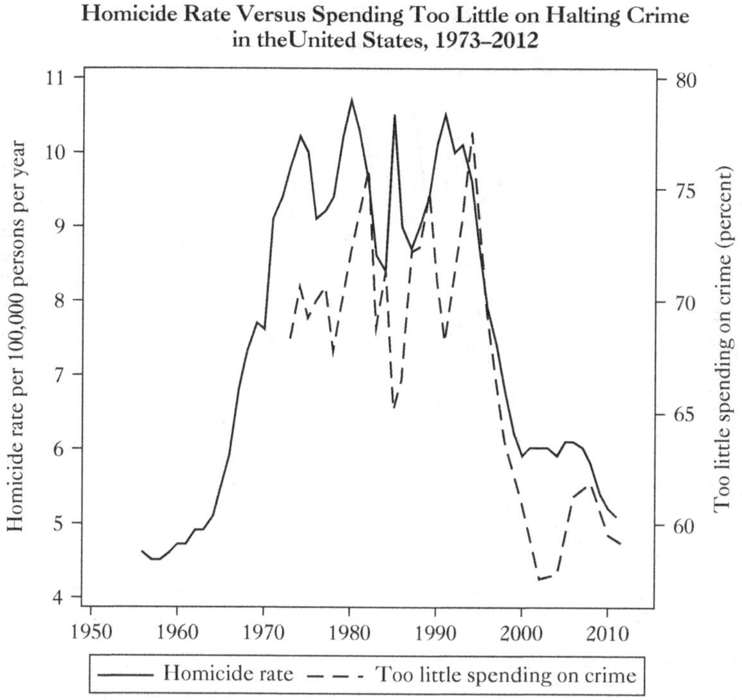

FIGURE 6.2 Homicide Rate versus Spending Too Little on Halting Crime in the United States, 1973–2012

Sources: Smith (2013), Bureau of the Census (1937–1967), and Centers for Disease Control and Prevention (2016).

annually—was by itself 3 to 15 times the homicide rate in other affluent nations, which had seen their homicide rates fall after World War II (LaFree 1998; Roth 2009a, 452–68).

Did punitiveness follow the same pattern? Tapio Lappi-Seppälä (2008, 2011) finds a close correlation cross-nationally in recent decades between distrust in government, lack of fellow feeling, national disunity, and high rates of incarceration. A similar pattern has appeared in the United States since World War II. According to Smith (2013) and Dugan (2014), the proportion of Americans who feel that too little was being spent by government on halting crime or who fear walking alone near their homes at night has gone up and down since World War II with the level of trust in government and with the murder rate (Figures 6.2 and 6.3). The same pattern holds for support for the death penalty, although only after a lag of a few years, which suggests that support for the death penalty responds to perceived differences in the rate of violent crime rather than to the feelings and beliefs which determine those rates.

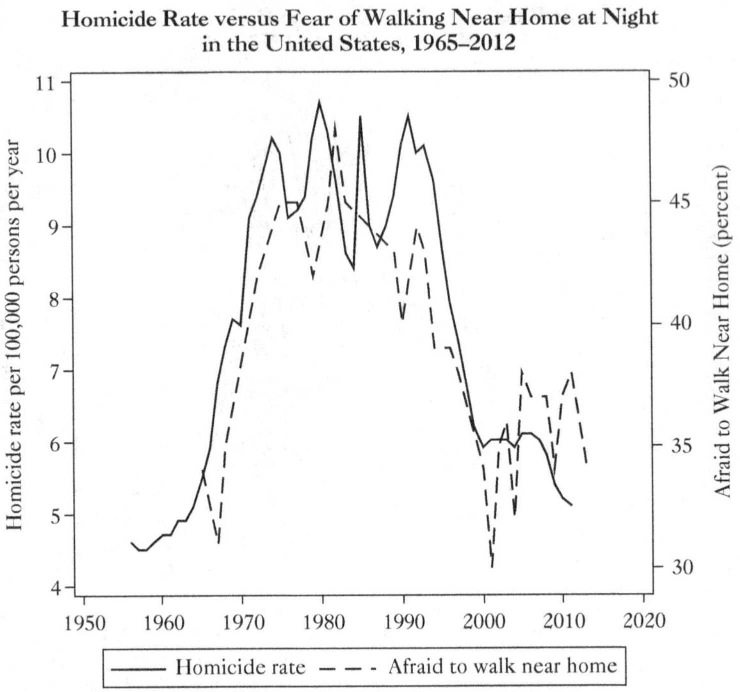

FIGURE 6.3 Homicide Rate versus Fear of Walking Near Home at Night in the United States, 1965–2012

Sources: Dugan (2014), Bureau of the Census (1937–1967), and Centers for Disease Control and Prevention (2016).

Support for the death penalty declined to 42 percent in the mid-1960s, rose to 80 percent by the mid-1990s, and has since fallen to 63 percent, a pattern that reveals a delayed reaction to changes in the homicide rate (Figure 6.4). Changes in incarceration rates and expenditures on law enforcement have also lagged since World War II behind changes in the homicide rate and in feelings toward government and society. The surge in incarceration and spending on law enforcement began in the 1970s, once it was clear that the level of violent crime had risen; and the surge continued for nearly a decade after the rate of violent crime began to fall in the mid-1990s. Punitiveness and homicide among unrelated adults appear to have had the same correlates in recent decades but at a remove of a few years.

But when we look back to the nineteenth century, it is not yet certain whether the same close relationships prevailed among punitiveness, expenditures on law enforcement, violent crime, and feelings toward government and society. The requisite data on capital punishment and incarceration have

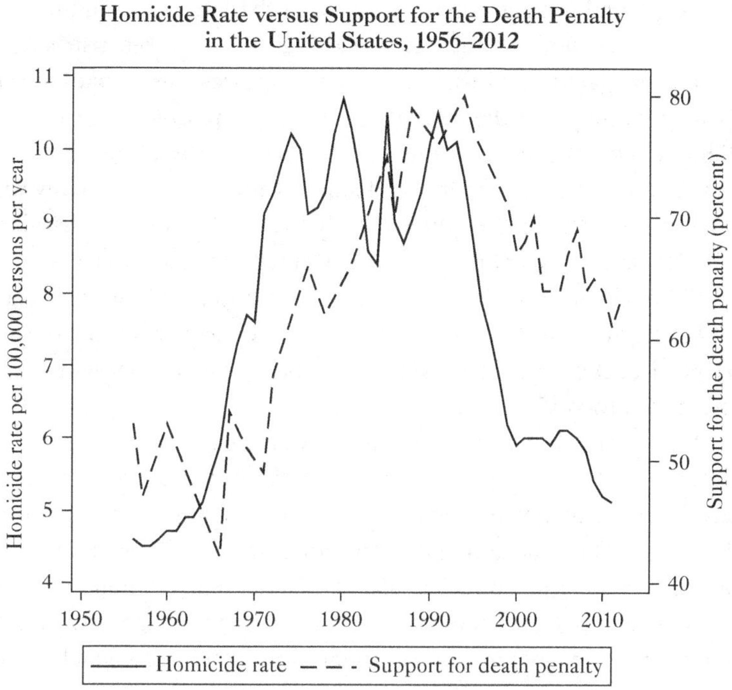

FIGURE 6.4 Homicide Rate versus Support for the Death Penalty in the United States, 1956–2012

Sources: Gallup (2015), Bureau of the Census (1937–1967), and Centers for Disease Control and Prevention (2016).

been gathered systematically for only a handful of states and the data on law enforcement for only a handful of cities. Data on incarceration and law enforcement are available in the federal census, but it is as yet unknown how reliable those data are. It appears that incarceration rates and expenditures on law enforcement rose between the early 1840s and the early twentieth century and that the execution rate, despite fluctuations, remained low; but it is difficult as yet to be precise.

The rate of executions appears to have increased in the 1850s and during the Civil War, after the homicide rate spiked beginning in the late 1840s (Figure 6.1). Several northern states that had suspended the use of the death penalty in the 1830s or early 1840s used it with a vengeance during and after the Civil War. From 1864 to 1882, New Hampshire carried out a third of the executions that have occurred in that state since the American Revolution, and Vermont carried out half. But the execution rate never rebounded nationally to the levels it had reached during the colonial, revolutionary, or early national eras; and it dropped substantially in the late 1860s and early 1870s, even though the homicide rate remained high through Reconstruction. And by the late nineteenth and early twentieth centuries, the execution rate was as low as it had been in the early 1840s, even though the homicide rate was much higher (and the data on capital punishment more complete). It is doubtful therefore that execution rates and support for the death penalty followed the same logic in the nineteenth and early twentieth centuries that they have since World War II, except perhaps in the late 1840s and 1850s. Opposition to the death penalty (or distaste for it) was so widespread that judges and jurors used it sparingly, even amid the worst homicide crisis that any Western nation experienced in the nineteenth century. Punitiveness did not win out in this instance (Roth 1997; Banner 2002, 208).

On the other hand, incarceration rates and expenditures on the police increased steadily from the mid-nineteenth century into the early twentieth century, whether or not the homicide rate was rising or the nation was in political crisis. The data gathered by the late Eric Monkkonen on the number of police officers per 100,000 persons in 23 cities show that the number rose gradually from a polished median of 90 in the 1850s to 180 after World War I (Figure 6.5), even though the homicide rate fluctuated considerably from

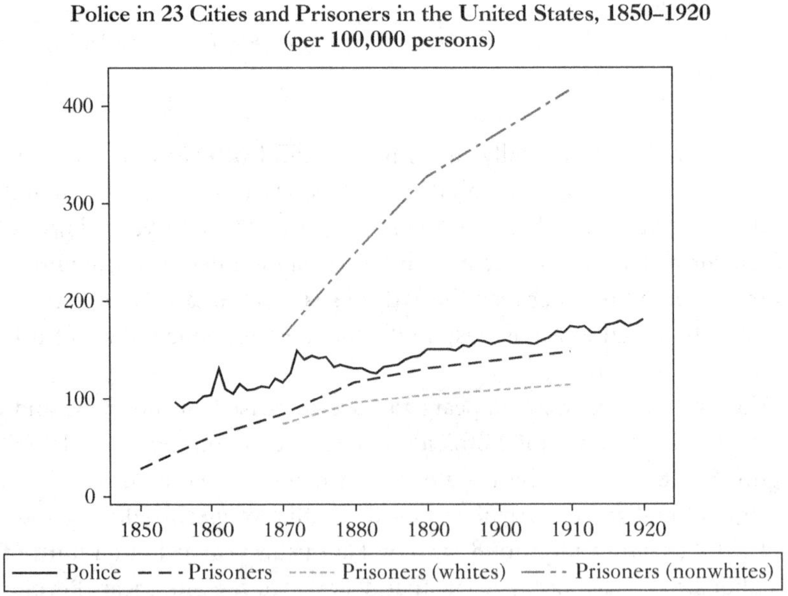

FIGURE 6.5 Police in 23 Cities and Prisoners in the United States, 1850–1920
Sources: Monkkonen (1981), Sec. of the Interior (1866), Census Office (1888, 1895), Bureau of Census (1907, 1918).

decade to decade in the North and South and declined steadily in the West. Indeed, in cities where data on both the homicide rate and the number of police per capita are available, there was no correlation from year to year or decade to decade between the homicide rate and the number of police per capita. The brief spike in the number of police per capita in the early 1870s and the drop over the next decade was an anomaly caused by the dramatic increase in expenditures on law enforcement by Republican administrations in southern cities during Reconstruction (Figure 6.6). The Republicans spent more on police in the South because they wanted to integrate blacks into their police forces; protect black and white Republicans against violence from white supremacists; provide social services to the poor and the homeless; enforce city codes aimed at improving sanitation, housing, and public health; ensure that justice was even-handed; and see to it that elections were orderly. The drop in expenditures on police in the mid- and late 1870s occurred as white supremacists regained control of city governments, dismissed black officers, and slashed budgets for law enforcement and social services. By 1880, the median proportion of blacks in the police forces of southern cities was zero. These changes had little to do with the homicide rate or with general attitudes toward government and society and everything to do with the battle between Republicans and conservative Democrats for control of the South after the Civil War. It seems, therefore, that cities large and small simply spent more and more on law enforcement from the late 1830s (when Boston and New

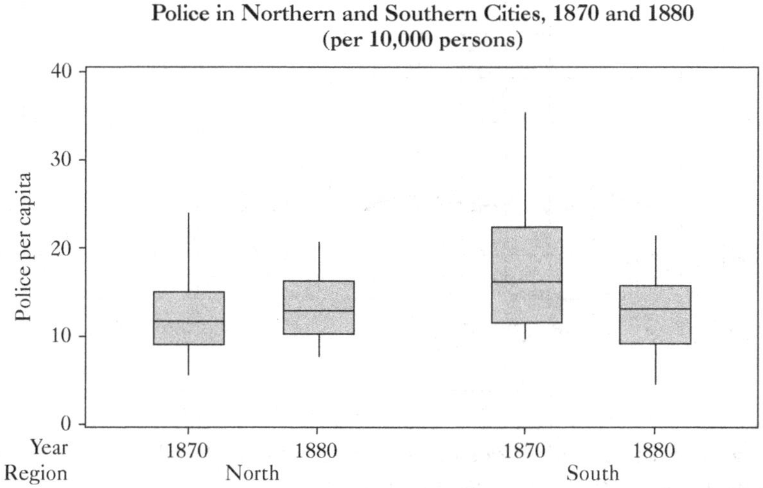

FIGURE 6.6 Police in Northern and Southern Cities, 1870–1880
Sources: Monkkonen (1981) and Roussey (1996).

Orleans organized the first modern police departments) into the early twentieth century, just as cities in other Western nations did, a process that was largely indifferent to changes in the rate of violent crime or to changes in the feelings toward government and society that determined the rate of violent crime (Monkkonen 1981; Roussey 1996).

The rate of incarceration also appears to have increased steadily until the end of the century, when it leveled off. Comprehensive data are not yet available except through the federal census.[7] Those data show that the number of prisoners per 100,000 persons (including prisoners in local jails and in juvenile facilities) rose substantially, from 29 in 1850 to 117 in 1880 and 148 in 1910—a rate that would persist into the early 1970s (Figures 6.5 and 6.7). It is probable that a similar, steady increase occurred between the late 1780s and 1790s, when the first state prisons were founded, to 1850. At the regional level, incarceration rates were highest in the Southwest and the Mountain West—then the most homicidal region in the United States—rather than in the South, which today has the highest rates of homicide and incarceration

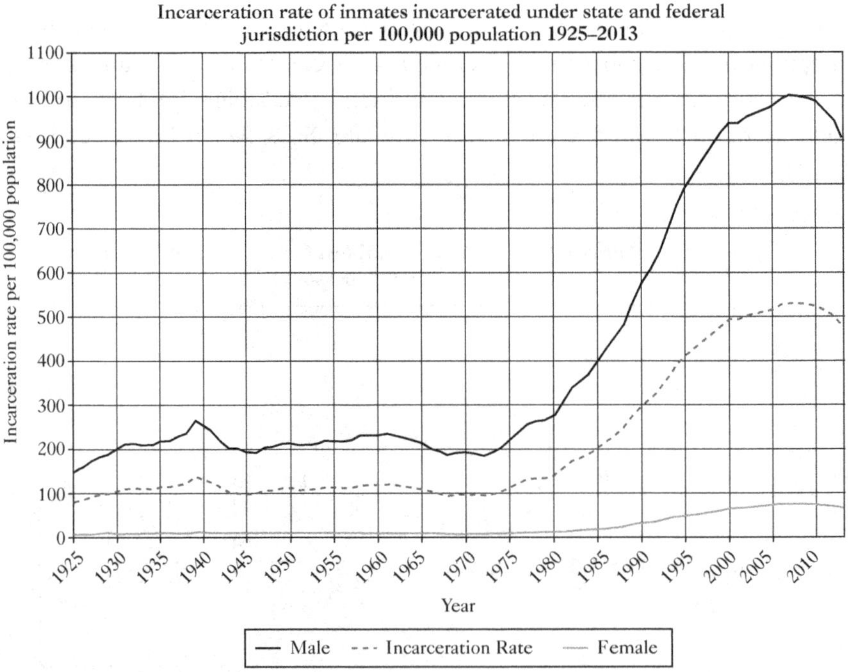

FIGURE 6.7 Incarceration Rate of Inmates Incarcerated under State and Federal Jurisdiction per 100,000 Population, 1925–2013

Source: Sourcebook of Criminal Justice Statistics Online (2017), Table 6.28.2012. http://www.albany.edu/sourcebook/pdf/t6282012.pdf.

(Figure 6.8). After the Civil War, most southern states leased most convicts to private contractors rather than send them to prison, which kept incarceration rates relatively low in the South until each state banned the practice in the early twentieth century (Ayres 1984, 185–222; Colvin 1997; Perkinson 2010, 83–214). The prairie states had the lowest rates of incarceration. But the most notable finding is that incarceration rates appeared to follow the same logic as expenditures on law enforcement: they increased steadily into the early twentieth century, then leveled off, regardless of trends in violent crime or in feelings toward government and society. Again, that may have been a common pattern among Western nations, including Great Britain and Canada, rather than a pattern unique to the United States. But we need better data on the United States and on other Western nations to be certain.

In sum, the historical data from the United States in the late twentieth and early twenty-first centuries support the idea that violence and punitiveness have similar causes and follow a similar logic, rooted in feelings and beliefs toward government and society. But the data available from the United States in the nineteenth and early twentieth centuries show strong secular trends away from capital punishment and toward more police and prisons that had little or nothing to do with changes in the level of violence or in feelings and beliefs toward government and society.

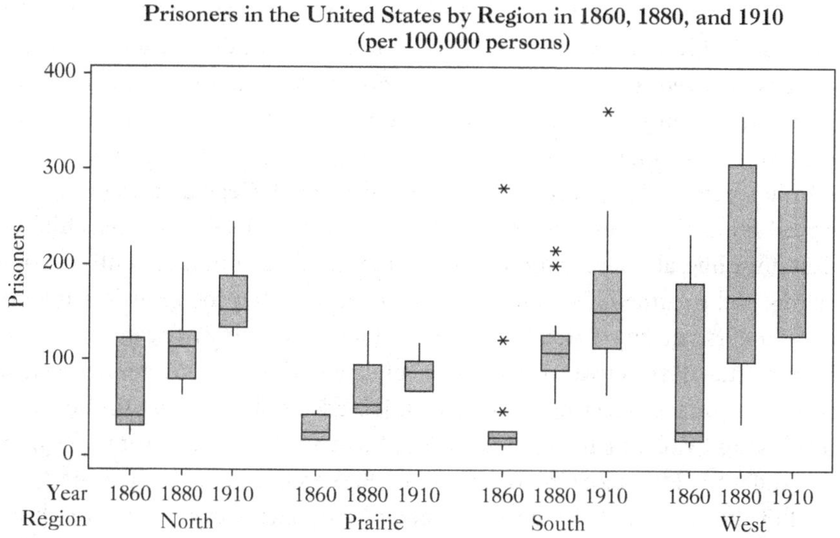

FIGURE 6.8 Prisoners in the United States by Region in 1860, 1880, and 1910
Sources: Secretary of the Interior (1866), Census Office (1888, 1895), and Bureau of Census (1907, 1918).

These patterns suggest that it would be wise to examine more closely, as a number of scholars have begun to do, the causes of the extraordinary rise in punitiveness in the United States since the mid-1970s. The strong lagged relationship between the level of violent crime and the degree of punitiveness, which was not readily apparent before World War II, may divert attention from the most important causes of the incarceration boom and the revival of capital punishment. The institutional infrastructure for the national War on Crime was already in place by the mid-1970s: well-funded prisons, well-funded law enforcement agencies, and growing federal involvement in the fight against drug crime, organized crime, and violent crime. And the rationale for the "punishment imperative" was also in place: a belief that rehabilitation had failed and that the only way to protect the public and deal with the small number of violators responsible for most crime was to arrest and convict felons at higher rates and send them to prison for longer terms. But the War on Crime of the late twentieth century was as much a product of political and cultural change as it was a response to violent crime, real or perceived (Gottschalk 2006, 7, 41–76; Clear and Frost 2014, 14–16).

In the opinion of most historians, the turn toward punitiveness was made possible above all by an unprecedented convergence of elite and popular opinion across the political spectrum. The initial impetus for the War on Crime came in the late 1950s and early 1960s from the far right, from white supremacists like Governor George Wallace of Alabama, who believed that African Americans were programmed by their very nature to commit the most "atrocious acts of humanity, such as rape, assault, and murder." Diehard segregationists believed that the only way to keep African Americans in check in a post-segregation society was to police and punish them more intensely. But they were in a minority among advocates of get-tough policies. Many liberals also supported more punitive policies as they took the lead in crusades against sexual assaults, domestic violence, gay bashing, and violence against children. Certainly, liberals were more likely to support education, intervention, counseling, and treatment for addicts and abusers; but they too grew less tolerant of offenders and supported tougher sanctions. And many African Americans, aware of the destructive consequences of drugs, violence, and property crime in the nation's poorest neighborhoods, joined the war against thieves, drug dealers, and violent gangs (Carter 1996, 8, 2000; Gottschalk 2006, 8–9, 115–64, and 2015; Phillips-Fein 2011; National Research Council 2014, 33–129).

But the bulk of the support for get-tough policies came from the broad middle of the political spectrum. Moderate, largely suburban Republicans rejected racism and segregation in favor of a "color-blind" philosophy that accepted limited integration. But they opposed welfare, busing, fair housing laws, affirmative action, and other measures that might benefit minorities disproportionately or force integration on unwilling whites in affluent neighborhoods; and they supported tough policies against criminals to ensure that drugs and street violence did not enter their communities. Centrist Democrats like President Bill Clinton supported government initiatives to advance the cause of social and racial equality, but they too supported welfare reform and punitive policies against street criminals because they wanted to strike what they perceived as a proper balance between generosity and accountability in public policy as they attacked poverty and crime. They called for more police, more prisons, mandatory sentences, and "truth-in-sentencing" laws that would require convicted felons to serve a minimum of 85 percent of their sentences. In short, the embrace of get-tough policies was so widespread that there were few dissenting voices, apart from a handful of opponents of the death penalty, proponents of rehabilitation, and skeptics who questioned the efficacy of punitive policies or observed their destructive impact on poor neighborhoods, on poor families, on drug addicts, on the mentally ill, on nonviolent offenders, on young men with little education and few legitimate prospects for employment, and on the budgets of the federal government and of state and local governments (Lassiter 2006; Gilmore 2007; Lynch 2010; Clear and Frost 2014, 47–136; National Research Council 2014, 130–319).

Rising expectations for a more peaceful, productive, and harmonious society might have led to harsher criminal sanctions in the 1970s and 1980s even if the crime rate had not risen in the late 1960s and early 1970s. There has been a fundamental shift in American culture since World War II toward a greater concern with the quality of life. Americans have become more aware of the need for a safe environment (cleaner air and water) and for safe products. They have become less tolerant of polluters, drunk drivers, dangerous toys, and unsafe cars; and their behavior has become more careful, more health- and safety-conscious, as shown by the decline in smoking and in all manner of accidental deaths, including deaths from guns, the only unsafe product in our society that has yet to be regulated. And an important component of the quality of life is freedom from street crime: murder, rape, robbery, burglary, carjacking, and home invasions. The fact that Americans are far less tolerant of such crime than they were in the nineteenth century is positive in most every way, but it has meant that Americans have sympathized and identified with victims of crime to a greater and greater degree and have demonized street criminals. Locking up persistent and violent offenders for long periods of time may not be the best way to improve everyone's quality of life, but the strategy has substantial support among Americans who care about making the world safe for themselves and others. What may be most exceptional therefore about the United States in the early twenty-first century is the ambition of its people for a better life, which can lead at times to frustration, anger, disappointment, intolerance, and finger-pointing, particularly at politicians and felons—categories that have merged in the minds of many Americans (Hays 1987; Gottschalk 2006, 77–114; Burnham 2009; Forman 2017).

History shows that the relationship between crime and punitiveness is far from simple. Culture matters, politics matters, aspirations matter. What has been exceptional in recent years is the way in which the stars have aligned in the United States, politically, culturally, and criminologically, to support the most punitive policies that have ever been witnessed in an affluent, democratic society.

NOTES

1. The estimates of the proportion of children who would be murdered are based on a life expectancy in 2014 of 78.8 years. See National Center for Health Statistics (2015: Table 15, p. 95). Zimring and Hawkins caution that the United States has not been exceptional in its rates of most crimes—only in its rates of homicide and armed robbery. The homicide data for the United States, 1900-present, are from Eckberg 1995, Bureau of Census 1900–1936, 1937–1967, and Centers for Disease Control and Prevention, 2016.
2. See also Wikipedia, "Incarceration in the United States" (http://en.wikipedia.org/wiki/Incarceration_in_the_United_States, accessed February 28, 2016).
3. See also "Use of Capital Punishment by Country" (http://en.wikipedia.org/wiki/Use_of_capital_punishment_by_country) and "Capital Punishment in the United States" (http://en.wikipedia.org/wiki/Capital_punishment_in_the_United_States, both accessed February 28, 2016). Since World War II, nearly 700 persons have been executed in Japan.
4. On the impact of modern emergency services and wound care on death rates from assaults, see Eckberg (2007) and Roth (2007). On the lethality of older firearms, see James (1999).
5. The data on inmates in the Ohio Penitentiary are courtesy of Nancy Tatarek of Ohio University, who gathered them.
6. The data on capital punishment are from Death Penalty Information Center (2016) and Espy and Smykla (2004).
7. The data are from Secretary of the Interior (1866, 512, 1872, 568–70); Census Office, Department of the Interior 1888, 479–83, 1895, 3); and Bureau of the Census, Department of Commerce (1918, 204–309). The data from the Bureau of the Census on the number of persons incarcerated on June 1, 1904, appear to be the most inadequate of any federal count because they were gathered during a separate survey of correctional institutions, rather than through the regular

census (Bureau of the Census, Department of Commerce and Labor 1907). For that reason, they are not included in the data for this chapter. They show an incarceration rate of only 99 per 100,000 persons—a rate that would be almost impossible to scale up to 148 per 100,000 by 1910.

REFERENCES

Archer, Dane, and Rosemary Gartner. *Violence and Crime in Cross-National Perspective.* New Haven, CT: Yale University Press, 1984.

Ayres, Edward L. *Vengeance and Justice: Crime and Punishment in the 19th-Century American South.* New York: Oxford University Press, 1984.

Banner, Stuart. *The Death Penalty: An American History.* Cambridge, MA: Harvard University Press, 2002.

Blaine, Quentin. "'Shall Surely Be Put to Death': Capital Punishment in New Hampshire, 1623–1985." *New Hampshire Bar Journal* 27 (1986): 131–54.

Bureau of the Census. *Mortality Statistics, 1900–1936.* Washington, D. C.: Government Printing Office.

Bureau of the Census. *Vital Statistics of the United States.* Washington, DC: Government Printing Office, 1937–1967.

Bureau of the Census, Department of Commerce and Labor. *Prisoners and Juvenile Delinquents in Institutions, 1904.* Washington, DC: Government Printing Office, 1907.

Bureau of the Census, Department of Commerce. *Prisoners and Juvenile Delinquents in the United States, 1910.* Washington, DC: Government Printing Office, 1918.

Burnham, John C. *Accident Prone: A History of Technology, Psychology, and Misfits of the Machine Age.* Chicago: University of Chicago Press, 2009.

Carter, Dan T. *From George Wallace to Newt Gingrich: Race in the Conservative Counterrevolution, 1963–1994.* Baton Rouge: Louisiana State University Press, 1996.

Carter, Dan T. *The Politics of Rage: George Wallace and the Origins of the New Conservatism, and the Transformation of American Politics.* 2nd ed. Baton Rouge: Louisiana State University Press, 2000.

Census Office, Department of the Interior. *Report on the Defective, Dependent, and Delinquent Classes of the Population of the United States.* Washington, DC: Government Printing Office, 1888.

Census Office, Department of the Interior. *Report on Crime, Pauperism, and Benevolence in the United States, 1890. Part II: General Tables.* Washington, DC: Government Printing Office, 1895.

Centers for Disease Control and Prevention. Compressed Mortality File: Underlying Cause-of-Death. 2016. http://wonder.cdc.gov/mortSQL.html.

Chenais, Jean-Claude. *Histoire de la Violence: En Occident de 1800 à Nos Jours.* Paris: Robert Laffont, 1981.

Clear, Todd R., and Natasha A. Frost. *The Punishment Imperative: The Rise and Failure of Mass Incarceration in America*. New York: New York University Press, 2014.

Colvin, Mark. *Penitentiaries, Reformatories, and Chain Gangs: Social Theory and the History of Punishment in Nineteenth-Century America*. New York: St. Martin's Press, 1997.

Cusac, Anne-Marie. *Cruel and Unusual: The Culture of Punishment in America*. New Haven, CT: Yale University Press, 2009.

Death Penalty Information Center. Executions by Year since 1976. 2016. http://www.deathpenaltyinfo.org/views-executions.

Dugan, Andrew. "In U.S., 37% Do Not Feel Safe Walking at Night Near Home." Gallup. November 24, 2014. http://www.gallup.com/poll/179558/not-feel-safe-walking-night-near-home.aspx.

Eckberg, Douglas L. "Estimates of Early-Twentieth-Century U.S. Homicide Rates: An Econometric Forecasting Approach." *Demography* 32 (1995): 1–16.

Eckberg, Douglas L. "Coroner's Records and Estimates of 'Excessive' Homicide Deaths in Charleston, South Carolina, 1879–1912." Paper presented at the Social Science History Association convention, Chicago, IL, November 16, 2007.

Edgerton, Keith. *Montana Justice: Power, Punishment, and the Penitentiary*. Seattle: University of Washington Press, 2004.

Eisner, Manuel. "Modernization, Self-Control, and Lethal Violence: The Long-Term Dynamics of European Homicide Rates in Theoretical Perspective." *British Journal of Criminology* 41 (2001): 618–38.

Espy, M. Watt, and John Ortiz Smykla. *Executions in the United States, 1608–2002: The Espy File*. 4th ed. Ann Arbor, MI: Inter-university Consortium for Political and Social Research, 2004.

Forman, James Jr. *Locking Up Our Own: Crime and Punishment in Black America*. New York: Farrar, Straus, and Giroux, 2017.

Gallup. Death Penalty. "Are You in Favor of the Death Penalty for a Person Convicted of Murder?" October 7–11, 2015. http://www.gallup.com/poll/1606/death-penalty.aspx.

Gartner, Rosemary. "The Victims of Homicide: A Temporal and Cross-National Comparison." *American Sociological Review* 55 (1990): 92–106.

Gilmore, Ruth Wilson. *Golden Gulag: Prisons, Surplus, Crisis, and Opposition in Globalizing California*. Berkeley: University of California Press, 2007.

Gottschalk, Marie. *The Prison and the Gallows: The Politics of Mass Incarceration in America*. New York: Cambridge University Press, 2006.

Gottschalk, Marie. *Caught: The Prison State and the Lockdown of American Politics*. Princeton: Princeton University Press, 2015.

Gould, Roger V. *Collision of Wills: How Ambiguity about Social Rank Breeds Conflict*. Chicago: University of Chicago Press, 2003.

Hadden, Sally E. *Slave Patrols: Law and Violence in Virginia and the Carolinas*. Cambridge, MA: Harvard University Press, 2001.

Hays, Samuel P. *Beauty, Health, and Permanence: Environmental Politics in the United States, 1955–1985*. New York: Cambridge University Press, 1987.

Hindus, Michael S. *Prison and Plantation: Crime, Justice, and Authority in Massachusetts and South Carolina, 1767–1878*. Chapel Hill: University of North Carolina Press, 1980.

Hirsch, Adam. *The Rise of the Penitentiary: Prisons and Punishment in Early America*. New Haven, CT: Yale University Press, 1992.

James, C. Rodney. "Firearm Lethality and Other Foolish Notions." *Ohio Association of Criminal Defense Lawyers (OACDL) Vindicator* 1999 (Spring 1999): 5–9.

Kahn, Mark E. *Punishment, Prisons, and Patriarchy: Liberty and Power in the Early American Republic*. New York: New York University Press, 2005.

LaFree, Gary. *Losing Legitimacy: Street Crime and the Decline of Social Institutions*. Boulder: Westview Press, 1998.

Lane, Roger. *Policing the City: Boston, 1822–1885*. Cambridge, MA: Harvard University Press, 1967.

Lappi-Seppälä, Tapio. "Trust, Welfare, and Political Culture: Explaining Differences in National Penal Policies." *Crime and Justice* 37 (2008): 313–87.

Lappi-Seppälä, Tapio. "Explaining Imprisonment in Europe." *European Journal of Criminology* 8 (2011): 303–28.

Lassiter, Matthew D. *The Silent Majority: Suburban Politics in the Sunbelt South*. Princeton, NJ: Princeton University Press, 2006.

Lewis, W. David. *From Newgate to Dannemora: The Rise of the Penitentiary in New York, 1796–1848*. Ithaca, NY: Cornell University Press, 1965.

Lieberson, Stanley. *Making It Count: The Improvement of Social Research and Theory*. Berkeley: University of California Press, 1985.

Lynch, Mona. *Sunbelt Justice: Arizona and the Transformation of American Punishment*. Stanford, CA: Stanford Law Books, 2010.

Meranze, Michael. *Laboratories of Virtue: Punishment, Revolution, and Authority in Philadelphia, 1760–1835*. Chapel Hill: University of North Carolina Press, 1996.

Miller, Wilbur R. *Cops and Bobbies: Police Authority in New York and London, 1830–1870*. 2nd ed. Columbus: Ohio State University Press, 1999.

Monkkonnen, Eric H. *Police in Urban America, 1860–1920*. New York: Cambridge University Press, 1981.

Montgomery, David. *Beyond Equality: Labor and the Radical Republicans, 1862–1872*. New York: Knopf, 1967.

Morris, Norval, and David J. Rothman, eds. *The Oxford History of the Prison: The Practice of Punishment in Western Society*. New York: Oxford University Press, 1995.

National Center for Health Statistics. *Health, United States, 2015: With Special Feature on Racial and Ethnic Health Disparities*. Hyattsville, MD: [publisher name], 2015.

National Research Council. *The Growth of Incarceration in the United States: Exploring Causes and Consequences*. Washington, DC: National Academies Press, 2014.

Nivette, Amy E., and Manuel Eisner. "Do Legitimate Polities Have Fewer Homicides? A Cross-National Analysis." *Homicide Studies* 17 (2013): 3–26.

Patterson, Orlando. *Slavery and Social Death: A Comparative Study*. Cambridge, MA: Harvard University Press, 1982.

Perkinson, Robert. *Texas Tough: The Rise of America's Prison Empire*. New York: Metropolitan Books, 2010.

Pestritto, Ronald J. *Founding the Criminal Law: Punishment and Political Thought in the Origins of America*. DeKalb: Northern Illinois University Press, 2000.

Phillips-Fein, Kim. "Conservatism: A State of the Field." *Journal of American History* 98 (2011): 723–43.

Rafter, Nicole H. *Partial Justice: Women in State Prisons, 1800–1935*. Boston: Northeastern University Press, 1985.

Roth, Randolph. *The Democratic Dilemma: Religion, Reform, and the Social Order of the Connecticut River Valley of Vermont, 1791–1850*. New York: Cambridge University Press, 1987.

Roth, Randolph. "The Other Masonic Outrage: The Death and Transfiguration of Joseph Burnham." *Journal of the Early Republic* 14 (1994): 35–69.

Roth, Randolph. "'Blood Calls for Vengeance!': The History of Capital Punishment in Vermont." *Vermont History* 65 (1997): 10–25.

Roth, Randolph. "The Impact of Modern Non-Emergency Medical Care on Homicide Rates." Paper presented at the Social Science History Association convention, Chicago, IL, November 16, 2007.

Roth, Randolph. *American Homicide*. Cambridge, MA: Belknap Press of Harvard University Press, 2009a.

Roth, Randolph. American Homicide: Supplemental Volume: Criminal Justice. Historical Violence Database, Criminal Justice Research Center, Ohio State University. 2009b. https://cjrc.osu.edu/sites/cjrc.osu.edu/files/AHSV-Criminal-Justice.pdf.

Roth, Randolph. "Biology and the Deep History of Homicide." *British Journal of Criminology* 51 (2011): 535–55.

Roth, Randolph. "Measuring Feelings and Beliefs that May Facilitate (or Deter) Homicide: A Research Note on the Causes of Historic Fluctuations in Homicide Rates in the United States." *Homicide Studies* 16 (2012): 197–216.

Rothman, David J. *The Discovery of the Asylum: Social Order and Disorder in the New Republic*. rev. ed. Boston: Little, Brown, 1980.

Roussey, Dennis C. *Policing the Southern City: New Orleans, 1805–1889*. Baton Rouge: Louisiana University Press, 1996.

Secretary of the Interior. *Statistics of the United States (Including Mortality, Property, &c.), 1860*. Washington, DC: Government Printing Office, 1866.

Secretary of the Interior. *The Statistics of the Population of the United States, 1870*. Ninth Census, v. 1. Washington, DC: Government Printing Office, 1872.

Smith, Tom W. *Trends in National Spending Priorities, 1973–2012. General Social Survey Trend Report*. Chicago: NORC at the University of Chicago, 2013.

Ward, Robert David, and William Warren Rogers. *Alabama's Response to the Penitentiary Movement, 1829–1865*. Gainesville: University Press of Florida, 2003.

Wilentz, Sean. *Chants Democratic: New York City and the Rise of the American Working Class, 1788–1850*. New York: Oxford University Press, 1984.

Zelinsky, Wilbur. *Nation into State: The Shifting Symbolic Foundations of American Nationalism*. Chapel Hill: University of North Carolina Press, 1988.

Zimring, Franklin E., and Gordon Hawkins. *Crime Is Not the Problem: Lethal Violence in America*. New York: Oxford University Press, 1997.

7

Making the State Pay

VIOLENCE AND THE POLITICIZATION OF CRIME IN COMPARATIVE PERSPECTIVE

Lisa L. Miller

Introduction

Katherine Beckett's essential reading *Making Crime Pay: Law and Order in Contemporary American Politics* (1997) drew social science attention to the politicization of crime after a long period of neglect.[1] Beckett's argument that elite manipulation of public fear largely explained the dramatic attention to crime in the postwar period (rather than crime rates or bottom-up political pressure) came to the conclusion that "crime pays." In this view, the crime issue, often independent of actual rates of crime, is a political opportunity, and lawmakers capitalized on it to send punishment and other repressive state practices skyrocketing. Since publication of this analysis, a wide range of scholarship in criminology, sociology, political science, and law has modified and built upon this story, highlighting the disconnect between crime and punishment, the manipulation of public fear by politicians, and the punitive impulses of mass publics (see Gottschalk 2015; Miller 2013, 2016 for a summary of this literature). In a related analysis, scholarly attention has focused on the dense electoral nature of the fragmented and highly localized American political system, where punitive publics and eager politicians converge, as explanations for the dramatically high rates of incarceration in the United States (Zimring and Johnson 2006; Tonry 2007; Lacey 2008). In this formulation, the United States is "exceptional" in that it carries democratic participation too far, resulting in an excessively punitive regime.

That the United States is the democratic world leader in imprisonment is well known. What is less frequently explored is the relationship between its exceptional rates of imprisonment, its exceptional rate of serious violent crime, and the political dynamics that may drive both (but see Zimring and Hawkins 1997 for an important exception, as well as Gallo, Lacey, and Soskice, this volume). At their peak in 1980, more than 10 Americans per 100,000 were murder victims, a risk more than five times as great as that of the Canadians and the English and 10 times as great as that of people in the Netherlands and Spain. This national average masked even more dramatic variations across states, localities, and demographic groups. Homicide rates were as high as 20 per 100,000 in states like Louisiana (in 1993) and a shocking 80 per 100,000 in cities such as the District of Columbia (in 1991).[2] And in 1972, as the homicide rate sped upward, black males were murdered at a rate of 76.6 per 100,000 compared to 7.7 for white males.[3]

Despite these dramatic disparities, few scholars seek to understand the relationship between violence, particularly homicide, and the *political* mechanisms that drive policy responses and legal reforms on crime and punishment (but see LaFree and Drass 2002; Western 2006; Zimring and Johnson 2006). This is a curious omission since violence is a serious political problem, a threat to the good society, and a core subject of the social contract (Scheingold 1984; Zimring and Hawkins 1997, 9–14; Loader 2008; Miller 2013). Furthermore, violence is not evenly or randomly distributed across the population but has deep racial, ethnic, and class disproportionality. The few works in the field of crime and punishment that do consider rates of violence generally find that homicide rates are an important contributing factor to punishment outcomes (Jacobs and Kleban 2003; Western 2006), but from there, they typically downplay the importance of violence because annual variation in the homicide rate leaves so much imprisonment unexplained (see also Lappi-Seppälä, this volume). Instead, the scholarly literature has largely untethered the *politicization of crime*—the salience of crime as a public and political issue—from rates of serious violence (Zimring, Hawkins, and Kamin 2001; Tonry 2007; Reiner 2007; Beckett 1997; Simon 2007; Lacey 2008; Barker 2009; Alexander 2010; Wacquant 2010; Page 2011).

In this chapter, I argue that a more complete understanding of the politics of punishment must attend to violence and that doing so can more accurately reveal the ways in which political institutions shape and channel public understanding of and reaction to violence. Furthermore, the analysis calls into question conventional understandings of the relationship between democratic politics and crime and punishment.[4] I suggest that politicization is more deeply connected to serious violence than we have heretofore determined and that politicization is, at least in part, a product of mass publics trying to "make the state pay," that is, forcing governments to offer policy responses that genuinely reduce violent victimization. This process can and does result in more punishing but does not necessarily exclude political attention to the causes and consequences of violence. The United States, I argue, is exceptional not because it is overly accountable to the public's punitive demands about crime and violence but because its highly fragmented political system leaves lawmakers largely *unaccountable* for actually reducing crime and a wide range of other social inequities. The result is a political process that decouples crime and violence from other social conditions and facilitates policies aimed narrowly at punishing offenders rather than reducing the likelihood of victimization.

I focus on three limitations to the current literature on crime, democratic politics, and punishment. First, on the whole, scholars stubbornly resist exploration of real rates of victimization; the tendency to dismiss crime as having any but the most marginal connection to punishment politics has become virtually de rigueur (but see Zimring and Hawkins 1997; Garland 2001; Western 2006; Zimring and Johnson 2006; Forman 2017; Fortner 2015). Tracking homicide rates in the postwar period, I illustrate how dramatically increasing rates of violence coincide with law-and-order issues coming on to public and political agendas.

Second, few analyses, even those that do take violence seriously, theorize the specifically *political causal mechanisms* that link crime or violence, mass publics, policy, and outcomes. The public is typically seen as monolithic, singularly punitive and easily manipulated; and repressive crime policies emerge like Athena, fully formed, and aimed exclusively at punishing. There are a number of excellent exceptions; but they are typically case studies with few opportunities for theorizing more generally, or they disproportionately rely on the US case and rarely explore real violence (see, e.g., Downes and Morgan 2002; Barker 2009; Page 2011; M. Campbell 2012). The assumption has been that the politicization of crime—regardless of its origins—means more punishment and the crowding out of policies addressing inequality or justice reforms. And yet, the lack of attention to specific institutional mechanisms in the wake of real violence has left many gaps in our understanding of these processes. As a result, we know little about the causal chains that link public attitudes, actions, and pressures to legal and policy dynamics and how those chains might vary across institutional designs (but see Barker 2009 for a related argument).

Finally, while the racial, ethnic, and class dynamics of punishment have been explored by many scholars, the political agency of low-income communities or racial and ethnic minorities and other groups that disproportionately experience violent victimization is almost entirely absent (Fortner 2015; Forman 2017), particularly in cross-national analyses, which tend to emphasize global shifts in economic systems—such as the rise of neoliberalism—or elite competition among political parties or governing coalitions (Betz 1990; Garland 2001; Downes and Morgan 2002; Balvig 2004; Newburn and Rock 2006; Lacey 2008). When victims are brought into the analytic picture, the emphasis is typically on the intersection of high-profile victims' groups and criminal justice actors, such as prosecutors or prison guard unions (Gottschalk 2006; Page 2011). The role of populations that are exposed to higher rates of violence and high rates of arrest and incarceration, such as minorities or the poor, is largely absent despite the fact that these populations often disproportionately suffer from a wide range of social insecurities, including homicide. There is a sizeable body of research into the variation in institutional designs that might incorporate minority interests into dominant political agendas, but it is rarely tapped for understanding the politics of crime and punishment (e.g., see Pontusson and Rueda 2010).

Here, I approach the politics of crime and punishment from the bottom up, rather than the top down. This emphasis on violence as the point of departure, rather than on policing or incarceration, contrasts with traditional studies of crime and punishment and recasts our understanding of the intersection of democratic politics and punishment. The chapter proceeds in four sections. First, I briefly lay out the dominant claims in the literature and argue that taking violence seriously poses problems for many of these claims. Second, I examine homicide rates cross-nationally, revealing exceptionally high rates of homicide in the United States and increases in violence in the postwar period. Third, I discuss three brief case studies—the United Kingdom, the United States, and the state of Pennsylvania—and explore the interconnection between levels of violence and the politicization of crime.

I conclude by assessing the institutional dynamics of crime and punishment in the United States and the United Kingdom in ways that highlight distinctions between the two political systems and call into question the highly responsive character of US democratic politics. In particular, I suggest that the fractured political landscape of the United States may *undermine*, rather than *promote*, democratic accountability on crime. In this formulation, the decoupling of crime from other social ills and the multilayered and overlapping legislative actors addressing crime make it difficult for the public to "make the state pay" for real suffering from serious violence and other forms of social and economic insecurity.

II. Extant Literature and Its Limitations

A large body of literature suggests that the politicization of crime is less likely to occur and less likely to result in high rates of punishing where institutional dynamics insulate governing officials from public pressure for moral-symbolic responses to crime (Garland 2001; Jacobs and Kleban 2003; Pettit 2004; Zimring and Johnson 2006; Tonry 2007; Lacey 2008). Indeed, though Beckett's causal narrative ascribed the massive buildup in punitive politics in the United States to the instrumental behavior of politicians, rather than bottom-up political pressure, a clear implication of this argument is that democratic systems that place institutional buffers between the public and electoral politics will create fewer opportunities for such behavior.

In this formulation, the politicization of crime—which may or may not be tethered to real rates of crime—necessarily results in political opportunities for public officials to respond with harsh law-and-order messaging and policies. When governing elites must stand for election, particularly in two-party systems, the political incentives all push toward more punishment because neither party wants to be seen as "soft" on crime. In contrast, corporatist systems coordinate both markets as well as social policy through more deliberative processes that insulate individual lawmakers from public anxiety (Jacobs and Kleban 2003; Zimring and Johnson 2006; Doob and Webster 2006; Lacey 2008). This leads to more measured responses to crime and, hence, less punishment. The United States is the iconic example of too much responsiveness and too much punishment. The Scandinavian countries, by contrast, function under tidier, more insulated political regimes that stave off the messy, often ugly, dynamics of mass publics and their troubling insecurities.

Put simply, the primary causal process of this framework can be visualized in Figure 7.1. Underlying social conditions (which may or may not be related to real rates of victimization) as well as routine electoral incentives for winning control of government put pressure on democracies in different ways, contingent on the type of political-economic system. In more insulated systems, these pressures are integrated into a political process where crime is less politicized, leading to fewer electoral incentives to use crime as a campaign issue or ratchet up punishment. In highly responsive systems, however (particularly those with two dominant parties), the same pressures lead to high levels of politicization—lots of public and elite attention to and responsiveness about crime—that leads to incentives for ever more punishing. Feedback loops in

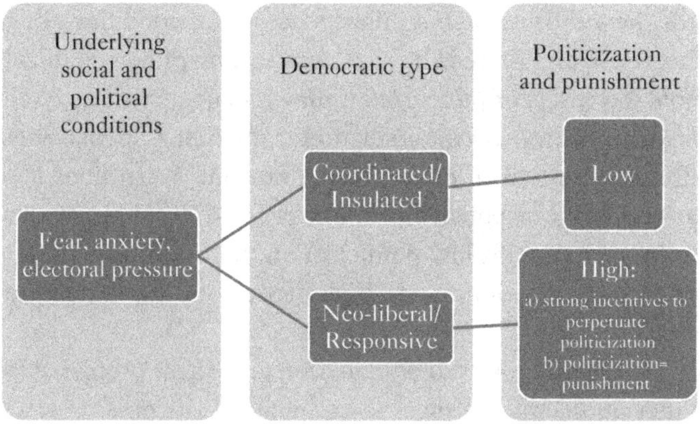

FIGURE 7.1 Extant Frameworks on Democracy and Punishment

the highly responsive systems generate more anxiety and, predictably, more pressure and incentives for punishment. Implicit in this dynamic process is the claim that law and order makes for "good politics" in highly responsive systems in that it is easy to maintain on the political agenda, regardless of crime rates, and that it has potentially powerful electoral payoff.

There is much insight in this framework. Most notably, as Lacey illustrates (2008), modern, industrialized democracies and their rates of punishment fit nicely into the model. Furthermore, Lacey's link between the political dynamics of punishment and the mechanisms through which other social policies are developed is a crucial component of understanding crime and punishment. This approach, particularly the linkage between constitutional systems and the politics of social welfare policy of many types, is an enormous contribution to the literature and one upon which I draw heavily here.

A glaring omission to the general body of work in this area, however, is that there is no clear role for real rates of violent victimization. And yet, predatory violence is real and, as illustrated in the next section, has risen and fallen dramatically in recent decades. Seen through the prism of violence, the framework in Figure 7.1 is substantially compromised for three reasons. First, while the United States and the United Kingdom both fall into the neoliberal, responsive democratic systems in most analyses, the rates of violence in both countries are dramatically different, in terms of both real rates as well as historic trajectories. Second, the coordinated market and social democratic systems, such as Denmark and the Netherlands, have extremely low crime rates. This poses a substantial endogeneity problem because the outcome of interest—punishment—may be highly correlated with other factors that explain both rates of punishment and the political-economic institutions. In other words, how those systems might react under conditions of high crime is undertheorized, and there is little understanding of how political dynamics that promote low levels of punishment may also generate low levels of crime. Finally, the distinction between insulation from, and responsiveness to, democratic publics suffers from conceptual confusion. What does it mean for a country to be highly responsive to mass publics? In short, we have tended to conflate low crime with low politicization, high politicization with highly responsive democratic politics, and high democratic accountability with high punishment.

A more systematic look can begin to overcome these problems by exploring crime, politicization, and the spectrum of political outcomes over a longer period of time. I do so in three ways. First, I use the matrix in Table 7.1 to explore rates of violence and rates of politicization and to categorize these dynamics over 30-year to 60-year periods across three jurisdictions (144 years of potential politicization). Much current scholarship would predict that democracies more responsive to political demand, such as the United States and the United Kingdom, will fall into the high politicization dimension, largely independent of rates of crime and that such democratic systems will exhibit high rates of politicization coupled with low crime. We would expect few highly responsive democratic systems to fall into the low-politicization category at all in the late twentieth century but particularly when crime is high or rising. In addition, the United States should exhibit high and sustained levels of politicization over the past, since the 1970s, with little relationship to real violence.

Secondarily, I explore whether the politicization of crime necessarily crowds out attention to other social problems. To the degree that the politicization of crime presents political opportunities, it has the potential to draw attention away from other issues, such as globalization, economic insecurity, neoliberal policies, and racial hierarchies. Thus, the politicization of crime should reduce attention to other, related social problems such as education, economic security, and social welfare.

Table 7.1 Matrix of Violence and Politicization and Predicted Outcomes Based on Extant Literature

		Homicide Rates	
		Low or Falling	High or Rising
Politicization	Low	Insulated (elite) democratic systems	
	High	Highly responsive (mass democratic) systems	

Finally, I distinguish between democratic responsiveness and democratic accountability and suggest that a more productive framework for measuring democratic politics and policy is the capacity of the general public to hold government accountable for a wide range of social insecurities, including, but not limited to, violence. In this formulation, the decentralization and fragmentation of the US political system provide multiple opportunities for decoupling crime from other social policies aimed at redistribution and reform, thus limiting political accountability and the capacity of mass publics to "make the state pay" for reducing violence, punishing, and other forms of social inequality and repression.

Violence in Cross-National Comparison

Figure 7.2 illustrates homicide rates across five industrialized democracies. Homicide rates are a crude measure for understanding crime trends generally, but I use them here for three reasons: they serve as a reliable proxy for *trends* in rates of violence more generally, especially violence accompanied by serious

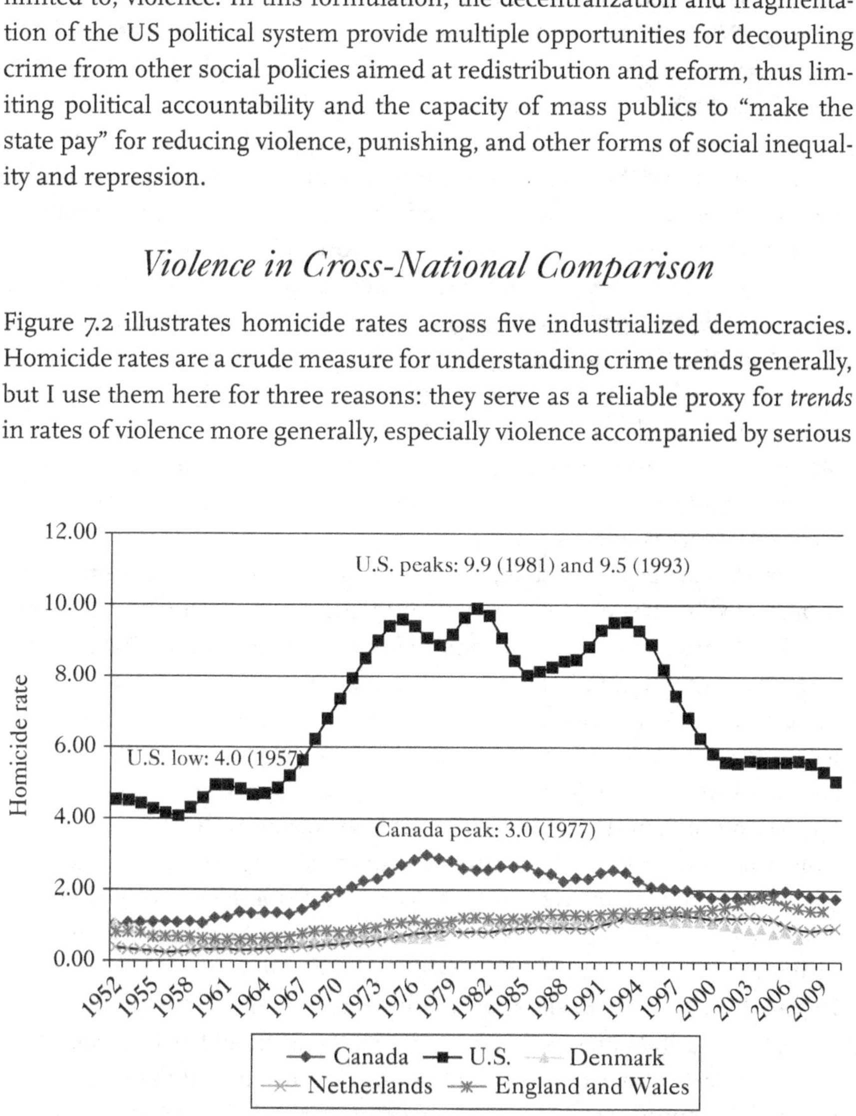

FIGURE 7.2 Homicide Rates per 100,000 (3-Year Moving Average), Select Countries, 1950–2008

Source: World Health Organization Mortality Database, category "homicide and injury purposefully inflicted, not war, " from ICD-7, ICD-8, ICD-9, ICD-10. http://www.who.int/healthinfo/statistics/mortality_rawdata/en.

injury; they are likely to be reliably recorded and reflect real rates of violence; and they represent the most feared type of criminal behavior (Zimring and Hawkins 1997; Fajnzylber, Lederman, and Loayza 2000).

Murder rates grew dramatically in the United States, the United Kingdom, Canada, Denmark, and the Netherlands in the second half of the twentieth century.[5] While the homicide rate increases and peaks came at different periods, every country experienced increases of at least twofold in the postwar period (see LaFree and Drass 2002 for a related discussion).

According to multiple data sources, the murder rate in the United States, for example, more than doubled between 1955 and 1980, from 4.1 persons per 100,000 to 10.2 per 100,000 (Fox and Zawitz 2005). The most significant increase in the homicide rate was between 1966 and 1972, and the initial peak was in 1980. The three-year moving average in 1980, however, was virtually indistinguishable from the rate in 1993.[6] Homicide, in other words, rose steadily *and remained high* for nearly 30 years with two clear high points, one in the late 1970s and one in the mid-1990s (see also Ruth and Reitz 2003). Equally as important, the lowest homicide rate in the postwar period for the United States (4.0 in 1957) was higher than any of the peak rates in the other countries (3.0 in Canada) and is more than an order of magnitude higher than some of the low-violence countries (such as Denmark).

A stark visualization of changes in homicide rates outside the United States is presented in Figure 7.3, which provides maximum, minimum, and average homicide rates across the eight countries, excluding the United States.[7] There is dramatic variation in homicide rates across countries, but the average rate more than doubles between 1959, with a mean of 1.1 per 100,000, and 1992, with a cross-national mean of 2.57 per 100,000. Homicide rates in England and Wales were at their lowest in the postwar period in 1961 (0.51 per 100,000) but had more than doubled by 1980 (1.27 per 100,000) (Chapin et al. 2011). After a decade of relatively steady rates, homicides again rose between 1985 and 2004, from 1.24 to 1.97 per 100,000. In the Netherlands, where homicide rates are extremely low, rates of homicide rose from less than 1 per 100,000 in 1976 to nearly 2 per 100,000 by the start of the twenty-first century. In Denmark, where homicide rates were a microscopic 0.48 per 100,000 in 1960, by 1980 the rate was nearly 1.5 per 100,000. In all five contexts, homicide rates rise and stay relatively high from the mid-1960s until the turn of the twenty-first century, at which point they remain roughly twice what they were in 1960 (see also LaFree and Drass 2002).

Comparisons across region, gender, age, and race reveal even more dramatic variation. In the United States, over this 30-year period, the rate of homicide victimization for adults under 35 was more than double that of those over

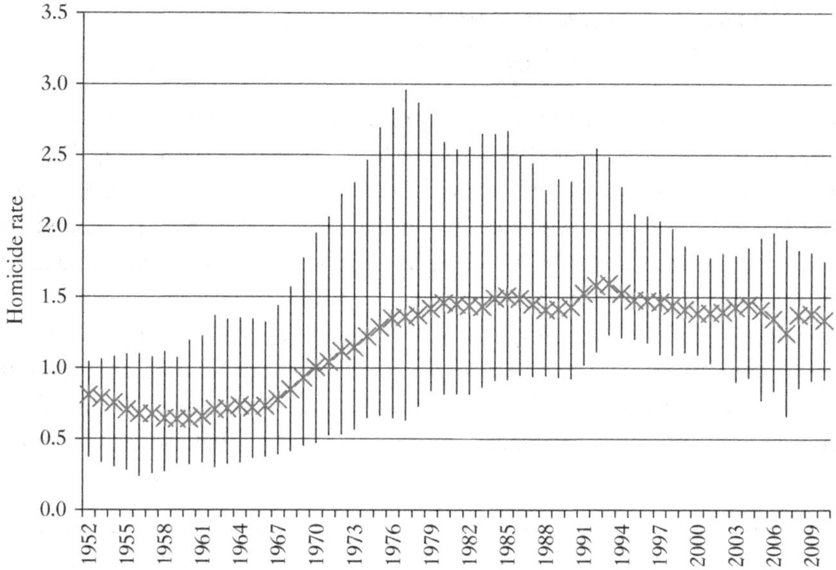

FIGURE 7.3 Maximum, Minimum, Average Homicide Rates (3-Year Moving Average) Select Countries, Excluding the United States, 1950–2008

Source: World Health Organization Mortality Database, category "homicide and injury purposefully inflicted, not war," from ICD-7, ICD-8, ICD-9, ICD-10. http://www.who.int/healthinfo/statistics/mortality_rawdata/en.

35 (Fox and Zawitz 2010).[8] Blacks and men also experienced these rising crime rates out of proportion to their population. In the 30 years between the mid-1970s and the first half-decade of the twenty-first century, the murder rate for blacks was six times that of whites and the rate for men was more than three times the rate for women (Fox and Zawitz 2010). In the United Kingdom, a 1998–1999 House of Commons report revealed that, despite black and Asian groups constituting only about 5 percent of the population at that time, they were 15 percent of victims of homicides (Homicide Statistics 1999).[9] In the Netherlands, young people were also victimized at high rates, and while time series data on the race or ethnicity of victims are not readily available, recent analysis suggests that a disproportionate number of victims of homicide in the Netherlands (as many as half) were not born in the Netherlands. People born in Morocco, the Dutch Antilles, Suriname, and Turkey were substantially overrepresented as victims of homicide in the early 2000s (Granath et al. 2011).

These rates of violence, it should be noted, were rising at the same time that rates of mortality from other causes in the democratized West were declining (Farley 1980). In other words, as democratic societies became more secure in the postwar period generally, acts of serious violence were on the rise.

Violence, Political and Public Attention to Crime in the United Kingdom and the United States

Does an increase in violent crime increase the politicization of crime? This section draws on several data sources to explore the relationship between homicide and public and political agendas on crime in the United Kingdom, the United States, and the state of Pennsylvania.[10] Figures 7.4, 7.5, and 7.6, illustrate the homicide rate as well as public and legislative attention to crime in the United Kingdom (1960–2008), the United States (1949–2008), and the state of Pennsylvania (1979–2010), as well as major crime events in each case, respectively.[11] Public attention is measured by public opinion polling on most important problems, and legislative attention is measured by the relative number of legislative hearings or amount of executive rhetoric about crime in

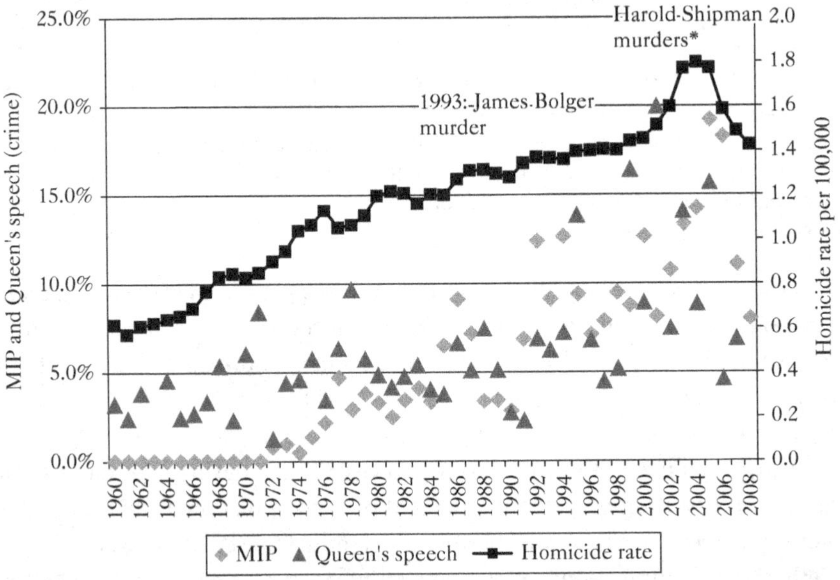

FIGURE 7.4 UK Homicide Rate (3-Year Moving Average), Queen's Speeches, "Most Important Problem," and Select Events (Percentages for Crime/Punishment), 1960–2008

*Harold Shipman, a doctor, was convicted of murdering 15 patients in 2000, though the actual number of deaths attributed to his actions was 172. These deaths are recorded as homicides in 2002 and 2003.

Source: Data are drawn from the UK Policy Agendas Project. Funded by the Economic and Social Research Council (ESRC Reference: RES-062-23-0872) as part of a European Science Foundation EUROCORES European Collaborative Research Projects (ECRP) application. Principal investigators are Dr. Will Jennings and Dr. Darren Halperin. Data and further details available at: http://www.policyagendas.org.uk.

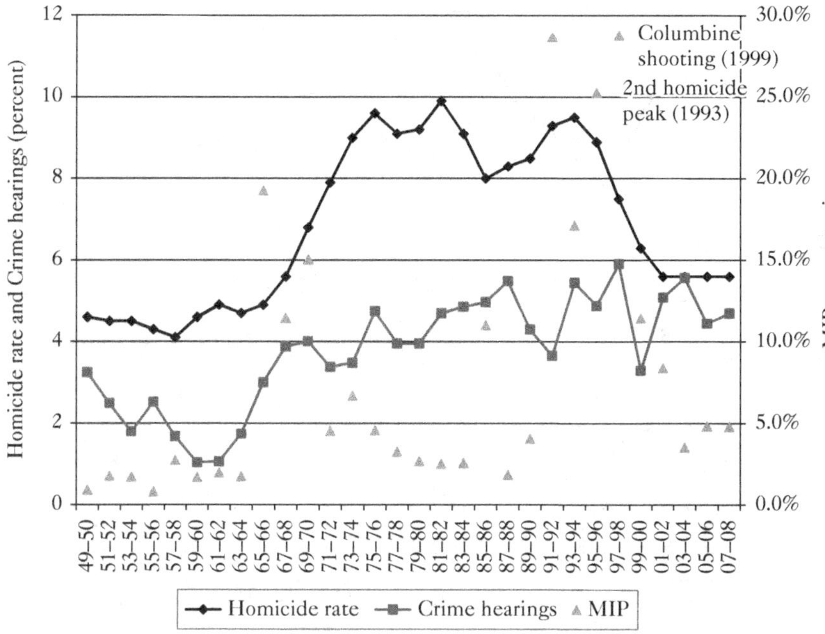

FIGURE 7.5 US Homicide Rate, Public and Legislative Agendas on Crime (Congressional Hearings and "Most Important Problem"), 1948–2010

Source: Data are drawn from the US Policy Agendas Project, originally collected by Frank R Baumgartner and Bryan D Jones with the support of the National Science Foundation (NSF) grant number SBR 9320922 and 0111611 and were distributed through the Government department at the University of Texas at Austin. Data and further details available at: http://www.comparativeagendas.net/us.

relation to other issues. In all three cases, public opinion, political attention to crime, and the homicide rate are positively correlated, often strongly.

The United Kingdom illustrates a robust and positive relationship between homicide rates and public attention to crime (.84). Surprisingly, though public attention is also positively correlated with the homicide rate (more modestly at .56), there is a long lag between the rising rates of violence and political attention, as measured by the amount of the annual speech from the government (known as the Queen's Speech) that focuses on crime issues of any kind. Between 1966 and 1996, crime is a remarkably small part of this agenda, despite gradual but steady increases in homicide rates, as well as outbursts of rioting in the 1980s in low-socioeconomic sections of London (Brixton) and other cities (see Downes and Morgan 2002). The homicide rate doubled during this time period, from .62 per 100,000 in 1960 to 1.27 per 100,000 in 1979, and the violent crime rate nearly quintupled from 38.1 violent crimes per

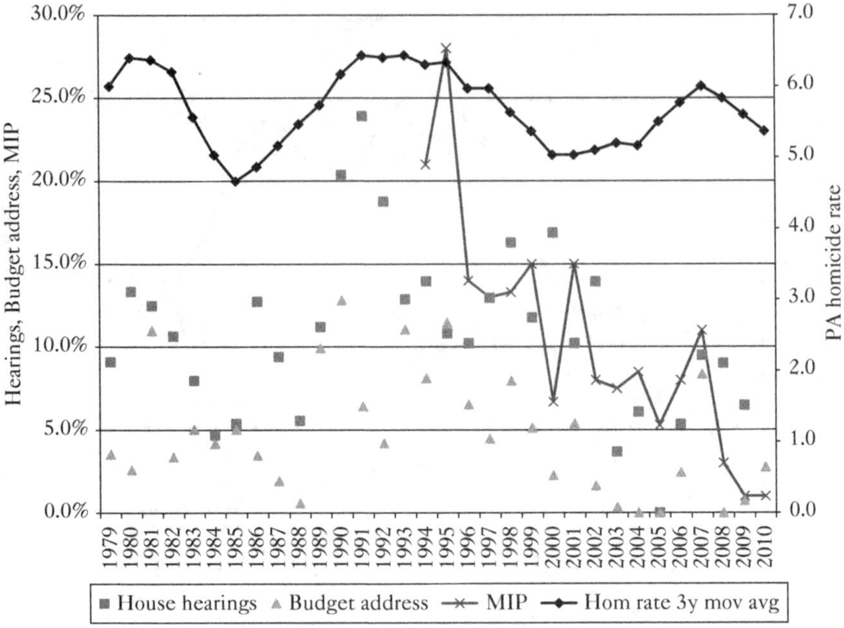

FIGURE 7.6 Pennsylvania Homicide Rate (3-Year Moving Average), Public ("Most Important Problem") and Legislative Attention to Crime (Governor's Budget Address and Legislative Hearings), 1979–2009

Source: Data are drawn from the State of Pennsylvania Policy Database Project, created by Temple University with funding support and cooperation of the Pennsylvania General Assembly and a grant from the Department of Community and Economic Development, and in-kind contributions from other participating universities in Pennsylvania. Data and further details available at: http://www.cla.temple.edu/papolicy/.

100,000 to 192.[12] The gruesome murder of three-year-old James Bolger in 1993 by two other prepubescent boys was a particularly dramatic news item and drew extensive public attention (see Morrison 1997). By the mid-1970s crime was gradually politicized, but well into the early 1990s the issue remained a minor part of the political agenda.

Perhaps most surprisingly, the Thatcher government (1979–1990) was relatively quiet on law and order; crime topics never reached more 10 percent of the agenda topics in Queen's Speeches, and most years hovered at or below a barely visible 5 percent. Analyses of other forms of political agenda setting during this period, such as party platforms and manifestos, show only modest attention to crime as well (Downes and Morgan 1997). Public concern about crime waxes and wanes, but the overall trajectory is increasing.[13] Policymakers, however, did not draw the issue onto the political agenda substantially for at least two decades.

The Thatcher government came to power with priorities other than crime, primarily in the area of housing, the economy, and local governance (see Downes and Morgan 1997).[14] In addition, though homicides had grown dramatically in the previous 20 years, by the start of Thatcher's 11-year tenure as prime minister, rates of predatory violence were relatively stable (see Farrall and Hay 2010 for a detailed discussion of this question).[15] There is little evidence that the Tories had "significant policy ambition" in the area of crime during this time period, despite what the literature might consider to be a prime opportunity for politicization (Farrall and Hay 2010, 563).

It was the conservative government of John Major that began a more sustained engagement with crime issues. By 1996, crime issues occupied nearly 14 percent of the topics in Queen's Speeches, more than any other year since World War II and more than 10 percent of the topics for only the second time since 1950 (the other was 1960, 10.5 percent). The Labour government of Tony Blair (1997–2007) continued this trend, and levels of attention to crime remained higher than under most previous governments in the postwar period, though there was enormous year-to-year variation.[16] By 2008, with the economic crisis on the horizon, crime and law topics barely edged up to 7 percent of speech topics. Indeed, public opinion polling confirms that crime is and has been quite low on the public agenda, with economic issues displacing it.[17]

Unfortunately, data that disaggregate rates of violence by race and ethnicity of victims are difficult to find. There is some evidence, however, that the disparities in violent victimization that are seen in contemporary reporting have been true for some time. The Brixton riots of 1981 in London, which spread to Liverpool, Manchester, and other urban areas, for example, involved a confrontation between a low-socioeconomic neighborhood with a significant Afro-Caribbean community and the Metropolitan police and were instigated in part because of growing frustration that the police were insufficiently attentive to violent victimization in the rioters' communities (Scarman 1982). In any case, in raw numbers, most victims of homicide in the United Kingdom are likely to be white, but the disparities in rates across racial groups are glaring and probably have been for some time (see Smith 1997). The class dimension is also important in the high-profile and brutal murder of James Bolger, a white child from a low-income and socially disadvantaged family and community in Liverpool (the perpetrators were also white) (see Downes and Morgan 1997).

In the US case, public and political attention to crime, as measured by congressional hearings on crime topics, rose dramatically with the significant increases in violence between the 1960s and 1980s. While the increase in homicides leveled off at this point and even declined slightly, a second peak occurred in the 1990s; and it was not until the turn of the twenty-first century that rates fell below 6.0 per 100,000, the rate of homicide in 1967. Indeed, the 1980 and 1993 three-year moving average homicide rates were virtually indistinguishable (9.9 and 9.3, respectively). With a one-year lag, homicide rates and congressional hearings on crime correlate positively and strongly at .62. Public declarations of crime as the most important problem are also positively correlated, though only weakly (.30). Notably, however, the percent of the public identifying crime as the most important problem decreased, even as homicide was increasing and very high. Only during a few years in the 1990s were homicides steady or declining and their perception as the most important problem high.

It is hard to know what to make of these most important problem trends. The Gallup "most important problem" question is a limited tool for identifying public priorities, primarily because it is heavily dominated by economic and national defense concerns. Indeed, during the period when homicide was rising and high but crime as the most important problem was falling, the United States was consumed by a series of issues, including Vietnam, Watergate, the Iran hostage crisis, the oil shortage, and the energy crisis. The percent of the public naming the economy or defense as the most important problem facing the country grew from 52 percent in 1973 to 84 percent in 1983 and remained above 60 percent through 1986. The crime issue, in other words, was displaced by economic and national defense crises in the poll.

In addition, the high percent of the public claiming that crime was the most important problem facing the country in the 1990s is less at odds with the trajectory of serious violence than it initially appears. As noted earlier, a second homicide peak occurred in the 1990s along with a number of high-profile violent events, including the riots after the Rodney King verdict in Los Angeles in 1992, the World Trade Center bombing in 1993, the bombing of the Oklahoma federal building in 1995, and the Columbine mass school shooting in 1999. In addition, President Clinton proposed a comprehensive crime bill during and after his election in 1992, and the bill was passed in 1994. Notably, the crime as the most important problem percent plummeted after 1998, dropping steadily to a barely noticeable 4.8 percent by 2010 as homicides reached a 50-year low.

In Pennsylvania, state legislative hearings on crime, mentions of crime in the Governor's Annual Budget address, and identification of crime as the most important problem again positively covary with the homicide rate (.46, .51, and .53, respectively). There are a few spikes in legislative attention to crime as homicide rates are declining, notably 1999 and 2001. The former comes on the heels of a decade of worsening homicides of African Americans in Pennsylvania's two major cities, Philadelphia and Pittsburgh. Homicide victimization rates for blacks in Philadelphia during this period were dramatically higher than the national average (Langley and Sugarmann 2015). While the extent of the drug and gang violence in the inner cities during the 1990s has been overstated in some cases, it is true that violence spiked during this time, particularly in those communities. My previous work, on the politicization of crime in Philadelphia and Pittsburgh in the 1990s, revealed strong and sustained attention to violent victimization and related issues during this time (Miller 2008).

Summary

These three brief analyses suggest important complicating dimensions to the dominant view of how crime is politicized. Reconsidering the high–low politicization and high–low violence matrix introduced in the last section, Table 7.2 disaggregates the years of exploration into periods of high and low politicization and violence.

Of the 144 combined years across the three cases, politicization occurs most frequently when homicide rates are high or rising (56/144, 39 percent). In one sense, this is not particularly revelatory; we know from an array of scholarship that when crime rates increased in the 1960s and 1970s, the issue became highly politicized (Garland 2001; Gottschalk 2006; Weaver 2007). However, because most studies have focused either on that period or on the later period,

Table 7.2 Homicide Rates and Political Salience of Crime: United Kingdom, United States, Pennsylvania, 1948–2010

		Politicization	
		Low/Falling	High/Rising
Homicide	Low/Falling	*31 years* UK: 1960–1965, 2008 USA: 1949–1964 PA: 1980–1985, 2009–2010	*15 years* USA: 1999–2008 PA: 1998–2002
	High/Rising	*42 years* UK: 1966–1995 PA: 2003–2008	*56 years* UK: 1996–2007 USA: 1965–1998 PA: 1986–1997

the late 1980s into the 1990s, when crime was decreasing, the connections between real rates of predatory violence and public anxiety about and political interest in crime and justice issues have gone largely unexplored. But the relationship between these conditions is consistent with a wide range of literature in public policy and comparative politics that sees underlying social conditions as reasonably connected to various measures of political attention (Burstein 2003; Brooks and Manza 2007; Baumgartner et al. 2009; Soroka and Wlezien 2010).

Perhaps most puzzling from the theoretical perspective on crime and punishment are the limited number of cases in the low violence/high politicization category and the numerous cases in the high violence/low politicization category. After high violence/high politicization, the next most common condition is high violence and low salience (42/144, 29 percent). This is particularly interesting given the alleged irresistible nature of crime as an electoral issue. What accounts for this?

The majority of case years in this category are in the United Kingdom between 1966 and 1995, and this period of relatively low politicization and rising rates of serious violence presents an interesting puzzle that cannot be easily accommodated by the dominant explanatory frameworks. When crime does become more politicized in the United Kingdom, we might say it arrives with a vengeance, given the intensity with which the Major government and, particularly, the Blair government remained attentive to and enacted policies and additional legislation on crime. Most analyses of the Blair years see this as evidence of the Labour Party's capitulation to law-and-order agendas on the crime issue. In his now-famous speech in the House of Commons in 1993, when he was the Labour shadow home secretary, Tony Blair set out the Labour Party's "tough on crime, tough on the causes of crime" program. Much scholarly analysis has argued that the former program came to flourish while the latter languished (Downes and Morgan 1997; Farrall and Hay 2010; Windelsham 1998).

Recall, however, that violence and public concern about it had been rising for three decades prior to its substantial politicization in the mid-1990s. Between 1966 and 1996, homicide rates had nearly doubled, public concern had increased sevenfold, and media coverage included far more stories about violence than in previous decades. Indeed, the growth in legislative attention to and action on crime needs to be grounded in the real violence experienced by an increasing segment of the British population. By this, I mean that violent crime was a serious and growing issue and one that affected multiple, traditional Labour constituencies, including working-class areas of London, Manchester, Birmingham, Liverpool, and other major cities, as well as low-income and minority communities in these areas. Seen in this light, the dramatic emergence of crime onto the British political agenda by both parties in the 1990s takes on a different characterization.

An additional puzzle is the low number of case years in the low/falling violence and high politicization box in the matrix (15/144, 10 percent), which presents a formidable challenge to the conventional wisdom. Though there are a few cases of legislative attention to crime even when serious violence is on the decline, there are essentially *no* cases of *high and sustained* politicization coupled with low or falling homicide rates that are comparable to the length of sustained high rates of violence and politicization. Arguably, the Blair government in the 2000s, President Clinton in the last three years of his presidency (1998–2000), and lawmakers in Pennsylvania in the late 1990s politicized crime during a period of stable or decreasing homicide rates. But, as noted earlier, in the United Kingdom serious violence rates remained extremely high relative to earlier time periods. Even in Pennsylvania, which I nonetheless count as falling homicide and high politicization, homicide rates in cities had been so high that political dynamics may not yet have registered the drop in violence. And in Congress, high politicization from the late 1990s into the first decade of the twenty-first century are complicated by new attention to security, justice, and law enforcement in the wake of the September 11, 2001, terrorist attacks.[18]

This exploratory analysis thus challenges several assumptions. First, though we may see the fact that there are few periods of high violence and low politicization in the United States as evidence of its highly reactive nature, there are lengthy periods of *low crime and low politicization*. This is a puzzle, given assumptions about crime as a relatively easy "go to" issue. Even in Pennsylvania, where we might expect lawmakers to capitalize on law-and-order issues, a traditional mainstay of state policy domains, there are substantial periods of low politicization, at least as measured by the attention of governors and the legislature and the public concern. In addition, the high levels of politicization in the United States need to be contextualized with very high relative rates of homicide.

Seen through the lens of serious violence, these outcomes are less puzzling than they at first appear. Homicide and violence are genuine political problems that the public and public officials can hardly ignore. But they are also difficult and at times intractable issues that lawmakers may wish to avoid. There is good evidence that politicians seek to avoid blame as much as gain credit, and crime is a difficult issue to tether oneself to, given its often intractable nature and the unpredictability, from the politicians' perspective, of high-profile and horrific crimes (Hood 2010; see also Miller 2013). From this perspective, it is less clear why public officials would seek to draw attention to serious crime when actual rates of crime are low.

Second, the United States and United Kingdom differ in important ways that defy conventional categorization. Given the relative nonreactiveness of the United Kingdom to rising rates of violence and public concern over several decades, we should think more systematically about the similarities and differences between the United States and the United Kingdom on the dimension of political responsiveness. One interpretation is to see the United Kingdom as more bureaucratic and insulated from underlying social changes and public concern about them than previously understood, particularly as judges and prosecutors are unelected and criminal justice planners are rarely directly accountable to mass publics. But rising rates of real violence call into question the normative assumptions that typically coincide with this claim. Where violence and public concern over it are on the rise but do not generate political attention to the issue, we might ask how politically accountable such a system is (see Dzur and Mirchandani 2007 for a related discussion). Moreover, the relatively low levels of politicization overall suggest that the issue is less electorally appealing than it may initially appear, perhaps until violence intrudes more dramatically on people's lives.

Finally, the public may be better risk assessors than we typically assume. While it is true that high rates of violence do not affect most people, particularly when those rates are concentrated among the worst off, this is also largely true of other crises, such as unemployment or communicable disease. But when these events occur, people are likely to hear more about them, from either friends and neighbors or media (or both), and, collectively, public concern rises. The threat of random violence, particularly violent death, is a sufficiently worrisome social problem that its dramatic increases can draw the issue onto public and political agendas.

Beyond Punishing?

Even if increased attention to crime does respond, at least in part, to rises in rates of violence rather than simple manipulation by political elites, according to conventional wisdom crime could still present an opportunity for public officials to give disproportionate attention to punishment, crowding out other social policy issues such as youth programs, labor/employment, social welfare provisions, civil rights, and housing (Simon 2007). This is particularly true if crime rates appear to be driven by minority populations or if public perception of the paradigm victim is a member of the dominant racial group (white) and that of the paradigm offender is of a racial or ethnic minority.

If the politicization of crime exclusively emphasizes punishing, ignores police and prison reform, and/or displaces attention to projects such as social welfare, education, community and economic development, and job creation, the populations facing the real risk of victimization may be doubly disadvantaged, both by high rates of violence and by low state investment in the kinds of policies that can reduce criminogenic conditions. How do other issues fare over these periods of low and high politicization?

Table 7.3 presents speech mentions and bills enacted in the United Kingdom over a range of issues during the 50-year period between 1957 and 2007, by governmental party control.[19] Though rudimentary, the comparison complicates conventional assumptions. During the Thatcher government, when politicization remained relatively low, constituting only 6–8 percent of speech mentions and acts, social welfare and civil rights legislation occupied a smaller portion of the political agenda than they had since the late 1950s, regardless of political party control. This is not surprising given the ideological orientation of the Thatcher government. As we move to greater politicization, with the government of John Major, also a Conservative, as we might expect, this trend continues, with the exception of crime legislation, which increases substantially. Acts addressing social welfare increase slightly as well.

By contrast, as measured by mentions in annual speeches to the government, the Blair government politicized crime substantially more than its predecessors; but, as Table 7.3 illustrates, Blair and New Labor also drew attention to other social issues, including civil rights, employment, housing, social welfare, and community development, substantially more than the Major government and more closely in line with previous Labour governments. Moreover, the Blair government's enactments reflect as much attention to social welfare as to crime. Of course, the content of those laws is not explored here, but these snapshots substantially complicate conventional wisdom about the colonization of political agendas by crime at the expense of other social policies. It is also worth noting that, though John Major and the Conservatives initiated the period of high crime politicization and fixated very narrowly on the punitive dimensions of the issue, his party decisively *lost* the 1997 election to a party that promised to confront crime *and* its causes.[20]

Pennsylvania

Some assessments of crime and punishment in the United States have suggested that crime comes to dominate state legislative agendas because states have few other policy areas in which they have sufficient political authority to enact legislation (Zimring and Johnson 2006). Indeed, states do engage in

Table 7.3 Speech Mentions and Acts, Crime and Social Welfare Provisions,[a] 1957–2010

		Speech mentions			Acts enacted			
		Crime	Social Welfare (All)	Civil Rights Only	Crime	Social Welfare (All)	Civil Rights Only	Peak Homicide Rate
MacMillan/Douglas-Home (1957–1963)	Conservative	26 (4.9%)	61 (11.4%)	3 (1.1%)	46 (9.7%)	56 (11%)	9 (1.9%)	.74 (1957)
Wilson (1964–1970)	Labour	24 (4.8%)	79 (16.0%)	15 (3.0%)	29 (7.1%)	57 (14.0%)	11 (2.7%)	.74 (1968)
Heath (1970–1974)	Conservative	16 (4.2%)	52 (13.8%)	12 (3.2%)	20 (7.2%)	42 (15.1%)	5 (1.8%)	.83 (1972)
Wilson/Callaghan (1974–1978)	Labour	26 (5.2%)	69 (13.8%)	16 (3.2%)	25 (8.2%)	45 (14.9%)	6 (2.0%)	1.07 (1978)
Thatcher (1979–1990)	Conservative	63 (6.6%)	85 (9.0%)	16 (1.7%)	63 (8.5%)	70 (9.4%)	15 (2.0%)	1.19 (1987)
Major (1990–1997)	Conservative	19 (4.4%)	26 (6.0%)	10 (2.3%)	51 (16.0%)	33 (10.3%)	6 (1.2%)	1.3 (1995)
Blair (1997–2008)	Labour	115 (13.2%)	122 (14.0%)	43 (5.0%)	46 (11.6%)	48 (12.1%)	18 (4.6%)	1.79 (2003)
Brown (2007–2010)	Labour	12 (7.1%)	26 (15.2%)		x	x	x	1.36 (2008)

[a]Civil rights, labor/employment, social welfare, community development/housing/planning.

the primary criminal enforcement mechanisms, and they have limited control over macroeconomic policy. But states can and do enact legislation on a wide range of other issues as well, including health care, education, agriculture, civil rights, banking and commerce, communications and technology, public lands and water, and even, occasionally, defense and immigration. Should they wish to do so, state lawmakers have ample opportunity to address (at least rhetorically or symbolically) a wide range of social problems related to crime.

In Figure 7.7 I compare legislative attention (acts) and spending on crime in Pennsylvania with traditional, core policy issues of state governments: social welfare and education.[21] Two observations are noteworthy. First, at least in terms of acts and spending, crime hardly dominates the Pennsylvania legislative agenda, even after it becomes highly politicized in the 1990s. Social welfare and education (primarily education) occupy a high portion of both political activities throughout the whole 30-year time period. Having said that, however, the period of high politicization of crime in Pennsylvania does coincide with reductions in attention to and spending on social welfare and education

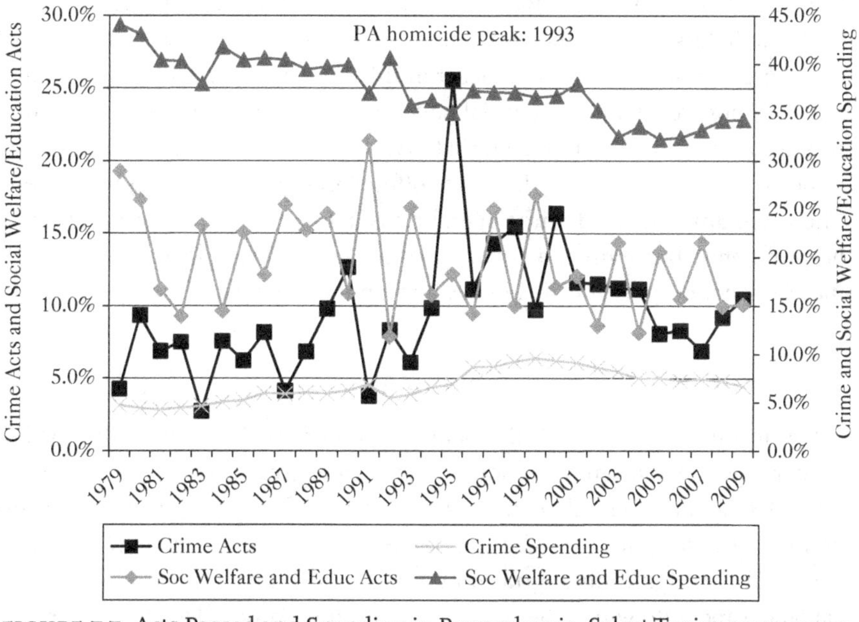

FIGURE 7.7 Acts Passed and Spending in Pennsylvania, Select Topics, 1979–2009
Source: Data are drawn from the State of Pennsylvania Policy Database Project, created by Temple University with funding support and cooperation of the Pennsylvania General Assembly and a grant from the Department of Community and Economic Development, and in-kind contributions from other participating universities in Pennsylvania. Data and further details available at: http://www.cla.temple.edu/papolicy/.

policies. As crime becomes more salient in legislative enactments and as a budget item, acts and spending on education and social welfare decline.

It is worth noting that, while there is a dramatic spike in criminal laws and spending on crime and justice in the mid-1990s that remains high, murder rates in Pennsylvania rose through the late 1980s and well into the 1990s, reaching a peak of 6.8 in 1993 and not falling below a rate of 5.0 until 1999. In 2010, rates continued to hover around 5.1, not remotely close to the low rate of 2.3 homicides per 100,000 Pennsylvania residents enjoyed in 1963. In addition, though violent crime in the state peaked earlier than homicide rates at 441.7/100,000 in 1991, they remained high throughout the 1990s, dropping only to 371.6 in 2001.[22]

These rates are dwarfed, however, by considering the murder rate of the state's most violent city, Philadelphia. In 2010, the murder rate remained high at 19.8/100,000, nearly four times as high as the state average of 5.2. Furthermore, fully 79.1 percent of the murder victims were African American, despite the city having a black population of 44 percent. Between 2007 and 2010, a staggering 91.3 percent of murder victims under the age of 18 were black and 82 percent of all homicide victims were killed with firearms.[23]

Nonetheless, the shifts in attention and spending between crime and social programs suggest that, at least in this one US state, while crime attention may not crowd out other social policy issues, crime spending is zero-sum. It is important to note, however, that states cannot run deficits, coin money, or borrow at the exceedingly low rates offered to the US national government. The zero-sum politics of crime spending is *not necessarily* a reflection of public preference but, rather, a function of limited state budgets that can only increase spending in one area by decreasing it elsewhere.

Summary

Taken in this larger context, the politicization of crime as the death knell of modern governance may be somewhat, if not greatly, exaggerated. In the United Kingdom, the lack of serious and sustained attention to crime for several decades, despite gradual but persistent increases in violence, including riots and the high-profile, gruesome murder of a toddler, provided a political landscape onto which the political parties moved rapidly beginning in the mid-1990s, particularly Labour. But the politicization of crime did not necessarily depoliticize other social policy concerns.

Interviews with ministers of Parliament who represented high-crime, heavily minority communities in London, as well as activists from these communities, provided some context in that they revealed political pressure for policy approaches to violence that combined strong law enforcement with economic development and police reform. In interviews with two Labour members of Parliament who represented diverse communities in London following the riots of August 2011, for example, both noted that a major cause of the riots was insufficient initial police response.[24] More broadly, however, both claimed that the majority of their constituents felt the dangers of serious violence acutely and wanted such activity removed from their communities, even as they also wanted the kind of community and economic development that can reduce criminal offending in the first place, such as a focus on youth employment and neighborhood quality. As one noted, "People don't want to live next to a crack house. They want to be safe. They want dangerous people locked up. But they also want fair police—they want a good relationship with the police. There is nothing inconsistent about this." He went on to say, "Historically, the right has been the party of law and order, which is daft because poor people are more often victims. Labour shouldn't be embarrassed about being tough on law and order."[25]

In Pennsylvania, by contrast, the politicization of crime coincided with a decline in attention to other social issues. Social welfare and education spending declined as crime became a more salient political issue. Recall, however, that rates of violence in Pennsylvania dwarfed those of Britain, even in its most dangerous places. Philadelphia's 19.8 murders per 100,000 residents in 2010 are almost incomprehensible in contrast to London's roughly 1.5. Pennsylvania's homicide and violent crime rate soared in the 1970s but peaked again during the period of high violence in the 1990s, and violence remained high in the state, particularly for African Americans who suffered from violent crime at far higher rates than whites.

At the same time, though the politicization of crime appears to be deeply connected to real rates of violence and crime and does not monopolize lawmaking to the degree predicted by the current literature, policy responses aimed at "root causes" or reform of justice institutions seem to decline during such periods. What explains these differences? I conclude with a discussion of institutional variation across the United States and the United Kingdom that might help to illuminate this variation.

Democratic Responsiveness or Accountability?

The contrast between the politicization of crime in the United Kingdom, the United States, and Pennsylvania presents important challenges to conventional understandings of the politics of punishing generally and US exceptionalism specifically. In this concluding section, I draw attention to distinctions between UK and US politics that can help us understand both high rates of violence and high rates of punishing and that call into question the claim that the US political system is *overly* responsive to the fickle masses.

First, the substantial differences in rates of serious violence between the United States and the United Kingdom require more attention. The relatively low rates of violence in the United Kingdom, as well as a politics of crime that does not *necessarily* separate crime from other social problems (or at least, less than we would think), draws us back to a more complex understanding of democratic systems and the politics of punishing. Though both the United States and the United Kingdom are (primarily) two-party, liberal economic market systems (per Lacey 2008), the levels of violence may reflect important differences in institutional dynamics that are underexplored.

Second, the multilayered nature of the US system, illustrated by attention to crime and a wide range of other social issues at both the national and state levels, poses problems for comprehensive policy reform and political accountability. Much of the literature has focused on the ways in which the decentralized and fractured nature of the US system promotes public participation and accountability (Jacobs and Kleban 2003; Zimring and Johnson 2006). But this also creates many veto points, and comparative research on political systems with many veto points reveals something else altogether: the challenge such systems pose to comprehensive social reform and welfare policies aimed at improving the conditions of large groups of people at the lower end of the socioeconomic scale (Stepan, 2001; Foweraker and Landman, 2002; Brooks and Manza 2007; Lijphart, 2008; see also Miller 2008). While some view veto points as potential safety valves for limiting reactive and repressive policy programs supported by the masses (e.g., Lacey 2008), such veto points also provide opportunities for elites and small groups to block redistribution and social reform. The United States is veto points to the *n*th degree. A classic illustration is gun control (see Goss 2006; Miller 2008), but the challenge of reforming racial hierarchy, policing, health care, and other policy areas also reveals substantial opportunity for small groups to block policies supported by majorities—sometimes large majorities (see Riker 1965; Lowi 1984; Robertson 2012).

The fragmented nature of the US system, then, may allow issues to be cleaved apart across the vertical and horizontal dimensions of the political landscape in ways that may make it harder, not easier, for citizens to hold the government accountable for security. Layers of jurisdictional overlap provide ample opportunity for single-issue politics and for sound-bite policy proposals with little impact and for which lawmakers in distant legislative venues have little accountability. In addition, there is good evidence that multiple electoral venues make it difficult for voters to know whom to hold accountable and generate voter fatigue and public confusion over political authority (Cutler 2004; Cameron 2006; see also A. L. Campbell 2012; Hacker and Pierson 2010). States in the United States address a substantial array of social issues but have little control over macroeconomic policy, long-term unemployment rates, poverty, and other social ills. As the Pennsylvania case briefly illustrated, single-issue politics may be more readily available in this fractured landscape where state governments have vast legislative authority over crime and punishment (through the criminal law and prisons) but less capacity to substantially alter underlying social conditions that give rise to violence. Though not explored here, the situation is even worse at the local level, where mayors and other elected officials have control over virtually none of the factors that contribute to high rates of violence *except* for policing and prosecutions. The incentives to promote punishing over comprehensive policymaking are strong since local lawmakers cannot promise much by way of the latter (see Peterson 1981 for a general discussion; see Lacey and Soskice, this volume and Miller 2008 for crime-specific discussions).

In fact, the combination of federalism and separation of powers may facilitate the rise of single-issue politics, divided government, fragmented political parties, and issue entrepreneurs. These factors combine to decouple crime and punishment from broader social conditions, generating opportunities to increase punitive policies against offenders without mitigating the harm of policing or socioeconomic marginalization. In the United Kingdom, the unitary, parliamentary system makes this more difficult. The centralization of power and party politics in the United Kingdom make single-issue politics less practical and promote more direct accountability. Advocates for more punishing must work their way into larger political platforms, and, as the brief investigation into the Blair government illustrated, untethering punishment from other issues may be more difficult.

Democratic systems can be broadly *responsive* to mass publics without being particularly *accountable* to them (see Miller 2013). What scholars have observed in the United States is a form of political responsiveness that may actually undermine accountability by making it harder for people suffering from real victimization and other forms of marginalization to link their concerns in the policy arena. This brief concluding discussion thus raises questions about the current literature's assessment of the United States as a highly responsive and excessive democracy. While there are many elections and many points of access, these features of American politics may conspire to limit, rather than enhance, the capacity of political leaders to adopt comprehensive responses to crime and violence and the opportunities for mass publics to respond.

Sample Speech Mentions

Major:

(1991) "They [government] will vigorously pursue their policies to combat drug trafficking and misuse of drugs, nationally and internationally."

(1992) "My Government will continue to give priority to law and order."

(1993) "A Bill will be introduced to improve the organisation and management of the police so that they are better able to combat crime, and to strengthen the administration of magistrates' courts."

Blair:

(1999) "A Bill will be introduced to modernise the youth courts and to give greater protection for vulnerable and intimidated witnesses in criminal cases."

(2001) "A Bill will be introduced to increase powers against money laundering, establish a criminal assets recovery agency, and make it easier to recover the proceeds of crime and drugs."

(2002) "My Government will introduce a Bill to tackle anti-social behaviour that damages communities."

Sample Acts:

Major:

Crime: Sex Offenses Act (1993)
Drug Trafficking Act (1994)
Criminal Injuries Compensation Act (1995)
Social Programs: Disability Discrimination Act (1995)
Trade Union Reform and Employment Rights Act (1993)

Blair:

Crime: Knives Act (1997)
Firearms Amendment Act (1997)
Crime and Disorder Act (1998)
Youth Justice and Criminal Evidence Act (1999)
Sexual Offences Act (2002)
Proceeds of Crime Act (2002)
Police and Justice Act (2006)
Social Programs: Race and Religious Hatred Act (2006)
Gender Recognition Act (2004)
Equality Act (2006)
Race Relations (Amendment) Act (2000)
Work and Families Act (2006)
Homelessness Act (2002)
Education Acts (2002, 205)

NOTES

1. A robust body of literature in political science in the 1970s and 1980s explored the impact of crime on urban politics and criminal justice institutions (e.g., Casper 1972; Eisenstein and Jacob 1977; Heumann 1978; Jacob 1980; Skogan and Maxfield 1981), but political science has been oddly slow to return to the topic (but see Gottschalk 2006; Weaver 2007; Miller 2008; Ewald 2012; Weaver and Lerman 2010; Murakawa and Beckett 2010).
2. FBI Uniform Crime Reporting Statistics: http://www.ucrdatatool.gov/Search/Crime/State/RunCrimeTrendsInOneVar.cfm.
3. Centers for Disease Control and Prevention, National Center for Health Statistics: http://www.cdc.gov/nchs/deaths.htm. see Zimring and Hawkins (1997) for a detailed analysis of violence in the United States and cross-nationally.
4. The analysis presented is drawn from my book, *The Myth of Mob Rule: Violent Crime and Democratic Politics*, Oxford University Press.
5. The selection of countries reflects the different types of political economies and institutional structures that are in the literature, for example, liberal market economies (United States, United Kingdom, Canada), corporatism (the Netherlands), and social democracies (Denmark).
6. Reported robbery rates also increased fourfold, from 60 per 100,000 in 1960 to 251 per 100,000 in 1980, though scholars dispute the extent of the increase (Ruth and Reitz 2003). Trends in robbery rates can be found on the FBI's Uniform Crime Reporting Statistics site (http://www.ucrdatatool.gov/index.cfm, accessed September 26, 2011).
7. I exclude the United States from this figure in order to illustrate the increases in homicide rates, independent of the extreme case of the United States.
8. See also Bureau of Justice Statistics, Homicide Trends in the United States (http://bjs.ojp.usdoj.gov/content/pub/pdf/htius.pdf, accessed September 26, 2011).
9. Also, a 2010 report from the Ministry of Justice found that between 2007 and 2010 the homicide rate for blacks was more than four times that for whites (49.7/million compared to 11.8) and for Asians, nearly double that of whites (18.3 per million). See Chapin et al. 2011.
10. The data are drawn from the US Comparative Agendas Project (www.policyagendas.org) and the UK Policy Agendas Project (http://policyagendasuk.wordpress.com/) data sets. The US data were originally collected by Frank R. Baumgartner and Bryan D. Jones, with the support of National Science Foundation grants SBR 9320922 and 0111611, and distributed through the Department of Government at the University of Texas at Austin. Neither the National Science Foundation nor the original collectors of the data bear any responsibility for the analysis reported here. The UK data were funded by the Economic and Social Research Council (reference RES-062-23-0872, Legislative Policy Agendas in the U.K.) as

part of a European Science Foundation EUROCORES European Collaborative Research Projects application, The Politics of Attention: West European Politics and Agenda-Setting in Times of Change, led by Professor Stefaan Walgrave, University of Antwerp. The UK project's principal investigator is Dr. Will Jennings at the University of Manchester, and Dr. Darren Halperin at Robert Gordon University is coinvestigator. The project is part of the Comparative Agendas Project directed by Professor Frank Baumgartner at the University of North Carolina. The Pennsylvania Policy Database Project "is a free, online resource that provides access to more than 180,000 state and news media records and enables users to trace and analyze with a few mouse clicks the history of public policy in the Commonwealth since 1979." The project was built by faculty-supervised students at Temple University and five other universities with the support and cooperation of the Pennsylvania General Assembly (http://www.cla.temple.edu/papolicy).

11. All public and legislative agenda measures come from the respective Policy Agendas Projects. Public opinion is measured as the "most important problem" (Gallup poll in United States; Ipsos MORI in United Kingdom; and Franklin and Marshall College Poll of Pennsylvania in Pennsylvania). Legislative attention in the United Kingdom is measured by sentence and partial sentences about crime and justice as a percent of all topics mentioned in the Annual Queen's Speech. The UK Policy Agendas Project (see note 10) collected and coded the full texts of the Speech from the Throne from 1911 to 2008. The speech is the statement "delivered by the monarch, on behalf of the government, at the beginning of each session of the U.K. Parliament. This sets out the executive and legislative priorities of the government in the forthcoming session" (see http://www.policyagendas.org.uk/ for more detail on the coding process). Acts refers to short and long titles of acts of the UK Parliament, which were also coded into topics, for which the topic code 12 (minus family issues) was extracted for this analysis. The US legislative agenda is measured by the percent of hearings in the House of Representatives about crime and justice. The Pennsylvania legislative agenda uses legislative hearings in the assembly as well as the Governor's Budget Address. For this analysis, I extracted topic code 12, Law, Crime and Family, and eliminated all text codes related to family issues that were not about criminal topics. Topics included in the data presented here are general references to crime, criminal justice issues; executive branch dealing with crime; white-collar crime; illegal drugs and drug trafficking; courts; prisons; juveniles; police and weapons control; criminal code/statutes; riots and crime prevention; domestic violence; sexual violence; and violence and sexual exploitation of children (excluding familial cases of child abuse and neglect, parental kidnapping, and incest).

12. Violent crime data in Britain are from Recorded Crime Statistics, provided to me by Will Jennings at the University of Southampton for providing the raw data.

13. Homicide rates are lagged one year behind measures of public and political attention.
14. Some have suggested that, while crime was a low-order priority in the Thatcher government (especially compared to economic reform, housing, and welfare state reform), the policies of the Thatcher years contributed to further increases in crime rates (Farrall and Hay 2010).
15. Obviously, the Queen's Speech is just one measure of the governing party agenda. Additional research is being conducted on party manifestos, bills introduced, and laws, which show similar patterns.
16. In 1998, for example, 4.5 percent of the speech was dedicated to crime topics. In 2000 it was 16.4 percent, and in 2001 it was back down to 9.0 percent. The highest percent of the speech that was dedicated to crime was in 2002, when a full 20 percent of the speech addressed these topics.
17. UK Policy Agendas Project, most important problem (see notes 10 and 11).
18. I removed the most overt congressional hearings that were related to the 2001 terrorist attacks; but many hearings took place on the creation of the Department of Homeland Security generally after 2001, and I removed only those that directly referenced September 11.
19. This analysis uses five topic codes in the Policy Agendas data to measure attention to social welfare issues: civil rights and civil liberties (2); employment, labor, and immigration (5); education (6); social welfare (13); and community development/housing (14).
20. Author's preliminary analysis of party manifestos from 1997.
21. Civil rights, employment, education, social welfare, and community development/housing.
22. Crime in Pennsylvania, Uniform Crime Report, Pennsylvania State Police. http://www.paucrs.pa.gov/UCR/Reporting/RptMain.asp.
23. Murder Analysis in Philadelphia, Philadelphia Police Department, (https://www.phillypolice.com/assets/crime-maps-stats/PPD.Homicide.Analysis.2007-2010.pdf).
24. Interviews with members of Parliament on February 12, 2012, and April 18, 2012.
25. Interview with member of Parliament on April 18, 2012.

REFERENCES

Alexander, Michelle. *The New Jim Crow: Mass Incarceration in the Age of Colorblindness.* New York: New Press, 2010.

Balvig, Flemming. "When Law and Order Returned to Denmark." *Journal of Scandinavian Studies in Criminology and Crime Prevention* 5 (2004): 167–87.

Barker, Vanessa. *The Politics of Imprisonment: How the Democratic Process Shapes the Way American Punishes Offenders.* New York: Oxford University Press, 2009.

Baumgartner, Frank R., Christian Breunig, Christoffer Green-Pedersen, Bryan D. Jones, Peter B. Mortensen, Michiel Nuytemans, and Stefan Walgrave. "Punctuated Equilibrium in Comparative Perspective." *American Journal of Political Science* 53, no. 3 (2009): 603–20.

Beckett, Katherine. *Making Crime Pay: Law and Order in Contemporary American Politics*. New York: Oxford University Press, 1997.

Brooks, Clem, and Jeff Manza. *Why Welfare States Persist: The Importance of Public Opinion in Democracies*. Chicago: University of Chicago Press, 2007.

Burstein, Paul. "The Impact of Public Opinion on Public Policy." *Political Research Quarterly* 56, no. 1 (2003): 29–40.

Cameron, David D. "Economic Voting and Multi-Level Governance: A Comparative Individual Analysis." *American Journal of Political Science* 50, no. 2 (2006): 449–63.

Campbell, Andrea Louise. "Policy Makes Mass Politics." *Annual Review of Political Science* 15 (2012): 333–51.

Campbell, Michael. "Ornery Alligators and Soap on a Rope: Texas Prosecutors and Punishment Reform in the Lone Star State." *Theoretical Criminology* 16 (2012): 289–311.

Casper, Jonathan. *American Criminal Justice: The Defendant's Perspective*. Englewood Cliffs, NJ: Prentice-Hall, 1972.

Chapin, Rubert, John Flatley, and Kevin Smith. "Crime in England and Wales." *Home Office Statistical Bulletin*. London: Crown, 2011.

Cutler, F. "Electoral Behaviour in a Federal Context: The Consequences of Confusion." *Publius* 34, no. 2 (2004):19–38.

Doob, Anthony N., and Cheryl Marie Webster. "Countering Punitiveness: Understanding Stability in Canada's Imprisonment Rates." *Law and Society Review* 40, no. 2 (2006): 325–68.

Downes, David, and Rob Morgan. "Dumping the 'Hostages to Fortune?': The Politics of Law and Order in Post-War Britain." In *The Oxford Handbook of Criminology*, edited by Mike Maguire, Rob Morgan, and Robert Reiner, 2nd edition, 87–134. Oxford: Oxford University Press, 1997.

Downes, David, and Rob Morgan. "Skeletons in the Cupboard: The Politics of Law and Order at the Turn of the Millenium." In *The Oxford Handbook of Criminology*, edited by Mike Maguire, Rob Morgan, and Robert Reiner, 286. Oxford: Oxford University Press, 2002.

Dzur, Albert W., and Rekha Mirchandani. "Punishment and Democracy: The Role of Public Deliberation." *Punishment and Society* 9 (2007): 151–75.

Eisenstein, James, and Herbert Jacob. *Felony Justice: An Organizational Analysis of Criminal Courts*. Boston: Little, Brown, 1977.

Ewald, Alec. "Collateral Consequences in the American States." *Social Science Quarterly* 93, no. 1 (2012): 211–47.

Fajnzylber, Pablo, Daniel Lederman, and Norman Loayza. "Crime and Victimization: An Economic Perspective." *Economia* 1 (2000): 219.

Farrall, Stephen, and Colin Hay. "Not so Tough on Crime? Why Weren't the Thatcher Governments More Radical in Reforming the Criminal Justice System?" *British Journal of Criminology* 50, no. 3 (2010): 550–69.

Forman, James. *Locking Up Our Own: Crime, Punishment and Black America.* New York: Farrar, Straus and Giroux, 2017.

Fortner, Michael. *Black Silent Majority: The Rockefeller Drug Laws and the Politics of Punishment.* Cambridge, MA: Harvard University Press, 2015.

Foweraker, J., and T. Landman. "Constitutional Democracy and Democratic Performance." *Democratization* 9, no. 2 (2002): 43–66.

Fox, James A., and Marianne W. Zawitz. *Homicide Trends in the United States.* Washington, DC: Bureau of Justice Statistics, Office of Justice Programs, 2010.

Garland, David. *The Culture of Control: Crime and Social Order in Contemporary Society.* Chicago: University of Chicago Press, 2001.

Goss, Kristin. *Disarmed: The Missing Movement for Gun Control in the U.S.* Princeton, NJ: Princeton University Press, 2006.

Gottschalk, Marie. *The Prison and the Gallows: The Politics of Mass Incarceration in America.* New York: Cambridge University Press, 2006.

Gottschalk, Marie. *Caught: The Prison State and the Lockdown of American Politics.* Princeton, NJ: Princeton University Press, 2015.

Granath, Sven, Johanna Hagstedt, Janne Kivivuori, Martti Lehti, Soenita Ganpat, Marieke Liem, and Paul Nieuwbeerta. *Homicide in Finland, the Netherlands and Sweden.* Research Report 2459/Finland, Research Report 2011:15/ Sweden. Stockholm: National Council for Crime Prevention; Leiden, the Netherlands: National Research Institute of Legal Policy, 2011.

Hacker, Jacob S., and Paul Pierson. "Winner-Take-All Politics: Public Policy, Political Organization, and the Precipitous Rise in the Top Incomes in the United States." *Politics and Society* 38, no. 2 (2010): 152–204.

Heumann, Milton. *Plea Bargaining: The Experiences of Prosecutors, Judges and Defense Attorneys.* Chicago: University of Chicago Press, 1978.

Hood, Christopher. *The Blame Game: Spin, Bureaucracy, and Self-Preservation in Government.* Princeton, NJ: Princeton University Press, 2010.

House of Commons. "Homicide Statistics, Research Paper 99/56." London: Parliamentary papers. http://www.parliament.uk.

Jacob, Herbert. *Crime and Justice in Urban America.* New York: Prentice Hall, 1980.

Jacobs, David, and Richard Kleban. "Political Institutions, Minorities, and Punishment: A Pooled Cross-National Analysis of Imprisonment Rates." *Social Forces* 82, no. 2 (2003): 725–55.

Lacey, Nicola. *The Prisoners' Dilemma: Political Economy and Punishment in Contemporary Democracies.* Cambridge: Cambridge University Press, 2008.

LaFree, Gary, and Kriss A. Drass. "Counting Crime Booms among Nations: Evidence for Homicide Victimization Rates, 1956–1998." *Criminology* 40 (2002): 769–800.

Langley, Marty, and Josh Sugarmann. "Black Homicide Victimization in the United States: An Analysis of 2012 Homicide Data." New York: Violence Policy Center, 2015.

Lijphart, A. *Thinking about Democracy: Power Sharing and Majority Rule in Theory and Practice*. New York: Routledge, 2008.

Loader, Ian. "The Anti-Politics of Crime." *Theoretical Criminology* 12, no. 3 (2008): 399–410.

Lowi, Theodore. "Why Is There No Socialism in the United States?: A Federal Analysis." *International Political Science Review* 5 (1984): 369.

Miller, Lisa L. "Power to the People: Violent Victimization, Inequality and Democratic Politics." *Theoretical Criminology* 17, no. 3 (2013): 283–313.

Miller, Lisa L. *The Myth of Mob Rule: Violent Crime and Democratic Politics*. New York: Oxford University Press, 2016.

Morrison, Blake. *As If*. London: Granta Publishing, 1997.

Murakawa, Naomi, and Katherine Beckett. "The Penology of Racial Innocence: The Erasure of Racism in the Study and Practice of Punishment." *Law and Society Review* 44, no. 3/4 (2010): 695–730.

Newburn, Tim, and Paul Rock. *The Politics of Crime Control: Essays in Honour of David Downes*. Oxford: Oxford University Press, 2006.

Page, Joshua. *The Toughest Beat: Politics, Punishment and the Prison Officers Union in California*. New York: Oxford University Press, 2011.

Peterson, Paul. *City Limits*. Chicago: University of Chicago Press, 1981.

Pettit, Philip. "Depoliticizing Democracy." *Ratio Juris* 17 (2004): 55.

Pontusson, Jonas, and David Rueda. "The Politics of Inequality: Voter Mobilization and Left Parties in Advanced Industrial States." *Comparative Political Studies* 43, no. 6 (2010): 675–705.

Reiner, Robert. "Political Economy, Crime, and Criminal Justice." In *The Oxford Handbook of Criminology*, edited by Mike Maguire, Rod Morgan, and Robert Reiner, 341–79. Oxford: Oxford University Press, 2007.

Riker, William. *Federalism: Origin, Operation, Significance*. Boston: Little, Brown, 1964.

Robertson, David Brian. *Federalism and the Making of America*. New York: Routledge Press, 2012.

Ruth, Henry, and Kevin Reitz. *The Challenge of Crime: Rethinking Our Response*. Cambridge, MA: Harvard University Press, 2003.

Scarman, Lord. *The Scarman Report: The Brixton Disorders, 10–12 April 1981*. London: Penguin Books, 1982.

Scheingold, Stuart A. *The Politics of Law and Order: Street Crime and Public Policy*. New York: Longman, 1984.

Simon, Jonathan. *Governing through Crime: How the War on Crime Transformed American Democracy and Created a Culture of Fear*. New York: Oxford University Press, 2007.

Skogan, Wesley C., and Michael G. Maxfield. *Coping with Crime: Individual and Neighborhood Reactions*. Thousand Oaks, CA: Sage, 1981.

Smith, David J. "Ethnic Origins, Crime and Criminal Justice in England and Wales." In *Crime and Justice. Ethnicity, Crime and Immigration: Comparative and Cross-National Perspectives*. Vol. 21. Edited by Michael Tonry, 101–18. Chicago: University of Chicago Press, 1997.

Soroka, Stuart, and Christopher Wlezien. *Degrees of Democracy: Politics, Public Opinion, and Policy*. Cambridge: Cambridge University Press, 2010.

Stepan, A. C. *Arguing Comparative Politics*. New York: Oxford University Press, 2001.

Tonry, Michael. "Determinants of Penal Policies." In *Crime and Justice. Crime, Punishment, and Politics in a Comparative Perspective*. Vol. 36. Edited by Michael Tonry, 1–48. Chicago: University of Chicago Press, 2007.

Wacquant, Loic. "Class, Race and Hyper-incarceration in Revanchist America." *Daedalus* 10 (2010): 74–90.

Weaver, Vesla Mae. "Frontlash: Race and the Development of Punitive Crime Policy." *Studies in American Political Development* 21 (2007): 230–65.

Weaver, Vesla Mae, and Amy Lerman. "Political Consequences of the Carceral State." *American Political Science Review* 104, no. 4 (2010): 817–33.

Western, Bruce. *Punishment and Inequality in America*. New York: Russell Sage, 2006.

Wilson, James Q. *Thinking about Crime*. New York: Vintage Press, 1975.

Windelsham, Lord. *Politics, Punishment and Populism*. Oxford: Oxford University Press, 1998.

Zimring, Frank E., and Gordon Hawkins. *Crime Is Not the Problem: Lethal Violence in America*. Oxford: Oxford University Press, 1997.

Zimring, Frank E., Gordon Hawkins, and Sam Kamin. *Punishment and Democracy: Three Strikes You're Out in California*. New York: Oxford University Press, 2001.

Zimring, Frank E., and David T. Johnson. "Public Opinion and the Governance of Punishment in Democratic Political Systems." *Annals of the American Academy of Political and Social Sciences* 605 (2006): 265–80.

8

Comparing Serious Violent Crime in the United States and England and Wales

WHY IT MATTERS, AND HOW IT CAN BE DONE

Zelia Gallo, Nicola Lacey, and David Soskice

Introduction

With half of the US prison population incarcerated for crimes of violence (Forman 2012, 25) and with evidence that levels of homicidal violence have been distinctively high through much of American history (Roth 2009), violent crime stands as possibly the single most important crime-related issue in any attempt to explain American exceptionalism in punishment. Yet comparative analysis of violent crime—by contrast to that of punishment—is hampered by a lack of reliable comparative statistics. This is a major problem even in a comparison between the United States and England and Wales, relatively similar societies, and the subject of this chapter. The only offense involving interpersonal violence for which reliable data are available is homicide; as is well known, the number of homicides per capita in the United States is at least five times the corresponding number in England and Wales. Data on violent crime are available from the International Crime Victimisation Survey (ICVS) for a number of societies, including the United States and England and Wales. Important though the survey is in relation to many offenses, it is widely argued to be misleading in relation to violent crimes.[1] Hence, there is some doubt over its finding that violent crime in England and Wales is greater than or equal to that in the United States. As will be seen, that doubt has not prevented such data being used in academic work. Thus, we believe that more carefully derived comparative data are needed. This may not be possible for the general category of violent crime because of intractable variations in both offense definition and recording practices in different countries (Aebi et al. 2010, 18, 22). We show in this chapter, however, that we can derive reasonably valid comparative data for the United States and England and Wales for the much narrower set of offenses constituting serious violent crime.

We show that the incidence of serious violent crime per capita is between 3.6 and 6.5 times as high in the United States as it is in England and Wales (Table 8.1). This very broadly parallels the comparative data on homicide between the two societies. There are, of course, many qualifications, which we set out at length: these relate to country differences in the statutory definitions of offenses, reporting of crimes to the police, and police recording practices[2]; and, for reasons we will explain (see "The Use of NCRS Data 2008–2009"), our comparative estimates relate only to the years 2008–2010. However, the New Zealand Ministry of Justice carried out a related exercise comparing serious violent crime in New Zealand with that in the United States for 2000, and their results (4.5 times higher in the United States)

Table 8.1 The Ratio of Serious Violent Crime and of Homicides, United States, England and Wales, Canada, and New Zealand: Offenses per 100,000 Population

	United States to England and Wales, 2008	United States to Canada, 2000	United States to New Zealand, 2000
Serious violent crime Ratio	3.6 (lower bound) 6.5 (upper bound)	2.3	4.5
Homicide ratio	4.6	3.1	3.2

Sources: The data are for the calendar years for the United States, Canada, and New Zealand and the "financial" years April 1 to March 31 for England and Wales. The US data are from Federal Bureau of Investigation (2013, table 1, col. 11). The data for England and Wales include possession of firearms with intent and are from Office of National Statistics (2012, rows 5A for lower and 8F for upper bound). The Canadian data are from Gannon (2001a, 2001b); the New Zealand data are from Segessenmann (2002).

are broadly comparable to ours (Segessenmann 2002). A similar comparison between Canada and the United States also for 2000 reported an incidence in the United States of serious violent crime 2.3 times that in Canada (Gannon 2001a, 2001b). These studies lend further weight to the claim that the United States experiences a distinctively higher level of serious violence compared with other relatively similar countries and, in doing so, provide important information relevant to the ongoing debate about the degree to which crime—and fear of crime—affects American patterns of punishment (Enns 2014; Miller 2016).

The chapter is arranged as follows. We first explain the significance of the issue. We then review the relationship between the legal definitions of serious violent offenses in the United States and in England and Wales. The main focus of our argument is in the following section, where we build robust comparative data based on police recording criteria in the two countries, using the detailed instructions and examples for recording given to police forces. Notwithstanding differences in offense definitions, it is possible to construct a persuasive argument that aggravated assault (or AA, based on the US Model Penal Code) operates in broadly similar ways to Sections 18 and 20 of the Offenses against the Person Act 1861 in England and Wales, along with certain smaller categories of interpersonal violent crime.[3] Next, we set our findings in the context of other comparative studies of serious violent crime in the United States, Canada, and New Zealand, before drawing conclusions.

Why This Chapter?

Recent years have seen a resurgence of interest in comparative criminal justice. Notwithstanding significant changes in both crime and punishment in most advanced democracies over the last half-century, scholars have begun to come to terms with differences in both the scale and the quality of these changes across different countries and to interest themselves in what can be learned from these differences about the underlying dynamics of crime and punishment (Downes 1988; Cavadino and Dignan 2006; Lacey 2008; Pratt and Eriksson 2013). Comparative studies inevitably raise problems of measurement in areas in which there are no internationally agreed criteria. But this is much less the case on the punishment side of the equation, where the crude but readily accessible measure of comparative imprisonment rates is widely used. While there are difficulties,[4] the problems in comparing levels and types of punishment pale into relative insignificance compared with those which arise in relation to crime.

In principle, the most straightforward way of comparing serious violent crime in the United States and England and Wales would be to use the large-scale and generally reliable victim surveys in the two countries, the National Crime Victim Survey (NCVS) in the United States and the Crime Survey of England and Wales (CSEW) in England and Wales. Unfortunately, although there are data on serious violent crime in the American survey, there are only data on a very much wider category of violence in the CSEW. We therefore developed a different approach using police-recorded crime data,[5] and we will show (see "Comparing the Detailed Rules for Recording Offenses in the United States and in England and Wales") that it is possible to put upper and lower estimates on levels of serious violent crime in England and Wales and in the United States. These data are summarized in Table 8.1 and justified in detail in the section "How the Data Are Compiled."

The US/England and Wales comparative measure of serious violence is a salient research question for a number of reasons. First, the most comprehensive comparative data on violent crime (ICVS) have been quite widely used in comparative work notwithstanding their methodological problems.[6] Similar questions can be raised about the United Nations Crime Trends Survey for 2013,[7] whose data for assaults give the England and Wales rate at about three times the US rate (US rate, 263; England and Wales rate, 724), suggesting that the US rate is based (correctly) on aggravated assault data, while the England and Wales rate is for a much wider category of assaults.[8] The more robust comparative data provided by the *European Sourcebook of Crime and Criminal Justice Statistics* (Aebi et al. 2010) do not, for obvious reasons, include the United States. The sourcebook uses a fruitful methodology—not dissimilar to the one used in this chapter—providing standard definitions of given offenses (for assaults "inflicting bodily injury on another with intent" (p. 350), approximating national data to that definition, and specifying when and how national data diverge from the definition (especially pp. 350–54; Aebi et al. 2009). However, sourcebook data for assaults in England and Wales are based on offenses of committing grievous bodily harm (GBH) with intent to commit GBH, roughly equivalent to section 18 of the Offenses against the Person Act 1861 or Home Office recording category 5A (Aebi et al. 2009, 136; compare Aebi et al. 2009, 112; Nicholas, Kershaw, and Walker 2007, 36, table 2.04). For the reasons set out (see "The Legal Background" and "How the Data Are Compiled," especially "Comparing the Detailed Rules for Recording Offenses in the United States and in England and Wales" and "The Definition of 'Serious Injury'"), we believe that *in a comparison with US aggravated assault*, offenses classed as 5A are not sufficient on their own but need to be combined with offenses categorized as 8F, including GBH without intent. We argue that the approach developed in this chapter is therefore the most promising way to refine our understanding of the relative rates of violent crime in the United States and England and Wales.

Second, there is a particular reason to focus on the comparison of serious violence between England and Wales and the United States.[9] Comparative data on most crimes are fraught with problems of definition and validity. It is, however, possible—for the reasons set out under "How the Data Are Compiled"—to construct very broadly comparative series of serious interpersonal violent crime for the two countries. This pushes the boundary of broadly reliable statistics out from homicide (or near-lethal violence; Zimring and Hawkins 1997) to a further and much larger category of crimes. From a political perspective, it can be argued that this category of offense is one about which voters in advanced countries are greatly concerned (Miller 2013, 2015, 2016; see also Miller, this volume)—a concern that is readily explicable when one contemplates the way in which American rates of serious violence translate into lifetime risks of violent victimization many times greater than that in otherwise comparable countries, not to mention the relevance of violent crime to race- and class-differentiated patterns of criminalization and victimization (Forman 2012, 25, 46–48, 68–69; Miller 2015). From a social science perspective, the particular benefit of comparisons between the United States and England and Wales (as well as Canada and New Zealand) is that these countries are "similar cases" in the way in which many political, economic, and legal institutions function, from the broad nature of the liberal capitalist system (Hall and Soskice 2001) to that of the safety net welfare state (Esping-Andersen 1990) and the competitive political system (Lijphart 1984), through to a common law legal system (Lacey 2008; Lacey and Soskice 2015).

Third, our data may be useful in current policy debates. One important debate concerns the role of crime in explaining the distinctive trajectory of American criminal justice since the 1970s. Some scholars have argued that when serious violence reaches a certain level (Peterson and Krivo 2012), it is of key concern to voters and hence acquires a new degree of political salience (Lacey and Soskice 2015; Miller 2013, 2015, 2016; Kleiman 2010; see also Miller, this volume); and one important study of homicide and "near-lethal violence" concluded that "America's special problem is violence and not crime" (Zimring and Hawkins 1997, 7).[10] By contrast, several leading scholars have argued that the exceptional level of American punishment in recent decades is a social and political phenomenon independent of high levels of violent crime (Tonry 2004, 2007; Western 2007; Wacquant 2010). Indeed, in Chapter 5 of this volume, Tappio Lappi-Seppälä argues that the fact that the rapid growth of imprisonment in the United States has coincided with periods of both rising and declining homicide provides evidence for the thesis that there is a "disconnect" between crime and punishment.[11] Recent work by political scientist Peter Enns (2014), however, has provided a sophisticated dynamic analysis which shows a strong correlation between homicide rates, public punitiveness, and the *rate of change in the incarceration rate in the United States* over a similar period. In support of the "disconnect" thesis, it is sometimes asserted that, in the United Kingdom, rates of violent crime are broadly similar to those in the United States, while incarceration rates are only a small proportion of American rates. This analysis loses force if rates of crime—particularly serious crime—are actually dissimilar. Reliable comparative data are therefore crucial to adjudicating between contrary positions on the diagnosis and meaning of American exceptionalism in punishment.[12]

Another policy issue relates to the debate over gun control. The Institute for Legislative Action of the National Rifle Association has claimed that violent crime rates are higher in the United Kingdom than in the United States, in support of the argument that high rates of gun ownership *reduce* violent crime. While the data source is not clear, it seems possible that the National Rifle Association's claim about relative crime rates may have been derived from a superficial interpretation of the ICVS data on violent crime.[13] This underlines a more general point about the need for transparency in methods of data collection and analysis, as well as a more general issue about the use of such data for political purposes. Strategies to combat serious violence are not well served by misleading comparative crime data, with potentially tragic consequences in the realms of public health and safety.

The Legal Background

As we have explained, our argument turns on the instructions to those recording crime issued by the Home Office in England and Wales and by the FBI in the United States. Since much of the debate thus far has turned on the legal definitions of the relevant offenses and since the recording instructions in each country refer to those offenses, we offer in this section a brief survey of the relevant offenses, as well as reasons for thinking that, despite technical differences, they may not be as legally divergent as generally assumed. The basic definitions of the main offenses in question are as follows.

Aggravated Assault under the Model Penal Code § 211.1(2) (US)

Statutory language requires that the offender (1) "attempts to cause serious bodily injury to another, or causes such injury purposely, knowingly or recklessly under circumstances manifesting extreme indifference to the value of human life" or (2) "attempts to cause or purposely or knowingly causes bodily injury with a deadly weapon" (American Law Institute 1980).[14]

Section 18 Offenses against the Person Act 1861 (England and Wales)—Wounding/Causing Grievous Bodily Harm with Intent

"Whosoever shall unlawfully and maliciously by any means whatsoever wound or cause any grievous bodily harm to any person . . . with intent, to do some grievous bodily harm to any person [*mens rea* i], or with intent to resist or prevent the lawful apprehension or detainer of any person [*mens rea* ii], shall be guilty."

Section 20 Offenses against the Person Act 1861 (England and Wales)—Malicious Wounding/Inflicting Grievous Bodily Harm

"Whosoever shall unlawfully and maliciously wound or inflict any grievous bodily harm upon any other person, either with or without any weapon or instrument, shall be guilty" (where the *mens rea* is foresight that the victim might suffer *some* harm).

It is apparent that, on the pure basis of the legal definitions of AA, on the one hand, and sections 18 and 20, on the other, there is a lack of precise fit between the two groups of assaults. Most obviously, Section 18 has a more stringent *mens rea* requirement (intent) than AA (knowledge or recklessness with extreme indifference), while Section 20 has a less stringent one than AA in that it can be committed recklessly as to some bodily harm (*R. v. Savage and Parmenter* 1992) and irrespective of extreme indifference to human life; furthermore it can be committed even where relatively trivial harm ensues given the very broad meaning which the courts have ascribed to the legal concept of a wound. Aggravated assault includes an attempted offense under § 211.1(2)(b), which requires proof of purpose to cause the specified injury or a belief that the injury will occur (American Law Institute 1980, § 5.01(1)(b)). However, this *mens rea* provision attaches to "bodily injury" and not "serious bodily injury," which would be required for an attempt under § 211.1(2)(a). *Prima facie* this is broader than Section 18; for example, using a gun in an attempt to bruise someone is not an offense under Section 18.[15] (We take up this definitional difference about attempts in the next section, explaining why it is unlikely to make a significant difference to the validity of our comparative data.)

Section 18, conversely, includes the offense with *mens rea* ii, which is not included under AA. This is a small category numerically. But in any case, given that the point we wish to establish is that the ICVS's finding of England's high levels of interpersonal nonfatal violence compared with the United States is exaggerated, the fact that including *mens rea* ii makes Section 18 larger is relatively unproblematic in that it makes our argumentative task harder rather than easier.

The key issue about the comparability of the *mens rea*, notwithstanding the possibility of recklessness as well as intent, is the inclusion in AA of the requirement that the offense is carried out "under circumstances manifesting extreme indifference to the value of human life." As we have noted, this is a much narrower test than in, say, Section 20 Offenses against the Person Act 1861, where the recklessness need only be as to some physical harm (*R. v. Savage and Parmenter* 1992). In fact, one might argue that it is not so different from the Section 18 test, in that it comes close to the definition of intention established in an important series of English cases from *Moloney* to *Woollin* (*R. v. Moloney* 1985; *R. v. Woollin* 1998). These held that where an outcome is so probable that the defendant must have realized it was virtually certain, juries are to be directed that they may infer that it was intended even if there is no direct intent—in other words, even if it is not proven to have been the offender's purpose to cause the (virtually certain) result. While only a tiny fraction of cases ever come before a jury and not all of these require a judicial direction on intent, this technical provision shows that, even in those rare cases where the defendant's intention becomes a key legal issue, evidential proxies short of clear proof of direct intention may be relied upon for the purposes of classification. As we shall see, this is yet more true of the norms that govern recording practices (see "Comparing the Detailed Rules for Recording Offenses in the United States and in England and Wales").

If a defendant charged with AA was indeed aware of what he or she was doing and did it "under circumstances manifesting extreme indifference to the value of human life," a natural interpretation—absent any mental incapacity excuse or other unusual circumstance—is that he or she was aware that serious injury or death was likely to result but was unconcerned. But the key comparative question is how an offense in which the defendant was aware that serious injury or death was likely to result from an action and knew that he or she was undertaking the action but did not explicitly have the intent to produce serious injury or death—a central case of AA in the United States—would be treated by the police who determine what goes into the official records in England and Wales. Here, we argue, the detailed administrative instructions issued to recording authorities in each country become crucial.

How the Data Are Compiled

In this section we explain in detail how police recording of serious violent crimes is structured in the United States and in England and Wales. This is on the basis of relatively precise instructions by the FBI to local police forces, contained in the *Uniform Crime Reporting Handbook* (UCRH) for the United States and by the Home Office in England and Wales in the periodically revised Home Office Counting Rules (HOCR). Both sources give a large number of examples which enable us to "match" categories of offenses in the two countries. Notably (apart from homicides) data on comparative crimes are bound to have substantial measurement error. However, as shown in the previous section, in both countries there are criminal assault offenses in which serious physical violence is present and/or intended, so categories of crime do exist that *prima facie* cover similar conduct. We argue that we can make meaningful comparisons of the American offense of AA and the English offenses of GBH, Section 18 (with intent, hence more serious) and Section 20 (less serious), based on police recording, at least giving upper and lower bounds in the period 2008–2010.

The main statistical problems in compiling a reliable basis for comparison come from the English, rather than the American, data. The UCRH has remained broadly consistent in coverage and recording procedures over a long period of time.[16] The framework for police recording of serious violent crime in England remained unchanged from 1960 until the early to mid–1990s. But at that point a political debate on violent crime developed, leading to a widespread view that serious violent crime was being heavily under-recorded by the police. The period from the mid-1990s to 2008 was accordingly one of a series of major and minor changes in recording procedures and HOCRs. Indeed, the major procedural changes in police recording of 2002–2003, under the National Crime Recording Standard (NCRS), are thought to have taken several years of "bedding-down." The year 2008–2009 is the first when the numbers of both Section 18 and Section 20 offenses are published; but it marks the high point of reliability as recent work suggests that police recording of offenses known to them has declined since then (although this is unlikely to have affected the recording of serious violent crime as much as more minor offenses).[17]

The criteria for police recording are broadly based on the legal definitions discussed in "The Legal Background." However, the precise instructions do *not* require that the police give a technical legal justification for their classification; indeed, US states have their own, somewhat idiosyncratic, definitions of criminal offenses,[18] but their police forces are still required to use the UCRH rules. Police recording must not be based on prosecution (or judicial) decisions if these differ from the recording criteria.[19]

Based on the instructions given in the FBI's UCRH and the Home Office's NCRS counting rules, we can be reasonably confident that the definition of AA has a wider reach than Section 18 offenses and a narrower reach than Section 20 offenses. In other words, if the English police applied the AA definition to assaults in England and Wales, they would record more assaults than would be recorded under the more serious Section 18 alone but fewer assaults than they would have recorded under Sections 18 and 20 together.[20]

To justify this claim, we make five points: (1) The HOCR for 2008–2009 under the NCRS for the first time explicitly record the number of Section 18 and of Section 20 offenses known to the police. By this date the NCRS procedures for recording serious violent crime were probably reasonably effective compared to previous periods. (2) The instructions for AA offenses in terms of "intent" are somewhat weaker than for Section 18 offenses, thus suggesting that at least some (but probably not most) offenses classified as Section 20 in the NCRS would be classified as AA in the UCRH. (3) The examples of injuries given in the UCRH and the HOCR show that the terms "grievous bodily harm" in Section 18 and Section 20 offenses and "severe or aggravated bodily injury" in AA offenses (or other similar phrases) are broadly interchangeable. (4) Reasonable upper bounds can be put on the relative rate of AA offenses in the United States and Section 18 and Section 20 offenses in England and Wales not recorded by the police, by drawing on the NCVS and the CSEW in relation to the UCRH and the NCRS. (5) The hierarchy rules and the counting rules in terms of offense per victim are similar for the UCRH and NCRS. Later, we note the need for some minor adjustments, for example, to take account of the fact that "attempted murder or killing" is part of AA offenses in the United States but not of Section 18 offenses in England and Wales.

The Use of NCRS Data 2008–2009

The Home Office has changed its counting rules used in compiling the NCRS on a number of occasions; since the late 1990s, in 1998–1999, in 2002–2003, in 2008–2009, and again in 2012–2013.[21] In addition, the procedural framework was changed in a major way in 2002–2003 with the introduction of the NCRS (see above). It is widely agreed, including by Home Office researchers, that each of these changes had the effect of increasing the numbers of recorded violent crimes in the first decade of the twenty-first century (Povey and Prime 1999; Simmons, Legg, and Hosking 2003; Hough, Mirrlees-Black, and Dale 2005; Walker, Kershaw, and Nicholas 2006; Reiner 2007, 70–71).

For instance, the Home Office estimated that the changes in 1998–1999 inflated the violence against the person count by over 120 percent (Hough, Mirrlees-Black, and Dale 2005, 28). Moreover, "changes would have taken several years to bed in. . . . [T]he changes will have artificially inflated the count of crimes each year, as officers across the country became more aware of, and compliant with, the new procedures" (Hough, Mirrlees-Black, and Dale 2005, 28). This seems of particular relevance for the major changes of 2002–2003. Thus, the NCRS data from 2002 onwards use counting rules that lead to the recording of a greater proportion of violent crime than do the data for previous years. For the purposes of our argument, the 2008–2009 HOCR are therefore the most suitable rules in that they provide the most rigorous benchmark for testing our claim.

In addition, and for our purposes most significantly, the 2008–2009 HOCR enable us (more or less) to distinguish Section 18 and Section 20 offenses from lesser Section 47 offenses, which was not previously possible. From 2008–2009 on, the Home Office classification 5A consists of Section 18 offenses together with a numerically insignificant number of other related offenses, and Home Office classification 8F consists of Section 20 offenses. Finally, the NCRS systematized procedure is believed to operate to catch a wide number of the most serious violent crimes; and as with the UCRH rules, there is no reason to believe that there are major discrepancies in recording practices across police forces (prosecutors play no role in the way the statistics are collected in either jurisdiction). Thus, we look at the 2008–2009 HOCR used in the NCRS data for classifying offenses in England and Wales involving GBH (broadly Section 18 and Section 20 offenses) and at the 2004 UCRH rules, still applicable from 2008 on, for classifying offenses in the United States involving serious bodily injury (AA).

Unfortunately, the HOCR were changed again from 2012–2013 onward. In HOCR 20012–2013, the division between Section 20 offenses and the less serious Section 47 offenses (assault occasioning actual bodily harm) is again dropped, so from now on it will not be possible to know the number of criminal assaults in which GBH was present. Whatever the Home Office's motivation, this is a most unhelpful change for research on serious violent crime in the United Kingdom; and, for the untutored reader of the data, crime involving GBH will appear to have been greatly reduced. Thus, we confine our attention to 2008–2009.[22]

Comparing the Detailed Rules for Recording Offenses in the United States and in England and Wales

We next set out the definitions of and guidance related to classifying the offenses, for the purpose of crime recording, using UCRH 2004 for AA and HOCR 2008–2009 for Section 18 and Section 20 GBH offenses. It is worth repeating that *in both crime-recording systems these definitions are independent of prosecutorial policy*. As the UCRH explains for the United States, "Prosecutorial policy in a jurisdiction must not dictate an agency's classification of an assault. Reporting agencies must examine and classify assaults according to the standard UCR definitions, regardless of whether they are termed misdemeanors or felonies by local definitions" (Federal Bureau of Investigation 2004, 27). Similarly, in HOCR 2010 the assault flow chart makes it clear that prosecutorial decisions play no part in the recording category (Home Office 2010).

Aggravated Assault

Aggravated assault is defined in UCRH 2004 as, "An unlawful attack by one person on another for the purpose of inflicting severe or aggravated bodily injury. This type of assault usually is accompanied by the use of a weapon or by means likely to produce death or great bodily harm" (Federal Bureau of Investigation 2004, 23).

The UCRH classifies AA into four groups, according to the type of weapon that is used:

- Aggravated Assault—Firearm (4a)
- Aggravated Assault—Knife or Cutting Instrument (4b)
- Aggravated Assault—Other Dangerous Weapons (4c)
- Aggravated Assault—Hands, Fists, Feet, Etc.—Aggravated Injury (4d)

In relation to the first three categories, "All assaults by one person upon another with the attempt to kill, maim, or inflict serious bodily injury with the use of any dangerous weapon are classified as Aggravated Assault. It is not necessary that injury result from an aggravated assault when a gun, knife, or other weapon that could cause serious personal injury is used" (Federal Bureau of Investigation 2004, 24). Given that all these assaults involve an "*attempt* to . . . inflict serious bodily injury," the classifying criteria appear to require intent. While no reference is explicitly made to intent in the eight examples given (pp. 23–24), it would be difficult to imagine intent not being present, though arguably the intent might have been to commit a less serious assault.

Agencies are further advised to take three factors into account in classifying the offense: (1) the type of weapon employed or the use of an object as a weapon, (2) the seriousness of the injury, and (3) the intent of the assailant to cause serious injury. "Often the weapon used or the extent of the injury sustained will be the deciding factor in distinguishing aggravated from simple assault. In only a limited number of instances should it be necessary to examine the intent of the assailant" (Federal Bureau of Investigation 2004, 27).

The language used in the UCRH is at times somewhat loose (as it is in the HOCR). The most straightforward reading of the last quotation is that if either a deadly weapon has been used (as specified under 4a–4c) or serious bodily injury resulted, that will normally be a sufficient condition for an AA classification. In 4d, "the seriousness of the injury . . . is the primary factor" (p. 25). It will not normally be necessary to examine intent because this will have been obvious from the circumstances. However, it follows that it is in principle possible that offenses in which a deadly weapon has been used without the intent to commit serious bodily injury are sometimes classified as AA.

Section 18 and Section 20 Offenses

Offenses in England and Wales involving GBH are classified into two categories, 5A and 8F, the two relevant categories in HOCR 2008–2009. Broadly, 5A corresponds to Section 18 offenses, GBH or wounding with intent to cause GBH, and 8F corresponds to Section 20 offenses, GBH or wounding without intent. In 5A and 8F, a small number of related offenses are included, to do with endangering life (Office for National Statistics 2013b, table A4, notes). Less serious assaults (occasioning actual bodily harm) correspond to Section 47 of the Offenses against the Person Act (1861) and are classified under 8G.

HOCR 2008–2009 (5A classification 2 of 3) gives the following recording instructions for Section 18 offenses:

> If there is intent to commit GBH, record under class 5A, otherwise record under 8F [Section 20 offenses] or 8G [Section 47 offenses of assault occasioning actual bodily harm]. The gravity of the injury resulting is not necessarily the determining factor.
>
> The following factors **may** indicate intent:
>
> - Use of a firearm
> - Use of a knife
> - Use of other made offensive weapons
> - Other object used as a weapon but not necessarily during instant arming
> - Glass-bottle smashed and used to assault

- Repeated kicks to the head
- Indication of pre-planning
- Words spoken by the assailant
- Ferocity and/or length of time of any assault

> . . . If any of these factors are present and the actions result in really serious bodily harm then record an offense under class 5A. If the elements of intent are present and the actions of the offender show a deliberate attempt to inflict serious bodily harm yet the resulting injury does not constitute serious bodily harm then record an offense under class 5A. (Home Office 2010)

The AA rules are couched somewhat differently from the Section 18 (5A) rules, but they have a very similar coverage. Both AA and Section 18 require intent to cause serious injuries, and the conditions for showing intent when serious injury is present seem similar: for Section 18 if any of the indicative factors are present (e.g., the use of a firearm), then serious injury constitutes a Section 18 offense, without further need to show intent. This is similar to AA.

In so far as there is a difference, it is this: in UCRH in the event of an assault without serious injury, the use of, for example, a firearm by itself constitutes an AA (Federal Bureau of Investigation 2004, 24); and, as we have seen, attempts are included. But these differences are unlikely to make a significant difference to the validity of our comparative figures, for the following reasons. Since AA requires intent, according to our reading of the UCRH, the presumption is that the use of a firearm is sufficient evidence of intent to commit serious bodily injury. In HOCR as in UCRH, in the *presence* of serious injury, the presumption is that the use of a firearm (or whatever other "element indicating intent") will generally be sufficient evidence of intent to commit serious injury. By contrast, however, if there is not serious injury, stronger evidence of intent appears to be called for in HOCR than UHCR: "If the elements of intent [e.g., use of a firearm] are present and the actions of the offender show a deliberate attempt to inflict serious bodily harm yet the resulting injury does not constitute serious bodily harm then record an offense under class 5A." In other words, there is an additional requirement that "the actions of the offender show a deliberate attempt to inflict serious bodily harm" in the case where the offense is classified as "attempt to inflict grievous bodily harm." In the practical context of decisions about recording crime, the use of a weapon such as a firearm is mandated as an evidential proxy for intent in both England and Wales and the United States. Thus, while nonharming threats involving weapons are explicitly covered by AA in the United States but not by class 5A in England and Wales, in practice such threats will generally be recorded under class 5A because they amount to attempts. There are exceptions to this practice, for example, in cases of instant arming (which Home Office rules specifically exclude from category 5A). We include attempted murder—separately recorded in England and Wales—in our comparative figures; and attempted GBH which results in minor injury is, as we have seen, comprehended by the recording instructions. This leaves just two technical differences: first, cases where an attempt to commit GBH results in no injury at all and where the proxy elements are not considered sufficient to establish intent to cause GBH; second, cases where an attempt specifically to wound, which causes no injury, may fall outside the recording instructions for Section 20 offenses. The second case is, however, rather unlikely to fit within the US criteria either, given the very broad (England and Wales) definition of wounding, which requires only a piercing of the skin (albeit all the layers of the skin). The first, too, seems unlikely to be very numerous as it would be difficult to imagine a case where the threatened use of a weapon (which is what the AA rules appear to cover) would not also be considered a proxy for intent under HOCR. However, we can account for a significant proportion of such offenses by including in our English figures the numbers of recorded offenses of possession of a firearm with intent (Home Office category 10A—an offense which does not require proof of intent to commit serious violence and which hence almost certainly deploys wider criteria for the English than the US data).[23] In fact, the addition of category 10A offenses changes our lower ratio only slightly, such that US rates of serious violence turn out to be at least 3.6, rather than 3.7, times higher than serious violence in England and Wales.

Thus, our view is that AA is close to Section 18 (5A) offenses when a serious injury is present; but it may be somewhat broader by not requiring additional proof of intent than the use of a weapon as described in Sections 4a–4c UCRH, where the injury is not sufficiently serious to itself be a proxy for intent. Thus, it may cover cases that in England and Wales would be classified as Section 20 (8F or 10A), where—in the absence of sufficiently serious injury—the relevant weapons are not sufficient for establishing intent in themselves. In those cases the UCHR uses more generous evidential presumptions to indicate intent (see Table 8.2). This means that Section 18 (5A) alone would be too narrow to directly compare to AA and, being unable to speculate just how many Section 20 (8F) events would be classed as AA were they recorded under UCHR, we use Section 20 offenses as an upper bound for our comparison. A quite conservative position, in terms of the point that we wish to establish, is therefore to say that Section 18 together with Section 20 offenses have at least as large a coverage as AA offenses. We now turn to this issue.

Table 8.2 Comparison of Detailed Rules for Recording Violent Offenses in the United States and England and Wales

		Factors to Consider When Classifying Offense			
		Serious Injury	Intent to Commit Serious Injury	Weapon and Serious Injury	Weapon
Offense categorization under US recording rules	Aggravated assault—UCRH	Class as AA if injury sufficiently serious and no further evidence of intent required.	Consider intent if injury/weapon not enough to define as AA. *AA is broader than HO category 5A, for which intent requirements are more stringent.*	Class as AA if injury sufficiently serious and/or deadly weapon used.	Class as AA if weapon evidence of intent. *If deadly weapon used, then AA may be broader than HO category 5A. Under UCRH deadly weapon is proxy for intent.*
Offense categorization under England and Wales HO rules	More serious wounding or other act endangering life—HO category 5A	Class as 5A if combined with intent to commit GBH.	Class as 5A if combined with serious injury *or* incident amounts to attempt to commit GBH with intent.	Class as 5A if weapon evidence of intent to commit GBH.	Class as 5A if weapon evidence of intent to commit GBH and incident therefore attempt to commit GBH with intent. *If there is no injury and weapon is not evidence of intent to commit GBH, AA may be broader than 5A and may spill over into HO 10A (possession of firearm with intent).*

(continued)

Table 8.2 continued

	Factors to Consider When Classifying Offense			
	Serious Injury	Intent to Commit Serious Injury	Weapon and Serious Injury	Weapon
GBH without intent—HO category 8F	Class as 8F if no intent to commit GBH. *Under UCRH rules this may be AA if injury is sufficiently serious and no further evidence of intent is required.*	Not required for 8F. If present, record as 5A.	Class as 8F if weapon is *not* evidence of intent to commit GBH, e.g., in instant arming. *Under UCRH this will be AA if weapon is sufficient evidence of intent, e.g., in cases of deadly weapons. Here AA may be broader than 5A and therefore spill over into 8F.*	Class as 8F if there is serious injury and weapon is not enough to make incident an attempt to commit GBH with intent. *Under UCRH this will be AA if weapon alone is sufficient evidence of intent. Here AA may be broader than 5A and therefore spill over into 8F.*

AA, aggravated assault; GBH, grievous bodily harm; HO, Home Office; UCRH, *Uniform Crime Reporting Handbook*.

The Definition of "Serious Injury"

The argument so far assumes that "grievous bodily harm" used in classifying Section 18 and Section 20 offenses is broadly comparable to "serious bodily injury" and related terms used in classifying AA offenses. We now examine the relation between the two definitions in the 2008–2009 HOCR and in the 2004 UCRH.

England and Wales

The relevant guidelines are contained in the HOCR 2008–2009. The definition (5A: "Wounding or Carrying out an Act Endangering Life Classification" 3 of 3) requires that, "to constitute grievous bodily harm, really serious bodily harm must be caused, 'grievous' means no more and no less than 'really serious,' and there is no distinction between the phrases 'serious bodily harm' and 'really serious bodily harm.' " The same section then gives six examples of "what would usually amount to serious harm":

- injury resulting in permanent disability or permanent loss of sensory function;
- injury which results in more than minor permanent, visible disfigurement; broken or displaced limbs or bones, included fractured skull;
- compound fractures, broken cheekbone, jaw, ribs, etc.;
- injuries which cause substantial loss of blood, usually necessitating a transfusion;
- injuries resulting in lengthy treatment or incapacity;
- psychiatric injury. As with assault occasioning actual bodily harm, appropriate expert evidence is essential to prove the injury. (Home Office 2010)

A series of examples is given about the boundary between wounds that should be classified as GBH and those that are more minor: "Great care should be taken when considering if the wound is minor. Class 8G (for more minor wounds than either S. 18 or S.20 offenses) should *only* [our italics] be used for wounds that require basic first aid or minimal hospital treatment" (Home Office 2010, 8G Classification, 3 of 3). In discussing Section 20 offenses (classified as class 8F), example 2 under 8F Counting Rules 1 of 1, a victim has a wound under her eye that "requires stitching at hospital." This is thus a sufficient condition for the wound to be "grievous bodily harm." In the assault flow diagram in the HOCR 2010 the two most serious injuries listed for the injury not to count as GBH are "a simple broken nose," "loss of or broken tooth," and "a broken finger or a broken toe with no intent to cause serious injury." These are given as examples of the injury only requiring "basic first aid or minimal hospital treatment."

The United States

The relevant counting rules are provided in the 2004 UCRH. This does not define serious bodily injury, but it gives examples: "[T]he personal injury is serious, for example, [if] there are broken bones, internal injuries, or stitches are required" (Federal Bureau of Investigation 2004, 25). In the two explicit examples given, "[a] man suffered an abrasion and a broken wrist" and "[a man] slapped [a woman] . . . and broke her jaw" (p. 25).

In conclusion, there does not seem to be a significant difference in the broad usage of "serious bodily injury" in AA and "grievous bodily harm" in Section 18 and Section 20 offenses. All of the examples of "serious bodily injuries" in the UCRH would be classified under 5A or 8F (in effect, Section 18 or 20) in the HOCR guidance, according to the assault flow chart.

Police Recording Practices

The next major issue is whether American and English police forces differ in the extent to which actual offenses are recorded under AA and under Section 18 and Section 20, respectively. In the absence of direct and detailed empirical research, we can get some critical purchase on whether our assumptions are robust by assessing the police recording data against the benchmark of the existing crime surveys. We do not, of course, know the number of offenses under these categories actually committed, but crime victim surveys provide a reasonable guide to the number of actual offenses. Using the NCVS in the United States, the rate per 100,000 population of AAs was 330 in 2008, 320 in 2009, and 280 in 2010 (Bureau of Justice Statistics 2009, 2010). This is relatively similar to the UCRH rates for the corresponding years, 277.5 in 2008, 264.7 in 2009, and 252.8 in 2010 (Federal Bureau of Investigation 2011, 2013).[24] The ratios of the UCRH rate to the NCVS rate are 84.1 percent in 2008, 82.7 percent in 2009, and 90.3 percent in 2010, or on average 83.2 percent over the three years. Hence, this suggests that the number of UCRH AAs is a reasonable ballpark estimate of the number of actual AAs, although underestimating the NCVS rate by around 15 percent.

In England and Wales, the CSEW does not have individual data on categories of Section 18 and Section 20 GBH assaults (5A and 8F, respectively, in the HOCR) but only a much larger category of violence against the person offenses. (This is presumably due to the sample size; if the CSEW did have such data, this chapter would be much shorter!) This is the category of "wounding" and notably includes, as well as Section 18 and Section 20 GBH offenses, the large actual bodily harm category (8G in HOCR), as interpreted by CSEW interviewers. For the reasons given earlier, we focus on 2008–2009 (see "The Use of NCRS Data 2008–2009"). The total number of "woundings" in the CSEW 2008–2009 survey is 498,000. If we add these categories up in the NCRS police recorded offenses, we get 414,077 (22,663 Section 18 and 5A in the HOCR; 17,159 Section 20 and 8F; and 374,255 Section 47 and 8G). In terms of rate per 100,000 population, CSEW woundings are 853 and NCRS, 760.4. The NCRS rate is 89.1 percent of the CSEW rate: so again these are in the same broad ballpark, with a shortfall of 11 percent.

The NCRS rate of Section 18 and Section 20 GBH offenses in 2008–2009 is 70.8, or 40.5 and 30.3, respectively. These are much smaller than the figure for the NCRS wounding rate of 760.4. These GBH offenses are for serious injuries, and it seems very probable that a high proportion would come to the attention of the police. There is clear evidence in the United States, from a study using NCVS microdata, that the probability of a victim reporting a crime to the police increases *inter alia* with the severity of injuries so that, for example, 88 percent of those hospitalised in the NCVS sample reported the crime to the police (Hart and Rennison 2003). We have not been able to find a similar study in England, perhaps because the sample size for very serious injuries is too small.[25] However, we do know, at least for 2008–2009, that of offenses that come to the notice of the police, the ratio of police recorded crimes of violence to a comparable subset of CSEW violent crimes reported to the police or which come to the notice of the police in other ways was 93 percent (Office for National Statistics 2013a, table UG10). Thus, we can have some confidence that the NCRS rates for Section 18 and Section 20 offenses are unlikely to be hugely short of the mark. There is no reason to believe that the shortfall is substantially different from the average 15 percent gap for 2008–2010 between the NCVS rate and the UCRH rate for aggravated assaults in the United States. Insofar as there are discrepancies in police recording of violent offenses and victimization levels, a comparison of victim surveys and police records in the United States and in England and Wales suggests that these discrepancies are roughly equivalent, further suggesting that AA and our constructed measure of serious interpersonal violence are indeed comparable.

Minor Adjustments

a. Both UCRH 2004 and HOCR 2008–2009 require one offense to be counted for each victim.
b. Hierarchical rules, which determine which offense is to be recorded where multiple offenses are committed against a single victim, are broadly similar.
c. AA includes "attempts to kill or murder" (Federal Bureau of Investigation 2004, 24). This is not included in 5A (or 8F) (Section 18 or 20) offenses, in HOCR 2008–2009 but in a separate category, HORC 2. There are no data available in the UCRH on the numbers of attempted murders alone. Hence, for comparability, we add this category, HOCR 2, to Section 18 offenses, Section 18 (5A). It is a small adjustment to Section 18 offenses as the rate in 2008–2009 increases by 1.3 from 51.2 to 52.4 per 100,000 of the population.
d. Threats and/or conspiracy to murder. This is a separate (large) category in the HOCR, with 9,448 offenses in 2008–2009; and it is not included in 5A or 8F. Nor is violence a part of such an offense. No such category is recorded in the UCRH; AAs require an assault; the only UCRH guidance ("threat to commit violence"—see Federal Bureau of Investigation 2004, 26) is that threats should be classified as simple assaults.[26] Hence these are excluded from our comparison.
e. As discussed, we include possession of a firearm with intent within the English figures, to (almost certainly over-) compensate for the definitional difference in terms of attempts.

Serious Interpersonal Violence in Other Liberal Market Countries

So far we have compared rates of serious interpersonal violence in the United States and England and Wales. Given that no ready comparators exist, we have done so by constructing broadly equivalent measures of violence in the two countries. The (simplified) conclusion of our analysis has been that rates of serious interpersonal violence are significantly higher in the United States than in England and Wales.

This section discusses existing studies that compare levels of recorded violence in the United States with two other liberal market systems: New Zealand and Canada. The studies, conducted by the New Zealand Ministry of Justice and the Canadian Centre for Justice Statistics, reveal that levels of interpersonal violence are higher in the United States than in either New Zealand or Canada.

New Zealand and the United States

The New Zealand Ministry of Justice report, *International Comparisons of Recorded Violent Crime Rates for 2000* (Segessenmann 2002), compares violent crime in New Zealand with violent crime in four other nations, including the United States and England and Wales. The report notes that country differences in legal definitions and definitions used for statistical recording make international comparisons particularly difficult (p. 1). To overcome this obstacle, the report constructs measures with which to compare rates of violent crime in New Zealand to rates of violent crimes elsewhere. For example, where the United States is concerned, the report uses the American definition of AA as its baseline and then selects the relevant New Zealand recorded crime data (coded under "police event type codes"). The constructed value includes attempted murder and all assaults that fall under the "grievous assault" category[27] (p. 13) such as assault with a weapon, wounding with intent, or injury with intent.[28]

Comparisons between US AAs and the New Zealand equivalent reveal that in 2000 the US rate was 323.6 per 100,000 compared to a New Zealand rate of 71.2 per 100,000 (p. 4). Rates of serious interpersonal violence were thus estimated to be approximately 4.5 times higher in the United States than in New Zealand.

The report's comparison between New Zealand and England and Wales uses a much broader category of "violence against the person."[29] For our purposes, it is nonetheless significant that rates of "violence against the person" were 1,131 per 100,000 in England, 1,140 in Wales, and 1,099.1 in New Zealand (p. 8). Assuming that the proportion of violent crimes in the two countries has remained unchanged between 2000 and 2008, this suggests that levels of recorded violence in England and Wales and in New Zealand are broadly comparable. This indirectly bolsters our findings that levels of serious violence are lower in England and Wales than in the United States.

Canada and the United States

The Canadian Centre for Justice Statistics has undertaken the *Feasibility Study on Crime Comparisons between Canada and the United States* to "determine if police-reported crime categories could be compared" between the two nations

(Gannon 2001a, 4). The report focuses on the eight US "index" crimes, including AA.[30] It concludes that comparisons can be made for seven out of the eight offenses, directly (for homicide) or with some modifications.

In order to compare the US category of AA with Canadian data, a new category was constructed aggregating three Canadian offenses: aggravated assault, assault with a weapon, and attempted murder (Gannon 2001a, 9). The Canadian Criminal Code defines an "aggravated assault" as one that "wounds, maims, disfigures or endangers the life of the complainant" (Section 268 (1)). As noted in the feasibility study, this definition "is remarkably similar" to the US definition of AA (Gannon 2001a, 8; compare Federal Bureau of Investigation 2004, 23). However, AA also includes assault with a weapon and attempted murder, which are recorded separately in Canada (Gannon 2001a, 8–9). When these two categories are added to aggravated assaults, they yield a comparable Canadian category that represents "the most serious form of assault, including actual and potential infliction of severe bodily harm" (Gannon 2001b, 5).

A comparison of US and Canadian serious interpersonal violence (Gannon 2001b) reveals that in 2000 the United States had an AA rate of 324 per 100,000 relative to Canada's rate of 143 per 100,000 equivalent assaults. The US rate was thus 2.3 times higher than the Canadian rate (Gannon 2001b, 5).

Comparisons between the United States and New Zealand and Canada therefore suggest that where constructed categories of (recorded) serious interpersonal violence are compared, the United States emerges as having far higher rates of violence than comparable countries such as New Zealand, Canada, and England and Wales. In 2000, US rates of violence were more than four times higher than rates in New Zealand and more than twice the Canadian rates. For the reasons explained earlier (see "The Use of NCRS Data 2008–2009"), comparisons between England and Wales and the United States are not readily available for the year 2000. However, on the basis of our calculations, US AA rates in 2008 were between 3.6 and 6.5 times higher than comparable rates in England and Wales—a finding which is substantially in line with the other studies analyzed in this section and with the broad differentials suggested by homicide rates.

Conclusion

In conclusion, on the basis of the best evidence available, there is strong reason to think that the scale of serious violent crime in the United States is significantly larger than that, not only in England and Wales but also other liberal market countries such as Canada and New Zealand. This confirms the basic comparative picture given by the homicide rates, which have featured as the standard comparator in much of the existing literature. The fact that only about 25 percent of AA offenses in the United States involve a firearm (Federal Bureau of Investigation 2011) gives further reason to think that the comparatively high levels of fatal and nonfatal violence in the United States are driven by factors more complex than the prevalence of firearms.[31]

We should be clear that we are not claiming to have found an accurate way of capturing comparative levels of interpersonal violence in the two countries. The complexities of offense definition and the vagaries of policy, resources, and the dynamics of the relevant bureaucracies in shaping recording practice over time in the two countries make any such aspiration unrealistic. What we do suggest is that our claims, made on the basis of the comparative measure that we have developed with its upper and lower bounds, need to be taken seriously. They are an important corrective to the misperceptions of comparative levels of serious violence which some have drawn from the ICVS.

This in turn, we claim, is of real significance to the broader debate about the role of violence and perceptions of violence in shaping the development of penal policy. Recent comparative commentary has focused on the fact that trends in homicide have been relatively similar between the United States and other countries (see Chapter 3, Figure 3.3). But given the evidence of the political salience of violent crime (Miller 2016; see Miller, this volume), it is crucially important to focus specifically on absolute levels of violent crime in the United States, as well as to have some sense of its scale compared with other countries, for the social and political significance of violence seems highly likely to be shaped by public perceptions of, for example, lifetime risks of violent victimization. These risks are so much higher in the United States than in comparator countries that one might reasonably suggest that violence represents a qualitatively as well as a quantitatively different social phenomenon (Miller 2015; Roth, this volume).[32] Without some reliable sense of the levels of serious violence in the United States and other liberal market countries, it is hard to see how meaningful comparative analysis can be achieved. Without that comparative analysis, our grasp of whether the United States is truly "exceptional"—and with it our understanding of crime and punishment in America—will remain radically incomplete.

NOTES

1. The latest iteration of the ICVS suggests that violence rates in the United States are broadly comparable with those in England and Wales (Van Kesteren, Mayhew, and Nieuwbeerta 2000; Van Dijk, van Kesteren, and Smit 2007). But many

scholars have questioned the validity of its findings on this point, identifying a number of methodological features of the survey that suggest that its results may be misleading (Reiner 2007, 104–05; Young 2004). Even leaving aside the relatively small samples (around 2,000 surveys per country), the use of a telephone survey may elicit responses skewed by a varying consciousness of violence in different countries, with those in low-violence countries exhibiting lower tolerance of violence and hence more likely to recall or identify an incident as involving violence than those in countries where violence is more common (Reiner 2007, 104–07). As Jackson et al. (2014, 174) describe the problem,

> One of the key methodological challenges in international surveys is the question of cross-national equivalence of measurement. Essentially the issue is, does a survey question measure the same concept and in the same way in all countries? If it does not, respondents from different countries can give different expected responses even if they have the same level of the concept of interest. Critically, lack of equivalence can compromise any substantive cross-national comparisons. It is quite plausible in surveys which cover many countries, perhaps because of cultural differences in how a question is understood, or variations in questionnaire translation.

2. For an evaluation of recording of violent crime, see the one-off analysis conducted by Her Majesty's Inspectorate of Constabulary (2009).
3. It is known that police in both countries depart from prescribed recording practices under a variety of conditions: we explain in the section "Serious Interpersonal Violence in Other Liberal Market Countries" why it is unlikely that these departures have a significant impact on the recording of serious violent crime. In the 2009 evaluation by Her Majesty's Inspectorate of Constabulary of 43 police forces in England and Wales, 30 were rated as having "excellent" and 6 as having "good" compliance in recording offenses of "most serious violence" (p. 25). More recording error was found in relation to recording of "assault with less serious injury," with 12 forces rated "excellent," 16 "good," 14 "fair," and 1 "poor" (p. 25). The primary error in relation to less serious assaults was recording as less serious those offenses that should have been included in the most serious violence category: 7.6 percent (290) of the 3,920 offenses audited were recorded as less serious when, on evaluation, they should have been recorded as most serious (p. 15). These figures should, however, be combined with the figures returned from auditing most serious violence, in which 6.9 percent (252) of the 3,675-offense sample was recorded as involving "grievous bodily harm" when "actual bodily harm" would have been more accurate (p. 12).
4. The main difficulties have centered on producing measures which capture, or act as reasonable proxies for, the qualitative severity of imprisonment and the evaluation of noncustodial sentences which are *prima facie* less punitive than prison sentences but nonetheless imply significant forms of surveillance (Cavadino and Dignan 2006; Tonry 2007; Wacquant 2009). Outside the domain of incarceration,

new efforts to generate comparative data concerning probation and parole supervision rates have begun to address problems of data compatibility (see Rhine and Taxman, this volume and van Zyl Smit and Corda, this volume). Comparative statistical data are almost totally lacking, however, on the subject of financial punishments and collateral consequences of conviction (Reitz 2015; see Demleitner, this volume).

5. Our approach works along the lines mapped out by one of the ICVS authors, John van Kesteren who, in a recent article, urges "future studies . . . to [supplement data from victimization surveys] with more detailed police-recording information on serious crimes of violence" (2014, 70).
6. A list of publications "completely or mainly based on ICVS data" can be found on the ICVS site (http://wp.unil.ch/icvs/key-publications/publications-completely-or-mainly-based-on-icvs-data/). The site also lists publications "in which ICVS data is used" (http://wp.unil.ch/icvs/key-publications/publications-in-which-icvs-data-is-used/), both accessed May 4, 2017.
7. Available at https://www.unodc.org/unodc/en/data-and-analysis/statistics/data.html (accessed June 10, 2014).
8. United Nations data are collected by means of surveys compiled by national criminal justice agencies. Until 2015, the relevant survey portion, directed to the police, defined assault as "physical attack against the body of another person, resulting in serious bodily injury, excluding indecent/sexual assault, threats and slapping." Assaults leading to death are also excluded. This classification is still in use by the Eurostat (Eurostat, 2016, available at ec.europa.eu/eurostat/cache/metadata/en/crim_esms.htm [accessed May 3, 2017]; United Nations Survey of Crime Trends and Operations of Criminal Justice Systems, available at https://www.unodc.org/unodc/en/data-and-analysis/statistics/crime/cts-data-collection.html [accessed June 10, 2014]). It has not been possible to identify what data were provided for England and Wales that match this definition.
9. The *European Sourcebook* (Aebi et al. 2010) differentiated in its fourth edition among assaults/bodily injuries ("inflicting bodily injury on another person with intent," p. 30) by adding categories of minor and aggravated bodily injury (pp. 42–44) but, unfortunately, was not able to provide these differentiated figures for England and Wales. From the definition of "aggravated assault" provided by the sourcebook it appears that the category would, in fact, encompass a subset of the offenses classed under category 5/Offenses against the Person Act S. 18: on our reading of the sourcebook, and the England and Wales data, it appears that the level of harm for sourcebook "aggravated assault" is more serious than that encompassed in the broader "grievous bodily harm" category (Aebi et al. 2010, 353–54). This also suggests that the sourcebook's "aggravated assault" is not in fact equivalent to *Uniform Crime Reporting Handbook*'s "aggravated assault."
10. Our findings are consistent with those of Zimring and Hawkins (1997) but substantially broaden the upshot of their analysis by moving beyond homicide and

lethal violence; moreover, our findings do not depend on survey evidence, with its attendant difficulties (see note 1).

11. Lappi-Seppälä (Chapter 5) in fact offers a range of data on the United States, some of which we would read as supporting a "connect" rather than a "disconnect" hypothesis.
12. A further obvious focus of interest in relation to this question would be comparisons of the levels of serious violence between US states. However, the existence of distinctive institutional arrangements in the US political, economic, and criminal justice systems quite generally means that it is also important to try to establish a clearer comparative picture at the national level.
13. See National Rifle Association (2011) and Mauser (2003) For recent analyses of the links between gun ownership and violence, also based on the ICVS but yielding different, more complex conclusions, see Van Kesteren (2014; for an overview of macrolevel studies on the gun–crime link, see p. 55).
14. The Model Penal Code (MPC) has not been adopted uniformly across the United States (Robinson and Dubber, 2007, 319). However, "since its introduction the MPC has served as the basis for wholesale replacement of existing criminal codes in almost three quarters of the states" (Robinson, 2010, 565) and has been adopted with only minor revisions in several more (Robinson, 2010, 565; see also Robinson and Dubber, 2007, 326–27). As such, the MPC offers the best available basis for our discussion of legal definitions of interpersonal violence. More significantly for our purposes, the MPC definition of AA is the basis for police recording guidelines (see "Serious Interpersonal Violence in Other Liberal Market Countries").
15. Under Section 1(1) of the Criminal Attempts Act 1981, an attempted GBH with intent requires the offender to do an act that is more than merely preparatory to the commission of a Section 18 offense, with the intent to commit the completed offense.
16. See Baumer and Lauritsen's cautionary note on US reporting rates over time (2010, 173).
17. The Office for National Statistics' view is that reliability of police recording fell again after 2007–2008, though the effect was probably small in 2008–2009 when the police data for the first time distinguish Section 18 and Section 20 offenses from less serious ones. Since then, reliability has fallen again; in January 2014 the UK Statistics Authority withdrew gold standard status from police recorded crime data; see Travis (2014).
18. See Robinson and Dubber (2007, 320) and Robinson (2010).
19. There is an alternative to the police recording system of estimating crimes in the two countries based on crime victim surveys: in the United States the NCVS and in England and Wales the CSEW. The NCVS is useful as it has the category of AA offenses. Unfortunately, the CSEW has no category of serious violent crime

but only a very much broader category of "wounding," leading us back to police recorded offenses as a better measure with which to compare violent interpersonal crimes across the two nations.

20. To the extent that part of the recording error identified by Her Majesty's Inspectorate of Constabulary (2009, 12) concerned offenses of GBH with intent being recorded as GBH without intent, aggregating Section 18 and Section 20 offenses also helps us iron out this specific recording inaccuracy.
21. On the importance of understanding counting rules and the breadth of the England and Wales definition of violent crime, see Lewis (2012, 11).
22. Though our chapter is focused on data for 2008–2009, we can nonetheless look at data from 2009–2010 and 2010–2011 for comparative purposes. Our calculations reveal that the ratio of US to England and Wales violent crime was between 6.3 and 3.5 in 2009–2010, while the ratio for 2010–2011 was between 7.0 and 3.9. These calculations, and their overall similarity to the 2008/9 data, seem to suggest that 2008–2009 was not an exceptional year.
23. From the HOCR we can see that category 10A in fact includes a multiplicity of offenses not limited to serious interpersonal violence. Examples include possession of a firearm or imitation firearm with intent to cause fear of violence (Firearms Act 1968, Section 16A) or being in possession of a firearm or an imitation firearm when committing or being arrested for the offenses specified under Schedule 2 of the Firearms Act 1968, including, for example, numerous sexual offenses (Section 17(2)). Category 10A also includes offenses under Section 18(1) of the Firearms Act 1968, whereby it is an offense to have a firearm or an imitation firearm with intent to commit an indictable offense. It appears that category 10A is thus likely to cover offenders who attempt Section 18 where no injury results, where the presence of the weapon is not judged to be sufficient evidence of intent for the incident to be recorded under 5A but where it is found that the offender intended to commit another indictable assault.
24. The population in the NCVS case is over the age of 12 and living in households, and the correct deflator since the survey is of those 12+ living in households. The population in the UCRH is total population, again the correct comparator.
25. The recent studies of accident and emergency admissions (Shepherd 1990; Sivarajasingam et al. 2012), which give valuable insights into trends in serious violence, only cover a sample of accident and emergency units.
26. Recall that threats with a weapon are recorded as aggravated assaults.
27. Police event type code 1400: see Segessenmann (2002, 14). Note also analogies with the *European Sourcebook*'s approach (Aebi et al. 2010).
28. For a full definition, see Segessenmann (2002, 1, 13–17). See also Statistics New Zealand (2006, 13).
29. Where the baseline for England and Wales includes not just HOCR categories 5 and 8 but also categories such as 105A (common assault). This reveals

the breadth of the England and Wales category of (undifferentiated) "violence against the person" (Segessenmann 2002, 15; Lewis 2012, 11).

30. Index crimes are criminal homicide, forcible rape, robbery, aggravated assault, burglary, larceny–theft, motor vehicle theft, arson.

31. The question of what contribution levels of gun ownership make to the amount and seriousness of violent crime is an independent and important one that cannot fully be addressed in this chapter, though we hope to work on it in the future. For a thoughtful analysis of the comparative victimization data in this area, see Van Kesteren's recent contribution to the debate (2014). Van Kesteren in effect draws the conclusion that significant forms of violent crime are higher in the United States than in England and Wales, or indeed New Zealand, Australia, and Canada, *even on ICVS measures.* Figure 2 of the article—mapping five-year prevalence rates for contact crimes involving firearms—schematically illustrates this conclusion (p. 61).

32. As Miller (2016) notes in the case of homicide, the lifetime risk in England and Wales at the peak of homicide rates in 2003 was 1 in 641—a significant increase on the lifetime risk in 1960 of 1 in roughly 2,300. But these risk figures pale in comparison with the US figures, which show a peak lifetime risk in 1980, on Miller's calculation of 1 in 132.

CASES CITED

R. v. Moloney (1985) 1 All ER 1025; (1985) Crim.L.R. 378; (1985) AC 905.
R. v. Savage and Parmenter (1992) 1 AC 699 HL.
R. v. Woollin (1998) 3 WLR 382.

REFERENCES

Aebi, M. F., Bruno Aubusson de Cavarlay, Gordon Barclay, Beata Gruszczyńska, Stefan Harrendorf, Markku Heiskanen, Vasilika Hysi, Véronique Jaquier, Jörg-Martin Jehle, Martin Killias, Olena Shostko, Paul Smit, and Rannveig Þórisdóttir. *Raw Data for the 4th Edition (2010) of the European Sourcebook of Crime and Criminal Justice Statistics 2003–2007*. The Hague, the Netherlands: Bibliotheek WODC, 2009.

Aebi, M. F., Bruno Aubusson de Cavarlay, Gordon Barclay, Beata Gruszczyńska, Stefan Harrendorf, Markku Heiskanen, Vasilika Hysi, Véronique Jaquier, Jörg-Martin Jehle, Martin Killias, Olena Shostko, Paul Smit, and Rannveig Þórisdóttir. *European Sourcebook of Crime and Criminal Justice Statistics—2010*. 4th ed. The Hague, the Netherlands: Bibliotheek WODC, 2010.

American Law Institute. *Model Penal Code and Commentaries*. Philadelphia: American Law Institute, 1980.

Baumer, Eric P., and Janet L. Lauritsen. "Reporting Crime to the Police, 1973–2005: A Multivariate Analysis of Long-Term Trends in the National Crime Survey

(NCS) and National Crime Victimization Survey (NCVS)." *Criminology* 48, no. 1 (2010): 131–85.

Bureau of Justice Statistics. *Criminal Victimization, 2008*. Washington, DC: US Department of Justice, 2009.

Bureau of Justice Statistics. *Criminal Victimization, 2009*. Washington, DC: US Department of Justice, 2010.

Cavadino, Michael, and James Dignan. *Penal Systems: A Comparative Approach*. London: SAGE Publications, 2006.

Downes, David. *Contrasts in Tolerance: Post-War Penal Policy in the Netherlands and England and Wales*. Oxford: Clarendon, 1988.

Enns, Peter K. "The Public's Increasing Punitiveness and Its Influence on Mass Incarceration in the United States." *American Journal of Political Science* 58, no. 4 (2014): 857–872.

Esping-Andersen, Gøsta. *The Three Worlds of Welfare Capitalism*. Cambridge: Polity Press, 1990.

Eurostat. *Crime and Criminal Justice Statistics–Reference Metadata at Country Level 2016 Version*. 2016. Accessed May 3, 2017. ec.europa.eu/eurostat/cache/metadata/en/crim_esms.htm ().

Federal Bureau of Investigation. *Uniform Crime Reporting Handbook*. Washington, DC: US Department of Justice, 2004.

Federal Bureau of Investigation. Crime in the United States 2011. Aggravated Assault, Types of Weapons Used. 2011. Accessed June 21, 2014. http://www.fbi.gov/about-us/cjis/ucr/crime-in-the-u.s/2011/crime-in-the-u.s.-2011/tables/aggravated-assault-table.

Federal Bureau of Investigation. Crime in the United States. 2013. http://www.fbi.gov/about-us/cjis/ucr/crime-in-the-u.s/2012/crime-in-the-u.s.-2012/tables/1tabledatadecoverviewpdf/table_1_crime_in_the_united_states_by_volume_and_rate_per_100000_inhabitants_1993-2012.xls.

Forman, James, Jr. "Racial Critiques of Mass Incarceration: Beyond the New Jim Crow." *New York University Law Review* 87 (2012): 21–69.

Gannon, Maire. *Feasibility Study on Crime Comparisons between Canada and the United States*. Ottawa: Canadian Centre for Justice Statistics, Statistics Canada. 2001a. http://www5.statcan.gc.ca/olc-cel/olc.action?objId=85F0035X&objType=2&lang=en&limit=0.

Gannon, Maire. *Crime Comparisons between Canada and the United States*. Ottawa: Canadian Centre for Justice Statistics, Statistics Canada, 2001b.

Hall, Peter A., and David Soskice, eds. *Varieties of Capitalism: The Institutional Foundations of Comparative Advantage*. Oxford: Oxford University Press, 2001.

Hart, Timothy C., and Callie Marie Rennison. *Reporting Crime to the Police*. Bureau of Justice Statistics NCJ 195710. 2003. Accessed May 5, 2017. https://www.bjs.gov/index.cfm?ty=pbdetail&iid=1142.

Her Majesty's Inspectorate of Constabulary. *Crime Counts. A Review of Data Quality for Offenses of the Most Serious Violence*. London: Her Majesty's Inspectorate of Constabulary, 2009.

Home Office. *Home Office Counting Rules for Recorded Crime—Violence against the Person*. London: Home Office, 2010. http://webarchive.nationalarchives.gov.uk/20110220160459/http://rds.homeoffice.gov.uk/rds/countrules.html

Hough, Mike, Catriona Mirrlees-Black, and Michael Dale. *Trends in Violent Crime since 1999/2000*. London: Institute for Criminal Policy Research, School of Law, King's College London, 2005.

Jackson, Jonathan, Jouni Kuha, Mike Hough, Ben Bradford, Katrin Hohl, and Monica Germber, Stefano Maffei, and Zsolt Boda. *Trust and Legitimacy across Europe: A FIDUCIA Report on Comparative Public Attitudes Towards Legal Authority*. Brussels, Belgium: EPLO, 2014.

Kleiman, Mark A. R. "Toward Fewer Prisoners & Less Crime." *Daedalus* 139 (2010): 115–25.

Lacey, Nicola. *The Prisoners' Dilemma: Political Economy and Punishment in Contemporary Democracies*. Cambridge: Cambridge University Press, 2008.

Lacey, Nicola, and David Soskice. "Crime, Punishment and Segregation in the United States: The Paradox of Local Democracy" *Punishment & Society* 17, no. 4 (2015): 454–81. doi: 10.1177/1462474515604042

Lewis, Chris. "Crime and Justice Statistics Collected by International Agencies." *European Journal of Criminal Policy Research* 18, no. 1 (2012): 5–12.

Lijphart, Arend. *Democracies: Patterns of Majoritarian and Consensus Governments in Twenty-One Countries*. New Haven, CT: Yale University Press, 1984.

Mauser, Gary A. *The Failed Experiment: Gun Control and Public Safety in Canada, Australia, England and Wales*. Public Policy Sources 71. Vancouver, Canada: Fraser Institute, 2003. Accessed June 21, 2014. https://www.fraserinstitute.org/sites/default/files/FailedExperimentGunControl.pdf.

Miller, Lisa L. "Power to the People: Violent Victimization, Inequality and Democratic Politics." *Theoretical Criminology* 17, no. 3 (2013): 1–13.

Miller, Lisa L. "What's Violence Got to Do with It? Rethinking Punishment, Inequality and the Modern State." *Punishment and Society* 17 (2015): 184–210.

Miller, Lisa L. *The Myth of Mob Rule: Violent Crime and Democratic Politics*. New York and Oxford: Oxford University Press, 2016.

National Rifle Association. UK Mayhem Leaves Disarmed Citizen at the Mercy of Criminals. August 12, 2011. Accessed June 21, 2014. http://www.nraila.org/legislation/federal-legislation/2011/8/uk-mayhem-leaves-disarmed-citizens-at-t.aspx.

Nicholas, Sian, Chris Kershaw, and Alison Walker, eds. *Crime in England and Wales 2006/07*. Home Office Statistical Bulletin 07. London: Home Office, 2007.

Office for National Statistics. Crime in England and Wales—Quarterly First Release. March 2012. http://webarchive.nationalarchives.gov.uk/20160106235326/http://www.ons.gov.uk/ons/publications/re-reference-tables.html?edition=tcm%3A77-265883.

Office for National Statistics. *User Guide to Crime Statistics for England and Wales*. London: Office for National Statistics, 2013a.

Office for National Statistics. *Appendix Tables—Focus on: Violent Crime and Sexual Offenses, 2011/12*. 2013b. Accessed May 5, 2017. http://webarchive.nationalarchives.gov.uk/20160106234922/http://www.ons.gov.uk/ons/publications/re-reference-tables.html?edition=tcm%3A77-290621.

Peterson, Ruth D., and Lauren J. Krivo. *Divergent Social Worlds: Neighborhood Crime and the Racial–Spatial Divide*. New York: Russell Sage Foundation, 2012.

Povey, David, and Julian Prime. *Recorded Crime Statistics England and Wales, April 1998 to March 1999*. London: Home Office Research and Statistics Directorate, 1999.

Pratt, John, and Anna Eriksson. *Contrasts in Punishment. An Explanation of Anglophone Excess and Nordic Exceptionalism*. London: Routledge, 2013.

Reiner, Robert. *Law and Order: An Honest Citizen's Guide to Crime and Control*. Cambridge: Polity Press, 2007.

Reitz, Kevin R. "The Economic Rehabilitation of Offenders: Recommendations of the Model Penal Code (Second)." *Minnesota Law Review* 99 (2015): 1735–77.

Robinson, Paul H. "United States." In *The Handbook of Comparative Criminal Law*, edited by Kevin Jon Heller and Markus D. Dubber, 563–92. Palo Alto, CA: Stanford University Press, 2010.

Robinson, Paul H., and Markus D. Dubber. "The American Model Penal Code: A Brief Overview." *New Criminal Law Review* 10, no. 3 (2007): 319–41.

Roth, Randolph. *American Homicide*. Cambridge, MA: Belknap Press of the Harvard University Press, 2009.

Segessenmann, Tanya. *International Comparisons of Recorded Violent Crime Rates 2000*. Wellington: New Zealand Ministry of Justice—Tāhū o te Ture, 2002.

Shepherd, Jonathan. "Violent Crime in Bristol: An Accident and Emergency Department Perspective." *British Journal of Criminology* 30 (1990): 289–305.

Simmons, Jon, Clarissa Legg, and Rachel Hosking. *National Crime Recording Standards (NCRS): An Analysis of the Impact on Recorded Crime*. London: Home Office Research and Statistics Directorate, 2003.

Sivarajasingam, Vaseekaran, John Wells, Simon Christopher Moore, Nicholas Page, Peter Huw Morgan, Kent Matthews, and Jonathan Shepherd. *Violence in England and Wales in 2012: An Accident and Emergency Perspective*. Cardiff, UK: Violence and Society Research Group, Cardiff University, 2012.

Statistics New Zealand. *Crime in New Zealand 1996–2005*. Wellington: Statistics New Zealand—Tatauranga Aotearoa, 2006.

Tonry, Michael. *Thinking about Crime: Sense and Sensibility in American Penal Culture*. Oxford: Oxford University Press, 2004.

Tonry, Michael. "Determinants of Penal Policy." In *Crime and Justice: Crime, Punishment, and Politics in a Comparative Perspective*. Vol. 36. Edited by Michael Tonry, 1–48. Chicago: University of Chicago Press, 2007.

Travis, Alan. "Police Crime Figures Lose Official Status over Claims of Fiddling." *Guardian*, January 15, 2014. Accessed February 4, 2014. http://www.theguardian.com/uk-news/2014/jan/15/police-crime-figures-status-claims-fiddling.

Van Dijk, Jan, John van Kesteren, and Paul Smit. *Criminal Victimisation in International Perspective: Key Findings from the 2004–2005 ICVS and EU ICS*. The Hague, the Netherlands: Ministry of Justice, 2007.

Van Kesteren, John N. "Revisiting the Gun Ownership and Violence Link." *British Journal of Criminology* 54, no. 1 (2014): 53–72.

Van Kesteren, John, Pat Mayhew, and Paul Nieuwbeerta. *Criminal Victimisation in Seventeen Industrialised Countries: Key Findings from the 2000 International Crime Victims Survey*. The Hague, the Netherlands: Ministry of Justice, 2000.

Wacquant, Loïc. 2009. *Punishing the Poor: The Neoliberal Government of Social Insecurity*. Durham, NC: Duke University Press, 2009.

Wacquant, Loïc. "Class, Race and Hyper-Incarceration in Revanchist America." *Daedalus* 10 (2010): 74–90.

Walker, Alison, Chris Kershaw, and Sian Nicholas. *Crime in England and Wales 2005/6*. London: Home Office Research and Statistics Directorate, 2006.

Western, Bruce. *Punishment and Inequality in America*. New York: Russell Sage Foundation, 2007.

Young, Jock. "Voodoo Criminology and the Numbers Game." In *Cultural Criminology Unleashed*, edited by Jeff Ferrell, Keith Hayward, Wayne Morrison, and Mike Presdee, 13–28. London: Glasshouse, 2004.

Zimring, Franklin E., and Gordon Hawkins. *Crime Is Not the Problem: Lethal Violence in America*. New York: Oxford University Press, 1997.

PART III

American Exceptionalism in Probation, Parole, and Collateral Consequences of Conviction

9

American Exceptionalism in Community Supervision

A COMPARATIVE ANALYSIS OF PROBATION IN THE UNITED STATES, SCOTLAND, AND SWEDEN

Edward E. Rhine and Faye S. Taxman

Introduction

Mass incarceration is viewed by many as the problematic hallmark of American exceptionalism in the justice system (Drucker 2011; Clear and Frost 2014; National Research Council 2014; Gottschalk 2015). Yet this falls far short of providing a complete accounting of penal severity within the United States, especially in light of the nearly 5 million adults on community supervision, more than twice the size of the nation's incarcerated population (Glaze and Kaeble 2014). It is estimated that 1 in 51 adults were under probation or parole (postrelease) supervision alone in 2013 (Glaze and Kaeble 2014). Several scholars have begun to focus on concepts of "mass probation" and "mass supervision" to draw attention to how penal severity is achieved through a myriad of controls and restrictions placed on offenders outside of prison walls (Taxman 2012; Klingele 2013; McNeill 2013; Phelps 2013; van Zyl Smit and Corda, this volume).

This chapter explores whether the concept of American exceptionalism applies to the discourse and conduct of community supervision in its main variant—probation—when comparing the United States with Europe. Community supervision in the United States does not serve merely as a stand-alone punishment. It functions frequently as a much-less-acknowledged "front door" to incarceration due to failures on its conduct. It is often used after incarceration terms (either short- or long-term periods of confinement) or as an "elastic frame" in which additional punishments—such as economic sanctions, liberty restrictions, and coerced treatment—can be levied (Klingele 2013).

The chapter's approach is to compare US and European probation through the use of five indicia, or "markers," to gauge the penal scope and shape of probation. The markers provide criteria to assess the liberty restrictions imposed on offenders. Probation generally includes numerous conditions affecting the psychological, spatial, and financial life of individuals. These constraints on liberty are all too often unrecognized, yet they define the experience and practice of supervision (Taxman 2012; Corbett 2015).

The five markers we identify are (1) the mission and goals of probation, (2) the length of supervision terms, (3) the intensity and restrictiveness of conditions of supervision, (4) the extent to which formal treatment programming is coercive rather than voluntary, and (5) the consequences of breaches or violations of probation. In the next part, these five markers will be used to compare variations and commonalities in probation practices in the United States, Scotland, and Sweden. In later sections, we will discuss the broader context of US–European comparisons in the uses of probation and propose an agenda for future comparative research.

Mass Probation and the Supervision Net in the United States and Europe

As Michelle Phelps (2013) notes, the period of growing mass incarceration in the United States was accompanied by an equivalent expansion of probation supervision. Probation witnessed a steady and, at times, dramatic increase from 1980 through 2008 (Maruschak and Parks 2012, 2).[1] From 1980 through year end 2013, probation started with 1.1 million and ended with just over 3.9 million adults under supervision (from 2003 to 2010 exceeding 4 million). One in every 62 adults was on probation in 2013, when the rate stood at 1,605 per 100,000 adults (Herberman and Bonczar 2014). In many states the breadth of probation increased as its jurisdiction changed to include prison releases, pretrial supervision, and specialized programming (Taxman, Perdoni, and Harrison 2007; Taxman 2012).

The year end 2013 probation population in the United States was higher than the remaining three components of the correctional population—prisons, jails, and parole—combined. The probation population equaled 3,910,600, while prisons, jails, and parole accounted for 1,574,700, 731,200, and 853,200, respectively (Glaze and Kaeble 2014). The majority of probationers were male (75 percent), were Caucasian (55 percent), had a felony offense (53 percent), and were placed on probation for property crimes (27 percent), followed by drug offenses (25 percent) and violent offenses (18 percent).[2] Like the prison system in the United States, probation has seen modest decreases in clientele over the past several years, though probation alone still accounts for roughly 57 percent of the adult correctional population (Glaze and Kaeble 2014).

The scale of US probation supervision appears to be orders of magnitude greater than in Europe. European data drawn from the Council of Europe SPACE II report offer information on noncustodial sanctions for year end 2013, including probation (Aebi and Chopin 2014). While the figures are incomplete, with data missing from several European states, they allow for some broad comparisons. The reporting nations represent 47 out of 52 probation services housed with the 47 Council of Europe member states. In 2013, a total of 2,145,289 individuals were under the supervision or care of probation agencies across Europe. The probation population rate at year end 2013 was 219.3 per 100,000 inhabitants, while the rates for 2012, 2011, and 2010 were, respectively, 214.3, 208.6, and 205.7 (with some variation in the number of countries reporting). The US probation rate (federal and state) in 2013 was 1,605 per 100,000 adults or, *when adjusted to account for the denominator used in SPACE II*, 1,219 per 100,000 general population, nearly six times the European rate.

The top five US states reveal the following rates in 2013 (again adjusted per 100,000 of the nation's population): Georgia 5,198, Ohio 2,138, Rhode Island 2,088, Idaho 2,009, and Indiana 1,886. These figures represent a stark contrast to the highest rates reported for European countries: Turkey 1,276, Latvia 859, Poland 540, Estonia 485, and Hungary 385. The five lowest US states across the spectrum include, in descending order, Maine 486, West Virginia 444, Nevada 437, Utah 429, and New Hampshire 296. Even New Hampshire at the lowest end exceeds the rates of probation in Europe with the exception of the nation states shown and Belgium 354. The difference becomes even more pronounced when the nations with the lowest rates across Europe are listed: Croatia 68, Italy 55, Finland 46, Norway 38, and Serbia 10.

Differences in the Bureau of Justice Statistics and SPACE II methodologies could affect the accuracy of these direct comparisons. Both data-collection systems rely upon their source data to define what is covered in each topic, which leaves open the potential for misspecification. In the United States, there could be variation in probation counts depending on whether probation includes alternatives to incarceration, specialty courts, pretrial supervision, postrelease supervision, intensive treatment programming, add-on incarceration time, and other variations of community sanctions. The same is true in Europe since probation is rather heterogeneous across the continent, and it is unclear what components are included in the SPACE II data-collection mode. Within both databases probation remains an elastic concept. Differences in measuring the use of probation across countries and continents require that those using such figures decide whether to be more inclusive or exclusive in what is included in the counts of probation. We have drawn on SPACE II's most expansive definition of probation, which encompasses the full range of supervision in the community, before and after sentence, and including specialized programming. This is in contrast to van Zyl Smit and Corda, who have adopted a more conservative calculation of what counts as probation in the SPACE II data, thereby arriving at a higher ratio between US and European rates of probation. Despite these caveats, collectively we agree there is a great difference in magnitude (whether the ratio is 10:1 or 6:1), which confirms that the probation supervision umbrella is far wider in the United States than in western Europe.[3]

Institutional Structure of Probation in the United States, Scotland, and Sweden

We now turn to a comparative evaluation of probation systems in the United States, Scotland, and Sweden using the five markers of punitive severity laid out earlier. First, however, we discuss the institutional structure and scope of probation in each country.

United States

American probation takes a multitude of different shapes across state, federal, and local jurisdictions. Probation is not a stand-alone sanction in most venues but is ordered as a concomitant to a "suspended" prison sentence. Typically, the prison term is considered the true sentence, but the "execution" of the prison sentence is suspended or "stayed" pending successful completion of the probation term. In a minority of states, probation may be imposed as a sentence "in its own right" without reference to a suspended or stayed prison term (Petersilia 1997, 1998; Taxman 2012; Klingele 2013; American Law Institute 2014; Mitchell et al. 2014). "Split sentences," or the use of incarceration prior to probation, is a frequent occurrence (Maruschak and Parks 2012). In some states, a relatively short jail term may be imposed as "a condition of probation" (Mitchell et al. 2014).

At the federal level, there are 94 different districts that supervise federal probationers. For state or local convictions, probation is administered by a state or local jurisdiction or, in some instances, a private company. Each state differs in its organizational structure, policies, and practices of probation (Taxman 2012). In total, 29 states administrator probation, parole, and prisons in a centralized fashion. Another 14 states are partially centralized with various probation administrators that coexist with other correctional agencies, while seven are part of the judiciary. In states with more than one organizational structure, probation can be administered by a state authority with various local offices, by the county government, or some combination. Interestingly, some states and/or local governments have two probation organizations—one for felony offenses and another for misdemeanor offenses, while a small number of states contract out for probation services, particularly for misdemeanor offenses (Stillman 2014). Given this diversity and complexity, little information is available on the full array of probation practices across the country.

Scotland

Scotland has a fragmented system of community and institutional corrections. Prisons and jails are part of institutional corrections administered by a nationalized prison service throughout the country. Probation commenced as localized services, run by local authorities or at the county/city level, until funding was nationalized in 1989. Criminal justice social work was positioned within child welfare services in the Social Work (Scotland) Act 1968, to facilitate community efforts and to reinforce an emphasis on social work. This act commingled child protective and welfare services with adult probation. The change was a product of efforts to reduce the unnecessary use of incarceration in Scotland, which has one of the highest incarceration rates in western Europe (McNeill 2005).

Continuous policy and legislative changes have affected the direction of probation in Scotland. Efforts have been made to increase the use of probation services for adult offenders (which declined after the merger with child welfare) and to position probation as an "alternative to incarceration." Over the course of changes, however, probation in Scotland has retained an emphasis on criminal justice social work (McNeill 2005).

In 2001–2002, there were 14,238 offenders ordered to probation supervision. The total increased to a high of 20,674 in 2008–2009 and dropped to 18,044 in 2010–2011. For the most part, offenders are placed on regular probation orders, but 16–20 percent of offenders during the last decade have received community service to pay back unpaid fines and fees. Another

3–5 percent were given drug treatment and testing orders. During the same time period, the courts in Scotland authorized 15,613 (2002–2003) to 15,303 (2010–2011) incarceration orders. Financial penalties have been imposed frequently (outside of probation), totaling 67,575 in 2010–2011. This results in 15 percent having probation orders, 67 percent receiving prison, and another 18 percent receiving other penalties (Scottish Government 2014a); but these are not mutually exclusive since people on probation may also receive prison.

In 2011–2012, around 84 percent of probation orders were for males of modal age 31–40. Most offenders were unemployed (nearly 61 percent), while another 11 percent were not seeking employment. Across various types of orders these percentages vary: employment rates for probationers serving drug testing and treatment orders were higher than for those under community service orders (Scottish Government 2014b). Scotland does not charge any fees for participation in probation or treatment services.

The emphasis on case management, as an informal process for assisting the probationer with his or her criminogenic needs and risk factors, means that very few revocations are due to breaches of social work–related requirements. The formal conditions mandated by court are the only bases for breaches other than new crimes (McNeill 2012).

Another responsibility of Scotland's criminal justice social workers is to address the issues of those returning from prison. In 2011–2012, nearly 5,600 individuals were required to participate in throughcare services managed by the Scottish Prison Service before being transitioned to the community (Scottish Government 2014a). Criminal justice social workers are responsible for home visits, diversion from prosecution, bail supervision, and home detention curfew. In addition, criminal justice social workers complete home circumstance reports to assess the residence for those on parole.

Sweden

Justice in Sweden is administered by national institutions. The Prison and Probation Service, prosecution services, and police are all housed within the Ministry of Justice. The courts operate with constitutional independence but are under the budgetary power of the Ministry of Justice.

Two main punishments are prescribed by the Swedish Penal Code: imprisonment and fines (Svensson 2016). Among Western democracies, Scandinavian rates of imprisonment are quite low. Imprisonment is reserved for more serious offenses, and lengths of terms are relatively moderate.[4] All other sanctions are alternatives to prison, authorized where a prison term is the stated penalty (Svensson 2016). The Penal Code specifies two alternatives to prison: the conditional sentence and probation. A conditional sentence represents a period of confinement which is not served, nor is its length indicated at sentencing. Rather, it is simply recorded by the court with the understanding that as a criminal sentence it may be revoked should the individual commit a new crime within two years. Fines remain the principal punishment in Sweden, though they may be combined with other sanctions such as conditional sentences and probation (Lappi-Seppälä 2007; Svensson 2016).

The Prison and Probation Service is responsible for implementing the full breadth of penal sanctions. Its jurisdiction includes probationers, prisoners, prison releasees, and offenders on electronic monitoring. The authority and range of duties of the Swedish probation service span the continuum of criminal justice system decision-making.[5] The agency enforces the terms and conditions of probation. It also conducts pretrial investigations, prepares social inquiry (presentence) reports, contacts offenders in their homes and other places (e.g., work, therapy centers, and prisons), and monitors the movements of offenders on electronic tagging (Lindholm and Bishop 2008; Persson and Svensson 2011, 2012).

Sweden reformed its Penal Code in 1965, heavily influenced by the positivist school of criminology and its commitment to treatment and rehabilitation. The late 1980s, nonetheless, witnessed a major shift in criminal justice policy, emphasizing just deserts, greater proportionality, and a redirection of focus on criminality rather than the offender (Svensson 2016). Yet probation has remained "the backbone of the Swedish community sanction system." As Lappi-Seppälä (2007, 224) points out, probation continues to serve as a "frame" penalty, one which creates a number of different combinations and treatment orders. In 1988, "contract treatment" was added, permitting probation to be combined with a regimen of designated treatment in the form of a contract. This translates most often into substance abuse care for offenders who committed a crime due to drug or alcohol use. In 1998, the Penal Code was amended to permit the use of probation combined with community service. Cumulatively, the growth in duties and responsibilities suggests that community sanctions play a prominent role within the framework of Swedish criminal justice policy (Lappi-Seppälä 2007; Lindholm and Bishop 2008).

Rates of probation in Sweden show some fluctuation. According to the Council of Europe's SPACE II report, Swedish rates of probation were 145.8 per 100,000 population in 2011, 153.3 in 2012, and 136.8 in 2013 (Aebi and Chopin 2014). The total number of persons under the supervision and care of probation services hit a peak of 14,539 in 2012, dropping in 2013 to 13,070. The Swedish probation supervision rate falls well below the US state with the country's lowest supervision rate (New Hampshire at 296). However,

Sweden's average probation supervision rate is at least twice the country's prison population rate (Aebi and Delgrande 2014).

Comparative Markers of the Penal Intensity of Probation

We now compare American, Scottish, and Swedish probation practices using the five markers of punitive severity set out earlier.

Marker 1: Mission and Goals of Probation

United States

In the United States, probation started as an alternative to jail for drunks when John Augustus invented the concept in 1841 and was clearly linked to a social work framework to address the ills of alcoholism. For nearly 150 years, probation focused on the social problems associated with mental illness, alcohol abuse, poverty, and other unmet needs. This was done through a social work approach where the probation official assumed that role (often as an agent of the court) (Petersilia 1997). The social work model later evolved into a brokerage model where probation officials would refer offenders to available services in the community (Taxman 2002, 2012).

Starting in the 1970s, the emphasis of probation supervision moved from social work and/or a brokerage model to one of enforcement and control. The shift was fueled by persistent high crime rates (Ruth and Reitz 2003) and a shift in penal approaches, the demise of rehabilitation theory exemplified by the "nothing works" message of Martinson's review of correctional treatment (Martinson 1974; Taxman and Belenko 2012), and the ascendancy of the just-deserts model (Von Hirsch 1976). The enforcement approach focused on compliance management where conditions of probation were viewed as binding expectations used to assess whether or not individuals were making progress. Community-based sanctions sometimes aspired to a "punishment without walls" framework that emphasized their retributive value—at lower cost than incarceration (Morris and Tonry 1990).

The tension between enforcement and other purposes of probation is reflected in the relationship between "managerial justice" and "individualized justice." As noted by Feeley and Simon (1992, 5),

> The new penology is markedly less concerned with responsibility, fault, moral sensibility, diagnosis, or intervention and treatment of the

> individual offender. Rather, it is concerned with techniques to identify, classify, and manage groupings sorted by dangerousness. The task is managerial, not transformative. . . . It seeks to regulate levels of deviance, not intervene or respond to individual deviants or social malformations.

An emphasis on the management of offender risk gives rise to surveillance-oriented, control-based strategies of supervision. The primary orientation is crime control effected through more contacts, more enforcement, and more sanctioning of noncompliance (Rhine 1997; Taxman, Soule, and Gelb 1999; Wodahl and Garland 2009).

The emergent risk-management framework has moved US probation away from its rehabilitative origins. The contemporary approach largely expects offenders to govern their own behavior and to address their own needs, even if they have no personal or financial resources to do so. Accountability is less about offenders making gains on individual change factors that may affect their behavior and more about compliance with the rules of probation. Essentially, "the message is voiced that [individual] reform is possible, if the right choices are made by the parolee" (Lynch 2000, 21).

In a study of the legislatively defined tasks for American probation officers, Steiner and colleagues (2004) reported that adult probation officers were prescribed 273 law enforcement tasks compared to 78 rehabilitation-oriented duties. This finding demonstrates the imbalance that might occur when officers are asked to wear the various hats of enforcer, social worker, and broker. This dilemma is exacerbated by tremendous workload pressures, in a nation in which caseloads of over 100 offenders per officer are commonplace—and where surveillance and control mechanisms are (increasingly) less costly than effective rehabilitative programming (American Law Institute 2014, § 6.03 and comment).

Scotland

In Scotland, probation is administered from a social work agency. The goals and mission of the larger agency have an impact on probation operations. "Probation social work" is the terminology used to symbolize the functions of probation, as well as its philosophical orientation. That is not to say that probation in Scotland has not endured the same pendulum swings as in other countries between enforcement and social work orientations. In fact, like most Western nations, Scotland has moved toward a "culture of control" in the last several decades (Garland 2001). The themes of probation range from enforcement supervision to treatment to welfare to responsibility to public protection to "payback" (McIvor and McNeill 2007). Contemporarily, Scotland is focusing on "four *R*'s"—rehabilitation, reparation, restrictions, and reintegration, although preference is given to reparation (McNeill 2012). Rehabilitation maintains a stronghold by virtue of prescribed national standards and the social work orientation of the workforce.

Most important to the delivery of probation services in Scotland are the 1989 National Standards for community service (McIvor 1993) and 1991 National Standards for other probation and rehabilitation-type services (Scottish Government 2010). A central goal of the standards was to increase judicial and public confidence in probation services by clarifying the role of probation as a primary sentence for nonviolent offenders. Criminal justice social work has the designated responsibilities for preparing presentence reports to courts, community sentences, and the postrelease supervision of offenders on statutory license and voluntary throughcare (a continuum of care). To ensure quality in services, the Scottish government mandated in 1993 that criminal justice social workers must have a master's degree (McNeill 2005). Probation embraces drug treatment and testing orders, liberty orders supervised by a contractual vendor, supervised release orders for both those who pose a serious risk of harm and nonviolent offenders, diversion from prosecution, bail releases, pre- and postrelease services for offenders coming from prison, and multiagency public protection arrangements for those offenders presenting the greatest levels of risk (see Scottish Government 2014b).

As part of the national standards, probation is expected to use a case-management system; deploy risk and needs assessments; "develop expertise" in risk management; use interventions that are based on "what works"; rely on accredited programs; emphasize service planning, delivery, and monitoring; and focus on public protection. The probation service has invested in the Level of Service/Case Management Inventory assessment tool to support these goals (Scottish Government 2014b). While the implementation of a standardized risk and needs assessment tool emphasizes the commitment to social work, it also suggests a movement toward more risk management in practice.

In 2010 "community payback order" legislation, the Scottish government again refocused supervision to include a new concept of "paying back." As noted by McNeill (2012), the effort had great significance:

> CPOs (Community Protection Orders) effectively replace a range of community sanctions (including probation and community service) with a single order, in respect of which judges can choose from a range of conditions relating to supervision, residence, compensation,

> programmes, unpaid work, drug treatment, alcohol treatment, mental health treatment and conduct requirements. Though this menu is similar to that which applies to community orders and suspended sentence orders in England and Wales, in the title of the order itself the Scottish Government seems to have signaled its acceptance of paying back as the defining purpose of community sanctions.

In essence, payback means finding constructive ways to compensate or repair harms caused by crime. It involves making good to the victim and/or the community. This might be through financial payment, unpaid work, engaging in rehabilitative work, or a combination of approaches. One way for offenders to pay back is by turning their lives around (Scottish Government 2008b, para. 3.28; McNeill 2012).

Under this new act, however, priority is given to reparation. Rehabilitation and restrictions are secondary goals, while the emphasis is on paying back to the community and public protection. The focus on repayment enhances probation's elements of offender accountability and responsibility. A major portion of this effort has been the establishment of "progress courts" where probationers are overseen by judges. The goal is to ensure that "specially trained judges who understand issues around compliance and desistance from crime would have mechanisms at their disposal for handling setbacks and lapses without undue recourse to custody" (McNeill 2012, 3).

The emphasis on repayment may signal an effort to pay less attention to "what works" or the service aspects of probation. The routine work of probation is embedded in the "what works" literature, however; and officers are required to use these components. Probation remains in local governments and, therefore, there is increasing demand for partnering with organizations such as nongovernmental entities (voluntary agencies) and statutory organizations. Since 2007, probation services agencies have been required to partner with local Community Justice Authorities to prepare jurisdictional plans for delivering public protection services. Essentially, Scotland has maintained the emphasis on social work but has integrated components of restorative justice and management of risky offenders into its probation frame. McNeill (2012) and other scholars of Scottish probation services argue that the added components are meant to strengthen probation orders but retain their emphasis on social work.

Sweden

Though Sweden has no single mission statement of the overarching goals of probation, it is understood that the main task of the Probation and Prison

Service is to address the steps offenders might take to refrain from further criminality (Flore et al. 2012) and to encourage actions that foster prosocial, law-abiding lives during the period of supervision. When translated from its Swedish, *skyddstillsyn*, probation means "protective care" (Svensson 2016). However, probation services have recently begun to move from the exercise of "caring power" toward a more managerial emphasis on structure and control, with probation now seeking to balance competing goals (Svensson 2010, 2016). The long-standing commitment to provide "assistance and support" has been augmented by the expectation that offenders will take steps to address the issues that resulted in their placement on probation. This is most evident in the steady growth and expansion of personal change programs targeting specialized offense behavior (e.g., domestic violence) or behavior that has a nexus to criminality (e.g., drug and alcohol misuse) (Lindholm and Bishop 2008). Some argue (Svensson 2016) that this is a nascent phase in the emergence of "managerial treatment" in Swedish community punishment (an issue we discuss in "Marker 4").

The probation service has at its disposal roughly 1,000 professionally trained probation officers, the majority of whom hold degrees in social work. They produce roughly 30,000 presentence investigation reports yearly and, depending on what is included in the count, supervise an average caseload of about 30 clients (Lindholm and Bishop 2008; Persson and Svensson 2011, 2012). Probationers are required to maintain regular contact with their probation officer, though the frequency varies depending on the offender's criminal history, the nature of the offense, the outcome of specialized risk and needs assessments, and personal and social circumstances.

The probation officer and, if there is one, the lay supervisor are required to meet the probationer within one month of the imposition of sentence to agree on a plan of action. There is an expectation that the initial supervision contact will be conducted as a personal meeting between the parties (Lindholm and Bishop 2008). If ordered by the court, the probation officer may be able to draw upon the Addiction Severity Index, the Spousal Assault Risk Assessment, and the Alcohol Drug Addiction Diagnosis, the latter for those under 21 years of age.

Normally, the frequency of contacts is expected to be most intensive during the first four months, ranging from two to four meetings per month. The schedule can be adjusted to once every three weeks should one or more of the following apply: the probability of offender relapse is low, the probationer is in regular interaction with social welfare services, or the offender is engaged in a treatment program or some type of comprehensive ambulant treatment. If geographic distance involves substantial travel time to required meetings and a lay probation supervisor has not been appointed, half of the contacts may be by telephone (Holmberg, Kindgren, and Bogestam 2012, 12).

Probation officers are assisted by lay supervisors—a key component of Swedish noncustodial care for over a century and one unique to Sweden. Appointed by the Prison and Probation Service, lay supervisors maintain close and supportive contact with roughly half of those placed on probation (Lindholm and Bishop 2008). Several years ago, the Prison and Probation Service established a national target of lay probation officers in 50 percent of all cases, a goal that has been exceeded each year since 2009 (Holmberg, Kindgren, and Bogestam 2012, 26–27). The probation officer is ultimately responsible for monitoring and control relative to conditions of supervision; lay supervisors are better positioned to give emphasis to rehabilitative and reintegrative priorities (Svensson 2016).

Summary

The shift in the mid-1980s toward greater crime control, surveillance, and risk management appears to have had a lasting effect on many probation agencies across the United States (Teague 2011) and has begun to influence—to a lesser extent—the practices of Scotland and Sweden. In all three jurisdictions, the rehabilitation movement has morphed into an emphasis on "what works" or "evidence-based" programs and practice (MacKenzie 2006; Taxman and Belenko 2012; Burrell and Rhine 2013). However, in the United States the setting for rolling out these tools has been the punitive era of mass incarceration, a context that ensures a continuing emphasis on offender accountability rather than offender change.

Probation in the United States is showing signs of inching toward evidence-based practices in some organizations, but risk-management policies and the "punishment imperative" remain influential (Clear and Frost 2014). The organizational culture in numerous agencies remains centered on "watching, catching, and sanctioning probationers when they don't follow the rules" (Burrell 2010, 730). Though there is a trend toward risk reduction and a growing accent placed on modifying probationer behavior, these goals align more closely with the new penology's risk-management approach than with an ethos of rehabilitation.

Scotland's history and evolution in mission clearly illustrate the tensions between rehabilitation and offender accountability (or social work and enforcement). The role of rehabilitation and the "what works" philosophy within these settings remain unclear, but the social work frame stresses individualized approaches. The recent efforts at adopting reparations through payback and progress courts may be setting the stage for more accountability-driven supervision.

Sweden has retained the goal of assistance and support in its supervision of probationers, but a more managerial phase appears to be emerging, centered especially on the design and implementation of treatment programs. Probation Services' commitment to "what works" principles, offender assessments, and evidence-based practices has triggered resistance from probation officers reluctant to embrace actuarial and other assessments in shaping their approaches to supervision (McNeill 2005). Regardless, probation officers are able to rely on volunteer laypersons to further a commitment to rehabilitation in the context of supervision.

Marker 2: Length of Supervision Terms

United States

The length of a sanction is one basic indicator of its penal severity—and there is an utter lack of consensus in the United States on the appropriate duration of probation supervision (Corbett and Reitz 2014). Overall, the era of incarceration explosion in the United States saw parallel increases in lengths of probation terms, contributing to exceptionally high supervision rates compared with other countries (Phelps 2013; Klingele 2013; Alper and Ruhland 2015). In comparative analysis of lengths of probation terms, it is necessary to address both the maximum supervision terms that may be handed down and, to the extent possible, the average time served by probationers.

Many states statutorily authorize terms of probation of 10 years or more (e.g., Hawaii and Alaska permit 10 years for felonies other than felony sex offenses, whose length is set at 25 years). And, for some sex offenses, lifetime terms of probation are increasingly common (e.g., Arizona, Colorado, Georgia, Michigan, Missouri, New York), while mandatory minimum probation sentences may likewise be given for specific offenses. Other states place lower ceilings on maximum probation terms for most offenses (e.g., Delaware specifies for violent felonies a two-year limit, while all other offenses are set at 12 or 18 months). Some states place a fixed limit on the term of probation independent of the maximum prison sentence that may be handed down for the conviction offense (e.g., in Ohio offenders are given a community control [probation] sanction for no more than five years), while other jurisdictions, like New York, do so for felony offenses generally; Mississippi limits terms to five years. A sizeable number of states impose probation terms whose length is coterminous with or determined in reference to the maximum prison sentence for the conviction offense (e.g., Indiana, Minnesota, Wisconsin). Several states distinguish the duration of probation based on whether the offender was convicted of a felony or a misdemeanor (e.g., Louisiana, New Hampshire).[6]

The average period of time actually served by offenders on probation in the United States is estimated to be 22 months (Maruschak and Parks 2012). This is more complicated than it appears because nearly 35–40 percent do not complete their term of probation; some are placed in half-way-back programs (such as residential treatment or short periods of incarceration) or in jail or prison due to violations. Sanctions including reincarceration or half-way-back programming often extend the total length of time a person is supervised by the probation system. Little data are available on such practices.

Scotland

The average probationer in Scotland is on supervision for about 14.6 months. This varies based on the type of order imposed. In 2010–2011, a regular probation order averaged 16.5 months and a drug treatment and testing order, 18.4 months. When there is unpaid work or other activity required, orders tend to indicate a number of hours included in the total probation length. For routine unpaid work or other activity, the community protection orders specify an average of 147 hours of work (whereas probation orders have around 138.9 hours). The supervised attendance orders (which are for those who do not fulfill their work commitments) average 47 hours, which is generally used to avoid revocation (McNeill 2005).

Sweden

In Sweden probationers receive three-year terms and are placed on active supervision for the first year. There is a presumption that the period of supervision will not be prolonged more than one year, unless the supervision board (discussed under "Marker 5") determines that the individual's behavior or adjustment to probation has been problematic. Otherwise, the remaining two years are served "on paper" in a manner similar to the conditional sentence in Sweden; it becomes a note in the register for two years. If the offender is charged with a new court case during this window of time, the judge may (but does not have to) revoke the old sentence and give a new sentence for both the old and the new crimes together (K. Svensson, personal correspondence).

Summary

The maximum lengths of probation terms in many US jurisdictions are exceptional, if not the average amount of time offenders spend on supervision. Individuals in Sweden and Scotland experience on average 12 months and 15 months of supervision, respectively, with outer limits that rarely exceed three years. In the United States, average probation terms are about one-third longer (22 months) and tend to feature conditions and financial penalties that keep probationers on an active caseload for even longer (see below). Unique to the United States, "probation without termination"—or lifetime terms of supervision—have become the community correctional analogue to "life without parole." There is no such sentence in Scotland and Sweden—or anywhere in Europe, to our knowledge.

Marker 3: The Intensity and Restrictiveness of Conditions of Supervision

United States

The conditions associated with US probation supervision have expanded over the past several decades. The statutory authority to impose conditions on probationers gives local judges enormous discretion, a practice grounded in the assumption that a community sentence, regardless of its components, is far less demanding than serving a sentence of incarceration. While some conditions placed on offenders have a nexus to their level of risk or criminogenic needs, the reality remains that there are few legal limitations on the conditions that may be required by the judge (American Law Institute 2014; Mitchell et al. 2014).

One study estimated that the average probationer can expect to have 13 conditions of supervision (Taxman 2012), including special conditions defined by the judiciary and the standard requirements of supervision (e.g., payment of fines, supervision and/or drug testing fees, curfews, notification of moves or change in location).[7] Another study reported an average of 30 conditions attached to offenders on probation or parole in Wisconsin (van Stelle and Goodrich 2009), while a recent case from the US Court of Appeals for the Seventh Circuit noted 30 conditions governing supervised releasees at the federal level (*U.S. v. Siegel* 2014). Over the last three decades, increasing emphasis has been placed on financial restrictions and obligations, heightening the punitiveness of the probation sanction (Peterson 2012).

Standard conditions of probation are typically imposed on all probationers, regardless of their offenses or their needs. The standard conditions are often supplemented by formal systems of classification and case management based on offenders' risk levels, but there is considerable variation across agencies (Fabelo, Nagy, and Prins 2011). Higher-risk offenders are generally required to meet with probation officers more frequently than lower-risk offenders. At any point in time, about 70 percent of offenders are required to report regularly (Taxman 2012). In some agencies, risk level determines the intensity and enforcement of conditions such as random drug testing, house arrest, and curfews.

Though actual figures are elusive, many American probation officers must cope with caseloads exceeding 100 offenders and, in some jurisdictions, 200–300 probationers (American Law Institute 2014).[8] Historically, probation officers conducted meetings in places frequented by offenders such as the home, place of employment, and other community locations. A shift toward use of the probation office as a place for meetings was part of the managerial justice movement, when the goals became the better management of probation staff's time and more effective tracking of face-to-face contacts. Taxman (2002) noted that office contacts became "check in" visits, giving officers little understanding of the environmental and individual pressures faced by each probationer.

Though their frequency varies, requirements surrounding the imposition of fines, community service, and treatment programs are the most frequently used supervision conditions (imposed 84 percent, 26 percent, and 41 percent, respectively; Bonczar 1995). Community service requirements have increased over the past several decades, although there is little research on this form of sanction in the United States.

Since the late 1980's, sophisticated technological tools have become an ever-greater part of probation strategies. Such tools include geographical spatial monitors (sometimes in smart phones) and electronic monitors. Other means, such as SCRAM (Secure Continuous Remote Alcohol Monitoring) and urinalysis testing, are often used to detect alcohol and drug use. The emergence of such tools has increased the importance placed on objective data to monitor offenders' progress, while expanding the tools of surveillance, monitoring, and control.

Drug testing through urine samples emerged in the late 1980s. Drug-testing policies vary considerably across probation agencies. In some settings, the court must specify the conditions under which an offender can be tested; in others, the probation agency may test freely without court permission. Some agencies drug test on a set schedule, while others use random testing procedures. Overall, more frequent drug testing in probation has resulted in more technical violations since officers are expected to respond to any violation of this court-ordered special condition (Taxman 2012).

Until recently, little attention has been given to the growing reliance on financial penalties as conditions of supervision. Although comparative data are not readily available, this may be another dimension of American exceptionalism in the sanctioning of criminals (Reitz 2015). In 44 states, offenders on probation (and parole) are now assessed supervision fees (Peterson 2012; Shapiro 2014). In some states, additional fees accompany drug testing, electronic monitoring or GPS, treatment participation, or other mandated conditions of release. All of this is added to offenders' other financial obligations, such as fines, restitution, court costs, and public defender fees. In some jurisdictions, the total burden of various criminal justice fees and assessments can easily run in the thousands of dollars.

The explosion of fines, fees, and assessments across the United States has not been rooted in mainstream criminal justice policies. Many fees are justified as providing badly needed resources for probation agencies, but this assumes that it is legitimate to treat criminal offenders as revenue sources or, as Reitz puts it, a special class of taxpayers who are subject to extraordinarily regressive taxation (Reitz 2015, 1749, 1763). It is likely that criminal justice debt works at cross-purposes with the core criminal justice policies of rehabilitation and successful re-entry—at least among the majority of criminal offenders who are near or below the poverty line (Pleggenkuhle 2012; Corbett 2015; Ruback 2015). High debt burdens make it harder to find and secure housing and pay for transportation that may be needed to sustain employment or meet supervision obligations. Criminal justice debt can strain family relationships if probationers are a net drain rather than contributors to their families' resources. It can also push probationers toward the illegal economy (Bannon, Nagrecha, and Diller 2010; Beckett and Harris 2011).

The enforcement of economic sanctions as conditions of probation can distort the mission and role of probation officers. In some states, probation officers now wear a "bill collector's hat" in addition to their traditional (and already problematic) "two hats" of social worker and cop.[9] Probation officers' performance in some agencies is now assessed by how much money they collect from their clientele. Many local probation departments rely on supervision fees for a considerable portion of their operating budgets, exceeding two-thirds of their total funding at the extremes (American Law Institute 2014; Alper and Ruhland 2015). The monetary incentives can create perverse practices, such as keeping offenders on supervision longer than otherwise justified, simply because the extended term is needed to assess and collect additional fees. This practice is sufficiently commonplace that it has been named "stay to pay" or "pay-only probation." Anecdotally, there have even been accounts of lenient enforcement of important sentence conditions by supervising officers—where violations are overlooked as long as the offender is otherwise keeping current with payments. In our judgment, the enlargement of economic requirements associated with probation deserves special mention as a potentially unique American phenomenon—subject to investigation of whether any other countries indulge in similar practices.

Scotland

The courts in Scotland are far less likely than US courts to assign large numbers of probation conditions. In 2010–2011, 43 percent of probation orders carried only one condition, 32 percent had two conditions, 21 percent had three conditions, 3 percent had four conditions, and less than .5 percent had five or more conditions. The type of conditions reveals an interesting pattern. For those assigned a requirement, under 8,000 (76 percent) orders included unpaid work or other activity (community payback that requires unpaid service), slightly over 6,000 (62.4 percent) received supervision only, around 800 (7.9 percent) received programs, around 600 (3.4 percent) received alcohol treatment, around 200 (2.3 percent) received drug treatment, around 300 (3.4 percent) were required to make compensation, and under 100 (0.7 percent) received mental health treatment (Scottish Government 2012, 13, chart 6). Specialized programming, such as drug treatment and testing orders, is rare and infrequently used. Again, Scotland does not have supervision fees like other countries.

Sweden

Sweden, like Scotland, attaches a small number of conditions to probation supervision. Only three measures may be imposed by the sentencing court. The probationer must (1) report on any place of residence or lodging; (2) report on any employment, education, or training; and (3) abide by the terms of medical care, treatment for alcoholism, or other related care whether in or out of a hospital or similar establishment. In most cases, only a single condition is required, usually calling for treatment intervention for drug abuse or psychiatric care (Holmberg, Kindgren, and Bogestam 2012; K. Svensson, personal correspondence). With respect to this condition, individuals may be monitored through various forms of substance abuse testing (Flore et al. 2012).

A sentence to probation carries the expectation that the probation officer will take steps to arrange for help and ensure control. Unless a condition is attached by the court directing participation in a specific program, probationers may decline to accept helping measures if they consider them too intrusive of their personal integrity. The control measures imposed by the court remain in force as long as the period of supervision continues (Lindholm and Bishop 2008).

There is nothing comparable within the Swedish system to the US trend that has thrust probation officers into the role of "bill collectors" via the enforcement of economic sanctions. Though fines may be combined with probation, supervision fees are unheard of as a period of community supervision is not considered a service for which offenders should pay. Nor are probationers required to provide remuneration for the costs of electronic monitoring, GPS, drug testing, or treatment-related financial obligations. Where a prison sentence is possible for six months or more, the offender must pay a fee into Sweden's Crime Victim Fund. However, the probation service is not involved in enforcing or collecting these fees or fines. They are administered through a completely separate system (K. Svensson, personal correspondence).

Summary

It is clear that the United States stands apart from Scotland and Sweden in its approach to the number of conditions and the myriad demands imposed as part of traditional supervision. These conditions, regardless of number, call for the enforcement of requirements that are intrusive to an individual's liberty interests, exact geographic and residential restrictions, and direct the payment of fees, often to offset the costs of supervision. Probationers in the United States experience an average of 13 conditions and may have 30 or more. This stands in stark contrast to Scotland, where 75 percent of probationers have two or fewer conditions, while Sweden relies routinely on no more than three. Within the United States, the number and restrictive dimensions of conditions of supervision place enormous expectations on probation agencies to ensure that offenders abide by these orders, which reinforces the extraordinary attention already devoted to surveillance, monitoring, and control.

Marker 4: Formal Treatment Programming

United States

In the United States, the trend has been to crystallize treatment-related conditions of supervision into formal treatment programs that combine both rehabilitative and punitive components. This reflects the shift in preferences that emerged in the 1990s toward a managerial approach. In essence, the program defines the requirements for participation to which probationers are subjected, which reduces the discretion of individual probation officers. A structured program provides for greater consistency in terms of the delivery of key components, promulgated under the "what works" philosophy. Formalized programs at their core represent coerced treatment models embracing the "spirit" of mass incarceration by imposing a greater breadth of penalties and intensity of structure, showcasing that offenders are being sanctioned even while receiving treatment.[10]

The formal programming model has gained favor in the United States due to the increasing recognition that certain types of programs are more effective than others, alongside the understanding that quality assurance is necessary to achieve reductions in recidivism. Martinson's "nothing works" mantra of the 1970s, which contributed to the demise of rehabilitation as a sentencing goal, was critical of correctional programming (Martinson 1974). So, too, meta-analyses have demonstrated that traditional supervision approaches with added conditions or requirements proved ineffective (Drake 2012; Drake and Aos 2012). The emergence of the "what works" or evidence-based treatment literature ignited a renewed focus on programs, particularly on models that are effective at improving offender outcomes (Andrews, Bonta, and Hoge 1990; Andrews and Bonta 1994; Cullen 2013). Systematic reviews and the evolving literature began to identify those programs and practices that reduce recidivism and improve offender outcomes, including cognitive behavioral therapy, therapeutic communities, contingency management, and drug-treatment courts (Taxman, Pattavina, and Caudy 2014), as well as the risk–need–responsivity paradigm for supervision (which embraces programming) (Drake 2012; Cullen 2013).

The emphasis on programming was fortified by quality standards. In Europe and Canada an accreditation process within the prison system emerged in the 1990s, requiring programs to be "certified" by an external body.[11] The United States did not adopt this accreditation process since decisions about programs are made at the local level where services are delivered. However, a trend emerged in the United States calling for the adoption of manualized or curriculum-based interventions. This offers the potential for the more deliberative provision of treatment, as well as a means of staff training. With a standardized curriculum, probationers can be exposed to consistency in the amount, intensity, and type of treatment provided. From a managerial perspective, formal treatment programs are easier to design, implement, deliver, and assess than a more individualized approach to supervision requirements.

Despite these shifts in outlook, most American probation agencies do not have the ability to provide formal programming to their clientele. Total program capacity is relatively low, with less than 10 percent of probationers able to participate on any given day (Taxman, Perdoni, and Harrison 2007). Many probation agencies do not offer services but instead rely on referrals or contracted services for probationers. By some lights, the shortage of correctional resources is a hallmark of probation services almost everywhere in the United States (American Law Institute 2014).

Scotland

Similar to other western European countries and Canada, Scotland has adopted an accreditation process for correctional programs. The Accreditation Panel for Offender Programs commenced in 2003, with one panel for prisons and one for probation. In 2006 the two panels were merged to foster continuity of programming across the systems. A manual of standards was produced to guide applicants (Scottish Government 2008). Like other European countries, the accreditation process uses an external panel to review the theory of the program, the manual, the techniques for delivering services, and the exercises. Scotland offers only accredited programs for its correctional populations. Since programming is infrequently ordered by the courts, its use is more often at the discretion of probation social workers.

Sweden

Support for probationers has increasingly taken the form of requirements that they address their offending behavior through formal programming. There has been a steady increase in personal change programs for particular kinds of offenses (e.g., domestic violence) or for behavior closely associated with offending (e.g., drug and alcohol misuse).[12] This reflects organizational efforts that began in the mid-1990s within the Prison and Probation Service to adopt more structured programs grounded in evidence-based literature and "what works" research. Imported mainly from Canada, cognitive skills programs were introduced, though this is most apparent in interventions targeting substance abuse and reoffending. The probation process allows the officer to recommend programming in the presentence report to the court so that it may be included in the conditions of the sentence. There is also a growing organizational commitment to apply standardized risk-assessment tools in presentence investigations to assist in matching offenders with suitable interventions. Doing so, however, is not mandatory (Persson and Svensson 2011, 2012). Nor is there an agreed-upon general risk–needs assessment tool.

In 2002, Sweden established an accreditation panel to review and approve reliance on correctional interventions. Since then, there has been an effort to identify and adopt programs that are evidence-based and can be evaluated. The panel certifies that programming is theoretically sound (Lindholm and Bishop 2008; Aarten, van der Heyden, and van der Laan 2011). In each probation office, one person has the designated responsibility for leading treatment board planning and approved offender program activities (Lindholm and Bishop 2008, 14).

There remains a disconnect between the probation service's commitment to evidence-based practice and professional resistance by some probation officers (the majority of whom have college degrees in social work), whose discourse does not naturally include the notion of risk (Persson and Svensson 2011, 2012). In a striking observation, one well-known Swedish scholar cautions that the larger embrace of restructuring programs in this manner has fostered a discernible shift toward an approach that is more managerial than rehabilitative or treatment-centered. Ever more detailed and "specific strict instructions" are attached to the implementation of prepackaged program curricula. Individuals under supervision are held responsible for their own actions and are expected to adjust to the demands placed on them by the requirements of the program, not the other way around (Svensson 2016).

Summary

Within the United States, as incarceration rates increased, the era of formalized program sanctions (under the mantle of rehabilitation programs) gained traction. These efforts function in reality as coerced treatment models, in effect, wrapping sanctioning around treatment or vice versa. Built on the premise that a formalized program structure defines the sanction in a manner that distinguishes it from standard probation, these control-based treatment interventions ensure that offenders are confronted with greater intrusiveness or penal severity while under community supervision. Sweden and Scotland, in contrast, do not rely excessively or even routinely on mandated conditions from the court. The most restrictive program in Scotland, the Drug Treatment and Testing Orders, are imposed on less than 5 percent of the offenders each year. In contrast, drug-treatment orders are generally included in over 35 percent of the probation cases in the United States (Glaze and Parks 2012), and the most structured programming, drug-treatment courts, attracts nearly 50,000 offenders a year. Svensson estimates that roughly one-quarter of Swedish probationers participated in programming in 2012 (personal correspondence). While court-ordered measures are not voluntary, they do not appear to be imposed with great frequency. If there is no specific condition set by the court, program involvement may be regarded as an opportunity and not a directive.

While program conditions are generally ordered by courts in the United States, Scotland and Sweden invest a greater degree of discretion in probation officers to work with offenders to identify needed programming and services. The tendency is to use more informal case-management processes, built on the relationship between the probation official (a social worker in Scotland and, for the majority of cases, in Sweden) and the offender, instead of coerced (judicial) mandates carrying myriad restrictions (Makiya 2007). The emphasis on judicially prescribed restrictions in the United States carries the clear potential for greater penal severity as failure to abide by these conditions may trigger the violations process and further justice system interventions.

Little information is available in any of the three countries on the actual availability of programs, their utilization rate, and outcomes achieved. A central problem in the United States is the low capacity of the system to offer good-quality treatment services. If only a small fraction of probationers are involved, interventions cannot have major effects on the activities of probation officers or supervision outcomes (Taxman 2014). Similar problems exist in Scotland and Sweden, where it is unclear whether necessary programming resources exist and whether they are of sufficient quality to address criminogenic factors.

The valence of punitive sentiment in a given probation system may also influence successful outcomes. Unanswered questions include whether novel programs clash with the penal severity underscoring probation programs, whether rehabilitative components can be delivered in an environment that emphasizes offender accountability, and whether periods of relapse can be addressed in a therapeutic rather than a retributive manner. All of these questions could be addressed if better data were available on programming in treatment agencies.

Marker 5: Consequences of Breaches or Violations of Probation

United States

Though there is some variation, most American states treat the violation of *any* probation condition as adequate legal ground for "revocation" and the imposition of a term of incarceration (Mitchell et al. 2014). So-called technical violations of probation are often treated as seriously as a new crime event. Probation agencies and judges often see technical breaches as willful disobedience—and view the enforcement of conditions as necessary to the legitimacy of probation sentences (Taxman 2012).

Studies of intensive-supervision probation routinely report that requirements of more contacts and conditions are associated with higher failure rates (Petersilia 1997, 2002). Violations are met with short and long periods of incarceration or residential treatment, enhanced supervision conditions, extended lengths of supervision (even lifetime supervision in extreme cases), and other punishments. Probation may be intended to serve primarily as a noncustodial sanction. Yet with its numerous if not unrealistic conditions, required programming, and expectations that probationers will pay supervision fees and other economic sanctions, probation all too often serves as a gateway to incarceration (Klingele 2013; Phelps 2013). Revocation numbers have fluctuated but remain significant. In 2004, 330,000 probationers were revoked and incarcerated in prison or jail—almost 50 percent more than the 222,000 probation revokees in 1990 (Pew Center on the States 2007). Although the federal government does not track probation revocation figures nationally, their contribution to American prison populations has been substantial. For example, a 2009 report found that 40 percent of new admissions to California prisons resulted from the revocation of probation—as opposed to new court commitments or parole revocations (Taylor 2009, 20).

The literature shows that around 60–68 percent of offenders successfully complete their term of probation or are discharged early (Taxman 2012; Maruschak and Bonczar 2013; Herberman and Bonczar 2014). Nationwide, from 2008 to 2013, approximately 15–17 percent were incarcerated for a new crimes or technical violations. Figures for year end 2013 indicate that 15 percent of probationers, totaling 319,695 individuals, were revoked either for a new offense or for violating their conditions of supervision (Herberman and Bonczar 2014). Unfortunately, the Bureau of Justice Statistics does not report the amount of time spent in incarceration by probationers who are subject to revocation. Nor do the federal statistics separately track technical violations; they mix them together with new crimes in the count of revoked and incarcerated probationers (Maruschak and Bonczar 2013).

It is noteworthy that many jurisdictions across the United States have begun to reexamine their revocation policies and practices, driven, in part, by decarceration efforts and the work of the Justice Reinvestment Initiative (JRI). This initiative, forged through a public–private partnership involving the Council of State Governments, the PEW Charitable Foundation, and the Bureau of Justice Assistance under the US Department of Justice, provides technical assistance to states committed to downsizing their prison population, achieving fiscal costs, and doing so in a manner that facilitates the reinvestment of the cost savings that are achieved toward recidivism-reduction efforts grounded in evidence-based policy and practice. Since its launching in 2002, roughly half of the states have received some form of JRI assistance. Though several states have enjoyed a measure of success, notably in relation to effecting changes in their probation (and parole) revocation policies sending fewer individuals to prison or jail, the objectives and outcomes sought by the JRI have been subject to criticism (Austin et al. 2013; Gottschalk 2015). Nonetheless, jurisdictions have begun to rethink their approach to probation violations policy, and decision-makers have begun to take steps to decrease the numbers of those who are subject to imprisonment by redefining what constitutes reasonable grounds for pursuing incarceration. Some states are considering half-back and other programs to address the system need for options for those who do not comply with the conditions of supervision.

Concurrent with the goals to reduce incarceration for violations, a rapidly growing trend in the United States is to use short periods of incarceration as part of a swift and certain response to violations. Modeled after Hawaii's Opportunity Probation with Enforcement program, the focus is on using short periods of incarceration in response to violations of probation conditions. The swift and certain jail time is considered a behavioral management tool to reduce revocations by providing for a response to noncompliance as it occurs instead of waiting until there are numerous infractions (Hawkins and Kleinman 2009). A recent study on the use of the swift and certain methodology by probation officers in Washington State found that this approach reduced revocations and reoffending, increased use of treatment services, and reduced costs to the system. The Washington State model relied upon probation officers to use short periods of jail to address noncompliance without pursuing a court hearing or revocation. This is a promising trend of responding to violations, though it positions jail time as the preferred method of intervention over other options (Hamilton et al. 2015).

Scotland

The completion rates of Scottish probationers vary by type of sentence. In 2010–2011, 74 percent of community service orders terminated successfully, 60 percent of probation orders, 60 percent of supervised attendance orders, and 46 percent of drug-treatment and -testing orders. More importantly, among the failures, only 14 percent were returned to custody. Other options to address probation violations include adding new conditions (15 percent), extending the probation term (7 percent), no action or change in conditions (17 percent), and the addition of varied community service hours (9 percent). Unpaid community service is typically the penalty, as determined by the Scottish government (2012) for violation of conditions, with an average of 47 hours added to the sentence. Incarceration is infrequently used, and the preference is to rely upon payback to the community for the added burden of violations of conditions (Scottish Government 2012).

Sweden

In Sweden, 30 independent supervision boards, appointed by local municipalities, address violations of probation conditions (Lindholm and Bishop 2008). Each board is headed by a judge; other members are drawn from welfare agencies and assisting organizations. Offenders who fail to maintain the agreed contact frequency, misuse drugs, or create an "irregular situation" may be found in breach of their conditions. Breaches viewed as nonserious can be dealt with through reminders to the probationer. More serious violations are reported to the supervision board within two weeks of their occurrence. The decision on what to do is made by the supervision board. The boards are empowered to issue warnings to probation violators, require their short-term arrest, modify supervision conditions, and recommend revocation (Lindholm and Bishop 2008, 6).

About half of the country's noncustodial care offices have local procedures for how noncompliance should be managed; there is no uniform national policy for when deviations from sentence requirements are to be regarded as noncompliance (Holmberg, Kindgren, and Bogestam 2012). The available research, of which there is very little, shows that roughly one-third of offenders subject to probation have new criminal proceedings taken against them in their first year of supervision. After three years, nearly 60 percent have had criminal proceedings taken against them. However, it is notable that only a very small percentage (3 percent) of probationers were ultimately revoked and had to serve their sentence in prison (Holmberg, Kindgren, and Bogestam 2012).

Summary

Rates of noncompliance by probationers shows some similarity and difference in the three countries, yet little is known about how any of the three probation systems manage compliance. Especially in the United States, it appears that noncompliance can lead to increased penal severity through increased requirements, extended supervision terms, and short stays in jail or prison. American probation officers and judges sometimes pursue punitive responses to violations to reinforce the message that being on probation is a "privilege" rather than a "right" and that abuse of the privilege will ultimately be met with incarceration. Scotland may be moving in a similar direction as judges are now involved in progress courts to review how well the offender is doing on probation (see "Marker 1"). In Scotland, the tendency has been not to use incarceration for breaches, but the new attention to payback and accountability may change how compliance-related issues are handled. Sweden, as observed, relies on independent supervision boards to respond to violation behavior, each chaired by a judge. The limited information available suggests these boards infrequently impose a prison sentence in response to probation violations.

Across the three systems, the most important generalization we can offer is that too little is known about how breaches of probation conditions are handled, what results are achieved by those responses, and how much punitive severity is added to probation sentences through violation and revocation processes.

Need for a Comparative Research Agenda

The five markers of penal severity in probation were developed to assess whether the machinery of probation services within the United States satisfies the criteria for "American exceptionalism." The use and refinement of these markers may also advance an understanding of how probation services are delivered across multiple jurisdictions. Many American and European scholars and policymakers have noted that there is a dearth of information on probation policy and practice (Taxman 2002, 2012; Durnescu 2008; van Kalmthout and Durnescu 2008; Daems, Snacken, van Zyl Smit 2013; McNeill 2013; McNeill and Beyens 2013; Phelps, 2013). To draw attention to the need for a better understanding of the penal severity of probation, the Confederation of European Probation helped launch the first World Congress of Probation held in London in 2013, with the second in Los Angeles in 2015. Academic writing on probation has been supported by a European Union Cooperation in Science and Technology (COST) grant funding the establishment of a COST research network (Action IS1106) on "offender supervision in Europe." The relatively recent establishment of the *European Journal of Probation* offers an additional forum for moving the understanding of probation policy and practice forward.

In the United States, the demand to understand probation is more muted. The Robina Institute of Criminal Law and Criminal Justice, housed at the University of Minnesota Law School, is currently conducting a five-year Probation Revocation Project, in partnership with multiple probation agencies around the country (see http://robinainstitute.umn.edu). The American Law Institute (2014) recently approved recommended legislation on probation and other community sentences, including provisions that address the five markers discussed in this chapter. Such efforts are rare within the United States, however, and are of recent origin. Given that the majority of offenders in the corrections system are serving sentences of probation, the subject receives far too little attention from the academic and research communities.

The remainder of this section will sketch a comparative research agenda for the study of probation systems, including inquiry into the five markers of penal severity laid out in this chapter.

Scale of Probation Services

Currently available statistics suggest that the United States dwarfs Europe in the scale of its probation supervision rates—but we do not have full confidence in the existing comparative data. For improved cross-national comparisons, it would be helpful to define consistent measurements of probation populations. The elastic term "probation" is now used in different systems to include those sentenced to supervision only, split sentences to jail or prison with probation, alternatives to incarceration or special programs, specialty courts, and administrative forms of probation that entail little or no supervision or services. Some agencies also manage pretrial and postrelease populations within their "probation" caseloads. The varying populations served by probation agencies affect the mission, services, violations procedures, and types of programming offered. More refined measures of probation populations and subpopulations would allow for compatible and nuanced assessments of comparative supervision rates and practices and their changes over time.

Mission and Goals Driving Probation

Rehabilitation across much of Europe and in the United States appears to be a goal in transition. While many probation systems have been investing in risk- and need-assessment instruments as a segue to rehabilitation, the degree to which these tools are used to create environments of managerial justice is an unanswered question. In light of the relatively new deployment of these tools, future research should look closely into their use and how they affect the liberty restrictions associated with routine probation supervision.

A major research effort should be devoted to understanding how the work of probation impacts the likelihood of offender recidivism and desistance from crime. The vision statement for probation in Ireland calls for the reduction of reoffending to create safer communities, while probation in the Netherlands aspires to effect a 10 percent reduction in crime (van Kalmthout and Durnescu 2008; Irish Probation Service 2012; Healy 2012). Some US jurisdictions clearly state that the goal of community supervision is public safety, with a focus on decreasing recidivism (Mitchell et al. 2014; Corbett 2015). Understanding how the historical, political, legal, and cultural milieus of individual probation systems affect the achievement of this goal should help foster greater comparative understanding of its efficacy within and across national boundaries.

Length of Supervision

Similar to incarceration, the length of supervision is a marker for American exceptionalism and an important subject of comparative study. There is no international consensus on the appropriate length of probation terms for different types of criminal conduct—or the considerations that are central to addressing the question. It is one of the least theorized questions in all of corrections—despite its obvious humanitarian, utilitarian, and financial importance. Probation terms in the United States can range from six months to life, with an average of 22 months and huge deviations in practice from state to state (Maruschak and Parks 2012). A review of countries in the European Union and its 28 member states (Flore et al. 2012) shows that the length of probation terms covers the gamut from as little as six months to an upper limit that typically hovers around three to five years. However, there are European countries where the cap is longer, such as France (seven years) and the Netherlands (10 years).[13] Research is required to better frame and understand how the legal codes of diverse nations, if not their different political and cultural histories, come to shape the significant variation that exists. And it is essential to have a better understanding of how length of supervision affects various outcomes and the achievement of sentencing goals.

Conditions of Supervision

The liberty restrictions attached to probation sentences represent another area that has received remarkably little research in the United States or Europe. It is difficult to assess whether the United States is exceptional in its use of conditions, although the rate and type of conditions have shifted over time. There is transnational diversity on the question of whether sentence conditions should be the judicial or the probation system's responsibility. While judges in some European countries operate within "written law systems," where probation measures or conditions are found in the law (e.g. France, Germany), judges across the United States enjoy a "broadly permissive" discretion to impose probation conditions (McNeil and Beyens 2013; Mitchell et al. 2014; American Law Institute 2014). The average probationer in the United States has 13 conditions, and many have 30 or more, while most European nations authorize the imposition of four to eleven probationary measures (Taxman and Thanner 2004; Flore et al. 2012). In the case studies of Scotland and Sweden, presented in this chapter, the average condition load was in the low single digits.

McNeill (2013) argues that not only has the scale of supervision and sanctions increased across the spectrum of probation but their intensity has as well. Though McNeill references Europe, Taxman and Thanner (2004) made a similar observation about probation in the United States, noting that onerous conditions can impede positive outcomes. McNeill (2013, 1) indicates that traditional measures of rehabilitation have now been greatly augmented "to include unpaid work, medical, psychological or substance misuse treatment, mandatory drug or alcohol testing, exclusion orders and residence conditions, curfews, house arrest and electronic monitoring." Though research has not been conducted to discern the standards and activities that constitute the actual content of day-to-day supervision and case management across Europe or even the United States, Durnescu's (2011) research into the "pains of probation" in Romania reveals significant liberty deprivations, a loss of autonomy, and other hardships associated with placement under community supervision. More such studies, if not ethnographies, are sorely needed.

Formal Programming

In the United States, formalized programming is synonymous with coerced programming given that individuals must participate in the programming as part of their conditions of release. Sweden and Scotland, in contrast, do not rely excessively or even routinely on mandated conditions from the court. These countries are more likely to depend on probation officers, working with offenders, to identify needed programs and services and make appropriate referrals.[14] More study is needed to understand the extent to which probation systems in the United States and Europe rely on formalized programming and whether this functions as a tool of coerced treatment. McNeill (2013) draws a contrast between a case-management process that allows for the development of therapeutic alliances and a judicial or system mandate that requires programming as part of a community sanction (such as drug court models in the United States). Of course, an under-researched area is the effectiveness of coerced rehabilitation during and beyond supervision terms (Young and Belenko 2002).

Violations or Breaches of Probation

In the United States and elsewhere, there is too little research on the critical question of how systems deal with noncompliance with probation conditions. The issue regarding noncompliance is whether some aspects are considered normal (that is, not everyone fulfills their obligations to the highest level) or whether any noncompliance warrants violation. In Europe, 13 provisions (out of 90) in the European Rules of Community Sanctions and Measures focus on the process for handling noncompliance. Imprisonment is considered the response of last resort (McNeill and Beyens 2013; van Zyl Smit and Corda, this volume). In the United States, there appears to be a preferred reliance on incarceration as a tool, albeit for short periods. Graduated sanctions and response systems are widely recommended to address noncompliance, but the implementation of these systems is fraught with difficulties, including active resistance to their use (see Steiner, Travis, and Makarios 2011; Rudes 2012). Even though a few states have altered policies to discourage the use of incarceration for violations of conditions, it is unclear how probation systems are handling these breaches. And some states now use half-back programs, small periods of incarceration, and residential treatment programs to address violations.

The complexity of collecting standardized data across countries is demonstrated by the Council of Europe's SPACE II data on the completion, revocation, and imprisonment of offenders for breaches of probation. There are sizeable difficulties associated with the use and interpretation of information from this database centering on the definitions of breaches, the collapsing of discrete data into broad categories (e.g., revocation), incomplete data, and the failure of countries to report their statistics consistently across time, or at all (van Zyl Smit and Corda, this volume). From the available information, it appears that a higher percentage of probationers in Europe successfully complete their terms of supervision than in the United States and that far fewer probationers are revoked and incarcerated. The variation may be due to notable differences in agency policies and practices, as much as differences in offenders' behavior. This represents research soil that has yet to be tilled.

Other Considerations

The five markers identified in this chapter are not the only criteria that may be used to contextualize or compare probation across systems. For example, the professionalism of the workforce might also be considered an important area. In many ways, the probation services in Scotland and Sweden place more attention on the professionalism of staff than agencies in the United States. Scotland requires criminal justice social workers to have a master's degree in social work. Sweden requires university credentials with a preference for a degree in social work. In fact, nearly two-thirds of Swedish probation officers have social work backgrounds (Persson and Svensson 2012). In the United States, there are very few standard credentials to become a probation officer, and few probation staff have graduate or master's degrees. A major challenge in probation services overall, and a critical area for comparative study, is the extent to which staff possess the necessary skills and education.

Another difference is in the area of requirements for the programs that are delivered. In Scotland, like Sweden, there is an Accreditation Panel for Offender Programs (or an equivalent body) which ensures that programs are theoretically sound. Accreditation panels also exist in many European systems, such as those of England and Wales, Denmark, Finland, the Netherlands, Norway, and Canada (Aarten et al. 2011). The presence of such oversight suggests a systemwide commitment to the quality and effectiveness of interventions. In the United States, there are no equivalent accreditation panels, and it is often left to individual treatment providers and probation systems to identify programming that is worthwhile and potentially useful. This is a major problem, and the quality of programming across the United States is generally considered low (Taxman, Perdoni, and Harrison 2007; Taxman 2014).[15]

A third area that may warrant discussion is the wide-ranging impact of collateral sanctions on offenders placed on supervision in a community, who are also expected to maintain full compliance with the conditions of supervision. In the United States, the enormous concern focused on mass incarceration and the death penalty has overshadowed the exponential creep of civil restrictions on citizenship, housing, education, employment, and other areas of civic and social responsibilities (e.g., parenting, voting). These "collateral sanctions of conviction" present daunting challenges during supervision and afterward—an area that requires further research to understand the sanctions' compound effects on probation outcomes and recidivism (Alexander 2010; Love, Roberts, and Klingele 2013; Lerman and Weaver 2014; Travis 2002; Uggen and Stewart 2015). Although little comparative study has been undertaken, there is reason to believe that the range and adverse impact of collateral consequences in the United States are far greater than in other nations—and thus another dimension of American exceptionalism (see Pinard 2010; Demleitner, this volume).

Probation, American Exceptionalism, and Europe

This chapter has considered whether probation supervision in the United States represents an unrecognized area of American exceptionalism in penal severity when compared to probation systems in Scotland, Sweden, and European probation more generally. We conclude that, on some key comparative markers, US probation exerts an exceptionally punitive reach. This is manifest in the daunting contrasts between the probation supervision rates in the United States and those throughout Europe. It is also evident in the authorized length of supervision terms that may be imposed under law and in the number, content, and impact of conditions that accompany placement on supervision. America's exceptional punitivism can be seen in the tendency to mandate treatment programs by court order, rather than leaving the question to the discretion of probation officers or the voluntary participation of probationers. In the United States, conditions of probation often include, rather remarkably, the collection of supervision fees and assessments for the costs of treatment, drug treatment, and electronic surveillance. American exceptionalism in probation may be found in its responses to sentences violations and the relatively high numbers of offenders who are revoked to prison or jail.

In other respects, the charge of American exceptionalism in probation practices requires an assessment of differing shades of gray. Probation supervision in the United States favors managerial justice, placing a strong emphasis on offender management through an escalating reliance on risk classifications and the enforcement of wide-ranging and intrusive liberty restrictions. European probation shows some of these same features, though their impact is mitigated by a more balanced approach to public protection and offender rehabilitation. Probation services in Scotland and Sweden appear to lean toward individualized justice, a supervision function that fosters offender inclusion and the values of social work over law enforcement. Both countries, however, show signs of edging toward the adoption of decision tools and supervision practices that we associate with managerial justice in the United States (Svensson 2016).

Overall, without a great deal more information, it is difficult to draw firm conclusions about the contrast in probation processes across America and Europe. The five markers in this chapter suggest a starting place for future research efforts, which become all the more crucial as some European nations drift in the direction of American punitivism. From a policy perspective, the study of American exceptionalism in probation may hold its greatest cautionary value for countries outside the United States, which have only begun down the same paths. Van Kalmthout and Durnescu (2008), in a survey of European probation, noted that probation's original mission—to "advise, assist and befriend"—is now being transformed into the primary correctional tasks of "supervision and control." Others have reported a dramatic net-widening in European community sanctions and measures from 1990 to 2010 (Aebi and Chopin 2015). Some have pointed to the increasing breadth and intrusiveness of probation sanctions beyond more traditional rehabilitative interventions

(McNeill 2013). Augmented by research, the comparative markers we have proposed (and perhaps others that may be developed) will provide a more complete mapping of probation as it is offered worldwide. Ultimately, such markers can expose areas of divergence and failure, while also identifying emerging convergences of approach and best practices.

NOTES

1. Despite its growth, probation's share of the overall correctional population has never been matched by proportionate budgetary support. Probation enjoys a small share (12 percent) of the funding allocated to adult corrections (Pew Center on the States 2009; Subramanian and Tublitz 2012).
2. The descriptive statistics in the text were generated using the Corrections Statistical Analysis Tool—Probation at www.bjs.gov/probation/ (accessed January 13, 2015), appendix table 3.
3. The analysis in the text draws from discussions with Kevin Reitz, reporter for the Model Penal Code, and American Law Institute (2014).
4. There has been, as Cavadino and Dignan (2006, 167) note, a "clear change of the crime policy climate in Sweden towards 'law and order', albeit mild by the standards of many other countries . . . the Swedish penal system is still characterized by serious ambitions to reform and rehabilitate its subjects within a sanctions framework defined by just deserts."
5. In 2005, the Prison and Probation Service became one authority for the country as a whole. The organization discharges its responsibilities at national, regional, and local levels of organization.
6. The survey of state laws in this paragraph is borrowed from research performed by reporters Kevin Reitz and Cecelia Klingele for the new Model Penal Code (summarized in American Law Institute 2014, § 6.03).
7. Though some of the conditions of supervision may address public safety and rehabilitation concerns, offenders may be placed on probation for the sole reason of ensuring they make victim restitution payments (Klingele 2013).
8. European systems also struggle with large or growing caseloads. Thus, in 2011 probation officers in France dealt with caseloads ranging from 80 to 130, while the comparable figures for Slovakia averaged 303 cases per probation officer (McNeill and Beyens 2013).
9. This can be especially pernicious when probation services are entrusted to private vendors (Stillman 2014).
10. More traditional treatment-type activities include treatments for drug or alcohol abuse, mental health, and sexual offending and other types of services. In a survey of probation and parole officers, Taxman, Perdoni, and Harrison (2007) found that few community correctional agencies operated treatment-type

programs but instead relied on other governmental or nonprofit organizations to provide services. Most strikingly, less than 10 percent of the community corrections population could participate in those services on any given day. As found by Mumola and Bonczar (1998) in a separate study, nearly half of probationers had drug treatment orders but less than 17 percent were enrolled in treatment during their term of supervision.

11. The accreditation process requires programs to define their target population, underlying theory, staffing requirements, core components, and implementation steps.
12. It is evident to both probation officers and lay supervisors that a majority of those sentenced to probation display personal problems and experience difficulties with their social situations. As part of its research, the Swedish National Council for Crime Prevention examined the enforcement plans of a random sample of 650 individuals receiving probation in 2008 (Holmberg, Kindgren, and Bogestam 2012). The sample was divided into those receiving regular probation and those with probation combined with either contract treatment or community service. Though there were sizeable gaps in the documentation captured in the enforcement plans for these individuals, the results indicated that three-quarters of the clients had a substance abuse problem (alcohol/drugs) and more than half were assessed as mentally ill. Finally, only 25 percent earned sufficient support from paid employment (pp. 10–11).
13. Aebi and Marguet (2013), in their annual SPACE II review for 2012, note that offenders are being placed under supervision for slightly longer periods of time (14.1 months on average in 2011 and 14.9 months in 2012).
14. Probation services in Sweden administer electronic monitoring, though offenders are not placed on electronic monitoring as a condition of probation. It is deployed to shorten conditional prison sentences or as an alternative to imprisonment. According to some (Nellis and Bungerfelt 2013), this reflects a "benign authoritarianism" masking a rather interventionist and disciplined form of state-sponsored penal liberalism.
15. In many respects, the "reinvention" or "transformation" of probation in the United States remains largely unfinished business. One indicator of partial movement is the publication of a special issue in 2011 of *Federal Probation* devoted to "Evidence-Based Practices in Action." Additionally, *Justice Research and Policy* published a special issue in 2013 on "Evidence-Based Practice in Community Corrections."

CASE CITED

U.S. v. Siegel, 753 F.3d 705, 708 (7th Cir. 2014).

REFERENCES

Aarten, Pauline, Thijs van der Heyden, and Peter van der Laan. *Accreditation of Offender Programmes: An Overview of Accreditation Panels and Procedures in Various Countries*. Amsterdam and The Hague: Netherlands Institute for the Study of Crime and Law Enforcement, 2011.

Aebi, Marcelo F., and Julien Chopin. *SPACE II—Persons Serving Non-Custodial Measures and Sanctions in 2013*. Strasbourg, France: Council of Europe Annual Penal Statistics, 2014.

Aebi, Marcelo F., and Julien Chopin. *SPACE II—Persons Serving Non-Custodial Measures and Sanctions in 2013*. Stasbourg, France: Council of Europe Annual Penal Statistics, 2015.

Aebi, Marcelo F., and Natalia Delgrande. *SPACE I—Prison Populations. Survey 2013*. Strasbourg, France: Council of Europe Annual Penal Statistics, 2014.

Aebi, Marcelo F., and Yann Marguet. *SPACE II—Persons Serving Non-Custodial Measures and Sanctions in 2012*. Strasbourg, France: Council of Europe Annual Penal Statistics, 2013.

Alexander, Michelle. *The New Jim Crow: Mass Incarceration in the Age of Colorblindness*. New York: New Press, 2010.

Alper, Mariel, and Ebony Ruhland. *Probation Revocation and Its Causes: Profiles of State and Local Jurisdictions: Bell County, Texas*. Minneapolis, MN: Robina Institute of Criminal Law and Criminal Justice, 2015.

American Law Institute. *Model Penal Code: Sentencing*. Tentative Draft 3 (approved May 19, 2014). Philadelphia: American Law Institute, 2014.

Andrews, Don A., and James Bonta. *The Psychology of Criminal Conduct*. Cincinnati, OH: Anderson Publishing, 1994.

Andrews, Don A., James Bonta, and Robert Hoge. "Classification for Effective Rehabilitation: Rediscovering Psychology." *Criminal Justice and Behavior* 17 (1990): 19–59.

Austin, James, Eric Cadora, Todd R. Clear, Kara Dansky, Judith Greene, Vanita Gupta, Marc Mauer, Nicole Porter, Susan Tucker, and Malcolm C. Young. *Ending Mass Incarceration: Charting a New Justice Reinvestment*. New York: Sentencing Project, 2013.

Bannon, Alicia, Mitali Nagrecha, and Rebekah Diller. *Criminal Justice Debt: A Barrier to Reentry*. New York: Brennan Center for Justice, 2010.

Beckett, Katherine, and Alexes Harris. "On Cash and Conviction: Monetary Sanctions as Misguided Policy." *Criminology and Public Policy* 10 (2011): 509–37.

Bonczar, Thomas P. "Characteristics of Adults on Probation, 1995." *Traffic* 4, no. 9 (1995): 10–12.

Burrell, William D. "Probation in the U.S." *Transnational Criminology* 3 (2010): 721–39.

Burrell, William D., and Edward Rhine. "Implementing Evidence-Based Practices in Community Corrections: A Review Essay." *Justice Research and Policy* 15, no. 1 (2013): 143–57.

Cavadino, Michael, and James Dignan. *Penal Systems: A Comparative Approach*. London: Sage Publications, 2006.

Clear, Todd R., and Natasha A. Frost. *The Punishment Imperative: The Rise and Failure of Mass Incarceration in America*. New York: New York University Press, 2014.

Corbett, Ronald P., Jr. "The Burdens of Leniency: The Changing Face of Probation." *Minnesota Law Review* 99 (2015): 1697–1733.

Corbett, Ronald P., Jr., and Kevin R. Reitz. "Introduction." In *Profiles in Probation Revocation: Examining the Legal Framework in 21 States*, edited by Mitchell, Kelly Lynn, Kevin R. Reitz, Alexis Watts, and Catherine A. Ellis, 3–9. Minneapolis, MN: Robina Institute of Criminal Law and Criminal Justice, 2014.

Cullen, Francis T. "Rehabilitation: Beyond Nothing Works." In *Crime and Justice: A Review of Research*. Vol. 42. Edited by M. Tonry, 299–376. Chicago: University of Chicago Press, 2013.

Daems, Tom, Sonja Snacken, and Dirk Van Zyl Smit. *European Penology*. Oxford: Hart Publishing, 2013.

Drake, Elizabeth K. "Reducing Crime and Criminal Justice Costs." *Justice Research and Policy* 14, no. 1 (2012): 97–116.

Drake, E. K., and S. Aos. *Confinement for Technical Violations of Community Supervision: Is There an Effect on Felony Recidivism?* Olympia: Washington State Institute of Public Policy, 2012.

Drucker, Ernest. *A Plague of Prisons: The Epidemiology of Mass Incarceration in America*. New York: New Press, 2011.

Durnescu, Ioan. "An Exploration of the Purposes and Outcomes of Probation in European Jurisdictions." *Probation Journal* 55, no. 3 (2008): 273–81.

Durnescu, Ioan. "Pains of Probation: Effective Practice and Human Rights." *International Journal of Offender Therapy and Comparative Criminology* 55, no. 4 (2011):530–45.

Fabelo, Tony, Geraldine Nagy, and Seth Prins. *A Ten-Step Guide to Transforming Probation Departments to Reduce Recidivism*. New York: Council of State Government Justice Center, 2011.

Feeley, Malcom M., and Jonathon Simon. "The New Penology: Notes on the Emerging Strategy of Corrections and Its Implications." *Criminology* 30, no. 4 (1992): 449–74.

Flore, Daniel, Stephanie Bosly, Amandine Honhon, and Jacqueline Maggio. *Probation Measures and Alternative Sanctions in the European Union*. Cambridge: Interstentia, 2012.

Garland, David. *The Culture of Control: Crime and Social Order in Contemporary Society*. Chicago: University of Chicago Press, 2001.

Glaze, Lauren E., and Danielle Kaeble. *Correctional Populations in the U.S., 2013*. Washington, DC: Bureau of Justice Statistics, Department of Justice, 2014.

Glaze, Lauren E., and Erika Parks. *Correctional Populations in the U.S., 2011*. Washington, DC: Bureau of Justice Statistics, Department of Justice, 2012.

Gottschalk, Marie. *Caught: The Prison State and the Lockdown of American Politics*. Princeton, NJ: Princeton University Press, 2015.

Hamilton, Zackary, Jacqueline van Wormer, Alex Kigerl, Brianne Posey, and Christopher Campbell. *Research Brief: Washington State Swift and Certain*. Seattle: Washington State University, 2015.

Hawkins, Angela, and Mark Kleinman. *Managing Drug Involved Probationers with Swift and Certain Sanctions: Evaluating Hawaii's HOPE*. Washington, DC: National Institute of Justice, 2009. https://www.ncjrs.gov/pdffiles1/nij/grants/229023.pdf.

Healy, Deirdre. "Advise, Assist and Befriend: Can Probation Supervision Support Desistance?" *Social Policy and Administration* 46, no. 4 (2012): 377–94.

Herberman, Erinn J., and Thomas P. Bonczar. *Probation and Parole in the U.S., 2013*. Washington, DC: Bureau of Justice Statistics, Department of Justice, 2014.

Holmberg, Stina, Johanna Kindgren, and Nadja Bogestam. *Non-Custodial Care in Sweden: A Summary of Three Evaluations*. Stockholm: Swedish National Council for Crime Prevention, 2012.

Irish Probation Service. *Annual Report 2012*. 2012. http://www.probation.ie/EN/PB/0/506892EA065F4F168025802E0035F0EB/$File/Probation+Service+Annual+Report+2012.pdf.

Klingele, Cecelia M. "Rethinking the Use of Community Supervision." *Journal of Criminal Law and Criminology* 103, no. 4 (2013): 1015–1070.

Lappi-Seppälä, Tapio. "Penal Policy in Scandinavia." In *Crime and Justice: A Review of Research*. Vol. 36. Edited by Michael Tonry, 217–95. Chicago: University of Chicago Press, 2007.

Lerman, Amy E., and Vesla M. Weaver. *Arresting Citizenship: The Democratic Consequences of American Crime Control*. Chicago: University of Chicago Press, 2014.

Lindholm, Margareta, and Norman Bishop. "Sweden." In *Probation in Europe*, edited by Anton van Kalmthout and Ioan Durnescu, 1025–46. Nijmegen, the Netherlands: Wolff Legal Publisher, 2008.

Love, Margaret C., Jenny Roberts, and Cecelia Klingele. *Collateral Consequences of Criminal Convictions: Law, Policy, and Practice*. Washington, DC: Thomson West, 2013.

Lynch, Mona. "Rehabilitation as Rhetoric: The Ideal of Reformation in Contemporary Parole Discourse and Practices." *Punishment and Society* 2, no. 1 (2000): 40–65.

MacKenzie, Doris L. *What Works in Corrections: Reducing the Criminal Activities of Offenders and Delinquents*. Cambridge: Cambridge University Press, 2006.

Makiya, Agnes. "Instead of Prison: A Study of the Rehabilitation of Offenders in Non-Institutional Sanctions, Sweden." Master's thesis, University of Goteborg, 2007.

Martinson, Robert. "What Works?—Questions and Answers about Prison Reform." *Public Interest* 35 (1974): 22–54.

Maruschak, Laura M., and Thomas Bonczar. *Probation and Parole in the U.S., 2012.* Washington, DC: Bureau of Justice Statistics, Department of Justice, 2013.

Maruschak, Laura M., and Erika Parks. *Probation and Parole in the U.S., 2011.* Washington, DC: Bureau of Justice Statistics, Department of Justice, 2012.

McIvor, Gill. "Community Service by Offenders: How Does the Community Benefit?" *Research on Social Work Practice* 3, no. 4 (1993): 385–403.

McIvor, Gill, and Fergus McNeill. "Probation in Scotland: Past, Present and Future." In *Handbook of Probation*, edited by Loraine Gelsthorpe and Rod Morgan, 131–54. Cullompton, UK, and Portland, OR: William Publishing, 2007.

McNeill, Fergus. "Remembering Probation in Scotland." *Probation Journal* 52 (2005): 23–28.

McNeill, Fergus. "Four Forms of 'Offender Rehabilitation': Towards an Interdisciplinary Perspective." *Legal and Criminological Psychology* 17, no. 1 (2012): 18–36.

McNeill, Fergus, and Kristel Beyens. *Offender Supervision in Europe.* New York: Palgrave Macmillan, 2013.

McNeill, Fergus. "Community Sanctions and European Penology." In *European Penology*, edited by Tom Daems, Sonja Snacken, and Dirk van Zyl Smit, 171–91. Oxford: Hart Publishing, 2013.

Mitchell, Kelly Lynn, Kevin R. Reitz, Alexis Watts, and Catherine A. Ellis. *Profiles in Probation Revocation: Examining the Legal Framework in 21 States.* Minneapolis, MN: Robina Institute of Criminal Law and Criminal Justice, 2014.

Morris, Norval, and Michael Tonry. *Between Prison and Probation: Intermediate Punishments in a Rational Sentencing System.* New York: Oxford University Press, 1990.

Mumola, Christopher J., and Thomas P. Bonczar. *Substance Abuse and Treatment of Adults on Probation.* Washington, DC: Bureau of Justice Statistics, US Department of Justice, 1998.

National Research Council. *The Growth of Incarceration in the United States: Exploring Causes and Consequences.* Edited by Jeremy Travis, Bruce Western, and Steve Redburn. Washington, DC: National Academies Press, 2014.

Nellis, Mike, and Jan Bungerfelt. "Electronic Monitoring and Probation in Sweden and England and Wales: Comparative Policy Developments." *Probation Journal* 60, no. 3 (2013): 278–301.

Persson, Anders, and Kerstin Svensson. "Signs of Resistance? Swedish Probation Officers' Attitudes toward Risk Assessments." *European Journal of Probation* 3, no. 3 (2011): 95–107.

Persson, Anders, and Kerstin Svensson. "Shades of Professionalism: Risk Assessment in Pre-sentence Reports in Sweden." *European Journal of Criminology* 9, no. 2 (2012): 176–90.

Petersilia, Joan. "Probation in the United States." In *Crime and Justice: A Review of Research*. Vol. 22. Edited by Michael Tonry, 149–200. Chicago: University of Chicago Press, 1997.

Petersilia, Joan. "A Decade of Experimenting with Intermediate Sanctions—What Have We Learned?" *Federal Probation* 62, no. 2 (1998): 3–9.

Petersilia, Joan. *Reforming Probation and Parole in the 21st Century*. Lanham, MD: American Correctional Association, 2002.

Peterson, Paul. "Supervision Fees: State Policies and Practice." *Federal Probation* 76, no. 1 (2012): 40–45.

Pew Center on the States. *When Offenders Break the Rules: Smart Responses to Parole and Probation Violations*. Washington, DC: Pew Charitable Trusts, 2007.

Pew Center on the States. *One in 31: The Long-Reach of American Corrections*. Washington, DC: Pew Charitable Trusts, 2009.

Phelps, Michelle S. "The Paradox of Probation: Community Supervision in the Age of Mass Incarceration." *Law and Policy* 35, no. 1–2 (2013): 51–80.

Pinard, Michael. "Reflections and Perspectives on Reentry and Collateral Consequences." *Journal of Criminal Law and Criminology* 100 (2010): 1213–24.

Pleggenkuhle, Breanne. "The Effect of Legal Financial Obligations on Reentry Experiences." PhD diss., University of Missouri–St. Louis, 2012.

Reitz, Kevin R. "The Economic Rehabilitation of Offenders: Recommendations of the Model Penal Code (Second)." *Minnesota Law Review* 99 (2015): 1735–77.

Rhine, Edward E. "Probation and Parole Supervision: In Need of a New Narrative." *Correctional Quarterly* 1, no. 2 (1997): 71–75.

Ruback, Barry R. "The Benefits and Costs of Economic Sanctions: Considering the Victim, the Offender, and Society." *Minnesota Law Review* 99, 5 (2015): 1779–1835.

Rudes, Danielle S. "Getting Technical: Parole Officers' Continued Use of Technical Violations Under California's Parole Reform Agenda." *Journal of Crime and Justice* 35, no. 2 (2012): 249–68.

Ruth, Henry, and Kevin R. Reitz. *The Challenge of Crime: Rethinking Our Response*. Cambridge, MA: Harvard University Press, 2003.

Scottish Government. *Manual of Standards: Scottish Accreditation Panel for Offender Programmes*. Edinburgh: Scottish Government, 2008.

Scottish Government. Scotland's Choice: Report of the Scottish Prisons Commission, July 2008. Edinburgh: Scottish Government, 2008. doi: http://www.gov.scot/Resource/Doc/230180/0062359.pdf.

Scottish Government. National Outcomes and Standards for Social Work Services in the Criminal Justice System. 2010. http://www.gov.scot/resource/doc/925/0103556.pdf.

Scottish Government. Criminal Justice Social Work Statistics, 2011–12. 2012. http://www.scotland.gov.uk/Resource/0041/00411735.pdf.

Scottish Government. High Level Summary of Statistics Data for Crime and Justice Trends. 2014a. http://www.scotland.gov.uk/Topics/Statistics/Browse/Crime-Justice/TrendData.

Scottish Government National Objectives for Probation Social Work. 2014b.

Shapiro, Joseph. "As Court Fees Rise, the Poor Are Paying the Price." *National Public Radio*, May 19, 2014. http://www.npr.org/2014/05/19/312158516/increasing-court-fees-punish-the-poor?utm_source=npr_email_a_friend&utm_medium=email&utm_content=20140520&utm_campaign=storyshare&utm_term=.

Steiner, Benjamin, Marcus Purkiss, Misty Kifer, Elizabeth Roberts, and Craig Hemmens. "Legally Prescribed Functions of Adult and Juvenile Probation Officers: Worlds Apart?" *Journal of Offender Rehabilitation* 39, no. 4 (2004): 47–67.

Steiner, Benjamin, Lawrence F. Travis, and Matthew D. Makarios. "Understanding Parole Officers' Responses to Sanctioning Reform." *Crime and Delinquency* 57, no. 2 (2011): 222–46.

Stillman, Sarah. "Get Out of Jail, Inc: Does the Alternatives-to-Incarceration Industry Profit from Injustice?" *New Yorker*, June 23, 2014.

Subramanian, Ram, and Rebecca Tublitz. *Realigning Justice Resources: A Review of Population and Spending Shifts in Prison and Community Corrections.* New York: Vera Institute of Justice, 2012.

Svensson, Kerstin. "Performing Caring Power in a Scandinavian Welfare State." *Social Work Review* 9, no. 3 (2010): 49–58.

Svensson, Kerstin. "Philanthropy, Welfare State, and Managerial Treatment: Three Phases of Community Punishment in Sweden." In *Community Punishment: European Perspectives*, edited by Gwen Robinson and Fergus McNeill, 209–27. New York: Routledge, 2016.

Taxman, Faye S. "Supervision—Exploring the Dimensions of Effectiveness." *Federal Probation* 66, no. 2 (2002): 14–27.

Taxman, Faye S. "Probation, Intermediate Sanctions, and Community-Based Corrections." In *The Oxford Handbook of Sentencing and Corrections*, edited by Joan Petersilia and Kevin Reitz, 363–85. New York: Oxford University Press, 2012.

Taxman, Faye S. "Second Generation of RNR: The Importance of Systemic Responsivity in Expanding Core Principles of Responsivity." *Federal Probation* 78, no. 2 (2014): 32–40. http://www.uscourts.gov/sites/default/files/fed_probation_sept_2014.pdf.

Taxman, Faye S., and Steven Belenko. *Implementation of Evidence-Based Practices in Community Corrections and Addiction Treatment.* New York: Springer, 2012.

Taxman, Faye S., April Pattavina, and Michael Caudy. "Justice Reinvestment in the United States: An Empirical Assessment of the Potential Impact of Increased

Correctional Programming on Recidivism." *Victims & Offenders* 9, no. 1 (2014): 50–75.

Taxman, Faye S., Matthew L. Perdoni, and Lana D. Harrison. "Drug Treatment Services for Adult Offenders: The State of the State." *Journal of Substance Abuse Treatment* 32, no. 3 (2007): 239–54.

Taxman, Faye S., David Soule, and Adam Gelb. "Graduated Sanctions: Stepping into Accountable Systems and Offenders." *Prison Journal* 79, no. 2 (1999): 182–204.

Taxman, Faye S., and Meredith Thanner. "Probation from a Therapeutic Perspective: Results from the Field." *Contemporary Issues in Law* 7, no. 1 (2004): 39–63.

Taylor, Mac. *Achieving Better Outcomes for Adult Probation*. Sacramento: California Legislative Analyst's Office, 2009.

Teague, Michael. "Probation in America: Armed, Private, and Unaffordable." *Probation Journal* 58, no. 4 (2011): 317–32.

Travis, Jeremy. "Invisible Punishment: An Instrument of Social Exclusion." In *Invisible Punishment: The Collateral Consequences of Mass Imprisonment*, edited by Marc Mauer and Meda Chesney-Lind, 15–36. New York: New Press, 2002.

Uggen, Christopher, and Robert Stewart. "Piling On: Collateral Consequences and Community Supervision." *Minnesota Law Review* 99 (2015): 1871–1910.

van Kalmthout, Anton, and Ioan Durnescu. *Probation in Europe*. Nijmegen, the Netherlands: Wolff Legal Publishers, 2008.

Van Stelle, Kit, and Janae Goodrich. "2008/2009 Study of Probation and Parole Revocation." University of Wisconsin Population Health Institute 158 (2009). Google Scholar.

Von Hirsch, Andrew. *Doing Justice: The Choice of Punishments*. Evanston, IL: Northwestern University Press, 1976.

Young, Douglas, and Steven Belenko. "Program Retention and Perceived Coercion in Three Models of Mandatory Drug Treatment." *Journal of Drug Issues* 32 (2002): 297–328.

Wodahl, Eric J., and Brett Garland. "The Evolution of Community Corrections: The Enduring Influence of the Prison." *Prison Journal* 89, no. 1 (2009): 81–104.

10

American Exceptionalism in Parole Release and Supervision

A EUROPEAN PERSPECTIVE

Dirk van Zyl Smit and Alessandro Corda

Introduction

Some discussions about American exceptionalism in criminal justice are relatively easy to conduct because practices in the United States are so clearly different from those of other Western countries. If one is talking about the death penalty (Steiker 2005; Garland 2010, 20–24) or incarceration rates (Downes 2001; Lacey 2010), it is obvious what is exceptional about the United States. Such exceptionalism provides a firm basis for a critique of American practices and suggestions for reform informed by comparative insights. Comparative discussions of other criminal justice institutions require more subtlety, however, for the specific phenomena being studied may not be significantly different. Exceptionalism has to be demonstrated before it can be discussed.

The subjects of this chapter, parole release and supervision, fall into the latter category. Observable differences between parole in the United States and equivalent institutions in Europe might be the product of factors other than American exceptionalism. For example, it is particularly difficult to isolate "parole" as an institution from the prison, as release from imprisonment lies at its core. The stresses placed upon systems for parole release and supervision by the exceptionally high rate of imprisonment in the United States could be expected to create differences in institutional standards and practices. However, if we are to develop the understanding of American parole specifically, we need to identify what, if anything, is exceptional about parole in the United States, other than it operating in the context of a penal system with an exceptionally large carceral component. This applies both to the way in which decisions in respect of release on parole are made and to the postrelease supervision of offenders that parole allows.

To introduce this investigation, we turn to establishing a clear understanding of what we mean by granting parole and parole supervision in the United States and Europe within the respective sentencing schemes and to giving a basic comparative statistical picture. The latter provides some evidence that parole remains important in the United States but is less freely granted and more harshly enforced than in Europe.

This exceptionalism does not reveal itself easily. The third part of the chapter considers the history of parole on both sides of the Atlantic, which provides some preliminary insights. It is a story of partially common historical roots but also of independent developments that suggests the possibility that American parole has had a different trajectory from that in Europe.

We then directly compare the general judgments on parole of the US Supreme Court and the European Court of Human Rights and find little to distinguish them in their hands-off attitude to the establishment of substantive standards for, and the enforcement of, procedural safeguards. Can one therefore conclude that the reformative project of revealing American exceptionalism in order to change the criminal justice system is doomed, at least as far as the twin processes of parole release and supervision are concerned? We think not.

In the fourth part of the chapter, much as James Whitman (2003) did in his historical comparative study of punishment in the United States and Europe (which focused mainly on France and Germany), we examine and compare current policies on the two sides of the Atlantic in more detail. In this regard we identify a vision of conditional release/parole that is now accepted in core western European countries and, to a lesser but important extent, at a pan-European level, and the very different vision that can be illustrated with examples of concrete practices in key American states. This distinction manifests itself in particular in the way the release of prisoners serving life imprisonment and other indeterminate sentences is considered. However, in many European countries there are also significantly more procedural safeguards than in the United States, which ensure that the granting and revocation of parole are fairly considered. Finally, European parole supervision serves different objectives from those in the United States.

In the next part of the chapter, our principal finding is that European parole, unlike its American counterparts, is dominated by a discourse that stresses human dignity and procedural justice rather than public safety. According to this discourse, postcustodial release and supervision should enable offenders to become full members of society by granting them enforceable legal rights and opportunities for reintegration. In other words, the European discourse recognizes that imprisonment is inimical to human dignity, and that it damages the ideal relationship between individual and society. Accordingly, it should be used to the most limited extent possible, and all prisoners should be assisted with reintegration into society after their release. This should be achieved, *inter alia*, by parole procedures that meet the substantive and formal due process requirements of a state governed by the rule of law. The ideals of dignity and parsimony should determine how parole is granted, the substantive conditions that are set in order to enable parolees to participate in society, and the way in which conditions are enforced and revocations handled.

In the American discourse, by contrast, there is less emphasis on the rights of parolees. Initially, this may have been because of an overoptimistic assessment of the reformative value of parole, under which officials enjoyed a largely unfettered discretion. In recent years concerns for public protection have continued to give unaccountable officials substantial discretion over the release of offenders and their supervision in the community, even as the legal possibilities for the granting of parole (ostensibly) decrease. In these respects parole in the United States is exceptional.

In the final part of the chapter we reflect on whether European ideals for parole may take root in the United States. We speculate that recent American developments may facilitate an approach that places greater emphasis on the dignity of potential parolees as well as of parolees subject to supervision.

American Parole and European Conditional Release: Definitional and Statistical Preliminaries

Before embarking, some definitional clarifications are necessary, for comparative analysis may be undermined by terms that sound similar but have subtly different meanings. Comparing statistics too requires clear, shared understandings of what is being compared across continents, where different jurisdictions do not necessarily use identical definitions.

Definition of Indeterminate/Determinate Sentences

In comparative analyses of prison-release systems, great confusion can be caused by what is meant by "determinate" and "indeterminate" sentences.

Despite using the same terminology, US and European penal systems have fundamentally different understandings of these categories. When sorting systems or individual sentences into one category or another, the American and European approaches disagree more often than not. Therefore, we pause to explain the different vocabularies.

The basic concept at work is that in America the word "determinate" focuses on the determinability (on the day of judicial sentencing) of a prisoner's actual release date, while in Europe the word attaches to the determinability (also at judicial sentencing) of the maximum possible prison stay. Because "determinacy" in the US lexicon requires prediction of future events that are difficult to know in advance and "determinacy" in Europe responds to a legally established element of the sentence that is easily discernable, a broader category of sentences is considered "determinate" in European usage than in American usage.

Within the United States, "determinate" and "indeterminate" sentencing systems are characterized by significant variations as to the foreseeability of prison-release decisions. In order to locate a particular system on a continuum of whether it is "indeterminate" or "determinate," it is crucial to understand whether and to what extent the offender's date of release can be forecast when a prison sentence is imposed. If a prison sentence is "determinate" in the American sense, then reasonably accurate predictions can be made—at the time of judicial sentencing—about what the actual "time served" will be. Both law and practice must be taken into account to classify a given sentence as "determinate" or "indeterminate"—or to characterize the degree of determinacy that exists in a given system. Under these conceptions, the majority of American states are considered to operate with indeterminate sentencing systems, at least with respect to the bulk of their prison sentences (Reitz 2015).

Europe, in contrast, is characterized, by and large, by what its scholars regard as "determinate" sentencing systems—but the European terminology is not linked exclusively to the predictability of actual time served. In European usage, the key element in deciding whether a sentence can be defined as "determinate" is whether the *maximum* term that the offender may serve is clearly indicated at the imposition of sentence. (It is important to note that the vast majority of sentences considered "indeterminate" in the United States would be classified as "determinate" in Europe. This is because prison sentences that do not carry a specified maximum term are very rare in America.) In Europe, the court's sentence is the maximum time the offender *could* spend in prison. The derivation of the word "determinate" in European usage, therefore, is the fact that the longest possible prison stay is "determined" on the day of judicial sentencing. The laws of European states do not routinely allow for judicially imposed minimum and maximum terms. However, offenders will not necessarily spend the whole of their sentences of imprisonment in prison. As we will see shortly, under most European sentencing schemes, inmates usually become eligible to be considered for conditional release after serving a defined portion of their imposed sentence. In some instances there is provision for automatic and unconditional early release as well, in particular for short sentences.

Therefore, from a European perspective, when a judge imposes a fixed-term sentence of, say, six years and the sentence is subject to reduction by parole or remission of a third or even a half, it is denoted a "determinate" sentence. The procedure by which parole may be granted is seen as separate from the process of setting a determinate (maximum) sentence. The fact that, in some European countries, an early release mechanism may operate after only one-half of the judicially pronounced sentence has been served does not move the sentence itself across the conceptual line that divides "determinate" from "indeterminate" prison terms.

There is also a difference of terminology for describing life imprisonment, which can promote additional confusion in comparative sentencing analysis. From the European perspective, a life sentence is fully indeterminate as the sentencer cannot know how long someone will live and does not set a fixed period to be served.[1] From the American perspective, in contrast, a life without parole sentence is regarded as fully determinate, for the offender knows that imprisonment will last until death. No one need guess about the timing of a release date that will never occur. For Americans, a life sentence is indeterminate only if, after a certain period in prison, a parole board or similar body can order the prisoner's release. For example, a maximum life prison term with parole eligibility at five years would be considered a *highly* indeterminate sentence by American criminal justice professionals. Thus, most life prison sentences in America would share with their European counterparts the categorization as "indeterminate" penalties—but for different reasons.

These definitions are not wholly static—in Europe or in America—so there are scenarios that might provoke disagreement in either setting (see, e.g., Wool and Stemen 2004; Weisberg 2012). Additional conceptual work is needed to enrich comparative analyses. For example, consider a sentence in which a judge at sentencing announces a penalty with, say, a minimum of one year and a maximum of 10 years and leaves it to a parole board to determine the actual time to be served in prison. From the US perspective, this is a classic example of an indeterminate sentence (Reitz 2015). In Europe, however, this example might prove difficult for many people to classify. Sentences of from one year to 10 years have never been common in Europe but, if they were, they might be regarded as "semi-determinate" as the 10-year maximum gives them the familiar marker of determinacy—even though the actual release date could be a small fraction of the maximum length of stay. The European language of criminal justice has not had to adapt to the phenomenon of low minimum sentences and low predictability of release dates, due to the historical fact that neither has been a widespread feature of the continent's criminal justice systems. In the absence of necessity, language does not evolve. In the American usage such a sentence would have no place in a "determinate" sentencing system—except in the highly unusual circumstance in which actual release dates were highly predictable despite the seemingly wide range of possibilities.

We speculate that the differences in language across these two loosely organized legal landscapes come from a key difference in approach to the restraints that ought to be placed on governmental power in the use of criminal penalties. In Europe, maximum sentences matter; in the United States, punitive severity is mediated to a much greater degree by release dates. In Europe, generally, the maximum prison term prescribed by law is meant to operate as a genuine protection against excessive punitiveness. In the United States, in contrast, statutory maximum penalties ceased to have much practical meaning in ordinary cases with the advent of highly indeterminate sentencing systems. In most states, it is not expected that judges will impose the statutory maximum except in the most extraordinary circumstances, and paroling systems contemplate early release after only a fraction of the significantly-below-maximum prison term chosen by the judge. In American indeterminate jurisdictions, therefore, authorized maximum sentences are not a useful barometer for gauging the overall severity or operation of the sentencing system in practice. Certainly at the dawn of indeterminacy in the United States, the important question was when a prisoner would be released, not the theoretical maximum term a prisoner could serve.

Definitions of Parole

Some discussion of what is meant by parole is also necessary. Here again, different understandings are found within and across systems. The term "parole" is common parlance in the English-speaking world, but has multiple and smudged-together meanings. It is typically regarded as the discretionary decision as to *when* to release sentenced prisoners prior to completion of their maximum sentences. The release decision is referred to as the "parole decision," and the relevant decision-maker is called the "parole board" or the "paroling" authority. Released prisoners, generally known as "parolees" or as being "on parole," are said to be placed "under parole" supervision and charged with obeying numerous "parole" conditions. That generally means that a parole supervision office (a different entity from the parole releasing agency) has the power to monitor releasees' behavior in the community for a specified or indefinite period. In the United States, therefore, the single word "parole" is used to denote the discretionary release decision but it also stretches across the entire period of postrelease supervision. This broad usage is potentially confusing. For example, when Americans speak of "abolishing parole," they mean removing the discretion to grant early release; they do not mean the abolition of postrelease conditional supervision (American Law Institute 2011).

In European criminal justice, "parole" is generally used only in the narrow sense of release from incarceration with conditions; it does not signal whether the release process was discretionary or mandatory. It derives from the French *parole*, meaning "word" or "promise." The leading pan-European text in this area, the 2003 Council of Europe *Recommendation on Conditional Release (Parole)*, defines its subject matter as "the early release of sentenced prisoners under individualized post-release conditions." One linguistic caveat should be added to this definition: the exact equivalent of the English legal term "parole" does not exist in all European languages. Statutes referring to early release subject to supervision usually employ the expression "conditional release"—for example, *liberación condicional* in Spanish, *libération conditionnelle* in French, *liberazione condizionale* in Italian. It is for this reason that the title of the key Council of Europe recommendation refers to "conditional release" and then adds "parole" in parentheses.

European early release systems can be divided in two main types, which are both explicitly recognized by the Council of Europe recommendation. First, under the "discretionary release" regime, inmates normally become eligible to be considered for conditional release after serving half to two-thirds of their sentence in the case of first offenders and two thirds to three quarters in the case of recidivists (Tonry 2004a, 59). Once an inmate becomes eligible, the decision to release is made based on a positive individual prognosis, taking into account factors such as restitution to the victim and good behavior in prison. Such (limited) discretionary release schemes are in force in most European countries (e.g., Germany, Austria, the Netherlands, France, Italy, Spain, and Poland). Second, in relatively recent years "mandatory" or "automatic" release systems have been encouraged by the Council of Europe[2] and have become increasingly popular across the continent. Such systems do not require an individual prognosis and simply set a point when offenders become legally entitled to release by virtue of having served a fixed period of their sentence. They can be identified as parole systems because conditions are attached to the release. Countries that follow this approach for most determinate sentences include England and Wales, Sweden, Finland, Greece, and Turkey. On closer examination, a middle-ground regime is also identifiable: some countries with a formally discretionary release system (e.g., Belgium, and Denmark) limit the requirements to be met to the *absence* of a negative prognosis so that early release becomes the norm unless significant factors or circumstances speak against it (Dünkel 2014, 1261).

Parole can be defined more broadly than what is typical in Europe. The US Bureau of Justice Statistics (BJS) does so by defining parole as "a period of conditional supervised release in the community following a prison term." The definition goes on to explain that it "includes parolees released through discretionary or mandatory supervised release from prison, those released through other types of post-custody conditional supervision, and those sentenced to a term of supervised release" (2014a, 2). Parole is distinguished from probation by the BJS, which it defines as "a court-ordered period of correctional supervision in the community, generally as an alternative to incarceration" (p. 2).

In the United States, the fact that a jurisdiction has a determinate sentencing scheme tells one nothing about the presence or absence of conditional release. Nearly all American states that have "abolished" parole as early release retain postimprisonment supervision. For example, there is provision for postrelease supervision sentences (PRS) in some states (and in the Model Penal Code, American Law Institute 2014, § 6.09). A PRS term is an independent phase of the sentence that occurs after the completion of a determinate prison sentence: it thus follows its own rules, first of all regarding its length, which is not measured by the unserved balance of the prison sentence but is determined independently by statute or the sentencing court (Travis and Stacey 2010, 605; Doherty 2013). At the federal level, it is estimated that more than 95 percent of offenders sentenced to a term of imprisonment are also sentenced to a term of supervised release—introduced in 1984 as part of the Sentencing Reform Act—to be served upon completion of the prison time (US Sentencing Commission 2010; Scott-Hayward 2013). PRS schemes as a "concomitant" component of determinate sentences in states that eliminated discretionary early release reveal the shift in the dominant ideology. While determinate sentencing reforms from the mid-1970s onward subscribed to a notion of punishment strongly influenced by desert considerations, according to which it was not defensible to subject offenders to supervision after the expiration of their fixed sentences, subsequently the new focus on surveillance and prevention favored the retention or enactment (e.g., New York Penal Law § 70.45 enacted in 1998.) of PRS terms that can exceed the length of the imposed incarceration term.

Statistical Comparisons

Statistical comparisons are not possible without applying the wide (American) definition of parole that the BJS uses. The figures provided by the BJS, most recently in its reports on probation and parole (2014a), correctional populations (2014b), and trends in admissions and releases (2014c) in the United States are invaluable for giving a picture of persons released from prison and subject to supervision.

For Europe it is hard to obtain similarly accurate overall data. The most complete quantitative data on imprisonment and early release in Europe as a whole are those provided by the SPACE surveys compiled by the Council of Europe.[3] The 2013 SPACE I survey on imprisonment (Aebi and Delgrande 2014) contains information from 50 out of 52 prison administrations in the 47 Council of Europe member states, whereas SPACE II on noncustodial sanctions and measures (Aebi and Chopin 2014) contains information from 47 probation services. The detailed figures in these reports are far less comprehensive than those of the BJS, particularly as far as "parole" is concerned. Given the problems of statistical comparison in this area, what useful information can nevertheless be extracted?

BJS statistics reveal that in 2013 about 6.9 million people (6,899,000) were under some form of adult correctional supervision in the United States: around 1.35 million were incarcerated in state prisons, 215,866 in federal prisons, and 731,200 in local jails. About 3.91 million offenders were on probation and 853,200 on parole (Bureau of Justice Statistics 2014a, table 1 and app. table 4, 2014b, table 1 and app. table 1).

During 2013 a total of 631,200 offenders were admitted to state or federal prisons: while state prison populations increased by about 6,300 from year end 2012, the federal prison population declined for the first time since 1980, with 1,900 fewer prisoners in 2013 than 2012. While 2013 federal figures regarding prison releases outnumbered admissions by 1,100 inmates, states admitted 9,000 more sentenced prisoners in 2013 than they released. Of the 573,212 prisoners released, 399,388 were conditionally released (Bureau of Justice Statistics 2014c, table 9). From the BJS reports we calculate that, at the end of 2013, 1,506.9 people per 100,000 US residents were supervised in the community, of whom 1,163.3 were on post-sentence probation[4] and 269.9 were on parole.[5]

In Europe the overall correctional population in 2013 amounted to roughly 3.8 million people: on September 1, 2013, there were 1,679,217 inmates held in penal institutions across Europe (Aebi and Delgrande 2014, table 1), while on December 31, 2013, there were 2,145,289 people under the supervision of the probation services of the responding countries before and after the imposition of a sentence. On December 31, 2013, the average rate of the population subject to some form of supervision or care of the parole and probation services in the responding countries was 219.3 persons per 100,000 inhabitants (Aebi and Chopin 2014, 1). In order to avoid any confusion with reference to Figure 10.1, which deals, with regard to probation and parole, exclusively with *sentenced* offenders, this number encompasses, in addition to people on parole and post-sentence probation, individuals on various forms of presentence probation and those who were not under some form of "active" supervision in the community. With respect to the latter, these are first and foremost persons serving fully suspended sentences without probation or whose criminal proceeding ended with a conditional suspension or a form of deferral, where the only condition was to abstain from the commission of a new offense.

At year end 2013 in Europe, 704,904 people were on probation after conviction,[6] while 314,228 people were on parole. For parole, the main focus of this work, these figures refer to persons out on "conditional release or parole with probation," as well as those serving partially suspended sentences and conditional pardons in a few individual European countries (Aebi and Chopin 2014, table 1.1). If combined, the result would be similar to those on parole as broadly defined by the BJS. The 314,228 persons on parole yield a figure

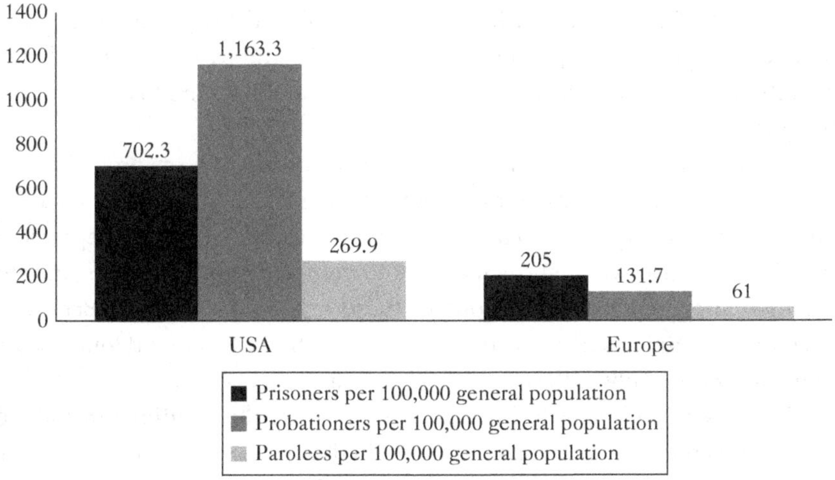

FIGURE 10.1 Prisoners (Including Jail Populations and Pretrial Detainees), Probationers, and Parolees per 100,000 General Population in the United States and Europe in 2013

of 61 persons per 100,000 of the general population of member states of the Council of Europe.

This relatively static picture needs to be brought to life. In Figure 10.1 we have reproduced the figures of people per 100,000 general population serving, respectively, terms of imprisonment (both sentenced inmates and pretrial detainees),[7] probation, and parole in the United States and in Europe.

The European numbers reported in Figure 10.1 require further explanation. The European prison rate is calculated for all Council of Europe member states—total prisoners per total Council of Europe population.[8] This overall prison rate may be higher than some readers would expect, primarily because it is a "weighted" average for Europe's entire population. Individual countries such as Poland and Russia have significantly higher confinement rates than the vast majority of other states (see Lappi-Seppälä, this volume), so a small number of high-incarceration jurisdictions—especially those with large resident populations—raise the overall average. If rates for individual Council of Europe countries are compiled separately and then averaged, the mean ("unweighted") incarceration rate is 140 per 100,000.

While all Council of Europe members are represented in European prison statistics, the SPACE II reports on probation and parole are seriously incomplete. Important states, including Russia, Iceland, and Ukraine (to which are to be added Andorra, Bosnia and Herzegovina, Liechtenstein, Macedonia, Montenegro, Slovenia, and the Slovak Republic), have not made any data available. Germany has never provided broken-down figures on probation and parole to SPACE II,[9] possibly because its official statistics do not distinguish between sentences of imprisonment that are fully and partially suspended on conditions. German scholars have recognized that the failure to draw this distinction is problematic (Dünkel 2010).

For the purposes of Figure 10.1, we used information on probation and parole only for European countries for which SPACE II included data that are reasonably comparable to probation and parole as defined and reported in the United States. We then calculated probation and parole supervision rates against the aggregated populations of those reporting countries. Because a dozen European jurisdictions are missing in the SPACE II report, our calculations may not be fully reflective of Europe as a whole.

One way to compensate for this is to compare the positions in individual American states with those in individual European countries, as we do in Figure 10.2. Taking a closer look at the US state figures,[10] at the high end[11] we have Pennsylvania (847.6 parolees per 100,000 general population), Arkansas (768.6), and Louisiana (656.4). At the opposite end, we have

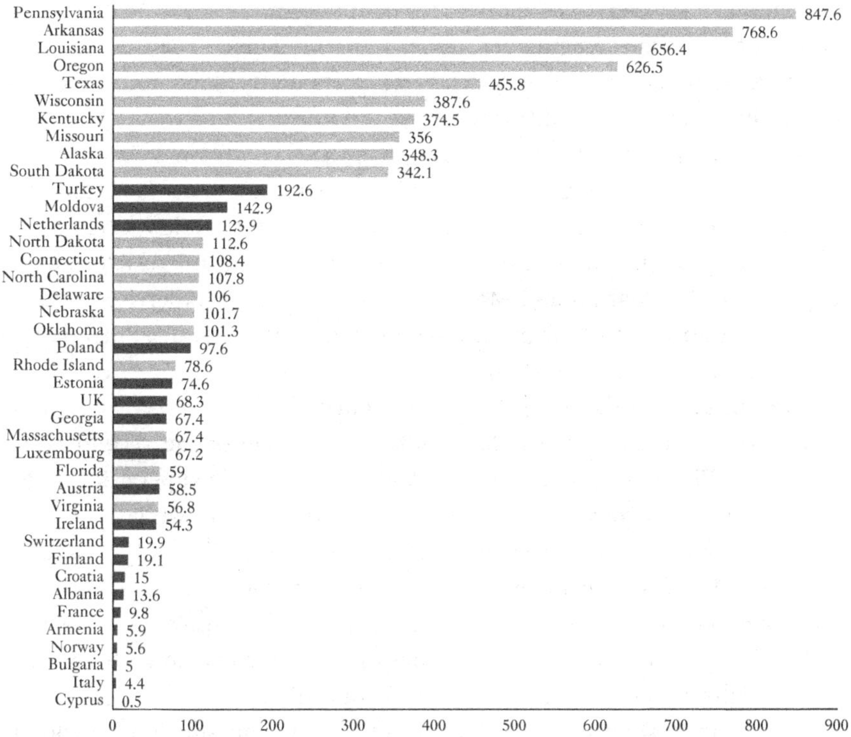

FIGURE 10.2 Parolees (under Bureau of Justice Statistics Definition) per 100,000 General Population, Selected US States and European Countries (10 Highest and 10 Lowest Rates), Year End 2013

Virginia (56.8), which abolished both parole release and supervision in 1995 (Allen 1995) but then five years later reinstated PRS for certain felonies (Code of Virginia §19.2-295.2.); Florida (59), which abolished discretionary early release in 1983 but has "controlled release" in order to maintain the state's prison population under 100 percent of its total capacity (Petersilia 1999, 482) and mandatory PRS under the name of "conditional release" for certain categories of serious offenders (Chapter 947.1405 Florida Statutes); and Massachusetts (67.4). These states reported the lowest numbers of offenders on parole per 100,000 of the general population among the US states with an operating parole system, meaning early release or/and PRS (Bureau of Justice Statistics 2014a, app. table 4). Even lower was Maine (36.6), which can fairly be considered as an outlier because in 1975 it became the first state to abolish early release and it has eliminated PRS for all offenders except egregious sex offenders (Maine Criminal Code § 1231). For this reason Maine is not included in Figure 10.2. From a European perspective, the imposition of a period of supervised release after imprisonment on offenders found guilty of gross sexual assaults resembles a post-sentence noncustodial "safety measure" tailored to a specific class of particularly dangerous offenders rather than a form of conditional release.

In Europe at the end of 2013, Turkey had 192.6 conditionally released persons per 100,000 of the general population, the highest rate among reporting Council of Europe countries. Also at the high end were Moldova (142.9) and the Netherlands (123.9). At the low end, not considering microstates like the Republic of San Marino and Monaco,[12] Cyprus had 0.5 supervised released persons per 100,000 of the general population, Italy (4.4), and Bulgaria (5.0) (Aebi and Chopin 2014, table 1.1).

We can say that the highest European rates of parole supervision, on the American BJS definition, would fit within the range of the second largest cluster of US states. Overall, 26 US states have a parole supervision rate of more than 200 parolees per 100,000 general population, while in 19 states the supervision rate is between 100 and 200. In Europe, in contrast, a rate of conditionally released persons of more than 100 per 100,000 residents is the exception, with only three countries above that threshold. At the same time, wide differences between US and European parole supervision rates are seen at the "highest" and "lowest" ends of the continuum.

Figure 10.2 shows this vividly. It selects 40 jurisdictions, including 10 with the highest supervision rates in the United States and in Europe (among reporting countries) and 10 in each region with the lowest rates. Most European jurisdictions do not overlap with the American rates, and when overlap does occur, it is at the lower end of the chart. While the 10 American states at the "high end" report supervision rates completely unmatched in the old continent, the leading European countries—with the sole visible exception of Turkey—present figures that tend to fold over the range of the lowest US rates, with only Virginia, Florida, and Massachusetts having rates comparable to the European mean.

In the United States in 2013, the average length of a parole supervision term was 22 months (Bureau of Justice Statistics 2014a, 8) compared to 14.9 months in Europe during 2012 (Aebi and Marguet 2014, 1).[13] Although this is a significant difference in duration (with US parole terms more than 47 percent longer than in Europe), it does not account for gross differences in parole supervision rates, where the US rate is over four times greater than the European rate among reporting states. Almost certainly, the bulk of the difference is attributable to much higher incarceration rates in the United States than in Europe—estimated as 3.4 times higher in Figure 10.1—resulting in much larger cohorts of prison releases.[14]

Finally, we explore the available statistics on parole revocation. In the United States at the federal level in 2013, about 9 percent (4,845 prisoners) of prison admissions were offenders returned for violating their conditional release. At the state level, there were 159,220, admissions due to parole violations. Parole violation admissions, including all conditional-release violators returned to prison for either violations of conditions of release or for new crimes, accounted for 27.5 percent of the total state prison entries (Bureau of Justice Statistics 2014c, table 9); and this is a low number in recent US history. Before the drop in California revocations due to the "realignment" plan in response to the 2011 Supreme Court decision in *Brown v. Plata*, about 35 percent of new admissions to state prisons were violators of conditional release. Moreover, approximately two-thirds of parole violators were sent back to prison for "technical" violations such as breaking curfew or failing to report to their parole officer (Clear et al., 2012, 405; Rhine 2012, 640).

In Europe, during 2012 (the most recent year for which information is available), prison entries after the revocation, suspension, or annulment of (or "recall" from) conditional release or probation amounted to a mean rate of only 7.4 percent of all prison admissions (Aebi and Delgrande 2014, table 8). A grain of salt is needed here, however. This statistic is incompatible with the BJS-reported figure. First, the SPACE I calculation is based on recalls of both probationers and parolees. The US calculation includes only parolees. Thus, for example, it is possible that only 5 or 6 percent of prison admissions in the reporting European countries were due to actions that are equivalent to parole revocations in the United States.[15] Second, calculations of percentages of "prison admissions" in Europe and the United States are based on very different denominators. In US jurisdictions, incarcerated populations are housed in both state prisons and local jails, with jails making up nearly one-third of the total confinement population. Jails admitted nearly 20 times more people than prisons in 2013 (Bureau of Justice Statistics 2014d, 2016, table 2). Besides pre-trial detainees and people convicted and sentenced for minor crimes, jail admissions include uncharged arrestees (including mentally ill and drug-addicted individuals), apprehended probation, parole, and bail bond violators awaiting a hearing on an alleged violation (thus, in regard to parole violators, with a risk of double counting if they are sent back to prison), as well as immigration and customs enforcement detainees pending deportation or adjudication (Subramanian et al. 2015; Bureau of Justice Statistics 2014d, 12). US jails are exceptional institutions. Prison population statistics in Europe, in contrast, are generally not similarly bifurcated: "prison" numbers as reported in Europe include the sum of prison and (much less eclectic and overused) jail confinement (Lappi-Seppälä, this volume). While available data do not allow precise comparisons, we suggest that the overall higher parole revocation rates in the United States seem to be attributable to the unusual scale of American prison and parole supervision populations, and also to the crime control approach to supervision adopted in American jurisdictions.

One provisional conclusion that can be reached from these statistics is that parole is a large-scale phenomenon in the United States compared to Europe on almost every measure. To the extent that America is "exceptional" in its confinement policies and practices, as measured by raw numbers, this exceptionalism carries forward to the postrelease stage. Yet one might argue that merely looking at differences in scale is not fully satisfactory. Although numbers vary significantly, they also show that parole is an important penal institution on both sides of the Atlantic. We should therefore also look at the "qualitative dimension" (Garland 2013, 500) of state power of release and supervision, as well as at the different ends toward which they are directed. Understanding what may be really exceptional about parole in the United States requires closer investigation.

Comparing the Similarities

In this part we consider the similarities between American and European systems of conditional release from prison. We first describe their common nineteenth century roots and the similar developmental paths they followed until the 1970s. We then discuss how the two models of conditional release parted ways after the indeterminate sentencing system came under attack in the United States beginning in the mid-1970s. Despite the misleading claim that parole has been "abolished" in the United States, we contend that it is still alive and well in today's America, even though parole policies and practices are substantially different from those of the "rehabilitative era." We also highlight some aspects of contemporary European systems of conditional release that echo the current approach to parole release and supervision in the United States. Finally, we turn to the evident similarities in the case law of the Supreme Court of the United States and the European Court of Human Rights concerning the procedural fairness of early release proceedings.

History: Until the 1970s

It is beyond the scope of this chapter to fully compare the evolution of parole in the United States and in Europe. It should be noted, though, that there was little that was exceptional in the United States about the very early ideas that led to the introduction of parole. Nineteenth-century American pioneers were in close contact with penal reformers in the English-speaking world, in particular with Sir Walter Crofton who introduced the first identifiable "parole" in Ireland, a system of early release based on points earned for good conduct in prison and community supervision thereafter, which was adopted shortly thereafter in England (Petersilia 2011a, 507). Ironically, given the subsequent evolution, an institution of this type was initially viewed with skepticism in the United States. It was considered contrary to the "American principles of freedom" to place someone under supervision after release. A person should either be in prison or at liberty. It seemed inconceivable to have a middle-ground regime where people were released without being completely free from official oversight. At this early stage, such supervision fell to the police, as it seemed unrealistic to delegate this task to any other body (Abadinsky 2012, 121).

This resistance was soon abandoned. In 1846, Massachusetts was the first state to create a form of parole, when a service was established under which an agent other than the police was appointed to assist and supervise released inmates. At this stage there was little difference between parole as it was emerging in the United States and in the United Kingdom, where prisoners released on a "ticket of leave" were also subject to supervision in the community (Wise 1950, 112).

US parole, however, gradually differentiated itself as a result of the adoption of a system of flexible sentences—"indeterminate" sentences, in the American usage. Such sentences were meant to allow prisoners to be *treated* by their expert custodians in ways that would rehabilitate them and released when their rehabilitation was better served by further treatment in the community. Of course, prisoners who did not respond to treatment would not be released.

The most famous early version of the US parole system was later developed by Zebulon Brockway, superintendent of the Elmira penitentiary in New York in 1877. Under the New York statute, after a certain period of good conduct, prisoners were released in the community, remaining under the supervision of the correctional system. They had to report monthly to a volunteer "guardian," the forerunner of today's parole officer, who would make a written report to the institution (MacKenzie 2002, 1212). The idea was to delegate supervisory powers to competent persons in the community (Abadinsky 2002, 1127), while encouraging prisoners to reform in order to "win their way out of prison" through good behavior (Petersilia 2011a, 507–508). This model of parole spread rapidly across the country, and in 1884, Ohio became the first state to create an official parole agency as part of a comprehensive sentencing law. Its members were prison officials in charge of setting up a plan under which any prisoner (except murderers) could be released (Travis 2005, 12).

The New York statute of 1877 was not only the first to use the term "parole" but also the first to introduce a highly indeterminate sentencing scheme limiting the duration of the sentence only by very high maximum terms (Lindsey 1925, 21).[16] In such structures, the first possible release dates for individual prisoners were typically set much earlier than their lengthy maximum terms, so that the parole board's authority over actual lengths of prison terms was greater than the power held by sentencing judges. Often, the judge's prison sentence was not even a pencil sketch of the actual time to be served but more of a blank canvass with constraints only at the extreme boundaries. In some American states, the parole board's power to release existed from the moment prison sentences began, yielding incarceration terms with maximum but no minimum durations under law.

The high–release discretion model of indeterminate sentencing spread quickly throughout the United States in the first half of the twentieth century. By the 1920s, 47 states (all but Florida, Mississippi, and Virginia) had adopted largely indeterminate sentencing systems (Taxman and Rudes 2011, 63), and by the 1940s all jurisdictions across the country had done the same, with Mississippi the last in 1944. At the federal level, in 1910 Congress established the US Federal Parole Commission and gave it the responsibility of evaluating and setting release dates for federal prisoners (Stinchcomb 2011, 214). Although each American jurisdiction adopted its own idiosyncratic configuration of the indeterminate model, the remarkable wave of system change in the early twentieth century, and the resulting congruity of philosophy and practice across the country, remained in place until the 1970s (Frankel 1973).

In continental Europe, the early history of parole release resembles the US history in many ways. The first form of modern early conditional release was introduced on an experimental basis for juvenile delinquents in France during the 1830s. Portugal was the first country to extend parole, in the sense of discretionary release followed by some supervision in the community, to adult prisoners in the penal code draft of 1861 (eventually enacted in 1893). Soon, many other countries passed similar legislation (e.g., Germany in 1871, France in 1885, the Netherlands in 1886, Belgium in 1888, Italy in 1889, Sweden in 1906, Spain in 1914, and Turkey in 1926) (Tak 1989, 22; O'Brien 1995, 189). Parole release systems thus spread across Europe a few decades earlier than their American counterparts, although in England a parole board with discretionary release authority (but with a relatively narrow scope) was not established until 1968 (Morris and Tonry 1990, 25). As in the United States, the conceptual superstructure of prison release prior to the maximum sentence, to be followed by a period of community supervision, became the dominant model throughout Europe.

At the same time, European legislatures remained skeptical about giving back-end decision-makers too much discretion. The high–release discretion model prevalent in the United States was never embraced with enthusiasm in Europe. From the earliest days of parole, European states have adopted a strict principle of legality, in the definition of punishment as well as crimes. The *nulla poena sine lege* principle, prominent in many classical European criminal codes, implied distrust of too much discretion in the imposition as well as the implementation of a sentence. Europeans saw indeterminacy, American style, as a danger to the rights of prisoners and as inclining toward severity (Morris 1967, 552). Further opposition to the full reception of parole release discretion was represented by the retributivist ideals that informed the classical European penal law doctrine since the end of the eighteenth century (Tak 1989, 19). Therefore, the uncertainty of highly indeterminate sentences was not only viewed as the possible resurgence of a dangerously unrestricted power to punish (Rothman 1980, 76; O'Brien 1995, 196) but also considered contrary to the principle of proportioning punishment to the gravity of the offense.

It is true that the final report of the 1887 International Prison Congress in Stockholm, at which both American and European representatives were present, acknowledged that conditional release was "not contrary to principles of penal law, not harming the judgment, and presenting advantages for society and for the convicted" (quoted in O'Brien 1995, 189). However, models of parole in Europe were generally characterized by less ambitious goals and by more limited discretion than their American counterparts. For instance, parole was seen as a useful tool, akin to the American good time, with which prison management could encourage good behavior in prison. The question of whether someone had behaved well in the institution was far less open-ended than a global inquiry into prisoner reformation.

Following from these differences in mission, the main distinction that developed between American and European parole systems was a far greater reliance in the former on highly indeterminate sentences and on "experts" for deciding when prisoners could safely be released. This distinction became prominent during the so-called Progressive era at the beginning of the twentieth century. David Rothman has explained that the optimistic American reformers of this era were far more trusting than their European counterparts that the state, as represented by the "experts" of the parole boards, would make "scientifically informed" decisions (1980, 68–70). According to Michele

Pifferi (2012), the broad historical differences of the late nineteenth and early twentieth centuries turned on subtly contrasting responses to the growing body of "scientific" support on both sides of the Atlantic for individualized treatment for offenders. In the United States, the response was to separate the trial from the sentence, giving parole boards considerable discretion in the post-sentencing phase to shape the term that would actually be served. In Europe the protection of individual liberty offered by the guaranteed release after determinate sentences following conviction remained important. At best, sentences could be reduced by early release/parole on the grounds of executive mercy (van Zyl Smit, Snacken, and Hayes 2015, 6), but wholesale reduction of effective sentences at the post-trial stage was not allowed.

In several jurisdictions, however, Europeans departed from these principles for a smaller class of "incorrigible" offenders, who through a parallel civil process of preventive detention could be detained indeterminately. The notion of incorrigible offenders was open to abuse and, in fact, widened and misused by Fascist governments in the 1930s. However, this was something of an aberration. Norval Morris' (1951) careful study of western European habitual criminal legislation in the immediate post-Second World War period reveals that most European countries adopted laws that limited the use of judicially imposed indeterminate preventive detention, to be served immediately after the completion of a determinate sentence, to a relatively small group of "dangerous offenders." Moreover, they retained judicial control over the enforcement of detention and the processes of release of such offenders for longer periods than their initial determinate sentences allowed. As will be explained, this has remained a source of tension in European law governing release.

In summary, by the late 1960s, although relative prison populations in the US and key European systems were broadly similar, significantly more use was being made of indeterminate sentences in the United States than in the United Kingdom and certainly more than in most continental European jurisdictions. At that time, decisions about parole had a more central role in the American penal process than elsewhere, with greater release discretion invested in back-end decision-makers. In the United States considerable deference was also paid to the "professional" expertise of parole officers assisting parolees.

The differences, however, were of degree rather than absolute. Confidence in parole boards when they were eventually introduced in 1968, and in those responsible for enforcing parole supervision, was high in the United Kingdom. Before the wave of crime-control legislation starting in the mid-1970s, parole in both the United States and the United Kingdom (where the decisive shift toward more populist and punitive policies occurred in the early 1990s; Newburn 2007, 426) could be characterized as a "hybrid, 'penal-welfare' structure, combining the liberal legalism of due process and proportionate punishment with a correctionalist commitment to rehabilitation, welfare and criminological expertise" (Garland 2001, 27). Increasingly in continental Europe, the social defense movement successfully advocated a wider use of specialists to supervise offenders in the community (Ancel 1965). By the late 1960s, concern with due process had not yet become a major issue in American or European parole release decisions, although in many European countries judges were already beginning to play a larger role in parole decision-making.

History: From the 1970s Onward

The relatively uniform picture of parole in the United States became considerably more complex from the 1970s forward. At the end of the twentieth century, Michael Tonry commented that "[a]fter a quarter century of changes, there is no longer anything that can be called 'the American system' of sentencing and corrections" (1999a, 1). Any national commitment to the rehabilitative ideal, genuine or rhetorical, had greatly weakened, and distinct regional traditions emerged (Dolovich 2012, 100–101).

From the 1970s to the 1990s, more than a dozen American jurisdictions adopted "determinate" sentencing schemes in order to modify "a system of sentencing in which there [had hitherto been] little understanding or predictability as to who would be imprisoned and for how long" (US Department of Justice 1996, 6). Legislators at the state and federal levels did so by eliminating altogether the release discretion of parole boards and by limiting, in some cases, judicial sentencing discretion through the adoption of sentencing guidelines. For many specific offenses, American legislatures sought to eliminate individualized sentencing discretion entirely through the creation of mandatory minimum penalties (although observers quickly complained that the chief effect of mandatory sentence provisions was to transfer sentencing discretion to prosecutors). Another component of the shift was the federal "truth in sentencing" legislation enacted in 1994. In order to qualify for federal funding, states were required to see that offenders served a substantial portion of their prison sentences, usually at least 85 percent for violent crimes, before being considered for release. As a result, parole and good-time credits were restricted or eliminated in a number of states (Mauer 1996; Ditton and Wilson 1999; Tonry 1999b).

The resulting picture is anything but clear. Notwithstanding bipartisan support for determinate sentencing, the enactment of determinate sentencing reforms has varied widely among the states (Dharmapala, Garoupa, and Shepherd 2010, 1045). The national picture has been shifting constantly. Maine was the first state to abolish discretionary parole release in 1975, soon followed by many others. Overall, 16 states[17] and the federal government have abolished discretionary release by a parole board. Some states abolished parole release only to restore it later for some or most criminal offenses. The 1976 California determinate sentencing legislation left release discretion in place only for offenders with life sentences, although massive changes in the California system following the Supreme Court's decision in *Brown v. Plata* (2011) have created numerous new avenues of early prison release. Other states abolished parole for certain violent crimes while maintaining it for less serious offenses (Reitz 2004, 199; Rhine 2012, 631–32).

Only one state (Maine) has entirely abolished parole release discretion and nearly all forms of PRS (Scott-Hayward 2011, 433–34). In most of the states that have adopted a "determinate" sentencing system there are still generous good-time credits. In Minnesota, for example, the PRS term usually amounts to one-third of the imposed prison sentence, with release generally occurring at the two-thirds mark. In Washington state, most offenders are eligible for a 50 percent good-time reduction (American Law Institute 2011).

A recent survey of the 50 US states has come to the conclusion that the overall picture of parole is "more complex than previously documented." According to this study, the division of parole systems according to whether sentencing in a state follows a "determinate" or an "indeterminate" approach is simply not valid since most states have mixed sentencing structures, blending features of both (Caplan and Kinnery 2010, 40). The overall conclusion is that there is no universal approach to parole in contemporary American correctional philosophy. As Kevin Reitz (2012, 289) has commented, "Despite the efforts of many sentencing 'reformers,' indeterminacy remains prominent on the American scene. It is still in place in half of the states, and may even be poised for resurgence." Perhaps this comeback is already on its way (O'Hear 2011, 1248).

The methodology of parole decision-making has also been subject to meaningful changes in the United States since the mid-1970s. Before the 1970s, the granting or denial of parole was based upon "the decision maker's subjective impressions from studying case records and reports, and perhaps from direct observations and interviews with the person" (i.e., the offender) (Glaser 1985, 367). In making their decisions, parole boards did not structure their discretionary power through rules, policy statements, or guidelines (Davis 1969, 126). Widespread discontent with the outcomes of unstructured "clinical" opinions and a growing concern for public safety triggered the development and adoption of explicit parole guidelines, which aimed to enhance the overall rationality, consistency, and accuracy of parole decisions (Palacios 1994, 579), which were often criticized as arbitrary, inconsistent, and inaccurate (Gottfredson et al. 1975; Carroll et al. 1982). American parole boards soon started to rely heavily upon risk-prediction instruments. As a result of these changes, parole officers became risk managers rather than facilitators of the personal rehabilitation and social reintegration of parolees. The institutional emphasis on risk, and even risk aversion, was reflected in the increasing ease with which American parolees could be subjected to recall (Kremling 2012, 95–96).

By contrast, European criminal justice has developed in very different ways since 1970. First, imprisonment rates across Europe as a whole have been relatively constant and have even declined slightly over the same period. This overall picture includes a great deal of regional variation, however. The dramatic decline in prisoner numbers in the countries of the former Eastern bloc more than compensated for the increases in some western European countries, such as the United Kingdom and, until relatively recently, the Netherlands (van Zyl Smit 2006; see Lappi Seppälä, this volume).

Second, there was no dislocation in Europe as dramatic as the move away from indeterminate to determinate sentencing in the United States. If anything, in a few countries there has been a small change in favor of sentences that allowed for imprisonment beyond the term that would otherwise be imposed. The most notable example is provided by the United Kingdom, where the 2003 Criminal Justice Act introduced the so-called extended sentence, consisting of a custodial period plus an extension period if the following requirements are met: an adult offender is found guilty of a specified violent or sexual offense, is deemed to pose a substantial risk of causing serious harm through re-offending, and has a previous conviction for an offense listed in the 2003 Act or the current offense justifies an appropriate custodial term of at least four years.

When all these conditions are met, the judge not only decides the length of the prison sentence but also fixes the extended period to be applied to the offender for the purpose of public protection (up to five years for a violent offense and up to eight years for a sexual offense). There is a further ceiling as the combined total of the prison term and extension period cannot be more than the maximum sentence for the offense committed. Under this scheme, the offender is entitled to apply for parole after having served two-thirds of the primary prison sentence. If parole is refused, the offender will be released at the expiration of the prison term. Following release, the offender will remain under supervision until the expiration of the extended period. If the imposed conditions are violated, the offender might be returned to prison to serve some or all of the extended period (Ashworth 2015, 242–43).

Interestingly, while recent European gestures toward indeterminate sentencing have been motivated by the perceived need to confine "dangerous" offenders for extended periods for purposes of incapacitation and public safety, in the United States the conventional (if questionable) belief is that indeterminate sentencing schemes are engines for the production of more lenient sentences overall (Reitz 2015).

Without fundamental system change, some European jurisdictions have moved in the direction of greater emphasis on punishment and control in the practice of post-release supervision. England and Wales has displayed the clearest manifestation of this trend: for instance, in the early 2000s it saw a significant increase in recalls of parolees to prison as a result of a "centrally led and politically driven transformation of the culture and practice" in parole (Padfield and Maruna 2006, 338). This shift, "from a social service orientation to a surveillance led focus on public protection," paralleled more extreme developments in the United States (Simon 1993).

The idea of "truth in sentencing" also has had some impact in western Europe. A Belgian study has observed that both judges and influential members of the political establishment were susceptible to criticism of conditional release as undermining the authority of the legislature and judiciary and as weakening the justice done in individual cases (Beyens, Snacken, and van Zyl Smit 2013). In March 2013, in response to the conditional release of the partner of Belgium's most notorious sex offender, Parliament quickly amended the law to extend the period during which parole could not be granted and to create procedural hurdles to the release of certain classes of offenders (Scheirs, Beyens, and Snacken 2013; Snacken, quoted in van Humbeeck 2013).

Even in eastern Europe, a region in which the overall penal climate is still more severe than the relatively mild conditions prevailing in western Europe (Krajewski 2014), there have been instances of policy shifts having a similar effect to those in the United States. Krzysztof Krajewski has used Poland as an example: between 2000 and 2007 the average time spent in prison by Polish inmates increased by more than one-fifth. However, "this probably resulted not from radical changes in sentencing patterns, but from more restrictive policies on conditional release" (Krajewski 2013, 317). As so often, the devil is in the details. Krajewski (2013, 317–18) explains,

> Conditional release in Poland is decided by the court, but on application either from the prison administration or from an inmate. An inmate's application always requires that an opinion must be provided to the

> court by the prison administration. In principle, conditional release is possible after half of the sentence has been served. These rules have not been changed since 1998. The government could not influence court decisions directly. Since 1999, however, the Ministry of Justice has tried by means of various guidelines to influence the prison administration to implement much more restrictive policies on conditional release. As a consequence the prison administration became much more reluctant to initiate conditional release procedures. Moreover, it has become much more reluctant to provide a positive opinion as required by the law if the application for conditional release is being initiated by the inmate. All of this probably had an impact on patterns of court decisions, although the final outcome resulted not from changes in judges' attitudes, but from courts' decisions being "structured" by the new policies of the prison administration.

Krajewski notes that from around 1996 the percentage of the motions for conditional releases granted (on average between 70 and 80 percent from 1990 until 1998) started to decline. In 1999 it fell below the 50 percent mark for the first time and, during the following decade, it has remained below 40 percent. In his view,

> This confirms that the growth of the prison population in Poland during the past decade is not primarily the result of changes in sentencing patterns by the courts, but of changes in patterns of conditional release, resulting in prisoners staying longer behind bars than during the preceding decade. (p. 318)

Due Process in Early Release Proceedings

If, as Krajewksi's study indicates, national courts that decide on conditional release in specific cases have little power to shape parole policy, what of more powerful courts that apply bills of fundamental rights? If one has regard only to the "apex courts" in the United States and in Europe, that is, the Supreme Court of the United States and the European Court of Human Rights (ECtHR), there are some striking similarities in the period from the 1970s onward in the cautious way in which they have approached legal standards governing the granting and withdrawal of parole. Of course, these courts have to deal with the very different legal regimes relating to parole in the states that fall within their jurisdiction. Nevertheless, both courts agree that in the normal course there is no fundamental right to early release before the maximum term of a prison sentence has expired, whether such release is conditional or not. The US Supreme Court made this explicit in 1979 in *Greenholtz* where it held that there is no "constitutional or inherent right of a convicted person to be conditionally released before the expiration of a valid sentence. . . . [T]he conviction, with all its procedural safeguards, has extinguished that liberty right" (at 7). The *Greenholtz* court held that even if the executive decided to set up a system of conditional early release and gave it a statutory basis, its constitutional obligations in this regard were limited. The court explained bluntly,

> Decisions of the Executive Branch, however serious their impact, do not automatically invoke due process protection; there simply is no constitutional guarantee that all executive decision-making must comply with standards that assure error-free determinations. This is especially true with respect to the sensitive choices presented by the administrative decision to grant parole release. (at 7)

This has continued to be the dominant view of the US Supreme Court.[18] In the 2011 case of *Swarthout v. Cooke*, the court again emphasized that when it came to the granting of parole, the prisoner was entitled only to the limited degree of due process required by the relevant state law (in this case, that of California). Only in cases where revocation of parole is involved has the Supreme Court stated that there are clear liberty interests involved requiring general due process protections. In 1972, in *Morrissey v. Brewer*, the Supreme Court determined that, although a parole revocation hearing is not part of the criminal proceedings that end with the adjudication of guilt, it might still result in the loss of liberty. Therefore, although it does not trigger "the full panoply of protective rights due a defendant" (*Morrissey*, at 480), the person's interest at stake implicates the recognition of a significant number of rights protected by the due process clause of the Fourteenth Amendment (in particular, advance and written notice of the alleged violation, full disclosure of the evidence against the offender, right to appear and present witnesses, neutrality and independence of the decision-maker).

In *Morrissey* and in the following year, in the case of *Gagnon v. Scarpelli* (1973), the Supreme Court set out a two-step process to be followed in revocation proceedings. The first step involves a preliminary hearing held at the time of arrest to determine whether probable cause exists with regard to the violation of the terms and conditions of parole. The second step is constituted by the final revocation hearing, a more extensive proceeding on the revocation of parole where a final decision on the merits is made. Finally, in *Scarpelli* (at 790) the Supreme Court has recognized only a limited right to counsel for the parolee in the revocation proceedings. The right to counsel applies when the parolee contests the allegations in a timely fashion or in cases in which relevant circumstances making the revocation inappropriate exist but are hard to develop or present.

Shifting our attention to Europe, we find a similar jurisprudence: where determinate sentences of imprisonment (those with designated maximum terms) are involved, the ECtHR has resolutely held that the protections relating to preventing wrongful detention and ensuring fair trials, contained in Articles 5 and 6 of the European Convention on Human Rights, do not apply to routine measures designed to allow for release prior to the completion of the full custodial term.[19] In *Dybeku v. Albania* (2007, para. 57), for example, the ECtHR stated clearly that "the Convention does not guarantee, as such, a right to conditional release or to serve a prison sentence in accordance with a particular sentencing regime." What this means in practice is that, where determinate sentences are involved, the ECtHR has consistently declined to review the procedural fairness of decisions to refuse early release (*Hudec v. Slovakia* 2006). Indeed, as far as the ECtHR is concerned, the absence of guaranteed procedural rights carries over to the recall of conditionally released offenders charged with infringing their conditions (*Ganusauskas v. Lithuania* 1999). In this respect, the ECtHR appears to be more conservative than the US Supreme Court. Whether this hands-off approach of the ECtHR is shared by other major European courts and whether the ECtHR applies the same approach to other aspects of the law that have an impact on parole will be considered more fully in what follows.

Comparing the Differences

Notwithstanding the partial similarities in history and law we have outlined in the previous part, we argue that Europe as a whole possesses a very different ideal notion of parole as conditional release, which contrasts substantially with the more law enforcement–oriented approach that dominates American penal policy, including parole release and supervision. Attempts to implement the essentially humanist ideal of conditional release, which recognizes the offender's capacity to change, can be identified both at the pan-European and at the national level and have had important practical consequences.

In this part we identify the broad contours of this ideal as it has emerged both at the European level and, in particular, in some key pronouncements of the German Federal Constitutional Court, arguably the most influential current national apex court in Europe. We pay particular attention to life imprisonment in this regard, as the very widespread acceptance in Europe that all persons serving life sentences should be considered for release stands in stark contrast to the American position and reflects a fundamentally different understanding of the roles of, and relationship between, the offender and the state. Subsequently, we look again at the approach adopted to the granting of parole to fixed-term prisoners and to the decision-making structures involving both the granting and revocation of parole. Finally, we highlight differing approaches to how parolees should be supervised.

Ideals about Parole

At the pan-European level there is evidence that, since the late 1980s, a particular notion of conditional release (parole) has been articulated by European institutions with growing strength. There is also evidence that it is still the dominant narrative (van Zyl Smit and Spencer 2010).

First, we offer some background on how penal policy is articulated in the European context. Regional penal policy has been principally developed by the Council of Europe, which has an overall brief to foster and protect human rights in Europe. Such policy is articulated directly in the recommendations and rules made by the Committee of Minsters of the Council of Europe. Technically, these recommendations and rules, although agreed unanimously by the member states of the Council, are merely soft law and not directly binding. However, they are often relied on specifically by two other key organs of the Council of Europe, the Committee for the Prevention of Torture and Inhuman or Degrading Treatment or Punishment (CPT) and the ECtHR. These institutions' powers are based on treaties that all European countries (except Belarus) have ratified and which therefore carry considerable legal weight.[20] More recently, council policy has been complemented by the emerging power of the European Union to set some criminal justice policy among its member states via directives, especially regarding the cross-border implementation of sentences (Baker 2013).

The 2003 Council of Europe's *Recommendation on Conditional Release (Parole)* closely represents the European ideal of parole. It begins by "recognising that conditional release is one of the most effective and constructive means of preventing reoffending and promoting resettlement, providing the prisoner with planned, assisted and supervised reintegration into the community [and that] it should be used in ways that are adapted to individual circumstances and consistent with the principles of justice and fairness."

Similarly, the 1992 *Rules on Community Sanctions and Measures*, which explicitly include parole, specify that parole "shall seek to contribute to personal and social development [of offenders that is] of relevance for [their] adjustment in society" and that its imposition and implementation must be guided "by the essential aim of treating the offender with respect as a responsible human being" (rule 55). These ends are also spelled out in the first of the general principles enumerated under the *Recommendation on Conditional Release (Parole)*:

> Conditional release should aim at assisting prisoners to make a transition from life in prison to a law-abiding life in the community through post-release conditions and supervision that promote this end and contribute to public safety and the reduction of crime in the community.

This point is underlined in the next principle:

> In order to reduce the harmful effects of imprisonment and to promote the resettlement of prisoners under conditions that seek to guarantee safety of the outside community, the law should make conditional release available to all sentenced prisoners, including life-sentence prisoners. (Council of Europe 2003)

Although these principles mention "public safety and crime reduction," it is clear from the recommendation as a whole that these objectives are contingent on fostering the human development of the persons placed on parole.

The 1999 *Recommendation Concerning Prison Overcrowding and Prison Population Inflation* also supports the use of parole, not only to reduce overcrowding but also as a positive means of managing the return of the offender to the community. It does not mention parole as a form of punishment to be continued in the community. At the core of the European conception of parole articulated in the various recommendations is the individual right to the possibility of parole as a means of achieving eventual social rehabilitation and reintegration into society.

This latter aspect is emphasized also in the 2008 Framework Decision on mutual recognition of judgments and probation decisions (including parole), which was developed by the European Union to enable sentences to be implemented across member states' national borders. The preamble to this Framework Decision explains that "the aim of mutual recognition and supervision of . . . decisions on conditional release is to enhance the prospects of the sentenced person's being reintegrated into society, by enabling that person to preserve family, linguistic, cultural and other ties," while its very first stated aim is to facilitate "the social rehabilitation of sentenced persons."

The CPT and the ECtHR have had relatively little to say about parole release policy in general, although the former has emphasized its importance as a means of restricting prison populations and thus reducing the overcrowding that jeopardizes the humanity and dignity of prison regimes (European Committee for the Prevention of Torture and Inhuman or Degrading Treatment or Punishment [CPT] 1992). The latter has made similar comments regarding overcrowding and has also recognized that conditional release has the legitimate aim of fostering the progressive social reintegration of persons sentenced to imprisonment (*Léger v. France* 2006, para. 70).

The thinking underlying the aforementioned European instruments is best illustrated by a remarkable decision of the German Federal Constitutional Court in the 1973 *Lebach* case (BVerfGE 1973), which explicated what offenders may expect with regard to conditional release as of (constitutional) right. At issue was whether a major German television could broadcast a sensational documentary about the offense committed some years previously by an offender who was about to be released on parole, if there was evidence that it would have the effect of undermining the successful reintegration of the offender into society.

In insisting on its right to do so, the television station relied on the explicit guarantee in the German Constitution of the media's right to free speech. In American constitutional law the right of freedom of speech may be expected to prevail. By contrast, the German Federal Constitutional Court ruled that this right had to be balanced against the constitutional rights of the offender, who retained personal rights to privacy and the protection of his or her reputation. These rights would always have to be considered and could outweigh even free speech rights. Crucial in this respect was what the court saw as a constitutional duty that the German state, as both a *Rechtsstaat* (a state bound by the rule of law) and a *Sozialstaat* (a state with constitutional obligations for the social welfare of all its inhabitants), had to manage in the implementation of a sentence of imprisonment in a way that would give a prisoner "the ability and the will to follow a responsible way of life; he should learn to maintain himself in a free society without breaking the law, to grasp its opportunities and to come to terms with its uncertainties" (BVerfGE 1973, para. 234). The court explained that this meant that the state was required to provide the offender with opportunities for resocialization, which the offender could exercise as of right. In the view of the German court,

> [T]he decisive stage began with release. Not only the offender must be prepared to return to free human society; society from its side must be prepared to take him up again. . . . From the point of view of the

> Constitution this requirement reflects the communal identity of a society that places human dignity at the center of its value system and is bound by the principle of the social state. As bearer of the guaranteed fundamental rights to human dignity the convicted offender must have the opportunity, after the completion of his sentence, to establish himself in the community again. (para. 234)

Having recognized this constitutional right to resocialization, the court weighed it against the right to free speech of the television station and concluded that, in this instance, the station's legitimate interest in making the public aware of a sensational but historical offense was less fundamental than the offender's constitutional right to resocialization.

The *Lebach* judgment, which is still good law in Germany, embodies the idealism of the various subsequent recommendations of the Council of Europe on conditional release. In stark contrast to what happens in the United States, its focus is principally on what is best for the individual offender. Risk management, so important in the American context, is not even mentioned directly in *Lebach*.

In the American context it is quite hard to find aspirational standards and regulations regarding parole that are comparable to those existing at the European level. Many US parole boards operate under a statutory set of goals, but they tend to be extremely broad and often "muddled and perplexing" (Reitz 2012, 278). In Arkansas, for example, the parole board is required to "establish written policies and procedures governing the supervision of parolees designed to enhance public safety and to assist the parolees in reintegrating into society" (A.C.A. § 16-93-712). According to the law of Pennsylvania, the US state with the highest figures of parolees per 100,000 inhabitants,

> [T]he parole system provides several benefits to the criminal justice system, including the provision of adequate supervision of the offender while protecting the public, the opportunity for the offender to become a useful member of society and the diversion of appropriate offenders from prison. [Yet, in] providing these benefits to the criminal justice system, the board and any other paroling entity shall first and foremost seek to protect the safety of the public. (Parole Act, 61 Pa.C.S. § 6102[1][2])

Although it is completely legitimate for a policy to pursue different objectives, whether there is a hierarchy of goals or not, the risk-averse American approach to parole (Raphael and Stoll 2013, 45) makes it predictable which goal will trump in case of a conflict between reintegration and public safety.

In sum, the language of European aspirational standards and most national case law is clearly focused on the reintegration of individual offenders into society and provides what is by and large a presumption in favor of release. In the United States, in contrast, the activity of parole boards seems to be primarily focused on the protection of the community. When public safety is at stake, even at the statutory level, US parole boards are more openly encouraged than the European ones to "err" on the side of safety.[21]

Life Imprisonment and Release Eligibility

The *Lebach* decision has not only continued to be influential in Germany but has also been complemented by other decisions. It has had particular impact on the law relating to the conditional release of offenders sentenced to life imprisonment. The willingness to consider even the worst offenders for conditional release underlines a key difference between the European and American approaches to parole.

European thinking on the law relating to life imprisonment, and to release from it, was shaped most dramatically by the German Federal Constitutional Court in 1977 (BVerfGE 1977). In that year it faced a direct challenge to the constitutionality of all life sentences. In response, the court built on the concept of human dignity that it had developed in the *Lebach* judgment and emphasized the importance of the right of all humans to develop their potential in a free society. It followed that it would be incompatible with human dignity for the state to arrogate to itself the power to deprive someone of his or her freedom, without at least the opportunity to be considered for release on the ground that he or she was fit to become part of free society again.

The German Federal Constitutional Court concluded that a life sentence could only be constitutional as a punishment for the most serious offenses if the requirements of human dignity were met. This entailed two elements. First, the prison regime had to be organized in a way that provided prisoners with a right to facilities that would enable them to resocialize themselves. Second, and more controversially, the court held that the existing system of release, where persons serving life sentences were considered for pardon by the premiers of the federal states in which they were being detained, contravened both the principle of legality and the dignity of the relevant offenders, who had a right to have such an important decision taken by a court. Accordingly, the court upheld the constitutionality of life sentences, but it instructed the government to enact legislation within three years of the judgment being adopted which would create an appropriate framework.

The government duly amended the Penal Code to provide that a court must consider the conditional release of everyone sentenced to life imprisonment after they have served 15 years (Art. 57a of the German Penal Code). The responsible court must consider the gravity of the offenders' guilt and whether it is likely that they will lead a law-abiding life outside prison. If, after 15 years, the court is of the view that an offender has not yet served a sufficient term as a proportionate punishment for the original offense or if the indication is that an offender would not lead a crime-free life on release, it can temporarily refuse release. However, as subsequent jurisprudence has made clear, as time passes, the significance to be attributed to the gravity of the initial offense declines and the importance of the fundamental dignity-based right to eventual freedom increases (BVerfGE 1992).

In contrast, American courts and policymakers have been quite prepared to accept that there are tens of thousands of prisoners who will never be considered for release. This category includes the increasingly common sentence of life without parole (LWOP) as well as other sentences from which there is no realistic prospect for release. LWOP sentences have been adopted by all states except Alaska, whose version is a 99-year sentence. Despite the large decline in violent crime across the United States from 1992 to 2008, the number of people sentenced to LWOP more than tripled from 12,453 to 41,095 (Nellis and King 2009, 9, fig. 2). In 2016 an estimated 53,290 people were held in prison with no possibility of early release (Nellis 2017, 9).

There is a wisp of hope of change: the US Supreme Court has affirmed the unconstitutionality of LWOP sentences for juveniles both in nonhomicide cases (*Graham v. Florida* 2010) and in homicide cases if such sentences are mandatory (*Miller v. Alabama* 2012). The underlying principle, that such sentences are disproportionately severe for offenders whose moral judgment may not be fully formed and who could mend their ways in the future, could arguably apply to older offenders too. Nevertheless, in the United States LWOP continues to be used for large numbers of adults. In theory this is because of the seriousness of the committed crime or because offenders are so dangerous that their release should never be considered; but research has revealed that in 2013 there were 3,278 prisoners in the United States serving LWOP for nonviolent offenses (American Civil Liberties Union 2013).

The contrast with Europe as a whole is stark. With only a few relatively minor exceptions, in the old continent all prisoners are in principle regarded as worthy of consideration for release, as a matter of right. The vast majority of European countries have laws, similar to the German model, that require the routine consideration by a court of parole for *all* prisoners serving life sentences after a fixed period ranging from 10 to 30 years (van Zyl Smit 2010). This is true even of Russia, which has a minimum of 25 years (Art. 79 of the Penal Code of the Russian Federation) and the Hague-based International Criminal Court, which must consider parole even for convicted genocidaires after 25 years (Art. 110 of the Rome Statute of the International Criminal Court).

In the United Kingdom, which in many respects is the most draconian of western European criminal jurisdictions (Tonry 2004b), the matter is approached somewhat differently: a minimum period is set in each case for almost all prisoners serving sentences of life imprisonment. This period reflects the minimum term necessary to meet the requirements of retribution and deterrence. After that, the prisoner should be released on parole unless he or she continues to pose a risk to society. The ECtHR has ruled that this decision has to be made by a court-like body, and therefore, the relevant panel of the parole board is always chaired by a high court judge (*Stafford v. United Kingdom* 2002). The law in England and Wales, however, provides that sentencing courts may set a whole-life tariff in exceptional cases, with no prospect for parole, where the offense is serious enough to necessitate that penalty for purposes of retribution and deterrence. In such a case release is only possible on compassionate grounds at the discretion of the secretary of state for justice, and the secretary has declared that this will be interpreted as limited to someone who is about to die.

In practice there are very few prisoners serving whole-life sentences (without prospect of consideration for parole as a result of legislation or the judge's sentence) in Europe as a whole—probably fewer than 200 prisoners across the entire continent (van Zyl Smit 2013), a total that can only pale in comparison to the reported US figures. Yet even that stark comparison is not the end of the story. In recent years the European legal position has changed considerably.

The Council of Europe's 2003 *Recommendation on Conditional Release (Parole)* states that the law should make conditional release available to *all* sentenced prisoners, including those serving life terms. Considerable weight was lent to this recommendation by the CPT, which in two 2012 national reports formally declared that imprisoning someone without a prospect of release infringed the prohibition on inhuman and degrading treatment (European Committee for the Prevention of Torture and Inhuman or Degrading Treatment or Punishment 2012a, 26, 2012b, 32).

In 2013 a near unanimous decision of the 17 judges of the Grand Chamber of the ECtHR in *Vinter and others v. United Kingdom* put the issue beyond doubt. It held that it was inhuman and degrading, and thus contrary to Article 3 of the European Convention on Human Rights (ECHR), to imprison someone for life without reasonable prospect of release. Such a prospect, the Grand Chamber ruled, had to exist at the time of sentence. The Grand Chamber made it clear that compassionate release for the terminally ill could not be considered release at all if all it meant was that a prisoner could die at home or in a hospice rather than behind prison walls. Foremost in the analysis of the Grand Chamber was the need to recognize the human dignity of even the worst offenders. All prisoners had a right to a realistic hope that they would be able to become full members of society again if the balance of penological justifications shifted so that their further incarceration was not justified. On this principle the Grand Chamber in *Vinter* essentially adopted the same position as the German Constitutional Court (van Zyl Smit, Weatherby, and Creighton 2014).

On the procedures that are required to underpin this hope, the ECtHR has been less emphatic. It indicated in *Vinter* that its preferred solution would be a review by a court after 25 years but recognized that European states have a (limited) "margin of appreciation" in this regard. This became clear in May 2014, when the ECtHR considered the release procedures of Hungarian prisoners serving life sentences for which no date for release was set in law (*László Magyar v. Hungary* 2014). Under Hungarian law, all release decisions in such cases fell to the president. The court did not object directly to the president being the decision-maker but rather to the lack of clarity of the procedure to be followed. It held that this procedural uncertainty infringed Article 3 of the ECHR. Hungary was,

> [R]equired to put in place a reform, preferably by means of legislation, of the system of review of whole life sentences. The mechanism of such a review should guarantee the examination in every particular case of whether continued detention is justified on legitimate penological grounds and should enable whole life prisoners to foresee, with some degree of precision, what they must do to be considered for release and under what conditions. (*László Magyar v. Hungary*, para. 71)

In the light of this judgment it is probably only a matter of time before the ECtHR develops comprehensive procedural standards for the evaluation of the continued enforcement of all whole life sentences. It has even be argued that the principle established in *Vinter* means that all prisoners, including those with fixed-term sentences, have a right in international law to be considered for parole (partly dissenting opinion of Judge Pinto de Albuquerque in *Öcalan v. Turkey* 2014). Whether this radical development will be accepted by the ECtHR as a whole remains to be seen.

There has been some resistance at the national level. The British government responded with great hostility to the decision in *Vinter* (Pettigrew 2015). In early 2014 a specially constituted English Court of Appeal ruled that the Grand Chamber had misunderstood the scope of the powers of release of the secretary of state for justice, which, in its view, were sufficient to give prisoners serving whole life sentences a realistic prospect of release (*R v. McLoughlin and Newell* 2014). In 2017 this somewhat strained reinterpretation of English law was upheld by the Grand Chamber of the ECtHR in *Hutchison v. United Kingdom* (2017), which ruled that the judgment of the English Court of Appeal had eliminated the lack of clarity in UK domestic law on how whole life sentences should be reviewed. However, the Grand Chamber emphasized that the secretary of state for justice still has a duty to exercise her release powers in a way that is compatible with the ECHR, as interpreted in *Vinter* and subsequent Grand Chamber decisions, such as *Murray v. the Netherlands* (2016) that further clarified the procedural requirements for the release of life sentenced prisoners.

Other European Indeterminate Sentences

The ECtHR has been equally scrupulous about protecting the rights of sentenced prisoners subject to other forms of what it regards as indeterminate sentences, namely custodial security measures (which may take different names such as "secure prevention detention" or "preventive supervision"), imposed instead of, or in addition to, other prison sentences because these offenders are deemed to be dangerous and a continuing risk to society. According to SPACE I statistics for 2013 (Aebi and Delgrande 2014, table 5.2), a total of 15,916 persons were detained under such postconviction preventive detention measures in responding European countries.[22]

At this point, a definitional caveat is required. In the European context, the divide between civil and criminal sanctions is different from its American counterpart. In most European penal codes, legislative safety measures coexist with traditional punishments, although formally labeled as "civil" or, more usually, "administrative" security measures. This type of sanction, advocated by Enrico Ferri in Italy and Franz von Liszt in Germany, is the most notable legacy of the positivist school of criminology of the late nineteenth century. Unlike classicists, who supported retributive punishments based on the notions of free will and moral responsibility, positivists were mostly concerned with the extent to which offenders could represent a danger to society in the future (Bottoms 1977, 75). Although the classical school of thought eventually prevailed in the European penal codifications of the twentieth century, a mixed system considering both moral responsibility and dangerousness (Ancel 1958, 369) is still in place in many countries (the so-called double track or dualistic system), allowing the sequential imposition of traditional punishment and security measures for dangerous offenders (e.g., a determinate prison sentence followed by an indeterminate term of secure preventive detention) (Battaglini 1933, 287–88; Mannheim 1935, 520; Corrado 2013, 55–57).

One example of ECtHR intervention with regard to security measures arose from the treatment of English prisoners sentenced to imprisonment for public protection (IPP).[23] IPP is a fully indeterminate sentence in the European sense of having no maximum term (that is, carrying a maximum of life imprisonment) and is often coupled with a relatively short minimum period after which the prisoners may be released if they can persuade the parole board that they no longer pose a risk to society. The officially expressed intention was that these prisoners should be offered training courses, which would enable them to rehabilitate themselves and thus present a good case for release after they had served their minimum terms. In practice the UK government underestimated the number of offenders who would be given IPP, with the result that far too few treatment programs were available. Without attending such programs, IPP prisoners were unable to show that they were no longer dangerous. The UK government had therefore failed to provide these prisoners with any reasonable prospect of expeditious release after their minimum term had expired. In the case of *James, Wells and Lee v. United Kingdom* (2012) the ECtHR not only held, as British courts did too (*R. [on the application of Wells] v. Parole Board*, 2009), that the UK government had failed in its public law duties but ruled further that IPP prisoners were entitled to compensation for not having expeditiously received the necessary courses in time. In December 2014 the UK Supreme Court reversed its previous view and somewhat reluctantly followed the ECtHR in awarding small amounts of monetary compensation to IPP prisoners who had not been given adequate training courses before the expiry of their minimum periods. Such courses would have enabled them to strengthen the cases that they were not dangerous anymore, which they put before the parole board (*R [on the applications of Haney, Kaiyam, and Massey] v. The Secretary of State for Justice* 2014).

The ECtHR has also challenged the detention of offenders who continue to be regarded as dangerous *after* they have served their criminal sentences and are then placed on a second track of *preventive* detention—a form of total confinement defined as outside the criminal justice system. In *M v. Germany* (2009) the ECtHR held that such detention is a criminal sentence in all but name[24]: the confinement followed a criminal conviction and was not (at least in M's case) based on diagnosed mental health concerns. The ECtHR ruled that "second track" punishments of this kind were prohibited by both Article 7 of the ECHR, which outlaws retrospective increases of punishment, and Article 5, the European equivalent of habeas corpus, which protects individuals against wrongful detention.

These decisions, taken together with those on life imprisonment, show the ECtHR's determination to move beyond its reluctance to intervene in release decisions generally by developing a principled approach to the release of those subject to all forms of indeterminate sentencing in order to protect them against the arbitrary exercise of state power. Exactly what the decisions' impact will be in European states that have similar provisions for post-sentence preventive detention remains to be seen. The German response to the decision in *M* was complex. In the light of *M v. Germany*, the Federal Constitutional Court reversed its earlier judgment and agreed that the 1998 amendment of the penal code had been unconstitutional (BVerfGE 2011). However, it did not accept that post-sentence preventive detention (*Sicherungsverwahrung*) was a form of punishment and therefore subject to the German constitutional prohibition on retrospective punishments. Instead, it found that general prohibitions against changing the law to the disadvantage of a citizen could be found in other provisions of the Constitution. The Constitutional Court also held that preventive detention was not sufficiently differentiated from imprisonment. The German legislature duly amended the penal code to make post-sentence preventive detention harder to impose without a full enquiry and to ensure that persons subject to it are held in institutions that are significantly differentiated from prisons. Thus, Germany has made significant changes to its law and practice as a direct result of the judgment of the ECtHR in *M*. However, it has contrived to keep a dual track system in place by amending German law to ensure that the second track meets all the due process protections of the criminal law while remaining conceptually outside of it (Drenkhahn, Morgenstern, and van Zyl Smit 2012). Whether this new regime will withstand a challenge in the ECtHR remains to be decided, as is the wider impact of *M v. Germany* on other European systems of indeterminate detention. What is significant is that the ECtHR has signaled stiff opposition to the development of such second track detention. This contrasts with the United States where 21 states and the federal government have passed civil commitment statutes providing for the further confinement of sex offenders after the completion of their prison sentences.[25]

Parole for Sentences with Fixed Maximum Terms

Although it has been noted that the ECtHR has not been as forthcoming as it could have been in giving overall principled guidance about how conditional release should be approached for sentences with fixed maximum terms (see the previous discussion on definitional issues in the second part of this chapter), such principles have been explored in several key national jurisdictions. This can be illustrated by a further German example, a lesser known case decided by the Federal Constitutional Court (BVerfGE 2009). The offender in this case had served two-thirds of his fixed-term sentence. Article 57 of the German Penal Code provides that at this point in their sentences offenders have a right to have their release considered by the chamber of the criminal court that has specialist responsibility for supervising the enforcement of sentences. The chamber must order their conditional release if they consent and if the "the release is appropriate considering public security interests."

In this case the relevant chamber of the criminal court had declined to release the offender as it held that his involvement in organized drug dealing as part of a Russian mafia (the offense for which he was convicted) precluded his release for public security reasons. The Federal Constitutional Court ordered the lower court to reconsider. It did so on the basis that the chamber had accepted uncritically the views of the prison authorities and had thus undermined its duty to come to an independent conclusion by failing to pay adequate attention to all the evidence that it could have considered. In particular, the chamber should have heard the evidence of a prison psychologist who had reported positively on the offender. In this way the court required clinical assessment of future behavior to be included in the decision-making process or, at least, that such evidence be weighed when it is available.

The Federal Constitutional Court stressed the importance of the prisoner's liberty interest even in cases where conditional release was being considered for the first time. In the words of the court,

> The freedom of the person may only be restricted on exceptionally weighty grounds and if strict formal conditions are met. From these are derived the minimum requirements for the penal law in respect of the reliable establishment of the truth, which have to be observed *not only in the initial trial but also in decisions that relate to the process of implementation of the sentence*. They set, amongst others, standards for the establishment of the facts and thus for a sufficient factual basis for judicial decisions. For it is a necessary condition for a procedure that meets the requirements of the *Rechtsstaat* that decisions that relate to the deprivation of human freedom be based on sufficient judicial fact finding and in practice have satisfactory bases that reflect the importance of the guarantee of [individual] freedom. (para. 26, emphasis added)

The contrast with US constitutional precedent is stark: in parole release proceedings American law does not recognize any liberty interest that would restrict the discretion of the parole authority, unless a given state has created it in the form, for example, of a presumptive right to parole release (*Morrissey* 1972; *Swarthout* 2011). Furthermore, the German judgment emphasized the continuity of procedural safeguards between the adjudication and sentencing phases, on the one hand, and the later release proceedings, on the other hand. This idea is shared by most European countries, as demonstrated by their using courts to make these decisions or, in the case of the United Kingdom, by high-level judicial intervention by the Supreme Court to strengthen parole board procedures in order to ensure that the board operates as a court-like body (*Osborn v. The Parole Board* 2013). It is very different from the US model where, after the adjudication of guilt, sentencing is governed by "second-class" procedures and parole release decision-making by "third-class" procedures (Reitz 2015).

The German Federal Constitutional Court also considered how the security interests of the public should be evaluated. In this regard the court made it clear that a prognostic evaluation of all relevant factors[26] was required, but that a release decision could *not* necessitate any certainty that the offender would not commit further offenses in the future. The court emphasized that the prison-release process must include the taking of an acceptable residual risk (para. 28). This decision illustrates a recognition of the tension between prisoners' liberty interests and the goal of public protection that is largely absent in the American law of parole release. While a German court may regard the "residual risk" to society as so severe that it is unacceptable and decline to release someone, the emphasis is on proportionality. Warnings on the need to limit consideration of risk abound in the German and European literature (Kunz 2004, 35).

The 2010 Council of Europe rules on probation, reflecting current best practices across the continent, make explicit that the assessment of the actual readiness for release must be made by focusing on the individual prisoner and not on any kind of actuarial generalization. Furthermore, they stress the importance of a direct and active involvement of the potential parolee in the release decision-making process. Rule 66 requires that an assessment of offenders be made "involving a systematic and thorough consideration of the individual case, including risks, positive factors and needs, the interventions required to address those needs and the offenders' responsiveness to the interventions." Most importantly, rule 67 maintains that "[o]ffenders should not only be made aware of the process and outcomes of the assessment, but they should also be enabled to make an active contribution to it, including by giving due weight to their views and personal aspirations, as well as their own personal strengths and responsibility for avoiding further offending." Finally, according to rule 68, "[t]he offenders shall be made aware of the process and outcomes of the assessment."

Contrary to the European approach, the current American position elevates risk of recidivism to primary stature in prison-release policy, with few compunctions and little quality control. In the United States, actuarial risk prediction, rather than clinical prediction, which is more prominent in Europe, now plays a central role in most parole authorities' decision-making. With the retreat of the "rehabilitative ideal" in favor of deterrence and incapacitation, the focus has moved decisively from reintegration to public safety. Only the best of the actuarial instruments used by American parole boards have been statistically validated on the state's offender populations, and the worst instruments have no credible claim of reliability whatsoever (Monahan and Skeem 2014, 162). The procedural interests of prisoners are given so little weight that they are afforded no opportunity to review or challenge the decisive risk scores that have been calculated in their cases—nor may they raise questions about the validity of the instrument (Rhine, Petersilia, and Reitz 2017, 299–305).

Although risk-prediction tools have been available since the 1920s, they were not widely adopted by American parole boards until the 1970s, with the advent of parole guidelines. In the mid-1970s only two states resorted to prediction tools. By 2004, 28 states relied on risk scale tools to guide their parole decisions—23 of those with an active parole system for new convictions (Harcourt 2007, 41). The majority of US indeterminate jurisdictions currently require parole boards to use these instruments to guide release decisions and to set conditions of supervision. This strongly suggests that "incapacitation policy predominates over any inquiry into prisoners' progress toward rehabilitation" (Reitz 2012, 278).[27] The two most common models of risk assessment are the so-called matrix model and the sequential model (Harcourt 2007, 84; Gottfredson et al. 1978). Under the matrix model, "parole authorities first use a risk-assessment instrument—the Salient Factor Score, for instance—and then use a grid based on the severity of the sentence and the risk assessment to determine length of sentence prior to parole." Under the sequential model, "parole authorities fill in a table with scores that relate to different factors for parole and tally the score to determine whether the inmate is likely or unlikely to be paroled" (Harcourt 2007, 85–86).

Risk instruments represent the core of parole guidelines, usually weighing static and dynamic factors associated with the offender's record. Through actuarial techniques, in the words of one commentator, the prisoner's individual identity is "fragmented and remade into a combination of variables associated with different categories and level of risk" (Robert 2005, 11).

Recently the US attorney general and a number of scholars have raised high-profile objections to risk-assessment tools as currently used. Critics have stressed the capacity of such tools to undermine the principle of equal justice that should inform the criminal justice system for they "have a disparate and adverse impact on offenders from poor communities already struggling with many social ills" (US Department of Justice 2014, 7). Resorting to socioeconomic factors such as employment, education, marital status, and residential stability would constitute a proxy for ethnicity and race, thus further worsening the distinctive racial disproportionality in American criminal justice decision-making (Tonry 2014, 173). Some have also expressed doubts about the constitutionality of current methods of risk assessment when they incorporate variables that indirectly implicate gender, race, or socioeconomic status as these refer to groups rather than individuals (Starr 2014a, 2014b). Finally, the use of risk-assessment instruments is perceived as unfair by prisoners applying for parole, who either are unaware of their existence or do not understand how they actually work. This is not surprising, since many such instruments are proprietary corporate products that cannot be accessed or challenged (Starr 2015, 871).

Decision-Making Processes for the Granting and Revocation of Parole

At first glance it seems hard to broadly characterize or identify trends in the procedural requirements that apply to parole decision-making in Europe. As we have noted, the ECtHR, like the US Supreme Court, gives relatively little guidance in this regard. Nevertheless, European procedures in most nation states reflect at their core a greater commitment than their American counterparts to *Rechtsstaatlichkeit*, a commitment not only to minimum requirements of due process but also to a procedural framework that can embody substantive underlying values such as human dignity, social reintegration, and the ability to change. Also, in contrast to the United States, European authorities tend to view all of the key decision points concerning parole release, supervision, and revocation as comparable in substance and consequence and as meriting equivalent procedural regularity. Thus, for example, there is no sharp differential in the procedural care taken in release and revocation decisions; both processes in Europe are often governed by identical standards.

The *Recommendation on Conditional Release (Parole)* of the Council of Europe (2003) provides a means for contrasting American and European approaches. In order to achieve pan-European applicability, the recommendation outlines two ways of granting conditional release, which it refers to as the mandatory and discretionary release systems, allowing for both automatic and considered conditional release procedures at the national level (paras. 16–24). There is some overlap between the two release systems. In both instances the period before release or consideration of release (respectively) must be set by law (paras. 22–23). Moreover, the recommendation sets procedural safeguards that apply to "decisions on granting, postponing or revoking conditional release, as well as on imposing or modifying conditions and measures attached to it" (para. 32). All such decisions should be taken by authorities established by law in accordance with the following procedures:

a. convicted persons should have the right to be heard in person and to be assisted according to the law;[28]
b. the decision-making authority should give careful consideration to any elements, including statements, presented by convicted persons in support of their case;
c. convicted persons should have adequate access to their file;
d. decisions should state the underlying reasons and be notified in writing. (para. 32)

In addition, under the procedures set out in the European *Rules on Community Sanctions and Measures* (Council of Europe 1992, para. 35), convicted persons should be able to make a complaint to "a higher independent and impartial decision-making authority established by law" against the substance of any such decision, as well as against a failure to respect these procedural guarantees (para. 33). As a result, the matter must also be referred to a judicial authority whenever the offender wishes to complain "that a restriction of his liberty or the decision is unlawful" (rule 15).

Around Europe, various arrangements are in place to ensure judicial supervision of decision-making regarding parole, thereby ensuring procedural fairness, while pursuing the principal post-sentence aims of rehabilitation and reintegration. These tend to position specialist judges, with expert knowledge about the implementation of both custodial and noncustodial sentences, in the conditional release decision-making process. Examples include the German *Strafvollstreckungskammern*—literally chambers (of the criminal courts) for the implementation of punishment (Dünkel 2010); the offices of the *juge de l'application des peines* and for prisoners serving imprisonment of more than three years, also the *tribunal de l'application des peines* in France (Reuflet 2010); the *tribunale di sorveglianza* in Italy (Gualazzi and Mancuso

2010); and the *juez de vigilancia* in Spain (De la Cuesta and Cordero 2011). Although there are important differences among these institutions, they each task a member or members of the judiciary, often sitting as a specialist chamber of a court, with safeguarding prisoners' rights and ensuring that prison conditions meet minimum standards. Such specialist chambers simultaneously decide on the early conditional release of prisoners as well as the potential revocation of such release.

These arrangements are not immune to criticism. While national critics recognize the value of the expertise of such specialist courts, they sometimes doubt their independence. Judicial independence can be threatened by structural factors or by more sociological processes by which judges arguably become "captured" by the priorities of the penal administrators upon whom they may depend for information and access (Dünkel 1997). In France, for example, such judges cannot give binding instructions to the authorities with respect to treatment in prison, which would facilitate eventual conditional release (Herzog-Evans 1997).

These specialist benches do, however, provide a way of regulating parole decision-making that carries with it the legitimacy attached to the judicial system as a whole: the judges have lifetime tenure and are in a relatively good position to resist public pressures to be more restrictive in times of moral panic about particular offenses (Garoupa and Ginsburg 2012). They are certainly better positioned to resist political pressure than their theoretical American counterparts—that is, parole board members—who are usually appointed for limited terms by state governors and have to be responsive to their political agendas and priorities (Rhine, Petersilia, and Reitz 2017).

Broadly speaking, European judicial bodies that make parole decisions meet the Council of Europe's requirements. However, there are mixed structures in some European countries that only meet this ideal in part: in England and Wales (Padfield 2010) the parole board is in many ways a court-like body (particularly when deciding on release in cases of life imprisonment, where the parole panel is always presided over by a high court judge), but its work until very recently has largely been restricted to deciding on the release of prisoners serving life and other indeterminate sentences. For the majority of offenders who are serving fixed-maximum sentences, no decision on release is required, as such prisoners are entitled to release on parole after having served half their sentences. Even this rule of automatic release in England and Wales is subject to an exception because prison authorities and not the parole board have the power to order release before the mandatory release point, without the due process guarantees expected by the 2003 recommendation when an element of discretion is involved.

Belgium too has a mixed system, for, although its legislation provides for prisoners' release to be considered by a sentencing implementation court, this regime currently only applies to prisoners serving more than three years, who are the only prisoners released conditionally. Those serving less than three years may be released early by the head of a prison and enjoy no due process guarantees. In practice, however, heads of prisons release prisoners sentenced to less than six months automatically and those sentenced to under a year after three months (Snacken, Beyens, and Beernaert 2010).

More fundamental exceptions to what we have described as the core model of the release process exist too. In Scandinavian countries, most decisions on conditional release are made by prison authorities. However, there is a strong presumption in favor of conditional release after a fixed portion of the sentence has been served, coupled with a heavy focus on social reintegration throughout the implementation of sentence, which generally means there are fewer issues of dispute. Even in Scandinavia, however, there appears to be a tendency to refer the most difficult cases to specialist courts, as has happened with the release of prisoners sentenced to life imprisonment in Sweden since 2006 (Schartmueller 2014) and as is also the case with the release of a limited number of dangerous offenders in Finland (Lappi-Seppälä 2010).

Finally, departure from the core model also exists where the procedure is formally judicial but lacks a distinction between the goals and objectives of parole and those of a criminal sentencing. In many post-Soviet countries, decisions on granting parole are taken by "ordinary" criminal courts, which have no general responsibility for the implementation of the sentence. In these countries the focus is more narrowly on whether there are grounds for reducing the sentence. Typically, cases are heard only when the prison administration, or in some instances the prisoner, applies to the court to have the conditional release considered. Supervision is conducted by the police. Although the outward form of judicially controlled conditional release exists, the frequency of parole being granted and the mode of supervision bear little resemblance to a western European parole system. This is only gradually beginning to change as reforms are implemented, often driven by the Council of Europe and the European Union and following the standards of the Council of Europe rules and recommendations (Seddon 2014).

These exceptions should not blind us to the core European model of judicially led parole decision-making undertaken in multidisciplinary sentence implementation courts led by skilled professional career judges, following the basic tenets of due process.

In the United States, in contrast, the overall framework as well as the rules of procedure regarding parole are far less strict. First of all, the decision-maker for release and revocation decisions, the parole board, is in most states made up of political appointees with no particular qualifications. Recent surveys report that in 43 out of 49 states retaining some form of parole in the United States, members of the paroling authority are appointed by the governor. Moreover, for the most part no particular expertise in the field of criminal justice, still less in specifics of implementation, is required. Indeed, only 15 states mandate members to have some kind of previous experience with the criminal justice system or related social and/or supervision services (Paparozzi and Caplan 2009, 411–15; Ruhland et al. 2016, 17–21).

Superficially, the issue of insulation from politics might appear more striking with regard to America's elected prosecutors (Ellis 2012) and judges (Swisher 2010) than for paroling authorities. Nevertheless, although members of parole boards do not directly run for office, they are usually chosen by the highest elected official in the executive branch and can be dismissed as easily as they were appointed. The requirements for removing parole board members vary from state to state, but while only few allow removal for cause only, many states "offer very little protection for parole board members and remind them that they serve at the pleasure of the Governor. This threat of removal introduces a political element into the parole process" (Bing 2012, 876). Indeed, parole board members are vulnerable to the loss of their livelihoods on every day of their tenure of service, whereas elected prosecutors and judges face ouster only at intervals of several years, depending on the length of their election cycles. Arguably, parole board members live with a degree of political insecurity more acute than other responsible officials in American criminal justice systems.

Small and politically vulnerable agencies, with vast systemwide power over the lengths of prison terms, can single-handedly effect large changes in a jurisdiction's overall prison policy. In the United States there is evidence that since the 1980s the institution of parole within indeterminate sentencing systems has not contributed to reducing incarceration rates. On the contrary, as a group, American indeterminate jurisdictions were the primary sites of the nation's massive prison expansion from 1980 through the first decade of the new century (Reitz 2012, 286–87). While until the mid-1970s discretionary parole release had served as "a back-end safety valve for the correctional system" (Clear and Frost 2013, 78), the policy shift toward increased punitiveness and risk aversion radically changed the functioning of existing institutions. As reported by the American Law Institute (2011, 147–48),

> Nine of 10 states with the highest standing imprisonment rates at year-end 2009 were indeterminate jurisdictions. The 10th state, Arizona,

> experienced most of its prison expansion prior to 1994, when it too was an indeterminate state. The five states with the largest per capita prison rates in 2009 included carceral powerhouses Louisiana, Texas, Oklahoma, and Georgia—all indeterminate jurisdictions. . . . If we ask which states have had the most per capita prison growth over time, the track record of indeterminate states is equally un-lenient. From 1980 to 2009, 9 of the "top" 10 prison-growth states were indeterminate jurisdictions.

Thus, one critical, but little recognized, source of American exceptionalism in prison population might well be the absence of effective, politically insulated back-end decision-makers able to release prisoners in a way that helps control prison population and prevents overcrowding.

As to procedural safeguards, American courts have traditionally afforded parole "only the most anemic procedural due process protections," as they "view parole decisions as 'equity-type' determinations" involving "predictive judgment[s]" about "what is best both for the individual inmate and for the community" (Bierschbach 2012, 1752). Often, prisoners have no meaningful opportunity to put their cases before the parole board, and decisions are not deliberative and are seldom adequately explained. Furthermore, there are no legally binding decision rules that have to be followed. One additionally important contrasting feature is the lack of enforceable decision rules and any significant possibility of appeal. In many systems, there is almost no right to participate in the first place, and when risk-assessment tools are used prisoners have very little real opportunity to challenge the outcomes. Reitz (2012, 283) speaks in this regard of "procedural shabbiness."

Ultimately, American parole is an executive, rather than a judicial, function of government, with profound effects on the personality and behavior of releasing agencies. The executive character of parole is especially pronounced in a handful of states. While a majority of states' parole boards have the final authority to authorize release, in some systems the governor retains the last word even after a positive recommendation has been issued by the parole board. In this way, parole release may become even more susceptible to policy choices that reflect a detachment from and lack of sympathy for offenders convicted of serious crimes: in Maryland, California, and Oklahoma, for example, the governor can overrule parole boards' decisions to free prisoners serving life sentences (Caplan and Kinnery 2010, 35). Between 1999 and 2011, California governors reversed or requested reviews for over 75 percent of the board's decisions to grant parole to lifers (Ghandnoosh 2017, 8).

The institutional shape and methods of prison release agencies have implications for their perceived legitimacy. The European insistence on procedural rectitude seems to have had a positive impact on the acceptance of parole decision-making. In Europe there are few general calls for "abolition" of parole as early release, although some clamor for limiting its scope in high-profile crimes against the person.

A good example is what happened in Belgium in the aftermath of the infamous Dutroux case. After being found guilty and sentenced for abducting and raping five young girls, in 1992 Marc Dutroux was released from prison by the Ministry of Justice (then in charge of release decisions) after serving half of his sentence. While under supervision, he abducted, raped, and eventually killed other teenage girls. After the discovery of these crimes in 1996, he was tried and sentenced to life imprisonment. The Dutroux case provoked a huge public outcry, which resulted in an overall institutional reform of the Belgian parole system with the main goal of enhancing public protection and reinforcing its transparency and legitimacy. The decision-making in such cases was first transferred to a specialist court for the implementation for sentences. Moreover, stricter criteria for granting release were introduced as well as conditions of supervision predominantly revolving around surveillance rather than reintegration (Snacken and Tournel 2014, 67; Bauwens, Robert, and Snacken 2012). In 2013, after serving 16 years, Dutroux applied for conditional release; but his request was denied. In general, however, European legislatures and supranational bodies have concentrated on increasing the rate of release on parole and focused on developing appropriate procedures for achieving it.

In contrast, the dire state of parole decision-making in the United States has led many influential voices to abandon discretionary release reform. Jeremy Travis, a prominent scholar of prisoner re-entry after release, has called for "an end to parole [release and supervision] as we know it" (2002, 1), mostly because of political and institutional realities. He has proposed abrogation of the release discretion of paroling agencies and a new approach to post-release supervision, recommending innovative incentives for early release and limited supervision conditions that would be set based on each prisoner's needs and risks (Travis 2005). Travis is far from being the only proponent of abolition of parole release discretion: other prominent scholars (Reitz 2004) as well as the American Bar Association (1994) and the American Law Institute's revised Model Penal Code sentencing provisions (2011) have called for the elimination of parole release authority in all American jurisdictions, while retaining post-release supervision that is reprioritized to focus on the successful reintegration of ex-offenders (see also American Law Institute 2014). Even those who favor the retention of discretionary release in American systems normally concede that a radical "reinvention" of the substance and procedures of release decisions is necessary (Petersilia 2003, 171; Chanenson 2005, 455; Burke and Tonry 2006).

Finally, as to the grounds for release decisions, in most US paroling systems, the parole board may take into account different factors—explicitly articulated in parole release guidelines in few states only—ranging from the severity of the current offense, the offender's criminal history, conduct in the institution while imprisoned, and risk assessment to the more amorphous question of whether the prisoner has been successfully rehabilitated. The seriousness of the current offense and the offender's criminal career tend to represent the most salient factors of the release decision-making process that seems to be largely characterized by risk aversion (Rhine 2012, 634–35; Cullen and Gilbert 2013, 138–39).

In contrast, in most European jurisdictions, where a strong presumption in favor of release at the initial parole eligibility is present, the current offense and criminal history, although certainly considered, are not at center stage in the decision-making of the sentence implementation court. Put differently, release decisions tend to be less backward and more forward-looking. Accordingly, they are mostly based on the evaluation of the prisoner's propensity to change and readiness for re-entry assessed at the time of application for release, taking into account factors such as good conduct in prison, reduced criminogenic needs, and participation in programs allowing the inmate to acquire skills and work experience. In addition, the satisfaction of certain obligations set out in law (primarily restitution for victims) is required (see, e.g., Cid and Tébar 2010, 370; Gualazzi and Mancuso 2010, 282–83).

The Approach to Supervision

The previously highlighted difference in revocation rates suggests a divergence in the approach to parole supervision in the United States and in Europe. While in Europe it is mostly structured as a rehabilitative tool aimed at facilitating the re-entry and resettlement of the offender in the community, in the United States parole tilts more heavily toward a punitive and managerial intervention, weakening or supplanting a commitment to the ideal of reintegrating parolees into society.

In comparison to Europe two distinctive characteristics of US parole are (1) longer terms of supervision and (2) more, and more intrusive, conditions of supervision. The latter add greatly to the burden placed on American parolees. Such impediments do not exist to the same extent in any European country, where conditions imposed on released offenders are first and foremost aimed at helping them to conduct law-abiding lives and to abstain from any illegal conduct.

Among others, conditions imposed in the context of US early-release schemes include extraordinary financial obligations placed on ex-offenders who are already struggling to resettle in the community. A recent report found that the 15 states with the highest prison populations in the country impose the payment of monthly supervision fees as a requirement for release, with no waiver for indigent offenders (Bannon, Nagrecha, and Diller 2010, 21). The ability to pay is often a precondition to be met in order to be released, and failure to make regular payments can constitute a violation leading to the revocation of parole. In addition, it is not unusual for profit-oriented private firms to become involved as contractors to provide supervision services (Logan and Wright 2014, 1193).

Very little of this can be encountered in Europe where conditional measures generally do not involve the imposition of financial burdens on offenders as part of a state-implemented penal sanction. In other words, besides the payment of fines and restitution to the victims, European offenders generally do not have to pay to be punished. Moreover, supervision services are usually provided by state-funded agencies. The involvement of private, paid-by-outcome firms and nonprofit organizations which receive referrals directly from the criminal justice system is limited for the most part to low-risk offenders (Robinson and Svensson 2013; Annison, Burke, and Senior 2014; Herzog-Evans 2014).

In the United States other conditions of supervision in the community can be very restrictive: for example, refraining from committing new crimes, reporting requirements, travel and residency restrictions, prohibition of association with known felons, curfews, prohibitions on the consumption of drugs and/or alcohol, and treatment (Rhine 2012, 637). In addition, a vast array of other burdens can be—and oftentimes are—imposed on parolees. As explained by Cecelia Klingele, this is possible Because "[l]aws governing the imposition of release conditions are broadly permissive . . . on the grounds that any conceivable term of release will be less punitive than the authorized term of confinement" (2013, 1032). In other words, given that parole is seen and conceived as an instrument of lenity and a milder mode of implementation of the sentence originally imposed as compared to serving time in prison, courts and correction agencies are granted a wide discretion in setting conditions of release. Regardless of how demanding they are, it becomes hard for parolees to challenge onerous and intrusive conditions, which may even infringe their constitutional rights: think, for example, of the tension between a condition allowing the parole officer to visit the parolee at any time at home or elsewhere and Fourth Amendment rights (Jacobi, Richardson, and Barr 2014, 897–98). This is because "courts typically treat such rights as 'diminished' during the period of supervision" (Klingele 2013, 1032), thus adopting a highly deferential approach with regard to those subjects setting the conditions of release.

From a longer view, parole supervision in the United States has experienced at least three radical shifts of purpose since its inception. Jonathan Simon (1993) has provided a useful conceptual guide to these shifts: parole was originally created as a technique for enabling people who met certain eligibility criteria to become "normal" members of society again. After the Great Depression, the original idea of disciplining (in the Foucauldian sense) the parolee by means of work was superseded by the belief that the goal of a durable re-entry could be better achieved through the resort to clinical expertise provided by the parole supervisor. The next radical shift in the nature of parole supervision from the 1970s onward was from the "normalization" of offenders (whether through work or treatment) to their management. In this regard parole has become a key part of the actuarial "new penology," which is aimed less at transforming people and returning them to society and more at regulating the risks posed by offenders to public safety and order (Feeley and Simon 1992).

The emphasis in American parole supervision has shifted over time from a rehabilitative to a law enforcement paradigm, although considerable attention is also being paid in some jurisdictions to re-entry and reintegration. American parole is experiencing a degree of "mission confusion," aggravated by the lack of a considered choice of parole conditions based on the careful assessment of individual cases, because of the over-reliance to standardized risk-assessment tools (Jannetta and Burrell 2014, 1312–13). While on paper US parole is still comprehensive in its scope, combining elements of both control and treatment (von Hirsch and Hanrahan 1979, 59–60), currently a preference for a punitive approach to the supervision of parolees can be identified, evidenced by the dramatic increase in revocations of parole over time, especially for technical violations (Lin 2010; Jacobson 2006, 140–49). Recent declines in parole revocation rates are not sufficient to alter the broader picture significantly. This reflects the widely held view that "offenders must be supervised closely and punished with incarceration" in case of misbehavior since "rehabilitation does not work" and there is no viable alternative (Kremling 2012, 95). As Travis (2007, 631) observed, "America now sends more people to prison for parole violations than were sent to prison in 1980 for any reason, including commitments on new convictions and parole violation."

Joan Petersilia (2003, 11) has vividly underlined the cultural implications of the shift to managerial parole in the United States:

> Parole departments in most large urban areas have developed a prevailing culture that emphasizes surveillance over services. Parole officers believe that their caseloads now contain more dangerous offenders, and they are now authorized to carry weapons in three-fourths of the states. Parole officer training often provides minimal training on casework practices and services referrals, but numerous classes on arrests, searches, and other topics stressing law enforcement. Such training increasingly reinforces the image of parole officers as police officers rather than social workers.

In the United States parole officers have been transformed from social workers, "who helped offenders find jobs or get drug treatment," to law-enforcement agents, "who are more concerned with surveillance, from electronic monitoring and curfews to drug tests" (Butterfield 1999, 11). The law enforcement model is endemic in the administration of parole, and it is particularly prominent in intensive supervision parole, a program that supervises parolees who are most likely to return to prison. The program requires a minimum of one contact per week and a more intense level of parole supervision than what other lower-risk parolees receive (Petersilia and Turner 1993; National Research Council 2008). While on paper intense supervision restricts free time and helps foster a structured environment, in practice "reintegration rarely flourishes in this type of environment" since it promotes continued institutionalization (Binnall 2007, 546). In the language of Michel Foucault, parole in the United States currently is more of a "carceral scheme" than a measure aimed at helping former inmates "resettle" as productive and law-abiding citizens in a free society. In so doing parole continues the penitentiary technique of surveillance and discipline outside prisons.

In Europe, in contrast, continuing efforts are being made to humanize the process of parole supervision, which is viewed as a transitional period aimed at facilitating a successful and enduring re-entry to the community of the offender. This is seen most clearly in the 2010 Council of Europe rules on probation, which were explicitly designed to complement the 2003 *Recommendation on Conditional Release (Parole)*. One of the drafters of the new rules has explained that they should be understood as a deliberate ethical constraint on a tendency for parole supervision to be driven primarily by concerns with punishment and public safety (Canton 2010). The rules emphasize, as their first principle, that they "aim to reduce reoffending by establishing positive relationships with offenders in order to supervise (including control where necessary), guide and assist them and to promote their successful social inclusion." They continue to set out detailed guidance to practitioners on how this ideal should be achieved.

Even in England and Wales, where risk avoidance has been emphasized most strongly, empirical data suggest that among practitioners there is a continued commitment to ideals about the possibility and value of individual change and development of persons subject to supervision in the community (Deering 2011). In Europe it is argued consistently, and with some considerable practical effect, that parole should be a means of enhancing the human dignity of sentenced offenders by enabling them to become full members of society and by giving them a legally enforceable right to the means to do so. Fergus McNeill (2013, 181) concluded that in Europe "an essentially humanitarian ethos" in community supervision practices (probation and post-release supervision) is probably "an important moderator of more punitive and exclusionary policy discourses."

General Conclusions, Recent Trends, and the Possibilities for Reform

Our general conclusion is that there are fundamental differences between approaches to parole in the United States and in Europe. We come to this conclusion notwithstanding some weaknesses in the available statistical evidence, the difficulties in comparing institutions that are not conceptually identical, and the apparent similarities in law and practice that we have identified. From a European perspective, the contemporary American approach is exceptional in failing to recognize the right of all offenders to be provided with a realistic opportunity to be reintegrated into society as full members with their human dignity intact.

This difference is illustrated by the continuing acceptance within the United States of LWOP sentences, which have the effect of permanently excluding many thousands of people from American society without any reasonable hope of release. The difference is also apparent in the greater weight that is attached to risk management and surveillance than to concerns about the human dignity of offenders in making release decisions in the United States. Other significant differences are to be found in the lesser commitment to due process in parole decision-making, as opposed to the European ideal, and in the approach to the management of parolees adopted by the supervising officials.

US parole practices have been the product, at the back end of the sentencing process, of the unprecedented popular punitiveness that, with the critical support of public opinion (Tonry 2004a, 11), has characterized American punishment policies from the mid-1970s onward. The rise of the use of victim impact statements at parole hearings, an example of what has been defined as "punitive victim rights," is telling. Currently, in many US jurisdictions, victims have a direct influence on whether parole is granted, and their input is considered very important to the parole board's decision-making process (Roberts 2009; Caplan 2012). Over the same period since the 1970s, the European commitment to the values of proportionality and dignity in sentencing matters, including parole decision-making, has not been substantially undermined. Emotional input from victims, where admitted at all, is largely discounted. This is not only due to the deep-seated belief that victims rarely possess information relevant to parole decision-making (BBC News 2014). European systems, while generally recognizing significant rights to victims in terms of participation in the criminal trial, protection, compensation, and restoration (Joutsen 1994; Kerner 2013), at the same time tend to resist populist trends toward granting victims a more active and central role at sentencing and in the sentence implementation phase (Tonry 2010).

According to Tonry (2013, 148, 150–51), after the end of the "tough on crime" era, the United States is currently experiencing a phase of "equilibrium" with regard to sentencing reforms and practices. In other words, in the current historical phase, law and policy would be inherently informed by a marked ambivalence as severity, compassion, and reintegration coexist within a picture in which "[n]o general theoretical logic is discernible in the crazy quilt of diverging policies." In this scenario it is hard to predict the future of parole in the United States. Will policymakers shift toward release mechanisms informed by the values of due process and long-term reintegration in the community or, rather, will they go even further toward the values of privatization, managerialism, and actuarial justice, embracing models like the "postconviction bail" through which prisoners can secure early release (Maruna, Dabney, and Topalli 2012) only on new, often privately enforced, conditions?

We were asked not only to consider American exceptionalism in respect of parole but also to suggest prescriptions for the future. Given that a key flaw in the American approach to parole lies in its failure to systematically address the underlying problems faced by parolees (Lynch 2000), it seems that thinking about how this could be achieved in practice would be a good place to start. However, in making this suggestion, we are alive to the fact that the United States and Europe differ on far more than just the arrangement of their penal systems. These underlying differences preclude a straightforward transplant of European systems, which have evolved in social, economic, political, cultural, and other conditions that are qualitatively distinct from the American experience (Tonry 2009; Nelken 2009, 293–94). It makes more sense in our view to develop existing American initiatives that have the potential to address at least some of the shortcomings we have noted.

Recent North American empirical studies have shown how new and more refined tools for implementing parole, such as specific forms of community partnerships, could be effective if well-implemented (Hipp, Turner, and Petersilia 2010; Petersilia 2011b). Furthermore, there is some evidence of a recent trend toward more room for judicial or parole board discretion, especially in the implementation of sentences for drug crimes. Several states are moving toward the bipartisan enactment of "smart on crime" laws aimed at reducing prison overcrowding, while also cutting the costs of keeping inmates incarcerated (Fairfax 2011; Gingrich and Nolan 2011; US Department of Justice 2013). More generally, there is consistent nationwide evidence of how parole in the narrow sense of conditional release before the end of a sentence is being reconsidered as a major tool to address prison overcrowding in an era of budget crisis. As noted by Ryan King,

> Between 2004 and 2006, at least twenty-two states enacted legislative reforms to their sentencing policies or adopted reforms affecting probation and parole revocation procedures. These developments were driven by a number of factors, including budget crises at the state level, the development and expansion of a range of programs offering alternatives to incarceration, and the falling crime rate. (King 2007, 124)

The legacy of the economic crisis is causing many US states to face difficult budget choices. Expanding parole eligibility has been proposed as a viable way to reduce spending by lowering prison populations, along with the adoption of early release programs, such as "earned time" or "good time," which are not regarded as "parole" (Klingele 2012; Eaglin 2013, 203–206). States have been strongly incentivized to refine risk-assessment instruments so that they can be used to make "evidence-based" decisions on how to expand the number of people released on parole without endangering the safety of the general public. From 2007 to 2012, 31 states have managed to cut their imprisonment rates, 14 of them by double-digit percentages (Pew Charitable Trusts 2014). Texas, traditionally considered as a law-and-order state, provides a good example of this trend: it managed to cut its imprisonment rate by 7 percent, having allegedly discovered how to "shrink the prison population without threatening public safety" (*New York Times* 2013). Major steps have been the investment in treatment and diversion programs as well as changing the way the parole board assesses risk.

In California, a state that is under court order to reduce its prison population and to maintain it below certain levels, post-release community supervision (PRCS) was established in 2011 by the Public Safety Realignment Act (AB 109) as a distinct form of county supervision replacing supervision by the state parole system for low-level offenders——people released from state prison who were serving a prison term for a nonviolent, non-serious non-sex felony, regardless of prior convictions (Lofstrom and Raphael 2016, 251; Petersilia 2014, 810–11, 815). Similarly, there are reports that the governor of California is now routinely approving recommendations from the parole board that prisoners sentenced to life with parole be released, while in the past his predecessors routinely declined to support such recommendations (Levin 2014; Ghandnoosh 2017, 16).

It is important to stress, however, that the language of public safety and risk management is still ubiquitous in much of the American debate on parole. A 2011 report by the National Institute of Corrections, entitled *The Future of Parole as a Key Partner in Assuring Public Safety*, emphasizes that paroling authorities "have immense potential to make a difference in terms of public safety and wise use of resources" (US Department of Justice 2011, 3). According to the report, it is therefore critical to use good, empirically based actuarial tools to assess risks and criminogenic needs.

However, not all American reform initiatives rely exclusively on actuarial calculations. The introduction of "reentry courts," convening "team-based efforts that typically involve a judge, a social worker, and a mental health professional, who design a diversionary social service supervisory regimen for parolees and help to facilitate access to employment and housing" (McLeod 2012, 1608), is designed to address the multiple needs of released prisoners, drawing upon the problem-solving strategies adopted by specialist drug courts. Re-entry courts have the potential to address the substantive requirements for reintegration of offenders, while also supervising the enforcement of parole conditions that have been set for offenders in a way that meets the standards of legality (Hamilton 2010). Arguably, re-entry courts could tap into the idealism of the American resettlement movement and the federal Second Chance Act of 2007 (H.R. 1593/S. 1060; O'Hear 2007; Green 2013),[29] which recognize the need to provide the means of reintegration to released prisoners (Maruna and LeBel 2003). However, although such courts have been discussed for a long time, their introduction seems not to have proceeded much beyond the pilot stage. Moreover, even the pilots seem largely to allow the parole system to operate side by side with the re-entry courts, rather than fully integrating the two systems (Lindquist et al. 2013). In other words, the conditional release decision is still often made under the traditional parole system, with the court operating within the parameters that the parole board has set. Moreover, reentry courts still lack a systemic role within the criminal justice system as well as consistent regulation capable of leading to predictable outcomes.

Integrating these decisions under the jurisdiction of a single specialist court or court-like body, as is done, for example, in France, Germany, and Italy, would be a better strategy. Such a court could combine substantive concerns about what is best for the parolee or potential parolee with the procedural safeguards that parole-related decision-making requires, including, but not limited to, the granting and revocation of parole.[30]

Some proposed American parole reform would proceed by restricting, not increasing, the powers of decision-makers in respect of conditional release. For example, Tentative Draft No. 2 of the *Model Penal Code: Sentencing* (American Law Institute 2011, app. B) argues for the removal of all initial release authority from parole boards both because of their perceived inadequacy at predicting the future behavior and because in their American guise such boards fail to meet minimum procedural standards.

While we share these criticisms of the current US system, we do not think that these weaknesses are inevitable. On the contrary, the European judicial model is routinely capable of making such decisions fairly and without political interference. The new Model Penal Code recommends a movement toward determinate sentencing, with a system to award good-time credits injecting a modest degree of indeterminacy, that will essentially eliminate the release authority of state parole boards but would allow a judicial authority (newly created agencies or tribunals or trial courts) to retrospectively adjust sentences of prisoners who have served 15 years (§ 305.6, the so-called "second-look provision") and modify a prison sentence at any time on compassionate grounds, or for other compelling reasons (§305.7). That is unobjectionable but still relatively limited. In our judgment an independent court with a wider remit to supervise the implementation of the sentence and to make a range of necessary decisions after the initial sentence has been imposed could undertake the whole process much more effectively. At the same time, the new Model Penal Code also endorses the imposition of a PRS term independent of the length of the prison term, but only if deemed necessary to further one or more of the following goals: holding offenders accountable for their criminal conduct, promoting their rehabilitation and reintegration into law-abiding society, reducing risk of re-offending, and addressing the offenders' needs during their transition from prison to the community (§ 6.09).

Recently, there have been proposals to reshape the institutional structure and composition of US parole boards with the goal of improving their decision-making by increasing their expertise and ensuring their independence from political pressure. According to such proposals, parole board members should be recommended for appointment by an independent special panel, although the recommendations of the panel would subsequently be subject to gubernatorial approval. The tenure of parole board members should be for a fixed term, with reappointment possible for only one further term. Conditions for removal should be governed by a protocol adopted and administered by the aforementioned special panel, thus by and large mirroring analogous protocols already in place for judges (Rhine, Petersilia, and Reitz 2017, 288–89).

While such reforms could certainly improve current US parole systems substantially, we think that in the long run a transition to a "judicial model" for parole boards would be advisable in order to achieve full independence from the executive branch of government. In other words, parole boards should be removed from the correctional environment and conceived anew as specialist sentence implementation courts squarely within the judicial branch. In this regard, the gradual evolution in England and Wales of the parole board from an advisory body squarely part of the Home Office (the government department responsible for immigration, security, and law enforcement) to a quasi-judicial, independent, nondepartmental public body board sponsored by the Ministry of Justice might represent a viable model for a common law jurisdiction such as the United States.[31]

To return to the wider issue of desirable changes, most recent parole reforms in the United States seem to have been driven by budgetary constraints rather than a real reconsideration of the appropriate role of parole in the criminal justice system. Nearly ten years ago, Marie Gottschalk noted,

> Evidence is growing that economic hardship may force a major change shift in penal policy that will significantly reduce the country's incarceration rate, for years the highest in the world. Dozens of states cut their corrections budgets in 2009, and many proposed closing penal facilities to cover gaping budget gaps. In 2008, 17 states enacted a slew of penal reforms aimed at shrinking their prison populations, including expanding the use of alternative sentences and drug courts, loosening restrictions on parole eligibility, and reducing revocations of parole and probation for minor infractions. (Gottschalk 2009, 42).

Joan Petersilia, in particular, has stressed the potential of hard times for reshaping an effective community corrections system:

> [I]f we use this crisis as an opportunity to implement evidence-based community correctional programs, we might finally demonstrate the

> critical role that community corrections agencies can play in the promotion of community safety, successful reintegration, and individual accountability. (Petersilia 2011a, 527)

A recent study has highlighted the increase in progressive legislative outcomes in the area of parole policy in the decade beginning with 2006, coupled with subtle yet notable shifts in the penal discourse surrounding their enactment. Such efforts peaked in the years immediately following the financial collapse of 2008. These reforms have been chiefly aimed at reducing the number of parole revocations due to technical violations and at facilitating the early release of prisoners (Beckett et. al 2016). However, the degree of irreversibility of these pieces of legislation is open to question:

> Some of these reforms entailed long-term changes to parole policy and practice, such as capping confinement lengths for parole violators, as lawmakers in Minnesota and Oregon did in 2009. Other reforms generated temporary prison release valves when budgets were especially tight, but were subsequently reversed. For example, in 2010, New Hampshire legislators enacted a reform requiring that inmates convicted of nonviolent offenses be released upon serving 120 percent of the minimum term, but repealed this reform in 2013. (247–48)

Are we experiencing the initial stages of a real shift in parole law and policy in the United States? It is too early to tell how deep the recent commitment to reform goes—in this and all other sectors of American criminal justice policy. Our concern is that public measures designed to reduce the use of imprisonment may be driven only by the economic crisis and budgetary problems (Aviram 2015; Alexander 2010, 14, 56). What if economic recovery enables a return to carceral excess and renewed denial of the role of parole within the penal system? Economic incentives are no guarantee of lasting penal improvement (Gottschalk 2015, 25). If the recent moves toward increased use of parole are to be maintained, they must be underscored by a clear commitment to the added value conditional release can bring not only to effectiveness but also to justice and humanity in the penal system. Our conclusion is that adoption of the best aspects of parole as it is practiced in Europe, but with an eye to the very different context of the United States, could ensure that this occurs. This approach would be preferable to the wholesale elimination of parole release discretion and could transform American parole supervision, moving it back toward its original aspirations of returning ex-offenders successfully to the community.

NOTES

1. We acknowledge that European penal codes usually list life imprisonment as a distinct category of penal sanction, without immediately setting a minimum period to be served before release can be considered. From a taxonomic perspective, therefore, a life sentence is a separate sanction, and to that extent it could be regarded as determinate. However, this does not change the fact that the sentencer cannot know how long offenders sentenced to life imprisonment will live and, thus, how much time they will spend in prison, regardless of possible early release schemes.
2. General Principle 7 of the Council of Europe's (2003) *Recommendation on Conditional Release (Parole)* provides, "Consideration should be given to the savings of resources that can be made by applying the mandatory release system in respect of sentences where a negative individualised assessment would only make a small difference to the date of release."
3. We use the Council of Europe membership as a proxy for Europe as a whole because it includes all European countries except Belarus. It thus encompasses more or less the whole of geographical Europe.
4. This chapter adopts a sentencing perspective. Thus, for probation, in Figure 10.1 we only took into account Council of Europe data that refer to post-sentence probationers and did not include forms of pretrial probation or deferred adjudication schemes. As for the United States, the BJS does not break down figures of different categories of pre- and post-sentence probationers. However, in the United States probation is mostly utilized as a *sanction*, and in the BJS data the focus is explicitly on people under probation as a sanction. The use of probation as an alternative to pretrial detention and in deferred adjudication and drug court schemes is of limited, although certainly growing, relevance. Moreover, in some states pretrial diversion programs run through prosecutors' offices are not included in the probation counts. For the purpose of Figure 10.1, we thus chose to use the overall number of probationers provided by the BJS's annual report on probation and parole minus the available counts from the BJS's *Annual Probation Survey* (2015) for the following categories: suspended imposition of sentence (persons not fully adjudicated, e.g., probation before verdict), forms of probation generally indicated as "other" than direct sentence to probation split sentence (incarceration combined with probation), and suspended execution of sentence to incarceration with probation. It must be noted that the question in the survey on how offenders are placed on probation does not have a good response rate. For this reason, the BJS does not produce official statistics on it.
5. While the US statistics on which Figure 10.1 is based are complete (all states are included), they have had to be converted from figures per 100,000 adults to per 100,000 of the total population to compare them with SPACE country statistics. To calculate the rate of parolees for 100,000 general population, we have made

the following calculation: (parole population at year end/estimated state population for the year) × 100,000.

6. For probation we counted fully suspended sentences with probation and community service sanctions, which historically grew as part of the probation scheme. Other postconviction measures like home arrest and semiliberty do not fit the US definition of probation and are not considered as parole. Rather, they are widely regarded across European jurisdictions as alternative forms of implementation of custodial sentences.
7. Available data did not allow us to break down figures: the BJS does not distinguish the jail population between pretrial detainees and those serving a custodial sentence for misdemeanors up to a year. For Europe, we had to rely on estimates for countries that did not report data (see note 8).
8. The source of these figures, SPACE I (Aebi and Delgrande 2014, table 1), is based in part on estimates for countries that did not submit their figures directly: 50 out of the 52 prison administrations under the control of member states reported data, while those for the remaining (Bosnia and Herzegovina and Ukraine) were retrieved from the SPACE website (http://www3.unil.ch/wpmu/space/space-i/prison-stock-2013-2014/).
9. Latvia, Malta, and Romania too did not provide any broken-down figures on individuals on parole at year end.
10. The converted federal rate per 100,000 adults, 35 per 100,000 general population, has been added to the converted single state numbers to (crudely) count federal supervised parolees for each state.
11. Due to its unique nature, we did not consider the District of Columbia, which in 2013 had 904.8 parolees per 100,000 of the general population.
12. Also, Serbia reported a total of only one person on supervised release and was not considered. In Serbia post-release supervision is authorized by law, but the country is struggling to implement it due to lack of resources (Zeleskov Djoric and Batricevic 2013).
13. Last measurement available, which, however, refers to persons placed under supervision in the community, with no distinction between probation and parole.
14. However, the scale of incarceration in the United States cannot account for its high probation supervision rates in comparison with European states. Indeed, one might expect a jurisdiction with an outsized confinement population to have lower than average numbers on probation, on the theory that probation is an "alternative" to prison—but no such relationship appears to exist within the United States or in US/European comparisons (Phelps 2013; Alper, Corda, and Reitz 2016; see Rhine and Taxman, this volume).
15. The share of prison admissions across the United States that are due to *probation* revocations is unknown as the BJS does not report this figure. Admissions to prison due to violations of probation are entered as "new court commitments"

in BJS reports, based on the legal fiction that a probation sentence is really a prison sentence whose execution has been suspended. In its turn, the Council of Europe's reports do not make it possible to distinguish parole revocations from total revocations. Given the available data, it is not possible to make a sensible estimate of the share of total recalls in Europe that originate in parole versus probation. Although probation populations in Europe are roughly twice as large as parole populations, we can expect prison releasees to be more prone to failure.

16. Interestingly, Brockway attempted to establish the country's first indeterminate sentencing system even earlier when in 1869 he drafted a law, passed by the Michigan legislature but then overturned by the state supreme court, that would allow for the conditional and discretionary release of "common prostitutes" (Lindsey 1925, 18; Gottschalk 2006, 117).
17. Maine, 1975; Indiana, 1977; Illinois, 1978; New Mexico, 1979; Minnesota, 1980; Florida, 1983; Washington, 1984; Oregon, 1989; Delaware, 1990; Kansas, 1993; Arizona, 1994; North Carolina, 1994; Mississippi, 1995; Virginia, 1995; Ohio, 1996; Wisconsin, 1999.
18. There have also been many attempts by constitutional lawyers to establish wider due process protections in the granting of parole. Some of these are built on the partial dissent by Justice Marshall in *Greenholtz*.
19. There may be exceptions for humanitarian reasons: for example, an illness that cannot be treated in prison may require release under the terms of Article 3 of the European Convention on Human Rights, even before the fixed-term sentence has expired. See *Mouisel v. France* (2002).
20. The CPT operates under the European Convention for the Prevention of Torture and Inhuman or Degrading Treatment or Punishment. It exists "to examine the treatment of persons deprived of their liberty with a view to strengthening, if necessary, the protection of such persons from torture and from inhuman or degrading treatment or punishment." The CPT may require European states to cooperate with its inspection visits and to pay heed to its policy recommendations. Similarly, the ECtHR applies the European Convention on Human Rights, which also prohibits "torture and inhuman or degrading treatment or punishment" (the "European Eighth Amendment") as well as guaranteeing a range of other civil and political rights.
21. To return to our earlier historical discussion, the current American outlook was very much a product of a cultural shift beginning in the 1970s. The landscape of risk aversion in US prison-release practices is a clear departure from the policy expressed in § 305.9 of the 1962 draft of the American Law Institute's Model Penal Code, which established a presumption favoring the prisoner's release at the initial parole eligibility.
22. Responding countries include Albania, Andorra, Austria, Belgium, Czech Republic, Denmark, Germany, Hungary, Iceland, Ireland, Italy, Liechtenstein,

Monaco, Montenegro, the Netherlands, Norway, Poland, Portugal, San Marino, Spain, and Switzerland. Note that with the exception of Albania, Andorra, Monaco, the Netherlands, and partly Germany, these persons are already included in the total number of the prison population.

23. The IPP sentence was abolished on December 3, 2012. However, the abolition was not retrospective, and about 4,000 prisoners sentenced to IPP before that date remained subject to its provisions in 2016 (Strickland 2016).
24. In order to ascertain whether a certain penalty constitutes a criminal sanction and, accordingly, conventional procedural safeguards provided for by Article 6 apply, the ECtHR set out three criteria, commonly referred to as the "Engel criteria" (see *Engel and others v. the Netherlands* 1976). The first criterion is the legal classification of the offense under national law, the second is the very nature of the offense, and the third is the degree of severity of the penalty that the person concerned risks incurring. The second and third criteria are alternative and not necessarily cumulative.
25. In most states committed individuals are detained indefinitely. They are evaluated on an annual basis but detained until they are no longer considered a danger to the community. Despite this forced deprivation of liberty, the Supreme Court has upheld state legislation that deems these commitment schemes to be civil commitment that is not punitive (*Kansas v. Hendricks* 1997). Most statutes allow committed persons to petition the court for conditional release if they have been "cured" so that they are no longer likely to engage in predatory acts of sexual violence. Because civil commitment schemes cannot hold sex offenders once treatment makes them no longer dangerous, it would seem that treatment is the premise to release. Yet the reality is quite different: states by and large provide inadequate treatment services and make it exceedingly difficult for committed persons to obtain release from civil commitment. In addition to this, "[r]ather than enable the offender to overcome his sexual deviancy, treatment often engenders further confinement by providing the prosecution with incriminating records" (Miller 2010, 2108).
26. Article 57 (1) provides that "The decision shall particularly consider the personality of the convicted person, his previous history, the circumstances of his offence, the importance of the legal interest endangered should he re-offend, the conduct of the convicted person while serving his sentence, his circumstances and the effects an early release are to be expected to have on him."
27. The other factor typically taken into account by American parole boards is the seriousness of the crime for which the offender has been convicted. This retributive consideration may be used to justify continued incarceration of prisoners who fall into low-risk classifications (Rhine, Petersilia, and Reitz 2017).
28. In contrast to the United States, where the right to counsel is almost unknown at the parole-release stage and some states bar participation of counsel retained

at the prisoner's expense, the right to assistance stated in the European rules refers first and foremost to the right of the prisoner to be represented by an attorney in parole proceedings. Furthermore, the right to assistance may also encompass, for instance, the presence of a translator for a prisoner who is not a native speaker of the country in which he or she is detained. However, at the national level the presence of a defense counsel in parole proceedings is usually not mandated by the law as a precondition for the validity of the procedure.

29. The Second Chance Act of 2007 (Pub. L. 110-199): Section 111 creates a grant program within the Department of Justice to fund re-entry courts. State and local adult and juvenile court systems may receive up to $500,000 to establish and maintain re-entry courts. Applicants must present a long-term strategy and implementation plan and identify government and community entities that the project would coordinate. In addition, grantees must submit an annual report to the Department of Justice. The bill authorized $10 million for fiscal years 2009 and 2010.

30. We are indebted to Martine Herzog-Evans for drawing to our attention the extent to which the French *juge de l'application des peines* can function as a problem-solving court in this dual sense.

31. English reformers would want the process to go further and have the parole board placed under the HM Courts and Tribunals Service, which would guarantee its independence even more fully (Creighton 2007).

CASES CITED

Brown v. Plata, 563 U.S. 493 (2011).

BVerfGE 35, 202 (June 5, 1973) (Lebach case).

BVerfGE 45, 187 (June 21, 1977) (Life imprisonment case).

BVerfGE 86, 288 (June 3, 1992).

BVerfG, 2 BvR 2549/08 (October 22, 2009).

BVerfGE, 2 BvR 2365/09, 740/10, 2333/08, 571/10, 1152/10 (May 4, 2011).

Dybeku v. Albania, ECHR, App. No. 41153/06 (2007).

Engel and others v. The Netherlands, ECHR, Apps. Nos. 5100/71; 5101/71; 5102/71; 5354/72; 5370/72) (1976).

Gagnon v. Scarpelli, 411 U.S. 778 (1973).

Ganusauskas v. Lithuania, ECHR, App. No. 47922/99 (1999).

Graham v. Florida, 560 U.S. 48 (2010).

Greenholtz v. Inmates of the Nebraska Penal and Correctional Complex, 442 U.S. 458 (1979).

Hudec v. Slovakia, ECHR, App. No. 4123/02 (2006).

Hutchinson v. United Kingdom. ECHR [GC], App. No. 57592/08 (2017).

James, Wells and Lee v. United Kingdom, ECHR, Apps. Nos. 25119/09, 57715/09 and 57877/09 (2012).

Kansas v. Hendricks 521 U.S. 346 (1997).
László Magyar v. Hungary, ECHR, App. No. 73593/10 (2014).
Léger v. France, ECHR, App. No. 19324/02 (2006).
M v. Germany, ECHR, App. No. 19359/04 (2009).
Miller v. Alabama, 567 U.S. 460 (2012).
Morrissey v. Brewer, 408 U.S. 471 (1972).
Mouisel v. France, ECHR, App. No. 67263/01 (2002).
Murray v. the Netherlands, ECHR [GC], App. No. 10511/10 (2016).
Öcalan v. Turkey (No.2), ECHR, Apps. Nos. 2406/03, 6201/06 and 10464/07 (2014).
Osborn v. The Parole Board [2013] UKSC 6.
R (on the applications of Haney, Kaiyam, and Massey) v. The Secretary of State for Justice [2014] UKSC 66.
R (on the application of Wells) v. Parole Board [2009] UKHL 22; [2010] 1 AC 553.
R v. McLoughlin and Newell [2014] EWCA Crim 188.
Stafford v. United Kingdom, ECHR [GC], App. No. 46295/99 2002.
Swarthout v. Cooke, 562 U.S. 216 (2011).
Vinter and others v. United Kingdom, ECHR [GC], App. Nos. 66069/09, 130/10 and 3896/10 (2013).

REFERENCES

Abadinsky, Howard. "Parole." In *Encyclopedia of Crime and Punishment*, edited by David Levinson, 1128–32. Thousand Oaks, CA: Sage Publications, 2002.

Abadinsky, Howard. *Probation and Parole: Theory and Practice*. 7th ed. Upper Saddle River, NJ: Prentice Hall, 2012.

Aebi, Marcelo F., and Julien Chopin. *SPACE II—Council of Europe Annual Penal Statistics: Persons Serving Non-Custodial Sanctions and Measures in 2013*. May 14, 2014. http://wp.unil.ch/space/files/2011/02/Council-of-Europe_SPACE-II-2013-E_Final_150205.pdf.

Aebi, Marcelo F., and Natalia Delgrande. *SPACE I—Council of Europe Annual Penal Statistics: Prison populations. Survey 2013*. December 15, 2014. http://wp.unil.ch/space/files/2015/02/SPACE-I-2013-English.pdf.

Aebi, Marcelo F., and Yann Marguet. *SPACE II—Council of Europe Annual Penal Statistics: Persons Serving Non-Custodial Sanctions and Measures in 2012*. April 29, 2014. http://wp.unil.ch/space/files/2011/02/Council-of-Europe_SPACE-II-2012_Final-report_140417.pdf.

Alexander, Michelle. *The New Jim Crow: Mass Incarceration in the Age of Colorblindness*. New York: New Press, 2010.

Allen, George. "The Courage of Our Convictions: The Abolition of Parole Will Save Lives and Money." *Policy Review* 72 (1995): 4–7.

Alper, Mariel, Alessandro Corda, and Kevin R. Reitz. American Exceptionalism in Probation Supervision. Probation Supervision Rates in the United States and Europe,

2013 Rates per 100,000 Adult Residents. March 2, 2016. http://robinainstitute.umn.edu/publications/data-brief-american-exceptionalism-probation-supervision.

American Bar Association. *Standards for Criminal Justice: Sentencing.* 3rd ed. Washington, DC: American Bar Association, 1994.

American Civil Liberties Union. *A Living Death: Life without Parole for Nonviolent Offenses.* New York: American Civil Liberties Union, 2013.

American Law Institute. *Model Penal Code—Proposed Official Draft.* Philadelphia: American Law Institute, 1962.

American Law Institute. *Model Penal Code: Sentencing.* Tentative Draft No. 2. Philadelphia: American Law Institute, 2011.

American Law Institute. *Model Penal Code: Sentencing.* Tentative Draft No. 3. Philadelphia: American Law Institute, 2014.

Ancel, Marc. "The Collection of European Penal Codes and the Study of Comparative Law." *University of Pennsylvania Law Review* 106 (1958): 329–84.

Ancel, Marc. *Social Defence: A Modern Approach to Criminal Problems.* London: Routledge and Kegan Paul, 1965.

Annison, Jill, Lol Burke, and Paul Senior. "Transforming Rehabilitation: Another Example of English 'Exceptionalism' or a Blueprint for the Rest of Europe?" *European Journal of Probation* 6 (2014): 6–23.

Appleton, Catherine, and Dirk van Zyl Smit. "The Paradox of Reform: Life Imprisonment in England and Wales." In *Life Imprisonment and Human Rights,* edited by Dirk Van Zyl Smit and Catherine Appleton, 217–40. Oxford: Hart Publishing, 2016.

Ashworth, Andrew. *Sentencing and Criminal Justice.* 6th ed. Cambridge: Cambridge University Press, 2015.

Aviram, Hadar. *Cheap on Crime: Recession-Era Politics and the Transformation of American Punishment.* Oakland: University of California Press, 2015.

Baker, Estella. "The Emerging Role of the EU as a Penal Actor." In *European Penology?* edited by Tom Daems, Dirk van Zyl Smit, and Sonja Snacken, 77–111. Oxford: Hart Publishing, 2013.

Bannon, Alicia, Mitali Nagrecha, and Rebekah Diller. *The Hidden Costs of Criminal Justice Debt.* New York: Brennan Center for Justice, 2010.

Battaglini, Giulio. "The Fascist Reform of the Penal Law in Italy." *Journal of the American Institute of Criminal Law and Criminology* 24 (1933): 278–89.

Bauwens, Aline, Luc Robert, and Sonja Snacken. "Conditional Release in Belgium: How Reforms Have Impacted Recall." *European Journal of Probation* 4 (2012): 19–33.

BBC News. "Family Hears Judge Say Victim Statements Make 'No Difference.'" August 5, 2014. http://www.bbc.com/news/uk-28644799.

Beckett, Katherine, Anna Reosti, and Emily Knaphus. "The End of an Era? Understanding the Contradictions of Criminal Justice Reform." *The Annals of the American Academy of Political and Social Science* 664 (2016): 238–59.

Beyens, Kristel, Sonja Snacken, and Dirk van Zyl Smit. "Truth in (the Implementation of) Sentencing: Belgium and Elsewhere." In *European Penology?* edited by Tom Daems, Dirk van Zyl Smit, and Sonja Snacken, 271–91. Oxford: Hart Publishing, 2013.

Bierschbach, Richard A. "Proportionality and Parole." *University of Pennsylvania Law Review* 160 (2012): 1745–88.

Bing, Stefan J. "Reconsidering State Parole Board Membership Requirements in Light of Model Penal Code Sentencing Revisions." *Kentucky Law Journal* 100 (2012): 871–93.

Binnall, James M. "They Released Me from My Cage . . . But They Still Keep Me Handcuffed: A Parolee's Reaction to *Samson v. California*." *Ohio State Journal of Criminal Law* 4 (2007): 541–53.

Bottoms, A. E. "Reflections on the Renaissance of Dangerousness." *Howard Journal of Criminal Justice* 16 (1977): 70–96.

Bureau of Justice Statistics. *Probation and Parole in the United States, 2013*. Washington, DC: US Department of Justice, 2014a.

Bureau of Justice Statistics. *Correctional Populations in the United States, 2013*. Washington, DC: US Department of Justice, 2014b.

Bureau of Justice Statistics. *Prisoners in 2013*. Washington, DC: US Department of Justice, 2014c.

Bureau of Justice Statistics. *Jail Inmates at Midyear 2013—Statistical Tables*. Washington DC: US Department of Justice, 2014d.

Bureau of Justice Statistics. *Annual Probation Survey, 2013*. Washington, DC: US Department of Justice, 2015.

Bureau of Justice Statistics. *Jail Inmates in 2015*. Washington DC: US Department of Justice, 2016.

Burke, Peggy, and Michael Tonry. *Successful Transition and Re-entry for Safer Communities: A Call to Action for Parole*. Silver Spring, MD: Center for Effective Public Policy, 2006.

Butterfield, Fox. "Eliminating Parole Boards Isn't a Cure-All, Experts Say." *New York Times*, January 10, 1999.

Canton, Rob. "European Probation Rules: What They Are, Why They Matter." *EuroVista* 1 (2010): 62–71.

Caplan, Joel M. "Protecting Parole Board Legitimacy in the Twenty-First Century: The Role of Victims' Rights and Influences. *Victims and Offenders* 7 (2012): 1–24.

Caplan, Joel M., and Susan C. Kinnery. "National Survey of State Paroling Authorities: Models of Service Delivery." *Federal Probation* 74 (2010): 34–42.

Carroll, John S., Richard L. Wiener, Dan Coates, Jolene Galegher, and James J. Alibrio. "Evaluation, Diagnosis, and Prediction in Parole Decision Making." *Law & Society Review* 17 (1982): 199–228.

Chanenson, Steven L. "The Next Era of Sentencing Reform." *Emory Law Journal* 54 (2005): 377–460.

Cid, José, and Beatriz Tébar. "Spain." In *Release from Prison: European Policy and Practice,* edited by Nicola Padfield, Dirk van Zyl Smit, and Frieder Dünkel, 358–92. Cullompton, UK: Willan Publishing, 2010.

Clear, Todd R., Michael D. Reisig, and George F. Cole. *American Corrections.* 10th ed. Belmont, CA: Wadsworth, 2012.

Clear, Todd R., and Natasha A. Frost. *The Punishment Imperative: The Rise and Failure of Mass Incarceration in America.* New York: New York University Press, 2013.

Corrado, Michael Louis. *Presumed Dangerous Punishment, Responsibility, and Preventive Detention in American Jurisprudence.* Durham, NC: Carolina Academic Press, 2013.

Council of Europe. *Recommendation No. R (92) 16 of the Committee of Ministers to Member States on the European Rules on Community Sanctions and Measures (Adopted by the Committee of Ministers on 19 October 1992 at the 482nd Meeting of the Ministers' Deputies).* Strasbourg, France: Council of Europe, 1992.

Council of Europe. *Recommendation No. R (99) 22 of the Committee of Ministers to Member States Concerning Prison Overcrowding and Prison Population Inflation adopted by the Committee of Ministers on 30 September 1999 at the 681st meeting of the Ministers' Deputies.* Strasbourg, France: Council of Europe, 1999.

Council of Europe. *Recommendation Rec(2003)22 of the Committee of Ministers to Member States on Conditional Release (Parole).* Strasbourg, France: Council of Europe Publishing, 2003.

Council of Europe. Council Framework Decision 2008/947/JHA of 27 November 2008 on the Application of the Principle of Mutual Recognition to Judgments and Probation Decisions with a View to the Supervision of Probation Measures and Alternative Sanctions. November 27, 2008. http://eur-lex.europa.eu/eli/dec_framw/2008/947/oj.

Council of Europe. Recommendation CM/Rec (2010) 1 of the Committee of Ministers to Member States on the Council of Europe Probation Rules, adopted 20 January 2010. Strasbourg, France: Council of Europe, 2010.

Creighton, Simon. "The Parole Board as a Court." In *Who to Release? Parole, Fairness and Criminal Justice,* edited by Nicola Padfield, 109–26. Cullompton, UK: Willan Publishing, 2007.

Cullen, Francis T., and Karen E. Gilbert. *Reaffirming Rehabilitation.* 2nd ed. Waltham, MA: Anderson, 2013.

Davis, Kenneth C. *Discretionary Justice: A Preliminary Inquiry.* Baton Rouge: Louisiana State University Press, 1969.

Deering, John. *Probation Practice and the New Penology.* Farnham, UK: Ashgate, 2011.

De la Cuesta, Juan Luis, and Isidoro Blanco Cordero. "Le système pénitentiaire espagnol." In *Les systèmes pénitentiaires dans le monde,* edited by Jean Paul Céré and Carlos Eduardo Adriano Japiassú, 123–48. Paris: Dalloz, 2011.

Dharmapala, Dhammika, Nuno Garoupa, and Joanna Shepherd. "Legislatures, Judges, and Parole Boards: The Allocation of Discretion under Determinate Sentencing." *Florida Law Review* 62 (2010): 1037–89.

Ditton, Paula M., and Doris James Wilson. *Truth in Sentencing in State Prisons*. Washington, DC: Bureau of Justice Statistics, 1999.

Doherty, Fiona. "Indeterminate Sentencing Returns: The Invention of Supervised Release." *New York University Law Review* 88 (2013): 958–1030.

Dolovich, Sharon. "Creating the Permanent Prisoner." In *Life without Parole: America's New Death Penalty?* edited by Charles J. Ogletree Jr. and Austin Sarat, 96–137. New York: New York University Press, 2012.

Downes, David. "The Macho Penal Economy: Mass Incarceration in the United States—A European Perspective." In *Mass Imprisonment: Social Causes and Consequences*, edited by David Garland, 51–69. London: Sage, 2001.

Drenkhahn, Kirstin, Christine Morgenstern, and Dirk van Zyl Smit. "What Is in a Name? Preventive Detention in Germany in the Shadow of European Human Rights Law." *Criminal Law Review* 3 (2012): 167–87.

Dünkel, Frieder. "Judicial Control and Supervision." In *Monitoring Prison Conditions in Europe*, edited by Penal Reform International, 109–14. Paris: Penal Reform International, 1997.

Dünkel, Frieder. "Germany." In *Release from Prison: European Policy and Practice*, edited by Nicola Padfield, Dirk van Zyl Smit, and Frieder Dünkel, 185–211. Cullompton, UK: Willan Publishing, 2010.

Dünkel, Frieder. "Early Release from Prison." In *Encyclopedia of Criminology and Criminal Justice*, edited by David Weisburd and Gerben Bruinsma, 1256–71. New York: Springer Verlag, 2014.

Eaglin, Jessica M. "Against Neorehabilitation." *Southern Methodist University Law Review* 66 (2013): 189–226.

Ellis, Michael J. "The Origins of the Elected Prosecutor." *Yale Law Journal* 121 (2012): 1528–69.

European Committee for the Prevention of Torture and Inhuman or Degrading Treatment or Punishment (CPT). *2nd General Report on the CPT's Activities Covering the Period 1 January to 31 December 1991*. CPT/Inf (92) 3. Strasbourg, France: Council of Europe, 1992.

European Committee for the Prevention of Torture and Inhuman or Degrading Treatment or Punishment. 2012. *Report on the Visit to Switzerland from 10 to 20 October 2011*. CPT/Inf (2012). Strasbourg, France: Council of Europe, 2012a.

European Committee for the Prevention of Torture and Inhuman or Degrading Treatment or Punishment. *Report on the visit to Bulgaria from 4 to 10 May 2012*. CPT/Inf (2012). Strasbourg, France: Council of Europe, 2012b.

Fairfax, Roger A., Jr. "From Overcriminalization to Smart on Crime: American Criminal Justice Reform—Legacy and Prospects." *Journal of Law Economics & Policy* 7 (2011): 597–616.

Feeley, Malcom M., and Jonathan Simon. "The New Penology: Notes on the Emerging Strategy of Corrections and Its Implications." *Criminology* 30 (1992): 449–74.

Frankel, Marvin E. *Criminal Sentences: Law without Order*. New York: Hill and Wang, 1973.

Garland, David. *The Culture of Control: Crime and Social Order in Contemporary Society*. Chicago: University of Chicago Press, 2001.

Garland, David. *Peculiar Institution: America's Death Penalty in an Age of Abolition*. Cambridge, MA: Harvard University Press, 2010.

Garland, David. "Penality and the Penal State." *Criminology* 51 (2013): 475–517.

Garoupa, Nuno, and Tom Ginsburg. "Hybrid Judicial Career Structures: Reputation vs. Legal Tradition." *Journal of Legal Analysis* 3 (2012): 1–38.

Ghandnoosh, Nazgol. *Delaying a Second Chance: The Declining Prospects for Parole on Life Sentences*. Washington, D.C.: Sentencing Project, 2017.

Gingrich, Newt, and Pat Nolan. "Prison Reform: A Smart Way for States to Save Money and Lives," *Washington Post*, January 7, 2011. http://www.washingtonpost.com/wp-dyn/content/article/2011/01/06/AR2011010604386.html.

Glaser, Daniel. "Who Gets Probation and Parole: Case Study versus Actuarial Decision Making." *Crime & Delinquency* 31 (1985): 267–378.

Gottfredson, Donald M., Peter B. Hoffman, Maurice H. Sigler, and Leslie T. Wilkins. "Making Paroling Policy Explicit." *Crime & Delinquency* 21 (1975): 34–44.

Gottfredson, Donald M., Colleen A. Cosgrove, Leslie T. Wilkins, Jane Wallerstein, and Carol Rauh. *Classification for Parole Decision Policy*. Washington, DC: National Institute of Law Enforcement and Criminal Justice, Law Enforcement Assistance Administration, US Department of Justice, 1978.

Gottschalk, Marie. *The Prison and the Gallows: The Politics of Mass Incarceration in America*. Cambridge: Cambridge University Press, 2006.

Gottschalk, Marie. "City on a Hill, City behind Bars: Criminal Justice, Social Justice, and American Exceptionalism." *Nanzan Review of American Studies* 31 (2009): 33–58.

Gottschalk, Marie. *Caught: The Prison State and the Lockdown of American Politics*. Princeton: Princeton University Press, 2015.

Green, David A. "Penal Optimism and Second Chances: The Legacies of American Protestantism and the Prospects for Penal Reform." *Punishment & Society* 15 (2013): 123–46.

Gualazzi, Alessandra, and Chiara Mancuso. "Italy." In *Release from Prison: European Policy and Practice*, edited by Nicola Padfield, Dirk van Zyl Smit, and Frieder Dünkel, 266–99. Cullompton, UK: Willan Publishing, 2010.

Hamilton, Zachary. *Do Reentry Courts Reduce Recidivism? Results from the Harlem Parole Reentry Court*. New York: Center for Courts Innovation. March 2010. http://www.courtinnovation.org/sites/default/files/Reentry_Evaluation.pdf.

Harcourt, Bernard E. *Against Prediction: Profiling, Policing, and Punishing in an Actuarial Age*. Chicago: University of Chicago Press, 2007.

Herzog-Evans, Martine. "Judicial Oversight on Prison Sentences." In *Monitoring Prison Conditions in Europe*, edited by Penal Reform International, 115–26. Paris: Penal Reform International, 1997.

Herzog-Evans, Martine. "French Third Sector Participation in Probation and Reentry: Complementary or Competitive?" *European Journal of Probation* 6 (2014): 42–56.

Hipp, John, Susan Turner, and Joan Petersilia. "Parolee Recidivism in California: The Effect of Neighborhood Context and Social Service Agency Characteristics." *Criminology* 48 (2010): 947–79.

Jacobi, Tonja, Song Richardson, and Gregory Barr. "The Attrition of Rights under Parole." *Southern California Law Review* 87 (2014): 887–976.

Jacobson, Michael. *Downsizing Prisons: How to Reduce Crime and End Mass Incarceration*. New York: New York University Press, 2006.

Jannetta, Jesse, and William D. Burrell. "Effective Supervision Principles for Probation and Parole." In *Encyclopedia of Criminology and Criminal Justice*, edited by David Weisburd and Gerben Bruinsma, 1308–18. New York: Springer Verlag, 2014.

Joutsen, Matti. "Victim Participation in Proceedings and Sentencing in Europe." *International Review of Victimology* 3 (1994): 57–67.

Kerner, Hans-Jürgen. "Establishing New Minimum Standards on the Rights, Support and Protection of Victims of Crime (Directive 2012/29/EU): A Promising Step Also for the Further Development of Restorative Justice Initiatives and Institutions in Europe." *Restorative Justice: An International Journal* 1 (2013): 430–37.

King, Ryan S. "Recent Developments in State Parole Reform, 2004–2006." *Federal Sentencing Reporter* 20 (2007): 124–27.

Klingele, Cecelia M. "The Early Demise of Early Release." *West Virginia Law Review* 114 (2012): 415–59.

Klingele, Cecelia M. "Rethinking the Use of Community Supervision." *Journal of Criminal Law & Criminology* 103 (2013): 1015–69.

Krajewski, Krzysztof. "Penal Developments in Poland: New or Old Punitiveness?" In *European Penology?* edited by Tom Daems, Dirk van Zyl Smit, and Sonja Snacken, 311–38. Oxford: Hart Publishing, 2013.

Krajewski, Krzysztof. "Different Penal Climates in Europe." *Kriminologijos Studijos* 1 (2014): 86–111.

Kremling, Janine. "Crime Control Model of Corrections." In *Encyclopedia of Community Corrections*, edited by Shannon M. Barton-Bellessa, 95–97. Thousand Oaks, CA: Sage Publications, 2012.

Kunz, Karl-Ludwig. *Kriminologie*. 4th ed. Bern, Switzerland: Haupt, 2004.

Lacey, Nicola. "American Imprisonment in Comparative Perspective." *Daedalus* 139, no. 3 (2010): 102–14.

Lappi-Seppälä, Tapio. "Finland." In *Release from Prison: European Policy and Practice*, edited by Nicola Padfield, Dirk van Zyl Smit, and Frieder Dünkel, 135–67. Cullompton, UK: Willan Publishing, 2010.

Levin, Matt. "Behind California's Dramatic Increase in Lifers Freed from Prisons." KQED News. May 15, 2014. http://blogs.kqed.org/newsfix/behind-californias-dramatic-increase-in-lifers-freed-from-prison/.

Lin, Jeffrey. "Parole Revocation in the Era of Mass Incarceration." *Sociology Compass* 4 (2010): 999–1010.

Lindquist, Christine, Jennifer Hardison Walters, Michael Rempel, and Shannon M. Carey. *The National Institute of Justice's Evaluation of Second Chance Act Adult Reentry Courts: Program Characteristics and Preliminary Themes from Year 1*. Washington, DC: US Department of Justice, 2013. https://www.ncjrs.gov/pdffiles1/nij/grants/241400.pdf.

Lindsey, Edward. "Historical Sketch of the Indeterminate Sentence and Parole System." *Journal of the American Institute of Criminal Law & Criminology* 16 (1925): 9–69.

Lofstrom, Magnus, and Steven Raphael. "Prison Downsizing and Public Safety Evidence From California." *Criminology & Public Policy* 15 (2016): 349–65.

Logan, Wayne A., and Ronald F. Wright. "Mercenary Criminal Justice." *University of Illinois Law Review* 2014 (2014): 1175–1226.

Lynch, Mona. "Rehabilitation as Rhetoric: The Reformable Individual in Contemporary Parole Discourse and Practices." *Punishment & Society* 2 (2000): 40–65.

MacKenzie, Doris Layton. "Probation and Parole: History, Goals, and Decision-Making." In *Encyclopedia of Crime & Justice*. Vol. 3. Edited by Joshua Dressler, 1210–19. New York: Macmillan Reference, 2002.

Mannheim, Hermann. "The German Prevention of Crime Act, 1933." *Journal of the American Institute of Criminal Law and Criminology* 26 (1935): 517–37.

Maruna, Shadd, Dean Dabney, and Volkan Topalli. "Putting a Price on Prisoner Release: The History of Bail and a Possible Future of Parole." *Punishment & Society* 14 (2012): 315–37.

Maruna, Shadd, and Thomas P. LeBel. "Welcome Home? Examining the 'Reentry Court' Concept from a Strengths-Based Perspective." *Western Criminology Review* 4, no. 2 (2003): 91–107.

Mauer, Marc. "The Truth about Truth in Sentencing." *Corrections Today* 58 (1996): 51–59.

McLeod, Allegra. "Decarceration Courts: Possibilities and Perils of a Shifting Criminal Law." *Georgetown Law Journal* 100 (2012): 1587–674.

McNeill, Fergus. "Community Sanctions and European Penology." In *European Penology?* edited by Tom Daems, Dirk van Zyl Smit, and Sonja Snacken, 171–91. Oxford: Hart Publishing, 2013.

Miller, Jeslyn A. "Sex Offender Civil Commitment: The Treatment Paradox." *California Law Review* 98 (2010): 2093–2128.

Monahan, John, and Jennifer L. Skeem. "Risk Redux: The Resurgence of Risk Assessment in Criminal Sanctioning." *Federal Sentencing Reporter* 26 (2014): 158–66.

Morris, Norval. *The Habitual Criminal*. London: Longmans, 1951.

Morris, Norval. "Introduction." *McGill Law Journal* 13 (1967): 534–52.

Morris, Norval, and Michael Tonry. *Between Prison and Probation: Intermediate Punishments in a Rational Sentencing System*. New York: Oxford University Press, 1990.

National Research Council. *Parole, Desistance from Crime, and Community Integration*. Washington, DC: National Academies Press, 2008.

Nelken, David. "Comparative Criminal Justice: Beyond Ethnocentricism and Relativism." *European Journal of Criminology* 6 (2009): 291–311.

Nellis, Ashley. *Still Life: America's Increasing Use of Life and Long-Term Sentences*. Washington, DC: Sentencing Project, 2017.

Nellis, Ashley, and Ryan S. King. *No Exit: The Expanding Use of Life Sentences in America*. Washington, DC: Sentencing Project, 2009.

Newburn, Tim. "Tough on Crime: Penal Policy in England and Wales." *Crime and Justice* 36 (2007): 425–70.

New York Times. "Shrinking Prisons, Saving Billions." March 24, 2013. http://www.nytimes.com/2013/03/24/opinion/sunday/shrinking-prisons-saving-billions.html?_r=0.

O'Brien, Patricia. "The Prison on the Continent: Europe, 1865–1965." In *The Oxford History of the Prison: The Practice of Punishment in Western Society*, edited by Norval Morris and David J. Rothman, 178–201. Oxford and New York: Oxford University Press, 1995.

O'Hear, Michael M. "The Second Chance Act and the Future of Reentry Reform." *Federal Sentencing Reporter* 20 (2007): 75–83.

O'Hear, Michael M. "Beyond Rehabilitation: A New Theory of Indeterminate Sentencing." *American Criminal Law Review* 48 (2011): 1247–92.

Padfield, Nicola. "England and Wales." In *Release from Prison: European Policy and Practice*, edited by Nicola Padfield, Dirk van Zyl Smit, and Frieder Dünkel, 104–33. Cullompton, UK: Willan Publishing, 2010.

Padfield, Nicola, and Shadd Maruna. "The Revolving Door at the Prison Gate: Exploring the Dramatic Increase in Recalls to Prison." *Criminology & Criminal Justice* 6 (2006): 329–52.

Palacios, Victoria J. "Go and Sin No More: Rationality and Release Decisions by Parole Boards." *South Carolina Law Review* 45 (1994): 567–615.

Paparozzi, Mario A., and Joel M. Caplan. "A Profile of Paroling Authorities in America: The Strange Bedfellows of Politics and Professionalism." *Prison Journal* 89 (2009): 401–25.

Petersilia, Joan. "Parole and Prisoner Reentry in the United States." In *Crime & Justice: A Review of the Research*. Vol. 26. Edited by Michael Tonry and Joan Petersilia, 479–529. Chicago: University of Chicago Press, 1999.

Petersilia, Joan. *When Prisoners Come Home: Parole and Prisoner Reentry*. Oxford and New York: Oxford University Press, 2003.

Petersilia, Joan. "Community Corrections: Probation, Parole, and Prisoner Reentry." In *Crime and Public Policy*. 2nd ed. Edited by James Q. Wilson and Joan Petersilia, 499–531. New York: Oxford University Press, 2011a.

Petersilia, Joan. "Beyond the Prison Bubble." *Federal Probation* 75 (2011b): 2–4.

Petersilia, Joan. "California Prison Downsizing and Its Impact on Local Criminal Justice Systems." *Harvard Law & Policy Review* 8 (2014): 327–57.

Petersilia, Joan, and Susan Turner. "Intensive Probation and Parole." In *Crime & Justice: A Review of the Research*. Vol. 17. Edited by Michael Tonry, 281–335. Chicago: University of Chicago Press, 1993.

Pettigrew, Mark. "A Tale of Two Cities: Whole of Life Prison Sentences in Strasbourg and Westminster." *European Journal of Crime, Criminal Law and Criminal Justice* 23 (2015): 281–99.

Pew Charitable Trusts. US Imprisonment Rate Continues to Drop Amid Falling Crime Rates. March 14, 2014. http://www.pewtrusts.org/en/about/news-room/press-releases/2014/03/14/us-imprisonment-rate-continues-to-drop-amid-falling-crime-rates.

Phelps, Michelle S. "The Paradox of Probation: Community Supervision in the Age of Mass Incarceration." *Law & Policy* 35 (2013): 51–80.

Pifferi, Michele. "Individualization of Punishment and the Rule of Law: Reshaping Legality in the United States and Europe between the 19th and the 20th Century." *American Journal of Legal History* 52 (2012): 325–76.

Raphael, Steven, and Michael A. Stoll. *Why Are So Many Americans in Prison?* New York: Russell Sage Foundation, 2013.

Reitz, Kevin R. "Questioning the Conventional Wisdom of Parole Release Authority." In *The Future of Imprisonment*, ed. Michael Tonry, 199–236. Oxford and New York: Oxford University Press, 2004.

Reitz, Kevin R. "The 'Traditional' Indeterminate Sentencing Model." In *The Oxford Handbook of Sentencing and Corrections*, edited by Joan Petersilia and Kevin R. Reitz, 270–98. New York: Oxford University Press, 2012.

Reitz, Kevin R. "Discretionary Prison Release Systems in the U.S.: A Comparative Framework." In *Offender Release and Supervision: The Role of the Courts and the Use of Discretion in Probation and Reentry*, edited by Martine Herzog-Evans, 81–107. Nijmegen: Wolf Legal Publishers, 2015.

Reuflet, Kim. "France." In *Release from Prison: European Policy and Practice*, edited by Nicola Padfield, Dirk van Zyl Smit, and Frieder Dünkel, 169–84. Cullompton, UK: Willan Publishing, 2010.

Rhine, Edward E. "The Present Status and Future Prospects of Parole Boards and Parole Supervision." In *The Oxford Handbook of Sentencing and Corrections*, edited by Joan Petersilia and Kevin R. Reitz, 627–55. Oxford and New York: Oxford University Press, 2012.

Rhine, Edward E., Joan Petersilia, and Kevin R. Reitz. "The Future of Parole Release: A Ten-Point Plan." In *Crime and Justice: Reinventing American Criminal*

Justice Systems. Vol. 46. Edited by Michael Tonry, 279–338. Chicago: University of Chicago Press, 2017.

Robert, Dominique. "Actuarial Justice." In *Encyclopedia of Prisons & Correctional Facilities*, edited by M. Bosworth, 11–14. Thousand Oaks, CA: Sage Publications, 2005.

Roberts, Julian V. "Listening to the Crime Victim: Evaluating Victim Input at Sentencing and Parole." *Crime and Justice: A Review of the Research*. Vol. 38. Edited by Michael Tonry, 347–412. Chicago: University of Chicago Press, 2009.

Robinson, Gwen, and Kerstin Svensson. "Practising Offender Supervision." In *Offender Supervision in Europe*, edited by Fergus McNeill and Kristel Beyens, 97–124. London: Palgrave Macmillan, 2013.

Rothman, David J. *Conscience and Convenience: The Asylum and Its Alternatives in Progressive America*. Boston: Little, Brown, 1980.

Ruhland, Ebony L., Edward E. Rhine, Jason P. Robey, and Kelly Lyn Mitchell, The Continuing Leverage of Releasing Authorities: Findings from a National Survey, Robina Institute of Criminal Law and Criminal Justice. August 22, 2016. https://robinainstitute.umn.edu/publications/continuing-leverage-releasing-authorities-findings-national-survey.

Schartmueller, Doris. "Too Dangerous to Get Out? The Use of Individualized Release Mechanisms for Lifetime Incarcerated Offenders in Sweden." *Criminal Justice Policy Review* 25 (2014): 407–31.

Scheirs, Veerle, Kristel Beyens, and Sonja Snacken. "De strafuitvoeringsrechtbanken buiten spel in de strijd voor een geloofwaardige justitie?" *De Morgen*, January 23, 2013, 19.

Scott-Hayward, Christine S. "The Failure of Parole: Rethinking the Role of the State in Reentry." *New Mexico Law Review* 41 (2011): 431–65.

Scott-Hayward, Christine S. "Shadow Sentencing: The Imposition of Federal Supervised Release." *Berkeley Journal of Criminal Law* 18 (2013): 180–229.

Seddon, Martin. "Not Far from Europe——But How Can We Make Our Penal Reform Messages Relevant?" In *Policy Transfer in Criminal Justice: Crossing Cultures, Breaking Barriers*, edited by Mary Anne McFarlane and Rob Canton, 275–89. London: Palgrave Macmillan, 2014.

Simon, Jonathan. *Poor Discipline: Parole and the Social Control of the Underclass, 1890–1990*. Chicago: University of Chicago Press, 1993.

Snacken, Sonia, Kristel Beyens, and Marie-Aude Beernaert. "Belgium." In *Release from Prison: European Policy and Practice*, edited by Nicola Padfield, Dirk van Zyl Smit, and Frieder Dünkel, 70–102. Cullompton, UK: Willan Publishing, 2010.

Snacken, Sonja, and Hanne Tournel. "Belgium." In *Long-Term Imprisonment and Human Rights*, edited by Kirstin Drenkhahn, Manuela Dudeck, and Frieder Dünkel, 61–81. London: Routledge, 2014.

Starr, Sonja B. "Evidence-Based Sentencing and the Scientific Rationalization of Discrimination." *Stanford Law Review* 66 (2014a): 803–72.

Starr, Sonja B. "Sentencing, by the Numbers." *New York Times*, August 11, 2014b, A17.

Starr, Sonja B. "The New Profiling: Why Punishing Based on Poverty and Identity Is Unconstitutional and Wrong." *Federal Sentencing Reporter* 27 (2015): 229–36.

Steiker, Carol S. "Capital Punishment and American Exceptionalism." In *American Exceptionalism and Human Rights*, edited by Michael Ignatieff, 57–89. Princeton, NJ: Princeton University Press, 2005.

Stinchcomb, Jeanne B. *Corrections: Foundations for the Future*. 2nd ed. New York: Routledge, 2011.

Strickland, Pat. "Sentences of Imprisonment for Public Protection." Briefing Paper No. 06086. London: House of Commons Library, 2016. http://researchbriefings.parliament.uk/ResearchBriefing/Summary/SN06086.

Subramanian, Ram, Ruth Delaney, Stephen Roberts, Nancy Fishman, and Peggy McGarry, *Incarceration's Front Door: The Misuse of Jails in America*. New York: Vera Institute of Justice, 2015.

Swisher, Keith. "Pro-Prosecution Judges: 'Tough on Crime,' Soft on Strategy, Ripe for Disqualification." *Arizona Law Review* 52 (2010): 317–93.

Tak, Peter J. P. "Concepts of Conditional Release in Western Europe." *Netherlands International Law Review* 36 (1989): 19–48.

Taxman, Faye S., and Danielle S. Rudes. "Early Release." In *Corrections*. Key Issues in Crime and Punishment, edited by William J. Chambliss, 61–70. Thousand Oaks, CA: Sage Publications, 2011.

Tonry, Michael. "The Fragmentation of Sentencing and Corrections in America." In *Sentencing and Corrections: Issues for the 21st Century*, 1–7. Washington, DC: US Department of Justice, National Institute for Justice, 1999a.

Tonry, Michael. "Parochialism in US Sentencing Policy." *Crime & Delinquency* 45 (1999b): 48–65.

Tonry, Michael. *Thinking about Crime: Sense and Sensibility in American Penal Culture*. New York: Oxford University Press, 2004a.

Tonry, Michael. *Punishment and Politics: Evidence and Emulation in the Making of English Crime Control Policy*. Cullompton, UK: Willan Publishing, 2004b.

Tonry, Michael. "Explanations of American Punishment Policies: A National History." *Punishment & Society* 11 (2009): 377–94.

Tonry, Michael. "'Rebalancing the Criminal Justice System in Favour of the Victim': The Costly Consequences of Populist Rhetoric." In *Hearing the Victim: Adversarial Justice, Crime Victims and the State*, edited by Anthony Bottoms and Julian V. Roberts, 72–103. Cullompton, UK: Willan Publishing, 2010.

Tonry, Michael. "Sentencing in America, 1975–2025." In *Crime and Justice in America, 1975–2025*. Vol. 42. Edited by Michael Tonry, 141–98. Chicago: University of Chicago Press, 2013.

Tonry, Michael. "Legal and Ethical Issues in the Prediction of Recidivism." *Federal Sentencing Reporter* 26 (2014): 167–76.

Travis, Jeremy. 2002. *Thoughts on the Future of Parole*. Washington, DC: Urban Institute, 2002. www.urban.org/UploadedPDF/410521.pdf.

Travis, Jeremy. *But They All Come Back: Facing the Challenges of Prisoner Reentry*. Washington, DC: Urban Institute Press, 2005.

Travis, Jeremy. "Back-End Sentencing: A Practice in Search of a Rationale." *Social Research* 74 (2007): 631–44.

Travis, Lawrence F., III, and James Stacey. "A Half Century of Parole Rules: Conditions of Parole in the United States, 2008." *Journal of Criminal Justice* 38 (2010): 604–608.

US Department of Justice. *National Assessment of Structured Sentencing*. Washington, DC: Bureau of Justice Assistance, 1996.

US Department of Justice. *The Future of Parole as a Key Partner in Assuring Public Safety*. National Institute of Corrections. July 2011. http://static.nicic.gov/Library/024201.pdf.

US Department of Justice. *Smart on Crime: Reforming the Criminal Justice System for the 21st Century*. August 2013. http://www.justice.gov/ag/smart-on-crime.pdf.

US Department of Justice. Letter to the Honorable Patti B. Saris, Chair, US Sentencing Commission. July 29, 2014. http://www.justice.gov/sites/default/files/criminal/legacy/2014/08/01/2014annual-letter-final-072814.pdf.

US Sentencing Commission. *Federal Offenders Sentenced to Supervised Release*. Washington, DC: US Department of Justice, 2010.

van Humbeeck, Humbert. "Gevangenissen geven burger vals gevoel van veiligheid." *Knack*, March 20, 2013. http://www.knack.be/nieuws/belgie/gevangenissen-geven-burger-vals-gevoel-van-veiligheid/article-normal-90179.html.

van Zyl Smit, Dirk. "Humanising Imprisonment: A European Project?" *European Journal of Criminal Policy and Research* 29 (2006): 107–20.

van Zyl Smit, Dirk. "Outlawing Irreducible Life Sentences—Europe on the Brink?" *Federal Sentencing Reporter* 23 (2010): 39–48.

van Zyl Smit, Dirk. "De levenslange vrijheidsstraf internationaal vergeleken." *Justitiële verkenningen* 39 (2013): 12–31.

van Zyl Smit, Dirk, Sonja Snacken, and David Hayes. "'One Cannot Legislate Kindness': Ambiguities in European Legal Instruments on Non-Custodial Sanctions." *Punishment and Society* 17 (2015): 3–26.

van Zyl Smit, Dirk, and John R. Spencer. "The European Dimension to the Release of Sentenced Prisoners." In *Release from Prison: European Policy and Practice*, edited by Nicola Padfield, Dirk van Zyl Smit, and Frieder Dünkel, 9–46. Cullompton, UK: Willan Publishing, 2010.

van Zyl Smit, Dirk, Pete Weatherby, and Simon Creighton. "Whole Life Sentences and the Tide of European Human Rights Jurisprudence: What Is to Be Done?" *Human Rights Law Review* 14 (2014): 59–84.

von Hirsch, Andrew, and Kathleen J. Hanrahan. *The Question of Parole: Retention, Reform, or Abolition?* Cambridge, MA: Ballinger, 1979.

Weisberg, Robert. "The Sentencing Commission Model, 1970s to Present." In *The Oxford Handbook of Sentencing and Corrections*, edited by Joan Petersilia and Kevin R. Reitz, 299–316. New York: Oxford University Press, 2012.

Whitman, James Q. *Harsh Justice: Criminal Punishment and the Widening Divide between America and Europe*. New York: Oxford University Press, 2003.

Wise, Randolph E. "Parole Progress." In *National Probation and Parole Association Yearbook*, 111–20. New York: National Probation and Parole Association, 1950.

Wool, Jon, and Don Stemen. *Aggravated Sentencing:* Blakely v. Washington: *Practical Considerations for State Sentencing Systems*. New York: Vera Institute of Justice, 2004.

Zeleskov Djoric, Jelena, and Ana Batricevic. *COST Action IS 1106: Offender Supervision in Europe: Country Report for Serbia*. 2013. http://www.offendersupervision.eu/wp-content/uploads/2013/10/Offender-supervision-in-Serbia.pdf.

11

Collateral Sanctions and American Exceptionalism

A COMPARATIVE PERSPECTIVE

Nora V. Demleitner

OVER THE LAST several years, the overall prison population in the United States has begun to decrease, albeit slowly and unevenly across the country (Carson 2015).[1] While some herald this development as a major policy change, others deem it solely an overdue fiscal response to depleted state budgets and, therefore, subject to reversal once state coffers have filled up again (cf. Cole 2011). The same may be said for collateral sanctions, the most widely debated of which—disenfranchisement of so-called ex-offenders—has come increasingly under attack while others continue to flourish. When these largely hidden, automatically imposed, additional postconviction sanctions are contrasted with comparable Western democracies, particularly in western Europe, the unique punitiveness that has become an integral part of American politics and law reveals itself (see Pinard 2010). Occasional reforms, especially in the area of re-enfranchisement, and a changing rhetoric have had greater symbolic than substantive impact yet have to some extent camouflaged the ongoing exclusion of ex-offenders.

Collateral sanctions, as they are called in the United States, encompass a broad array of restrictions on offenders during the time they are under a criminal justice sanction and often well beyond. They arise under local, state, and federal law and tend to flow from the type of crime for which the offender is sentenced rather than being individually tailored. Many impinge dramatically on an individual's freedom and ability to participate effectively in political, social, and economic life. Nevertheless, most collateral sanctions flow automatically from a conviction, usually without being announced at sentencing and often without knowledge of any of the players in the criminal justice system (Klingele, Roberts, and Love 2013).[2] Administrative tribunals and other bodies, such as licensing authorities, may impose yet another set of sanctions, often called "disqualifications," which are assessed on an individual basis (American Bar Association 2003).[3] Generally under US law, collateral sanctions are viewed as civil or regulatory measures rather than "punishments" and, therefore, are not covered by the protections and rules that govern the imposition of criminal penalties.[4]

The European Union calls collateral sanctions, which it deems preventive, "disqualifications arising from a criminal conviction." They are defined as "measure[s] which [restrict], for a limited or unlimited period, a natural or legal person from exercising certain rights, occupying certain functions, engaging in certain activities, going to certain places or carrying out certain measures" (Commission of the European Communities 2006, para. 6). A wide variety of such disqualifications exist in EU member states, arising from EU directives as well as a host of national laws, only some of which are part of the criminal code. Some of these restrictions are tied to specific types of convictions, while others are based on more general standards, akin to those often used for disqualifications in the US context.[5]

In the United States the sheer number of collateral sanctions has become staggering, and it has been almost impossible to detail all the sanctions potentially befalling an offender.[6] In the EU countries it has been equally difficult to ascertain disqualifications as they affect offenders in different ways and national criminal record registries vary in terms of their comprehensiveness (Commission of the European Communities 2006, para. 28). Nevertheless, the impact of collateral sanctions in the United States far outpaces that of disqualifications in Europe. This is in part due to the total number of offenders with criminal records in the United States, as well as the panoply of such sanctions and their impact on all aspects of an offender's life.

Dramatically different philosophies about the treatment of those with criminal records are at work in the United States as opposed to Europe. As the chapter will show, punitiveness, attitudes of exclusion, and fear of the risk of reoffending lead to offenders virtually "exiting" American society, often without hope of re-entry from outside this virtual—and for immigrant offenders physical—border. The European model, on the other hand, remains based on assumptions of reintegration and rehabilitation of those with a criminal record. European states do, however, increasingly exercise control over select offender groups assumed to be particularly dangerous or to pose a high risk of reoffending.

This chapter first provides an overview of the development of collateral sanctions in Europe and the United States over time, up to the present. It then discusses specific groups of collateral sanctions. Under the political rights category the focus is on the right to vote during imprisonment and after release. While the franchise connotes a crucial right of citizenship, formal and informal restrictions on participation in the labor market can effectively amount to an exclusion from legitimate employment. In contrast to western European countries in particular, the United States selectively denies social and welfare benefits to particular offender groups, often making it difficult for them to re-enter society successfully. The web of collateral sanctions restricts US offenders from functioning as full members of society based solely on their criminal record to a substantially greater extent than is the case in most European countries.

The chapter then turns to two groups of collateral sanctions that exemplify the increasing harshness of such consequences. Noncitizen offenders face deportation and a long-term re-entry bar upon certain criminal convictions. Sex offenders may be subject to public ostracism because of US notification and registration laws and to potentially lifelong detention in the form of civil commitment. While deportation and preventive detention based on criminal offenses also exist in western Europe, their breadth, scope, and length render them qualitatively different.

The situation in the United States is aggravated because of limited relief provisions, many of which have also become increasingly outdated because conviction records are easily and often permanently accessible. Even though differences between the US and European sanctioning systems have been well documented, little attention has been given to collateral sanctions. Differences between such sanctions, however, provide yet another glimpse into the distinct attitudes toward offenders and goals of punishment on both sides of the Atlantic.

Collateral Sanctions in Mobile, Information-Based Societies: The Impact of Values

Collateral sanctions have changed throughout history. Initially their goals were to punish, often severely, and to publicize wrongdoing. Following a period of decline which has continued in Europe, in the United States today these goals play a dominant role, though the sanctions are often justified as incapacitative measures.

Collateral Sanctions over Time

Under Roman law, conviction of a capital offense destroyed full citizenship. Any judgment that included a corporal penalty or imprisonment, especially convictions for larceny, fraud, and robbery, triggered *infamia*, which generally lasted a lifetime. These so-called honor penalties were not imposed but came into effect automatically. Some crimes, for example, led to the person's inability to operate as a witness to a contract. For others, the convicted could not be mentioned honorably after death. When a male offender was sentenced to working in the mines, he was also automatically marked (Kühne 1931, 3–4).

Even though Germanic law originally viewed honor as intrinsic—rather than extrinsic—to the individual, corporal punishments and the death penalty also carried automatic loss of rights with them. Among the public law consequences were loss of the active and passive right to vote and restricted rights to appear in court. Further loss of rights, which flowed directly from an action rather than a conviction, could lead to the total destruction of the person by denying him home and protection. This particular penalty also amounted to a death sentence for the offender's family. In some cases, honor penalties could lead to removal from a guild, with devastating professional and financial consequences. At the same time canon law developed its own honor consequences, such as excommunication or denial of a religious funeral (Fröhling 2014, 35, 47; Kühne 1931, 5). At the time, honor penalties served largely retributive and deterrent purposes. Still, there was also a security component to them. For example, public humiliation at the pillory assured that everyone in town knew about the offender, especially when he or she returned after being banned (Fröhling 2014, 58).

On the Continent, the Enlightenment led to changes that tied automatic collateral sanctions to specific offenses, such as lying under oath, and limited the number of honor penalties substantially. Prussian land law decreed that, for nonenumerated crimes, loss of rights could occur only if explicitly imposed at sentencing (Fröhling 2014, 19).[7] Some sentences remained tied to the loss of citizenship rights.[8] A few German states embedded collateral sanctions in parts of the law other than the criminal code. Saxony's election law, for example, prescribed denial of the right to vote for crimes considered dishonorable (Kühne 1931, 6–7).

In the nineteenth century, honor penalties decreased substantially, and those remaining emphasized public safety. By the middle of the nineteenth century demeaning honor penalties, including the public use of the pillory, had been abolished. Instead, the goal in Germany was to keep serious offenders out of the military and the civil service, which followed upon convictions with aggravated prison sentences. In clearly delineated cases the court could individually declare the denial of such rights but not for longer than 10 years (Fröhling 2014, 69–70, 78–80).

Starting in 1871, the German judge had to impose all collateral sanctions at sentencing, even if they flowed automatically from the conviction. The loss of election rights, loss of rights to serve as a witness and a custodian, and loss of the right to hold government offices were part of these sanctions but could not last longer than 10 years. The court also could impose additional sanctions, such as a prohibition on holding public office, generally for up to five years. In only a few cases could public office be lost forever (Kühne 1931, 17). Under French law, on the other hand, loss of citizenship rights was tied to the type of primary sentence imposed and lasted for the rest of life (p. 43). The loss of this cluster of rights was explicitly classified as a penalty. As they deprive an offender of the ability to participate in public life, their loss amounted to "civil death" (p. 17).

In German law, not much is left of these honor penalties. Only an offender convicted of a crime and sentenced to more than one year will be automatically excluded from access to certain positions, including those in the administration of justice, to protect the public. Loss of the right to vote has to be specially imposed and is permitted only for a narrow category of offenses against the state, the Constitution, and elections (Demleitner 2000; Demleitner 2009).

Historically, England treated convicted criminals as outlaws, which later morphed in Anglo-Saxon law into attainder, which resulted from a felony conviction that led to the forfeiture of all possessions and "civil death." This (lack of) status implied the absence of all civil rights, which included the loss of family rights and freedom of movement (Easton 2006, 443–44).

By the nineteenth century, English law recognized the loss of civil rights upon conviction for treason or any felony with a minimum sentence of 12 months. Among the rights forfeited for life were access to public office and pension benefits, similar to the continental practice, together with the loss of rights over one's property and election rights. In addition to having to give up these public rights, in many countries the convicted lost a host of private rights, such as the ability to inherit or to have a will honored (Kühne 1931, 46).

While many countries have recognized the loss of rights upon a criminal conviction, the goals have differed among nations and over time, though they appear to have always been mixed. In some nations the loss of honor has been dominant; in others it has been public safety (Kühne 1931). Increasingly the latter rationale has become controlling, though in the United States some denials of rights are only tangentially related to public safety and appear instead to be animated by punitive impulses.

Collateral Sanctions Today

While many of the features of "civil death" have long been abolished in all countries, others not only survive stubbornly but play a more pernicious role, with greater long-term impact, in modern society. Much of the US literature on rehabilitation, reintegration, and recidivism includes discussions on the vast array of such disabling sanctions as they are widely believed to inhibit successful reintegration.

These sanctions came under substantial attack in the 1960s, an era focused heavily on rehabilitation, and subsequently decreased in scope and impact. They almost disappeared from public view until the mid-1990s. In the intervening years, the United States witnessed the onset of the "War on Drugs" and the growth not only in the prison population but in the overall number of individuals under a criminal justice sanction and with prior criminal convictions. It was not until the mid- to late 1990s that some focus on debilitating collateral sanctions returned (Klingele, Roberts, and Love 2013). In light of the annual release of large numbers of inmates from prisons and the impact of recidivism on incarceration rates, the role of collateral sanctions has been questioned, though their numbers have continued to expand. The impact of collateral sanctions on an offender has also been criticized as exclusionary. Unless the breadth and effects of collateral consequences are addressed, even broad-based efforts at rehabilitation are likely to be hindered, if not condemned to fail (Maruna 2011, 98).

Recidivism-based arguments indicate that the greatest concern of policymakers and of criminal justice officials remains with the management of the risk ex-offenders potentially pose (Harcourt 2006; Slobogin 2011; see Webster and Doob, this volume). Collateral sanctions that have been promoted as effective at reducing risk—despite some evidence to the contrary in many cases—will not easily be modified, let alone abolished.

As the US criminal justice system has spearheaded a relentless movement toward greater harshness and punitiveness, a number of European countries have followed that lead, albeit with much greater restraint (see Lappi-Seppälä, this volume), which likely reflects historical, religious, and social differences. Most European countries continue to emphasize resocialization and reintegration as they focus on providing a helping hand after a (temporary) failing (Field 2006, 538). Since the United States and European countries started in the 1960s with a similar degree and level of imprisonment and collateral sanctions, the distinctions have become more pronounced, reflecting largely divergent attitudes toward offenders, rehabilitation, and the role those with criminal records can and should play after completing their criminal justice sanctions. These differences have been heightened in light of developments in information technology that increasingly limit privacy and subject personal information, including criminal records, to public scrutiny.

In earlier times criminal offenders in the United States could usually leave their past behind. Records of criminal convictions were only accessible at the courthouse, and a move across state or international boundaries allowed offenders an opportunity to reinvent themselves. Modern technology, however, has made this much more challenging. In the United States criminal records are easily accessible, in some cases directly through websites and in others through private providers and state agencies (Jacobs 2015). European countries are generally unwilling to hold offenders out to the type of public shaming that is occurring in the United States. Spain, for example, prohibits the public distribution of the names of convicted offenders, on the theory that this would violate the offender's "constitutional rights of honor, privacy, and rehabilitation" (Jacobs and Larrauri 2012, 10).

These philosophical differences are particularly jarring in the case of sex offenders. The United States mandates sex offender registries to be put on websites to provide the public with an opportunity to protect themselves against a group of offenders that is (erroneously) considered to have a high recidivism rate.[9] Many Spanish legal scholars consider such publication degrading (Jacobs and Larrauri 2012, 12). German police agencies keep databases on select groups of offenders, including sex offenders, yet those are not publicly accessible. Even though such publication has occasionally been considered, it has been rejected as a violation of the offender's right to resocialization and right to informational self-determination (Fröhling 2014, 408–09).

Increasingly even leaving one's home country temporarily has become more challenging for some categories of offenders, let alone starting a new once abroad. Both the United States and England require sex offenders, including those with foreign convictions, to notify the police of their whereabouts and any changes to their residence. England and Ireland may bar convicted child sex offenders from traveling abroad, to prevent them from targeting children there (McAlinden 2012, 173–74). So-called football hooligans may also be barred from leaving their home countries during major international soccer matches abroad and from attending games in England. These football banning orders, which last from three to ten years, can be imposed upon convictions for a select group of offenses connected to a soccer game (Kidza 2014, 318–23).[10] The English government has used this procedure regularly to deny those convicted (or otherwise suspected) of violence during a soccer match from traveling to other EU member states for a fixed number of years, with the ban restricted to the times of major soccer matches (Beckham 2001).

In light of overall increasing mobility of people, within the European Union but also globally, transferability of criminal records as well as recognition of collateral sanctions by the receiving countries have become salient issues. In the United States, state law governs the imposition of collateral sanctions on those who were convicted in another state (Ewald 2009, 543–44). In the European Union, a series of directives have led to partial mutual recognition of collateral sanctions, with other directives considering more closely the results of disqualifications (Commission of the European Communities 2006, para. 13). The European Union has struggled with mutual recognition of disqualifications in light of the diversity of sanctions in member states. Frequently, member states that do not impose certain sanctions on domestic offenders refuse to be put in a position where they would have to enforce such sanctions in their territories when imposed by another member. Also, "extending the territorial effect of disqualifications could be seen as aggravating the sanction, and raises the issue of the rights of the individual who will see the territorial scope of the disqualification extended to the whole territory of the European Union" (para. 22). This statement is indicative of European concern for the rights of the offender and the impact of these disqualifications in light of the ultimate goal of rehabilitation, which continues to govern at least the continental European regimes. In US states, however, those considerations appear to play little role as collateral sanctions will be imposed territorially so that those with a criminal record may be liberated from or restricted by collateral sanctions if moving to a different state.

The starkest differences between collateral sanctions in Europe and the United States are the breadth, automaticity, and often the length of the consequences that befall offenders in the United States even after they have served a criminal justice sentence. The most prominent indicator of the distinct philosophies and approaches to offenders prevalent on both sides of the Atlantic may be the debate about access to the ballot box by those with a criminal record.

Political Rights during and after Release from Imprisonment

Once the franchise became more widely available to different groups within the citizenry in Europe, for convicted offenders the loss of civil rights generally also entailed disenfranchisement for good. As early as the late nineteenth century, however, a major liberalization in England legally restricted the loss of prisoner voting rights as well as the ability of prisoners to run for office to those serving 12 months or longer.[11] All prisoners nevertheless remained effectively disenfranchised as the administrative apparatus did not provide for those serving a shorter sentence to cast a ballot (Murray 2013, 515–16).

Around the same time in the United States, in the aftermath of the Civil War many of the former Confederate states restricted the franchise, largely to exclude African Americans from the ballot not only during imprisonment but well beyond. The types of convictions that led to disenfranchisement varied widely, often based on a perception of the crimes African Americans would commit.[12] In 1974 the US Supreme Court upheld disenfranchisement based on criminal convictions as constitutional based on a provision in Section 2 of the Fourteenth Amendment, unless racial animus could be proven.[13]

Automatic and broad-based prisoner disenfranchisement lacks any coherent philosophical underpinning (Pettus 2013). Nevertheless, it tends to be justified either on a social contract or on a Republican citizenship theory. Under the former, the offender, having "broken" the social contract, may no longer participate in the political process. Under the latter, the "purity of the ballot box" concept requires that offenders be removed from the vote. Both theoretical constructs appear misplaced at a time of ever broader voting rights. Occasionally one also finds the claim that disenfranchisement adds to deterrence,[14] though others argue that it impedes rehabilitation and reintegration because of its exclusionary character (Easton 2011; Miller and Spillane 2012).

For most detainees in the United States, voting rights are effectively restricted during pretrial detention, though legally the denial of voting rights becomes effective upon admission to prison. Only two states remain that allow imprisoned inmates to cast their ballot,[15] which means that over 2.2 million people currently held in prisons and jails are effectively denied the right to vote (Kaeble et al. 2015). A vast array of states also disenfranchise anyone under a criminal justice sentence; and some disenfranchise anyone with a felony conviction, even if such a conviction is far in the past.

In light of a 1998 report by Human Rights Watch and The Sentencing Project (Fellner and Mauer 1998), much of the collateral sanctions reform efforts in the United States that followed have focused on voting rights, an emphasis that increased after the 2000 presidential election in which Florida's disenfranchisement law may have had an impact on the outcome of the vote (Uggen and Manza 2006). As state rather than federal law governs voting rights, these reform efforts have led to piecemeal changes in individual states, though millions of Americans with felony records remain unable to vote as some of the states that disenfranchise everyone or a broad group of people with felony records make it virtually impossible to regain the franchise (see, e.g., Ewald 2009; Mauer 2011, 533; Eisenberg 2012).[16]

Much of the franchise-reform effort was the result of studies indicating a stark racial impact of felon disenfranchisement (Mauer 2011, 553–54). With the focus on racial disparity, other advocacy arguments—the potential impact of exclusion on recidivism and the reintegration of offenders, especially those who had proven themselves to be law-abiding citizens (Uggen, Van Brakle, and McLaughlin 2009, 74), the dignity rights of offenders, or the franchise as a crucial civil or human right—carried comparatively little weight. Relatively little academic or advocacy discourse on voting as a human rights issue or a matter of human dignity surrounds re-enfranchisement efforts in the United States, though it has been a major focus of election-related litigation around the globe (Mauer 2011).

In a number of countries prisoner disenfranchisement has been increasingly challenged in domestic courts or regional and international human rights fora. The theories behind such court challenges are frequently based either on an argument of voting rights as (strong) human rights or on the claim that disenfranchisement constitutes a serious impediment to the full integration and rehabilitation of offenders (Easton 2011, 220–22; Mauer 2011, 562–63).

A study by the Quaker Council for European Affairs indicates that in 2011 eight of the European countries imposed no restrictions on voting rights during imprisonment, while three excluded some categories of prisoners from the franchise and continued to do so upon release (Quaker Council for European Affairs 2011, 101–02)—Belgium, Estonia and Luxembourg (Home and White 2015, app.).[17] In Belgium such disenfranchisement ranges from five years to life; in Luxembourg a prison sentence of 10 years or more carries with it lifetime disenfranchisement, while a 5- to 10-year sentence leads to disenfranchisement generally from 10 to 20 years, with a lifetime denial possible. Another 10 countries disenfranchise prisoners (Quaker Council for European Affairs 2011, 102–03). A 2013 study by the Prisoner Trust showed that only seven of the countries that have signed on to the European Convention on Human Rights prohibit all prisoners from voting (London School of Economics 2013, 18).

As Sweden, Denmark, and Finland do not appear to recognize any so-called honor sanctions, they do not permit disenfranchisement based on a criminal conviction. The predominant argument favoring retention of voting rights is resocialization as those who do not have any civil rights also lack any incentive to recognize civil duties (Weinrich 2009, 204). Switzerland, Ireland, and Spain allow all prisoners to vote,[18] while Russia denies that right to all inmates. In France a select group of offenses leads to automatic disenfranchisement.[19]

In Germany judges can specifically impose deprivation of voting rights as an additional sanction but only for specific offenses against the state (Demleitner 2000, 86).[20] When inmates are enfranchised, the interest in casting a ballot seems robust, with 20–60 percent of them voting.[21] While in the United States disenfranchisement provisions are closely tied to geography and race history (Quaker Council for European Affairs 2011, 103), in Europe largely eastern European countries have retained extensive prisoner disenfranchisement (Home and White 2015, app.).

Even though the legal landscape may be somewhat checkered in Europe, over the last decade the Committee of Ministers of the Council of Europe and the European Court of Human Rights (ECHR) have staked out baseline requirements for inmate voting. In 2005 the ECHR held an English ban on voting imposed on any prisoner to be in violation of the European Convention of Human Rights' requirement that member states provide for free and fair elections.[22] Despite granting member states a margin of appreciation with respect to the rules governing free elections, the court deemed automatic disenfranchisement upon incarceration disproportionate as it was not tied to the seriousness of the offense, the offender's background, or the length of the sentence. Therefore, the ban may be unjustifiable, especially in light of jurisprudential changes in the value attached to the right to vote. As the court affirmed in a later case, "[a] general, automatic, and indiscriminate restriction on all detained convicts' rights to vote was considered by the Court as falling outside the acceptable margin of appreciation."[23] The court also noted that the English Parliament had never substantively debated the blanket ban, indicating that it failed to evaluate the proportionality or the impact of this sanction.

The decision implies that "[d]isenfranchisement may only be envisaged for a rather narrowly defined group of offenders serving a lengthy term of imprisonment; there should be a direct link between the facts on which a conviction is based and the sanction of disenfranchisement; and such a measure should preferably be imposed not by operation of a law but by the decision of a judge following judicial proceedings."[24] Even though blanket prisoner disenfranchisement in the United Kingdom is a relatively recent phenomenon,[25] it has been fiercely defended in Parliament, often with the argument that voting is a privilege rather than a human right, which makes it easier for the legislature to consider the denial an appendage to imprisonment rather than an additional sanction. In fact, much of the justification of a blanket ban appears to be tied to populist retributive notions of punishment. In addition, British resistance stems from the perception that a "foreign" court imposed its decision on Parliament (Murray 2013, 513). The obstinacy of British lawmakers to change has led the ECHR to rule repeatedly against the United Kingdom on this issue.[26] The United Kingdom still has not adopted new election legislation (Home and White 2015).

In other cases the ECHR seemed to retreat from its reading of Article 3 somewhat, perhaps to be conciliatory toward the United Kingdom. For example, in another English case it indicated that voting rights do not have to be extended to referendums or the election of local government.[27] In *Scoppola v. Italy (No. 3)*, the Grand Chamber appeared to draw back from the positions that a judge has to impose the denial of the franchise and that there has to be a direct connection between the offense and disenfranchisement.[28] As long as it is closely tied to the offense and the sentence imposed, disenfranchisement will be permissible. The court upheld an Italian law that permitted lifetime disenfranchisement upon imposition of a sentence of at least five years imprisonment.[29] Similarly, the Australian Supreme Court rejected a blanket ban on prisoner voting but resurrected the previous policy, which prohibited from voting only those who serve three years or more in prison (Victorian Electoral Commission 2012, 3).

The ECHR also struck down a Turkish disenfranchisement law that applied once offenders were released conditionally and to those whose sentences were suspended.[30] In a case against Russia, the court declared even a constitutionally based blanket ban on voting in violation of the Convention.[31]

Not unlike some of the discourse in the United States, European prison reformers have argued that at best blanket disenfranchisement of prisoners serves no purpose and that at worst it will lead to social exclusion, which will perpetuate criminality and lead to recidivism (Quaker Council for European Affairs 2011, 105; Ölbermann 2011, 261–62). The Canadian Supreme Court, in striking down Canadian disenfranchisement legislation, which applied only to those serving a sentence of more than two years, as violating the proportionality principle under the Canadian Charter of Rights and Freedoms, went even further, claiming that loss of voting rights by prisoners "undermines the legitimacy of the government, the effectiveness of the government, and the rule of law."[32] It viewed the government's avowed objectives as unconnected to disenfranchisement and perhaps even counterproductive. Retaining voting rights may play a salutary role for prisoners as it allows them to "maintain . . . connections to society and . . . have some say in the laws that affect them" (Quaker Council for European Affairs 2011, 105). The court, therefore, considered disenfranchisement akin to an attribution of "moral unworthiness," a notion inconsistent with democracy and "the constitutional command to respect everyone's right to dignity and respect."[33] Ultimately, "[p]rison should not seek to remove what defines us as people and citizens" (Quaker Council for European Affairs 2011, 105). This decision may be one of the most inclusive, attempting to establish that imprisonment should not exclude individuals from society and the polity, even if it removes them physically. The court also deemed the measure to have a highly negative impact on the aboriginal population, which Canada imprisons in disproportionate numbers, as is also true for Native populations in Australia, New Zealand, and the United States.

The South African Constitutional Court also upheld prisoners' rights to vote against challenges.[34] The 1963 Kenyan Constitution, on the other hand, barred prisoners from participating in elections for president and the national assembly.[35] The High Court of Kenya, however, interpreted the provision narrowly so as to allow prisoners, sans those convicted of an electoral offense, to vote in a referendum.[36] It held that voting in a referendum is substantively different from voting in elections as it only occurs when the constitution is approved or altered. In its decision, the court looked toward the jurisprudence of both the United Nations Human Rights Committee and the ECHR.[37] It concluded that the right to vote is a basic human right as it is part of the people's power so that "[o]n the balance of proportionality . . . there is no legitimate governmental objective or purpose that would be served by denying the inmates the right to vote in a referendum." This court focused on the guarantee of voting rights as a human and political rights issue rather than on the impact of disenfranchisement on the offender. Similarly, the Israeli Supreme Court upheld the right of prisoners to vote in the case of Prime Minister Rabin's assassin.[38]

The International Covenant on Civil and Political Rights (ICCPR), one of the two fundamental human rights documents, guarantees citizens the right to vote "without unreasonable restrictions." The general comment on this provision, issued by the United Nations Human Rights Committee, states that "[t]he grounds for such deprivation should be objective and reasonable." It specifically notes that if a conviction is the cause of disenfranchisement "the period of suspension should be proportionate to the offence and the sentence." Nevertheless in 1993 the Human Rights Committee, in considering a Luxembourg law that mandated disenfranchisement for anyone convicted of a "serious crime," merely suggested that Luxembourg consider abolishing the law as disenfranchisement was to be viewed as an additional sanction. When addressing the US situation in 2006, the committee declared that "the general deprivation of the right (to) vote for persons who have received a felony conviction, and in particular those who are no longer deprived of liberty, do[es] not meet the requirements of [the ICCPR]." The committee's analysis has evolved over time, though it seems to distinguish between those denied the franchise while imprisoned and those released from prison.[39] Even though the jurisprudence of national and regional courts and international fora differs in the rationales and justifications for their decisions, ultimately they are unified in their rejection of a blanket ban on prisoner voting in fundamental elections.

The position of most US states has, therefore, increasingly become an outlier, especially with respect to nonproportionate inmate and postincarceration disenfranchisement. In America, even though many have argued for lifting or at least shortening the bans on offenders upon their release from prisons, there is virtually no advocacy for even a limited enfranchisement of those imprisoned.[40] The ready acceptance of prisoner disenfranchisement, even by those who otherwise promote limitations on collateral sanctions and the restoration of voting rights upon release from incarceration, is telling. Despite its overall restrictive approach on collateral sanctions, a cautionary example of this acquiescence may be the 2003 American Bar Association's standards on collateral sanctions. In contrast to the 1981 edition, which indicated that prisoners should be authorized to vote, the current standard explicitly states that "[j]urisdictions should not impose the following collateral sanctions: (a) deprivation of the right to vote, except during actual confinement" (American Bar Association 2003, standard 19-2.6 and 35–38). This change in the standard reflects the wider societal climate on punishment and the American approach to prisons and inmates. The general approach is to locate prisons far from public view and to assume that inmates are correctly excluded from virtually any participation in outside life other than on the most personal level. Despite state budget cuts that also impact corrections budgets and counsel in favor of smaller inmate populations and a greater efficacy of rehabilitative measures, the goals of normalizing life in prison to make it resemble life on the outside and beginning the reintegration of prisoners while in prison effectively remain largely absent.[41]

The franchise is an important marker of citizenship. Restricting or removing such a marker is likely to imply to offenders that they are not full members of this community and perhaps can never be such.[42] Economic and social rights, however, may have a more dramatic impact on the ability of someone with a criminal record to reintegrate effectively and quickly upon release from imprisonment. In that area, US restrictions are broad and lengthy and hinder re-entry efforts.

Economic and Social Rights

Economic and social rights are designed to guarantee everyone at least the opportunity to live a decent life. These are generally considered to include rights to an education, food, health, housing, social security, and work.

Access to Employment

Employment restrictions on those with a criminal record may be legally mandated, arise from legal provisions that make it inefficient or unreasonably costly to hire such a person, or arise from an employer's preference. The latter informal restrictions may stem from employers who fear being sued if the employee were to commit a criminal act while in their employ or who are biased. As offenders often have less schooling and employment market experience than other applicants, not hiring them may also reflect a rational response to the available human capital.[43] In addition to these barriers, outright restrictions on employment are increasingly common in Europe and the United States. Many of these pertain to convicted sex and drug offenders, mainly to restrict them from occupations that would bring them in regular contact with children.[44] These restrictions are substantially broader in the United States, however (Jacobs and Larrauri 2012).

Entire areas of work have become off limits to individuals with select convictions because of outright governmental bans, licensing restrictions, or other limits on governmental funding or contracting that make it illegal or at least inefficient for an employer to hire someone with any or a particular criminal conviction. Examples of indirect governmental influence on hiring are restrictions on a company's ability to receive public reimbursement for services provided or to bid on public contracts if a particular type of former offender is in its employ. Such prohibitions are in place in both the European Union and the United States. The EU Public Procurement Directive, for example, provides that someone convicted of participation in a criminal organization, corruption, fraud on the European Union, or money laundering may be precluded from participating in a public contract (*Official Journal of the European Union* 2004, 114).[45] The select restrictions, usually based on particular types of convictions, must be rational and appropriately limited to high-risk offenders.

In addition to restrictions that emanate—automatically or in some cases after consideration of individual cases—from administrative and civil law on both sides of the Atlantic (Sobota 2015), German criminal law explicitly recognizes an employment prohibition as a part of the criminal sanctioning system, albeit as not a penalty but rather a security-based measure.[46] It can be imposed from one to five years, though it includes the possibility of a lifetime ban. The sanction can be inflicted only if the employment was used explicitly in connection with the criminal offense or the offender recklessly violated the job duties. There must be a reasoned likelihood of continuing abuse of such position to inflict substantial danger on the public. The sanction is used relatively rarely and largely in the white-collar context upon commission of fraud or environmental offenses (Hellwig 2008, 222).

When imposed at sentencing, the offender will be informed about the consequences of his or her conviction. Many of these restrictions, in Germany and the United States, follow from other, noncriminal areas of the law and are therefore regularly unknown to the convicted. In addition, often they do not impact an offender until many years after his or her conviction at a time when the person is fully rehabilitated. This is particularly likely to occur in the United States, where employment prohibitions are frequently not tied to the length of time that has passed since the conviction and criminal records cannot be sealed or expunged (Bowes 2015).[47] Under German law, some prohibitions are automatic but limited in most cases to five years. In addition, criminal convictions—and the ensuing employment restrictions and other limitations—entered into the federal central register are regularly expunged, based on statutory rules (Bundesamt für Justiz 2016). In the United States, on the other hand, the combination of lack of sufficient notice of the full impact of a criminal conviction with the lifelong existence of such a record provides substantial hurdles for those with a criminal conviction.

Access to the labor market may be indirectly restricted through other types of collateral sanctions, including denial of a driver's license and loss of the right to carry a weapon. In addition, as discussed in the next section, many offenders have been deprived of even a minimum social safety net because of their criminal record.

Access to Social Welfare and Other Benefits

Continental lawyers are regularly astounded to learn of US restrictions on social welfare rights and entitlements. The Council of Europe declared the successful social integration of prisoners an important part of a functioning democracy (Council of Europe 2006). To accomplish this goal, vocational training and employment are crucial elements, and social benefits are important reintegration investments that ultimately facilitate employment.[48] As part of the War on Drugs, the United States, on the other hand, allows states to exclude automatically any offender convicted of a single felony drug crime from financial and other social welfare assistance.

As part of the 1996 welfare overhaul, Congress included a provision banning those with a felony drug conviction from the receipt of Temporary Assistance to Needy Families and the Supplemental Nutrition Assistance Program. There was virtually no discussion of the exclusion, which apparently was meant to be punitive, though occasionally it is defended on deterrent grounds or as a pre-emptive strategy against welfare fraud. Even though states have the opportunity to opt out of the ban, the vast majority of them have not done so or have qualified their participation only in minor ways (Sentencing Project 2014).

In addition, the federal government allows for broad discretion in exclusions of offenders from a variety of other benefits, such as public housing for those engaged in drug or violent activity that would have a detrimental impact on the premises, and encourages states, through financial incentives, to enact restrictive hiring policies (Demleitner 2002; Salzmann and Love 2009; Blumstein and Nakamura 2009). Under certain conditions educational loans are also prohibited under the 1998 Higher Education Act for some of those convicted of drug offenses (US Department of Education 2016).[49]

Drug convictions can also lead to the suspension of an offender's driver's license, even if they are unconnected to driving.[50] Many states have abolished or amended the suspension, but some retain it (Subramanian and Moreno 2014; Schoenberg 2016). In Pennsylvania, for example, any drug conviction leads to a six-month license suspension, which may go up to two years, depending on the offender's criminal record.[51] Collateral sanctions based on drug convictions may be waning generally as the country appears to be re-evaluating its attitude toward drugs and at least nonviolent and minor drug offenders (Subramanian and Moreno 2014).

Only a limited amount of academic literature exists in the United States on driver's license restrictions, while in some European countries substantial justification and analysis have gone into this limitation, which some commentators consider an infringement on personal liberty. German law, for example, recognizes two forms of prohibitions on driving: a temporary ban and a longer and more burdensome license confiscation.[52] Both of these arise only from traffic violations and indicate different levels of a driver's inability to conduct himself or herself responsibly as a traffic participant, as determined by a court (Halecker 2008). The economic impact on many offenders may be more dramatic in the United States, where public transportation tends to be more limited than in Europe.

Despite efforts in the United States that extended from the 1950s to the mid-1980s to limit collateral sanctions with respect to social rights and licensing provisions, the tide turned at that point, leading to more restrictions on convicted offenders (Love 2011, 764–71). While many of the restrictions are in some way risk-based, they are often unnecessarily broad in the types of offenses that trigger them and expansive with respect to length. That seems to reflect legislators having become increasingly risk-averse. The underlying philosophy appears to be a belief that a former offender will pose a constant threat and therefore can never be trusted—or will never be deserving of any benefits. Denial of welfare benefits resembles a return to the times when benefits were given only to the "deserving" (Katz 1989).

The lack of support, especially for those released from prison, contributes to the high recidivism rate, which reaffirms those who are suspicious of anyone with a criminal record. Ultimately, the number and severity of these restrictions imply a gradual move back toward "civil death," especially as a more transparent society allows instant access to personal data and therefore interference with an individual's right to privacy and choice.

In addition to impacting these rights and benefits, a criminal record can trigger a host of other collateral sanctions. There are two types of collateral sanctions legislators and courts have singled out as particularly severe and potentially detrimental to a person's life and well-being. The first is deportation arising from a criminal conviction. While not deeming it a penalty, the US Supreme Court acknowledged its unique character when mandating in *Padilla v. Kentucky* (2010) that criminal defense attorneys inform their clients of immigration consequences before accepting a plea bargain. The second is civil confinement based on a sex offense. In the states that allow for this possibility, the laws provide for criminal procedure–type protections.

Are Some Collateral Sanctions Truly Penalties?

Two collateral sanctions are particularly life-altering. One—deportation—befalls many convicted noncitizen offenders automatically, though it may also occur through an administrative process. A number of states reinstituted the other—civil commitment for sex offenders—in the 1990s. It is always subject to heightened procedural protections, including the right to counsel. For sex offenders, however, civil commitment is merely the most severe of a tight web of collateral sanctions. Deportation and civil commitment ultimately amount to exiling the person with a criminal record from our society.

Noncitizens: Deportation

Even though criminal offenders have been deported from the United States because of their criminal convictions for decades, since the mid-1990s the deportation regime has become much harsher. A larger number of offenses, many relatively minor, now lead to automatic deportation upon conviction (Human Rights Watch 2007). Deportations, therefore, do not include any proportionality considerations, making them formally devoid of limitations on retribution (Stumpf 2009) and consequently perhaps better understood solely as a utilitarian instrument, though perhaps with questionable effectiveness. With increasing funding for immigration enforcement, the number of deportations increased manifold between 1990 and 2014 but declined in 2015 and again in 2016 (Rosenblum and McCabe 2014; US Immigration and Customs Enforcement 2015; see also *Padilla*).

As no constitutional provisions assure noncitizens of substantive rights against deportation, litigants have taken refuge in procedural mechanisms. Many celebrated the Supreme Court's *Padilla* decision, which requires that criminal defense counsel inform their clients whether their plea carries a risk of immigration consequences. They deem the decision a helpful step against the harshness and spread of collateral sanctions and an effective way of protecting criminal defendants against the imposition of such sanctions (Love 2011, 756–58). The last revolution with respect to the expansion of criminal procedural rights, which occurred during the 1960s, however, seems to have precipitated, perhaps even allowed for, the subsequent rush to ever greater punitiveness (Stuntz 2011). Ultimately, an increase in procedural rights allows for enhanced penalties and harsher collateral sanctions at the back end.

Notification requirements do not prohibit ever more draconian or ever broader sanctions,[53] though at least they lay out the panoply of consequences to be expected. The *Padilla* court's demand that accused noncitizens be counseled regarding potential immigration consequences does not prohibit Congress from further expanding the sway of those provisions, even if their initial harshness led to the increase in procedural guarantees.

While European countries also permit and in some cases strongly encourage the deportation of noncitizen offenders,[54] the regimes are generally less restrictive and more discretionary, with a focus on the individual offender's circumstances rather than merely the offense committed. The new German residency law, for example, notes explicitly that deportation will result if the facts in the individual case indicate that the public's interest in the foreigner's departure is higher than in his or her stay in Germany because he or she presents a danger to public order and safety, the democratic order, or other important state interests. Listed among the *especially* important state interests in departure is the commission of intentional offenses that resulted in a prison sentence of more than two years or the imposition of civil (preventive) detention after the last conviction. A state interest favoring deportation, albeit to a lesser degree, exists when the conviction led to a prison sentence of at least one year or a youth sentence of the same length that was not suspended. These rules are largely more restrictive than earlier legislation but explicitly recognize the discretionary character of a deportation even if a criminal conviction counsels in its favor (Sobota 2015, 184–88). The goal of such deportation is in the protection of public order and may also serve general and specific deterrence functions.

The European Court of Human Rights has frequently prevented deportations based on the Convention's protection of family life, which includes family unity.[55] Here, a substantive right has been used to prevent deportations, especially for long-term residents who have little or no ties to their country of citizenship but strong ties to the country of destination and a spouse and children in whose best interest it would be to stay in the country that tries to deport him or her. Nevertheless, the gravity of the crime of conviction may outweigh all of those interests (Agostino 2015). In contrast to the mandatory nature of deportations from the United States based on select criminal convictions, all members of the European Convention are asked to weigh the proportionality of deportation against a Convention right.

Collateral sanctions on the immigration side may be the ultimate "civil death" as they (almost) permanently exile the person with the criminal record from the community. In the United States deportation reflects a perception of the offender as a solitary individual, whose removal presumably will not impact his or her family or community. It also accords with the prevailing spirit of offenders as risks whose incapacitation—perhaps quarantine-like status—should continue even beyond release from incarceration. In Europe, on the other hand, rehabilitative and reintegrative measures generally dominate, even with respect to those who might be removable as long as they have earned some membership in the community or who might suffer hardship upon removal. The ECHR has provided recourse for some of these otherwise deportable individuals. The court's rulings have, however, been attacked in some members states, most notably Great Britain.

Under the 2012 amendments to the immigration rules, deportations of criminal offenders from the United Kingdom will be easier as deportation is now mandatory for non–European Economic Area offenders with a sentence of 12 or more months in custody and those from European Economic Area countries with twice that sentence length. Appeals are impossible unless a human rights or international obligation is at issue (Ashworth and Zedner 2014, 237–38). In the latter case British courts have asserted their obligation to conduct a proportionality review despite attempts to restrict such review.[56] Public approval of deportations for criminal offending is high, presumably because the public strongly disapproves of those it considers abusive of its hospitality (Gibney 2013, 218–19). Deportations of offenders appear to reaffirm the values and the significance of citizenship.

In the end, protections under the European Convention will mitigate any draconian deportation regime in its member states (Gibney 2013, 232–33), in contrast to the United States where a right to family life is not constitutionally protected and the prohibition on "cruel, inhuman or degrading treatment" has been found inapplicable. The sole protection emanates from the non-refoulement provision in the Refugee Convention. The assumption of membership in the political community has become more attenuated and more fragile in the United States where the state will sever its relationship with a noncitizen even upon relatively limited criminal conduct and despite prior valuable—and even valiant—service to the country or the community and without weighing the equities.

The other category of offenders who have been increasingly vilified and are considered irredeemable are sex offenders. Because of their allegedly high recidivism rate, they are viewed as a constant risk that must be labeled, watched, contained, and banned, if necessary (Mancini 2014; *Kansas v. Hendricks* 1996).

Sex Offenders: A Web of Collateral Sanctions

Since the 1990s in many countries sex offenders are treated as *sui generis*, though only the United States and England and Wales have uniquely "singled [sex offenders] out as a special class of offenders" (McAlinden 2012, 172). After long incapacitative prison terms, "intensive and restrictive measures [follow] in the community" (Hebenton and Seddon 2009), creating extensive supervision well beyond the prison walls (McAlinden 2012, 172). Lurid media accounts of sex crimes against children and concerns about the ongoing risk sex offenders pose drive much of this policy response on both sides of the Atlantic, though still to a lesser extent in continental Europe.

While high-profile sex offenses have strengthened the criminal justice response, including collateral sanctions, in all of Europe, "a number of historical as well as contemporary social structural factors have prevented the diffusion of punitive and exclusionary penal policies on sex offending across much of Western Europe" (McAlinden 2012, 183). Even though the assessment of recidivism risks plays a role in all countries, in much of western Europe broader confidence exists that the state can protect the community against such risk, as expressed in greater faith in expert rather than populist decision-making on criminal justice issues. The state's ability to provide more effectively for its citizens in social welfare than in neoliberal states may lead also to confidence in the state's security and safety guarantees (Freiberg 2000, 66–68; Hummelsheim et al. 2011).

Prevalent on both sides of the Atlantic are sex offender notification and registration statutes, though their scope and impact vary widely. The United States and England and Wales require sex offenders, including those with foreign convictions, to notify the police of their whereabouts and any changes to their residence.[57] The English registry includes a wide variety of offenses, but some exceptions to the requirement exist based either on specific offense considerations or on the sentence imposed. The length of the notification period depends on the penalty.[58] While some continental European countries have also created sex offender registries and imposed restrictions on the movement of sex offenders, others have rejected this approach as a violation of the rights of individuals (McAlinden 2012, 174).[59] England's highest court declared lifetime registration, without periodic review, in violation of the protection of privacy under the European Convention on Human Rights.[60] Such reviews, which will be conducted by the police rather than the court, will start 15 years after the beginning of the notification period.[61] In contrast, the US Supreme Court has upheld a retroactive lifetime registration period in *Smith v. Doe I* (2003).[62]

Neither the United States nor the United Kingdom considers notification or registration requirements part of the criminal punishment. In neither country, therefore, do sentencing courts impose the requirements or factor them into the sentence. Sentencing judges typically *notify* covered defendants of sex offender requirements, however (Richardson and Clark 2014, 507–08), which contrasts with many other collateral sanctions.

The US public strongly supports sex offender registries, in part because of an empirically unsupported belief that they decrease sexual recidivism.[63] About one-third of the US population has accessed sex offender registries, and fewer have acted upon their findings (Mancini 2014, 110–11).

In general, many European countries are unwilling to hold sex offenders out to the public shaming that has occurred in the United States. Some European countries prohibit the public distribution of the names of offenders, while the United States requires such disclosures (Jacobs and Larrauri 2012, 10).[64]

Other restrictions also exist for sex offenders. In some US states sex offenders are required to have indication of their status as registered offenders on their driver's license. About 30 US states and many counties extensively regulate the location, type, and occupancy of housing for sex offenders (Mancini 2014, 226–28). In addition, offenders may be restricted from frequenting places in which children congregate. Convicted child sex offenders can be barred from traveling abroad to prevent them from targeting children outside the United States. Such travel restrictions also exist in some European countries, including England and Ireland (McAlinden 2012, 173–74).[65] The United Kingdom has a civil preventative order, the so-called Sexual Offense Prevention Order, designed to protect the public from substantial harm committed by a convicted offender (Richardson and Clark 2014, 110–15).[66]

Employment restrictions with respect to sex offenders are widespread and generally connected to work with children or vulnerable adults. While sex offenders are mandated to reveal their conviction status, employers are also tasked with background checks on potential hires. Spanish employers with positions that are potentially closed to sex offenders, for example, must require applicants to provide an official statement indicating either the absence of relevant criminal convictions or a summary of them (Jacobs and Larrauri 2012, 15). England requires all those who work with children or vulnerable adults to be preapproved (McAlinden 2012, 168). Sex offenders whose crimes are connected to children are banned or disqualified from such positions, which may occur automatically based on the crime of conviction or upon an administrative decision.[67] At conviction the court is to advise convicted offenders of these bans or their possibility. In the United States prior conviction information is easily available through government agencies or private vendors. Licensing agencies are required to obtain such records (Jacobs and Larrauri 2012, 17–18).

Collateral sanctions on sex offenders in the United States exist in all states. Even though the federal government has asked states, through funding largess or threats of denial of funds, to impose some of these disqualifications, substantial differences remain even among community notification and registration laws (Mancini 2014, 215–29). European Union member states lack uniformity in terms of types of positions from which sex offenders are barred and the level of availability of criminal records (McAlinden 2012, 175). Only in a few areas has the European Union adopted directives that require member states, for example, to take measures to temporarily or permanently prevent those convicted of sexual exploitation of children or possession of child pornography from supervising children in any professional capacity.[68]

The ultimate sanction for sex offenders is civil commitment, which is an individualized court-imposed sanction that prevaricates between a civil and a criminal sanction (Ashworth and Zedner 2014, 164–65). Currently it is available in 19 US states for the purpose of detaining dangerous sex offenders indefinitely or until treatment has decreased their risk of reoffending (Mancini 2014, 216–18). As a long-standing practice for certain types of offenders—often those found not legally responsible by reason of insanity—this sanction has been imposed in select US states and some European countries—Belgium and Germany in particular—on those whose sentences have run but who are viewed as too dangerous to release. Both the US Supreme Court and the ECHR have declared the practice constitutional, albeit with some restrictions.[69] Primarily the civil commitment must provide the opportunity for therapy, must be regularly reviewable, and must separate those convicted from the ones under civil commitment.[70]

Despite decreasing commitments throughout the 1980s, starting in the 1990s civil commitments designed for those with psychiatric disorders have increased substantially in Austria, Germany, and Switzerland (Birklbauer 2014, 95, 98–99, 102).[71] In addition to *Sicherungsverwahrung*—preventive detention—they can take the form of commitment to a psychiatric hospital upon findings of both reduced responsibility (or insanity) and ongoing dangerousness (Kinzig 2013, 73–75). Switzerland has introduced a virtually mandatory lifelong commitment for offenders who are considered not amenable to treatment.[72] Since 2004 the Netherlands also recognizes a security measure for repetitive offenders of petty crimes that allows for an additional two-year imprisonment upon a finding of likelihood of recidivism (van der Wolf 2013, 97–98).

Release from civil commitment poses a major challenge for governmental authorities and the medical profession as they are asked to certify that the offender is not likely to reoffend. Risk aversion has increasingly limited such relief, especially as belief in effective treatment and rehabilitation of sex offenders has declined, often despite evidence to the contrary. Problematic and characteristic of civil commitment for sex offenders are "the confused manner in which contemporary laws contain a promiscuous combination of desert and danger, of preventive measures and punishment, and of civil and criminal procedures." Ultimately, this sanction shows the same weakness, albeit with higher stakes, as other collateral sanctions. It remains unclear what its ultimate purpose is—treatment, individual deterrence, incapacitation—which also makes it difficult to categorize it legally (Ashworth and Zedner 2014, 164, 167).

Relief from Collateral Sanctions

"Once a criminal, always a criminal" appears to be the motto of the United States. Forsyth (1987) distinguished between "rehabilitation" and "reform," with the latter denoting a change in an individual's character, while the former implies restoration of a person's full citizenship and reputation. At a time when those with criminal records encompassed a smaller slice of US society and criminal records were relatively inaccessible, it was easier to obtain an official pronouncement of rehabilitation (Love 2011, 755). That holds true no longer, even though successful reintegration demands such forgiveness through a relief mechanism that would allow for the full restoration of rights. At present, even those policies that allow for a restoration of rights require too many years of crime-free behavior to impact reintegration effectively (Maruna 2011, 98), though they may ultimately acknowledge true reform.

In many ways expungement of criminal records and relief from preventive measures must philosophically be—and is—an integral part of the European system. As the ECHR and national legal orders recognize the preeminent role of the state—and its obligation—in offering rehabilitative measures, relief from a sanction implies that the system has worked as intended. The overarching systemic aim dictates both the individual character of sanctions and safety-based measures, their time limitations in most cases, their focus on improvement, and ultimately the ability to receive usually automatic relief from them in the form of an expunged record (van Kempen and Young 2014, 1).

Judicial rehabilitation can take many forms. Australia has a carefully structured regime of excluding sex and violent offenders from employment or volunteering in select positions. Exclusions range from mandatory to an individual risk assessment flowing from the type of conviction. An individual can appeal discretionary limitations, with a reversal of such a decision functioning "as a form of judicial rehabilitation" (Naylor 2011, 79, 87–88). A few US states now permit offenders to petition a court to lift individual employment bars and bans on professional licenses (Palazzolo 2015).

As pardons have increasingly atrophied and expungement has become difficult and anachronistic in a world in which no record can ever be fully erased (Jacobs 2015; Demleitner 2016), certificates of restoration of rights would acknowledge the prior conviction but at the same time free the individual from all collateral sanctions (American Law Institute 2017, § 6x.06). Alternatively, sentencing judges could be granted the power to grant relief from specific sanctions, on an individual basis (National Conference of Commissioners on Uniform State Laws 2010; Love 2011, 783–88; Maruna 2011; American Law Institute 2017, § 6x.04).

Some European countries, such as France, still partake regularly in acts of clemency (Novak 2016, 8–9). In many others, however, official recognition of either reform or rehabilitation may be of lesser concern as sanctions are imposed in a more individualized manner and are generally time-limited. Therefore, they are more carefully targeted and allow for full rehabilitation and reintegration within a relatively short time frame. Expungement of criminal records also occurs in most instances regularly (Stacey 2015, 17, 20–24).

It has been the existence and growth of the criminal record system and the development of national—and now regional and international—registries that has made further supervision and monitoring in the community possible (McAlinden 2007, 74). In light of special concerns about the roaming criminal, officials may be reluctant to give up or dilute technological advances they—and the public—consider crucial deterrents and investigatory tools.

Conclusion

Collateral sanctions now constitute the dark underbelly of the US sanction regime. They have proliferated and often operate automatically on the convicted offender, with long-term consequences. In many cases the offender knows little about them when they are imposed yet may face criminal consequences for violating them. Ultimately, such sanctions are the extreme result of a society whose fear of crime and rejection of offenders lead to greater difficulties in rehabilitating offenders and possibly even to higher rates of recidivism. These sanctions contradict the goals of re-entry and rehabilitation, which should be the ultimate aims of sentencing.

Many of the new collateral sanctions in the United States seem to be punitive, driven by retribution. However, they lack any sense of proportionality and are stacked. While deterrence plays a part in justifying some of the more targeted sanctions, there is little empirical support for many of them (Mears and Cochran 2014, 131–33).

Even though sanctions generally have also become harsher in Europe in recent decades, collateral sanctions remain more narrowly targeted, less comprehensive, usually imposed directly and publicly, not retroactive, and time-limited. Some are part of the panoply of sanctions available to a court, in which case they tend to be bounded by principles of proportionality. Many of the others stem from the global desire to control risk, especially in the employment sector, and to assure public safety. With an ultimate goal of offender reintegration, however, some of the most exclusionary forms of US-type collateral sanctions remain inconceivable.

While less publicized than differentials in incarceration rates and the application of the death penalty, the striking differences in scope, breadth, manner of imposition, and length of collateral sanctions in the United States, as opposed to Europe, exemplify distinct cultural perceptions of criminal offenders and their future in society. They contrast a society focused on exclusion of criminal offenders with countries driven by a belief in the ability to include even those who once failed. If the United States were able to accept collateral sanctions either as part of proportionate retributive punishment or as non-prison-based incapacitative sanctions, based on empirical risk-control assessments, they could become an effective and integral part of our punishment regime, as they are partially used in other countries. At this point, however, they are merely a stark reminder of the continued existence of the "scarlet letter" in the fabric of American society.

NOTES

1. Much of the decrease in state prison populations has been due to developments in California, following the Supreme Court's decision in *Brown v. Plata* (2011).
2. The American Bar Association's online inventory of collateral sanctions has done much to document the broad array of such restrictions in individual states (American Bar Association 2016).
3. This chapter will not address disqualifications based on "good character" or "good repute," which are substantially broader than sanctions and disqualifications based on a conviction (see, e.g., Lapp 2012).
4. Examples are the protections against double jeopardy and against *ex post facto* laws (see, e.g., *Smith v. Doe* 2003; but see *Padilla v. Kentucky* 2010, requiring defendant's counsel to inform him or her prior to a guilty plea of immigration consequences). Whether *Padilla* will lead to the expansion of criminal justice–like protections to other collateral sanctions remains an open question.
5. The European Union's directives on the financial sector also require "good repute" for managers of financial institutions but without detailing what types of convictions, if any, may be (automatically) disqualifying (Commission of the European Communities 2006, para. 11c).
6. See, for example, American Bar Association (2016). Regular updating of such an inventory presents an ongoing challenge.
7. For discussion of collateral sanctions in the Prussian land law and the Bavarian Criminal Code, see Kühne (1931, 5–6).
8. Even though Prussian land law prohibited automatic sanctions to flow from a sentence of imprisonment, it did permit them to result from an aggravated prison sentence to the so-called *Zuchthaus* (Kühne 1931, 5–6).
9. See Adam Walsh Child Protection and Safety Act of 2006, 42 U.S.C.A. § 16918 (2006) (mandating that "each jurisdiction shall make available on the Internet, in a manner that is readily accessible to all jurisdictions and to the public, all information about each sex offender in the registry"). For examples of such state registries, see http://www.criminaljustice.ny.gov/nsor/ (New York), http://sexoffender.vsp.virginia.gov/sor/index.html (Virginia).
10. Such orders can also be imposed without a domestic conviction (Kidza 2014, 323–25).

11. Forfeiture Act, 1870 Chapter 23, 33, & 34 Vict., sec. 2 [4th July 1870] (http://www.legislation.gov.uk/ukpga/Vict/33-34/23/enacted) See also Murray (2013, 515–16) and Home and White (2015, 5–6), indicating that the 1870 Forfeiture Act "denied offenders their rights of citizenship" but that "there had been a partial enfranchisement of prisoners between 1948–1969" (Home and White 2015, 5).
12. See *Hunter v. Underwood* (1985) (striking down disenfranchisement provisions that evidenced an intent to discriminate based on race).
13. *Richardson v. Ramirez* (1974); see also *Hunter v. Underwood* (1985).
14. This appears to be a curious claim in light of the widespread lack of knowledge and confusion about disenfranchisement and the often severe prison sanctions that already exist at least in the United States.
15. Only Maine and Vermont permit prison inmates to vote. Massachusetts abolished that right, by referendum, in 2000.
16. In spring 2016 Virginia's governor ordered the restoration of voting rights to all those with a criminal record who had served their criminal justice sentence. He also committed to restoring the franchise on an ongoing basis. Up until that point Virginia had had one of the most restrictive disenfranchisement laws among US states (Governor and Secretary of the Commonwealth of Virginia 2016; Commonwealth of Virginia 2016). In the summer of 2016 the Virginia Supreme Court declared the governor's action in violation of the state constitution. The governor proceeded to restore the rights of citizens who had served their entire criminal justice sanction on an individual basis. By April 2017, 150,000 people had regained their right to vote (Brennan Center 2017).
17. But see Ispahani (2009, 25), indicating that Belgium and Luxembourg allow some prisoners to vote, while European countries that disenfranchise all prisoners are largely located in eastern Europe, with the addition of Spain and the United Kingdom.
18. Ireland, together with two other European countries, changed its domestic law in light of the European Court of Human Rights decision in *Hirst, infra* (*see* London School of Economics 2013, 19).
19. For a listing of European disenfranchisement regimes, see Home and White (2015, app., 52–65).
20. For a critical assessment of this practice, see Ölbermann (2011). In recent years the number of such denials has ranged between none and four (p. 228).
21. See Mauer (2011, 564) and Ölbermann (2011, 110–11) (numbers from one German prison indicate very high participation in national and somewhat lower participation in local/state elections).
22. *Hirst v. United Kingdom* (2005). The law at issue is the Representation of the People Act 1985 Sec. 3(1), which mandates disenfranchising a "convicted person" while being "detained in a penal institution in pursuance of his sentence."
23. *Ždanoka v. Latvia* (2006, para. 105).

24. *Frodl v. Austria* (2010) (striking down blanket disenfranchisement for those sentenced to prison terms of more than one year for an intentional offense). For a discussion of this decision in light of *Hirst, Sauvé,* and US case law on the issue, see Murray (2011).
25. See Murray (2013) (discussing the broad exception to disenfranchisement occurring after World War II).
26. *Greens and MT v. United Kingdom* (2010).
27. *McLean and Cole v. United Kingdom* (2013).
28. *Scoppola v. Italy* (2011). Italy's disenfranchisement provision extends to those sentenced for specific offenses and anyone sentenced to more than three years of imprisonment; for a prison term between three and five years, disenfranchisement is limited to five years; for higher sentences, it lasts for life (see Home and White 2015, 12–13). Italy's ban on offender voting even continues after the person completed the sentence.
29. *Scoppola v. Italy* (2012).
30. *Söyler v. Turkey* (2013); see also *Murat Vural v. Turkey* (2014) (ECHR affirms its earlier decision against Turkey, with facts again arising from a suspended sentence).
31. *Anchoguv and Gladkov v. Russia* (2013).
32. *Sauvé v. Canada* (2002, para, 58).
33. *Sauvé v. Canada* (2002, para. 44).
34. *August and Another v. Electoral Commission and Others* (1999); *Minister of Home Affairs v. NICRO and Others* (2004) (court holding that governmental assertion of cost and an anticrime agenda are insufficient rationales for denial of the franchise to prisoners).
35. Constitution of Kenya, S.43.
36. *Priscilla Nyokabi Kanyua v. Attorney General & Another* (2010).
37. Curiously, the ECHR determined in *McLean and Cole v. United Kingdom* (2013, § 4) that only elections to national and the European parliaments are covered by its prisoner jurisprudence but not referenda and local elections.
38. *HCJ 2757/06 Alrai v. Minister of the Interior* (1996).
39. International Covenant on Civil and Political Rights, Dec. 16, 1966, art. 25, 999 U.N.T.S. 171.k.
40. The American Law Institute's recently revised Model Penal Code recommends that prisoners and jail inmates be afforded the right to vote during their terms of incarceration but leaves it open to state legislatures that "an individual serving a custodial sentence as a result of a felony conviction may be disqualified while incarcerated" (American Law Institute 2017, § 6x.03(1)). The official comment to this provision states that "there are few principled or practical arguments in favor of disenfranchising prisoners" (comment *b* at 245).
41. These principles are outlined in the United Nations *Standard Minimum Rules for the Treatment of Prisoners* (2015), now called the "Nelson Mandela Rules."

German law, for example, following the Nelson Mandela Rules and the European Prison Rules, mandates the so-called *Angleichungsprinzip* under which life in prison is supposed to resemble life on the outside as much as is feasible. *See* Strafvollzugsgesetz (Penitentiary Act) § 3 Abs. 1 and the laws of individual German states (*Länder*), such as Bavaria's Penitentiary Act (Bayerisches Strafvollzugsgesetz Art. 5(1)). For a critical analysis, see Laubenthal (2015).

42. For a discussion of the negative impact of disenfranchisement on the polity and the democratic structure of government, see Pettus (2013).
43. Many communities and governmental agencies have signed on to the international "Ban the Box" movement, which urges employers to remove from job applications the question about a prior criminal record. See bantheboxcampaign.org.
44. A search through the American Bar Association's National Inventory of the Collateral Consequences of Conviction provides state-by-state information on employment restrictions for different types of offenders, including drug and sex offenders. Still, the database is unlikely to include all such limitations (Palazzolo 2015). For an example of opposition to increased employment restrictions on those convicted of sexual crimes, see New York Civil Liberties Union (2011).
45. The Convention of May 26, 1997, on the fight against corruption involving officials of the European Communities or officials of member states of the European Union (*Official Journal of the European Union* 1997, 2), however, does not contain any such provision.
46. German criminal law distinguishes between penalties and measures for (self) improvement and (public) safety (Albrecht 2004, 200, 2013, 213).
47. See *Stephenson v. U.S.* (2015) (federal judge denied request for expungement based on full rehabilitation and desire to get a nursing license, which would likely be denied based on prior conviction, because petitioner could not show required "exceptional circumstances").
48. For support available to those leaving prison in the United Kingdom, see a fact sheet provided by the Government of the UK (2016).
49. The Obama administration defined the restriction more narrowly than prior administrations did where any drug offense, not just any committed while receiving federal student aid, triggered the ban. Compare the legal situation in 2006, as described in Students for Sensible Drug Policy (2006) with the federal government's information materials under President Obama (Office of National Drug Control Policy, US Department of Education).
50. 23 U.S. Code § 159 (withholding of percentage of federal highway funds unless the state imposes at least a six-month suspension on driver's licenses upon a drug conviction or the legislature votes not to impose such a ban). For a critique of the Massachusetts license suspension law which applies to everyone with a drug conviction that carries at least a six-month sentence, see Sakala (2014).

51. Pennsylvania Statutes Title 75 Pa.C.S.A. Vehicles Sec. 1532(c).
52. See Strafgesetzbuch (German Penal Code), Arts. 44 and 69 (2016).
53. See American Bar Association (2003) (requiring that defendants be informed of all collateral sanctions that may befall them).
54. See Aufenthaltsgesetz §§ 53(1) & 54(1)(1)-(2), (2)(1)-(2) (adopted July 27, 2015, effective as of Jan. 1, 2016) (German residency law).
55. European Convention of Human Rights, Art. 8.
56. See *MF (Nigeria) v. Secretary of State for the Home Department* (2013) (Court of Appeals adopts general proportionality review). For a discussion of the case law in the United Kingdom and the relative limited numerical impact of the European Convention provision even before the law change, see Human Rights Futures Project (2013).
57. Sexual Offences Act 2003 §§ 97–101. The notification requirement applies only to convictions that would be covered under English law and as long as the notification period would not have already expired upon arrival in England.
58. See Sexual Offences Act 2003 §§ 80–92; also Richardson and Clark (2014: 503–04, 506–07).
59. South Africa created a national sex offender registry in 2008. Criminal Law (Sexual Offences and Related Matters) Amendment Act 32 of 2007, as amended by Judicial Matters Amendment Act 66 of 2008, Regulations under this act, Ch. 6 National Register for Sex Offenders (§§ 40–53).
60. *R (on the application of F and Thompson) v. Secretary of State for the Home Department* (2010). The act requires a host of parties to report a sex offense conviction. It allows for removal from the register if the sentence did not exceed a maximum of 18 months imprisonment.
61. After the initial 15-year period, the offender can petition in eight-year intervals (Richardson and Clark 2014, 507).
62. In that case the court declared the *ex post facto* clause inapplicable to registration requirements for sex offenders.
63. The public is apparently also willing to support sex crimes legislation even if informed that it is ineffective (Mancini 2014, 121).
64. Adam Walsh Child Protection and Safety Act of 2006, 42 U.S.C.A. § 16918 (2006).
65. Sexual Offences Act 2003, §§ 114–22.
66. Sexual Offences Act 2003 §§ 104–13.
67. These bans include crimes of violence generally (Richardson and Clark 2014, 113, 523–25).
68. Directive 2011/92/EU (13 December 2011) on combating the sexual abuse and sexual exploitation of children and child pornography, and replacing Council Framework Decision 2004/68/JHA. *Compare* Framework Decision 2003/568/JHA on combating corruption in the private sector. See also McAlinden (2012, 173) (describing English laws).

69. *Kansas v. Hendricks* (1996). For examples of critiques of the decision, see Steiker (1998) and Morse (1998). *M. v.* Germany, ECHR, Judgement of 17 December 2009, 5th section, App. No. 19359/04; *Kallweit v. Germany*, ECHR, Judgement of 13 January 2011, 5th Section, App. Nos. 17792/07, 20008/07 (*Mautes v. Germany*), 27360/04, 42225/07 (*Schummer v. Germany*), and 6587/04 (*Haidn v. Germany*); BVerfG (German Constitutional Court), 2 BvR2365/09 (May 4, 2011) (all cases holding in violation of ECHR and German Constitution, respectively, Germany's extension of preventive detention beyond 10 years when at the time of its imposition the legal limit was at 10 years). See also Slobogin (2012) and Demleitner (2003). Some European countries also impose chemical castration as a sanction (McAlinden 2012, 174).
70. While the US Supreme Court considers civil commitment nonpunitive, the ECHR has found it to be a sentence, a penalty (Vars 2013, 158).
71. These countries also recognize lifelong commitment for those with a psychiatric disease (Birklbauer 2014, 108). See also Kinzig (2013, 78–80).
72. Strafgesetzbuch (German Penal Code) Art. 64 Abs. 1bis; see also Pieth (2015, 139).

CASES CITED

Anchoguv and Gladkov v. Russia [2013] ECHR 638.

August and Another v. Electoral Commission and Others (CCT8/99):1999 (3) SA.

Brown v. Plata, 563 U.S. 493 (2011).

BVerfG (German Constitutional Court), 2 BvR2365/09 (May 4, 2011).

Frodl v. Austria, 52 EHRR 5, App. No. 20201/04, Eur. Ct. H.R. (Apr. 8, 2010).

Greens and MT v. United Kingdom, Apps. Nos. 60041/08 & 60054/08, Eur. Ct. H.R. (Nov. 23, 2010).

HCJ 2757/06 Alrai v. Minister of the Interior 50(2) PD 18 [1996] (Isr.).

Hirst v. United Kingdom (No. 2), ECHR 681, App. No. 74025/01, Eur. Ct. H.R. (Oct. 6, 2005).

Hunter v. Underwood, 471 U.S. 222 (1985).

Kallweit v. Germany, ECHR, Judgement of 13 January 2011, 5th Section, App. Nos. 17792/07, 20008/07 (*Mautes v. Germany*), 27360/04, 42225/07 (*Schummer v. Germany*), and 6587/04 (*Haidn v. Germany*).

Kansas v. Hendricks, 521 U.S. 346 (1996).

M. v. Germany, ECHR, Judgement of 17 December 2009, 5th section, App. No. 19359/04.

McLean and Cole v. United Kingdom, [2013] ECHR 1368, applications 1262613 & 2522/12, Eur. Ct. H.R. (June 11, 2013) (http://hudoc.echr.coe.int/eng?i=001-122352).

MF (Nigeria) v. Secretary of State for the Home Department [2013] EWCA Civ 1192 (8 October 2013).

Minister of Home Affairs v. NICRO and Others, CCT 03/04 (2004).

Murat Vural v. Turkey (2014) ECHR 1113.
Padilla v. Kentucky, 559 U.S. 356 (2010).
Priscilla Nyokabi Kanyua v. Attorney General & Another (2010) eKLR, http://kenyalaw.org/Downloads_FreeCases/75044.pdf.
Richardson v. Ramirez, 418 U.S. 24 (1974).
R (on the application of F and Thompson) v. Secretary of State for the Home Department [2010] UKSC 17.
Sauvé v. Canada, [2002] 3 S.C.R. 519 (Can.).
Scoppola v. Italy (No.3) [2011] ECHR 2417.
Scoppola v. Italy (No. 3), App. No. 126/05, Eur. Ct. H.R. (May 22, 2012).
Smith v. Doe, 538 U.S. 84 (2003).
Söyler v. Turkey [2013] ECHR 821.
Stephenson v. U.S., 139 F. Supp.3d 566 (E.D.N.Y. 2015).
Ždanoka v. Latvia, App. No. 58278/00, Eur. Ct. H.R. (Mar. 16, 2006).

REFERENCES

Agostino, Alexandra. *Deportation of Foreign Criminals and Article 8 of the European Convention on Human Rights: What Does the Strasbourg Court Really Say?* London: René Cassin, 2015.

Albrecht, Hans-Jörg. "Security Gaps: Responding to Dangerous Sex Offenders in the Federal Republic of Germany." *Federal Sentencing Reporter* 16 (2004): 200–07.

Albrecht, Hans-Jörg. "Sentencing in Germany: Explaining Long-Term Stability in the Structure of Criminal Sanctions and Sentencing." *Law and Contemporary Problems* 76 (2013): 211–36.

American Bar Association. *ABA Standards for Criminal Justice: Collateral Sanctions and Discretionary Disqualifications of Convicted Persons*. 3rd ed. Chicago: American Bar Association, 2003.

American Bar Association. *National Inventory of the Collateral Consequences of Conviction*. 2016. https://niccc.csgjusticecenter.org.

American Law Institute. *Model Penal Code: Sentencing. Proposed Final Draft*. Philadelphia: American Law Institute, 2017.

Ashworth, Andrew, and Lucia Zedner. *Preventive Justice*. Oxford: Oxford University Press, 2014.

Bayerisches Strafvollzugsgesetz. 2007 (updated 2009). https://www.justiz.bayern.de/media/baystvollzg.pdf.

Beckham, Geoff. "The Price of Passion: The Banishment of English Hooligans from Football Matches in Violation of Fundamental Freedoms." *Hastings International & Comparative Law Review* 25 (2001): 41–61.

Birklbauer, Alois. Wenn das Urteil die Dauer des Freiheitsentzuges nicht festlegt. In *Strafverteidigung und Sicherheitswahn*, edited by Niklaus Ruckstuhl, 95–134. Vienna: Neuer Wissenschaftlicher Verlag, 2014.

Blumstein, Alfred, and Kiminori Nakamura. "Redemption in the Presence of Widespread Criminal Background Checks." *Criminology* 47 (2009): 327–59.

Bowes, Daniel C. *Summary of North Carolina Expunctions 2015*. Raleigh: North Carolina Justice Center, 2015.

Brennan Center for Justice. *Voting Rights Restoration Efforts in Virginia*. 2017. https://www.brennancenter.org/analysis/voting-rights-restoration-efforts-virginia.

Bundesamt für Justiz. Häufige Fragen zum Bundeszentralregister. 2016. https://www.bundesjustizamt.de/DE/Themen/Buergerdienste/BZR/Inhalt/Fragen/FAQ_node.html.

Carson, Ann E. *Prisoners in 2014*. Washington, DC: Bureau of Justice Statistics, 2015.

Cole, David. "Turning the Corner on Mass Incarceration?" *Ohio State Journal of Criminal Law* 9 (2011): 27–51.

Commission of the European Communities. *Communication from the Commission to the Council and the European Parliament: Disqualifications Arising from Criminal Convictions in the European Union*. Eur. Parl. Doc. (COM (2006) 73 final, 21.2.2006). Brussels, Belgium: Commission of the European Communities, 2006.

Commonwealth of Virginia. Summary of the Governor's Restoration of Rights Order. April 22, 2016. https://commonwealth.virginia.gov/media/5843/restore_rights_summary_4-22.pdf.

Council of Europe. *Parliamentary Assembly, Social, Health and Family Affairs Committee, Report: Social Reintegration of Prisoners (7 Feb. 2006)*. Doc. 10838. Strasbourg, France: Council of Europe, 2006.

Demleitner, Nora V. "Continuing Payment on One's Debt to Society: The German Model of Felon Disenfranchisement as an Alternative." *Minnesota Law Review* 84 (2000): 753–804.

Demleitner, Nora V. "'Collateral Damage': No Reentry for Drug Offenders." *Villanova Law Review* 47 (2002): 1027–54.

Demleitner, Nora V. "Abusing State Power or Controlling Risk? Sex Offender Commitment and Sicherungverwahrung." *Fordham Urban Law Journal* 30 (2003): 1621–69.

Demleitner, Nora V. "U.S. Felon Disenfranchisement: Parting Ways with Western Europe." In *Criminal Disenfranchisement in an International Perspective*, eds. Alec C. Ewald and Brandon Rottinghaus, 79–108. Cambridge: Cambridge University Press, 2009.

Demleitner, Nora V. "Judicial Challenges to the Collateral Impact of Criminal Convictions: Is True Change in the Offing?—A Response to Jason Cade." *New York University Law Review Online* 91 (2016): 150–70. http://www.nyulawreview.org/sites/default/files/NYULawReviewOnline-91-Demleitner_0.pdf.

Easton, Susan. "Electing the Electorate: The Problem of Prisoner Disenfranchisement." *Modern Law Review* 69, no. 3 (2006): 443–52.

Easton, Susan. *Prisoners' Rights: Principles and Practice.* Abingdon, UK, and New York: Routledge, 2011.

Eisenberg, Lynn. "States as Laboratories for Federal Reform: Case Studies in Felon Disenfranchisement Law." *New York University Journal of Legislation and Public Policy* 15 (2012): 539–83.

Ewald, Alec C. "Criminal Disenfranchisement and the Challenge of American Federalism." *Journal of Federalism* 39, no. 3 (2009): 527–56.

Fellner, Jamie, and Marc Mauer. *Losing the Vote: The Impact of Felony Disenfranchisement Laws in the United States.* New York: Human Rights Watch; Washington, DC: Sentencing Project, 1998. https://www.hrw.org/legacy/reports98/vote/.

Field, Stewart. "State, Citizen, and Character in French Criminal Process." *Journal of Law and Society* 33 (2006): 522–46.

Forsyth, William James. *The Reform of Prisoners, 1830–1900.* New York: St. Martin's Press, 1987.

Freiberg, Arie. "Guerillas in Our Midst? Judicial Responses to Governing the Dangerous." In *Dangerous Offenders—Punishment and Social Order,* edited by Mark Brown and John Pratt, 51–70. London and New York: Routledge, 2000.

Fröhling, Mareike. *Der Moderne Pranger.* Marburg: Tectum Verlag, 2014.

Gibney, Matthew J. "Deportation, Crime, and the Changing Character of Membership in the United Kingdom." In *The Borders of Punishment: Migration, Citizenship, and Social Exclusion,* edited by Katja Franko Aas and Mary Bosworth, 218–36. Oxford: Oxford University Press, 2013.

Government of the UK. Leaving Prison. 2016. https://www.gov.uk/leaving-prison/support-when-someone-leaves-prison.

Governor and Secretary of the Commonwealth of Virginia. Order for the Restoration of Rights. 2016. https://commonwealth.virginia.gov/media/5848/order_restoring_rights_4-22-16.pdf.

Halecker, Dela-Madeleine. *Der "Denkzettel" Fahrverbot.* Baden-Baden, Germany: Nomos, 2008.

Harcourt, Bernard E. *Against Prediction: Profiling, Policing, and Punishing in an Actuarial Age.* Chicago: University of Chicago Press, 2006.

Hebenton, Bill, and Toby Seddon. "From Dangerousness to Precaution: Managing Sexual and Violent Offenders in an Insecure and Uncertain Age." *British Journal of Criminology* 49, no. 3 (2009): 343–62.

Hellwig, Bernhard-Martin. *Entziehung der Fahrerlaubnis gemäss § 69 StGB und der Verhältnismässigkeitsgrundsatz.* Berlin: Logos, 2008.

Home, Alexander, and Isobel White. *Prisoners' Voting Rights (2005 to May 2015).* SN/PC/01764. London: Library House of Commons, 2015.

Human Rights Futures Project. *Deportation and the Right to Respect for Private and Family Life under Article 8 HRA.* London: London School of Economics, 2013.

Human Rights Watch. *Forced Apart: Families Separated and Immigrants Harmed by United States Deportation Policy*. July 2007. Accessed January 20, 2016. https://www.hrw.org/reports/2007/us0707/index.htm.

Hummelsheim, Dina, Helmut Hirtenlehner, Jonathan Jackson, and Dietrich Oberwittler. "Social Insecurities and Fear of Crime: A Cross-National Study on the Impact of Welfare State Policies on Crime-related Anxieties." *European Sociological Review* 27, no. 3 (2011): 327–45.

Ispahani, Laleh. "Voting Rights and Human Rights: A Comparative Analysis of Criminal Disenfranchisement Laws." In *Criminal Disenfranchisement in an International Perspective*, edited by Alec C. Ewald and Brandon Rottinghaus, 25–58. Cambridge: Cambridge University Press, 2009.

Jacobs, James B. *The Eternal Criminal Record*. Cambridge, MA: Harvard University Press, 2015.

Jacobs, James B., and Elena Larrauri. "Are Criminal Convictions a Public Matter? The USA and Spain." *Punishment and Society* 14 (2012): 3–28.

Kaeble, Danielle, Lauren Glaze, Anastasios Tsoutis, and Todd Minton. *Correctional Populations in the U.S., 2014*. Washington, DC: Bureau of Justice Statistics, 2015.

Katz, Michael. *The Undeserving Poor: From the War on Poverty to the War on Welfare*. New York: Pantheon, 1989.

Kidza, Zacharias. *Hooliganismus und Gewalt beim Fussball in Deutschland und Grossbritannien*. Berlin: Wissenschaftlicher Verlag, 2014.

Kinzig, Jörg. The ECHR and the German System of Preventive Detention: An Overview of the Current Legal Situation in Germany. In *Preventing Danger: New Paradigms in Criminal Justice*, edited by Michele Caianiello and Michael Louis Corrado, 71–106. Durham, NC: Carolina Academic Press, 2013.

Klingele, Cecelia, Jenny Roberts, and Margaret Colgate Love. *Collateral Consequences of Criminal Convictions: Law, Policy and Practice*. New York: Thomson West, 2013.

Kühne, Emil. *Die Ehrenstrafen: insbesondere auch rechtsvergleichend und rechtsgeschichtlich dargestellt*. Würzburg, Germany: Triltsch, 1931.

Lapp, Kevin. "Reforming the Good Moral Character Requirement for U.S. Citizenship." *Indiana Law Journal* 87 (2012): 1571–1637.

Laubenthal, Klaus. *Strafvollzug*. 7th ed. Heidelberg: Springer, 2015.

London School of Economics. Prisoner Voting and Human Rights in the UK. June 2013. http://www.lse.ac.uk/humanRights/documents/2013/PrisonerVotes.pdf.

Love, Margaret. "Paying Their Debt to Society: Forgiveness, Redemption, and the Uniform Collateral Consequences of Conviction Act." *Howard Law Journal* 54 (2011): 753–93.

Mancini, Christina. *Sex Crime, Offenders, and Society: A Critical Look at Sexual Offending and Policy*. Durham, NC: Carolina Academic Press, 2014.

Maruna, Shadd. "Judicial Rehabilitation and the 'Clean Bill of Health' in Criminal Justice." *European Journal of Probation* 3, no. 1 (2011): 97–117.

Mauer, Marc. "Voting Behind Bars: An Argument for Voting by Prisoners." *Howard Law Journal* 54 (2011): 549–66.

McAlinden, Anne-Marie. *The Shaming of Sexual Offenders*. Oxford and Portland, OR: Hart Publishing, 2007.

McAlinden, Anne-Marie. "The Governance of Sexual Offending across Europe: Penal Policies, Political Economies and the Institutionalization of Risk." *Punishment and Society* 14 (2012): 166–92.

Mears, Daniel P., and Joshua C. Cochran. *Prisoner Reentry in the Era of Mass Incarceration*. Los Angeles: Sage Publications, 2014.

Miller, Bryan Lee, and Joseph F. Spillane. "Civil Death: An Examination of Ex-Felon Disenfranchisement and Reintegration." *Punishment & Society* 14, no. 4 (2012): 402–28.

Morse, Stephen J. "Fear of Danger, Flight from Culpability." *Psychology, Public Policy and Law* 4 (1998): 250–67.

Murray, Colin R. G. "Playing for Time: Prisoner Disenfranchisement under the ECHR after Hirst v United Kingdom." *King's Law Journal* 22 (2011): 309–34. ssrn.com/abstract=1718992.

Murray, Colin R. G. "A Perfect Storm: Parliament and Prisoner Disenfranchisement." *Parliamentary Affairs* 66, no. 3 (2013): 511–39.

National Conference of Commissioners on Uniform State Laws. Uniform Collateral Consequences of Conviction Act (Last Amended or Revised in 2010). 2010. http://www.uniformlaws.org/shared/docs/collateral_consequences/uccca_final_10.pdf.

Naylor, Bronwyn. "Criminal Records and Rehabilitation in Australia." *European Journal of Probation* 3 (2011): 79–96.

New York Civil Liberties Union. Legislative Memo: In Relation to Limiting the Type of Employment Convicted Sex Offenders Can Seek. June 15, 2011. http://www.nyclu.org/content/legislative-memo-employment-sex-offenders.

Novak, Andrew. *Comparative Executive Clemency: The Constitutional Pardon Power and the Prerogative of Mercy in Global Perspective*. London/New York: Routledge, 2016.

Office of National Drug Control Policy, US Department of Education. FAFSA Facts. https://obamawhitehouse.archives.gov/sites/default/files/ondcp/recovery/fafsa.pdf.

Official Journal of the European Union. Council Act of 26 May 1997. OJ C 195. June 25, 1997.

Official Journal of the European Union. Directive 2004/18/EC of the European Parliament and of the Council 134. April 30, 2004.

Official Journal of the European Union, Directive 2011/92/EU of the European Parliament and of the Council. December 17, 2011.

Ölbermann, Jan. *Wahlrecht and Strafe*. Baden-Baden, Germany: Nomos, 2011.

Palazzolo, Joe. "For Americans Who Served Time, Landing a Job Proves Tricky." *Wall Street Journal*, May 17, 2015.

Pettus, Katherine Irene. *Felony Disenfranchisement in America.* 2nd ed. Albany: State University of New York Press, 2013.

Pieth, Mark. *Strafrechtsgeschichte.* Basel, Switzerland: Helbing Lichtenhahn Verlag, 2015.

Pinard, Michael. "Collateral Consequences of Criminal Convictions: Confronting Issues of Race and Dignity." *New York University Law Review* 85 (2010): 457–534.

Quaker Council for European Affairs. The Social Reintegration of Ex-Prisoners in Council of Europe Member States. May 2011. www.qcea.org/wp-content/uploads/2011/05/rprt-reintegration-full-en-may-2011.pdf.

Richardson, Nigel, and Peter Clark. *Sexual Offences: A Practitioner's Guide.* Haywards Heath, UK: Bloomsbury Professional, 2014.

Rosenblum, Marc R., and Kristen McCabe. *Deportation and Discretion: Reviewing the Record and Options for Change.* Washington, DC: Migration Policy Institute, 2014.

Sakala, Leah. Suspending Common Sense in Massachusetts: Driver's License Suspensions for Drug Offenses Unrelated to Driving. May 14, 2014. http://www.prisonpolicy.org/driving/report.html.

Salzmann, Kelly, and Margaret Love. *Internal Exile: Collateral Consequences of Conviction in Federal Laws and Regulations.* Chicago: American Bar Association, 2009.

Schoenberg, Shira. Massachusetts Repeals Automatic License Suspension for Drug Crimes. Mass Live. March 30, 2016. http://www.masslive.com/politics/index.ssf/2016/03/massachusetts_repeals_automati.html.

Sentencing Project. *A Lifetime of Punishment: The Impact of the Felony Drug Ban on Welfare Benefits.* Washington, DC: Sentencing Project, 2014.

Slobogin, Christopher. "Prevention as the Primary Goal of Sentencing: The Modern Case for Indeterminate Dispositions in Criminal Cases." *San Diego Law Review* 48 (2011): 1127–71.

Slobogin, Christopher. Preventive Detention in Europe, the United States, and Australia. June 27, 2012. http://papers.ssrn.com/sol3/papers.cfm?abstract_id=2094358.

Sobota, Sebastian. *Die Nebenfolge im System strafrechtlicher Sanktionen.* Berlin: Duncker & Humblot, 2015.

Stacey, Christopher. Rehabilitation & Desistance vs Disclosure. April 2015. http://www.wcmt.org.uk/sites/default/files/report-documents/Stacey%20C%20Report%202014%20Final.pdf.

Steiker, Carol. "The Limits of the Preventive State." *Journal of Criminal Law and Criminology* 88 (1998): 771–808.

Strafvollzugsgesetz (Germany, federal). 1976 (last updated 2015). https://www.gesetze-im-internet.de/stvollzg/BJNR005810976.html.

Students for Sensible Drug Policy. Harmful Drug Law Hits Home: How Many College Students in Each State Lost Financial Aid Due to Drug Convictions?

April 17, 2006. http://www.prisonpolicy.org/scans/ssdp/red_052605_ssdp-state-report.pdf.

Stumpf, Juliet. "Fitting Punishment" *Washington and Lee Law Review* 66 (2009): 1683–1741.

Stuntz, William J. *The Collapse of American Criminal Justice*. Cambridge, MA: Harvard University Press, 2011.

Subramanian, Ram, and Rebecka Moreno. *Drug War Détente? A Review of State-Level Drug Law Reform, 2009–2013*. New York: Vera Institute of Justice, 2014.

Uggen, Christopher, and Jeff Manza. *Locked Out: Felon Disenfranchisement and American Democracy*. New York and Oxford: Oxford University Press, 2006.

Uggen, Christopher, Mischelle Van Brakle, and Heather McLaughlin. "Punishment and Social Exclusion: National Differences in Prisoner Disenfranchisement." In *Criminal Disenfranchisement in an International Perspective*, edited by Alec C. Ewald and Brandon Rottinghaus, 59–78. Cambridge: Cambridge University Press, 2009.

United Nations. *United Nations Standard Minimum Rules for the Treatment of Prisoners (the Nelson Mandela Rules)*. A/Res/70/175. New York: United Nations, December 17, 2015.

US Department of Education. Federal Student Aid: Students with Criminal Convictions Have Limited Eligibility for Federal Student Aid. 2016. https://obamawhitehouse.archives.gov/sites/default/files/ondcp/recovery/fafsa.pdf.

US Immigration and Customs Enforcement. *ICE Enforcement and Removal Operations Report—Fiscal Year 2015*. Washington, DC: Department of Homeland Security, 2015.

van der Wolf, Michiel. "Comment on Kinzig." In *Preventing Danger: New Paradigms in Criminal Justice*, edited by Michele Caianiello and Michael Louis Corrado, 96–101. Durham, NC: Carolina Academic Press, 2013.

van Kempen, Piet Hein, and Warren Young. "Obligations and Means to Prevent Reoffending: Introduction, Context and Conclusions." In *Prevention of Reoffending: The Value of Rehabilitation and the Management of High Risk Offenders*, edited by Piet Hein van Kempen and Warren Young, 1–22. Cambridge; Antwerp, Belgium; Portland, OR: Intersentia, 2014.

Vars, Fredrick E. "Comment on Slobogin." In *Preventing Danger: New Paradigms in Criminal Justice*, edited by Michele Caianiello and Michael Louis Corrado, 158–60. Durham, NC: Carolina Academic Press, 2013.

Victorian Electoral Commission. Prisoners and Voting. 2012. http://www.vec.vic.gov.au/files/RP-PrisonersVoting.pdf.

Weinrich, Christoph. *Statusmindernde Nebenfolgen als Ehrenstrafen im Sanktionensystem des StGB 204*. Baden-Baden, Germany: Nomos, 2009.

Index

9/11 terrorist attacks, 315, 327n18

Aaltonen, Mikko, 261n20
Accreditation panels for offender programs, 388, 399
actuarial risk assessment
  for prison diversion, 5
  parole release decisions, 449–50, 471n27
  racial disparities, 5, 31n11
Adams, Michael, 134, 169–70n11
Adam Walsh Child Protection and Safety Act of 2006, 513n9
Aebi, Marcelo F., 402n13
AECP. *See* American exceptionalism, in crime and punishment
African Americans.
  homicide rates, 273–4, 282, 299, 307, 325n9
  incarceration rates, 4, 5, 74, 138, 145, 245–6
  male children, lifetime risk of incarceration, 4
  probationers in the US, 32n23
  racial disparity, incarceration in the US (2006), 64
aggravated assault
  compiling data on, 341, 343–50
  under the MPC, 337–9
  rates, 23, 37n55
  US *vs.* Canada, 353–4
Albuquerque, Pinto de, 443
Alexander, Michelle, 76–7, 241
American Bar Association standards on collateral sanctions, 500
American creed, 110
American exceptionalism
  broad vs. narrow definitions, 1–2
  capital punishment as instance of American exceptionalism, *see* American exceptionalism, capital punishment
  collateral sanctions as instance of American exceptionalism, 20–1
  contrastive concepts, specifying compared phenomenon, 106
  correlates of incarceration rates in US vs. other nation states, 226–56
  correlates of incarceration rates in US states vs. other nation states, 226–56
  "crime spike" period in US, 1962–1974, 23–4
  ecconomic sanctions as instance of American exceptionalism, 16–7
  "high-crime mentality" in American culture, 27–8

American exceptionalism (*cont.*)
high parole-release discretion as American exceptionalism, 13–15
high serious violent crime rates as American exceptionalism, 2, 22–4
ideological/evaluative use of the term, 107–8
mass incarceration as instance of American exceptionalism, 2–4, 12, 196–8, 256
negative exceptionalism, 107
parole supervision rates as instance of American exceptionalism, 12
probation supervision rates as instance of American exceptionalism, 9–11
racial disparities in incarceration as instance of American exceptionalism, 4–5
"scissors effect" in 1960s US (liberal crime polices and spiking crime rates), 24–6
sociological/historical use of the term, 107, 109
US criminal record exceptionalism, 37n52
American exceptionalism, capital punishment. *See also* capital punishment; death penalty, United States
abolition in Europe and the US, 108–9, 112, 115
abolition of, 108–9, 112, 182
actual use of, 113
American creed, 110
America's distinguishing characteristics, 110
capital punishment as a product of American exceptionalism, 110–1
divergence from the rest of the Western nations, 108
failure to qualify as, 117
framing the question, 113–8
historical/comparative view, 109, 112
justification for use, 116
lethal injections, 116
means of, 116
Michigan, abolition of capital punishment, 115
vs. other Western nations, 114
positive *vs.* negative exceptionalism, 107–8
public support for, 116
reform in the US, 115
retention of, 112
Rhode Island, abolition of capital punishment, 115
speeding death and reducing pain, 115, 116
stages of decline, 115–6
standard view of, 111–13
Supreme Court declares unconstitutional, 116
viewed along a continuum, 114–15
Wisconsin, abolition of capital punishment, 115
American exceptionalism, claims that America is
distinctive, 106
exceptional, 105
in an extreme position, 106
an outlier, 105, 118n2
unique, 105
American exceptionalism in crime and punishment. *See also* American exceptionalism, capital punishment, collateral consequences of conviction, crime rates, economic sanctions, imprisonment, incarceration,

probation, parole release, parole supervision
adverse social outcomes, 56
in coordinated market economies, 55
in liberal market economies, 53–7, 60
liberal *vs.* coordinated market economies, 59
serious violent crime rates, 1, 22–8
American exceptionalism, study methodology
cultural determinism, 111
historical variations, 104
identifying a norm from which to be an exceptional departure, 118n1
internal variations, 104
misplaced depth, 111
precise descriptions, 104–5
sociological explanations of punishment, 111
specifying the phenomenon under study, 106
trends, trajectories, and processes of change, 104
twin fallacies, 111
American optimism, post-progressive era. *See also* Canadian pessimism; penal pessimism, Canada
conservative optimism, 149
death knell for rehabilitative model, 145
determinate sentencing, 146
eliminating crime through punishment, 146
incapacitating and deterring crime, 143
indeterminate sentencing, 146
predicting the end of crime, 150, 170n13
punishing illegal drug use, 144
Rockefeller drug laws, 145
segregating offenders from society, 144
warehousing crime, 144
War on Poverty, 145
American optimism, progressive era. *See also* Canadian pessimism; penal pessimism, Canada
as cause of American faith in parole boards, 33n29
controlling crime, 140–1
curing criminals, 141–2
improving the correctional system, 142–3
President's Commission on Law Enforcement and Administration of Justice, 141–2
root causes of crime, 141
social causes of crime, 142, 147–9
War on Poverty, 143
America's distinguishing characteristics, 110
Anchoguv and Gladkov v. Russia (2013), 515n31
Angleichungsprinzip, 515–16n41
Anglosphere, incarceration trends, 198–202
Annual Probation Survey, 468n4
Arkansas, parole boards, 439
Asian Americans, homicide rates, 273–4
Asians, homicide rates, 325n9
August and Another v. Electoral Commission and Others (1999), 515n34
Augustus, John, 374
Australia
history and politics of race, 78
homicide rates *vs.* US, 23
incarceration trends, 201
Austria
homicide rates *vs.* US, 37n54
incarceration rates, 199
automatic release, 416

Baldus, David, 7
"ban the box" movement, 516n44
Barker, Vanessa, 62, 265n45, 265n51
Barr, Bob, 30n4
Baumer, Eric P., 358n16
Baumgartner, Frank R., 325–6n10
Bearden v. Georgia (1983), 36–7n50
Beck, Allen J., 145
Beckett, Katherine, 84, 85–6, 137, 298, 302
Belarus, homicide rates, 215–16
Belgium
- Dutroux case, 456
- incarceration trends, 201
- parole boards, 453, 456
- voting rights for prison inmates, 496, 514n17

Bennett, William J., 30n4
Beyle, Thad, 265–6n52
BJS (Bureau of Justice Statistics)
- *Annual Probation Survey*, 468n4
- parole, definition, 417
- parole supervision, America *vs.* Europe, 418–24
- probation, definition, 417

black gangs, 72
Blair, Tony, 311, 314–15, 317, 324
Blumstein, Alfred, 145
Bolger, James, 310
Bonczar, Thomas, 402n10
Bontems, Roger, 112
books and publications
- *Annual Probation Survey*, 468n4
- *Canadian Charter of Rights and Freedoms*, 152
- *The Challenge of Crime in a Free Society*, 142
- *The Collapse of American Criminal Justice*, 81–2
- *The Contradictions of American Capital Punishment*, 185
- *Criminal Code* of Canada, 152, 163, 171n18, 173nn27–8
- *European Sourcebook of Crime and Criminal Justice Statistics*, 335, 357n9
- *The Future of Parole as a Key Partner in Assuring Public Safety*, 464
- *Harsh Justice*, 62
- *International Comparisons of Recorded Violent Crime Rates for 2000*, 353
- *Making Confinement Decisions*, 149–50
- *Making Crime Pay: Law and Order in Contemporary American Politics*, 298, 325n1
- *The Myth of Mob Rule: Violent Crime and Democratic Politics*, 325n4
- *The New Jim Crow*, 76
- *Our Criminal Law*, 159
- *The Prisoners' Dilemma*, 58–9, 61, 63, 65, 90n4
- *The Public Interest*, 145
- *Recommendation Concerning Prison Overcrowding and Prison Population Inflation*, 437
- *Recommendation on Conditional Release (Parole)*, 416, 436–7, 442, 450–1
- *Rules on Community Sanctions and Measures*, 436–7, 451
- *Thinking about Crime*, 147
- *UCRH (Uniform Crime Reporting Handbook)*, 340

Bottoms, Anthony, 195
breaching probation, 390–4, 397–8
Bright, Stephen, 32n16
British Isles, incarceration trends, 201
Brixton riots, 311
Brockway, Zebulon, 425, 470n16
Brown v. Plata (2011), 423, 513n1
Buffet, Claude, 112

Bureau of Justice Statistics (BJS)
Annual Probation Survey, 468n4
parole, definition, 417
parole supervision, America *vs.* Europe, 418–24
probation, definition, 417
Bush, Jeb, 30n4

California
drop in crime rate, 146
parole boards, 455
parole supervision, 464
prison population, 513n1
sentencing severity, 146
Campbell, Michael C., 83, 91n10, 146
Canada
crime rates, recorded crimes, 212
Criminal Code, 125, 163, 171n18, 173nn27–8
disenfranchisement, 498–9, 515nn32–3
homicide rates, 216–19, 305–7, 333–4
homicide rates *vs.* US, 23
imprisonment rates, 212
incarceration rates, 160, 162–3, 216–19
incarceration trends, 260n8
index crimes, 168n3
patterns of crime growth, 122
penal pessimism, 151, 153, 165 (*see also* penal pessimism, Canada)
punitive loss of welfare benefits, 135, 137
reported crime rates, 123
total crime, 168n3
whipping prisoners, 171–2nn21–22
Canada *vs.* US, serious violent crime
aggravated assault, 353–4
Feasibility Study on Crime Comparisons between Canada and the United States, 353–4
index crimes, 354, 360n30
Canadian Charter of Rights and Freedoms, 152
"Canadian exceptionalism," 202
Canadian pessimism
Canadian Charter of Rights and Freedoms, 152
Criminal Code, 152, 163, 171n18, 173nn27–8
determinate sentencing, 151, 170n15
emergence of, 153
indeterminate sentencing, 170n15
life imprisonment, 170–1nn16–17
proportional sentencing, 152, 156, 171n19
purpose of sentencing, 171n19
sentencing dangerous offenders, 170–1nn16–17
vs. US punishment philosophy, 151–3
Canadian pessimism, post-progressive era
adverse effects of imprisonment, 158
costs of criminal law, 159
hate-motivated crime, 173n27
imprisonment as a last resort, 159, 161, 164, 172–3n26
incarceration, failure of, 159
incarceration rate, 160, 162–3
mandatory minimum sentences, 161
proportional sentencing, 161, 164
sentencing habitual sex offenders, 161
solving the drug problem, 157–8
"tough-on-crime" issues, 173n29
Canadian pessimism, progressive era
capital punishment, 154, 171n20–171n21
corporal punishment, 154
crime deterrence, 155–6, 160–1
fixed sentences, 155
fundamental goal of the correctional system, 172n24
harsh sanctions, 153

Canadian pessimism, progressive era (*cont.*)
imprisonment as a last resort, 156, 172n23
penitentiaries, 153–4 (*see also* imprisonment; incarceration)
punishment, certainty *vs.* severity, 153
rehabilitation of offenders, 156–7
rehabilitative model as crime control, 156
sentencing structure, 153–5
whipping prisoners, 171–2nn21–22
capital punishment. *See also* death penalty
abolishment of, 276
American exceptionalism (*see* American exceptionalism, capital punishment)
Canada, 154, 171n20–171n21
executions in the US (1772–2002), 277
France, 114
for heresy, 279
India, 118n3
Japan, 118n3
late 1960s through early 1970s, 25
for moral offenses, 279
pre and post Civil War, 276
as a product of American exceptionalism, 110–11
Saudi Arabia, 116
for sedition, 279
social policies affecting, 134–6
Sudan, 116
for treason, 279
for whites, 276
for witchcraft, 279
carceral approach to parole supervision, 460
caseloads of probation in the US, 383, 401n8
Cavadino, Michael, 401n4
The Challenge of Crime in a Free Society, 142
Charles, Camille Zubrinsky, 77
child support debt, 35n42
China, death penalty, 7–8
Chiricos, Ted, 138
Chrétien, Jean, 160
Christie, Nils, 195
city trenches, 79
civil commitment of sex offenders, 509–10, 518nn69–71
civil death, 37n51, 492–4, 506
civil rights movement, 25
Clark, Ramsey, 143
Clements, Dianne, 107–8
Clinton, Bill, 89, 136–7, 291, 312, 315
The Collapse of American Criminal Justice, 81–2
collateral consequences of conviction. *See* collateral sanctions
collateral sanctions
American Bar Association standards, 500
civil and regulatory measures, 19
civil death, 37n51, 492–4, 506
compiling relevant laws, 21
description, 487–8, 513n2
development of, 489–94
disenfranchisement, 494–500, 514nn12–14
disqualifications, 488, 494, 513n3
effects of the War on Drugs, 492–4
effects on American lives, 21
in English law, 491
in the European Union, 488, 513n5
expunging, 502, 516n47
felon disenfranchisement, 136–7
football banning orders, 493–4
granting relief from, 21
hallmarks of AECP, 20

honor penalties, 490–1
imposition of criminal penalties, 488, 513n4
informal discrimination against those with criminal histories, 37n52
as instance of American exceptionalism, 20–1
against international travel, 493–4
loss of welfare benefits, 135, 136–7
in mobile, information-based societies, 489–94
modern, 492–4
need for comparative research, 399
number of in the US, 488
persistence of, 37–n53
pervasive harm, 20–1
political rights, 494–500
racial disparity, 20
relief from, 510–12
severtity compared with criminal sentences, 19–20
societal effects, 20
transferability, 494
US *vs.* Europe, 494
voting rights (*see* voting rights for prison inmates)
welfare reform bill, 136–7
collateral sanctions, drug offenders
employment restrictions, 501, 516n47, 516nn44–5
revealing criminal history on job applications, 503
suspension of driver's license, 516n44, 516nn49–50
collateral sanctions, economic and social rights
access to employment, 501–2
average severity of, 16
"ban the box" movement, 516n44
child support debt, 35n42
deportation of noncitizens, 504–7
drug offenders, 501, 503, 516n44, 516n47, 516nn44–5, 516nn49–50
Ferguson, MO, 17
German criminal law, 501–2, 516n46
Germany, 35n41
incarceration for nonpayment, 36–7n50
increase in the US, 34n38
mass fines, 34n36
means testing, 18–19, 36n48
negative effects of, 18, 36n46
outside the US, 17, 34n39
overdoing, 18, 35–6n45
in Pennsylvania, 34n37
probation revocation for nonpayment, 35–6n45
proportionality, 35n43
questioning criminal record on employment applications, 516nn43–4
reforming, 18–19, 36n49
for rehabilitation, 18
reintegration services, 502, 516n48
as retributive justice, 35n40
role in offender reintegration, 18
Scandinavian countries, 17
in the service of criminal justice, 18
sex offenders, 501, 516n44
social welfare and other benefits, 501–4
supervision fees, 9
suspension of driver's license, 503
in the US, 16–18, 35n43
War on Drugs, 502
collateral sanctions, in German law
honor penalties, 491
sex offenders, 493
collateral sanctions, sex offenders
Adam Walsh Child Protection and Safety Act of 2006, 513n9

collateral sanctions, sex offenders (*cont.*)
  civil commitment, 509–10, 518nn69–71
  civil confinement, 504
  employment restrictions, 501, 509, 516n44, 517n67
  in England and Ireland, 493
  in German law, 493
  notification requirements, 517n57
  registration statutes, 508, 517n57
  registries, 493, 517nn59–63
  Sexual Offenses Act (2003), 517n57
  in Spain, 493
Colson, Chuck, 30n4
Committee for the Prevention of Torture and Inhuman or Degrading Treatment or Punishment (CPT), 436, 470n20
Committee of Ministers of the Council of Europe, voting rights for prison inmates, 497
community supervision. *See* parole; probation
compiling data on serious violent crime
  aggravated assault, 341, 343–50
  classifying offenses, 344
  definition of serious injury, 349–50
  definitions of criminal offenses, 341
  GBH, 344–50
  HOCR (Home Office Counting Rules), 340, 342, 359n22
  involving firearms, 355, 359n23
  NCRS (National Crime Recording Standard), 341–2
  role of gun ownership, 355, 359n23
  sample size for serious injuries, 351, 359n25
  Section18 Offenses against the Person Act, 344, 351
  Section20 Offenses against the Person Act, 344, 351
  statistical problems, 340
  threats with a weapon, 352
  UCRH (Uniform Crime Reporting Handbook), 340
  US reporting rates over time, 358n16
compiling data on serious violent crime, police recordings
  alternatives to, 358–9n19
  criteria for, 340
  English *vs.* American, 350–2, 359n24
  recording error, 359n20
  reliability of, 358n17
  rules for, 343–8
comprehensive crime bill (1992), 312
conditional release. *See also* parole
  automatic release, 416
  discretionary release, 416
  Germany, 438
  mandatory release, 416
  Recommendation on Conditional Release (Parole), 416, 468n2
conditions of supervision, need for comparative research, 396–7, 402n13
confinement. *See also* imprisonment; incarceration
  controlling drug crimes, 145
  US *vs.* other countries (*see* incarceration trends)
congressional hearings on crime topics, 311–12
connectedness hypothesis, 205, 209, 219, 222, 261n20, 358n11. *See also* disconnectedness hypothesis
connectedness via policy effects, 263n28
consensual democracy
  imprisonment rates, worldwide, 239–40, 265n45
  vs. majoritarian democracy, 239–40
conservative optimism, 149

The Contradictions of American Capital Punishment, 185
conviction, collateral consequences of. *See* collateral sanctions
Corda, Alessandro, 12, 125, 370
corporal punishment, Canada, 154
correctional free lunch, 240
correctional systems
  fundamental goal, Canada, 172n24
  improving in the progressive era of American optimism, 142–3
counter arguments to local autonomy thesis. *See also* local autonomy, political dynamics of punishment
  elites and law and order, 85–7
  federalization in the context of local power, 81–5
  history and politics of race, 73–81
  limited impact of federalization, 81–5
CPT (Committee for the Prevention of Torture and Inhuman or Degrading Treatment or Punishment), 436, 470n20
Crafts, Samuel, 276–7
Crime. *See also* violence
  controlling in the progressive era of American optimism, 140–1
  costs of, 159
  democracy and punishment, 303
  effects of punitiveness on, 276
  eliminating through punishment, 146
  extant literature, 302–5
  freedom from street crime, 291–2
  hate-motivated, 173n27
  impact on urban politics and criminal justice, 325n11
  as the most important problem, 312
  patterns of growth, Canada, 122
  politicizing, 302–5
  predicting the end of, 150, 170n13
  root causes of, 141
  social causes of, 142, 147–9
  violent victimization, rates of, 303–4
crime rates. *See also specific crimes*
  Canada *vs.* US, 122–3
  Denmark, 211–13
  England and Wales, 211–13
  Finland, 211–13
  and imprisonment, 147, 211–13
  and incarceration policies, 205–6
  influence on incarceration rates (*see* incarceration rates, and crime rates)
  Norway, 211–13
  serious violent crime spike (1960s–1970s), 22
  Sweden, 211–13
  for US states, 220–2
crime rates, recorded crimes
  Canada, 123, 212
  Canada *vs.* US, 123
  England and Wales, 212, 261–2n21
  Germany, 212
  Netherlands, 212
  Nordic countries, 212
  robbery, 325n6
  United States, 212
  US *vs.* Canada, 123
crime rates, United States
  crime spike, 262n22
  high-crime plateau, 262n22
Criminal Code of Canada, 125, 152, 163, 171n18, 173nn27–8
criminal offenses, definitions of, 341
criminal penalties, as collateral sanctions, 488, 513n4
criminal record on employment applications, 516nn43–4
criminals, curing in the progressive era of American optimism, 141–2
Crofton, Walter, 425

Crowley, Monica, 30n4
Cuba, incarceration rates, 197, 259n3
culture of control, 195
Czech Republic, imprisonment rates, 186

dangerous offenders, sentencing, 170–1nn16–17
DDB Needham Lifestyles Survey, 264–5nn42–44
death penalty. *See also* capital punishment
  China, 7–8
  Iran, 7
  Japan, 32n19
  opposition to, 286
  Pakistan, 32n20
  Saudi Arabia, 32n20
  support for, 283–4
  support for *vs.* homicide rates, 285
death penalty, United States. *See also* American exceptionalism, capital punishment
  abolition of, 8
  America's standing in the world, 6, 7
  vs. China, 8
  The Contradictions of American Capital Punishment, 185
  distribution among US states, 184–5
  executions, 1976–2012, 181
  executions per capita, 6, 31n13
  executions per million, 182
  Missouri, 7
  race of the victim as a factor, 7, 32n17
  racial disparity, 6–7, 91n19
  risk of, 6
  scale of, 6, 7, 31–2n15
  support for, 273
  Texas, 7, 32n16
Delaware, imprisonment rates, 186
Delgrande, Natalia, 402n13
Demleitner, Nora, 20
democracy, effects on imprisonment rates
  apportioning power, 240–1
  consensual democracy *vs.* majoritarian democracy, 239–40, 265n45
  political structures and democracy, 239–45
Democratic states *vs.* Republican, imprisonment rates, 244
Denmark
  crime rates, 211–13
  disenfranchisement, 496
  homicide rates, 214–15, 305–7
  incarceration rates, 199
Denton, Nancy A., 77
deportation of noncitizens, 504–7
determinate sentencing
  and American optimism in the post-progressive era, 146
  America *vs.* Europe, 412–15, 429, 435, 468n1
  and Canadian pessimism, 151, 170n15
  definition of, 13, 15, 412–15
  vs. indeterminate, 412–15, 430
deterrence, Canada, 155–6, 160–1
deterrence through
  harsh penalties, 149, 170n14
  incapacitation, 143
  sentencing, 155–6, 160–1
Deukmejian, George, 146
Dickens, Charles, 114
Dignan, James, 401n4
DiIulio, John J., Jr., 30n4
disconnectedness from crime rates, 224–6
disconnectedness hypothesis, 204, 207, 337, 358n11. *See also* connectedness hypothesis
discretionary release, 416

disenfranchisement. *See also* voting rights
- Canada, 498–9, 515nn32–3
- collateral sanctions, 494–500, 514nn12–14
- South Africa, 515n34, 515n36

disenfranchisement, racial impact of
- on Canada aboriginal population, 499
- franchise-reform efforts, 496

disparity ratios *vs.* absolute levels, incarceration rates in the US, 5
disqualifications, collateral sanctions, 488, 494, 513n3
District of Columbia
- homicide rates, 299
- parolees, 469n11

distrust in government, effects on punitiveness, 283
Doob, Anthony N., 189–90, 220
Downes, David, 137
downsizing, incarceration rates, 3–5
driver's license suspension, collateral sanctions, 503
drug crime
- controlling through confinement, 145
- imprisonment of African Americans, 145
- punishing in the post-progressive era of American optimism, 144
- punishment *vs.* rehabilitation, 144
- Rockefeller drug laws, 145
- solving, Canada, 157–8

drug offenders
- collateral sanctions (*see* collateral sanctions, drug offenders)
- employment restrictions, 516n47, 516nn44–5
- incarceration, 91n18

drug testing, mass probation in the US, 383
Dugan, Andrew, 283
Dutroux, Mark, 456
Dybeku v. Albania (2007), 435

early release, due process, 433–5
early release programs, 463–4. *See also* parole; probation
earned time, 463
ECHR (European Court of Human Rights)
- on disenfranchisement, 497–9, 515n37
- voting rights for prison inmates, 497–9, 515n37

economic sanctions.
- and disadvantaged communities, 17
- and growth of US income inequality, 17
- as instance of American exceptionalism, 16–17
- as revenue generation, 9, 17–18, 384
- day fines, 17, 35n41
- effects on reintegration, 18
- expansion since 1980s, 16–17
- greater use in US than elsewhere, 17
- means testing at sentencing, 18–19
- Model Penal Code recommendations, 18–19
- probation supervision fees, 9, 384–6, 390, 400, 458

ECtHR (European Court of Human Rights), 436
Eisner, Michael, 278
EIU (Economist Intelligence Unit), 241, 265nn47–8
electronic monitoring
- need for comparative research, 402n14

elites and law and order, 85–7
El Salvador, incarceration rates, 259n3
emergency services and wound care, effects on homicide rates, 292n4

employment access, collateral sanctions, 501–2
employment restrictions, on sex offenders, 509, 516n44, 517n67
Engel and others v. the Netherlands (1976), 471n24
England, homicide rates *vs.* US, 23, 37n54
England and Ireland, collateral sanctions of sex offenders, 493
England and Wales. *See also* United Kingdom
  crime rates, 211–13
  crime rates, recorded crimes, 212, 261–2n21
  homicide rates, 214, 305–7
  homicide rates, influence on incarceration, 214–19
  imprisonment rates, 53, 212, 261–2n21
  incarceration rates *vs.* the US, 31n8
  parole boards, 452, 461, 466
  serious violent crime (*see* serious violent crime, US *vs.* England and Wales)
  sex offender registration, 508
Engle criteria, 471n24
Estonia
  homicide rates, 215–16
  voting rights for prison inmates, 496
ethnic segregation of migrants, 79
Europe
  disenfranchisement, 498
  imprisonment rates, *vs.* US states, 202–3, 260n9
  incarceration rates, 202–3
  mass probation, 369, 401n8
  mass probation *vs.* US, 399–401
  parole supervision, *vs.* America (*see* parole supervision, differences between America and Europe; parole supervision, similarities between America and Europe)
  probationers, *vs.* the US, 10–11
  trends in imprisonment rate, 54, 55
European colonists in British North America (1675–1693), homicide rates, 279
European Court of Human Rights (ECHR)
  on disenfranchisement, 497–9, 515n37
  voting rights for prison inmates, 497–9, 515n37
European Court of Human Rights (ECtHR), 436
European Sourcebook of Crime and Criminal Justice Statistics, 335, 357n9
European Union, collateral sanctions, 488, 513n5
evidence-based parole decisions, 463
executions, United States. *See also* capital punishment; death penalty
  1772–2002, 277
  1976–2012, 181
  nineteenth century, 285–6
  per capita, 6
  per million of population, 182
exile. *See* deportation of noncitizens
expunging collateral sanctions, 502, 516n47. *See also* relief from collateral sanctions

fear of crime, ICVS (International Crime Victims Survey), 238–9
fear of walking near home at night, *vs.* homicide rates, 284
fears and punitivity, effects on imprisonment rates worldwide, 233–9

Feasibility Study on Crime Comparisons between Canada and the United States, 353–4
federal court involvement, serious violent crime spike (1960s–1970s), 25
federalization, in the context of local power, 81–5
Feeley, Malcom M., 374–5
fees. *See* collateral sanctions, economic and social rights
felon disenfranchisement, 136–7
Ferguson, MO, economic sanctions, 17
Ferri, Enrico, 444
financial obligations on ex-offenders, 458
fines. *See* collateral sanctions, economic and social rights
Finland
  crime rates, 211–13
  disenfranchisement, 496
  homicide rates, 214–15
  incarceration rates, 199, 260n6
firearms
  compiling data on serious violent crime, 355, 359n23
  gun control, 322
  gun control movement, serious violent crime spike (1960s–1970s), 25
  gun ownership, compiling data on serious violent crime, 355, 359n23
fixed sentences, Canada, 155. *See also* determinate sentencing
Florida, homicide rates, 274
football banning orders, 493–4
Fordism, collapse of, 56, 63, 71, 76, 80, 90n1
Fordist production regimes, 56, 63, 71, 90n1
forfeitures. *See* collateral sanctions, economic and social rights
formal programming
  mass probation in the US, 386–7, 401–2nn10–11
  need for comparative research, 402n14
  during probation, 386–90
Forman, James, Jr., 74, 91n18
Foucault, Michael, 460
France
  homicide rates *vs.* US, 37n54
  incarceration trends, 201
  juge de l'application des peines, 451, 472n30
  parole boards, 451
  tribunal de l'application des peines, 451
freedom of speech, Germany, 438
Frodl v. Austria (2010), 515n24
Furman v. Georgia (1972)., 108, 112, 116
The Future of Parole as a Key Partner in Assuring Public Safety, 464

Gagnon v. Scarpelli (1973), 434–5
gangs
  black, 72
  development in the late 1970s, 72
  Hispanic, 72
  within prisons, 72
  in urban localities, 72
Ganusauskas v. Lithuania (1999), 435
Garland, David, 8, 62, 195
GBH (Grievous Bodily Harm), 338, 344–50, 358n15, 359n20
Georgia, imprisonment rates, 132
German law, collateral sanctions, 493, 501–2, 516n46
Germany
  crime rates, recorded crimes, 212
  deportation of noncitizen offenders, 505–6

Germany (*cont.*)
disenfranchisement, 497
economic sanctions, 35n41
freedom of speech, 438
homicide rates, 214–15
homicide rates *vs.* US, 37n54
imprisonment rates, 212
incarceration rates, 199
license suspension resulting from drug convictions, 503
life imprisonment, 440–4
parole boards, 451
parole for sentences with fixed maximum terms, 446–50
Rechtsstaatlichkeit (commitment to due process), 450
right to conditional release, 438
second track punishments, 445–6, 448, 471n24, 471n26
Strafvollstreckungskammern (chambers of the criminal courts), 450
voting rights for prison inmates, 515–16n41
get-tough policies, 290–1
Gingrich, Newt, 30n4
Gini index, 228, 264n36, 264n38
GIP (governor's institutional power), 241, 265n51
Glorious Revolution of 1688, 279
Glueck, Bernard, 141
Goldwater, Barry, 83
good time, 463
Gottschalk, Marie, 62, 83, 466
Gould, Roger, 278, 279
Graham v. Florida (2010), 441
Greenholtz v. Inmates of the Nebraska Penal and Correctional Complex (1979), 470n18
Greens and MT v. United Kingdom (2010), 515n26
Gregg v. Georgia (1976), 108
Grievous Bodily Harm (GBH), 338, 344–50, 358n15, 359n20
gun control, 322. *See also* firearms
gun control movement, serious violent crime spike (1960s–1970s), 25
gun ownership, compiling data on serious violent crime, 355, 359n23

Harsh Justice, 62
Hartz, Louis, 109
hate-motivated crime, 173n27
Hawaii
imprisonment rates, 132
racial disparity, incarceration, 64
Hawkins, Gordon, 149–50, 240, 336, 357–8n10
Herbert, Steve, 84
heresy, capital punishment for, 279
Herzog-Evans, Martine, 472n30
high-release discretion model, indeterminate sentencing, 426
American optimism as cause of, 33n29
high risers *vs.* low risers, 219–26, 262n26
Hirst v. United Kingdom (2005), 514n22
Hispanic gangs, 72
Hispanics
imprisonment rates, 74, 245–6
probationers in the US, 32n23
historical/comparative view of American exceptionalism, 112
Hochschild, Jennifer, 92n26
HOCR (Home Office Counting Rules), compiling data on serious violent crime, 340, 342, 359n22
homicide
imprisonment rates, US states, 222, 263n27
murder of James Bolger, 310

homicide rates
across eight countries, 306–7 (*see also specific countries)*
adaptation of humans to group living, 278
Asians, 325n9
Belarus, 215–16
for blacks, 282, 299, 307, 325n9
Canada, 216–19, 305–7
Canada *vs.* US, 333–4
correlation with punitiveness and incarceration in the US, 337
crime-spike period, 23
cross-national comparison, 305–7
curves, 225
Denmark, 214–15, 305–7
early 1960s to early 1970s, 23
effects on punishment outcomes, 299
England and Wales, 214, 305–7, 360n32
English-speaking countries, 22–3
Estonia, 215–16
European colonists in British North America (1675–1693), 279
vs. fear of walking near home at night, 284
feelings toward government and society, role of, 278
Finland, 214–15
Germany, 214–15
Glorious Revolution of 1688, 279
influence on incarceration, 214–19
Japan, 214–15
lagged policy effects, 218–19
legitimacy, 278
for men, 307
and nation building, 278–9
Netherlands, 305–7
New Zealand, 214, 333
nineteenth century, 280–1, 284–6
North America *vs.* western Europe, 278
and number of police per capita, 286
political stability, 278
property owners, 281
role of indeterminate sentencing, 124–5
Second Reform Act, 279
vs. spending on halting crime, 283
vs. support for the death penalty, 285
Third Reform Act, 279
trends, 55
UK, by race and ethnicity of victims, 311
vs. violence politicization, 313–14
whites, 282, 325n9
homicide rates, United States
African Americans, 273–4
Asian Americans, 273–4
on contested frontiers, 274
cross national comparison, 305–7
District of Columbia, 299
emergency services and wound care, effects of, 292n4
exceptional low rates, 280
Florida, 274
fluctuation over time, 273–4
lifetime risk, 272, 292n1
Louisiana, 299
for Native Americans, 273
northern states *vs.* southern states, 274
Pennsylvania, 315
for racial minorities, 273
since the Civil War era, 281
in the slave South, 274, 281
Texas, 274
trends, 216–19
US states (*see specific states*)
for white Americans, 273

homicide rates, US *vs*
  Australia, 23
  Austria, 37n54
  Canada, 23, 90n3, 124, 168n4
  England, 23, 37n54
  France, 37n54
  Germany, 37n54
  Ireland, 23
  Italy, 37n54
  Netherlands, 37n54
  New Zealand, 23
  Portugal, 37n54
  Scotland, 23
  Spain, 37n54
  Switzerland, 37n54
  western Europe, 37n54
homicide rates *vs*. political agenda
  Pennsylvania, 310
  UK, 307–10
  in the US, 309, 311–12
honor penalties, 490–1. *See also* collateral sanctions
Hudec v. Slovakia (2006), 435
Hungary, life imprisonment, 443
Hunter v. Underwood (1985), 514n12
Hutchinson, Asa, 30n4
Hutchison v. United Kingdom (2017), 444

ICCPR (International Covenant on Civil and Political Rights), voting rights for prison inmates, 499
ICVS (International Crime Victims Survey)
  comparative levels of serious violence, 335
  crime rates and incarceration policies, 205–6
  European Sourcebook of Crime and Criminal Justice Statistics, 335, 357n9
  fear of crime, 238–9
  limitations of, 332–3
  NRA claims about crime rates, 337
  publications based on, 357n6
Idaho, imprisonment rates, 226
ideological/evaluative use of American exceptionalism, 107–8
imprisonment. *See also* confinement; incarceration; prison
  adverse effects of, 158
  African Americans, 145
  and crime rates, 22–8, 147
  for drug crimes, 145
  harsh penalties as deterrent, 149
  imprisonment for public protection (IPP), 445, 471n23
  isolating offenders, 148
  as a last resort, 156, 159, 161, 164, 172–3n26, 172n23
  recidivism, 148
  state, patterns of, 189
imprisonment rates.
  for African Americans, 74, 138, 145
  black males, 74, 138
  Canada, 212
  Czech Republic, 186
  definition, 30n5
  England and Wales, 212, 261–2n21
  Germany, 212
  Hispanic males, 74
  history and politics of race, 74
  incarcerated population, 197
  vs. incarceration rate, 30–1n5
  Latino males, 74
  Latvia, 186
  Maori population, 75, 91n21
  measurement of, percentage growth *vs*. absolute-change approach, 126–8, 130, 169n7, 179–80, 190–1, 219–20, 262n25
  Netherlands, 212

Nordic countries, 212
penal optimism, US, 121, 168n2
per million population, 185–6
punitiveness as cause of, 137–9
racial makeup, 138
scale of measurement, 190
Seychelles, 30n3, 168n2
social policies affecting, 134–8
stability, 168n5
Thailand, 186
total US, 122
trends in Europe, 54, 55
trends in the US, 55
uniform growth, 191
uniformity, 185–91
variability, 185–91
white males, 74
imprisonment rates, Canada
cultural underpinnings, 134
provincial/territorial rates, 168–9n6
research on, 126
social policies affecting, 134–8
vs. US, 122, 139–40, 169–70n11
imprisonment rates, United States
African Americans, 245–6
Hispanics, 245–6
judicial selection methods, 245–6
minority threat hypothesis, 246
vs. other countries, 212
imprisonment rates, US states
absolute change, 128–9
basis for, 262n24
compared to Canada, 169–70n11
comparison chart, 179–80
connectedness hypothesis, 222
connectedness via policy effects, 263n28
Delaware, 186
disconnectedness from crime rates, 224–6
vs. Europe, 202–3, 260n9
Georgia, 132
growth rate, 188–9
Hawaii, 132
highest rates, 134
high risers *vs.* low risers, 219–26, 262n26
homicide, 222, 263n27
homicide rate curves, 225
Idaho, 226
judicial selection methods, 244
Louisiana, 127, 186, 224–5
lowest rates, 134
Maine, 127, 186, 226
Massachusetts, 132, 186
Minnesota, 127, 132, 186, 224–5
Mississippi, 127
Missouri, 224
Montana, 132
Nebraska, 127
New Hampshire, 132
New Jersey, 186
New York, 186, 225–6, 263n29
North Carolina, 132
North Dakota, 132
northern *vs.* southern, 244
policy effects, 225
prison growth, 220–2
prison rates, 130–1
property crime, 223
punitiveness as cause of, 137–9
Republican *vs.* Democratic, 244
Rhode Island, 132
size of increase, 132–3, 169n10
social policies affecting, 134–8
Utah, 186, 224–5
variation across states, 127
Vermont, 132
violent crime, 222–3
volume effects, 225
Washington, 186
West Virginia, 225–6, 263n29

imprisonment rates, US *vs*
Canada, 122, 127, 139–40
England and Wales, 53, 74–5
New Zealand, 75
imprisonment rates, worldwide
consensual democracy *vs.* majoritarian democracy, 239–40, 265n45
correctional free lunch, 240
data and methods, 226–8, 263nn31–3
DDB Needham Lifestyles Survey, 264–5nn42–44
EIU (Economist Intelligence Unit), 241, 265nn47–8
fears and punitivity, effects of, 233–9
GIP (governor's institutional power), 241, 265n51
global samples, 241–4
income inequality, effects of, 229–32
Legatum Prosperity Index of Educational Performance, 228
Lijphart index, 266n54
OECD countries, 227–8, 263n32
political structures and democracy, effects of, 239–45, 265n46
Polity IV index, 241, 241–4, 265n7, 266n53
regression analyses, 246–56, 266nn55–6
SEP indicator, 241, 265–6n52
TANF (Temporary Assistance for Needy Families), 228
trust and legitimacy, effects of, 233, 264–5nn40–43
US states, 244–5
wealth and prosperity, effects of, 229, 264n39
welfare policy and social inclusion, 228–33, 263–4nn34–37
incarceration. *See also* imprisonment; mass incarceration; prison
constitutional politics, state *vs.* federal, 91n8
cost-benefit ratio, 149
drug offenders, 91n18
failure of, 159
for nonpayment of economic sanctions, 36–7n50
under state and local government, 181
violent offenders, 91n18
incarceration, lifetime risk of
black male child, 4
white male child, 4–5
incarceration policies, and crime rates, 205–6
incarceration rates
700 Club, 3
African Americans, 4, 5
Austria, 199
Canada, 160, 162–3, 216–19
combining prison plus jail, 3
comparison of US states, 220–2
Cuba, 197, 259n3
Denmark, 199
downsizing, 3–5
effects on punitiveness, 283
El Salvador, 259n3
Europe, 202–3
Finland, 199, 260n6
Germany, 199
vs. imprisonment rates,30–1n5 (*see also* imprisonment rates)
Latinos, 4
links to political systems, 3
measurement of, percentage growth *vs.* absolute-change approach, 126–8, 130, 169n7, 179–80, 190–1, 219–20, 262n25
Native Americans, 4
nineteenth century, 286
North Dakota, 169nn7–9
Norway, 199

per capita, 3
percentage growth *vs.* incremental change, 190
political view on, 2–3
prisoners by US region (1860, 1880, 1910), 289
racial disparity, 4–5
ratio of rates, 127, 169nn7–9
regional comparisons, 197–8, 202–3, 259n4
Russian Federation, 197
Seychelles, 197, 259n3
since WWII, 284
St. Kitts and Nevis, 197, 259n3
state, 126–31, 169nn7–9
state and federal jurisdictions, per 100,000 persons (1925–2013), 288
state by state, 187
by states and select nations, 187
status of the expert bureaucracy, 90–1n7
sunbelt states *vs.* Northeast and Midwest, 91n10
Sweden, 199
Switzerland, 199
Turkmenistan, 259n3
United States, 216–19, 272–3
US states, 202–3
Virgin Islands, 197, 259n3
incarceration rates, and crime rates
annual changes *vs.* absolute values, 261n18
connectedness hypothesis, 205, 209, 219, 261n20
cross sectional snapshots, 205–9
data availability and reliability, 204–5
disconnectedness hypothesis, 204, 207
homicide data, 207, 261n15
lethal violence, 204, 209–11, 260n13, 261n20
negative correlations, 261n19
policy effects, 203–4, 260nn11–12
recorded crime *vs.* actual crime, 204, 260n14
Simpson's paradox, 261n18
United States data, 207, 261n16
US states, 207
volume effects, 203–4, 207
incarceration rates, in the US
actuarial risk assessment, 5, 31n11
criticism of, 30n2
disparity ratios *vs.* absolute levels, 5
vs. England and Wales, 31n8
federalization of criminal justice policy, 91n11
vs. New Zealand, 31n6
vs. other countries, 3, 30n3, 90n6
racial disparity, 31n11
vs. Russia, 3, 31n7
vs. western Europe, 4
incarceration trends
2011–2013, 197–8
the Anglosphere, 198–202
Australia, 201
Belgium, 201
British Isles, 201
Canada, 260n8
France, 201
Netherlands, 201, 260n7
New Zealand, 201
regional patterning, North America, 201–2
United States, 198–202
western Europe, 198–202
income inequality, effects on imprisonment rates worldwide, 229–32
indeterminate release systems, 13, 33n29

indeterminate sentencing
  and American optimism, post-progressive era, 33n29, 146
  and Canadian pessimism, 170n15
  as cause of mass incarceration, 15
  America *vs.* Europe, 412–15, 429, 435, 468n1
  definition of, 13, 15, 412–15
  degree of indeterminacy, 13
  vs. determinate sentencing, 412–15
  high degree of indeterminacy as American exceptionalism, 13–15
  high-release discretion model, 426
index crimes, 354, 360n30
India, capital punishment, 118n3
Inglehart, R., 241
institutional racism, 75–6
institutional structure, mass probation in the US, 370–1
intensity and restrictiveness, mass probation in the US, 382–5, 401n7
International Comparisons of Recorded Violent Crime Rates for 2000, 353
International Covenant on Civil and Political Rights (ICCPR), voting rights for prison inmates, 499
International Crime Victims Survey (ICVS)
  comparative levels of serious violence, 335
  crime rates and incarceration policies, 205–6
  European Sourcebook of Crime and Criminal Justice Statistics, 335, 357n9
  fear of crime, 238–9
  limitations of, 332–3
  NRA claims about crime rates, 337
  publications based on, 357n6
international travel, collateral sanctions against, 493–4
IPP (imprisonment for public protection), 445, 471n23
Iran, death penalty, 7
Ireland
  homicide rates *vs.* US, 23
  voting rights for prison inmates, 496, 514n18
Italy
  homicide rates *vs.* US, 37n54
  parole boards, 451
  tribunale di sorveglianza, 451
Iversen, Torben, 59

Jacobs, James B., 37n52
jail figures for US states, 121, 168n1
James, Wells and Lee v. United Kingdom (2012), 445
Japan
  capital punishment, 118n3
  death penalty, 32n19
  homicide rates, 214–15
Jennings, Will, 326n12
Jim Crow system, 73
Johnson, Devon, 137–8
Johnson, Lyndon B., 83, 141, 145
Jones, Bryan D., 325–6n10
judicial selection methods
  effects on imprisonment rates, 245–6
  and imprisonment rates, 244
juge de l'application des peines, 451, 472n30

Kallweit v. Germany, 518n69
Kansas v. Hendricks (1996), 518n69
Kansas v. Hendricks (1997), 471n25
Katzenbach, Nicholas deB., 141–2
Katzenbach Report, 145
Katznelson, Ira, 79
Kelling, George, 30n4

Kesteren, John, 357n5
King, Desmond S, 77
King, Rodney, 312
King, Ryan, 463
Klingele, Cecelia, 401n6, 458
Kohler-Hausmann, Julilly, 144–5
Krajewski, Krzysztof, 432–3
Krivo, Lauren J., 70, 77, 79

Lacey, Nicola, 90n4, 90n6, 91n12, 303
lack of fellow feeling, effects on punitiveness, 283
LaFree, Gary, 278, 282
lagged policy effects, 218–19
Lappi-Seppälä, Tapio, 137, 139, 283, 336–7, 358n11, 373
László Magyar v. Hungary (2014), 443
Latino males, imprisonment rate, 74
Latinos, incarceration rates, 4
Latvia, imprisonment rates, 186
Lauritsen, Janet L., 358n16
law enforcement
- expenditures, nineteenth century, 286
- expenditures since WWII, 284
- LEAA (Law Enforcement Assistance Administration), 83
- police, per 100,000 persons (1850–1920), 286
- police in northern and southern cities, per 10,000 persons (1870–1880), 287
- police per capita and homicide rates, 286
- President's Commission on Law Enforcement and Administration of Justice, 141–2
- in the slave South, 277

Lawrence, Stephen, 92n22
LEAA (Law Enforcement Assistance Administration), 83
Lebach case (BVerfGE 1973), 438–40
Le Dain, Gerald, 157–8
legal citations
- *Anchoguv and Gladkov v. Russia* (2013), 515n31
- *August and Another v. Electoral Commission and Others* (1999), 515n34
- *Bearden v. Georgia* (1983), 36–7n50
- *Brown v. Plata* (2011), 423, 513n1
- *Dybeku v. Albania* (2007), 435
- *Engel and others v. the Netherlands* (1976), 471n24
- *Frodl v. Austria* (2010), 515n24
- *Furman v. Georgia* (1972)., 108, 112, 116
- *Gagnon v. Scarpelli* (1973), 434–5
- *Ganusauskas v. Lithuania* (1999), 435
- *Graham v. Florida (2010)*, 441
- *Greenholtz v. Inmates of the Nebraska Penal and Correctional Complex* (1979), 470n18
- *Greens and MT v. United Kingdom* (2010), 515n26
- *Gregg v. Georgia* (1976), 108, 184
- *Hirst v. United Kingdom* (2005), 514n22
- *Hudec v. Slovakia* (2006), 435
- *Hunter v. Underwood* (1985), 514n12
- *Hutchison v. United Kingdom* (2017), 444
- *James, Wells and Lee v. United Kingdom* (2012), 445
- *Kallweit v. Germany*, 518n69
- *Kansas v. Hendricks* (1996), 518n69
- *Kansas v. Hendricks* (1997), 471n25
- *László Magyar v. Hungary* (2014), 443
- *Lebach* case (BVerfGE 1973), 438–40
- *Léger v. France* (2006), 438
- *M. v.* Germany, 518n69
- *McCleskey v. Kemp* (1987), 7, 32n18

legal citations (*cont.*)
McLean and Cole v. United Kingdom (2013), 515n37
McLean and Cole v. United Kingdom (2013), 515n27, 515n37
MF (Nigeria) v. Secretary of State for the Home Department (2013), 517n56
Miller v. Alabama (2012), 441
Minister of Home Affairs v. NICRO and Others (2004), 515n34
Morrissey v. Brewer (1972), 434, 448
Mouisel v. France (2002), 470n19
Murat Vural v. Turkey (2014), 515n30
Murray v. the Netherlands (2016), 444
M v. Germany (2009), 445–6
Öcalan v. Turkey (2014), 443
Osborn v. The Parole Board (2013), 448
Padilla v. Kentucky (2010), 504–5, 513n4
Priscilla Nyokabi Kanyua v. Attorney General & Another (2010), 515n36
R. (on the application of Wells) v. Parole Board, (2009), 445
R. v. Ipeelee (2012), 125
R. v. Moloney (1985), 339
R. v. Savage and Parmenter (1992), 339
R. v. Woollin (1998), 339
R [on the applications of Haney, Kaiyam, and Massey] v The Secretary of State for Justice (2014), 445
R v. McLoughlin and Newell (2014), 444
San Antonio Independent School District v. Rodriguez (1973), 81, 92n25
Sauvé v. Canada (2002), 136, 515nn32–3
Scoppola v. Italy (2011), 515n28
Scoppola v. Italy (2012), 515n29
Scoppola v. Italy (No. 3), 498
Söyler v. Turkey (2013), 515n30
Stafford v. United Kingdom (2002), 442
Stephenson v. U.S. (2015), 516n47
Swarthout v. Cook (2011), 434, 448
United States v. Burns (2001), 136
Village of Euclid, Ohio v. Ambler Realty Co. (1926), 91n15
Vinter and others v. United Kingdom (2013), 442–4
Ždanoka v. Latvia (2006), 514n23
Legatum Prosperity Index of Educational Performance, 228
Léger v. France (2006), 438
legitimacy, effects on homicide rates, 278
lethal injections, 116
lethal violence, effects on incarceration rates, 204, 209–11, 260n13, 261n20
liberalization of justice policies, serious violent crime spike (1960s–1970s), 24–5, 38n59
life imprisonment
American *vs.* European definition, 414
Canadian pessimism, 170–1nn16–17
differences between America and Europe, 440–4
Germany, 440–4
lifetime risk of homicide
England and Wales, 360n32
United States, 272, 292n1
lifetime risk of incarceration
black male child, 4
white male child, 4–5
lifetime supervision, 10
life without parole (LWOP), 441, 461
lightning strikes, death by, 31n14
Lijphart, Arend, 60–1, 239–40
Lijphart index, 266n54

Lipset, Seymour Martin, 109, 110
Liszt, Franz von, 444
local autonomy, political dynamics of punishment. *See also* political structures
  administration of federal grants, 80
  banishment of the poor or undesirable, 84
  Byrne Grant program, 83
  counter arguments (*see* counter arguments to local autonomy thesis)
  criminogenic effects, 69–72
  disorganization theory, 70
  electoral competition, 65
  federalization, 81–5
  fragmentation of America's political system, 71
  Gautreaux litigation, 81
  hourly wages and crime rate, 71
  implementing national policies, 68–9
  infrastructure of gangs, 71–2
  law as guarantor of common standards, 80
  levels of decision making on criminal justice policy, 85, 92n27
  limits of federalization, 81–5
  loss of skilled jobs, 71 (*see also* Fordist production regimes)
  median voter effect, 66, 88
  nationalization of crime policy, 83
  overall cost of the prison system, 66
  political decentralization, role in patterns and levels of crime, 66
  poor policing, 70
  prisoners' dilemma effect, 65
  pros and cons, 88–9
  racial integration, 71
  violence rates, 70
  War on Drugs, 82–3
loss of welfare benefits, 135, 136–7
Louisiana
  homicide rates, 299
  imprisonment rates, 127, 186, 224–5
Loury, Glenn C., 77
Love, Margaret, 19
low risers *vs.* high risers, 219–26, 262n26
Luxembourg, voting rights for prison inmates, 496, 514n17
LWOP (life without parole), 441, 461

M. v. Germany, 518n69
Macdonald, John A., 153
MacGuigan, Mark, 160
Macpherson, William, 92n22
main distinction, parole supervision, 427–8
Maine
  abolishing discretionary parole release, 430
  imprisonment rates, 127, 186, 226
Major, John, 311, 317, 324
majoritarian democracy, imprisonment rates worldwide, 239–40, 265n45
majoritarian democracy *vs.* consensual democracy, 239–40
Making Confinement Decisions, 149–50
Making Crime Pay: Law and Order in Contemporary American Politics, 298, 325n1
Malicious Wounding/Inflicting Grievous Bodily Harm, 338
managerial justice *vs.* individualized justice, 374–5
managerial parole, 460
mandatory minimum sentences, 161
mandatory release, 416
Maori population
  imprisonment rate, 75, 91n21
  integration of, 78

Marshall, Thurgood, 470n18
Martinson, Robert M., 145
Martinson Report, 145, 158
Maryland
  parole boards, 455
  racial disparity, incarceration, 64
Massachusetts
  imprisonment rates, 132, 186
  parole supervision, 425
  voting rights for prison inmates, 514n15
Massey, Douglas S., 77
mass fines, 34n36
mass incarceration
  in America, history and politics of race, 77
  in cross-national perspective, 196–8, 202–3
  parole as a cause of, 15
  race, history and politics of, 77
  relationship to crime rates, 203–4, 205–7, 214–26
  relationship to homicide rates, 205–6, 207, 209–11, 214–26
  state-by-state comparisons, 202–3
  in US, 2–3, 196–8
mass probation, markers of penal severity
  consequences for breaches or violations, 390–4
  formal treatment programming, 386–90
  intensity and restrictiveness, 382–5, 401n7
  length of supervision terms, 380–2
  mission and goals of probation, 374–80, 395–6
mass probation in Europe
  caseloads, 401n8
  vs. US, 369, 399–401
mass probation in Scotland
  consequences for breaches or violations, 392
  formal treatment programming, 388
  institutional structure, 371–2
  intensity and restrictiveness, 385
  length of supervision terms, 381
  mission and goals of probation, 375–7
mass probation in Sweden
  consequences for breaches or violations, 392–3
  formal treatment programming, 388–9, 402n12
  institutional structure, 372–4, 401nn4–5
  intensity and restrictiveness, 385–6
  length of supervision terms, 381
  mission and goals of probation, 377–9
  probation as protective care, 378
mass probation in the US
  caseloads, 383, 401n8
  consequences for breaches or violations, 390–2
  drug testing, 383
  electronic monitoring, 384
  vs. Europe, 369, 399–401
mass probation in the US, need for comparative research
  Accreditation panels, 399
  collateral sanctions, 399
  conditions of supervision, 396–7, 402n13
  consequences for breaches or violations, 397–8
  electronic monitoring, 402n14
  formal programming, 402n14
  length of supervision, 396
  mission and goals of probation, 395
  professionalism of the workforce, 398–9

requirements for programs, 399
scale of probation services, 395
mass punishment, 8
matrix model of risk assessment, 449
Mauser, Gary A., 358n13
McCleskey v. Kemp (1987), 7, 32n18
McLean and Cole v. United Kingdom (2013), 515n27, 516n37
McNeill, Fergus, 396–7
means of execution
lethal injections, 116
speeding death and reducing pain, 115, 116
means testing for economic sanctions, 18–19, 36n48
Meese, Edward, III, 30n4
men, homicide rates, 307
MF (Nigeria) v. Secretary of State for the Home Department (2013), 517n56
Michigan, abolition of capital punishment, 115
Miller, Lisa, 62, 81, 85
Miller v. Alabama (2012), 441
minimum wage, 135, 137
Minister of Home Affairs v. NICRO and Others (2004), 515n34
Minnesota, imprisonment rates, 127, 132, 186, 224–5
minority threat hypothesis, 246
mission and goals of probation, 374–80, 395–6
Mississippi, imprisonment rates, 127
Missouri
death penalty, 7
imprisonment rates, 224
Mitchell, Kelly Lyn, 33n30
Model Penal Code: Sentencing, 465
Monkkonen, Eric, 286
Montana, imprisonment rates, 132
moral offenses, capital punishment for, 279
Morrissey v. Brewer (1972), 434, 448
Mouisel v. France (2002), 470n19
MPC (Model Penal Code). *See also* serious violent crime, US *vs.* England and Wales
aggravated assault, 337–9
GBH (Grievous Bodily Harm), 338, 358n15, 359n20
Malicious Wounding/Inflicting Grievous Bodily Harm, 338
means testing for collateral sanctions, 18–19, 36n49
Section18 Offenses against the Person Act, 338
Section20 Offenses against the Person Act, 338
voting rights for prison inmates, 515n40
Wounding/Causing Grievous Bodily Harm with Intent, 338
Mumola, Christopher J., 402n10
Murat Vural v. Turkey (2014), 515n30
murder. *See* homicide
Murray v. the Netherlands (2016), 444
M v. Germany (2009), 445–6
The Myth of Mob Rule: Violent Crime and Democratic Politics, 325n4

national disunity, effects on punitiveness, 283
National Rifle Association (NRA), 337, 358n13
nation building
effects on homicide rates, 278–9
key elements, 278
Native Americans
homicide rates, 273
incarceration rates, 4
NCRS (National Crime Recording Standard), compiling data on serious violent crime, 341–2

Nebraska, imprisonment rates, 127
Needham Lifestyles Survey, 264–5nn42–44
negative exceptionalism, 107
Nelson Mandela Rules, 515–16n41
Netherlands
  crime rates, recorded crimes, 212
  homicide rates, 305–7
  homicide rates *vs.* US, 37n54
  imprisonment rates, 212
  incarceration trends, 201, 260n7
Newburn, Tim, 91n9
New Hampshire, imprisonment rates, 132
New Jersey, imprisonment rates, 186
The New Jim Crow, 76
New York
  imprisonment rates, 186, 225–6, 263n29
  parole supervision, 425–6
New Zealand
  history and politics of race, 78
  homicide rates, 214
  homicide rates *vs.* the US, 23
  incarceration rates *vs.* the US, 31n6
  incarceration trends, 201
New Zealand, homicide rates
  influence on incarceration, 214–19
  vs. the US (*see* serious violent crime, US *vs.* New Zealand)
New Zealand, Maori population
  imprisonment rate, 75, 91n21
  integration of, 78
New Zealand, serious violent crime
  vs. England and Wales, 353, 359–60n29
  vs. US, 333, 353
9/11 terrorist attacks, 315, 327n18
Nolan, Pat, 30n4
nonwhite prisoners, per 100,000 persons (1850–1920), 286
Nordic countries
  crime rates, recorded crimes, 212
  imprisonment rates, 212
Norquist, Grover, 30n4
North America *vs.* western Europe, homicide rates, 278
North Carolina, imprisonment rates, 132
North Dakota
  imprisonment rates, 132
  incarceration rates, 169nn7–9
Norway
  crime rates, 211–13
  incarceration rates, 199
notification requirements, sex offenders, 517n57
NRA (National Rifle Association), 337, 358n13
nulla poena sine lege principle, 427

Öcalan v. Turkey (2014), 443
OECD countries, imprisonment rates worldwide, 227–8, 263n32
offender reintegration, role of economic sanctions, 18
Ohio, parole supervision, 425–6
Oklahoma, parole boards, 455
on parole. *See* parole
Osborn v. The Parole Board (2013), 448
Our Criminal Law, 159
outlier, definition, 118n2
overcrowded prisons, 438–9

Padilla v. Kentucky (2010), 504–5, 513n4
Pakistan, death penalty, 32n20
Parole. *See also* conditional release
  as a cause of mass incarceration, 11, 15
  decision making, methodology of, 430–1
  definition, American *vs.* European, 415–17
  European (*see* conditional release)

exceptionally severe practices, 12
granting, decision making, 450–7
ideals, 436–40, 470n21
indeterminate release systems, 13, 33n29
managerial parole, 460
vs. probation, 417
public perceptions of, 12
release eligibility, 440–4
release for humanitarian reasons, 470n19
release policies, 436–40
revoking, 450–7
right to conditional release, 434, 470n18
right to counsel, 450–1
for sentences with fixed maximum terms, Germany, 446–50
setting minimum terms based on offenses, 33n30 (*see also* indeterminate release systems)
supervision rates, 12, 33n26
parole, decision making
abolition of release discretion, 456–7
definition, 415
differences between America and Europe, 450–7
granting parole, 450–7
lack of procedural safeguards, 14
relitigation of judicial sentence, 14
revoking parole, 450–7
United States, 456–7
unpredictable and changeable, 14
parole board members
appointing, 454, 466
high turnover rates, 14–15
removing, 454
tenure of, 466
parole boards
Arkansas, 439
Belgium, 453, 456
California, 455
definition, 415
England and Wales, 452, 461, 466
France, 451
Germany, 451
grounds for release decisions, 457
gubernatorial overrides, 455
Italy, 451
Maryland, 455
Oklahoma, 455
procedural safeguards, 455
political vulnerability of, 14–15
combined with great power, 15
power to influence imprisonment rates, 33n32
reforming, 466–7, 472n31
risk aversion, 15
romanticized vision of, 15
Scandinavian countries, 453
Spain, 452
strengths and weaknesses, 14–15, 34n34
turnover rates, 14–15
United States, 453–4
victim input to, 14
parole conditions, definition, 416
parolees
definition, 415–16
District of Columbia (2013), 469n11
number of US (2013), 418–19
selected US states and European countries, 421
US *vs.* Europe (2013), 419–20
parole release
abolition of parole release discretion, 16, 430, 470n17
crimes committed by the released, 15, 34n35
decision makers, 14
eligibility for, 441–2

parole release (*cont.*)
  high parole release
    discretion as American
    exceptionalism, 13–15
  and prison growth, 34n33
  romantic vision of, 15
  and state election cycles, 33n31
parole revocation, resulting in prison
    admission, 423, 469–70n15
parole revocation rates
  parolees *vs.* probationers, 33n27
  revocation decisions, 33–4n32
  US *vs.* Europe, 13, 33n28, 423–4
parole supervision
  differences between America and
    Europe, 435–61
  early release programs, 463–4
  earned time, 463
  evidence-based decisions, 463
  The Future of Parole as a Key Partner in
    Assuring Public Safety, 464
  good time, 463
  LWOP (life without parole), 441, 461
  Model Penal Code: Sentencing, 465
  Pennsylvania, 439
  possibilities for reform, 461–7
  PRCS (post-release community
    supervision), 464
  PRS (post release supervision), 417
  punitive victim rights, 462
  recent trends, 461–7
  re-entry courts, 464, 472n29
  risk assessment tools, 463
  Second Chance Act of 2007, 472n29
  similarities between America
    and Europe (1970s
    onward), 429–33
  similarities between America and
    Europe (pre-1970s), 424–9
  team-based efforts, 464
  "tough on crime" era, 462
  trend to judicial and parole board
    discretion, 463
  victim impact statements, 462
parole supervision, differences between
    America and Europe
  actuarial risk prediction,
    449, 471n27
  American rates *vs.* European rates,
    12, 469n14
  approaches to supervision, 457–61
  community supervision, 458–9
  CPT (Committee for the Prevention
    of Torture and Inhuman
    or Degrading Treatment or
    Punishment), 436, 470n20
  ECtHR (European Court of Human
    Rights), 436
  eligibility for release, 441–2
  Engle criteria, 471n24
  financial obligations on
    ex-offenders, 458
  freedom of speech, 438–9
  granting parole, decision making,
    450–7 (*see also* parole boards)
  indeterminate sentences, 444–6,
    470–1n22, 470–1n25, 471n25
  IPP (imprisonment for public
    protection), 445, 471n23
  life imprisonment, 440–4
  LWOP (life without parole), 441
  matrix model of risk
    assessment, 449
  number of US parolees
    (2013), 418–19
  overcrowded prisons, 438–9
  parole for sentences with fixed
    maximum terms, 446–50
  parole ideals, 436–40, 470n21
  parole release policy, 436–40
  preventive detention, 445–6
  preventive supervision, 444

protecting rights of sentenced prisoners, 444–6
Recommendation Concerning Prison Overcrowding and Prison Population Inflation, 437
Recommendation on Conditional Release (Parole), 436–7, 442, 450–1, 460
release eligibility, 440–4
revocation rates, 13, 33n28, 423–4
revoking parole, decision making, 450–7 (*see also* parole boards)
right to counsel, 450–1
risk assessment, 449, 471n27
risk assessment tools, 449–50
Rules on Community Sanctions and Measures, 436–7, 451
second track punishments, 445–6, 471n24
secure prevention detention, 444
sequential model of risk assessment, 449
Serbia, 469n12
SPACE II, 418
SPACE surveys, 418
statistical comparisons, 418–24 (*see also* BJS (Bureau of Justice Statistics)).
parole supervision, similarities between America and Europe (1970s onward)
abolishing discretionary release, 430, 470n17
determinate sentencing, 429, 435
determinate *vs.* indeterminate approach, 430
due process in early release, 433–5
European criminal justice, 431–2
Poland, 432–3
release for humanitarian reasons, 470n19
right to conditional release, 434, 470n18
truth in sentencing laws, 429, 431–2
parole supervision, similarities between America and Europe (pre-1970s)
carceral approach *vs.* resettlement approach, 460
continental Europe, 426–7
indeterminate sentencing, 426
main distinction, 427–8
managerial parole, 460
Massachusetts, 425
New York, 425–6
nulla poena sine lege principle, 427
Ohio, 425–6
US Federal Parole Commission, 426
parole supervision rates, American *vs.* European, 469n14
paroling authority, definition, 415
patterns
of crime growth, Canada, 122
punishment, over time, 59
Patterson, Orlando, 275
Pattillo-McCoy, Mary, 80
penal confinement. *See* imprisonment; incarceration
penal disparity, US and other liberal market economies, 74
penal optimism, US. *See also* American optimism; penal pessimism, Canada
history of, 165–6
imprisonment rate, 121, 168n2
jail figures for US states, 121, 168n1
prison and jail population, 168n2
three-strikes sanctions, 167
penal pessimism, Canada, 151, 153, 165. *See also* penal optimism, US

penitentiaries, Canadian, 153–4. *See also* imprisonment; incarceration
Pennsylvania
economic sanctions, 34n37
license suspension resulting from drug convictions, 503
parole and supervision, 439
violence politicization (*see* violence politicization in Pennsylvania)
percentage growth, state-level imprisonment *vs.* absolute growth, 190
Perry, Rick, 30n4
Petersilia, Joan, 460, 466
Peterson, Ruth D., 77, 79
Pew Charitable Trusts, 3, 4
Phelps, Michelle, 368
Phillips-type curve, 217–18
Pickett, Justin T., 138
Pinard, Michael, 19
Poland, parole supervision, 432–3
police recordings
alternatives to, 358–9n19
compiling data from (*see* compiling data on serious violent crime, police recordings)
criteria for, 340
English *vs.* American, 350–2, 359n24
recording error, 359n20
reliability of, 358n17
rules for, 343–8
policing. *See* law enforcement
policy effects
connectedness via, 263n28
incarceration rates, 203–4, 260nn11–12
lagged policy effects, 218–19
on US states, 225
political decentralization. *See* local autonomy, political dynamics of punishment
political rights, collateral sanctions, 494–500
political stability, effects on homicide rates, 278
political structures. *See also* local autonomy, political dynamics of punishment
consensus-based *vs.* competitive, 61
and democracy, effects on imprisonment rates worldwide, 239–45, 265n46
effects on criminal justice, 58–64
first-past-the-post systems, 60
floating voters, 61
links to incarceration rates, 3
penal state *vs.* welfare state, 62
in the South, 79–80
Polity IV index, 241, 241–4, 265n47, 266n53
Portugal, homicide rates *vs.* US, 37n54
positive *vs.* negative exceptionalism, 107–8
post release supervision (PRS), 417
Poveda, Tony, 109
Powell, Lewis, 32n18
PRCS (post-release community supervision), 464
President's Commission on Law Enforcement and Administration of Justice, 141–2
pretextual racism, 76
preventive detention, 445–6
preventive supervision, 444
Priscilla Nyokabi Kanyua v. Attorney General & Another (2010), 515n36
prison and jail population, 168n2
prisoners
nonwhite, per 100,000 persons (1850–1920), 286
per 100,000 persons (1850–1920), 286
protecting rights of, 444–6

treatment of, 275
US *vs.* Europe (2013), 419–20, 469n7
white, per 100,000 persons (1850–1920), 286
The Prisoners' Dilemma, 58–9, 61, 63, 65, 90n4
prison gangs, 72
prison growth
measurement of, percentage growth *vs.* absolute-change approach, 126–8, 130, 169n7, 179–80, 190–1, 219–20, 262n25
per capita growth among US states by sentencing system type, 16
uniformity, 189
in US states, 16, 220–2, 274–5
prison population
California, 513n1
United States, 487, 513n1
prison rate, *see* incarceration rate
prisons. *See also* incarceration
corporal punishment, 275
disenfranchisement of inmates (*see* voting rights for prison inmates)
living conditions, 275
overcrowding, 438–9
voting rights (*see* voting rights for prison inmates)
probation
as an alternative to prison, 8
average length of terms, 10, 32–3n24
budgetary support, 401n1
day-to-day experience of, 9
declining, 33n25
definition, 417
history of, 8–9
length of term, 9–10
lifetime supervision, 10
mass (*see* mass probation)
vs. parole, 417
racial disparity, 9, 32n23
scale of, 9
supervision rates, 9, 32n21
surveillance and control, 9
probationers in Europe (2013), 419, 469n6
probationers in the US
African Americans, 32n23
vs. Europe, 10–11, 419–20
fees collected from (*see* supervision fees)
Hispanics, 32n23
number of, 32n21
some probationers' preference for incarceration, 33n25
whites, 32n23
probation revocation, 9, 32n22, 33n25, 35–6n45
probation supervision rate
mass probation in the US, 369
vs. Europe, 9–11
professionalism of the workforce, need for comparative research, 398–9
property crime, and imprisonment rates, 223
proportional sentencing
Canada, 125, 152, 156, 161, 164, 171n19
economic sanctions, 35n43
sentencing, 152
PRS (post release supervision), 417
The Public Interest, 145
public support for capital punishment, 116
punishing in the post-progressive era of American optimism, 144
punishment. *See also* punitiveness
certainty *vs.* severity, 153
patterns over time, 59
vs. rehabilitation for drug crimes, 144
punishment imperative, 290
punishment in Pennsylvania
crime spending, 319

punishment in Pennsylvania (*cont.*)
legislative attention, 319
murder rates in Philadelphia, 320, 321, 327n23
single-issue politics, 323
punishment in the UK
bills enacted, 317–18, 324
lack of attention to crime, 320–1
murder rates in London, 321
serious violence rates, *vs.* US, 322
single-issue politics, 323
social welfare provisions, 317–18
speech mentions, 317–18, 324
punishment in the US
problems caused by the US political system, 322–3
serious violence rates, *vs.* UK, 322
punitiveness. *See also* collateral sanctions; prison growth; punishment; sentencing
as cause of imprisonment rates, 137–9
distrust in government, 283
effects on crime, 276
get-tough policies, 290–1
harsh penalties as deterrent, 149, 170n14
high rates of incarceration, 283
lack of fellow feeling, 283
loss of welfare benefits, 135, 137
national disunity, 283
populist punitiveness, 195
punishment imperative, 290
rise since the 1970s, 290
truth in sentencing laws, 291
War on Crime, 290
punitive victim rights, 462

Queen's Speech, 308–9, 326n11, 327nn15–16

R. (on the application of Wells) v. Parole Board, (2009), 445
R. v. Ipeelee (2012), 125
R. v. Moloney (1985), 339
R. v. Savage and Parmenter (1992), 339
R. v. Woollin (1998), 339
race, history and politics of
Australia, 78
city trenches, 79
comparative measures of racism, 92n22
ethnic segregation of migrants, 79
imprisonment rates, 74
institutional racism, 75–6
Jim Crow system, 73
linkage between race and class, 77
mass incarceration in America, 77
New Zealand, 78
penal disparity, US and other liberal market economies, 74
pretextual racism, 76
racial caste system, 76
racial institutional orders/alliances, 77
racial residential segregation, 78
residential sorting, 79
segregation and violence, 79
segregation of the disadvantaged, 78–9, 92n23
United Kingdom, 78
race and class, 77
race of the victim
as a factor in the death penalty, 7, 32n17
lack of data in non-capital criminal cases, 32n17
racial caste system, 76
racial disparity
collateral consequences of conviction, 20
death penalty, 6–7
incarceration rates, 4–5, 31n11
probation, 9, 32n23

racial disparity, incarceration in the US (2006)
  African Americans, 64
  Hawaii, 64
  Maryland, 64
  South Dakota, 64
  Washington, D. C., 64
  Wisconsin, 64
racial institutional orders/ alliances, 77
racial makeup of imprisonment rates, 138
racial minorities, homicide rates, 273
racial residential segregation, 78
racism
  comparative measures of, 92n22
  institutional, 75–6
  pretextual, 76
rape rates, 23, 37n55
Raphael, Steven, 5
ratio approach *vs.* absolute-change approach, 219–20, 262n25
ratio change, *vs.* absolute change, 190
Reagan, Ronald, 146, 401n6
Rechtsstaatlichkeit (commitment to due process), 450
Recommendation Concerning Prison Overcrowding and Prison Population Inflation, 437
Recommendation on Conditional Release (Parole), 416, 436–7, 442, 450–1, 460, 468n2
recorded crime *vs.* actual crime, 204, 260n14
re-entry courts, 464, 472n29
reforming
  economic sanctions, 18–19, 36n49
  parole boards, 466–7, 472n31
  parole supervision, 461–7
registries for sex offenders, 493, 508, 517n57, 517nn59–63
rehabilitation
  death knell for rehabilitative model, 145
  emphasis on, 25
  factors contributing to, 18, 36n47
  failure of, 148
  of offenders, 156–7
  vs. punishment for drug crimes, 144
  role of economic sanctions, 18
rehabilitative model as crime control, 156
reintegration services, 502, 516n48
Reitz, Kevin R., 24, 147, 149, 259n1, 262n22, 401n3
relief from collateral sanctions, 510–12. *See also* expunging collateral sanctions
reported crime rates. *See* crime rates, recorded crimes
Republican states *vs.* Democratic, imprisonment rates, 244
requirements for programs, need for comparative research, 399
resettlement approach to parole supervision, 460
residential sorting, 79
restitution costs. *See* collateral sanctions, economic and social rights
retributive justice, role of economic sanctions, 35n40
revocation of probation, mass probation in the US, 390–1
revoking parole, decision making, 450–7
Rhine, Edward E., 33n30
Rhode Island
  abolition of capital punishment, 115
  imprisonment rates, 132
Right on Crime
  members of, 30n4
  views on incarceration rates, 3

risk assessment, parole decisions, 449–50, 463, 471n27
risk aversion among parole boards, 15
risk of death penalty, 6
robbery rates, serious violent crime spike (1960s–1970s), 23, 37n55
Robey, Jason P., 33n30
Robina Institute of Criminal Law and Criminal Justice, 9
Rockefeller, Nelson, 144, 146
Rockefeller drug laws, 145, 158
R [on the applications of Haney, Kaiyam, and Massey] v The Secretary of State for Justice (2014), 445
Roth, Randolph, 1, 207
Rothman, David, 140–1, 170n12
Ruhland, Ebony L., 33n30
Rules on Community Sanctions and Measures, 436–7, 451
Russia
  disenfranchisement, 498, 515n31
  incarceration rates *vs.* the US, 3, 31n7
Russian Federation, incarceration rates, 197
Ruth, Henry, 24, 147, 149, 262n22
R v. McLoughlin and Newell (2014), 444

Sampson, Robert J., 77
Saudi Arabia
  capital punishment, 116
  death penalty, 32n20
Sauvé v. Canada (2002), 136, 515nn32–3
scale of probation services, need for comparative research, 395
Scalia, Antonin, 108–9
Scandinavian countries
  economic sanctions, 17
  parole boards, 453
Scheingold, Stuart, 85–6
Scoppola v. Italy (2011), 515n28
Scoppola v. Italy (2012), 515n29
Scoppola v. Italy (No. 3), 498
Scotland. *See also* United Kingdom
  homicide rates *vs.* US, 23
  mass probation (*see* mass probation in Scotland)
SCRAM (Secure Continuous Remote Alcohol Monitoring), 383
Seattle, WA, banishment of the poor or undesirable, 84, 92n26
Second Chance Act of 2007, 472n29
Second Reform Act, 279
second track punishments, 445–6, 448, 471n24, 471n26
Section18 Offenses against the Person Act, 338, 344, 351
Section20 Offenses against the Person Act, 338, 344, 351
secure prevention detention, 444
sedition, capital punishment for, 279
segregating offenders from society, 144
segregation
  of the disadvantaged, 78–9, 92n23
  and violence, 79
sentencing. *See also* determinate sentencing; indeterminate sentencing
  cost-benefit ratio, 149
  dangerous offenders, 170–1nn16–17
  habitual sex offenders, 161
  life imprisonment in Canada, 170–1nn16–17
  mandatory minimum sentences, 161
  proportional (*see* proportional sentencing)
  purpose of, in Canada, 171n19
  severity, California, 146
sentencing structure, Canada, 153–5
SEP indicator, imprisonment rates worldwide, 241, 265–6n52
sequential model of risk assessment, 449

Serbia, parole supervision, 469n12
serious injury, definition of, 349–50
serious violent crime, across US states, 358n12
serious violent crime, England and Wales *vs.* New Zealand, 353, 359–60n29
serious violent crime, US *vs.* Canada
  aggravated assault, 353–4
  Feasibility Study on Crime Comparisons between Canada and the United States, 353–4
  index crimes, 354, 360n30
serious violent crime, US *vs.* England and Wales
  aggravated assault, 337–9
  compiling data (*see* compiling data on serious violent crime)
  CSEW (Crime Survey of England and Wales), 335
  data for assaults, 335, 357n8–357n9
  establishing comparable measures, 334–5, 356–7n4
  GBH (Grievous Bodily Harm), 338, 358n15, 359n20
  gun control issues in the US, 337
  and gun ownership, 337, 358n13
  incidents per capita, 333, 355–6n1
  legal background, 337–9 (*see also* MPC (Model Penal Code)).
  MPC (Model Penal Code), 358n14
  NCVS (National Crime Victims Survey), 335
  per the ICVS, 335
  police recording practices for offenses, 356n3
  relevant offenses, 337–9
  role of crime in American justice, 336
  United Nations Crime Trends Survey, 335
serious violent crime, US *vs.* New Zealand
  aggravated assault, 353
  homicides per 100,000 persons, 333
  International Comparisons of Recorded Violent Crime Rates for 2000, 353
serious violent crime spike (1960s–1970s). *See also* homicide rates
  aggravated assault rates, 23, 37n55
  changes in case processing and court procedures, 25
  civil rights movement, 25
  crime rates, 22
  emphasis on rehabilitation, 25
  federal court involvement, 25
  gun control movement, 25
  liberalization of justice policies, 24–5, 38n59
  memorable disruptions, 37–8n57
  rape rates, 23, 37n55
  relaxation of public order laws, 25
  robbery rates, 23, 37n55
  types of, 22
700 Club, 3
sex offenders
  collateral sanctions (*see* collateral sanctions, sex offenders)
  lifetime supervision, 10
  registering, South Africa, 517n59
  registration statutes, 508, 517n57
  registries, 493, 517nn59–63
  sentencing, 161
Sexual Offenses Act (2003), 517n57
Seychelles
  imprisonment rates, 30n3, 168n2
  incarceration rates, 197, 259n3
Simon, Jonathan, 62, 374–5, 459
Simpson's paradox, 261n18

single-issue politics
punishment in Pennsylvania, 323
punishment in the UK, 323
slavery, and the government structure of the South, 79–80
Smith, Rogers M., 77
social policies, affecting imprisonment rates, 134–8
social policies affecting imprisonment rates, 134–8
social welfare and other benefits, collateral sanctions, 501–4
societal effects, collateral consequences of conviction, 20
sociological/historical use of American exceptionalism, 107, 109
Sombart, Werner, 109
Soskice, David, 59, 91n12
South Africa
disenfranchisement, 515n34, 515n36
sex offender registration, 517n59
South Dakota, racial disparity in incarceration, 64
Söyler v. Turkey (2013), 515n30
SPACE II, 369–70, 418
SPACE surveys, 418
Spain
collateral sanctions on sex offenders, 493
employment restrictions on sex offenders, 509
homicide rates *vs.* US, 37n54
juez de vigilancia, 452
parole boards, 452
voting rights for prison inmates, 496
spending on halting crime, *vs.*. homicide rates, 283
St. Kitts and Nevis, incarceration rates, 197, 259n3
Stafford v. United Kingdom (2002), 442
Standard Minimum Rules for the Treatment of Prisoners (2015), 515–16n41
Steiker, Carol S., 109
Stephenson v. U.S. (2015), 516n47
Strafvollstreckungskammern (chambers of the criminal courts), 450
Stuntz, William, 81–2
Sudan, capital punishment, 116
supervision, post-parole release. *See* parole release
supervision fees, 9
supervision rates, probation, 9, 32n21
support for the death penalty, *vs.* homicide rates, 285
surveillance and control, 9
Swarthout v. Cook (2011), 434, 448
Sweden
crime rates, 211–13
disenfranchisement, 496
incarceration rates, 199
mass probation (*see* mass probation in Sweden)
Switzerland
homicide rates *vs.* US, 37n54
incarceration rates, 199
voting rights for prison inmates, 496

TANF (Temporary Assistance for Needy Families), 228
Tatarek, Nancy, 292n5
Taxman, Faye S., 397
team-based efforts, 464
Texas
death penalty, 7, 32n16
homicide rates, 274
parole supervision, 463
Thailand, imprisonment rates, 186
Thanner, Meredith, 397
Thatcher government, 310–11, 317, 327n14

Thinking about Crime, 147
Third Reform Act, 279
three-strikes sanctions, 167
Tocqueville, Alexis de, 109, 114
Tonry, Michael, 61, 167, 429, 462
"tough-on-crime" era, 462
"tough-on-crime" issues, 173n29, 314
transferability of collateral sanctions, 494
Travis, Jeremy, 456
treason, capital punishment for, 279
tribunal de l'application des peines, 451
trust and legitimacy, effects on imprisonment rates worldwide, 233, 264–5nn40–43
truth in sentencing laws, 291, 429, 431–2
Turkey, disenfranchisement, 498, 515n30
Turkmenistan, incarceration rates, 259n3
turnover rates of parole boards, 14–15

UCRH (Uniform Crime Reporting Handbook), 340
UN HDI (United Nations Human Development Index), 198–202
United Kingdom. *See also* England and Wales; Scotland
  history and politics of race, 78
  life sentences, 442
  punishment in (*see* punishment in the UK)
United States. *See also specific topics*
  crime rates, recorded crimes, 212
  crime reporting rates over time, 358n16
  homicide rates, 216–19, 305–7
  imprisonment rates, 212
  incarceration rates, 216–19
  incarceration trends, 198–202
  mass probation (*see* mass probation in the US)
  parole boards, 453–4
  punishment in (*see* punishment in the US)
United States v. Burns (2001), 136
US Federal Parole Commission, 426
US states. *See also specific states*
  incarceration rates, 202–3, 220–2 (*see also* imprisonment rates, US states)
Utah, imprisonment rates, 186, 224–5

van Zyl Smit, Dirk, 12, 125, 370
Vermont
  imprisonment rates, 132
  voting rights for prison inmates, 514n15
victim impact statements, 462
victim input to parole boards, 14
Vinter and others v. United Kingdom (2013), 442–4
violating probation, 390–4, 397–8
violence politicization
  avoiding blame *vs.* gaining credit, 315–16
  crime rates *vs.* politicization rates, 315
  cross-national comparison, 305–7, 313
  vs. homicide rates, 313–14
violence politicization in Pennsylvania
  9/11 terrorist attacks, 315, 327n18
  crime as the most important problem, 312
  data sources, 325–6nn10–12
  homicide rates, 315
  homicide rate *vs.* political agenda, 310
violence politicization in the UK
  data sources, 325–6nn10–12
  homicide rates *vs.* political agenda, 307–10

violence politicization in the UK (*cont.*)
vs. politicization in the US, 316
Queen's Speech, 308–9, 326n11, 327nn15–16
Thatcher government, 310–11, 327n14
violence politicization in the US
comprehensive crime bill (1992), 312
congressional hearings on crime topics, 311–12
crime as the most important problem, 312
data sources, 325–6nn10–12
vs. politicization in the UK, 316
violence rates, UK
Brixton riots, 311
by race and ethnicity of victims, 311
violent crime, and imprisonment rates, 222–3
violent crime victimization, rates of, 303–4
Virginia, voting rights for ex-offenders, 514n16
Virgin Islands, incarceration rates, 197, 259n3
Vogel, Matt, 91n10
volume effects, 203–4, 207, 225
voting rights for prison inmates. *See also* disenfranchisement
Angleichungsprinzip, 515–16n41
Committee of Ministers of the Council of Europe, 497
disenfranchisement, racial impact of, 496
ECHR (European Court of Human Rights), 497–9, 515n37
ICCPR (International Covenant on Civil and Political Rights), 499
MPC (Model Penal Code), 515n40
Nelson Mandela Rules, 515–16n41
overview, 496–7, 514nn15–17
restrictions on convicted offenders, 135, 136–7
Standard Minimum Rules for the Treatment of Prisoners (2015), 515–16n41

Wacquant, Loïc, 62, 195
Walgrave, Stefan, 325–6n10
Wallace, George, 290
warehousing crime, 144
War on Crime, 290
War on Drugs
collateral sanctions, 502
effects on collateral sanctions, 492–4
War on Poverty, 143, 145
Washington, D. C., racial disparity, incarceration, 64
Washington, imprisonment rates, 186
wealth and prosperity, effects on imprisonment rates worldwide, 229, 264n39
Webster, Marie, 189–90, 220
welfare policy and social inclusion, effects on imprisonment rates worldwide, 228–33, 263–4nn34–37
welfare reform bill, 136–7
Welzel, C., 241
Western, Bruce, 63, 77, 137
western Europe
homicide rates *vs.* US, 37n54
incarceration rates *vs.* the US, 4
incarceration trends, 198–202
vs. North America, homicide rates, 278
West Virginia, imprisonment rates, 225–6, 263n29
white Americans, homicide rates, 273
white male child, lifetime risk of incarceration, 4–5

white males, imprisonment rate, 74
white prisoners, per 100,000 persons (1850–1920), 286
whites
  homicide rates, 282, 325n9
  probationers in the US, 32n23
  rates of capital punishment for, 276
Whitman, James Q., 61, 109, 167
Williams, Joshua, 91n10
Wilson, James Q., 38n60, 76–7, 77, 80, 147–50
Wisconsin
  abolition of capital punishment, 115
  racial disparity, 64
witchcraft, capital punishment for, 279
Wounding/Causing Grievous Bodily Harm with Intent, 338

Zackin, Emily, 91n8
Ždanoka v. Latvia (2006), 514n23
Zimring, Franklin E., 62, 109, 149–50, 167, 240, 336, 357–8n10